What Was Bolshevism?

Historical Materialism Book Series

The Historical Materialism Book Series is a major publishing initiative of the radical left. The capitalist crisis of the twenty-first century has been met by a resurgence of interest in critical Marxist theory. At the same time, the publishing institutions committed to Marxism have contracted markedly since the high point of the 1970s. The Historical Materialism Book Series is dedicated to addressing this situation by making available important works of Marxist theory. The aim of the series is to publish important theoretical contributions as the basis for vigorous intellectual debate and exchange on the left.

The peer-reviewed series publishes original monographs, translated texts, and reprints of classics across the bounds of academic disciplinary agendas and across the divisions of the left. The series is particularly concerned to encourage the internationalization of Marxist debate and aims to translate significant studies from beyond the English-speaking world.

For a full list of titles in the Historical Materialism Book Series available in paperback from Haymarket Books, visit: www.haymarketbooks.org/ series_collections/1-historical-materialism.

What Was Bolshevism?

Lars T. Lih

Haymarket Books
Chicago, IL

First published in 2023 by Brill Academic Publishers, The Netherlands
© 2023 Koninklijke Brill NV, Leiden, The Netherlands

Published in paperback in 2024 by
Haymarket Books
P.O. Box 180165
Chicago, IL 60618
773-583-7884
www.haymarketbooks.org

ISBN: 979-8-88890-329-2

Distributed to the trade in the US through Consortium Book Sales and
Distribution (www.cbsd.com) and internationally through Ingram
Publisher Services International (www.ingramcontent.com).

This book was published with the generous support of Lannan
Foundation, Wallace Action Fund, and the Marguerite Casey Foundation.

Special discounts are available for bulk purchases by organizations and
institutions. Please call 773-583-7884 or email info@haymarketbooks.org
for more information.

Cover art and design by David Mabb. Cover art is a detail of *Leftover*
(Cross VI, Monument to the Third International), oil paint and acrylic on
canvas (2017).

Printed in the United States.

Library of Congress Cataloging-in-Publication data is available.

For Julie

I' benedico il loco, e 'l tempo, e l'ora
che sí alto miraron gli occhi mei,
e dico: "Anima, assai ringraziar dei,
che fosti a tanto onor degnata allora."

⁞

Contents

Acknowledgements

Since *What Was Bolshevism?* contains writings that span over three decades, any effort to give proper acknowledgement to all those who helped me intellectually or materially would be futile. I can only give a very hearty thanks to all those who commissioned these essays, published them, read them, and supported or challenged my arguments. Putting this book together made me realize how much my own intellectual path has been influenced by investigating topics suggested by others. My Introduction contains more specific thank-yous to those who commissioned or published individual essays.

For the last decade, many essays of mine have been published online. Although the present volume contains only one of these efforts, all of my research has hugely benefitted from the immediate feedback that the internet has made possible. In particular, for giving me an online platform, I want to thank the *Weekly Worker* in the UK and John Riddell in Toronto. I also thank them for their support, publicly and personally, during all the controversies of the decade.

The last stages of preparation of this volume were darkened by the news that my teacher, mentor and friend Stephen Cohen died in October 2020. Before I learned of his passing, I had already written a tribute to him and Robert Tucker as part of my Introduction.

Sebastian Budgen and Danny Hayward are to be thanked for their faith in this project despite long delays – a faith expressed most often by prodding me to finish. And here it is! The parts of the present volume not previously published have greatly benefitted from the expert eyes of Emelyn Lih and Ariadne Lih. As always, my family made possible the productive working environment of an independent scholar – just one of the things for which I love them.

A note to the reader. Three guides to the contents of *What Was Bolshevism?* have been provided. 1. The Introduction discusses the origins and aims of each chapter. 2. An Appendix contains an Analytical Table of Contents for each chapter and its sections. 3. An Index of Proper Names follows the Appendix. (If the subject of an index entry is mentioned in the title of a chapter, that chapter is not included in the entry. For example, the index entry for Stalin does not include references to the chapter 'Stalin at Work'. The Appendix gives the relevant information.)

Original Publication

1. 2015, 'Ordinary Miracles: Lenin's Call for Revolutionary Ambition', in *Revolutionary Moments: Reading Revolutionary Texts*, edited by Rachel Hammersley, London: Bloomsbury Academic.

2. 2006, 'The Soviet Union and the Road to Communism', in *Cambridge History of Russia, Vol. III, The Twentieth Century*, edited by Ron Suny, Cambridge: Cambridge University Press.

3. 'Tsiurupa's White Beard', previously unpublished.

4. 1997, 'The Mystery of the ABC', *Slavic Review*, 56, no. 1: 50–72.

5. 1999, '*Vlast* from the Past', *Left History*, 6, no. 2: 29–52.

6. 1997, 'Grain Monopoly and Agricultural Transformation: Ideals and Necessities', in *Critical Companion to the Russian Revolution*, edited by Edward Acton and William Rosenberg, London: Arnold.

7. 1986, 'Bolshevik *Razverstka* and War Communism', *Slavic Review*, 45, no. 4: 673–89.

8. 1990, *Bolshevik Sowing Committees of 1920: Apotheosis of War Communism?*, Carl Beck Papers No. 803, University of Pittsburgh Center for Russian and East European Studies.

9. 2015, 'Bolshevism's "Services to the State": Three Russian Observers', *Revolutionary Russia*, 28, no. 2: 118–39.

10. 2007, ' "Our Position is in the Highest Degree Tragic": Bolshevik "Euphoria" in 1920', in *History and Revolution: Refuting Revisionism*, edited by Mike Haynes and Jim Wolfreys, London: Verso.

11. 2008, 'Zinoviev: Populist Leninist', *The NEP Era: Soviet Russia, 1921–1928*, 2: 1–23.

12. 1991, 'Political Testament of Lenin and Bukharin and the Meaning of NEP', *Slavic Review*, 50, no. 2: 241–52.

13. 2000, 'Bukharin's "Illusion": War Communism and the Meaning of NEP', *Russian History*, 27, no. 4: 417–60.

14. 1995, 'Introduction', in *Stalin's Letters to Molotov, 1925–1936*, edited by Lars T. Lih, O.V. Naumov and Oleg Khlevniuk, New Haven: Yale University Press.

15. 'Bukharin's Bolshevik Epic: The Prison Writings', previously unpublished.

16. 2002, 'Melodrama and the Myth of the Soviet Union', in *Imitations of Life: Two Centuries of Melodrama in Russia*, edited by Joan Neuberger and Louise McReynolds, Durham, NC: Duke University Press.

17. 'Vertigo: Masks and Lies in Stalin's Russia', previously unpublished.

18. 2016, 'Who Is Stalin? What Is He?', *Crisis and Critique*, 7.

19.   2009, 'Perestroika's Revival of NEP: A Contemporary Chronicle, 1985–
1990', *The NEP Era: Soviet Russia 1921–1928*, 3: 1–34.

What Was Bolshevism?

What was Bolshevism? This book presents, not my own answer to this question, but rather the answers given by authoritative and authorized Bolshevik spokesmen. In what way authoritative? First, because of their record of long service as Bolshevik leaders from its beginning, and second, because of their official status after October. In other books and articles, I have examined Lenin's outlook, and Lenin's voice is also heard in the present volume. Nevertheless, the focus here is on the top tier of Bolshevik leaders: Nikolai Bukharin, Iosif Stalin, Grigorii Zinoviev, Lev Trotsky, Lev Kamenev, Aleksandra Kollontai, and many others.

During the Soviet era, not only political leaders answered the question 'what was Bolshevism?' Soviet artists were also authorized to define Bolshevism: Soviet Realist playwrights such as Aleksandr Afinogenov, composers such as Sergei Prokofiev and Dmitri Shostakovich, Stalin-era filmmakers such as Mikhail Chiaureli, Thaw-era novelists such as Vladimir Dudintsev, and even singer-songwriters from the Brezhnev era such as Vladimir Vysotsky. All find their place here. While of course their answers had to be acceptable to the powers that were, each of them displays an individual take on the Bolshevik narrative of identity. And, to add to the mix, we will hear from some unusual Russian supporters of Bolshevism who were situated a considerable distance away on the political spectrum, such as the very moderate socialist Alexei Peshekhonov and the right-wing Russian nationalist Sergei Lukianov.

The essays collected here span a scholarly lifetime, from my first published article in 1986 to new pieces written for this volume. Although they were written under various circumstances and inspired by various stimuli, they were all written with the same question in the back of my mind: what was Bolshevism? They come together here as a unified and comprehensive argument.

The reader will not find here a narrative history of Bolshevik doctrine, but rather a series of case studies – some short, some extensive – showing Bolshevism as it engaged with some of the central issues of Soviet history. Perhaps we can think of these case studies as snapshots of Bolshevism, each at a particular time and place. When placed side by side, the snapshots reveal both an underlying continuity and a gradual metamorphosis. The case studies that follow begin in 1902, before the term 'Bolshevism' was invented, and they end in 1991, when the question 'what was Bolshevism?' had become once more the focus of impassioned public debate. The individual case studies that follow focus on the dramatic period from the 1917 revolution to the eve of World War II. At the beginning of the book is an overall survey of the entire period of Soviet history ('The Soviet Union and the Path to Communism'), while at the end of the book a final essay shows Soviet society assessing its past, present and imagined future ('Perestroika Looks Back'). These bookend essays put the intervening snapshots into a wider context.

The individual case studies are further unified by an approach that sees Bolshevism, not as a doctrine constructed out of abstract propositions, but as a narrative with a central theme of inspiring class leadership. The party inspires the Russian workers who inspire the Russian peasants to create together a worker-peasant *vlast* that will inspire the world by building socialism – this is the heart, the emotional core, of Bolshevism. Before the revolution, the Bolsheviks self-identified as the Russian branch of 'revolutionary Social Democracy', the name given by its adherents to the left wing of the Second International. Karl Kautsky, the acknowledged spokesman of revolutionary Social Democracy, was seen by the Russian Bolsheviks – and rightfully so – as their own mentor. And indeed, the essentials of the Bolshevik narrative come from the Europe-wide movement of Social Democracy. This narrative was presented in many forms during the Soviet period, from political speeches to popular songs, but it also guided the party as it faced an unending series of real-world crises. In order to properly tell the story of the Bolshevik story, both dimensions – imaginative projections and policy decisions – must be included.

Since an overview of my argument can be found in 'The Soviet Union and the Path to Communism', the present introduction will limit itself to providing a guide to the case studies that follow. Besides indicating each essay's place in my overall argument, I will add a few remarks on when and why it was written. All the previously published essays have been slightly re-edited for clarity (in particular, titles are often modified), but they are substantially as they first appeared, except as noted. For those readers who remain suspicious of some of my more iconoclastic arguments, this introduction contains a multitude of references to other writings of mine that pursue various topics in more detail.

Part 1: Overview

According to my original concept for exploring 'what was Bolshevism?', a central aim was to 'decentre' Lenin by looking at a much wider range of Bolshevik sources. But I quickly found that decentring Lenin was only possible *after* giving him some very detailed attention, owing to strongly entrenched distortions of his outlook. Therefore, when Sebastian Budgen suggested that I contribute a commentary and new translation of *What Is to Be Done?* to the *Historical Materialism* series, I was happy to accept.[1] I later balanced this very long book on a couple of years in Lenin's life with a very short book on Lenin's whole career.[2]

In *What Was Bolshevism?*, I finally return to my original aim of decentring Lenin – not, of course, by minimizing his huge importance as a leader but by widening the focus to include a much larger cast of characters. To act as a preface to the present volume, I chose a short essay which gives the essence of my reading of Lenin's message in 1902, when he wrote *What Is to Be Done?* 'Ordinary Miracles: Lenin's Call for Revolutionary Ambition' was written for an innovative series by Bloomsbury called *Textual Moments in the History of Political Thought*. For the volume in this series devoted to *Revolutionary Moments*, edited by Rachel Hammersley, contributors were asked to examine one representative passage from a classic text about revolution as an emblem of the whole text. My assignment was to take a passage from Lenin's 1902 work *What Is to Be Done?* For anyone not inclined to plough through my book-length commentary on *What Is to Be Done?* (although you really should), this essay is an acceptable substitute.[3]

As preparation, I indulged myself in a little fantasy: if I were appointed tsar of the textbooks, what passages would I choose to be the ones endlessly cycled and recycled in the one or two paragraphs devoted to Lenin and Bolshevism? Dating from the 1950s – owing more, I believe, to Harvard political scientist Adam Ulam than to any other scholar – some misleading and wrongly interpreted phrases became the core of the educated public's understanding, not only of one particular book, but of Lenin, Bolshevism, Communism as a whole. And academic specialists have done very little to disabuse their readers of these notions.[4] So I chose a passage that represents much more accurately the spirit of Lenin's book – not dour 'worry about workers', but enthusiastic confidence in the power of the Social Democratic message.

---

1 *Lenin Rediscovered: What Is to Be Done? in Context* (Lih 2006); this volume contains a new full translation of Lenin's book. See also 'Lenin and the Great Awakening' (Lih 2007) for a brief statement of my interpretation.

2 *Lenin* in the Critical Lives series of Reaktion Press (Lih 2011b).

3 Or consider the following compromise: the core of my interpretation is set out in chapters 1, 2, and 7 of *Lenin Rediscovered* (Lih 2006).

4 A notable exception to the academic consensus was Robert Tucker; see his 'Lenin and Revolution', first published as the introduction to his classic collection of Lenin's writings, *The Lenin Anthology* (Tucker 1975). For the story of how this incorrect consensus was formed, see 'How a Founding Document was Found, or One Hundred Years of Lenin's *What Is to be Done?*' (Lih 2003).

'Ordinary Miracles' (I stole the title from the classic Evgeny Shwartz play *Oby-knovennoe chudo*) shows us the heart of what I often call 'the narrative of class leadership': the confident expectation that the Social Democratic message represents exciting 'good news' that will be eagerly received by the Russian workers and points beyond. The power of the message enables ordinary Social Democratic *praktiki* (rank-and-file activists) to achieve 'miracles' (Lenin's word) of inspiring leadership. The standard textbook interpretation of *What Is to Be Done?* is the direct opposite: Lenin is pictured as pessimistically, even cynically, *worried* that workers are permanently deaf to the message. This misleading cliché renders the actual world of Bolshevism a closed book. In response to the prevailing textbook interpretation of *What Is to Be Done?*, 'Ordinary Miracles' presents the emotional heart of Bolshevism.

In this essay and in this book as a whole, I assume the essential continuity of Bolshevism's message from its beginnings. The reader should be aware that this assumption is highly controversial, since prevailing views of Lenin and Bolshevism from both academics and activists are fascinated with *rupture*: a rupture in 1902 between Lenin and 'the Marxism of the Second International', a rupture in 1914 between Lenin and Kautsky as the main spokesman of 'revolutionary Social Democracy', and a rupture in 1917 when Lenin 'rearmed the party', to name just the most popular examples. Much of my writing over the last decade or so has examined the case for the alleged ruptures in 1914 and 1917 and found them wanting.[5] Luckily, these controversies about pre-October Bolshevism, important as they are, are separate from the account of post-October Bolshevism contained in the present book.

The short prefatory essay on a single passage from *What Is to Be Done?* is followed by a large-scale survey of the Bolshevik outlook throughout the Soviet period. 'The Soviet Union and the Path to Communism' was written in 2006 as the concluding survey article in *Cambridge History of Russia, Vol. III, The Twentieth Century* (edited by Ron Suny). One reviewer praised the volume as a whole but not my essay: 'A couple of chapters, it might be noted, [including] Lars T. Lih on "The Soviet Union and the Road to Communism", leave the reader somewhat baffled by their postmodern methodology with its jargon of "discourse", "con-

---

5   For 1914, see Lih 2009, Lih 2014a, Lih 2019b; for 1917, see Lih 2011a, Lih 2014b, Lih 2015, Lih 2017, Lih 2020a, Lih 2020b, Lih 2021. I have been commissioned by the French publisher Editions Sociales to present an overview of my argument for essential continuity in 1902, 1914, 1917 and 1920 (the book is provisionally entitled *Lenin and the Bolshevik Message: A Historical Investigation*, to appear in 2024). This study will serve as a prequel to *What Was Bolshevism?*

struction", and "narrative", but the rest of the volume is fortunately free of these innovations."[6] Gosh – I hardly know what a post-modernist is and now I find I am one!

In actuality, the search for meaningful metaphors is a completely conventional technique of traditional history. But this comment gives me an opening to talk about the source material used in this volume. Almost the exclusive source base that historians have used to answer the question 'what was Bolshevism?' is Lenin's articles and books, all conveniently available in both Russian and English. I have tried to expand this base in a number of directions. In contrast to the polemics that dominate in his articles and book, Lenin's speeches when in power have been neglected as a source, even though they starkly present the message he was trying to bring home to his (usually) party audiences. I have also looked at the articles and books, not only of Lenin, but also of Stalin, Bukharin, Zinoviev, Trotsky. Despite the fame of these leaders, and despite the availability of their writings in published collections, much of what they have to say has simply been overlooked. Each of these prominent leaders have individual essays dedicated to them, but readers will also hear a variety of other Bolshevik voices: Lev Kamenev, Aleksandra Kollontai, Evgenii Preobrazhensky, Vyacheslav Molotov, and many others. Karl Kautsky, who can be thought of as almost an honorary Bolshevik during the decade before the war, is not neglected.

Pamphlets and leaflets are other political genres essential to understanding the Bolshevik worldview in action; conference resolutions and decrees were also used to deliver the message.[7] But beyond these directly political channels, the reader will find in these pages discussions of novels, plays, literary criticism, photographs, statues, poetry, history textbooks, songs, choral cantatas and film.

'The Soviet Union and the Path to Communism' is organized around the metaphor of the path, and practically every quotation in the essay has a 'path' or 'road' reference. But, as the reader will see, another metaphor is just as fundamental: the leader, the guide, the 'inspired and inspiring activist'.[8] In these essays, written over a number of years, I have labelled this underlying narrative in different ways: the class narrative, the heroic scenario, the hegemony scenario, and others. These terms all point to the same essential worldview.

Bolshevik 'hegemony' (to be sharply distinguished from the myriad other meanings given to this word) refers to class leadership of the peasantry by the

---

6   Robert V. Daniels in *Slavic Review* Vol. 67, No. 1 (Spring, 2008), pp. 231–232.

7   On the importance of political pamphlets as a primary source, see Thatcher 2016, pp. 1635–53.

8   I use the quoted phrase to describe Lenin's outlook as expressed in *What Is to Be Done?* See the discussion in Lih 2006.

socialist proletariat. Back in 2006, when I wrote 'Path to Communism', I did not use the word 'hegemony' and restricted my discussion of the peasantry to the NEP period in the 1920s. As a result, as I now see, the essay underplays a central part of the Bolshevik outlook.[9] This theme nevertheless plays a major role throughout the present book.

Another vocabulary item that is missing in this essay (because I only coined it later) is 'campaignism'.[10] Nevertheless, the essential argument justifying the term is here adumbrated: Ferdinand Lassalle invented the 'permanent campaign' which became an intrinsic part of the SPD model; the Bolshevik drive to overthrow absolutism was primarily fuelled by its desire to attain the political freedom needed for SPD-style campaignism; sadly, 'state monopoly campaignism' after October was a prime incentive to shut down political freedom in the Soviet Union; the rhythm of the campaign saturated Soviet life in large ways and small.

'The Soviet Union and the Path to Communism' also shows that the famous phrase *kto-kovo*, who-whom – popularly supposed to be one of Lenin's favourite phrases – was barely used by him, and then only at the end of his career. When he did use it, his meaning was close to the direct opposite of the hard-line meaning it acquired during Stalin's collectivization. In my mind, the true story of *kto-kovo* is a small parable of scholarship's failure to take Lenin seriously as an object of historical study.

'The Soviet Union and the Path to Communism' goes beyond the Stalin era to look at the Khrushchev and Brezhnev eras. Perhaps the question 'what was Bolshevism?' is not so relevant to this stretch of time. One is reminded of a well-known *anekdot*: Brezhnev's mother is visiting him, and he is proudly showing off his truly impressive collection of fancy cars. 'That's all right, sonny', she says, 'but what if the Bolshies come back?'[11] Nevertheless, during these years Soviet citizens continued to ponder the meaning of their unique experiment – and they did so with greater and greater independence from the official message. The Khrushchev-era novel *Not by Bread Alone* serves as a window into the age of 'the thaw' after Stalin. This novel briefly introduced returnees from the camps;

---

9   In my essay 'The Proletariat and its Ally: The Logic of Bolshevik "Hegemony"' (entry in Lih 2017, 'All Power to the Soviets!'), I document the enthusiastic endorsement by Lenin, Trotsky and Stalin of Kautsky's 1906 presentation of the logic of 'hegemony', that is, proletarian leadership of the Russian peasantry as a means of carrying the Russian revolution 'to the end'.

10 'Campaignism and the Fate of Political Freedom in Russia' (Lih 2019a); 'Campaignism: An Essential Theme in the History of the Left' (Review-Essay of Kevin Callahan, *Demonstration Culture: European Socialism and the Second International*) (Lih 2013).

11 My thanks to Ian Thatcher for reminding me of this *anekdot*.

two works recently available in English bring out the complex human realities of this monumental process: Stephen F. Cohen's *The Victims Return* and a new English translation of Vasily Grossman's *Everything Flows*.[12] Vladimir Vysotsky's song 'Morning Gymnastics' is used in a similar way for the Brezhnev era. I mention in my essay that '"Morning Gymnastics" was not an underground song – it can be found on a record sold in Soviet stores around 1980'. And that was where I first came across the song, when I purchased a Vysotsky LP in my IREX-supported year of research (1980–1981).[13]

Part 2: Deferred Dreams: Against the Myth of 'War Communism' (1918–1921)

In Part II, I document the strong commitment of historians to what I call the myth of war communism and then I lay out my case against the myth. Refuting the standard story was my first priority, partly because I had to convince myself as well as others. At a certain point, I successfully convinced myself and no longer felt the urge to refute (or rather, the urge moved on to other topics). Whether I have succeeded in convincing anybody else is still an open question.

The first item in Part II – 'Tsiurupa's White Beard' – is based on a Power-Point talk presented to the Historical Materialism annual conference in London 2018 as well as to the annual conference of the Study Group on the Russian Revolution held at Cardiff in January 2019. My thanks to the organizers and participants of both memorable conferences. I have retained much of the original PowerPoint format, because it is well adapted to bringing out the dramatic contrast between what the Bolsheviks said vs. what the historians claimed the Bolsheviks said.

One question that came up at the conferences was whether the myth of war communism in the version documented in 'Tsiurupa's White Beard' is still dominant. Library restrictions due to the pandemic do not allow a detailed answer at time of writing, but I will give my impression (as of September 2020) for what it is worth. The myth of a leap into communism, of euphoria-induced hallucination, of a 'short-cut to communism', of glorification of coercion as the royal road to communism, etc., is still dominant in most works that reach the larger reading public. Academic monographs these days do not usually endorse the

---

12   Cohen 2010; Grossman 2009.
13   The International Research & Exchanges Board (IREX) was established in 1968 and sponsored many generations of research by US graduate students in the Soviet Union. My IREX year resulted in some lifelong friendships.

myth in the vivid dramatic terms of an earlier generation of historians, but neither do they bother to refute it or offer anything to take its place. Absent from these monographs is the central point that needs to be brought out: the civil war was a time, not of Bolshevik euphoria over instant communism, but rather of a resigned acceptance of deferred dreams. Indeed, the most original theoretical work produced by Bolshevik spokesmen during this period – Bukharin's *Economy of the Transition Period* (1920) – set out to generalize the Bolshevik experience by arguing that *any* proletarian revolution would inevitably lead to a short-term but sharp social crisis, forcing dreams of socialist transformation to be put on hold.

One essential task for historians is to distinguish Bolshevik attitudes toward two very different challenges: the imperative of establishing and defending a worker-peasant *vlast*, and the imperative of transforming society in a socialist direction. Many of the misleading assertions in present-day scholarship come from confusing these two themes, although they are quite different. From the Bolshevik point of view, the *political* imperative of establishing a worker-peasant *vlast* is *either-or*: a *vlast* is either dominated by the bourgeoisie or by a proletarian-peasant alliance, and not somewhere in between. Thus the Bolshevik story about establishing the worker-peasant *vlast* is about opening up the very possibility of any socialist transformation of society, not about 'instant socialism'.[14] In contrast, the story about socialist transformation is *more-or-less*: a gradual journey toward socialist society, with the possibility of halts, detours and retreat never ruled out. We can hardly say anything sensible about, say, the Bolshevik attitude toward coercion, unless we are aware of this distinction. The Bolshevik leaders were triumphal about the first imperative: they had successfully defended the worker-peasant *vlast* against all comers. They were much more subdued about the second: they were ruefully aware that they had hardly begun to travel along the road to a socialist society.

The rest of Part II consists of two essays that challenge various avatars of the myth of 'war communism'. The first has the melodramatic title 'The Mystery of the *ABC*' and examines the most comprehensive and influential statement of the Bolshevik outlook in the years immediately following October: *The ABC of Communism* by Nikolai Bukharin and Evgenii Preobrazhensky. This article was originally published in 1997, and looking back at it now, I see how it pointed the way for my later scholarly trajectory. It was directly inspired by a remark about

---

14   In his letter to *Slavic Review* quoted below, Martin Malia writes: 'instant socialism following the proletarian seizure of power was the creed, not only of the young Bukharin and Lenin, but also of the "moderate" German SDs – indeed of all Marxists back to Marx himself.' This confident assertion is wildly off-base, as the essays in this volume will show.

'war communism' that Martin Malia made in his book *The Soviet Tragedy*: 'In a veritable ideological delirium, the most colossal economic collapse of the century was transmogrified into really-existing Communism, the radiant future *hic et nunc*, a vision projected in Bukharin's and Preobrazhenskii's once famous *ABC of Communism*.'[15]

I had recently familiarized myself with the *ABC* in order to write a small item on it for a reference work.[16] After reading Malia's comment, I was upset and even indignant at the blithe way he turned the book on its head. I sat down and feverishly wrote my article in a white heat – easy enough to do, since all I had to do was find quotes from a single 200-page book. I do not think I wrote another article that moved so quickly from conception to publication.

As sometimes happens, the original impetus behind the article – Malia's mischaracterization – faded away to a single footnote. Malia himself, however, picked up on this footnote and wrote a letter to *Slavic Review* that contained the following remark: 'Is Lih so certain that my reading of Bukharin (like Andrzej Walicki's and Leszek Kolakowski's – two pretty big guns, after all) is mistaken?'[17] I have often reflected on this response. The *ABC of Communism* (authored, please remember, by Bukharin *and* Preobrazhensky) is not an obscure document and not particularly hard to obtain, even in its original Russian text. An afternoon at any good research library would have given Malia a very secure sense of the strength of my case. Young and unknown I may have been, but certainly I had documented a solid *a priori* case that Malia's published description was dead wrong. So why didn't Malia take off a couple of hours and see for himself? Instead, he wrote in to *Slavic Review* to say that Lih can hardly be right if he dares to disagree with various big guns of the profession.

My *ABC* essay contains a short methodological credo that informs much of my later research. 'A point of method: I do not make the claim that any text "speaks for itself" or that the surface meaning is the only significant one. My objection is to interpretations that present themselves as unproblematic yet ignore crucial and abundant textual evidence.' Let me expand briefly on this credo. Teachers of Greek and Latin have been known to complain that there is no absurdity so far-fetched that a schoolboy would not be ready to attribute it to a classical author. Why? Because the schoolboy's grasp of Greek and Latin is shaky, and because he thinks of classical authors as strange beings capable of saying just about anything. Many of my colleagues are in the same position as these schoolboys when it comes to 'reading Bolshevik'. They read a text by a

---

15   Malia 1994, p. 130.
16   Lih 1995, pp. 5–9.
17   *Slavic Review*, Vol. 56, No. 4 (Winter, 1997), pp. 850–1.

Bolshevik spokesman, extract an absurd implication and hold it up for display. Then they lose interest. One result is that massive textual evidence is simply ignored. Another result for those of us who dig deeper is that even when we report a finding that outsiders will find banal and commonsensical, specialists view us as paradoxical contrarians – for example, if we point out that Lenin the dedicated Marxist did *not* despise the proletariat as incorrigibly reformist.

Another methodological challenge is a widespread assumption that we cannot take Bolshevik texts at face value, because the speakers were wearing masks and not saying what they really thought. Both those hostile and those friendly to Lenin accuse me of impermissible naivete when I point to actual statements that challenge a prevailing interpretation. 'Well of course Lenin (or Bukharin, or Stalin) would *say* that – but, obviously, that's not what he really thought.'

I admit that my default position is scepticism when presented with these hidden meanings and secret messages. Certainly, however, there is always a real possibility of hypocrisy, of insincerity, of 'Aesopian language' (coded formulations to fool the censor) and the like. I have argued for such interpretations myself, in particular cases. But here's the problem. Such interpretations can be defended only *after* the surface meaning – the official argument, as it were – has been firmly established. This is rarely done. The result is very often circular reasoning in support of *a priori* interpretations: here's what Lenin meant, and if it's different from his actual words, that's not my problem. And we need hardly bother to call this contrary evidence to our readers' attention.

Finally, we must remember that our Bolshevik texts are public statements, intended to persuade a large audience. The speaker as an individual may be highly hypocritical, but his actual arguments have an independent reality in the minds of his listeners. If we focus exclusively on Lenin's putative secret meanings, we make all other Bolsheviks either minions (those in on the con) or dupes (those taken in by the con). But that's not how it works. Recently I saw a sign at a construction site here in Montreal: *excavation profonde*. I immediately adopted the phrase as something I aspire to. And sometimes an *excavation profonde* is just what is needed to accurately establish the surface meaning of a text.[18]

'*Vlast* from the Past', the final essay in Part II, demonstrates how some top Bolshevik spokesmen viewed the course of events after October. Here I try to replace the myth of war communism with a better sense of the actual 'stories told by Bolsheviks' – the stories that defined who they were, what they thought they were doing, and where they were going. '*Vlast* from the Past' retells five

---

18   For further discussion, see my engagement with the work of one of the premier North American Lenin scholars, the late Carter Elwood: 'The Non-Geometric Elwood' (Lih 2012).

stories that influenced or strived to represent early Bolshevism, by Kautsky, Bukharin, Trotsky, Kollontai and Zinoviev. Later essays in this volume that are specifically devoted to Bukharin, Trotsky, and Zinoviev go into more detail. But to those readers who wish to read straight through the present volume, I should note that over the years I have tried not to duplicate supporting evidence, even if the overall argument remains the same. Of course, there are a few eloquent quotations that show up more than once in this volume – for example, Zinoviev on the little old lady.

The essays and case studies in this volume contain a wide and massive amount of documentation about the Bolshevik outlook during the time of troubles. Three of the myth's weightiest proof texts – Bukharin and Preobrazhensky's *ABC of Communism*, Bukharin's *Economy of the Transition Period*, and Trotsky's *Terrorism and Communism* – are addressed in detail. Lest anyone think that in any way these essays come close to exhausting the available evidence, I will mention here some of the sources I consulted but for one reason or another (*not* including lack of support for my thesis) were never fully presented in published form.

1. Vladimir Mayakovsky's *ROSTA* Windows and his play *Mystery-Bouffe*. The great poet put his talents to work for the Bolshevik cause in 1920 by drawing propaganda posters – called ROSTA Windows after the acronym for the official press agency – and composing little jingles to accompany them. He put out two or three a week all during the year, thus providing a unique (and highly entertaining) window into Bolshevik concerns and self-presentation during this period. Here is a sample:

The text says: 'Do you want to fight against the cold? Do you want to fight against famine? Do you want to eat? Do you want to drink? Hurry to enrol in a shock group of exemplary labour.'

Mayakovsky also rewrote portions of his 1918 play *Mystery-Bouffe* for a production in early 1921. A new character was introduced, the demon-queen *Razrukha*, whose name comes from the expressive and ill-boding word used during the time of troubles to denote Russia's social and economic collapse. What all this Mayakovsky material shows should hardly be a surprise: uppermost in Bolshevik minds was survival and meeting the challenges of civil war, foreign intervention, and combatting the *razrukha* – *not* a euphoric leap into communism.

2. The Second Comintern Congress in summer 1920. The records of this congress are easily available in an excellent English edition.[19] Communists

---

19   *Workers of the World and Oppressed Peoples, Unite!: Proceedings and Documents of the Second Congress, 1920* (Riddell 1991).

gathered from around the globe to (among other things) admire the achievements of the Bolsheviks. And what were these achievements, as presented by the Russians and accepted as such by the delegates? Having the audacity to carry off a revolution, having the smarts and stamina to fend off enemies of the worker-peasant *vlast*, fighting a successful (as it seemed at the time) war against Polish invaders, dictating correct tactics to Communist parties everywhere, and so on. The socialist transformation of Russia was *not* included.

3. Larin and Kritsman on the Soviet economy. In the summer of 1920, two top Soviet economists, Iurii Larin and Lev Kritsman, were asked to write a guide to the Soviet economy for the foreign comrades. The result is an essential source. The following passage would be an excellent epigraph for a book on the civil-war economy in Russia:

> The genuine economic history of Soviet Russia will begin only with 1921, since only in the second half of 1920 does Russia exist as a unified economic organism. The first three years of the proletarian revolution up to now are only a preface, only an introduction to this history. This preface consists of the struggle to create the first presupposition for the possibility of normal economic development: gathering together into one whole all the parts [of pre-revolutionary Russia] ripped apart by the bourgeois-landlord counterrevolution and by the countries of the Entente, namely, Ukraine, Great Russia, Siberia, Turkestan, the Don.[20]

4. Lev Kritsman's magnum opus *Heroic Period of the Great Russian Revolution* was written in the early 1920s. To date, only short excerpts are available in English, although Kritsman's book is not only the best treatment – both empirically and analytically – of the Russian economy during the civil war, but is also a substantial contribution to a Marxist theory of revolution.[21] Bringing the book to wider attention is unfinished business on my part.

5. Bukharin's *Economy of the Transition Period* (1920). The *Ekonomika* is discussed in a number of essays here, but a full and complete decoding of his argument remains highly desirable. I say 'decoding', because, although Bukharin was talking about and justifying very concrete Bolshevik policies, he chose to

---

20   Iu. Larin and L. Kritsman 1920, *Ocherk khoziaistvennoi zhizni i organizatsiia narodnogo khoziaistva Sovetskoi Rossii, 1 noiabria 1917–1 iiulia 1920 g.*, pp. 100–1 (available online).

21   L. Kritsman, *Geroicheskii period velikoi russkoi revoliutsii (opyt analiza t. n. 'Voennogo Kommunizma'*), 2nd edition (Gosizdat: Moscow, 1926) (first edition 1924) (available online). For an English translation of Kritsman's Foreword and first chapter ('Mechanics of Revolution'), see Ronald Kowalski 1989.

do so by describing them in highly abstract, generalizing language. Even so, the book is an excellent guide to the grim realities of the time of troubles, a.k.a. 'transition period'.

6. Debates at the 9th Party Conference in September 1920.[22] This party gathering, held at the supposed high point of supposed 'war communism', reflects not euphoria, but a sense of deep crisis. Special attention was given to a malaise within the party: the growing split and mutual alienation between the *verkhi* and the *nizi*, the 'higher-ups' (leaders) and the 'lower-downs' (rank and file). Some of the issues from this debate are briefly mentioned in *'Vlast'* from the Past'.

7. Informed outside observers, writing prior to NEP. The introduction of NEP in early 1921 was billed by both friend and foe as something of a retreat. This perception subtly (and later not so subtly) distorted people's memory of the civil war period. If NEP was a retreat, then the preceding 'war communism' must have been an offensive – a frontal assault aimed at building communism. But objective investigations into the Soviet economy written prior to NEP tell a very different story. In these works, the emphasis is on how *little* the Bolsheviks had been able to achieve of their program, how *meagre* the attempts at socialist transformation. Those hostile to the Bolsheviks blasted them for cynical compromises and for abandoning their earlier promises – *not* for blindly leaping into the unknown in a hallucinatory haze of revolutionary romanticism.

Many of these writers were remarkably well-informed and they produced studies that are still valuable today. Russian émigré economists such as Leo Pasvolsky had direct access to Soviet economic decrees and policy statements.[23] Other writers, such as the American socialist John Spargo, were able to rely on a mass of primary material made accessible to him by anti-Bolshevik socialists in emigration. Spargo was an American pro-war socialist whose general take on the Bolsheviks can be guessed at from the title of one of his books: *'The Greatest Failure in All History'* (his quotation marks). Due to his contacts in the emigration, Spargo was able to produce a well-documented act of indictment against the Bolsheviks. His conclusion is very germane to debates over 'war communism':

There is a still more important reason why the Bolshevist regime continues, namely, its own adaptability. Far from being the unbending and

---

22   *Protokoly desiatoi vserossiiskoi konferentsii* RKP (*bol'shevikov*) 1933.
23   Leo Pasvolsky 1921, *The Economics of Communism, with Special Reference to Russia's Experiment.*

uncompromising devotees of principle they are very generally regarded as being, the Bolshevist leaders are, above all else, opportunists. Notwithstanding their adoption of the repressive and oppressive methods of the old regime, the Bolsheviki could not have continued in power had they remained steadfast to the economic theories and principles with which they began. No amount of force could have continued for so long a system of government based on economic principles so ruinous.

As a matter of fact, the Bolsheviki have continued to rule Russia because, without any change of mind or heart, but under pressure of relentless economic necessity, they have abandoned their theories. The crude communism which Lenin and his accomplices set out to impose upon Russia by force has been discarded and flung upon the scrap-pile of politics. That this is true will be abundantly demonstrated by the testimony of the Bolsheviki themselves.[24]

Thus, Spargo, writing without the benefit of hindsight, paints a picture of the Bolsheviks completely opposite to the one evoked by those who believe in the myth of 'war communism'. He condemns them, not as blind utopians, but rather as cynical opportunists who openly admit the failure of their original hopes.

In this category we can also point to accounts by foreign visitors who are often sympathetic to the Bolshevik cause and thus give us the portrait that the Bolsheviks themselves wanted to present. This self-portrait certainly did not include anything like a fully socialist society in the near future. George Lansbury, a British pacifist socialist, visited Soviet Russia in February 1920 and commented:

Lenin and his colleagues found themselves with a nation of over one hundred million people and a country of thousands of square miles to administer, with nearly all the old rulers and leaders of the people hostile. In spite of this, the country is slowly being organized and made safe from the evils arising out of the blockade and foreign wars ...

Once the townspeople are able to give the peasants what they need in the way of clothes, seeds, tools and other necessaries of life, all friction will have passed away between artisan and peasant; once the advocates of

---

24   John Spargo 1920, *'The Greatest Failure in All History': A Critical Examination of the Actual Workings of Bolshevism in Russia*, p. 5 (according to the copyright notice, this book was published in August 1920). This book is available online and I strongly recommend it.

mass production are able to demonstrate the superiority of their system in giving a fuller life to all, there will be no question as to which system will carry the day.[25]

More hostile observers, such as the anarchists Emma Goldman and Alexander Berkman, also document from their point of view the Bolshevik failure to carry out meaningful socialist transformation.[26]

I would now like to offer some advice to any historian who finds this voluminous evidence to be persuasive. First, drop the term 'war communism' altogether. It is guaranteed, at the very least, to produce confusion and miscommunication. There is not even consensus about when it occurred. Some push it back to the start of the civil war in spring 1918, others push it forward to the last months of 1920. Usually the term is thrown around with only a vague sense of its chronological limits.

There is no consensus on the policy content of 'war communism'. There is no consensus on its relation to overall Bolshevik policy. Does 'war communism' refer to all of Bolshevik policy? To a subset that for some reason requires special attention? To an outlook that permeates policies, either as a whole or in part? Does it refer solely to alleged 'euphoria'? And when I say 'no consensus', I may give a false impression of actual debate and attention to definitions. Most often the term is tossed off carelessly and without thought.

Historians should be aware that the term 'war communism' was originally coined in order to further an ideological agenda and has continued to do so ever since. No one had any consciousness of any such entity during 1918–1921 – the period when it is supposed to have existed. Lenin himself coined the term in 1921 as part of his efforts to justify and popularize NEP. In my essay 'Bukharin and Bolshevik Illusions', included in this volume, I illustrate how Bukharin modified the meaning of 'war communism' during the 1920s as his polemical needs dictated. And, in our time, 'war communism' was again employed in the service of Soviet economic reform.

Usually the 'debate about war communism' is framed in something like these terms: what was the cause of Bolshevik euphoria in 1920? Were the crazy policies of 1920 motivated directly by a long-term Marxist commitment to bring about 'instant socialism'? Or did these crazy policies arise out of pragmatic

---

25   George Lansbury, *What I Saw in Russia* (Lansbury 1920), pp. 54, 58–9; see also Arthur Ransome, *Russia in 1919* (Ransome 1919). [Update: For a full discussion of outside observers, see my chapter in the upcoming volume in the HM series dedicated to the Tenth Party Congress (Clayton Black and Alexis Pogorelskin, editors).]

26   Alexander Berkman, *The Bolshevik Myth* (Berkman 1925).

responses to the national emergency that somehow transmogrified into 'an ideological construct that mistook the egalitarianism of poverty and wartime brotherhood not only for that of socialism, but also for that of communism'?[27] But this whole debate about how to explain Bolshevik euphoria is pointless, since in point of fact neither the Bolsheviks nor their 'ideological construct' made this hallucinatory error.

We don't need the term 'war communism', we don't need a debate about how it came to be, we don't need to generate confusion by using it as (so we think) convenient shorthand. The historical category 'civil war' does all the necessary work in a more enlightening way. I further think that historians would be well advised – even if they don't agree with my own description of the period – explicitly to distance themselves from the extreme formulations found in the very eminent and influential historians quoted in 'Tsiurupa's White Beard'. Precisely because we all honour and respect (most of) them, we cannot let their authoritative voices inculcate error.

Historians should also drive home the crucial distinction between the goal of *founding and protecting a worker-peasant vlast* and the goal of *transforming society in a socialist direction*. They should be aware of and bring to the attention of their readers the Bolshevik leaders' actual pronouncements on the subject. Precisely because the Bolsheviks are alien and far distant from us socially and psychologically, historians should bend over backwards *not* to dismiss them as irrational fanatics, but rather seek diligently the rational kernel in their doings. Thus endeth the sermon.

Part 3: Time of Troubles: Policies (1914–1921)

My first book – *Bread and Authority in Russia, 1914–1921* – came out in 1991. In this book, I looked at the years 1914–1921 as a 'time of troubles', a term with a specific and ominous meaning for Russians. The first time of troubles in Russia began when Tsar Boris Godunov died in 1605. For the following decade, the country was without a settled and recognized sovereign authority, a situation giving rise to civil war and foreign intervention. For Westerners, Modest Mussorgsky's opera *Boris Godunov* best conveys the atmosphere of the seventeenth-century time of troubles. This period came to an end in 1613, when the first Romanov was crowned.

---

27   Lewin 1974, p. 79. See also Deutscher 1954, p. 489: 'The Bolshevik was therefore inclined to see the essential features of fully fledged communism embodied in the war economy of 1919–20.'

The last Romanov abdicated in early March 1917, thus sparking off a second time of troubles: no firmly established *vlast* (sovereign authority), civil wars, foreign intervention, and finally a battered return to something approaching normality. 'Time of troubles' is the standard translation of the Russian expression *smutnoe vremia*, but the Russian words bring out better the element of murkiness and confusion. Many Russian observers at the time and since have applied this term to the upheaval of 1914 to 1921 – and, closer to our times, to the 1990s after the fall of another established *vlast*.

I took over the Russian term to use as an analytic tool to describe a complex process of breakdown and reconstitution in Russia from 1914 to 1921. The growing weakness of all essential coordinating institutions – economic, social and political – led to 'an elemental whirlpool' (an expression borrowed from a food supply official in 1917) that accelerated the country's breakdown. I can remember the exact place I was standing – in the stairway of the Princeton University library – when it occurred to me that someone should really look at food-supply policy (*prodovolstvennyi vopros*) throughout this period, since it was such a sensitive barometer of the stresses and strains of the time of troubles, and furthermore, that 'someone' was me.

The underlying aim of *Bread and Authority* – and the aim of the essays in Part 3 and the following Part 4 – is to bring out the constraints and pressures of a situation difficult for us in more settled societies to imagine. My sympathies went to people that posterity tends to look down upon, even though they worked to restore the broken ties of society. As I wrote in my final paragraph: 'If this study has any heroes, they are unlikely ones – the bureaucrats and middlemen of the entire period. Whatever their motives, they helped to overcome the disintegration and demoralization that showed themselves so powerfully in the food-supply crisis.'[28] Even though I included the bureaucrats and middlemen from all three governments – tsarist, Provisional Government, Soviet – I quickly found out that only the implied compliment to the Bolsheviks was considered controversial.

A comic routine I once read in Walt Kelly's *Pogo* has much influenced the way I think about these issues (I quote from memory):

Bunrab: Phew! This coffee is awful!
Pogo: It's not coffee, it's paint. We mixed it in the coffee pot.
Bunrab: Oh! (Slurp) Well, for paint it's not too bad.

---

28   Lih 1990, p. 273.

Many observers looking back from both left and right are disdainful of early Bolshevik Russia because of the metaphorical (and literal) absence of good coffee. It was neither a liberal republic nor a socialist commune-state. 1917 (either February or October, depending on one's stance) was a state of grace, the calamities and emergencies of the following period a fall from grace. As a character in a play by the perestroika playwright Mikhail Shatrov put it, 'October was a pure stream; it was the civil war that muddied it.'[29] And one can understand this point of view. Nevertheless, I aim to bring out the constructive energy that was *also* present during the time of troubles, even though by normal standards the results were unimpressive to say the least. It wasn't coffee, but for paint, it wasn't too bad.

As I wrote in *Bread and Authority*, 'we who live in normal times can have little conception of what is required to restore the structure of everyday life and return efficacy and meaning to social activity. We should be more ready than we often are to extend our compassion and admiration.'[30] Or, to put it in more social-sciency terms, we need to be aware of the powerful constraints, the daunting cost-benefit choices, and the meagre alternatives before we judge. Or, to put it more colloquially, if we walk imaginatively a mile or two in their shoes, we might be inclined to cut these guys more slack.[31]

Part 3 on actual Bolshevik policies during the time of troubles comes first, so the reader can receive a hands-on sense of the challenges facing policy-makers in real time. The broader views of Bolshevik leaders and others are set out in Part 4, 'Time of Troubles: Outlook'. Any reader who feels it would be useful to get an overview of the unique constraints imposed by a time of troubles before reading about concrete policies will benefit from 'Bolshevism's "Services to the State": Three Voices', especially the long excerpt by Alexei Peshekhonov.

The three essays in Part 3 focus on the most crucial and fraying tie in Russia during the time of troubles, the one between town and country. Grain deliveries, land redistribution, hunger first in the cities and then in the villages – all are considered in these three essays. The first essay is a summary of the overall trends of policy ('Grain Monopoly and Agricultural Transformation: Ideals and Necessities'), the second is a more detailed study of one of the iconic policies of the civil war ('Bolshevik *Razverstka* and War Communism'). The original title of the third case study was 'Bolshevik Sowing Committees of 1920: Apotheosis of War Communism?' (I answered the question in the negative). I have changed

---

29   See the essay 'Perestroika Looks Back', included in this volume.

30   Lih 1990, p. 273.

31   For a broader look at these issues, see 'All Power to the Soviets: Marx Meets Hobbes' (Lih 2018a).

the title to 'Bolsheviks at Work: The Sowing Committees of 1920' in order to make a connection with an essay later in the book entitled 'Stalin at Work'. The present essay, an intensely detailed case study of an almost forgotten and transitory policy, will give a sense that is hard to find elsewhere of how the Bolsheviks in the early days of Soviet power went about making important policy decisions.

An appendix to this case study contains the preamble to the legislation passed in late 1920 on the sowing committees. The preamble vividly portrays how the Bolsheviks saw the time of troubles. Like other governing authorities, they were quick to blame others for the problems that confronted them (and, like other governing authorities, they had a point). But, given the stereotypes of historians about the 'euphoria' of the Bolsheviks during so-called 'war communism', what stands out is the sober and unadorned evocation of the desperate crisis facing society:

> The victorious but burdensome struggle of the workers and peasants with Russian and foreign landowners, kulaks and capitalists, demanded great sacrifices from the labouring peasants. They endured the ravages of the pillaging White Guards. They suffered from the mobilization of workers and horses for the Red Army, the defender of worker-peasant freedom.
>
> They have received too few machines, scythes, iron, nails and the rest from the factories and workshops destroyed by Kolchak and Denikin and deprived by them of coal and raw materials. The import of goods from abroad necessary for the peasantry was stopped by the foreign landowners and capitalists. Despite all the efforts of the worker-peasant authority [*vlast*] and its concern for the toiling peasantry, sown acreage in the last years has shrunk, the cultivation on the land has worsened, and livestock has fallen onto a decline.
>
> Due to the efforts of the heroic Red Army, the last dangerous internal enemy, General Wrangel, has been crushed. For a time the pressure of the external enemy has slackened. The soviet authority [*vlast*] again turns its main attention to peaceful construction and in the first place to the strengthening and development of peasant agriculture.

Part 4: Time of Troubles: Outlook

In Part 4, I let five eloquent people take centre stage. Only one of the five, Lev Trotsky, is famous for his eloquence. Two of the others (Alexei Peshekhonov and Sergei Lukianov) are pretty much unknown. Bukharin is certainly known, but his treatise *Economy of the Transition Period* (1920) remains something of a closed book. In my essay, although I tease him for the dense jargon invented specifically for this treatise, I grant him an austere sort of eloquence, since all the generalizing abstractions reflect some very concrete realities. Zinoviev is certainly remembered, but respected or admired by few. Yet in his day, Zinoviev was the Bolshevik orator of choice when a particularly tough audience was expected. His two-hour speech in Germany at the Halle Congress in late 1920 successfully incited a split among the Independent Social Democrats of Germany, perhaps the premier rhetorical feat of the period.[32] No wonder that when Mikhail Levidov wrote a book in the mid-twenties about Bolshevik eloquence in 1917, not only Trotsky but Zinoviev get chapters to themselves.[33]

All this to say that these essays are full of quotable one-liners and riveting perorations. I have had to restrain myself from quoting too much of this material in my introduction. Enjoy!

'Bolshevism's "Services to the State"' is a homage of sorts to three marginal voices who I encountered early on in my scholarly travels and who influenced me perhaps more than such unknown writers should. My thanks to *Revolutionary Russia*, the journal of the Study Group on the Russian Revolution (SGRR), for letting me go public about these voices in my head. After he was expelled from Soviet Russia in 1922, Alexei Peshekhonov was alienated both from the émigré community and Soviet Russia. Sergei Lukianov wrote a disregarded essay in a disregarded collection – *Smena vekh* (*Change of Signposts*), put together in the early twenties by Russian nationalists who urged support for the Bolshevik regime. Yet these two writers capture something essential about the time of troubles that I have found very rarely elsewhere.

Very early on in my studies I purchased a reprint edition by Prideaux Press of Bukharin's *Economy of the Transition Period* – if memory serves, in a bookstore in Hamburg. This chance encounter led to a permanent swerve in my scholarly interests, since I literally spent years learning to decipher Bukharin's text. The *Ekonomika* surfaces in a number of essays in this book, but in 'Bolshevism's "Services to the State"', I set out its underlying message about the grievous but nevertheless justifiable costs of revolution. One person who immediately picked up on Bukharin's message was Trotsky. Shortly after the appearance of

---

32 For this speech and Iulii Martov's counter-speech, see *Zinoviev and Martov: Head to Head in Halle*, edited by Ben Lewis and myself (London: November Publications, 2011).

33 Mikhail Levidov 1925, *Oratory oktiabria: siluety, zapisi*. Included in this book is Levidov's own intriguing account of the October days, which he penned at the time as an informed but nonpartisan observer. My thanks to Clayton Black for calling my attention to this book and providing me with an electronic copy.

the *Ekonomika* in 1920, he argued that a fall in productivity and in quantity of products after the revolution was to be expected, 'given the transition of the national economy onto new rails ... We know from experience and should have predicted from Marxist theory the inevitability of the deepest crises during the epoch of revolutions. [Society's development] is not a straight one but a zigzag one.' A couple of years later, Trotsky deployed his talent for aphorism: 'Revolution opens the door to a new political system, but it achieves this by means of a destructive catastrophe.' This dour message – not the euphoria and the hubris depicted by the myth of war communism – shows the true impact of the time of troubles on the Bolshevik outlook.

The essay ' "Our Position is in the Highest Degree Tragic": Trotsky and Bolshevik "Euphoria" in 1920' is devoted entirely to Trotsky's pronouncements during the year usually seen as the climax of 'war communism'. It originally appeared in *History and Revolution: Refuting Revisionism*, edited by Mike Haynes and Jim Wolfreys and published in 2007 by Verso. The reader will hardly be surprised at this point to hear that the corpus of Trotsky's writings and speeches in 1920 reveals not the slightest resemblance to later scholarly descriptions of 'war communism'. Half of my essay is devoted to the policies of 'militarization' in 1920, and the other half to Trotsky's thoughts about how far Soviet Russia had already travelled on the path to socialism. A coda offers an explanation why distortions of Trotsky's record that are so harmful, one would think, to Trotsky and to the left in general have not been challenged by historians on the left: the distortions were introduced by these very same historians to advance other agendas, in particular, the cause of economic reform in the Soviet Union.

Although my essay 'Zinoviev: Populist Leninist' was published in 2008 (in the useful journal *The NEP Era: Soviet Russia, 1921–1928*), it was originally drafted much earlier. In fact, it was one of my first forays into the topic of 'what was Bolshevism?' after completing *Bread and Authority*. When writing my study of food-supply policies, I found that Zinoviev's speeches to various worker and peasant audiences were very useful for grasping how the Bolsheviks wanted to present themselves and their policies. And also, somewhat to my surprise, I found some attractive human features in Zinoviev's speeches that I miss in those of his fellow leaders. Zinoviev actually seemed to listen to what was bothering the people in his audience and to respond in an empathetic way. There is a breath of real life that is harder to find in the more abstract exhortations of more famous Bolshevik spokesmen.

When I wrote my Zinoviev essay, I presented his take on Lenin as something of an anomaly: look, here is a Lenin disciple who does *not* 'worry about workers' but who optimistically expects the Bolshevik message to resonate in wider and wider circles. Since then, I have discovered that Zinoviev was right, and the rest of us wrong, about Lenin's outlook. I unapologetically admit that my understanding of Lenin and the Bolshevik outlook comes in large part from Lenin's closest allies and life-long *soratniki*: Zinoviev, Kamenev, Krupskaya, and even the young Stalin. In particular, these leaders have made me see the centrality of the hegemony scenario to Bolshevism. Despite my changed understanding, I have let this essay stand as written. 'Populism' is now a considerably more charged political term than it was back then, so please heed my specific definition for purposes of my essay.

Part 5: NEP (1921–1930)

In Part 5, the views of Lenin and Bukharin about NEP – and therefore, about 'war communism' – are put under the microscope. 'Political Testament: Lenin, Bukharin, and the Meaning of NEP' was written for a conference held in 1989 in Moscow that represented one of the first times Russian and Western historians met together for a joint discussion. At the conference – rather cockily, as it now seems to me – I disputed the message attributed to Lenin's so-called 'political testament' by the ideologists of perestroika. Thus, in my very small way, I participated in the drama described in the final essay in this volume about perestroika and its use of NEP as a symbol.

The other essay in this section – 'Bukharin on Bolshevik "Illusions": "War Communism" vs. NEP' – was first published in 2000. The original article consisted of four mini case studies of Bukharin's rhetorical definition of 'war communism' and 'NEP'; for this volume, two of the case studies are summarized only. I originally set out only to examine Bukharin's view of 'war communism', but I quickly found out that these two concepts almost always appear in tandem. 'War communism' was only brought up in order to define and defend NEP. Did Bukharin need to shed his war-communist 'illusions' (his term) in order to become the most prominent defender of NEP? I show that Bukharin himself did not think so – and I tend to agree with him.

This seems like a good place to discuss the outsize role played by Bukharin in this volume. Rare is the essay where he does not make an appearance. His voice is heard at every stage of his career: his first published book in 1915, newspaper articles in 1917, Left Communist opposition in 1918, the *ABC of Communism* in 1919, his magnum opus *Economy of the Transition Period* in 1920, voluminous writings on NEP in the twenties, opposition and then solidarity with Stalin in the late twenties and early thirties, prison writings in the mid-thirties. Even his ghost returns in the late eighties as a patron saint of perestroika.

And yet in no way do I aim at a biographical sketch of Bukharin. There already exists a magisterial biography of Bukharin that situates him as an individual and a political leader in the history of his time.[34] My scholarly interest is not in Bukharin as an individual but Bukharin as *the* authoritative spokesman of Bolshevism. He appears so often in this book because he took on, or was given, the semi-official role of providing the specifically Bolshevik take on the problems of the day and the Bolshevik response to them. As the French scholar Maurice Andrieu points out:

> Bukharin is the main drafter and the main writer of all the communist programs, for Soviet Russia as well as for world communism ... He gives a Platform to the first congress of the Communist International (1919) and three drafts for a Program of the CI in 1922, 1924 and 1928 (with three reports to the congresses of the CI). He is also in charge of mass media (*Pravda*) and of the training for ideological managers (the 'red professors'). If there is one leading Bolshevik who develops the Bolshevik heroic scenario, he is Bukharin.[35]

Let me make a comparison that both sides would reject with indignation: Bukharin was the Karl Kautsky of Bolshevism. Just as Kautsky was *the* authoritative spokesman of revolutionary Social Democracy over several decades, Bukharin played the same role for the post-war heir of revolutionary Social Democracy. Both writers made their name with book-length commentaries on the party programme (*Erfurt Program* vs. *ABC of Communism*, co-authored with Evgenii Preobrazhensky). Both wrote on a wide variety of issues, with global scope, and always from the party point of view. Neither one was in any way a hack who put a spin on whatever was handed to them. On the contrary, they each had principled and consistent views that often prompted them to harsh criticism of this or that trend in party affairs. But each had an outlook that put *the mission of the party* front and centre. My party, may she always be right – but my party, right or wrong.

Given the nature of my research, then, I have ended up reading just about everything Bukharin wrote. Like the other top Bolshevik leaders, Bukharin expressed the common Bolshevik outlook with a personal inflection that stayed constant over the years. Here is a list of themes and emphases consistently displayed throughout his career that strike me as idiosyncratic:

---

34 Stephen F. Cohen, *Bukharin and the Bolshevik Revolution* (Cohen 1971).
35 'What Was Bolshevism? The Case of N.I. Bukharin' (Andreu 2012); see also Andreu 2003.

- An almost apocalyptic sense of a world in deep crisis, with only one way out, a way that necessarily entails deep suffering but offers entry into a new world of freedom. In my essay on Bukharin's prison writings included in this volume, I look closely at Bukharin's apocalyptic sensibility.
- An angry and indignant rejection of the 'philistine' who sees only the immediate chaos and does not realize that these costs (*izderzhki*) are painful necessities. Bukharin did not want to deny or minimize the human cost, even for revolution – he is often eloquent on its huge dimensions. Nevertheless, he insists, we cannot let ourselves be daunted or ultimately dismayed. (One cannot help speculating that one reason Bukharin is so angered by this kind of sceptical pessimism is that he is also arguing with himself.)
- An expectation that the modern world is headed for a mono-organizational society in which a central authority coordinates everything and there are no really independent institutions.[36] Social evolution is moving toward this same end-goal in both capitalist and socialist society. And, in and of itself, this prospect of a completely organized society is a good thing. The future society will be 'a triumphant symphony of creativity, a chorale ascending from earth to heaven' (as Bukharin put it in his prison writings).
- The continual use of what I call the 'same but different' topos. Socialist and capitalist institutions are in many respects the same, but also totally different. Why? Because the question of class rule makes *all* the difference. A straightforward example is the army: all armies must observe the same essential rules of military effectiveness, they must be centralized and disciplined whether they defend bourgeois governments or proletarian governments, yet the class content of the army's goals, the relations between ranks, and the nature of its political leadership means that structural similarity hides essential difference. The ultimate example of 'same but different' is the drive toward the mono-organizational society: diabolical when capitalists are in control, emancipatory when the proletariat is in control.

If there is such a thing as Bukharinism – and there probably isn't – these are its characteristic features.

In 1991, when 'Political Testament: Lenin, Bukharin, and the Meaning of NEP' was published, a footnote at the beginning stated the following: 'This essay is dedicated to my teachers Robert Tucker and Stephen Cohen, who, long before perestroika, emphasized the importance both of Lenin's testament and Nikolai Bukharin to the Soviet reform tradition.' I would like to expand,

---

36   I have taken over the term 'mono-organizational' from T.H. Rigby, who used it to describe the Soviet political system; see Rigby 1977, 'Stalinism and the Mono-Organizational Society'.

all too briefly, on this dedication. Most of the items in this volume were published by academic journals or university presses, following all the rules of academic respectability. Yet I have not had a full-time academic job since the early nineties.[37] One reason why I was able to survive and thrive as a published historian is the support and help that my Princeton teachers Robert Tucker and Steve Cohen provided, both psychologically and materially. They shoved many a commission in my direction, but more importantly, they showed a stubborn faith in my potential. Thank you.

Tucker and Cohen showed me the narrow path between the Scylla and Charybdis that beset a project like mine. Some academic historians tend to automatically assume that Lenin (other Bolsheviks barely exist) was a liar and a conman, and one shouldn't waste one's time trying to perceive some rational justification for his views. Some writers on the left tend to swoon over the unrivalled insight of their particular revolutionary hero. Many writers tend to describe 'communist ideology' as abstract propositions detached from the real hurly-burly of Soviet history. In their biographies and essays, Tucker and Cohen showed me the narrow path between these extremes by presenting Bolshevik leaders in deep context, without neglecting either long-term outlooks or real-life challenges.

The above paragraphs were written just before I learned of the unexpected death of Stephen Cohen in September 2020. I have lost a friend and mentor, and this book has lost a penetrating but sympathetic reader. One of the central themes in Steve's scholarly career was his passionate involvement with Russian society and its fight to find and travel down the path to its own unique destiny. As Russian historian Gennady Bordiugov wrote in a commemorative article, 'Stephen Cohen loved Russia, responded to its travails with all his heart, and played his direct part in its history.'[38] Steve was an iconoclast's iconoclast, ready to take on anything and anybody. I can only hope that some of these qualities are reflected in the following essays.

---

37 Since moving to Montreal in the mid-nineties, I have taught a number of courses at the Schulich School of Music at McGill University on the history of opera. The dividends of this experience for the present volume can be seen directly in my discussion of the Stalin-era cantatas of Prokofiev and Shostakovich, and indirectly throughout.

38 *Novaia gazeta*, 21 September 2020. Bordiugov and Katrina vanden Heuvel are co-editors of a volume of tributes to Steve Cohen published in Moscow to which I contributed: *His Way/Ego Put'* (AIRO-XX: 2021). For Cohen's large role in Russian discussions during the 1980s, see 'Perestroika Looks Back', included in this volume. My essay on Bukharin's prison writings ('Bukharin's Bolshevik Epic', included in this volume) depends entirely on material that Steve Cohen was instrumental in bringing to public view.

Part 6: The Stalin Era (1925–1953)

One of the first English-language publications of post-Soviet archival discoveries was *Stalin's Letters to Molotov, 1925–1936* by Yale University Press in 1995. The Yale publication was based on the superb Russian edition prepared by Oleg Naumov and Olev Khlevniuk. As American editor, I was de facto translator (the original draft of the translation needed much repair) and contributed a long Introduction along with an appendix about the kerfuffle over Max Eastman's *Since Lenin Died* (1925). *What Was Bolshevism?* contains the Introduction, now entitled 'Stalin at Work'. My aim was to write a stand-alone essay on the main themes revealed by Stalin's correspondence with Molotov and other Politburo members.

My thanks to Jonathan Brent at Yale University Press for taking me on board in my first major post-academic project. Our book was published with much hoopla, owing to its pioneer status as one of the first 'now it can be told' archival publications. I still remember with enjoyment the press conferences and other such publicity events. Nevertheless, I was no more than a supporting actor in this show. The spotlight fell on the companion volume published at the same time that had 'sensational new revelations' about Soviet spies in America – a topic of great interest to right-wing columnists in local newspapers across the land (those were the days when there *were* local newspapers across the land).[39]

The bulk of the letters in the Stalin-Molotov collection come from the 1920s. At first I planned to put this essay into the previous section about NEP, but, on reflection, I decided that the Stalin era really should be dated from 1925. The Stalin-Molotov letters show why: by that time, Stalin was the leader of the Soviet Union, and acknowledged as such by his comrades.

One of these comrades was Nikolai Bukharin, an ally of Stalin's in the twenties, an opponent at the end of the decade, and then a public figure tolerated but viewed suspiciously during the thirties. He was arrested in 1937 and executed after a show trial in 1938. We now know that during the many months in prison awaiting trial, Bukharin continued to express his own view of the world. His output during this period, both in quantity and quality, is astounding: an autobiographical novel, one book-length set of musings on cultural issues and another on philosophic issues, and over 170 poems. Thanks to the team of Stephen Cohen and Bukharin's widow Anna Larina, these writings became public in the 1990s, and they are now available in good English-language edi-

---

39   Harvey Klehr, John Earl Haynes, F.E. Firsov, *The Secret World of American Communism* (New Haven: Yale University Press, 1995).

tions. Bukharin also became a prominent presence in the Stalin-era imaginary as the archetypal *dvurushnik* or 'double-dealer' who wears a mask in order to wreak incalculable damage.[40] Paradoxically, his strongest defenders today also picture him as a *dvurushnik*, but a heroic one, whose surface loyalty was a disguise for subversive messages.

My essay on Bukharin's prison writings in this volume is based on a previously published review of his *Philosophical Arabesques* plus a previously unpublished study of the epic, indeed apocalyptic, view of the world found in his prison poem cycle *Transformation of the World*. I came across George Shriver's translation of the poem cycle in Open Books, a Seattle bookstore completely dedicated to poetry – an unexpected place to find a source for an essay on Stalinist politics.[41] Nevertheless, this poem cycle, which seems to be available only in English translation, is an unappreciated guide to Bukharin's view of Soviet history. This essay forced me to take up the vexed question of Bukharin's sincerity. While realizing that the question will never be definitely settled, I lean toward what I call the Horton school of Bukharin interpretation: like the Dr Seuss character of that name, Bukharin by and large meant what he said and said what he meant.

When I heard that my friends Louise McReynolds and Joan Neuberger were preparing a collection of essays on melodrama in Russia both before and after the revolution, I eagerly invited myself in, due to my interest in the aptly-named 'show trials' of the Stalin era, and, more broadly, to my feeling that the classical melodrama of the nineteenth century had much to tell us about political attitudes.[42] And indeed, the running *Pravda* account of the trial of the 'Anti-Soviet Bloc of Rights and Trotskyites' in 1938 does read like the play script of an unusually lurid melodrama. Taking the metaphor of 'show trial' seriously, I put these trials into the context of Soviet 'socialist realist' plays of the early 1930s ('Show Trials in the Stalin Era, on Stage and in Court'). At the time when this essay first appeared, very little had been written in English about the theatre of socialist realism, as opposed to novels, art, and film. This is unfortunate, because theatrical drama is an irreplaceable gateway to the emotional heart of cultural myths. In the Soviet case, as Russian theatrical historian Violetta Gudkova argues, the dramatists of the late twenties and early thirties were the originators of some

---

40 Instead of refusing to wear a mask, to wreak incalculable damage (written September 2020).

41 *The Prison Poems of Nikolai Bukharin* (Bukharin 2018).

42 *Imitations of Life: Two Centuries of Melodrama in Russia* (McReynolds and Neuberger 2002).

of the essential tropes of the Stalin era.[43] The importance of Soviet theatre is being increasingly recognized, and so this essay is the only one where I have added a few pages with updated references to more recent Western and Russian discussions.

One addition to our knowledge of the period is the publication of the first version of *Lies* by Aleksandr Afinogenov, the premier playwright of the Stalin era. Afinogenov sent this version of his play to Stalin, who responded first with constructive criticism, but later with dismissive disapproval. Thus *Lies* had only a few performances in Kharkov in 1933 before it was removed from the repertory. When I wrote 'Show Trials in the Stalin Era' in the 1990s, my knowledge of *Lies* and its fate was perforce based on a few quotations in secondary sources. A new essay entitled 'Vertigo: Masks and Lies in Stalin's Russia' takes advantage of more recent archival publications to document this revealing episode in more detail. Both the play and Stalin's reaction to it provide an unsettling entry into the vertiginous world of the Stalin era.

The final essay in this section was commissioned by the online periodical *Crisis and Critique* for a special issue on Stalin. My thanks to editors Agon Hamza and Frank Ruda for giving me the opportunity to present this material. As is my wont, I built 'Who Is Stalin? What Is He?' around three mini case studies: a special issue of *Life Magazine* on the wartime Soviet Union, patriotic cantatas composed during the period of 'the cult of personality', and Stalin's own self-mythologizing. Back in the days when I taught Soviet politics, I used the *Life Magazine* issue dated 29 March 1943 as a teaching tool about changing American attitudes toward what was then its great Other. *Life Magazine* throughout its life span provides an excellent introduction to the role of the Soviet Union in the American imaginary. The US attitude alternated between fear of a powerful rival and contempt for its lack of a consumer culture – between Sputnik and the dowdy attire of Nina Khrushcheva.

I still remember rummaging around the Montreal used bookstore Encore and stumbling on a CD of Gennady Rozhdestvensky's performance of Prokofiev's *Cantata on the Twentieth Anniversary of the Russian Revolution* (1938). At that time, I had barely heard of it. I looked at the text of the cantata found in the liner notes, and realized with a shock that one movement was taken straight from Lenin's *What Is to Be Done?*, a book I had recently translated and annotated. I also observed that whoever wrote the liner notes had no clue about the origin and significance of this text. I later discovered that the

---

43   Violetta Gudkova, 'Osobennosti "sovetskogo siuzheta": k tipologii rannei rossiiskoi dramy
      1920-x gg' (Gudkova 2006).

major academic examination of the cantata, while useful for tracking down the sources for the libretto, also showed very little understanding of the political and historical meaning of the passages from Marx, Lenin, and Stalin that Prokofiev chose to set.[44] And so, a personal mission was born – partially fulfilled by the present essay – to provide proper historical context to a great piece of music. Along with the *Anniversary Cantata*, I also look at Prokofiev's *Birthday Ode* (1939) and Shostakovich's *Song of the Forests* (1949).

The third mini case study in 'Who Is Stalin? What Is He?' delves into Stalin's own mythology about two subjects he saw as inseparable: Bolshevism and himself. Here I was able to benefit from some remarkable recent archival publications, in Russian and English, about Stalin's own long-time and very personal involvement in Soviet history-writing. This involvement climaxed in the legendary *Short Course* of 1938, which Stalin effectively authored by means of a massive rewrite of a committee draft. My thanks to David Brandenberger for an early look at this enormously revealing material.[45] As I show, Stalin's sense of self was very much wrapped up in his vision of the Bolshevik party line and in his own status (not without factual foundation) as its lifelong champion.

Readers who come to the Stalin era after reading through the earlier history of Bolshevism will ask themselves: to what extent was the official narrative of the Stalin era based on the earlier Bolshevik narratives presented here? My own answer uses Bukharin's favourite topos: the same but different. The core theme of class leadership remains, but painted in more grandiosely emotional colours and at the same time more violent and threatening. The spectrum of Stalin-era narratives is bounded by the Oath vs. the *Short Course*: the Oath taken by Stalin in his eulogy for Lenin after his death in 1924 that remains a classic exposition of the Bolshevik sense of mission and remained a potent symbol throughout the Stalin era vs. the *Short Course* of party history in 1938, with its rather dreary polemics of intra-party squabbles into whose dry bones Stalin sought to breathe his own passionate and self-absorbed involvement.

Prokofiev set Stalin's Oath to memorable music. In my discussion of the Prokofiev Cantata on the Anniversary of the Revolution, I make the follow-

---

44   Simon Morrison and Nelly Kravetz, 'The Cantata for the Twentieth Anniversary of October, or How the Specter of Communism Haunted Prokofiev' (Morrison and Kravetz 2006).

45   David Brandenberger and Mikhail Zelenov have edited two irreplaceable collections: *Stalin's Master Narrative: A Critical Edition of the* History of the Communist Party of the Soviet Union (Bolsheviks): Short Course, (Brandenberger and Zelenov 2019) and *'Kratkii kurs istorii VKP(b)': Tekst i ego istoriia v 2 chastiakh*, Chast' 1 (Brandenberger and Zelenov 2014).

ing contrast between the Lenin half and the Stalin half of the cantata: 'All of the Lenin movements carry a great sense of forward movement, but the two Stalin choral movements are much more static. [In Prokofiev's cantata,] Stalin appears as hierophant, as high priest, one who represents the sacred to the community and the community to the sacred.' This contrast has wider application. In the Stalin era, the Bolshevik narrative becomes more sacralized and also more paranoid, less dramatic and more melodramatic, less polemical and more dogmatic.

The essays in this section waver between the empirical Stalin and the mythologized Stalin, as well as these two in combination, the self-mythologizing Stalin. They also seem to waver between personal narratives – not only from Stalin, but from Bukharin – and the official narratives of the period. And perhaps this wavering between perspectives makes the section as a whole a not inaccurate reflection of an era. As I remark at the end of 'Stalin at Work', 'it would take the powers of a Dostoyevsky to fully describe the combination of cynicism and belief, of manipulation and sincerity, that resulted in the tragedy of Stalin and his times'.

Part 7: Perestroika (1984–1919)

Like several other essays in this volume, 'Perestroika Looks Back' was published long after it was written, as explained in a note at the beginning of the essay. 'Perestroika Looks Back' provides an appropriate endpiece for *What Was Bolshevism?*, since it shows one of the last avatars of the Bolshevik narrative (perestroika) defining itself by looking back to one of the earliest ones (NEP). Although the focus of the essay is primarily on the outsize role played by the NEP experience in the debates of the late 1980s, underneath we find Soviet society trying to come to terms with its Bolshevik origins and trying to decide, as a society, what Bolshevism really was.

The essay is thus the end of the road in more than one sense. With the detachment of hindsight, we can see that the perestroika reformers found NEP attractive, not as a pathway *toward* the mono-organizational society, as Bukharin did, but rather *away* from it. Or, more accurately, the lively and high-level public discussion of these issues led the reformers themselves to this conclusion. Thus my essay is, I hope, a reflection of the positive energy of late – very late – Soviet society.

Perhaps a good subtitle for *What Was Bolshevism?* would be 'The Story of a Story'. Like many another divine being, the Bolshevik narrative was strong and powerful as long as people believed in it. It faced many challenges, refurbished itself to meet new realities, inspired heroism and crimes. In many ways it defined the twentieth century. When the time came, it was freely abandoned by Russian society. The perestroika reformers asked themselves and asked society: which path leads to the temple? At the end, the answer consisted simply of a loss of faith in paths and in temples.

PART 1

Overview

∵

Ordinary Miracles: Lenin's Call for Revolutionary Ambition

1   Lenin's Text from *What Is to Be Done?*

[1] But a circle of inspiring leaders [*korifei*] such as Alekseev and Myshkin, Khalturin and Zheliabov are capable of political tasks in the most genuine and practical sense of the word – precisely because their impassioned preaching meets with an answering call from the masses awakening in an elemental fashion, and the leaders' seething energy is taken up and supported by the energy of the revolutionary class. [2] Plekhanov was a thousand times right when he not only identified the revolutionary class, not only proved the inevitability and unavoidability of its elemental awakening, but also presented to the 'worker circles' a great and noble political task. [3] But you refer to the mass movement that arose afterwards in order to lower this task – in order to narrow the energy and sweep of the activity of the 'worker circles'. [4] What is this, except an artisan's infatuation with his own artisanal limitations? [5] You brag about your practicality and you don't see (a fact known to any Russian *praktik*) what miracles for the revolutionary cause can be brought about not only by a circle but by a lone individual. [6] Or do you think that our movement can't produce real leaders [*korifei*] like those of the seventies? Why? Because we're unprepared? [7] But we are preparing ourselves, we will go on preparing ourselves – and we will not stop until we are prepared!

[8] True, over the stagnant waters of 'an economic struggle against the owners and the government', a layer of slime has unfortunately formed – people appear among us who get down on their knees and pray to elementality, gazing with beatitude (as Plekhanov put it) on the 'posterior' of the Russian proletariat. [9] But we will be able to free ourselves from this slime. [10] And it is precisely at the present time that the Russian revolutionary, guided by a genuinely revolutionary theory and relying on the class that is genuinely revolutionary and that is undergoing an elemental awakening, can at last – at last! – draw himself up to his full stature and reveal all his heroic [*bogatyrskii*] strength.

1.1   *Commentary*

The process by which certain passages from a famous book become emblems of the book as a whole and its author is not a straightforward one. In the Western academic tradition, Lenin's *What Is to Be Done?* has come to be represented by two or three passages where Lenin seems to be expressing his worries about lack of revolutionary fervour among the workers.[1] The rest of the book might as well not exist. In Russia, the passages regarded as central in the West are the ones that do not exist. In 2005, a book of Russian political quotations was published in which Lenin has the most extensive entry – 216 items – but his famous (in the West) remarks about the limitations of the 'spontaneous worker movement' do not appear.[2]

The quotations that constitute the Russian memory of *What Is to Be Done?* create a dramatically different sense of Lenin's outlook – not worry about workers but exhilaration about their elemental awakening, combined with a call for revolutionaries to think big.[3] One of these familiar quotations begins with the words 'in a tight little band, hands firmly joined, we are treading a steep and narrow way'. This passage was set to music by Sergei Prokofiev in his Cantata for the 20th Anniversary of the October Revolution; the propulsive energy of Prokofiev's setting is an excellent commentary on the spirit of *What Is to Be Done?*[4]

If I had to choose one passage from *What Is to Be Done?* to be ceaselessly recycled in textbooks and histories of Russia, I would pick the textual moment analysed here. It helps us understand why the young underground activists who were the book's first readers were so thrilled by it. One such activist, N. Valentinov, broke with Lenin soon thereafter. Yet he later reminisced that in his youth, he and his fellow activists were attracted by 'struggle, risk and danger'; just for this reason, '*What Is to Be Done?* struck just the right chord with us and we were

---

1   Lars T. Lih, 'How a Founding Document was Found, or One Hundred Years of Lenin's *What Is to Be Done?*' (Lih 2003). For an extended critique of the standard 'worry about workers' interpretation, see Lih, *Lenin Rediscovered* (Lih 2006); this book contains a new translation of *What Is to Be Done?* and the passage analysed here can be found on pp. 770–1.

2   Konstantin Dushenko, *Tsitaty iz russkoi istorii: spravochnik: 2200 tsitat ot prizvaniia variagov do nashikh dnei* (Dushenko 2006).

3   The phrase 'worry about workers' is taken from Reginald Zelnik, 'Worry about Workers: Concerns of the Russian Intelligentsia from the 1870s to *What Is to Be Done?*' (Zelnik 2003).

4   An excellent performance of Prokofiev's Cantata conducted by Gennady Rozhdestvensky can be found on Chandos CD 9095; live performances of the Cantata can also be found on YouTube. For more discussion, see 'Who Is Stalin, What Is He?', included in this volume.

only too eager to put its message into practice'.[5] Any interpretation of Lenin's book must account for this enthusiastic reaction.

Our passage also shows Lenin's idiosyncratic blending of aggressive polemic with what another early reader (Aleksandr Potresov, who also later became a determined foe of Lenin) called political poetry. In order to understand the impact of *What Is to Be Done?* on its target audience, we must have a sense of this poetry. In order to have a sense of the poetry, we must first wade into the polemical context.

What Is to Be Done? was written in late 1901 and early 1902 in order to propagate Lenin's plan for achieving a widely held goal: creating a nationwide party structure out of the existing scattered and isolated underground organizations of Russian Social Democracy. Lenin was a prominent member of the *Iskra* group, named for an underground newspaper printed in Western Europe and smuggled into tsarist Russia. The *Iskra* editorial board represented a coalition between the founders of Russian Social Democracy (Georgii Plekhanov, Vera Zasulich, Pavel Axelrod) and younger activists who had practical experience in underground work (Lenin, Iulii Martov, Aleksandr Potresov).

Iskra's highly ambitious political programme was to create a national party structure, secure for it a strong base in the burgeoning mass worker movement and thus give Russian Social Democracy an important role – perhaps even a leading role – in the imminent overthrow of the tsarist system. In support of these optimistic perspectives, Lenin and his comrades could point to an upsurge of politicized worker protest that had taken place in the early months of 1901.

By the time Lenin sat down to drafting his book, *Iskra's* programme had been subjected to withering criticism by a rival group of Social Democratic émigrés associated with the journal *Rabochee delo*. This group argued that *Iskra's* political aims were too ambitious, since 'political tasks in the actual and practical sense of the word – that is, in the sense of a rational and practical struggle for political demands – are not in general accessible to worker circles' (see sentence 1 for Lenin's paraphrase). In a way extremely typical for Lenin, he seeks to refute *Rabochee delo's* 'no we can't' with his own 'yes we can'.

In the passage we are analysing, Lenin rhetorically addresses these critics with an argument that can be paraphrased as follows:

You say that small underground circles cannot rally the Russian workers around the banner of an all-out fight against tsarism? This is true, perhaps, of an

---

5   Lih 2006, p. 13.

underground organization made up of people like yourself: people who whine about the difficulties facing them and use the workers as an excuse for their own lack of ambition and refusal to think big. But what if the underground organization was made up of genuinely inspiring leaders such as those who created *Narodnaia volia* (People's Will) in the 1870s? Those were true heroes with ambitious aims, although the situation they faced back then prevented them from achieving their full potential. But today we have exactly what they lacked: a mass movement that is looking for us – the revolutionaries of today – with the same energy that we revolutionaries have always sought out the workers.

Yes, there are practical difficulties that confront a persecuted, illegal underground organization that is trying to reach out to the masses. But instead of treating these difficulties as a challenge, you let them overwhelm you. You use the presence of the mass movement as an excuse to lower your ambitions. Precisely at the present time, even a lone activist who thinks big and who is able to convey to his audience the grandeur of his revolutionary dreams can achieve miracles!

The above paraphrase gives the logical outline of Lenin's argument. He wants to show that his opponents have set their sights too low, and he points to the heroic revolutionaries of the 1870s who accomplished great things (Lenin assumes that his audience agrees with this characterization). He then argues: think how much more they could have accomplished with the advantage we enjoy, namely, support from a growing mass movement full of energy and enthusiasm.

To back up his argument and inspire his readers, Lenin deploys an extensive battery of rhetorical devices, all of which rely on the contrast between high and low – between great and noble tasks vs. stagnant lack of ambition. A review of these devices will help put our passage in its full context.

One of Lenin's favourite techniques throughout his writings is to take a formulation of his opponents and turn it against them. One of the *Rabochee delo* group, Aleksandr Martynov, had advanced as a tactical slogan the idea of 'an economic struggle against the owners and the government', that is, using economic grievances to stoke anti-tsarist sentiment among the workers. The *Iskra* group objected that workers were already capable of responding to directly political appeals. Lenin loves to take a slogan like Martynov's and repeat it so often that it begins to lose meaning and appear ridiculous. The appearance of Martynov's slogan in our passage (sentence 8) is due to this rhetorical technique. The words 'worker circles' and 'practicality' are also taken directly from *Rabochee delo* (sentences 3, 5). Lenin wants to expose his critics as people who talk about 'practicality' as a way of condescending to the *praktik*, that is, the activist out on the frontlines of local underground organizations. In contrast, Lenin evokes the paradoxical image of the *praktik* as miracle-worker (sentence 5).

A more subtle and fundamental example of this ideological jiu-jitsu is Lenin's use of 'elemental' (*stikhiinyi*). Anyone picking up *What Is to Be Done?* will get the impression that Lenin was obsessed with the concept of *stikhiinost*. Indeed, scholarly consensus regards such an obsession as established fact.[6] Nevertheless, this impression is an illusion, due entirely to Lenin's habit of sarcastic repetition of his opponent's phrases. The only reason *stikhiinost* is prominent in *What Is to Be Done?* is because the term was used in September 1901 by Boris Krichevsky, a leading member of *Rabochee delo*. Lenin showed very little interest in the topic of *stikhiinost* either before or after this particular polemical joust.

The best English translation of *stikhiinyi* is 'elemental'. The etymological origin of the Russian word is the Greek *stoikheion* or 'element'; both the Greek and its Latin equivalent became associated with 'force of nature', a connotation that *stikhiinyi*, its Russian descendant, still retains. Nevertheless, in English translations of *What Is to Be Done?*, *stikhiinyi* is most often (but never consistently) translated as 'spontaneous'. There were practical reasons for this rendering. The polemics of *What Is to Be Done?* gave rise to constant use of the noun form *stikhiinost* (otherwise a rather rare word in Russian when compared to the adjective). Unfortunately, 'elemental' has no familiar noun form ('elementality' is the best I could come up with), whereas 'spontaneous' does. Furthermore, the phrase '*stikhiinyi* element' is a common one in *What Is to Be Done?* And so, out of a purely practical translation problem arose a great subject of theoretical debate: Lenin's attitude toward 'spontaneity'.[7]

As mentioned, the word 'elemental' is centrally connected to the idea of a force of nature – a metaphor that can go in many directions. A force of nature can be seen as unfocused, unorganized, violent and destructive. When this set of connotations is in the forefront, Lenin is 'against' elementality – as was Russian Social Democracy as a whole, which saw its task precisely as organizing and channelling originally chaotic worker protests. In fact, the Menshevik wing of Russian Social Democracy was considerably more focused on the need to overcome elementality than was the Bolshevik wing.[8]

---

6   For example see Leopold Haimson, 'Lenin's Revolutionary Career Revisited' (Haimson 2004).
7   In my translation of *What Is to Be Done?*, I avoided these difficulties by retaining the Russian word (Lih 2006). In this shorter translation, I have used 'elemental' and 'elementality'. For a full word history of *stikhiinost*, see Lih 2006, pp. 616–28.
8   For example, in a Menshevik comment from April 1917, we read that Lenin is dangerous

The metaphor of a force of nature can also be mobilized to evoke the idea of a mighty and irresistible power that is working, not against you, but for you. To understand our passage, we have to see that Lenin uses 'elementality' in both negative and positive senses. The negative sense is associated with his polemical opponents, who (according to Lenin) pray to elementality, that is, they not only passively accept the given situation, the current limitations, but they do so almost as a matter of principle. Lenin relays Plekhanov's joke about idealizing the proletariat from behind, with no sense that the proletariat itself is moving on (sentence 8).

The positive connotations of 'force of nature' – as inevitable, unstoppable, transformative power – are mobilized in the image of the 'elemental awakening' of the workers, an image used three times in our passage (sentences 1, 2, 10). This particular force of nature is working for us, so we should have the confidence to think big – this is the heart of Lenin's message, not only in *What Is to Be Done?* but throughout his writings.

Lenin repeated ad nauseam not only his opponents' formulations but his own newly-minted polemical coinages. One example that resounds throughout *What Is to Be Done?* is 'kowtowing to elementality', a variant of which is found in our passage (sentence 8). Another example is *kustarnichestvo*, which I have translated as 'artisanal limitations' (other renderings include 'amateurism', 'primitivism'). A *kustar* is a traditional Russian craftsman, working for a local market with little or no division of labour. When applied to party organization, the *kustar* metaphor referred to local party committees that were isolated and separated from each other, due to absence of nation-wide organizational structures. With this meaning, Lenin's coinage became part of the standard lexicon of Russian Social Democracy. In our passage, *kustarnichestvo* plays an additional role as yet another evocation of thinking small and unambitiously (sentence 4).

Opposed to the *kustar* in Lenin's system of images is the *korifei*, an exalted word for 'leader' (sentences 1, 6). Its etymological origin is the coryphaeus, the leader of the chorus in Greek tragedy.[9] As examples of *korifei*, Lenin lists 'Alekseev and Myshkin, Khalturin and Zheliabov'. These populist revolutionaries

---

because 'he can recruit new supporters from among the revolution's unconscious and spontaneous [*stikhiinye*] elements' (Michael Hickey, *Competing Voices from the Russian Revolution* [Hickey 2011, p. 115]).

9   The word and its exalted overtones are used in an ironic way in one version of a well-known prison-camp song by Yuz Aleshkovsky: 'Tov. Stalin, vy bol'shoi uchenyi, V iazykoznanii prosto korifei' (Com. Stalin, you are a great scholar, just a really great leader in linguistics). One of Stalin's last writings was *Marxism and Linguistics* (1950).

from the 1870s have specific connotations that are mobilized by Lenin in his argument. First and foremost, they were 'inspiring' due to selfless dedication and their 'impassioned preaching' of ambitious revolutionary goals (sentence 1). The four leaders evoked by Lenin symbolize the union of workers and intelligentsia that was a key aspect of the new mass movement Lenin saw arising. These leaders also represent a shift in populist thinking from aiming at purely economic revolution to working for a political one, even if this new commitment was expressed first of all in the dead-end tactic of individual terrorism (the assassination of Alexander II in 1881). Finally, all of these *korifei* ended badly, personally and politically: death in Siberia or on the scaffold, combined with a stalled and demoralized revolutionary movement.

There is an autobiographical aspect to Lenin's evocation of populist *korifei* that might have resonated with some of his readers. Lenin's older brother Aleksandr Ulyanov was himself an inspiring and dedicated revolutionary leader who got embroiled in a futile attempt to assassinate the tsar in 1884 and died on the scaffold. Where Aleksandr failed, Vladimir was determined to succeed – because in the following two decades, a genuine mass movement had sprung up, and Russian revolutionaries had also discovered Marxism, a 'genuinely revolutionary theory' (sentence 10). This evolution in the Russian revolutionary tradition is vividly incarnated in Plekhanov, whom Lenin cites not only as an authority but as a living link between the *korifei* of the 1870s and the *praktiki* of the new century.

Lenin's rhetorical opposition between high ambition and low routine even finds expression in sound effects. Alliteration of v and k adds to the solemnity of 'great and noble' tasks (*vysokii i velikii*) (sentence 2). In contrast, the hissing z's and i's of 'to lower' (*prinizit*) and 'to narrow' (*suzit*) strengthen the imagery of reptilian sloth (sentence 3). An even lower life form is evoked by the image of slimy pond scum (sentence 8). In contrast to all this creeping, crawling stagnation is the heroic *bogatyr* who strides forth to do battle in the final sentence. The *bogatyri* were the giant marvellous heroes of the Russian folk epics. Lenin could have chosen no better word to evoke his romantic conception of the Social Democratic *praktik* as people's hero.

The scholarly consensus that Lenin's central theme was worry about workers arises from focusing all attention on a few of Lenin's formulations about *stikhinost*/elementality/'spontaneity', while completely ignoring the overall system of images that governs Lenin's rhetoric throughout *What Is to Be Done?* – a rhetoric that continually contrasts high ambition to low routine, to the decided advantage of the former. If our passage had been chosen as the exemplary textbook quote from *What Is to Be Done?*, we would have a very different and much more accurate idea of Lenin's outlook.

'It is precisely at the present time that the Russian revolutionary ... can at last – at last! – draw himself up to his full stature' (sentence 10). The repeated 'at last' reveals the emotional investment that Lenin put into his argument and that so impressed the first readers of *What Is to Be Done?* The same emotional investment is manifest throughout Lenin's career. We will conclude our consideration of his 1902 book with a passage from early 1919, when Lenin still thought the Russian revolution would quickly spread to Western Europe (he was soon to be disillusioned):

> Comrades, behind us there is a long line of revolutionaries who sacrificed their lives for the emancipation of Russia. The lot of the majority of these revolutionaries was a hard one. They endured the persecution of the tsarist government, but it was not their good fortune to see the triumph of the revolution. The happiness that has fallen to our lot is all the greater. Not only have we seen the triumph of our revolution, not only have we seen it become consolidated amidst unprecedented difficulties, creating a new kind of government and winning the sympathy of the whole world, but we are also seeing the seed sown by the Russian revolution spring up in Europe.[10]

Lenin's hopeful words in 1919 provide a gloss on our passage from *What Is to Be Done?*, a gloss that brings out the essential political poetry without the dross of momentary polemics. In both passages, the ongoing force of history has made meaningful the sacrifices of earlier generations of Russian revolutionaries (including Lenin's brother Aleksandr Ulyanov). In 1919, Lenin asserts that the isolated *praktiki* of 1902 had in fact accomplished miracles: the Russian proletariat, led by the party, had carried out a revolution that is now inspiring the whole world. No wonder so many of the first readers of *What Is to Be Done?* were themselves inspired by Lenin's injunction to think big.

---

10   Lenin 1958–1965: 38:215 (March 1919).

CHAPTER 2

The Soviet Union and the Path to Communism

The heart of the governing ideology of the Soviet Union was an image of itself as a traveller on the path to communism. This image was embedded in the narrative of class struggle and class mission created by Karl Marx and first embodied in a mass political movement by European Social Democracy. When Russian Social Democrats took power in October 1917, they founded a regime that was unique in its day because of their profound sense that the country had embarked on a journey of radical self-transformation.

Throughout its history, the Soviet Union's self-definition as a traveller on the road to socialism coloured its political institutions, its economy, its foreign policy and its culture. The inner history of Soviet ideology is thus the story of a metaphor – a history of the changing perceptions of the road to communism. In 1925, Nikolai Bukharin's book *Road to Socialism* exuded the confidence of the first generation of Soviet leaders. Sixty years later, the catch-phrase 'which path leads to the temple?' reflected the doubts and searching of the perestroika era. Right to the end, Soviet society assumed that there *was* a path with a temple at the end of it and that society had the duty to travel down that path.

1   Marxism and the Class Narrative

The Soviet Union's vision of the journey's end – socialist society – was in many respects the common property of the European left as a whole. The distinctive contribution of the Marxist tradition to the new revolutionary regime in Russia was a narrative about how socialist society would come to be. Marxism provided a description, not only the protagonists whose interaction would result in socialism, but also of their motivations, the tasks they set themselves and the dramatic clashes between them that propelled society forward.

Marx shaped the Soviet Union's constitutive narrative in three crucial ways. First, the narrative was about *classes*. The Marxist understanding of 'class' is deeply shaped by seeing classes as characters in a narrative, with motivations, will, purposes and the ability to perceive and overcome obstacles. The role of 'scientific socialism' was to give a strong underpinning to this narrative. The doctrine of surplus value, for example, implied the unavoidable conflict between proletariat and bourgeoisie and this in turn gave the proletariat as a class its essential motivation.

Second, the central episode in Marx's world-historical narrative portrays the process by which the industrial proletariat recognizes, accepts and carries out the *historical mission* of taking political power as a class and using it to introduce socialism. This central episode is summed up by the phrase 'dictatorship of the proletariat'. The proletariat needs *political* power in order to carry out its mission for two sets of reasons: the defensive/repressive need to protect socialism from hostile classes and the constructive need for society-wide institutional transformation. Although a class dictatorship is only possible when the class in question was in a position to carry out its class interest fully and without compromise, Marx always assumed that the proletarian class dictatorship would rest securely on the voluntary support of the other non-elite classes.

Third, Marx brought the world-historical narrative home by assigning a mission here and now to dedicated socialist revolutionaries. 'The emancipation of the working classes must be conquered by the working classes themselves.' The famous motto of the First International can be understood in two ways. On one reading, the motto tells revolutionaries from other classes to butt out: the emancipation of the working class is the business of the workers and no one else. The motto was understood in this way by the French Proudhonists who were perhaps the most important constituency within the First International.

On another reading, the motto not only refuses to close the door to non-proletarian revolutionaries but actually invites them in. If only the workers themselves can bring about their liberation, then it is imperative that they come to understand what it is they need to do and that they obtain the requisite organizational tools. This mission of preparing the working class for its mission was incumbent upon *any* socialist who accepted the Marxist class narrative, no matter what his or her social origin.

2   Revolutionary Social Democracy: 'The Merger of Socialism and the Worker Movement'

The basic self-definition of the Bolsheviks was that they were the Russian embodiment of 'revolutionary Social Democracy'. Their angry rejection of the label 'Social Democracy' in 1918 was meant to be a defiant assertion of continued loyalty to what the label once stood for. When the pioneers of Russian Social Democracy looked west in the 1890s, they saw a powerful, prestigious and yet still revolutionary movement. They saw mass *worker* parties, inspired by the Marxist class narrative, that continued to advance despite the persecutions of such redoubtable enemies as Chancellor Bismarck. They saw a set of innovative institutions – a party of a new type – that set out to bring the message to the workers and instil in them an 'alternative culture'.[1]

The man who gave canonical expression to the elaborated class narrative of Social Democracy was Karl Kautsky. Kautsky is remembered as the most influential theoretician of international Social Democracy, but in certain key respects – particularly in the case of the fledgling Russian Social Democracy – Kautsky's role went beyond influence. In 1892, Kautsky wrote *The Erfurt Program*, a semi-official commentary on the recently adopted programme of the Social Democratic Party of Germany (SPD). This book *defined* Social Democracy for Russian activists – it was the book one read to find out what it meant to be a Social Democrat. In 1894, a young provincial revolutionary named Vladimir Ulianov translated *The Erfurt Program* into Russian just at the time he was acquiring his life-long identity as a revolutionary Social Democrat.

In *The Erfurt Program*, Kautsky defined Social Democracy as 'the merger [*Vereinigung*] of socialism and the worker movement'. This slogan summarised not only the proletarian mission to introduce socialism, but also the Social Democratic mission of filling the proletariat with an awareness of its task. Kautsky's formula also provided Social Democracy with its own origin story. According to the merger formula, Social Democracy was a *synthesis*. As Kautsky put it, each earlier strand of both socialism and the worker movement possessed '*ein Stückchen des Richtigen*', a little bit of the truth.[2] This little bit of truth could be preserved, but only if its one-sidedness was transcended. In this way, the merger formula implied a two-front polemical war against all who defended the continued isolation of either socialism or the worker movement – against anarchism as well as reformism. The technical term within Social Democratic discourse for the effort to keep the worker-class struggle free from socialism was *Nurgewerkschaftlerei*, 'trade-unions-only-ism'. (Since England was the classical home of this anti-Social Democratic ideology, the English words 'trade union' were used by both German and Russian Social Democrats to make an '-ism' that was equivalent for *Nurgewerkschaftlerei*. To render Lenin's epithet *tred-iunionizm* as 'trade-unionism' is really a mistranslation, since it implies that Lenin was hostile toward trade unions rather than toward a specific ideology that denied the need for a Social Democratic worker party.) A corresponding '*Nur*' term could have been coined for bomb-throwing revolutionaries who continued to think that it was a waste of time to propagandize and educate the working class as a whole prior to the revolution.

---

1 Vernon Lidtke, *The Alternative Culture: Socialist Labor in Imperial Germany* (Lidtke 1985).
2 Karl Kautsky, *Die historische Leistung von Karl Marx* (Kautsky 1908, p. 36).

By assigning the task of introducing socialism to the working class itself, the merger formula implied an exalted sense of a world historical mission. The most powerful source for this aspect of the Social Democratic narrative was Ferdinand Lassalle, the forgotten founding father of modern socialism. The cult of Lassalle that was an integral part of the culture of the German Social Democratic party was based on his thrilling insistence during his brief two years of proto-Social Democratic agitation (1862–1864) that the workers, the despised fourth estate, must accept the noble burden of an exalted mission. 'The high and world-wide honour of this destiny must occupy all your thoughts. Neither the load of the oppressed, nor the idle dissipation of the thoughtless, nor even the harmless frivolity of the insignificant, are henceforth becoming to you. You are the rock on which the Church of the present is to be built.'[3] Anyone who pictures Social Democracy as based on dry and deterministic 'scientific socialism' and overlooks the fervent rhetoric of good news and saving missions has missed the point.

The merger formula also reveals the logic that drove the creation of the party-led alternative culture. The fantastic array of newspapers, the sporting clubs, the socialist hymns, all under the leadership of a highly organized national political party – this entire innovative panoply was meant to merge in the most profound way possible the new socialist outlook with the outlook of each worker.

Social Democracy's self-proclaimed mission of bringing the good news of socialism to the workers meant that it had a profound stake in political democracy and particularly in political liberties such as freedom of speech, press, and assembly. Political liberties were only a means – but they were an absolutely essential means. In an image that profoundly influenced Russian Social Democracy, Kautsky asserted that political liberties were 'light and air for the proletariat'.[4] The vital importance of political liberties was a key sector in the two-front polemical war again both isolated trade-union activists and isolated revolutionaries, both of whom tended to ignore or even scorn the need for fighting absolutism and broadening political liberties.

Indeed, Social Democracy pictured itself, accurately enough, as one of the principal forces sustaining political democracy in turn-of-the-century Europe. The reasoning behind this claim is the basis for the political strategy to which the Russian Social Democrats gave the name of 'hegemony in the democratic revolution'. The bourgeoisie does indeed have a class interest in full parliamen-

---

3   Ferdinand Lassalle, *The Workingman's Programme* (*Arbeiter-programm*) (Lassalle 1899, p. 59).
4   Karl Kautsky, *Das Erfurter Programm* (Kautsky 1965, p. 219).

tary democracy and political liberties, but as time goes by, the bourgeoisie is less and less ready to act on this interest. The same reason that makes Social Democracy eager for democracy (political liberties make the merger of social-ism and the worker movement possible and therefore inevitable) douses the enthusiasm of the bourgeoisie. Thus Social Democracy becomes the only con-sistent fighter for democracy. In fact, some major democratic reforms will prob-ably have to wait until the dictatorship of the proletariat and the era of socialist transformation. In the meantime, bourgeois democracy is much too important to be left to the bourgeoisie.

The defence of democracy was a *national* task in which Social Democ-racy saw itself as a fighter for the here-and-now interests of *all* the non-elite classes. In the Social Democratic narrative, the proletariat did not look on all the other labouring classes with 'contempt' (as is often stated). The proletariat was rather pictured as the inspiring leader of what might be called follower classes. As Kautsky explained in a section of *The Erfurt Program* entitled *Das Sozialdemokratie und das Volk*, the leadership role of the proletariat had two aspects. In the long run, peasants and urban petty-bourgeoisie would see that their own deepest aspiration – to assert control over their productive activ-ity – could only be attained through the 'proletarian socialism' that aimed for centralized social control rather than small-scale individual ownership. In the short run, the non-elite classes would realize – sooner rather than later – that nationally organized and militant Social Democracy was the only effective defender of their current perceived interests. In the Marxist texts that most influenced Lenin, the dominant note is not pessimism and fear of, say, the peasants but rather an unrealistic optimism that they would soon accept the leadership of the organized workers.

3   Russian Social Democracy

From the point of view of a young Russian revolutionary in the 1890s choosing a political identity, what was the greatest obstacle to choosing to be a revolution-ary Social Democrat? A Social Democrat had to reject the pessimistic horror that capitalist industrialization had inspired in earlier Russian revolutionaries, but this rejection was hardly an obstacle – on the contrary, it was an impetus for optimistic energy in the face of what seemed by the 1890s to be inevitable economic processes. The minuscule dimensions of the new Russian industrial working class also hardly constituted an obstacle, since organizing and propa-gandizing even the relatively few Russian workers offered plenty of scope for activity.

The greatest obstacle – the crucial distinction between Russia and the countries where Social Democracy flourished – was the *lack of political liberties*. The tsarist autocracy seemed to make 'Russian Social Democrat' something of an oxymoron. The whole meaning of Social Democracy revolved around propaganda and agitation on a national level. What then was the point of even talking about Social Democracy in a country where even prominent and loyal members of the elite were prohibited from publicly speaking their mind?

Accordingly, many revolutionaries adopted severely modified forms of Social Democratic ideas. Some accepted the importance of achieving political liberty but concluded that a mass movement was a non-starter as a way of overthrowing tsarism and obtaining needed liberties. Others accepted the importance of organizing the working class but felt that political liberties were not *so* fundamental that overthrowing the autocracy needed to be a top priority task for the workers.

The central strand of Russian Social Democracy – the strand that ran from the Liberation of Labour group (Georgii Plekhanov, Pavel Akselrod and Vera Zasulich) in the early 1880s through the *Iskra* organization of 1900–1903 and then through both the Menshevik and Bolshevik factions that emerged from *Iskra* – tried to be as close to western-style Social Democracy as circumstances would allow. The guiding principle of Russian Social Democracy can be summed up as: Let us build a party as much like the German SPD as possible under absolutist conditions so we can overthrow the tsar and obtain the political liberties that we need to make the party even more like the SPD!

As worked out by the polemics of the underground newspaper *Iskra* at the turn of the century, this basic principle led to the following assertions. The Russian working class *can* be organized by revolutionaries working in underground conditions. The workers *can* understand the imperative of political liberty both for the sake of immediate economic interests and for the long-run prospects of socialism. Their militant support of a democratic anti-tsarist revolution will instigate other non-elite classes and even the progressive parts of the elite to press home their own revolutionary demands. Thanks primarily to the militancy of the working class, the coming Russian democratic revolution will have a more satisfactory outcome than, say, the half-baked German revolution in the middle of the nineteenth century, since it will attain the greatest possible amount of political liberty. And these political liberties will allow the education and organization of the Russian working class on an SPD scale, thus creating the fundamental prerequisite of socialist revolution: a class ready and able to take political power.

Compared to the trends they were combating, the *Iskra* team stands out by its *optimism* about the potential of the Russian working class to organize and become an effective and indeed leading national political force under tsarism. *Iskra* believed that this potential could only be realized given the existence of a well-organized and highly motivated Social Democracy – a lesson they learned from the astounding success of German Social Democracy. Many readers of Lenin's *What Is to Be Done?* have concluded that Lenin wanted a nationally organized party of disciplined activists because he had pessimistically given up on the revolutionary inclinations of the workers. In reality, Lenin wanted an SPD-type party – that is, a party with a national centre and a full-time corps of activists – because of his optimistic confidence that even the relatively backward Russian proletariat living under tsarist repression would enthusiastically respond to the Social Democratic message. Lenin's opponents were the sceptical ones on this crucial issue.

It is completely anachronistic to see Lenin assuming in 1902 that the party could accomplish its task only if it had control of the state and a monopoly of propaganda. His idea of an effective party in 1902 was an organization that was efficient enough to publish and distribute a national underground newspaper in regular fashion and that was surrounded by a core of activists who were inspired by and could inspire others with the good news of Social Democracy. Thus the key sentence in *What Is to Be Done?* is: 'You brag about your practicality and you don't see (a fact known to any Russian *praktik*) what miracles for the revolutionary cause can be brought about not only by a circle but by a lone individual.'[5]

Given later events, it is difficult to remember that a central plank in the *Iskra* platform was the crucial importance of political liberties. *Iskra* insisted to other socialists that achieving political liberty had to be an urgent priority. It insisted to other anti-tsarist revolutionaries that only proletarian leadership in the revolution would ensure the maximum achievable amount of political liberty. They drummed home in their propaganda and agitation the vital importance of what might be called the four S's: *svoboda slova, sobraniia, stachek,* freedom of speech, assembly and strikes. The Social Democratic narrative absolutely required these freedoms to operate.

Overthrowing the autocracy was a *national* task that would advance the interests of almost every group in Russian society. Following the logic of the Social Democracy class narrative, *Iskra* assumed that a socialist party could and should assume the leadership role in achieving a democratic republic. They engaged in a complicated political strategy whereby they supported anti-tsarist liberals, fought with the liberals for the loyalty of the non-elite classes and tried

---

5   *What Is to Be Done?* (Lenin 1958–1965); for an analysis of the quoted passage, see 'Ordinary Miracles: Lenin's Call For Revolutionary Ambition', included in this volume.

to make the non-elite classes aware of the necessity of conquering as much political liberty as possible in the upcoming revolution.

Iskra conducted the usual Social Democratic two-front polemical war. The prominence of *What Is to Be Done?* means that we see only one front of the war, namely, the attack against the 'economists' who allegedly wanted to keep the workers aloof from the great merger. In *Iskra*'s activity (and in Lenin's writings) as a whole during this period, the other front in the war was just as prominent or even more so: the attack against the terrorists who allegedly believed that an organized mass worker movement was a pipe-dream that would only delay the revolution.

After 1903, the *Iskra* organization broke up into two Social Democratic factions. The Menshevik/Bolshevik split has achieved mythic status as the place where two roads diverged and taking one rather than the other made all the difference. Counterintuitive as it may seem, the Menshevik leaders originally dismissed Lenin as someone who put *too high* a priority on achieving political liberties, who would therefore allow Social Democracy to be exploited by bourgeois revolutionaries and who neglected the specifically *socialist* task of instilling hostility between worker and capitalist.

Similarly, Bolshevism prior to World War I can almost be defined as the Social Democratic faction most fanatically insistent on the importance of political liberties. Lenin's precepts were: *don't* be satisfied with bourgeois leadership of the bourgeois revolution because the liberals will not push the revolution to achieve its maximum gains. *Don't* be satisfied with the meagre liberties provided by the post-1905 Stolypin regime. *Search* for the most radically democratic allies among the non-elite classes. *Preserve* at all costs a party base in the illegal underground that is the only space in Russia for truly free speech, the only place where socialists could proudly unfurl their banner.

4   The Class Narrative in a Time of Troubles

In 1914 a group of Bolsheviks – the party's representatives in the national legislative Duma – met to compare impressions about the stunning news that the German SPD had voted in favour of war credits for the German government. This news shook them profoundly because 'all Social Democrats had "learned from the Germans" how to be socialists'. The deputies agreed on one thing: the erstwhile model party had betrayed revolutionary socialism.[6]

---

6   Aleksandr Shliapnikov, *Kanun semnadtsatogo goda, Semnadtsatyi god* (Shliapnikov 1992–1994, 1:61).

Six years later at the Second Congress of the Third International, another party presented itself as an international model: the Bolsheviks themselves. This new Bolshevik model, profoundly marked by the intervening six years of war and civil war, could not have been predicted from knowledge of pre-war Bolshevism. A party that had put the achievement of 'bourgeois democracy' in Russia at the centre of its political strategy now angrily rejected bourgeois democracy and all its works. A party that had propagandized the crucial importance of political liberties had become notorious for dictatorial repression and a state monopoly of mass media.

And yet, despite all these changes, the Bolsheviks claimed to remain loyal to the old class narrative – indeed, they claimed to be the *only* loyal ones. Bolshevism as a factor in world history – as an alternative model for socialist parties and as the constitutive myth of the Soviet Union – was based on the Social Democratic class narrative as it emerged from the severe and distorting impact of an era of world crisis.

Three major developments influenced the new version of the class narrative. The first was the sense that western Social Democracy had betrayed its own cause. Before 1914, the western European party leaders had announced in solemn convocation that they would make war impossible by using the threat of revolution – and now they not only refused to make good on this threat but turned into cheerleaders for their respective national war machines! The next influence was the apocalyptic world war. The adjective is hardly too strong: the war seemed to the Bolsheviks to present mankind with a choice between socialism and the collapse of civilization.

The third influence was the Bolshevik experience as a ruling party. The Bolsheviks understood the October revolution as the onset of the central episode of the class narrative – the long-awaited proletarian conquest of power. All of their experiences in power were deeply informed by this narrative framework. In turn, the rigors and emergencies of the civil-war period modified their understanding of the framework. Just as fundamentally, the very concept of a class in power was discovered in practice to contain a host of hitherto unsuspected consequences and implications.

The experience of being a ruling party responsible for all of society meant dealing with other classes. This necessity intensified a fear already latent in the class narrative – the fear of becoming infected by contact with other classes and losing the proletarian qualities needed to accomplish the great mission. A group often hailed as the conscience of the party, the Worker Opposition of 1920–1921, was also the one that most energetically followed out the resulting logic of purge, purification and suspicion.

When the Bolsheviks closed down the bourgeois and even the socialist press, they shocked many socialists into realizing their own commitment to 'bour-

geois democracy'. The short-term justification offered by the Bolsheviks was
that coercion was needed to complete any revolution, as shown by the history
of bourgeois revolutions. This argument was not as fateful as the decision to create an exclusive state monopoly of the mass media. This decision paradoxically
had strong roots in the pre-war class narrative. The central reason that Social
Democracy required freedom of speech was to be able to raise the consciousness of its worker constituency, and Social Democrats had always envied the
tools of indoctrination at the command of the elite classes. If one mark of an
SPD-type party was the massive effort to inculcate an alternative culture, then
one possible path for an SPD-type party in power was to create what has been
called the 'propaganda state'. Grigorii Zinoviev explained why the Bolsheviks
chose this path:

> As long as the bourgeoisie holds power, as long as it controls the press,
> education, parliament and art, a large part of the working class will be
> corrupted by the propaganda of the bourgeoisie and its agents and driven
> into the bourgeois camp ... But as soon as there is freedom of the press
> for the working class, as soon as we gain control of the schools and
> the press, the time will come – it is not very far off – when gradually,
> day by day, large groups of the working class will come into the party
> until, one day, we have won the majority of the working class to our
> ranks.[7]

The Bolshevik self-definition as the proletariat in power implied that the new
regime had begun the process of socialist transformation. It did not necessarily imply anything definite about the depth of that transformation at any one
time nor even about its tempo. Unfortunately, there are two deep-rooted misunderstandings about what the Bolsheviks actually did claim about the road
to socialism in the early years of the regime. The first misunderstanding is
associated with the phrase 'smash the state'. Many have felt that Lenin's use
of this phrase in *State and Revolution* (written in 1917) was a promise (whether
sincere or not) to bring about an immediate end to any repressive or centralized state. Some writers have gone further and posited a genuine if temporary
conversion to anarchism that led to a massive attempt in 1917–1918 to create
a 'commune-state' that was the polar opposite of the 'dictatorship of the proletariat'.[8] The other misunderstanding is associated with the phrase 'short cut

---

7   *Workers of the World and Oppressed Peoples, Unite!: Proceedings and Documents of the Second
    Congress, 1920* (Riddell 1991, p. 153).
8   Neil Harding, *Leninism* (Harding 1996).

to communism'. Although the Bolsheviks never used this phrase, scholars too often employ it when describing the policies of 'war communism' in 1917–1920. According to the short-cut thesis, the Bolsheviks thought that measures put in place to fight the civil war had accelerated the pace of social transformation to the point of bringing Russia to the brink of a leap into full socialism.

These two myths obscure the real innovation in the Bolshevik version of the class narrative – one which the Bolsheviks leaders themselves insisted upon. This innovation was the thesis that a proletarian revolution was *necessarily* accompanied by a massive, society-wide political and economic crisis. As Lev Trotsky summed it up in an epigram from 1922: 'Revolution opens the door to a new political system, but it achieves this by means of a destructive catastrophe.'[9] Far from implying any acceleration of socialist transformation – as suggested by both 'smash the state' and 'short cut to communism' – this quasi-inevitable crisis meant that the new era in world history would be inaugurated by a series of severe challenges to any meaningful transformation.

Lenin's use of 'smash the state' in 1917 was conducted entirely within the framework of the class narrative: the proletariat wrests political power away from the bourgeoisie and uses it to gradually remove the class contradictions that make a repressive state necessary. In his celebrated epigram about the cook running the affairs of the state, Lenin promised only that the new regime would set about *teaching* the cook how to administer society. 'Smash the state' always meant 'smash the bourgeois state *in order to* replace it with a proletarian state'. The new proletarian state might have many of the same institutions and even many of the same personnel – and yet class rule would have changed hands and this made *all* the difference.

Bukharin drew out another implication of the 'smash the state' scenario. If the bourgeois state had to be smashed and the proletarian state had to be built up, a time of breakdown would have to be endured – and therefore social breakdown was no argument against revolution. The paradigmatic instance of this process was the army. Naturally the old bourgeois army *had* to disintegrate, since its use as a weapon against the revolution had to be forestalled, its officers could not be trusted and anyway soldiers in a revolutionary period would simply no longer obey orders. The army thus falls apart, but 'every revolution smashes what is old and rotten: a certain period (a very difficult one) must pass before the new arises, before a beautiful home starts to be built upon the ruins of the old pig-sty'. Eventually a new proletarian army arises. This army would fight according to the standard rules for an effective war machine and it would

---

9   Lev Trotsky, *Sochineniia* (Trotsky 1925–1927, 12: 327–31).

recruit as many 'bourgeois military specialists' as possible – of course, under the watchful eye of the commissars appointed by the new proletarian state authority.[10]

Much confusion will be avoided once we realize that the Bolsheviks saw the mighty Red Army not as a refutation but as a paradigm of the 'smash the state' scenario. When the Bolsheviks took stock as the civil war wound down in 1920, they were proud that they had successfully defended their right to go down the road to socialism, and they certainly felt they were moving in the right direction – but they also realized that the civil war had set them back in a major way. The Bolshevik economist Iurii Larin told foreign visitors in 1920 that the real economic history of the new regime would begin *after* the civil war. In December 1920 (supposedly the height of the 'euphoria' of 'war communism'), Trotsky put it this way: 'We attack, retreat and again attack, and we always say that we have not traversed even a small portion of the road. The slowness of the unfolding of the proletarian revolution is explained by the colossal nature of the task and the profound approach of the working class to this task'.[11]

Thus, remarkably, the Bolsheviks had committed themselves to promising the workers a vast social crisis in the event of a successful proletarian revolution. This strand of Bolshevism only makes sense when seen in the context of the all-embracing disaster of the world war. What reasonable worker or peasant would refuse the sacrifices needed to put into practice the only possible escape from a recurrence of this tragedy?

The new themes and emphases that Bolshevism brought to the old class narrative during this time of troubles were not ironed out into a completely consistent whole. Underneath the aggressive defiance, some embarrassment can be detected on issues such as freedom of speech. Still, the heart of this new amalgam was the same as the old class narrative: the proletariat's mission to conquer state power and to use it to construct socialism, and, just as important, the inspired and inspiring leadership that fills the proletariat with a sense of its mission. This underlying faith that the proletariat could and would respond to inspiring leadership informed what outsiders could hardly help seeing as a cynical and manipulative strategy. It was this same faith that became the real constitution of the new regime and a central influence on its institutions and policies.

---

10   Bukharin, *Programma kommunistov (bol'shevikov)* (Bukharin 1918b, pp. 5–8).
11   Trotsky 1925–1927, p. 428 (2 December 1920).

5   'Who-Whom' and the Transformation of the Countryside

Nowhere is the influence of the class narrative more evident than in the crucial
decisions made in the 1920s about the best way to effect the socialist transformation of the countryside. The link between the class narrative and Bolshevik
thinking about the peasantry is the scenario summarized by the phrase *kto-
kovo* or 'who-whom'.

Kto-*kovo* – usually glossed as 'who will beat, crush or dominate whom?' – is
widely seen as the hard-line heart of Lenin's outlook. Eric Hobsbawm writes:
'"Who whom?" was Lenin's basic maxim: the struggle as a zero-sum game in
which the winner took, the loser lost all'.[12] This understanding of *kto-kovo* fits
in with a standard account of the origins of Stalin's collectivization drive that
goes like this: the Bolsheviks tried to force communism on the peasants during the period of 'war communism' but found that the task was beyond their
strength. Harbouring a deep contempt and resentment of the peasantry, they
retreated in 1921 by introducing NEP (New Economic Policy), after which they
waited for the day when they would have the strength to renew their assault on
the countryside.

Given the almost folkloric status of *kto-kovo* as Lenin's favourite phrase, it is
something of a shock to discover that Lenin's first and only use of the words *kto-
kovo* is in two of his last public speeches given at the end of his career and that
his aim in coining the phrase was to explain the logic of NEP. After the Bolsheviks legalized various forms of capitalist activity at the beginning of NEP, they
had to demonstrate – to themselves as well as to their audience – that per-
mitting capitalist activity could actually redound to the ultimate advantage of
socialism. In speeches of late 1921 and early 1922, Lenin put it this way: yes, we
are giving the capitalists more room to manoeuvre in order to revive the economy – and therefore it is up to us to ensure that this revival strengthens socialist
construction rather than capitalist restoration. The question therefore is, who
will outpace whom (*kto-kovo operedit*), who will take ultimate advantage of the
new economic policies? This question in turn boiled down to a problem in class
leadership:

> From the point of view of strategy, the essential question is, who will
> more quickly take advantage of this new situation? The whole question is,

---

12   Eric Hobsbawm, *The Age of Extremes: A History of the World, 1914–1991* (Hobsbawm 1996,
      p. 391).

whom will the peasantry follow? – the proletariat, striving to build socialist society, or the capitalist who says 'Let's go back, it's safer that way, don't
worry about that socialism dreamed up by somebody'.[13]

Lenin pounded this basic point home in a great many formulations and the
phrase *kto-kovo* would have passed unnoticed if it had not been picked up by
Zinoviev when he gave the principal political speech at the Thirteenth Party
Congress in 1924. Zinoviev glossed the phrase as follows: '*Kto-kovo*? In which
direction are we growing? Is the revival that we all observe working to the
advantage of the capitalist or is it preparing the ground for us? ... Time is working – for whom?'[14]

Thus the *kto-kovo* scenario was indeed built around the class struggle, but the
enemy class was not the peasantry but NEP's 'new bourgeoisie'. Victory would
be achieved by using the economic advantages of socialism to win the loyalty of the peasantry. This scenario was not a product of NEP-era rethinking,
but rather a variant of the class leadership scenario essential to Bolshevism
from its beginnings. Basing themselves on the characterization of the peasant found in Marx, Engels and Kautsky, the Bolsheviks saw the peasants as
a wavering class but just for that reason a crucial one: the fate of the revolution would be decided by which class the peasants chose to follow. As the
Bolsheviks saw it, they had been compelled during the civil war to place heavy
burdens on the peasantry. Nevertheless, when push came to shove, the mass
of the peasantry realized that the Bolsheviks were defending peasant interests as the peasants themselves defined them and therefore they gave the Bolsheviks just that extra margin of support that ensured military victory. This
scenario meant that far from looking back at the civil war as a time of fundamental conflict between worker and peasant, leaders like Bukharin urged
Bolsheviks to look back at the successful military collaboration of the two
classes during the civil war as a model for the economic class struggle of the
1920s.

Official Bolshevik scenarios assumed that complete socialist transformation
of the countryside – large-scale collective agricultural enterprises operating as
units in a planned economy – would not be possible without an extremely
high level of industrial technology. The transformative power of technology
was symbolized by the slogans of electrification and tractorization that Lenin

---

13   Lenin 1958–1963, 44: 160. For other uses of *kto-kovo*, see 44:161, 163 (speech of 17 October
      1921) and 45: 95 (speech of 27 March 1922).
14   *Tridnadtsatii s'ezd RKP(b)* (*Tridnadtsatii* 1963, pp. 45, 88).

coined prior to NEP. This task of economic transformation was so gargantuan that many Bolsheviks assumed it would not occur until a European socialist revolution released resources unavailable to Russia alone. As good Marxists, the Bolsheviks felt that the use of force to create fundamentally new production relations (as opposed to defending the revolution) was not so much wrong as futile. Precisely in 1919, when the Bolsheviks were putting extreme pressure on the peasantry in order to retain power, can be found Lenin's most eloquent denunciations of any use of force in the establishment of communes or collective farms.

The NEP-era *kto-kovo* scenario is thus an application of an underlying scenario of class leadership of the peasants to the new post-1921 situation of a tolerated market and a tolerated 'new bourgeoisie'. The Bolshevik understanding of the dynamics of this situation was based heavily on pre-war Marxist theories of the evolution of modern capitalism. According to Bolshevik theorists, these evolutionary trends were immanent in *any* modern economy, whether capitalist or socialist – although of course the socialist version would be more democratic and less socially destructive. General European capitalist trends could thus serve the Bolsheviks as rough guides to their own near future. One such trend was the steady movement toward organized and monopolistic forms and the consequent self-annulment of the competitive market. The Bolsheviks also took over Kautsky's assertion that the city was always the economic leader of the countryside. These two factors together implied a steady process of 'squeezing-out' (*Verdrangung, vytesnenie*) of small-scale forms by more efficient and larger ones – petty traders by large-scale trading concerns, small single-owner farms by large-scale collective enterprises (which could be either capitalist or socialist).

These perceived trends informed the Bolshevik scenario of class leadership during the 1920s. The Bolsheviks had no doubt that the countryside would eventually be dominated economically by large-scale, urban-based and society-wide monopolistic institutions. The perceived challenge was not here but in the *kto-kovo* question: what class would be running these institutions? To use another term coined by Lenin at the same time as *kto-kovo*: what kind of *smychka* would be forged between town and country? *Smychka* is usually translated 'link' but this can be misleading if it is taken to imply that the Bolsheviks were unaware prior to NEP of the need for town-country economic links. The *smychka* slogan is specific to NEP because it evokes the economic aspect of the *kto-kovo* struggle against a tolerated bourgeoisie for the loyalty of the peasants. As Bukharin put it in 1924: 'The class struggle of the proletariat for influence over the peasantry takes on the character of a struggle against private capital and for an economic *smychka* with the peasant farm through co-operatives and state trade'.[15] The Bolsheviks assumed that 'the advantages of socialism' – the efficiencies generated by large-scale, society-wide institutions in general and *a fortiori* by the planned and rationalized socialist version of such institutions – would steadily come into play and fund the class leadership struggle by providing economic benefits to the peasants.

Stalin presented the mass collectivization of 1929–30 as the triumphal outcome of Lenin's *kto-kovo* scenario. *Kto-kovo* acquired its aura of hard-line coercion from Stalin's use of it during this period: 'we live by the formula of Lenin – *kto-kovo*: will we knock them, the capitalists, flat and give them (as Lenin expresses it) the final, decisive battle, or will they knock us flat?'[16] Yet Stalin's claim to embody the original spirit of *kto-kovo* contains some paradoxes. Lenin and the Bolshevik leaders who picked up on his phrase had used *kto-kovo* to justify an *economic* competition with the *nepmen* who dominated trade activities – a competition that would result in new forms of agricultural production only *after* an extremely high level of industrial technology was available. Stalin used *kto-kovo* to justify a policy of mass *coercion* against *peasant* kulaks to implant collective farms *long before* industry reached a high level.

These paradoxes make the often-heard claim that Stalin was simply carrying out Lenin's plan a bizarre one. Nevertheless, a close reading of Stalin's speeches in 1928–1929 shows that the rationale – and perhaps even the real motivation – for his radical strategy was strongly based on the narrative of class leadership. His key assertion was that 'the socialist town can *lead* the small-peasant village in no other way than by *implanting* collective farms [*kolkhozy*] and state farms [*sovkhozy*] in the village and transforming the village in a new socialist way'. This was because class leadership would be qualitatively different *within* the collective farms than in a countryside dominated by single-owner farms:

> Of course, individualist and even kulak habits will persist in the collective farms; these habits have not fallen away but they will definitely fall away in the course of time, as the collective farms become stronger and more mechanized. But can it really be denied that the collective farms as a whole, with all their contradictions and inadequacies but existing as an *economic fact*, basically represent a new path for the development of the village – a path of *socialist* development as opposed to a kulak, *capitalist* path of development?[17]

---

15   Bukharin, *Izbrannye proizvedeniia* (Bukharin 1990b, p. 256).
16   Stalin, *Sochineniia* (Stalin 1947–1952, 12:37, see also 12:144).
17   Stalin 1947–1952, 12:162–5 (December 1929).

The role of the collective farms as an incubator of the new peasantry helps account for dekulakization, the most brutal aspect of Stalin's strategy. If the kulaks were not removed from the village or, even worse, they were allowed into the collective farms, they would simply take over and continue to exercise leadership in the wrong direction. As Stalin lieutenant Mikhail Kalinin put it, excluding the kulaks was a 'prophylactic' measure that 'ensures the healthy development of the *kolkhoz* organism in the future'.[18]

In Kalinin's defence of Stalin's murderous form of class leadership, we still hear a faint echo of the original meaning of *kto-kovo*: 'You must understand that dekulakization is only the first and easiest stage. The main thing is to be able to get production going properly in the collective farms. Here, in the final analysis, is the solution to the question: *kto-kovo*.' Nevertheless many Bolsheviks were appalled by Stalin's version of *kto-kovo*. In the so-called 'Riutin platform' that was circulated in underground fashion among sections of the Bolshevik elite in 1932 (it is unclear how much of the 100-page document was written by Martemian Riutin himself), it is argued that the Leninist path toward liquidation of the class basis of the kulak meant showing the mass of peasants 'genuine examples of the genuine advantages of collective farms organized in genuinely voluntary fashion'. But Stalin's idea of class leadership of the peasants had the same relation to real leadership as Japan's Manchuria policy did to national self-determination. As a result, 'pluses have been turned into minuses, and the best hopes of the best human minds have been turned into a squalid joke. Instead of a demonstration of the advantages of large-scale socialist agriculture, we see its defects in comparison to the small-scale individual farm.'[19]

We have traced the path of *kto-kovo* starting with Lenin's coinage of the term to express the logic of NEP and ending with Stalin's contested claim that mass collectivization was the decisive answer to the *kto-kovo* question: who will win the class allegiance of the peasantry? *Kto-kovo* establishes a link between Lenin and Stalin but it also demonstrates the inadvisability of turning that link into an equation. Most importantly, *kto-kovo* refers us back to the narrative of class leadership and the basic assumptions guiding the Bolsheviks as they tackled their most fateful task, the socialist transformation of the countryside.

18   *Pravda*, 21 January 1930.
19   The title of the Riutin platform is 'Stalin and the Crisis of the Proletarian Dictatorship'; it can be found in *Reabilitatsiia: Politicheskie protsessy 30–50-kh godov* 1991, pp. 334–442.

6   From Path to Treadmill: The Next Sixty Years

Out of the turmoil of the early thirties emerged the system that remained intact in the Soviet Union until near the very end: collective farms, centralized industrial planning, monopolistic party-state. The construction of this system entailed a fundamental shift in the nature of the authoritative class narrative. Stalin officially declared that no hostile classes still existed in the Soviet Union nor were there any substantial amount of still unpersuaded waverers. This new situation meant that, although there still existed a long road ahead to full communism, the heroic days of class leadership were over.

In one sense, the new class narrative of the early thirties remained unchanged for the next six decades. Within its framework, there were various attempts to realize 'the advantages of socialism', either in frighteningly irrational attempts to rid the system of saboteurs or more reasonable attempts to tinker with the parameters of the planning system. This 'treadmill of reform' (as the economist Gertrude Schroeder famously described the process) was bathed in an atmosphere of constant celebration about the achievements and prospects of the united Soviet community as it journeyed toward communism. But underneath this resolutely optimistic framework we can discern a real history of the changes in the way people related to the narrative emotionally and intellectually – a history in which uncertainty and anxiety play a much greater role. By focusing on certain key moments in the presentation of the authoritative class narrative, we can provide an outline of this history.

In March 1938, the big story in *Pravda* was the trial of the Right-Trotskyist bloc – the last of the big Moscow show trials at which Bukharin, Rykov and other luminaries were condemned as traitors and sentenced to death. But alongside transcripts and reports 'from the courtroom' were continuing stories on topics such as Arctic exploration, the party's attempts to apply the Plenum resolution of January 1938, campaigns to fulfil economic targets and the crisis-ridden international situation.

The Moscow show trial was intended to dramatize the need for 'vigilance' and for a 'purification' of Soviet institutions from disguised saboteurs and spies. The terror of 1937–1938 was paradoxically explained and justified by the premise that there no longer existed hostile classes and undecided groups in the Soviet Union. Therefore, if the 'advantages of socialism' were not immediately apparent, the problems were not caused by the understandable interests of an identifiable group – and certainly not by structural problems – but only by *individual* saboteurs who were wearing the mask of a loyal Soviet citizen or even party member. Stalin insisted that the danger of isolated saboteurs was potentially immense. Class leadership was therefore no longer described as persuading wavering groups to follow the lead of the party but simply as 'vigilance', as ripping the mask off two-faced *dvurushniki* or 'double-dealers'.

But on the same *Pravda* pages as the coverage of the Moscow trials were other stories that stressed the *damage* done by the vigilance campaign. In January 1938, the Central Committee passed a resolution that tried to cool down the prevailing hysteria – and yet the leadership proved singularly unable to move past the metaphor of the hidden enemy within:

> All these facts show that many of our party organizations and leaders still to this day haven't learned to see through and expose the artfully masked enemy who attempts with cries of vigilance to mask his own enemy status ... and who uses repressive measures to cut down our Bolshevik cadres and to sow insecurity and excessive suspicion in our ranks.[20]

Pravda also printed resolutions from economic officials that say in effect: 'Yes, we know we have problems fulfilling our plan directives, but what can you expect, with all those wreckers running around? But now the wreckers have been caught and we promise to do better'. One can perhaps see in these stories the beginnings of a new approach to improving poor economic performance: tinkering with reforms rather than catching wreckers.

March 1938 was also the month of the Nazi take-over of Austria. *Pravda* stories about international tension were used to underscore the necessity of vigilance. But the shadow of the looming war also strengthened the desire of many to move beyond the internecine paranoia of the purification campaign.

The pages of *Pravda* were not exclusively devoted to the anxiety-provoking evils of two-faced wreckers, super-vigilant party officials, poor economic performance and international tension. Its pages in March 1938 were also filled with a symbolic triumph of Soviet society: the return of Arctic explorers Ivan Papanin and his team from a dangerous and heroic expedition. As Papanin and his men travelled closer and closer to the capital, the stories about them become bigger and bigger. With exquisite timing, they hit Moscow only a few days after the trial closed and several issues of *Pravda* were entirely devoted to the ecstatic welcome they received. A smiling Stalin made an appearance in order to greet the heroes.[21]

---

20 Richard Kosolapov, *Slovo tovarishchu Stalinu* (Kosolapov 1995, pp. 151–2, 148–9).

21 For background on this striking theme in Soviet culture, see John McCannon, *Red Arctic: Polar Exploration and the Myth of the North in the Soviet Union, 1932–1939* (McCannon 1988).

This sense of a triumphal progression after overcoming heroic difficulties was for many participants – including the top leaders – as much or more a part of the meaning of the 1930s as the traumas associated with collectiviza-tion or the purification campaign. This way of remembering the 1930s should be kept in mind when we approach the speech given by Andrei Zhdanov in September 1946 which denounced the alleged pessimistic outlook of the great literary artists Anna Akhmatova and Mikhail Zoshchenko. More than just a clamp-down on literature, this speech served as a signal that the political lead-ership was going to try to recreate the triumphal mood that it remembered from before the war. The complex of hopes and illusions, disappointments and strivings generated in Soviet society by the anti-Nazi war stood in the way of this project and were therefore perceived as an unsettling and dan-gerous threat. Thus the key passage in the speech – undoubtedly reflecting Stalin's own preoccupations – is: 'And what would have happened if we had brought up young people in a spirit of gloom and lack of belief in our cause? The result would have been that we would not have won the Great Fatherland war.'

Zhdanov presented the Soviet Union as a traveller on a long journey in which the present moment lacked meaning: 'We are not today what we were yester-day and tomorrow we will not be what we were today'. Writers were enlisted as guides and leaders on the journey whose job was 'to help light up with a search-light the path ahead'. In this version of the constitutive Soviet narrative, 'class' has almost dropped out while 'leadership' remains. Thankfully, the spotlight is not directed toward searching out hidden enemies. Yet an atmosphere of doubt and anxiety emanates from the speech: can we meet the difficulties ahead if the coming generation does not see itself as participants in a triumphal progres-sion? Thus the core of the attack on Akhmatova was her concern with her own 'utterly insignificant experiences', her 'small, narrow, personal life' – a tirade in which 'personal' (*lichnaia*) is a synonym for 'small' and 'narrow'. The Stalin era is often called the era of the 'cult of personality [*lichnost'*]', but it might just as well be called the era of the *fear* of a personal life.[22]

When the Stalin era drew to a close in early 1953, things immediately started to change, and the leadership came face to face with a task which it never really solved: how to account for these changes within the framework of the overar-ching narrative? The key problem was brought up as early as June 1953 at the Central Committee Plenum in which the Politburo (called Presidium during

---

22   *The Central Committee Resolution and Zhdanov's Speech on the Journals* Zvezda *and* Leningrad 1978, pp. 19–20, 35–6, 16.

this period) announced and justified to the party elite the arrest of Lavrentia Beria, head of the NKVD. The archival publication of these deliberations in 1991 showed how the leadership had to face up to an embarrassing question (as formulated by Lazar Kaganovich): 'It's good that you [leaders] acted decisively and put an end to the adventurist schemes of Beria and to him personally, but where were you earlier and why did you allow such a person into the very heart of the leadership?'[23] The question is here a narrow one about individual leaders, but the same question was bound to expand to the much more difficult issue of why the Soviet system as a whole allowed Stalinism.

The June Plenum revealed two different narratives about the downfall of Beria, one mired in the past and the other struggling toward the future. The paradigmatic examples of these contrasting narratives can be found in the speeches by Kaganovich and Anastas Mikoyan. Kaganovich insistently defined the present situation as another 1937. More than once he approvingly referred to Stalin's 1937 speech 'On Inadequacies in Party Work', a speech that served as a signal for the terroristic purification campaign of 1937–1938. Using 1937 rhetoric, Kaganovich condemned Beria as a spy in the pay of imperialist powers. Accordingly, Kaganovich called for renewed 'vigilance' and 'purification'. 'Much of what was said in 1937 must be taken into account today as well.'

Mikoyan also employed 1937 rhetoric such as 'double-dealerism' (*dvurushnichestvo*). But the spirit behind his use of such terms is almost comically opposed to the spirit of 1937. Here is Mikoyan's proof of Beria's double-dealerism: 'I asked him [after Stalin's death]: why do you want to head the NKVD? And he answered: we have to establish legality, we can't tolerate this state of things in the country. We have a lot of arrested people, we have to liberate them and not send people to the camps for no reason'. Mikoyan had no problem with this statement as a policy goal, but he argued that Beria was a *dvurushnik* because – he did not move fast enough during the three months since Stalin's death to introduce legality and release prisoners!

Kaganovich was genuinely angry at Beria, who 'insulted Stalin and used the most unpleasant and insulting words about him'. Beria's insulting attitude toward Stalin did not seem to bother Mikoyan – indeed, in his low-key way, Mikoyan made it clear that Stalin was mainly responsible for Beria's rise to power. Mikoyan rejected the 1937 scenario as simply irrelevant: 'We do not yet have direct proof on whether or not [Beria] was a spy, whether or not he received orders from foreign bosses, but is this really what's important?' He was

---

23   The Plenum proceedings were first published in *Izvestiia TsK KPSS* 1991, Nos. 1 and 2. Lazar Kaganovich's remarks are in No. 1, pp. 187–200 (the quoted hypothetical question found on p. 188), Anastas Mikoyan's remarks in No. 2, pp. 148–56.

clearly anxious to get past Beria and talk about issues of economic reform. He described the ludicrous situation in which the government offered unrealistically low prices for potatoes, the *kolkhozniki* had therefore no economic interest in growing them, and government institutions sent out highly paid white-collar workers every year to plant them while 'the *kolkhozniki* look on and laugh'.

The same only partially successful struggle to shed the old language in order to present new concerns can be seen in many of the literary works of the 'thaw' that took place in the period 1953–1956. A novel such as Vladimir Dudintsev's *Not By Bread Alone* (1956) resembles in many respects the old narrative of unmasking evildoers who carry a party card. The noble inventor Lopatkin is thwarted at every turn by officials such as Drozdov. Drozdov is not a spy who should be shot or sent to the camps, but he *is* an enemy of the people who should be purged.

The historic originality of *Not by Bread Alone* and other literary productions of the 'thaw' does not come from its muck-raking narrative but rather from its mode of being. The novel is a personal statement by an individual, Vladimir Dudintsev, who wrote it to express *his* views on the country's situation. For the first time in Soviet history, the party-state's monopoly on shaping the authoritative narrative was challenged. This aspect was magnified by the enormous and unprecedented public discussion generated by the book. Again for the first time in Soviet history, an autonomous public opinion used public channels to hear and deliberate, pro and con, on vital issues.

The narrative of *Not by Bread Alone* also affirmed an autonomous space for 'small, narrow, personal life'. Lopatkin has an affair with Drozdov's estranged wife who has left Drozdov partly because of his inability to have any sort of personal life. Indeed, even Lopatkin, the counter-Drozdov, has trouble accepting his own need and right to have such a personal life. The real climax of the novel is not when Lopatkin's invention is officially introduced but when he decides to ask Nadia to marry him – or rather, when he decides he *can* ask her to marry him.

Some aspects of Dudintsev's novel are more evident today than they could have been to contemporary observers. In a brief episode toward the end of the novel, Dudintsev touches on another great turning-point in Soviet history: the return of Gulag inmates to Soviet society. In hindsight we can also see that Lopatkin is a proto-dissident. He survives on the margin of society, outside of state service, and he relies on the support of fellow eccentrics, odd jobs, material aid from sympathizers and finally on occasional patronage from people within the system. Given the new possibility of independent material existence and armed with a ferocious self-righteousness, Lopatkin sets out to reform the system.

The last lines of the novel evoke the path metaphor. 'Although Lopatkin's machine was already made and handed over to the factories, he again suddenly saw before him a path that lost itself in the distance, a path that most likely had no end. This path awaited him, stretched in front of him, luring him on with its mysterious windings and with its stern responsibility'.[24] Lopatkin's personally chosen and mysterious road without an end accepts yet subverts the narrative of society's triumphal journey to communism.

Yet the triumphal official version of the path metaphor still had some life in it. One of the most exuberant, optimistic and inclusive speeches in Soviet history is Nikita Khrushchev's comments on the new party programme at the 22nd Party Congress in 1961. Here Khrushchev updated the path metaphor in an allusion to the successful exploits in space that appeared to validate Soviet claims to leadership: 'The Programs of the Party [1903, 1919, 1961] may be compared to a three-stage rocket. The first stage wrested our country away from the capitalist world, the second propelled it to socialism, and the third is to place it in the orbit of communism. It is a wonderful rocket, comrades! (*Stormy applause*)'.

The new Programme ratified a fundamental shift in the conception of class leadership within the narrative. The official formula that summarized this shift was the replacement of the 'dictatorship of the proletariat' by the 'state of the whole people'. The proletarian dictatorship was defined as not only a time of repression but also of class leadership:

> The workers' and peasants' alliance needed the dictatorship of the proletariat to combat the exploiting classes, to transform peasant farming along socialist lines and to re-educate the peasantry, and to build socialism ... The working class leads the peasantry and the other labouring sections of society, its allies and brothers-in-arms, and helps them to take the socialist path of their own free will.

In essence, this shift had been announced already in the early 1930s, but Khrushchev now drew the full implications without obsessing about the enemy within. 'The transition to communism [in contrast to the transition from capitalism to socialism] proceeds in the absence of any exploiting classes, when all members of society – workers, peasants, intellectuals – have a vested interest

---

24   V. Dudintsev, *Ne khlebom edinom* (Dudintsev 1957a, p. 296). An English translation by Edith Bone was published in 1957 (Dudintsev 1957b).

in the victory of communism, and work for it consciously'. The transformative function of class leadership was now transferred to the more or less automatic results of economic growth.[25]

On the basis of this combination of class collaboration and institutional tinkering, Khrushchev promised the realization of full communism within twenty years. But this less dramatic and more inclusive version of the path metaphor ran into trouble when the expected 'advantages of socialism' failed to materialize. During the post-Khrushchev period, the journey to communism seemed stalled. The Brezhnev period is now known to history as the era of stagnation, but an even more sardonic label can be found in a song by Vladimir Vysotsky. Vysotsky was a figure scarcely conceivable in earlier phases of Soviet society – a hugely popular actor and singer who was also famous for his contribution to the genre of *magnitizdat*, the guitar poetry that circulated unofficially on tape cassettes.

One of his more hilarious songs is entitled 'Morning Gymnastics'. Sung uptempo with manic cheerfulness, the song urges us to preserve our health by doing push-ups every morning until we drop.[26] The climactic final verse is given special emphasis:

> We don't fear any bad news.
> Our answer is – to run in place!
> Even beginners derive benefits.
> Isn't it great! – among the runners, no one is in first place and no one is
> backward.
> Running in place reconciles everybody!

'Morning Gymnastics' was not an underground song – it can be found on a record sold in Soviet stores around 1980. To read the final verse as a satirical comment on Soviet society may be over-interpreting a highly entertaining comic song (although this kind of over-interpretation was also a feature of this complex and ambiguous period). Nevertheless, whether Vysotsky meant it this way or not, his image of 'running in place' is a highly appropriate symbol of the class leadership narrative in its last days. A sense of frantic activity without real movement, a loss of the earlier dynamic arising from a vanguard seeking to inspire backward strata, a 'hear-no-evil' refusal to acknowledge problems –

---

25   *The Road to Communism* 1962, pp. 292, 250, 194, 247.
26   The text to 'Morning Gymnastics' (*Utrenniaia gimnastika*) can be found in Vladimir Vysotsky, *Pesni i stikhi* (Vysotsky 1981, pp. 230–1). A clip of Vysotsky singing 'Morning Gymnastics' can be found on YouTube, along with various post-Soviet cover versions.

many Soviet citizens, even the most loyal, saw their society increasingly in these terms. Khrushchev had called for conflict-free progress toward communism, and what was the result? 'Running in place reconciles everybody!'

When the perestroika era began in 1985, there was a widespread feeling that running in place could now finally be transformed into real movement forward. Instead, the perestroika era was marked by an ever-intensifying feeling that no one really knew any more *where* society should go. This de-enchantment of the narrative of the path to socialism took place in two interlocking processes. The first process was the development of reform thinking away from the question 'how do we realize the advantages of socialism?' and toward the question 'how do we avoid the disadvantages of socialism?' The other process was a painful rethinking of Soviet history. How and when did we lose the true way and what must we do to get back on track?

Now that the lid was off, Soviet society had to face up to the full implications of the question that Kaganovich dimly perceived back in 1953. Mikhail Gorbachev tried to give an answer that fully acknowledged the disasters of Soviet history while preserving the sense that Soviet society still had a mission to complete the great journey. 'Neither flagrant mistakes nor the deviations from socialist principles that were allowed could turn our people or our country off the road on which they set out when they made their choice in 1917. The impulse of October was too great!'[27]

The two processes – the rapid evolution of reform thinking and the agonizing reappraisal of Soviet history – came together in the use of NEP as a symbol of the path not taken. On the one hand, NEP represented a type of socialism that co-existed with market elements and that could therefore be used to de-legitimize the 'administrative command system' associated with the Soviet planned economy. On the other hand, NEP seemed to represent a genuine alternative *within* Soviet history to Stalinist crimes and inefficiency.

But NEP provided only a temporary barrier between the glory of the revolution and the taint of Stalinism. The actual NEP had meant the short-term toleration of the market on the road to socialism. If the reformers of perestroika were indeed on the same road, they were travelling in the opposite direction. And the more closely the reformers looked at the political institutions of NEP, the less it looked like a genuine alternative to Stalinism. As the novelist Fazil Iskander wrote sadly in 1988, 'the awful thing is that, remembering the Party arguments of the time, I somehow cannot remember one man who put forward a programme for the democratization of the country. There were arguments

---

27   Gorbachev 1987.

about inter-party democracy but I don't remember any others ... In such conditions Stalin, naturally, proved to be the best Stalinist, and won.'[28]

The feeling grew stronger that perhaps 'the impulse of October' opened up a fundamentally false path and made it impossible to get off that path – or even that the path metaphor is simply not a useful way of thinking about a society's development. When in 1991 the Soviet Union collapsed not with a bang but a whimper, this unexpected outcome was partly the result of the previous de-enchantment of the narrative of class leadership. The Soviet Union had always been based on fervent belief in this narrative in its various permutations. When the binding power of the narrative dissolved, the Soviet Union itself dissolved.[29]

---

28   *Moscow News*, 1988, No. 28, p. 11.
29   For debates over Bolshevik identity in this period, see 'Perestroika Looks Back', included in this volume.

PART 2

Deferred Dreams: Against the Myth of 'War Communism' (1918–1921)

∵

CHAPTER 3

Tsiurupa's White Beard

1   Victor Serge Tells a Story (from *Memoirs of a Revolutionary*)[1]

I remember a conversation I had [during the Russian civil war, 1918–1920] with the People's Commissar for Food, Tsiurupa, a man with a splendid white beard and candid eyes. I had brought some French and Spanish comrades to him so that he could explain for our benefit the Soviet system of rationing and supply. He showed us beautifully-drawn diagrams from which the ghastly famine and the immense black market had vanished without trace.

'What about the black market?' I asked him.

'It is of no importance at all', the old man replied. No doubt he was sincere, but he was a prisoner of his scheme, a captive within offices whose occupants had obviously all primed him with lies.

2   Serge's Story Illustrates 'the Myth of War Communism'

Aleksandr Tsiurupa, a prominent member of the Bolshevik party and government:

- is a complete 'prisoner of his scheme'
- believes that an ideal system is already a reality
- ignores the harsh realities of life in Russia at the time
- is repellingly complacent about the sufferings of the people.

3   His Story Tells Us about the Myth in Other Ways

- The story has absolutely no basis in reality.
- The idea that Aleksandr Tsiurupa, the man responsible for food-supply policy at the highest level, was unaware of the famine, was dismissive of the scope of the black market, and mistook beautifully drawn diagrams for reality, is laughable.

---

1   This essay is based on a PowerPoint presentation given to the Historical Materialism annual conference in London 2018 as well as the annual conference of the Study Group on the Rus-

– The falsity of Serge's portrait is easily documented. I've written a book on
  food-supply politics in Russia from 1914–1921, so I know what I'm talking
  about.

4   Was Tsiurupa Really an Arrogant Fanatic Blind to Reality?

Tsiurupa speaking on food-supply policy at the Seventh Congress of Soviets in
December 1919:

> There are only two possibilities: either we perish from hunger, or we
> weaken the [peasant] economy to some extent, but [manage to] get out
> of our temporary difficulties … I can say about myself that I am at fault
> as well. I've worked for five years on food-supply procurement, but that
> is not enough in such a difficult moment. It must be admitted that we
> do not know how to work – but the fact that we are aware of this is also
> important.

5   Was Tsiurupa Really 'an Old Man with a Splendid White Beard'?

Figure 1 shows Aleksandr Tsiurupa (b. 1870, same year as Lenin) in the early
1920s.

6   'War Communism': A Vague Historical Term

In various historical accounts, 'war communism' can mean:
– The entire period between the 1917 revolution and NEP (1921–1929)
– Only the period from about late 1919 to late 1920
– Only the economic policies during this or that period
– Only one subset of Bolshevik economic policies
– The mindset of the Bolsheviks vis-à-vis any of these
– Or some unclear mixture of the above.

---

sian Revolution held at Cardiff in January 2019. I have retained a similar format as a dramatic
way of exposing the myth of 'war communism'. Quotations are not footnoted here; reference
information can be found in the relevant essays in this volume. The opening anecdote from
Victor Serge can be found in Serge 1963, p. 117.

FIGURE 1 Aleksandr Tsiurupa (b. 1870, same year as Lenin) in the early 1920s
HTTPS://EN.WIKIPEDIA.ORG/WIKI/ALEXANDER_TSIURUPA, LAST ACCESSED
11 JUNE 2023)

7   The Real Definition of War Communism, according to a Strong and
     Wide Consensus of Historians

War communism was the time when the Bolsheviks went crazy. As shown by:
- Bolshevik 'euphoria' and criminal complacency
- Belief in 'short-cuts to full communism'
- Belief in an imminent 'leap into communism'
- A *principled* preference for coercion over material incentives
- An inability to grasp the most simple facts, for example, the damage civil war
  policies were doing to the peasant economy
- A morally reprehensible indifference to suffering.

8   A Pantheon of Historians in Support

The myth of war communism rests on a strong, mostly unchallenged consensus
among the stars of the field across the whole political spectrum.
   Historians who endorse the myth of war communism, listed impressionisti-
cally in a political spectrum from left to right:
- Isaac Deutscher, Moshe Lewin
- E.H. Carr, S.A. Smith
- Stephen Cohen, Sheila Fitzpatrick
- Alec Nove, Andrzej Walicki
- Leszek Kołakowski, Orlando Figes
- Robert Conquest, Martin Malia

9   What Did the Bolsheviks Themselves Say during 1919–1920?

- Russia is facing a grave, life-and-death economic emergency of tragic proportions.
- Russia has taken only a pitifully few steps on the long path to socialist society.
- Material incentives are crucial, but at present they are in desperately short
  supply. We must therefore use what we have to maximize their effect, despite
  the injustices and inequalities involved. The use of force is justified if it
  prevents complete economic breakdown and in this way preserves the possibility of using material incentives in the future.
- Looting the peasant economy to feed the army and urban industry is a miserable necessity imposed upon us by the need 'to achieve victory over the
  generals'. Obviously, this situation cannot go on too much longer.

- We must all be aware of the sufferings of the Russian population – they threaten to make a mockery of revolutionary promises – and act with the indicated urgency.

10   Who Is Hallucinating, the Bolsheviks or the Historians?

Let us compare
- Assertions by prominent historians
versus
- Actual pronouncements from late 1919 to late 1920 by Bolshevik leaders such as
  - Lev Trotsky
  - Grigorii Zinoviev
  - Nikolai Bukharin
  - Evgenii Preobrazhensky

11   Alec Nove vs. Nikolai Bukharin

ALEC NOVE:

Bukharin in 1917–1920 was one of those who suggested an extremely radical line of instant socialism ... a Utopian and optimistic set of ideas concerning a leap into socialism, which would seem to have little to do with the reality of hunger and cold.

NIKOLAI BUKHARIN:

Of course, it would be absurd to think that within a brief space of time, when hunger and cold are rife, when there is a lack of fuel and raw materials, it is possible to rapidly achieve permanent and satisfactory results ... Unfortunately, we cannot leap [*skaknut*] right away into communism. We are making only the first steps toward it.

12   Moshe Lewin vs. Lev Trotsky

MOSHE LEWIN:

The term "war communism" implied that the most progressive system on earth was just installed *deus ex machina* by the most expedient, unexpected but irreversible leap to freedom ... a shortcut to socialism.

LEV TROTSKY (December 1920):

We always say that we have not traversed even a small portion of the road. The slowness of the unfolding of the proletarian revolution is explained by the colossal nature of the task and the profound approach of the working class to this task.

13   Isaac Deutscher vs. Grigorii Zinoviev

ISAAC DEUTSCHER:

The Bolshevik was therefore inclined to see the essential features of fully fledged communism embodied in the war economy of 1919–20 ... Silently, with a heavy heart, Bolshevism parted with its dream of war communism.

GRIGORII ZINOVIEV (early 1920):

[Yes, the peasants had received land:] 'But you know, the peasant can't scrape the earth with his teeth. The peasant can't work the land because he has no horses. We declared mobilization after mobilization. The village is short of everything necessary. [Taking peasants away from the field for two weeks at harvest time is] appalling and a real torture. But still – it was unavoidable ... With a weary heart, we were forced literally to loot half of Russia, but achieve victory over the generals.'

14   E.H. Carr vs. Tsiurupa and Others

E.H. CARR:

The mood of 1920 remained on the whole one of complacency. [The Soviet leaders were] obstinately slow to recognize the hard fact that the main difficulty in securing supplies of food for the towns was ... that no adequate return could be offered to the peasants.

P.K. KAGANOVICH (food-supply official):

What do you think, the People's Commissariat does this [takes grain without proper exchange] for its own satisfaction? No, we do it because there's not enough food.

ALEKSANDR TSIURUPA [People's Commissar of Food Supply]:

There are only two possibilities: either we perish from hunger, or we weaken the [peasant] economy to some extent, but [manage to] get out of our temporary difficulties.

15   Andrzej Walicki vs. Bukharin

ANDRZEJ WALICKI:

Bukharin spoke glowingly about the collapse of the Russian economy.

NIKOLAI BUKHARIN:

The foundation of our whole policy must be the widest possible development of productive forces. The breakdown [*razrukha*] is so vast, the post-war scarcity [*golod*] is so conspicuous, that everything must be subordinated to this one task. More products! More boots, scythes, barrels, textiles, salt, clothing, bread and so on – these are our primary need ... This is what we need now, if we are to avoid dying of hunger amid the post-war breakdown, if we are to be clothed, if we are to regain our strength, if we are to proceed more swiftly along the road of constructing a new life.

16   Moshe Lewin vs. Lev Trotsky

MOSHE LEWIN:

[War communism is] an ideological construct that mistook the egalitarianism of poverty and wartime brotherhood not only for that of socialism, but also for that of communism.

LEV TROTSKY:

As long as we are poor and beggarly, as long as we have insufficient food for supplying even a minimum of our needs, we are not able to distribute it equally to all toilers. We are going to direct consumer items to the central branches of labour and to the most important enterprises. And we are obliged to do this – obliged in the name of saving the toiling masses and the future of the country. We will be able to dress the worker more warmly, give him better nourishment, if he works conscientiously and energetically. That's why we are applying the bonus system [of differential wages] ... Without this injustice within the working class itself – without feeding some and letting others go hungry – we won't be able to cope.

17   The Historians Sum Up

MARTIN MALIA:

In a veritable ideological delirium, the most colossal economic collapse of the century was transmogrified into really-existing Communism, the radiant future *hic et nunc*, a vision projected in Bukharin's and Preobrazhenskii's once famous *ABC* of Communism.

ROBERT CONQUEST:

[Grain requisitioning by force was] regarded by the Party, from Lenin down, as not merely socialism, but even communism.

SHEILA FITZPATRICK:

The Bolsheviks' perception of the real world had become almost comically distorted in many respects by 1920.

18   Trotsky Sums Up

[From his speech on the third anniversary of the October Revolution, November 1920:]

'We went into this struggle with magnificent ideals, with magnificent enthusiasm, and it seemed to many people that the promised land – the new kingdom of justice, freedom, contentment and cultural uplift – was so near it could be touched ... If back then, three years ago, we were given the opportunity of looking ahead, we would not have believed our eyes. We would not have believed that three years after the proletarian revolution it would be so hard for us, so harsh to be living on this earth.'

19   Importance of Getting the Story Straight

– The Bolsheviks were not clueless idiots.
– The actual policies of the Bolsheviks during the civil war were for the most part *conscious retreats* from ideal socialist policies.
– NEP was not a sharp reversal of Bolshevik thinking, but an adjustment to peacetime conditions and just one more retreat.
– Bolshevik attitudes and policy toward the *peasants* have been especially distorted by the myth of war communism. For the Bolsheviks, the civil war was an example of successful wartime partnership between the classes, and as such a source of inspiration for NEP's programme of economic partnership.
– For the Bolsheviks, the main achievement of the civil war was the successful defence of soviet power, that is, a shift in class power as manifested in a worker/peasant *vlast* – *not* policies of socialist transformation.

20   Who Created the Myth?

– Left activists and historians first created the myth for intra-left polemical purposes (in particular, supporting economic reform within the Soviet Union).
– Historians on the right gratefully accepted the myth for their own purposes.
– When left and right agree on a position, it must be uncontroversially correct – right?

21   Questions for Historians

- Why didn't alarm bells go off?
- Has the unfounded consensus around 'the myth of war communism' ever been seriously challenged?
- What are the prospects for real change on this issue?

CHAPTER 4

The Mystery of the *ABC*

Bukharin in 1917–1920 was one of those who suggested an extremely radical line of instant socialism ... a Utopian and optimistic set of ideas concerning a leap into socialism, which would seem to have little to do with the reality of hunger and cold.

ALEC NOVE, *An Economic History of the USSR*, 1969

• • •

Unfortunately, we cannot leap [*skaknut*] right away into communism. We are making only the first steps toward it.

NIKOLAI BUKHARIN, *ABC of Communism*, 1919

• •
•

Let us imagine a community of scholars that seeks to understand Marxism but cannot be bothered to read the *Communist Manifesto*. A widespread impression exists among these scholars that Marx and Engels argued in the *Manifesto* for amity and cooperation between classes. Occasionally someone quotes a passage from the *Manifesto* and notes with a vague sense of surprise that this particular passage seems to be an exception to the general theme of class partnership. A long-standing debate divides these scholars: Is the *Manifesto*'s insistence on class partnership consistent with other writings by Marx and Engels? Or should it be explained mainly by the circumstances of 1848?

Fortunately, no such community of scholars exists. But a close parallel does exist: the *ABC of Communism* and the community of scholars that seeks to understand Bolshevism. The *ABC* was written in 1919 by Nikolai Bukharin and Evgenii Preobrazhensky as a popular commentary on the new programme that the Bolshevik party had adopted at the Eighth Party Congress in March of that year. It was the most extensive, the most authoritative, and the most widely read exposition of the Bolshevik outlook. As Sidney Heitman states, 'It became a veritable Bible of communism, enjoying greater currency and authority than any of the works of such well-known figures as Lenin and Trotsky.'[1]

---

1 Heitman's comment comes from his unpaginated introduction to the 1966 Ann Arbor paper-

Yet the *ABC* is often ignored in scholarly discussions of Bolshevik ideology. Worse still, when it is invoked, it is turned on its head.

In this essay, I will provide an elementary description of this crucial document: the *ABC*s of the *ABC*. At the same time, I will demonstrate the misuse of the *ABC* by advocates of three widely accepted hypotheses about the Bolshevik outlook prior to the New Economic Policy (NEP): the 'stress-induced vision' thesis (the Bolshevik utopia was created in reaction to the difficulties of the civil war), the 'socialism now' thesis (the Bolsheviks euphorically saw the tragic realities of 1919–1920 as the realization of their dreams), and the 'disingenuous Bolshevik' thesis (the Bolsheviks justified the coercive burdens of 1919–1920 as an emergency measure only in hindsight). In each case, authoritative voices have assured us that the *ABC* strongly supports the hypothesis. In each case, the *ABC* actually speaks strongly against it.[2] What I call the mystery of the *ABC* is the discrepancy between the text and the image enshrined in our scholarship: how did we end up with a picture of this crucial document that is as inaccurate as the claim that Marxism preaches class partnership?

---

back reprint of the 1922 English translation of the *ABC* by Eden and Cedar Paul. (Heitman's introduction is one of the best available discussions of the *ABC*, although he does not take up any of the issues addressed in this essay.) The original publication was *Azbuka kommunizma* (Bukharin and Preobrazhensky 1920). At the time of the original publication of this article, the Russian edition was rare and difficult to obtain, and none of the scholars cited in this essay seemed to have consulted it. Now, of course, it is easily available online, for example, at the MIA site: https://www.marxists.org/russkij/bukharin/azbuka/azbuka_kommunizma.htm. Because of the variety of editions, I have identified passages by section number. Since Bukharin and Preobrazhensky wrote separate chapters, I have noted the author of a particular passage where convenient. My admiration for the vigorous translation by Eden and Cedar Paul has grown as I have worked with the text, and I have used it as the basis for my own translations presented here. Nonetheless, serious comment on the *ABC* requires consulting the original. For example, the Pauls translate the passage cited in the epigraph as follows: 'Unfortunately, however, we cannot reach communism in one stride. We are only taking the first steps towards it' (sec. 101). There is nothing wrong with this translation, but Bukharin's anti-leap imagery has been obscured.

2   By identifying these hypotheses, I hope to sidestep the unproductive debate on 'war communism' and focus on more specific and manageable issues concerning the Bolshevik outlook prior to 1921. A point of method: I do not make the claim that any text 'speaks for itself' or that the surface meaning is the only significant one. My objection is to interpretations that present themselves as unproblematic yet ignore crucial and abundant textual evidence.

1   The 'Stress-Induced Vision' Thesis

The most influential and indeed the only detailed discussion of the ABC is E.H. Carr's essay 'The Bolshevik Utopia,' written in the mid-sixties as an introduction to a reprint of the ABC.[3] Carr presents the ABC as an emblem of utopianism: 'The introduction of NEP in 1921 [marked] the end of the Utopian period in Soviet history ... of which The ABC of Communism is an outstanding memorial'. In periods of storm and stress such as the civil war, 'the utopian elements inherent in any revolutionary doctrine are thrown into relief' and at the same time there arises 'a contempt for hardships and suffering incurred'. In stark contrast to this utopianism is NEP, characterized by 'the shelving of revolutionary ideals and revolutionary aspirations under the crude impact of Stalinist [sic] realism'. Practical problems became more pressing than 'utopian visions of a future that now seemed inconceivably remote'.[4]

Carr's argument is that there is something distinctly odd about the ABC's version of a future society – something that can only be explained by the storm and stress experienced by Bolsheviks in 1919. I will call this the 'stress-induced vision' thesis. I will not ask whether it is really true that utopian thinking flourished more during the civil war than during NEP.[5] I also will not dwell on the curious contradiction between Carr's concluding remarks and his detailed discussion of the actual text, which he describes as a 'striking amalgam of the practical with the utopian' (and yet Carr chooses to give exclusive emphasis to just one aspect of this amalgam in his title and conclusion).[6]

---

3   E.H. Carr, 'The Bolshevik Utopia', in his October Revolution: Before and After (Carr 1969); a slightly different version of Carr's essay can be found in the Penguin edition of the ABC (Bukharin and Preobrazhensky 1969). Carr had little to say about the ABC in his general history; I have found only three passing references to it in The Bolshevik Revolution (Carr 1950–1955, vol. 2, pp. 152, 208, 262). On the influence of Carr's essay, see Sheila Fitzpatrick, The Russian Revolution, 1917–1932 (Fitzpatrick 1982, p. 171) and Silvana Malle's positive citation in Economic Organization of War Communism, 1918–1921 (Malle 1985, p. 20).

4   Carr 1969, pp. 83–5. As Carr himself points out, 'for ten years [the ABC] was constantly reprinted and translated, circulating widely in many countries as an authoritative exposition of the "aims and tasks" of communism' (p. 62). This fact is hard to explain if the ABC's alleged utopianism seemed 'inconceivably remote'.

5   The flourishing of utopian thinking during the 1920s is copiously documented by Richard Stites, Revolutionary Dreams: Utopian Visions and Experimental Life in the Russian Revolution (Stites 1989). Compare Trotsky's genuine utopian fervour at the end of Literature and Revolution (Trotsky 1924) with his Terrorism and Communism (Trotsky 1920).

6   In Carr's discussion of specific issues, the practical aspect seems uppermost. For example, he writes about national self-determination: 'In this question, as in others, The ABC of Communism combines a utopian vision of the future ... with concessions to the expediencies

Let us turn instead to the ABC itself. The ABC is divided into two parts. Part One (written entirely by Bukharin) tells the larger historical story of how the development of capitalism led in the end to destructive imperialist wars and thus to the revolution. Part Two (written by both Preobrazhensky and Bukharin) portrays the building of socialism in Russia. After a brief introduction, Part Two presents a series of chapters describing what the Bolsheviks are doing to achieve socialist goals in each area of Bolshevik policy.[7]

The broad world-historical narrative of Part One contains Bukharin's vision of 'full communism'.[8] In a passage that has struck many commentators, Bukharin tells us that 'the main direction [of the economy] will be entrusted to various kinds of bookkeeping offices or statistical bureaus ... Inasmuch as, from childhood onwards, everybody will have been accustomed to social labour and will understand its necessity, seeing how life goes easier when everything is done smoothly [po maslu] according to a prearranged plan, everybody will work in accordance with the indications of these statistical bureaus' (sec. 21).[9]

---

of current policy' (Carr 1969, p. 82; see also pp. 63, 66, 80 for comments on other issues). Carr's discussion of the nationality issue is rather peculiar. He writes that 'Bukharin's personal standpoint on the national question adds a special interest' to this chapter, even though, as he notes, the chapter was written by Preobrazhensky. Carr goes on to discuss the issue as if Preobrazhensky did not exist. But Preobrazhensky was not Bukharin's amanuensis, and the chapter in question defends a position that Bukharin strongly attacked at the Eighth Party Congress. (The tendency to regard Bukharin as the sole author of the ABC is symbolized by the Ann Arbor paperback reprint, which simply leaves Preobrazhensky off both front and back covers.)

7 In its construction, the ABC appears to be based on *Grundsätze und Forderungen*, one of the basic propaganda works of the German Social Democratic party. The first half of this work is Karl Kautsky's summary of his *Das Erfurter Programm*, while the second half consists of Bruno Schoenlank's discussion of immediate party demands (Kautsky and Schoenlank 1899). The importance of this work is shown by publication figures given by Gary Steenson in *'Not One Man! Not One Penny!': German Social Democracy, 1863–1914* (Steenson 1981, p. 139).

8 According to Carr, Part One is more 'utopian' than Part Two. This should have made Part One less popular during NEP, but in fact Part One dated less rapidly than the second half of the book. In 1923, it was issued in a separate edition (see the Bukharin bibliography in Bukharin, *Put' k sotsializmu* [Bukharin 1990a], p. 270, item 513).

9 In the Pauls' translation, we find the words 'when the social order is like a well-oiled machine'; these appear to be an expansion of Bukharin's phrase *kak po maslu*. Stites cites the phrase added by the translators; possibly this has led him to overemphasize the theme of 'order and mechanics' in the ABC (Stites 1989, pp. 47–8). Bukharin did compare production to a machine during his discussion of labour discipline in his 1918 manifesto *Program of the Communists*: see Bukharin, *Izbrannye proizvedeniia* (Bukharin 1990b, p. 74). Both in 1918 and later, however, the dominant metaphor in Bukharin's discussion of labour discipline is 'the army of labour'; see the ABC, sec. 100.

Sheila Fitzpatrick uses this passage to support the 'stress-induced vision' thesis. She cites it at length and comments that this 'depersonalized, scientifically regulated world ... was the antithesis of any actual Russia, past, present or future; and in the chaos of the Civil War that must have made it particularly appealing'.[10] Was this vision of statistical bureaus in fact produced in reaction to the environment of the civil war and 'war communism'? A clue is provided by a crucial feature of the ABC text: the reading lists appended to each chapter. Among the works recommended to the diligent student of Bolshevism are earlier evocations of socialist society, including Bukharin's *The Program of the Communists (Bolsheviks)* (1918), Aleksandr Bogdanov's *Red Star* (1908), and August Bebel's *Die Frau und der Sozialismus* (first published 1883).

What do these earlier works tell us about the ABC's statistical bureaus? In *Program of the Communists*, dated May 1918, Bukharin himself writes that communist society is 'one great labour association [*artel*]; no man is master [*khoziain*] over it ... The work is carried out jointly, according to a pre-arranged lab or plan. A central bureau of statistics calculates how much it is required to manufacture in a year: such and such a number of boots, trousers, sausages, blacking, wheat, cloth, and so on ... working hands will be distributed accordingly'.[11]

In Bogdanov's pre-war novel *Red Star*, a picture of a socialist society on Mars, we find an extensive description of the work of these statistical bureaus. The Martian guide informs the narrator that 'two hundred years ago, when collective labour just barely managed to satisfy the needs of society, statistics had to be very exact, and labour could not be distributed with complete freedom'. Now, however, 'the statistics continually affect mass transfers of labour, but each individual is free to do as he chooses'.[12]

Going even further back and moving out of Russia, we arrive at Bebel's *Die Frau und der Sozialismus*, a book that can be called the ABC of German Social Democracy. Bebel writes that in the society of the future 'statistics play the chief role. They become the most important applied science of the new order; they furnish the measure for all social activity'. Statistics play a powerful role even in the crisis-ridden contemporary world, but in a socialist society 'the whole

---

10   Fitzpatrick continues: 'The Civil War was a time when intellectual and cultural experimentation flourished' (Fitzpatrick 1982, p. 77). In his discussion of the ABC's vision of full communism, Stites ties it not only to 'the appalling uncertainty and hardship' of war and revolution, but also to a 'deep Russian tradition of phobia toward anarchy, chaos, disorder, and panic' (Stites 1989, pp. 47–8).

11   Bukharin 1990b, p. 47. I have used the translation made by 'The Group of English Speaking Communists in Russia' and published in 1918 (Bukharin 1918).

12   Alexander Bogdanov, *Red Star: The First Bolshevik Utopia* (Bogdanov 1984, pp. 65–8). (Stites notes the relevance of *Red Star*; see Stites 1989, pp. 47–8.)

society is organized and everything proceeds according to plan [*nach Plan und Ordnung*] ... With a little experience, the thing is as easy as play'.[13] Examples could be multiplied, but the point is clear: the famous statistical bureaus are an integral part of the traditional socialist utopia – a necessary feature of a world without bosses and without crises. It would have been impossible to write a description of communist society without them. The point can be generalized: the *ABC*'s vision of a future society, right down to its details, is taken straight out of the Social Democratic tradition.[14] Bukharin and Preobrazhensky were not trying to be original and in tune with the times, they were remembering their future. The Bolshevik utopia was an affirmation of orthodoxy, a retelling of old tales in a time of troubles.

In response to scholarly debates, we have focused our attention on Bukharin's sketch of communist society. But it would be a mistake to assume that the utopian vision is a particularly prominent part of the epic story presented in Part One. On the contrary, it is a small section sandwiched in the middle of a much more dramatic presentation of the titanic collapse of the old order and the anguished birth of the new. If we want to account for the continuing appeal of Part One, we need to see how it provided a way of making sense of the mind-numbing and globe-shaking events of the world war.[15] Bukharin's world-historical narrative is much more focused on the horrors of the imperialist war than on the usual evils denounced by Marxism, such as oppression in the factory or tsarist absolutism.[16] Bukharin pictures the war as the climax of the age of imperialism: the high point of capitalism's achievement and the low point of its failure. Capitalism's achievement is rational organization, extended by war-time imperatives to a nationwide scope and carried to an unheard-of intensity. Capitalism's failure is social conflict, carried to the demonic pitch of the mass destruction of life and of civilized values.

---

13 August Bebel, *Die Frau und der Sozialismus* (Bebel 1891, pp. 266–8). On the unique importance of Bebel's book in Germany, see Vernon Lidtke, *The Alternative Culture: Socialist Labor in Imperial Germany* (Lidtke 1985, p. 186); for its influence in Russia, see Stites 1989, pp. 31, 261.

14 On utopian writing during the Second International, see Marc Angenot, *L'utopie collectiviste: le grand récit socialiste sous la Deuxième Internationale* (Angenot 1993).

15 David Joravsky has recently stressed the importance of the war and the protest against it for understanding Bolshevism; see his insightful article 'Communism in Historical Perspective' (Joravsky 1994).

16 In the debates over the party programme at the Eighth Party Congress, Bukharin wanted to drop the part of the older programme that examined the pre-imperialist age; these sections were kept only at Lenin's insistence.

Bukharin draws a very definite moral from his story: 'Universal disintegration or communism' (sec. 34). In Bukharin's narrative, revolutionary socialism proves itself correct not by learned demonstrations of the doctrine of surplus value or even by the inherent attractiveness of its future society. No, Bolshevism's claim to authority arises from its instinctive and uncompromising opposition to the war; it arises from capitalism's obvious inability to put back together the social order it has torn apart. The emotional climax of Bukharin's narrative is the following outburst (sec. 33):

The costs [*izderzhki*] of revolution are not a conclusive argument against revolution.[17] The capitalist system, the growth of centuries, culminated in the monstrous imperialist war, in which rivers of blood were shed. What civil war can compare in its destructive effects with the brutal disorganization and devastation, with the loss of accumulated wealth of mankind, that resulted from the imperialist war? Manifestly it is essential that humanity shall make an end to capitalism once and for all. With this goal in view, we can endure the period of civil wars and can pave the road to communism, which will heal all our wounds and quickly lead to the development of the productive forces of human society.[18]

The 'stress-induced vision' thesis only obscures the sources of Bukharin's analysis. His central indictment of imperialism – increasing rationalization intertwined with increasing aggression – can be found in such pre-war writers as Karl Kautsky and Rudolf Hilferding.[19] Bukharin's achievement is not so much

---

17   The theme of the *izderzhki* of revolution was constant throughout Bukharin's career; see 'Bukharin's Bolshevik Epic: The Prison Writings', included in this volume.

18   The Pauls were aware of the importance of this passage: they put the last two sentences in capitals, even though they are not so distinguished in the Russian text. In 1918, Bukharin wrote: 'He who defers [the decisive and final victory of the workers] and calls the struggle for this victory an "adventure" when it is the sole exit from the bloody impasse – that person goes against socialism' (*Kommunist*, 1918, no. 3, reprint edited by Ronald Kowalski [Kowalski 1990], p. 174).

19   If we look at the *ABC* reading lists for titles issued prior to 1910, we find that Kautsky is cited more often than any other author, far outstripping Marx, Engels, and the pre-war Lenin. On Kautsky's influence, see the path-breaking book by Moira Donald, *Marxism and Revolution: Karl Kautsky and the Russian Marxists, 1900–1924* (Donald 1993). See also Lih, 'The Proletariat and its Ally: The Logic of Bolshevik "Hegemony"' (entry in Lih 2017, 'All Power to the Soviets!') and Lih 2018b, 'The Tasks of Our Times: Kautsky's *Road to Power* in Germany and Russia'. Hilferding's *Das Finanzkapital* (Hilferding 1910) is also mentioned as a difficult but basic work.

theoretical innovation as the effective presentation of standard Social Democratic themes in a coherent and compelling narrative.

From another angle, we can see that the 'stress-induced vision' hypothesis is not so much wrong as highly misleading, due to its restricted focus on 'war communism' and the trials of 1919. Bukharin's story is not a response to one passing episode but to the global calamity of 1914–1919 as a whole. The fact that the ABC's narrative was provoked by a worldwide time of troubles is not an occult feature to be uncovered by later generations. It is the whole point of the story, loudly insisted on by Bukharin himself. Can the ABC then be called 'a supremely optimistic document'?[20] Yes, but only the gritted-teeth variety of optimism evoked by Preobrazhensky in a pamphlet on the third anniversary of the October revolution: 'Beggarly, devastated, labouring Russia, flowing with blood, will have a reward for its great sufferings.'[21]

2 The 'Socialism Now' Thesis

Part Two of the ABC drops from the heights of the world-historical narrative to tell the story so far of socialism in Russia. Part Two thus offers valuable evidence about what gap, if any, the Bolsheviks saw between their ultimate socialist goals and the realities of Russia in 1919. The most widely accepted hypothesis on this issue is succinctly stated by Isaac Deutscher: 'The Bolshevik was therefore inclined to see the essential features of fully fledged communism embodied in the war economy of 1919–20.'[22] I call this the 'socialism now' thesis.

The ABC is regularly invoked to make this hypothesis seem plausible. Andrzej Walicki points to its 'triumphalistic' tone; Martin Malia tells us that 'in a veritable ideological delirium, the most colossal economic collapse of the century was transmogrified into really-existing Communism, the radiant future hic et nunc, a vision projected in Bukharin's and Preobrazhensky's once famous ABC of Communism'.[23] Leszek Kołakowski is appalled by the criminal utopi-

---

20   Stephen F. Cohen, *Bukharin and the Bolshevik Revolution* (Cohen 1971, p. 100).

21   Evgenii Preobrazhensky, *Trekhletie Oktiabr'skoi revoliutsii* (Preobrazhensky 1921, pp. 15–16).

22   Isaac Deutscher, *The Prophet Armed: Trotsky, 1879–1921* (Deutscher 1954, p. 489).

23   Andrzej Walicki, *Marxism and the Leap to the Kingdom of Freedom: The Rise and Fall of the Communist Utopia* (Walicki 1995, p. 376); Martin Malia, *The Soviet Tragedy: A History of Socialism in Russia, 1917–1991* (Malia 1994, p. 130). Malia's misreading of the ABC does heavy (in my personal view, irreparable) damage to a central thesis of his book, namely, that the 'deep structure' of Marxism permitted or even mandated a leap into socialism, even in the beggarly, devastated Russia of 1920. As far as I know, however, Malia's critics have not challenged the accuracy of his portrait of 'war communism'.

anism he finds in the *ABC*: 'In 1920 the idea of a planned economy belonged to the realm of fantasy: Russia's industry lay in ruins, there was barely any transport, and the one pressing problem was how to save the towns from imminent starvation, not how to bring about a Communist millennium'.[24] Sheila Fitzpatrick uses the *ABC* to document the existence of Bolsheviks who got so carried away that they thought that Russia was approaching communism. She writes that 'in 1920, as the Bolsheviks headed towards victory in the Civil War, a mood of euphoria and desperation took hold. With the old world disappearing in the flames of Revolution and Civil War, it seemed to many Bolsheviks that a new world was about to arise, phoenix-like, from the ashes [and that] the transition to communism was imminent, possibly only weeks or months away'.[25]

In his more balanced and nuanced account of Bolshevik beliefs prior to NEP, Stephen Cohen does not fully endorse the 'socialism now' thesis. In his brief discussion of the *ABC* itself, however, he sees it as a manifestation of the alleged 'general euphoria' of the civil war: the *ABC* was 'a statement of Bolshevik aspirations and utopian hopes in 1919, of party innocence, not Soviet reality'.[26] It should be noted that all of the authorities cited here correctly assume that their reading of the *ABC* is uncontroversial; they certainly feel no need to document their interpretation at any length.

The real message of Part Two is not difficult to uncover. Bukharin and Preobrazhensky believed that the Bolsheviks had the right and the duty to begin constructing socialism in Russia; they believed that in some areas the foundation had already been laid; they believed that progress in Russia would be much swifter after the inevitable world revolution.[27] But they also believed, and repeatedly emphasized, that Russia in 1919 had made only the first steps in a long and difficult journey. They looked around them and saw what anybody would see: poverty, disorganization, tragedy. They did not see achieved socialism.

---

24 Leszek Kołakowski, *Main Currents of Marxism*, 3 vols (Kołakowski 1978, 3, p. 29).
25 Fitzpatrick 1982, pp. 71, 77. Even though the *ABC* was written in 1919 and the climax of Bolshevik foolishness is located in 1920, Fitzpatrick supports her remarks with a reference to Carr's 'Bolshevik Utopia' essay that is exclusively devoted to the *ABC* (the Carr reference has been dropped from the second edition of Fitzpatrick's *The Russian Revolution*).
26 Cohen 1971, pp. 87, 84.
27 See sec. 41. In the Pauls' translation of this section, we read 'our party has made the prompt establishment of communism its definite aim'. 'Prompt establishment' translates *nemedlennoe stroitel'stvo*; as the argument of the section and of the chapter shows, the sentence is better translated as 'our party sees its task as getting down to the job of building socialism right away'.

Bukharin and Preobrazhensky's insistence on this point is not merely a casual admission, not some parenthetical qualification, but rather a constant and prominent theme that is impossible to miss. Part Two sometimes seems little more than a long string of excuses about why 'years and years will go by before things are set up properly' and why there are 'enormous [*velichaishei*] difficulties' in constructing communism in Russia (sec. 42). High on the list is the government's helplessness in the face of appalling poverty. All that soviet power can do about, say, the very severe [*tiagchaishee*] housing crisis during the civil war is to guarantee fair distribution (sec. 126).[28] Although there are plenty of decrees about labour protection, 'it happens very often that reality has nothing to do with the decree, which exists on paper and not in real life' (sec. 134). After describing 'our final goal' of full and effective social protection, Bukharin notes that 'of course, this bears not the slightest resemblance to our present condition. We are now an impoverished country, thanks to the tender mercies of the international robbers' (sec. 130). The closing words of the ABC leave the reader with an impression of devastating poverty:

> It is necessary to assure that the population be able to receive free medicines and medical help. The difficulty at present is the absolute shortage of medicines. This shortage is not caused so much by the collapse [*razrukha*] of our own production as by the blockade. The 'humane' Allies want to crush us not only by cutting us off from raw materials and fuel – not only by the 'bony hand of hunger' – but by epidemics. This brings us back to our general struggle with world imperialism (sec. 138).

Another enormous barrier to Bolshevik transformational goals is cultural backwardness: 'the petty-bourgeois character of Russia, the lack of extensive organizational experience on the part of the proletariat, and so on' (sec. 45). A better understanding of these realities led Bukharin to temper the optimism of 1917. 'In one of his pamphlets, published before the October revolution, Comrade Lenin wrote very truly that our task was to see that every cook should be taught to take her share in the administration of the state. Of course, this task is very

---

28   In the ABC and other writings of this period, the term soviet power (*sovetskaia vlast*)
      wavers between designating a type of political system (as opposed, for example, to a par-
      liamentary republic), and designating a specific state or country (as in 'Soviet Russia'). In
      order to keep alive the more unfamiliar nuance of 'a sovereign authority based on the sovi-
      ets', I will refrain from capitalizing 'soviet'. For the record, Bukharin and Preobrazhensky
      usually write *Sovetskaia vlast*; the Pauls translate this as 'Soviet Power'.

difficult and a mass of obstacles exist on the path to its realization. First among such obstacles comes the low cultural level of the masses' (sec. 47).

In a similar vein, Preobrazhensky laments the difficulty of fighting 'the religious prejudices that are already deeply rooted in the consciousness of the masses and that cling so stubbornly to life. The struggle will be a long one, demanding much steadfastness and great patience' (sec. 92). The abolition of classes will not in itself solve these problems, since 'class psychology always lives on after the social relations that gave birth to it'. Indeed, 'even the abolition of classes may prove a lengthy process [*mozhet silno zatianutsia*]' (sec. 75).

According to the 'socialism now' thesis, the Bolsheviks believed that the transition to socialism was being accelerated by the imperatives of struggle.[29] The authors of the *ABC* saw these same imperatives as another excuse for delay. In the chapter on finance, Preobrazhensky writes that 'so long as the civil war continues and the bourgeoisie's resistance has not been broken, the proletarian state is forced to some degree to be an organ standing apart from production ... But what is really characteristic of the proletarian state is not these things, the ones that make it similar to an exploiter state – rather, it is that this organization will gradually be transformed from an unproductive organization to an organization for economic administration' (sec. 122). Preobrazhensky sounds the same note of apology about the delay in replacing the barrack system with a territorial militia: 'Although the circumstances of the civil war often compel the party to make the best of old methods of organization, the essential aspiration is toward something different' (sec. 66). The reader of the *ABC* learns that bureaucratism – in the opprobrious sense of 'a detachment from the masses, on the one hand, and from the party, on the other' – is 'the common lot of almost all important organizations of soviet power'. Preobrazhensky lamented that the system of army commissars has turned into 'a harbour of refuge for lazy and incompetent party and war office *chinovniki*' (sec. 65). Bukharin remarks that

---

29 For example, Moshe Lewin writes that 'there was even a stronger sedative for whoever might have had qualms about this or other harsh practices: the belief that something more than the war economy justified them. The term "war communism" implied that the most progressive system on earth was just installed *deus ex machina* by the most expedient, unexpected but irreversible leap to freedom' (*Political Undercurrents in Soviet Economic Debates* [Lewin 1974, p. 79]). In the reprint edition of 1991, Lewin adds that 'it is worth reminding the reader that the term war-communism was not used during the events but was applied by Lenin after the civil war. But other similar terms, expressing this same content, were current' (*Stalinism and the Seeds of Soviet Reform* [Lewin 1991, p. xxvii]). Unfortunately, Lewin does not inform us what these 'similar terms' were.

bureaucratism 'is a grave danger for the proletariat, [which] did not destroy the old official-ridden state in order for bureaucratism to grow up again from below' (sec. 54).[30]

The *ABC* does show that party officials 'in the provinces' had been forcing the pace of socialist transformation. Rather than being carried away by a wave of revolutionary enthusiasm, Preobrazhensky in particular seems appalled:

> It makes no sense for the soviet power to simply prohibit petty trade when it is not in a position to replace that trade completely with the activity of its own organs of distribution. There have been cases when local soviets (especially in regions from which the White Guards have recently been cleared out) have prohibited free trade without having created their own food-supply organs or, what is even more important, without assuring themselves of having enough food to give the population via these organs. As a result, private trade is made illegal, and prices multiply by many times (sec. 115).

Similarly with housing: 'The nationalized houses, both large and small, had no one to care for them properly; they fell into disrepair and in many cases there was no one willing to live in them. Meanwhile, all this stirred up anger and indignation against the soviet power on the part of the owners of small houses' (sec. 126).

---

30   In 'Bukharin and the State', Neil Harding has used the *ABC* to strengthen the contrast he sees between Bukharin's political outlook in 1917–1918 and his outlook in 1919–1920 (Harding 1991, see especially pp. 102–3). According to Harding, in the earlier period Bukharin wanted to 'smash the state' and leap immediately into a realm of freedom, but by 1919 Bukharin had reverted to defending the repressive 'dictatorship of the proletariat' that copied the imperialist state. The contrast Harding is trying to establish founders on material he does not take into account. First, there is much evidence from 1917–18 that Bukharin wanted a repressive dictatorship of the proletariat that would use the imperialist state machine for the benefit of the people (besides the *Program* already cited, see the articles from 1917 reprinted in *Na podstupakh k oktiabriu* and, in particular, Bukharin's speech to the Constituent Assembly [Bukharin 1926, pp. 177–85]). Second, there is much evidence in the *ABC* itself that Bukharin still saw 'soviet power' as a state form distinguished by high and growing mass participation. (Harding also erroneously attributes some passages written by Preobrazhensky to Bukharin.) It should be noted that Bukharin's discussion of bureaucratism was not his individual warning to the party. It is a reflection of the official party programme that was adopted in spring 1919: the programme recommends combating the menace of bureaucratism by going further down the path opened up by the Paris Commune. The Bolshevik conception of the dictatorship of the proletariat cannot be grasped unless we see that it was meant to be both repressive and participatory.

Poverty, cultural backwardness, the imperatives of struggle, undisciplined enthusiasm – the list of excuses is a long and compelling one. Did Bukharin and Preobrazhensky think that the Bolsheviks had achieved nothing by way of socialist construction? No, but even here their claims are carefully hedged. Bukharin announced that a basic task of the soviet power was the unification of all economic activity under one state plan, and he furthermore claimed that the foundation and basic framework [kostiak] of the planned economy had already been created, at least in the large-scale industrial sector. Lest any reader get the wrong idea about the concrete results of this achievement, Bukharin is quick to add that 'of course, it would be absurd to think that within a brief space of time, when hunger and cold are rife, when there is a lack of fuel and raw materials, it is possible to rapidly achieve permanent and satisfactory results. But while it is true that people do not live in the foundations of their house, and that they cannot live in the house at all until it is completed and the scaffolding removed, nevertheless the foundation is indispensable' (sec. 95).

Walicki informs us that 'Bukharin spoke glowingly about the collapse of the Russian economy'.[31] Bukharin's actual words leave a different impression:

The foundation of our whole policy must be the widest possible development of productive forces. The breakdown [razrukha] is so vast, the post-war scarcity [golod] is so conspicuous, that everything must be subordinated to this one task. More products! More boots, scythes, barrels, textiles, salt, clothing, bread and so on – these are our primary need ... This is what we need now, if we are to avoid dying of hunger amid the post-war breakdown, if we are to be clothed, if we are to regain our strength, if we are to proceed more swiftly along the road of constructing a new life (sec. 94).

Preobrazhensky's claims for socialist transformation in agriculture are even more modest. He lists what the Bolsheviks had already accomplished by way of sovkhozy, communes, and the more primitive forms of collective agriculture. But the bottom line is that 'the Russian Communist Party is forced to fight for socialism in agriculture under the most unfavourable conditions ... whatever successes we may achieve in this matter of organizing soviet farms and com-

---

31   Walicki 1995, p. 596. Alec Nove remarks: 'Of course Bukharin and his friends were well aware of the appalling shortage of goods of every kind, and did emphasize the necessity of increasing production' (An Economic History of the USSR [Nove 1969, p. 66]). It is unclear how Nove reconciled this observation with the views cited in the passage used as an epigraph for the present article.

munes, small-scale peasant farming will continue to exist for a long time to come; it will remain the predominant form of agriculture in Russia, both in terms of area cultivated and quantity of agricultural produce' (secs. 104, 112). Preobrazhensky goes on to discuss state aid to peasant agriculture. All in all, the ABC paints a vivid picture of Russia in 1919 – a picture that is the exact opposite of what the 'socialism now' thesis would lead us to expect. Indeed, what is distinctive about the ABC as a political platform is not its promise of pie-in-the-sky at some unspecified future date but rather its almost obsessive emphasis on the present costs to be endured, on Russia's poverty and its enforced distance from the goals of the revolution. The ABC by itself does not refute the 'socialism now' thesis; perhaps some other Bolsheviks at some other time thought that the millennium was only a few weeks away.[32] We are still left with the mystery of the ABC: How can this text leave anyone with an impression of 'euphoria', 'contempt for hardships and suffering', or 'the glorious future *hic et nunc*'? More to the point, why has this indefensible reading been left unchallenged? Can it be that the scholarly community interested in the Russian revolution and its consequences simply does not have a very sound grasp of Bolshevik doctrine?

3   The 'Disingenuous Bolshevik' Thesis

We can divide Bolshevik policies prior to 1921 into two broad categories: policies aimed at socialist transformation and policies aimed at meeting the emergencies of civil war and economic breakdown. 'We' can divide up policies in this manner, but did the Bolsheviks? It is widely believed that they did so only after 1921 as a way of covering up their ideological tracks. I call this the 'disingenuous Bolshevik' thesis after Malia's vivid formulation: although in actuality 'the Bolsheviks escalated the military communism of the Civil War emergency into a militant and millenarian communism, one that was designed to endure', they were afterwards 'somewhat disingenuous in disowning their handiwork once they were forced to embark on the NEP'.[33]

---

32   See, for example, Bertrand Patenaude, 'Peasants into Russians: The Utopian Essence of War Communism' (Patenaude 1995). In what is by far the best effort to document the 'socialism now' thesis, Patenaude explicitly limits his case to the latter part of 1920. Patenaude argues that at this time a Bolshevik consensus had emerged that the peasants had already attained socialist consciousness even though agricultural production was still untransformed. I find the existence of this consensus highly implausible because (among other reasons) it blatantly contradicts the party programme of 1919 and the ABC. See also 'Bolsheviks at Work: The Sowing Committees of 1920', included in this volume.

33   Malia 1994, p. 132.

According to this thesis, the Bolsheviks failed to justify their policies in 1919–20 as temporary responses to military and economic emergencies; any later claim to the contrary is disingenuous. Fitzpatrick invokes the ABC as an emblem of this disingenuousness:

> Once War Communism had failed, the less said about its ideological underpinnings the better. But from an earlier Bolshevik perspective – for example, that of Bukharin and Preobrazhensky in their classic ABC of Communism (1919) – the opposite was true. While War Communism policies were in force, it was natural for Bolsheviks to give them an ideological justification – to assert that the party, armed with the scientific ideology of Marxism, was in full control of events rather than simply struggling to keep up.[34]

Let us test the 'disingenuous Bolshevik' thesis by means of two important policies of the pre-NEP period: the frantic inflation and the burdens placed on the peasantry. The ABC's chapter on currency policies was written by Preobrazhensky. Did he see the runaway inflation as either good in itself or as a desirable tool in the rapid abolition of money?

The brief chapter gives contradictory impressions. On the one hand, Preobrazhensky seems intent on delaying the abolition of money. For the first and only time in the ABC, we hear of socialism as a stage prior to full communism. Why? Presumably so Preobrazhensky could make the point that money will still be around in the socialist stage. 'Commodity production' – production for the market – will still exist at this intervening stage, if only because of the 'huge dimensions' of private trade and the economic weight of peasant agriculture. Furthermore, 'it will be disadvantageous to abolish money right away insofar as the issuing of paper money is a substitute for taxation and gives the proletarian state the possibility of holding out in unbelievably difficult circumstances'. Thus money will continue to exist as long as the state is unable to assume the market's role in providing consumer items, that is, not until 'the restoration of industry and its expansion' (sec. 121). On the other hand, we find a passage such as the following: 'The gradual abolition of money will also be aided by the enormous issuing of paper money, in association with the enormous reduction in the exchange of commodities caused by the disorga-

---

34   Fitzpatrick 1982, p. 71. If the Bolsheviks wanted to hush up the ideological underpinnings of earlier policies, and these underpinnings were revealed by the ABC, it is something of a puzzle why the ABC was widely reprinted and hugely popular during the 1920s.

nization of industry. The increasing depreciation of the currency is in essence its spontaneous cancellation [*stikhiinoe annulirovanie*]' (sec. 121). Well, which is it? Does the abolition of money have to wait until Russia has obtained a flourishing industrial base, or is money now being abolished by the collapse of industry?

At this point it is legitimate to look ahead to summer 1920 and the much more extensive discussion of currency policies contained in Preobrazhensky's *Paper Money in the Era of the Proletarian Dictatorship*.[35] This book should provide a strong reinforcement for the 'disingenuous Bolshevik' thesis, since in general the Bolsheviks are supposed to have gotten more and more carried away during 1920. Indeed, according to Carr's translation, Preobrazhensky dedicated his book to the printing press in these terms: 'that machine-gun of the Commissariat of Finance which poured fire into the rear of the bourgeois system and used the currency laws of that regime in order to destroy it'. Carr mistranslated this sentence and overlooked what Preobrazhensky said in the rest of the dedication.[36] He thus is able to present this statement as a deluded claim to be in full control: 'The thesis that the depreciation of the rouble was engineered or tolerated by the Soviet Government in order to compass the ruin of the bourgeoisie by destroying the bourgeois monetary system was an ex post facto justification of a course which was followed only because no means could be found of avoiding it.'[37]

Preobrazhensky's real attitude could have been expressed by quoting Abraham Lincoln: 'I claim not to have controlled events, but confess plainly that events have controlled me.'[38] Preobrazhensky's main purpose for looking back at previous policy is to hold up Soviet policy as an example of how not to do it. The financial decisions of the Soviet government were not based on any scientific insight, but rather were carried out chaotically [*sovershenno stikhiino*], under the pressure of day-to-day circumstances. Future revolutionary governments should look back at the Bolshevik experience mainly to find out what to avoid.[39]

---

35   Evgenii Preobrazhensky, *Bumazhnye dengi v epokhu proletarskoi diktatury* (Preobrazhensky 1920) (hereafter referred to as *Paper Money*).

36   In reality, Preobrazhensky did not say 'in order to destroy' but 'as a means of destroying' (*v sredstvo unichtozheniia*). The dedication itself explains how the printing press was used: it was a 'source of financing for the revolution' that saved soviet power 'in the most difficult period of its existence, when no possibility existed of using direct taxes to pay for the costs of the civil war' (*Paper Money*, 4).

37   Carr, *Bolshevik Revolution*, 2:261.

38   Lincoln's comment comes from a letter written to A.G. Hodges on 4 April 1864.

39   Preobrazhensky 1920, p. 69.

Preobrazhensky examines at length the destructive social consequences of using the unlimited issuing of paper money as a way of taxing the population. The salaried office workers are the worst hit, since they have nothing material to exchange. The workers are not far behind: because wages are not adjusted in timely fashion to rising prices, the burden imposed by the inflationary tax falls heavily on all wage earners. Peasants may benefit in the short term by charging exorbitant prices, but inflation then proceeds to destroy the value of the money they have hoarded. In fact, the only one to really benefit from the inflation is the speculator – a figure that in hindsight we might call the proto-nepman. 'In general, this stratum of the population succeeds in adapting to the Soviet system, to the issuing of paper money, to money's loss of value; it manages to evade any tax burden and to throw the burden back either on the naive peasant or on the workers and salaried employees.'[40]

Despite all these unpleasant consequences of the inflation, Soviet power deserves credit for one thing and for one thing only: when the printing press was the only method for taxing the population and thus saving the revolution, Soviet power did not spare the printing press.

Still, the usefulness of the inflationary tax was now (summer 1920) coming to an end; the immediate future required new approaches. Preobrazhensky compares the situation to tapping wine from a barrel that is rapidly filling up with water as well as losing wine through another hole.[41] Revolutionary upheaval had destroyed the economy, there was small hope of getting aid from abroad, so that in order to get desperately needed resources, the state was forced to adopt a variety of crudely direct methods. In line with official policy, Preobrazhensky suggests a number of such methods, ranging from 'labour obligation' (that is, state-imposed corvée) to belt-tightening by the proletariat.[42]

Despite his earlier comments in the ABC about the self-abolition of money, Preobrazhensky now (1920) advocates the introduction of a new currency

---

40   Preobrazhensky 1920, pp. 56–7.
41   Preobrazhensky 1920, p. 60.
42   In this discussion, Preobrazhensky uses for the first time the term for which he later became famous – primitive socialist accumulation – although he confines it to undoing the damage done by war and revolution. Ironically, he took the term from Bukharin's *Economy of the Transition Period* (1920). The assumption that Russia was necessarily confined to its own resources represents a change of emphasis from the ABC or perhaps simply a difference between Preobrazhensky and Bukharin. In September 1920, even after the defeat in Poland, Bukharin was still prepared to assert that 'the [international] revolutionary wave has never been so high as it is now' (*Deviataia konferentsiia RKP(b)* 1972, p. 59; see also the ABC, secs. 41–2).

backed by silver. This more secure currency would ward off a disastrous peasant boycott of money and thus a relapse into barter that would leave the cities
defenceless. Even if by some chance the state managed to collect enough grain
to feed the urban population during the upcoming year, money would still be
required to obtain products that the state could not yet supply. Even after the
economy revived, money would still be a very useful 'corrective' to planned distribution.[43]

By now, Preobrazhensky's long-term scenario for the elimination of money
will not surprise the reader: 'When the state is gradually in a condition to give
the peasant everything that local industry [*kustar*] now gives, and to give it
with higher quality and under better conditions, then the dying out of the free
market will begin; there will be a decrease in its economic significance for peasant farms as well as a squeezing-out of local industry by the socialist factory.'
Preobrazhensky therefore criticizes Iurii Larin for his 'completely unjustified
optimism' in claiming that money will die out in the next few years.[44]

Let us take stock. It would be incorrect to view *Paper Money* as representative
of a Bolshevik consensus, since Preobrazhensky is engaged in lively polemics
with other Bolshevik economists such as Larin. That said, *Paper Money* is still
one of the most extensive and authoritative Bolshevik comments on financial
questions. In it we find that the inflation is already justified as a painfully costly
emergency measure, prior to NEP, at the height of so-called war communism.
In 1920, Preobrazhensky seems even less inclined than he was in the ABC to
see the inflation as a tool for abolishing money; he now argues for retaining a
useful currency for the foreseeable future. As a method of taxation, the main
advantage of the inflation was that it minimized the direct use of coercion.
Coercive 'labour obligation' policies are also firmly tied to the economic crisis
facing Russia in 1920. Preobrazhensky does not advocate coercion instead of
material interest: he advocates coercion for the sake of material interest.

At the Tenth Party Congress in March 1921, Preobrazhensky gave strong support to Lenin's proposal to introduce a tax-in-kind and cited *Paper Money* in

---

43 Preobrazhensky 1920, pp. 83–4. See also Preobrazhensky's words in the ABC, sec. 116: 'Pre-
    cisely in view of the high degree of centralization, this [socialist apparatus of distribution]
    can easily degenerate into a cumbrous and dilatory machine in which a great many arti-
    cles rot before they reach the consumer.'
44 Preobrazhensky 1920, pp. 82–3. Despite Preobrazhensky's polemic with Larin, despite his
    advocacy of a silver-backed currency, despite his scepticism about the results of the *razver-
    stka* in the near future, despite his warning that a premature abolition of money would be
    'catastrophic', Malle writes on the basis of this text and without qualification that Pre-
    obrazhensky 'affirmed that the time for abolishing paper money was near' (Malle 1985,
    p. 184).

order to demonstrate the need for a more secure currency. Was he being disingenuous? I rather think he understood his own previous arguments and attitudes better than scholars do today.[45]

We now turn to an even more fundamental issue: the coercive burdens placed on the peasantry by means of the *prodrazverstka* and the seemingly endless 'obligations' (*povinnosti*) ranging from compulsory cartage to removal of snow from railroad tracks. Did the Bolsheviks see the coercive backup to these policies as distasteful emergency measures or as a permanently valid way of achieving socialism and assuring the normal functioning of the economy? Did coercion replace material interest out of necessity or out of perceived socialist principle?[46] According to Kolakowski, the ABC shows that 'Bukharin, like Lenin, regarded the system of basing economic life on mass terror not as a transient necessity but as a permanent principle of socialist organization ... Socialism – as conceived by both Trotsky and Bukharin at this time – is a permanent, nation-wide labour camp.' Walicki tells us that the ABC justified Stalin-type policies of coercive collectivization a decade ahead of time.[47]

My reading of the ABC suggests that Bukharin and Preobrazhensky remained loyal to the orthodox Social Democratic scenario of socialist transformation (after a forcible revolution) as a gradual and voluntary process based on per-

---

45 Contrary to our general picture of accelerating Bolshevik radicalism in 1920, Preobrazhensky seems to have sobered up somewhat between the ABC and *Paper Money*. After writing the above, I came across a contemporary review of *Paper Money* that confirms this general picture. Mikhail Olminsky's review (clearly written before the end of 1920) argued that Preobrazhensky had arrived at a more reasonable position during the process of writing the book itself. Olminsky therefore recommended it strongly as an antidote to the 'popular stupidities' current in the party about the quick disappearance of money. Olminsky's endorsement of Preobrazhensky is in striking contrast to his harsh 1921 review of Bukharin's *Economy of the Transition Period*, in which he argues (in my view, erroneously) that Bukharin seemed to think that the transition to full socialism was actually happening. (Olminsky's review of *Paper Money* was originally published in *Proletarskaia revoliutsiia*, 1921, no. 1: 181–5; Olminsky's review of Bukharin's *Economy of the Transition Period* is discussed in 'Bukharin on Bolshevik Illusions', included in this volume).

46 In the words of László Szamuely: 'This thesis [that the main tool of building and controlling the socialist economy is state coercion] can perhaps not be found *expressis verbis* in contemporary literature, but we can draw well-founded conclusions from the measures and methods that were discussed by the contemporary ideologues and from the methods that were not mentioned', that is, material incentives. See *First Models of the Socialist Economic Systems: Principles and Theories* (Szamuely 1974, pp. 38–9, 44).

47 Kolakowski 1978, 3: 28–9; Walicki 1995, pp. 404–11. Kolakowski's remarks are based not only on the ABC but also on Bukharin's *Economy of the Transition Period* (1920). I agree that the two works express essentially the same outlook – an outlook, however, that is the complete opposite of what Kolakowski claims.

ceived material advantage.[48] In the case of Russia, this view translated into the following axiomatic assumptions that pervade the entire argument of the ABC:

- Large-scale centralized economic units are vastly more productive than scattered, small-scale ones.
- Only direct perception of material interest – not coercion – can induce people to adopt these higher economic forms. The legitimate use of coercion is to 'expropriate the expropriators', defend worker power against its enemies, and deal with the emergency situations created by civil war and economic breakdown. The organs created in order to win the civil war – the revolutionary tribunals, the Red Army, the Cheka – 'have no future' after the end of hostilities.[49]
- Even in the best of circumstances, preparation of higher forms will take time, and the sacrifices imposed by the civil war have made this preparatory work even more difficult and time-consuming. Lower economic forms should not be eliminated until higher forms are ready to replace them.
- It will therefore be necessary to rely during the foreseeable future on lower economic forms such as single-owner peasant farms, wage differentials, and petty trade.

Did the ABC's justification of policies toward the peasantry conform to these guidelines? Most writers today see the *prodrazverstka* as the centrepiece of Bolshevik relations with the peasantry. As far as I can discover, however, the words *razverstka* or *prodrazverstka* do not occur in the ABC. I explain this by observing that *razverstka* was the name of a method of grain collection, a method borrowed from a tsarist minister of agriculture, A.A. Rittikh. As such it was not

---

48   The orthodox Social Democratic scenario insisted that a gradual transformation of society was possible only after a forcible revolution gave state power to the proletariat. The classic account of the reasoning behind this scenario is Karl Kautsky, *Die soziale Revolution* (Kautsky 1902), a work that is cited in the ABC's reading lists. Even in *State and Revolution*, Lenin says that this book contains 'very much that is exceedingly valuable' and makes no objection to its overall argument (*Polnoe sobranie sochinenii*, 5th ed., 33: 107).

49   Preobrazhensky writes: 'As far as the revolutionary tribunals are concerned, this form of proletarian justice also has no future, just like the Red Army after its victory over the White Guards, or the extraordinary commissions, or all the organs created by the proletariat during the period of the not-yet-completed civil war. With the victory of the proletariat over the bourgeois counterrevolution, these organs will fall away as unneeded [*za nenadobnost'iu*]' (sec. 75). According to Walicki, 'The authors insisted that under a proletarian dictatorship the resistance of the bourgeoisie would intensify' (Walicki 1995, p. 377). In his effort to forge links between the ABC and Stalin, Walicki has forced the text: the authors offer no opinion on whether bourgeois resistance will intensify (sec. 23). As noted below, the ABC assumes permanent hostility from the kulaks; in other passages, the projected scenario seems to be the opposite (for example, sec. 101 on 'bourgeois specialists').

THE MYSTERY OF THE ABC

a matter of great doctrinal significance.[50] The issues symbolized for us by the *prodrazverstka* were separated by the authors of the *ABC* into two overlapping concerns: the long-term goal of abolishing private trade and the short-term goal of maintaining some kind of revolutionary alliance with the peasantry.

Preobrazhensky's scenario for abolishing private trade in the long run is straightforward:

> Petty trade will be finished off [*ubita*] only gradually, in proportion as a larger and ever larger quantity of products needed for the supply of the population passes through the hands of the state. If today Narkomprod exists side by side with a luxuriantly blooming Sukharevka, it means only one thing: the war between capitalism and socialism in the realm of distribution still goes on ... Petty trade will continue to exist until large-scale industry in the towns has been restored and the provision of basic consumer items can be genuinely accomplished by state monopolies (sec. 115).[51]

Of course, these pleasing long-term scenarios did not help the Bolsheviks very much at a time when they were putting immense burdens on the peasantry. These burdens confronted the Bolsheviks with some life-or-death questions of political strategy and class relations. In the *ABC*, the key discussion of these matters is by Preobrazhensky in a section entitled 'The Tactics of the Communist Party in Relation to the Peasantry' (sec. 114).[52] He takes the traditional Bolshevik division of the peasantry into kulak, middle peasant, and poor peasant and turns these categories into characters in a narrative of class relations.

Preobrazhensky begins his discussion with the kulaks, who supported the October revolution as long as it was aimed principally at the landlords. They

---

50 On the tsarist origins of the *razverstka* system, see Lih, *Bread and Authority in Russia, 1914–1921* (Lih 1990, chap. 2) and 'Bolshevik *Razverstka* and War Communism', included in this volume. An alternative explanation is that the *razverstka* had only become official policy at the beginning of 1919, and the authors of the *ABC* did not foresee that it would become ideologically central in 1920. This seems unlikely to me.

51 The image of the war between Narkomprod (the government food-supply agency) and Sukharevka (the Moscow bazaar that was a symbol of the underground market) as a war between socialism and capitalism was a commonplace. Preobrazhensky's understanding of 'petty trade' obviously does not include the grain trade. For more on the need to provide goods for the countryside, see Bukharin in section 42.

52 A full discussion of Preobrazhensky's views would place them in the context of his other writings on the peasantry from this period, particularly his remarkable *Pravda* articles of 1918 and 1919. If these writings were better known, there would be a fundamental modification in the stereotypical view of Preobrazhensky as somehow anti-peasant.

started to lose their enthusiasm when they were forced to undergo egalitarian land redistribution. More and more they realized that the Bolsheviks stood in the way of their own treasured goal of a bourgeois transformation of the countryside, and so they adopted a stance of 'unremitting hostility' toward the new regime. Preobrazhensky's conclusion is bleak: 'The possibility is not excluded that the soviet power will be forced to carry out a systematic expropriation of the kulaks, mobilizing them for socially useful work and above all for the task of improving peasant and state land.'

Middle peasants constitute the vast majority of the countryside. Torn as they are between the labouring side of their nature and the 'small property-owner' side, the central characteristic of the middle peasant is vacillation. This 'wobbling' between the two contending sides is intensified 'by the necessity to share their grain surpluses with the urban worker [and to do this] ahead of time without the hope of immediately receiving the products of town industry in exchange'.[53] In response, the Bolsheviks must 'emphasize the specifically peasant motives for participation in the civil war. The peasant is not interested in the fact that we are fighting for socialism as such, but rather in the fact that we are depriving imperialism of the power to exploit the small-scale property owner in barbarous fashion' by reinstating the landlords. Therefore, 'while struggling for the socialist transformation of agriculture, we must not irritate the middle peasant by ill-considered and premature measures; we should avoid in every way any coercive enlistment [*pritiagivanie*] into communes and artels'.

Preobrazhensky casts the poor peasants as the regime's main prop in the countryside, but he is forced to note that at present they are in disarray. The correct strategy in the future is to show the economic superiority of collective farming methods. The poor peasant can truly undermine the kulak's influence only by out-producing him, since 'the kulak is powerful in the village because he is a good *khoziain*'. This strategy stands in direct contrast to the committees of the poor (*kombedy*) in 1918. Preobrazhensky's distaste for the *kombedy* is so strong that he even has a kind word for the kulaks: 'This will not be a dictatorship of the poor peasants in the strict sense of the term, not the domination of "paupers and loafers," as the kulak used to complain during the time of the *kombedy*, and not always without reason.'[54]

---

53   Unfortunately, the Pauls' translation drops the key word 'immediately' (*nemedlenno*). The term *wobbling* is taken from the Pauls' translation of *mechetsia* in section 25, which contains Bukharin's account of relations with the peasantry.

54   Preobrazhensky continued to sneer at the *kombedy* in 1922, for which he was rebuked by Lenin (see Lenin, *Polnoe sobranie sochinenii*, 3d ed., 27: 440–6). Unfortunately, the main

To Preobrazhensky's discussion we may add a crucial passage from Bukharin's *Economy of the Transition Period*, published only a few months after the ABC [Bukharin's emphasis]:

> It is obvious that only a real process of 'exchange of objects' between town and country can provide a strong and stable base for the decisive influence of the town. *The renewal of the productive process in industry*, the rebirth of industry in its socialist form, is thus a necessary condition for the more or less swift enlistment [*vtiagivanie*] of the village into the organizing process. But since the rebirth of industry itself requires that a stream of goods flow into the towns, the absolute necessity of this stream no matter what is utterly clear.

This minimal 'equilibrium' can only be achieved (a) by using some of the resources that remain in the town and (b) with the help of state-proletarian coercion. This state coercion (forced collection of grain surpluses, tax-in-kind, or any other such policy) has an economic foundation: in the first place, directly, since the peasantry is itself interested in the development of industry that gives it agricultural machinery, artificial fertilizer, electrical energy, and so forth; in the second place, indirectly, since the proletarian state power is the best means of protection against the restoration of economic repression by the large landowner, the usurer, the banker, the capitalist state, and so on.

Bukharin has a footnote to this discussion in which he responds to Karl Kautsky's criticism of the Bolsheviks for taking grain surpluses: 'The "intelligent" Kautsky does not even understand the significance of the war against Denikin, does not understand what is understandable to the most benighted peasant.'[55]

---

secondary description of this revealing and symptomatic exchange is E.H. Carr's unreliable account (*The Bolshevik Revolution*, 2: 291–3; see also p. 152).

55 Bukharin, *Ekonomika perekhodnogo perioda* (Bukharin 1920, pp. 83–4). On pages 132–3, it is stated in abstract but unambiguous language that obtaining goods from the countryside by noneconomic methods is an emergency measure that cannot be continued for any length of time. In the notorious chapter on 'extra-economic coercion', Bukharin notes that peasant resistance is understandable 'insofar as the exhausted towns are unable at first [*v pervikh porakh*] to give an equivalent for grain and for [labour] obligations' (146). Nowhere does Bukharin suggest any modification of the ABC's prohibition against coercive enlistment into communes and the like. It should be noted that there is no contradiction between Bukharin's pre-NEP justification of coercion applied to the peasantry and his later views during NEP. In any event, Bukharin himself saw none: he consistently affirmed the basic argument of *Economy of the Transition Period* about the costs of revolution; he consistently defined 'war communism' as a policy that would always be justified under similar circumstances of class struggle and external intervention; he consistently

Let us take stock of what the preceding material has to tell us. Bukharin and Preobrazhensky take for granted that town-country relations should be based, when possible, on mutual material advantage. Coercion did not replace perceived material advantage as the main motor of their transformation strategy. The coercive burden placed on the peasantry during the civil war is already described as an unfortunate emergency measure *prior* to NEP, during the height of so-called war communism. The standard scholarly claim to the contrary must be rejected.

The most ominous note is struck by Preobrazhensky's threat of retaliation against the kulaks. This threat reveals the real source of danger in the Bolshevik outlook: the narrative of class struggle and the self-fulfilling prophecy of 'unremitting hostility'. The 'disingenuous Bolshevik' thesis gets in the way of proper analysis of this danger when it insists that the Bolsheviks saw coercion as a tool of socialist transformation. The ABC is not a charter for Stalin's coercive collectivization; on the contrary, it demonstrates why Stalin had to lie so grandiosely about the 'voluntary' nature of collectivization.[56]

Of course, the Bolsheviks changed their mind about some of the arguments made in these passages (and admitted they had done so): the private market was legalized and the economic leadership of the poor peasants proved a disappointment. Yet none of these modifications touched on the main strategy of transformation: the private market would eventually be 'squeezed out' by the superior performance of state and cooperative trading organs, and a restored industrial sector would provide the basis for the socialist transformation of

---

described the Russian civil war as a time of worker-peasant alliance – in contradistinction, for example, to the Hungarian revolution of 1919. He stated these views with great explicitness during the programme debates at the Sixth Comintern Congress in 1928: see Bukharin, *Problemy teorii i praktiki sotsializma* (Bukharin 1989), pp. 213–14, 244–6, 248–50. See also 'Bukharin on Bolshevik "Illusions", included in this volume. (For similar remarks made by Preobrazhensky in late 1920 on the emergency nature of the *razverstka* burdens, see Preobrazhensky 1921, pp. 13–16.)

56   The extent to which the Bolshevik tradition forced Stalin to deny (perhaps even to himself) the real nature of what he was doing is revealed in a hitherto unpublished circular sent out from the Central Committee to party organizations on 2 April 1930, which condemns in no uncertain terms the violation of 'the most important principle of collectivization – the voluntary principle' (*Dokumenty svidetel'stvuiut* [Danilov and Ivnitskii 1989, pp. 387–94]). In section 141 of the ABC, Preobrazhensky argues that the socialist road out of peasant backwardness will be much more peaceful than the capitalist road. Walicki takes a phrase from the very sentence in which Preobrazhensky makes this point (as the Russian text shows) and connects it by means of an ellipsis to Preobrazhensky's earlier remark about the kulaks. This procedure enables Walicki to present the ABC as an advocate of violent collectivization (Walicki 1995, p. 409).

agricultural production. The scholarly search for reprehensible illusions in the ABC only distracts attention from the less reprehensible illusion that was never rejected: the automatic assumption that the state could economically outperform the private market.

The 'disingenuous Bolshevik' thesis makes a good story. Bukharin and Preobrazhensky are portrayed either as amusing fools who thought they controlled events or Mephistophelean figures of evil who dreamed of a utopia of permanent labour camps. The ABC and other works from 1920 reveal much more ordinary human beings: two men who were intolerantly certain of the rightness of their cause and who were using all their insight (no doubt much inferior to our own) to get Russia out of the mess it was in. It may be that a story that features these more ordinary human beings will turn out to be more satisfactory than the one we are used to. Such a story would be a genuine Soviet tragedy instead of a Soviet melodrama.

4   Case Closed?

In this article, I have sketched out the beginnings of an alternative interpretation of the ABC of Communism that at least has the merit of not being blatantly contradicted by numerous passages. The ABC tells two stories, an epic story on the world-historical level and a smaller but intensely dramatic story about the construction of socialism in Russia. The two stories together portray socialism as the only path out of the ruinous crisis created by capitalism. They are further connected by the presentation of the Bolshevik party as the collective hero that alone remains true to the revolutionary traditions of pre-war Social Democracy. Only this party had the courage and resourcefulness to lead Russia out of the war; only this party had the courage and resourcefulness to begin the long and painful journey to socialism. Coercion is required during this journey to protect the revolution against its enemies (a category that expands to include significant sections of the population). Still, only perceived material advantages can really transform people's outlook, and socialist methods will reveal these advantages, once the present emergency is over. Despite the poverty and suffering of the present, the socialist organization of society will eventually lead to a democratic, prosperous, and self-respecting Russia.

If this is an accurate account of the message of the ABC, it speaks strongly against some widely accepted theses concerning 'war communism' and the Bolshevik outlook prior to NEP. The scholarly community remains unaware of this fact partly because authoritative voices have invoked the ABC in support of these claims. These theses are not only inaccurate in themselves, but they distract us from the questions we should be asking. Instead of the 'stress-induced vision' thesis, we should be examining the connections between Bolshevik doctrine and European Social Democracy as well as Bolshevism's appeal as a plausible account of a world turned upside down. Instead of the 'socialism now' thesis, we should examine Bolshevik excuses about their deferred dreams. Instead of the 'disingenuous Bolshevik' thesis, we should examine the real sources of danger in Bolshevik doctrine: the self-fulfilling prophecy of unremitting class hatred and the unquestioned assumption that socialist methods would not only be economically advantageous but be seen as such.

What I call the mystery of the ABC has unsettling implications. The ABC is a basic text that has long been available in a serviceable English translation. If misreading of the magnitude documented here has been allowed to stand without challenge in the case of the ABC, what assurance do we have that we really understand other standard texts or that we really know anything about more obscure and hard-to-find statements? How can we interpret the exciting new archival finds if we do not have a secure understanding of the doctrinal basis of the Soviet system? The mystery of the ABC is part of a larger mystery that can only be solved by reopening questions long thought laid to rest. The clues are everywhere, and the solution is as simple – and as complex – as the ABC.

Vlast from the Past: Stories Told by Bolsheviks

Central to the self-representation of the Bolsheviks was the claim that October 1917 gave rise to a proletarian *vlast*. It is hard for us to grasp today the rich meanings of this term. The difficulty is partly a matter of translation, since the usual rendering of *vlast* by 'power' can be misleading: the Russian word signifies the sovereign authority in the political system and it is therefore closer to German 'Macht' or French 'pouvoir' than to English 'power'. But the difficulty goes deeper than this. For the Bolsheviks, the term *vlast* was embedded in a narrative which they took over from pre-war Social Democracy and applied as best they could to their own unprecedented situation. The best way for us to understand the multiple meanings of *vlast* is to listen attentively to the narratives in which it was used.

Attention to the narrative context of a basic term can bring out themes missed or misunderstood by those who see political doctrine as primarily propositional. Indeed, the core of a political doctrine is much more likely to be its narratives than its theoretical propositions. In order to demonstrate this, I shall examine a standard thesis about Bolshevik beliefs during the early years of the revolution: the 'shortcuts to communism' thesis about so-called war communism in 1920. After presenting this thesis in the words of its original and most influential exponent, Isaac Deutscher, I will test it by looking at doctrinal narratives produced by Karl Kautsky, Nikolai Bukharin, Lev Trotsky, Aleksandra Kollontai and Grigorii Zinoviev. I will argue that one of the reasons that this thesis has not been adequately assessed earlier is a deep-seated underappreciation of the narrative element in doctrine.

1   The Nature of Political Doctrine

Doctrine is used here to mean an explicit, self-consciously controversial set of beliefs that claims authoritative status. Doctrine can be presented either as a narrative or as a set of propositions. For present purposes, narrative can be defined as a plot-structured relationship among characters; the characters can be large social groups such as classes that for narrative purposes are treated as individual agents. In contrast, a set of propositions is held together by claims to logical entailment and consistency rather than by plot.[1]

To illustrate the difference between these two forms, let us consider the Marxist term 'petty bourgeois'. If we view Marxism as a set of propositions, we

will come up with a definition of 'petty bourgeois' something like this: 'someone who owns the means of production but does not exploit others'. But if we
base ourselves on the tales told by Marxists in which the petty bourgeoisie plays
a prominent role, we will emphasize characteristics such as vacillation, the
need to accept leadership from others, and gradual polarization. It is these features that allow peasants, intellectuals and shop-owners (the disparate social
categories that make up the petty bourgeoisie) to be melded into a usable and
consistent character in Marxist doctrine.

Recent work in cognitive psychology and allied fields has brought out just
how much easier it is to think with narrative modes of thought than with propositional modes. Narrative is an evolved cognitive tool provided by evolution to
help us make our way around the social environment. It is a device for focusing
attention on the features of a social situation that impinge most directly on our
choices and for recalling relevant information from the past.[2] The primordial
importance of narrative for both attention and memory is brought out by suggestions that narrative is not a potentiality opened up by language, but rather
that language itself was created as a tool in the evolutionary drive for more and
better narratives. As a result, 'language in a preliterate society lacking the apparatus of the modern information-state is basically for telling stories'.[3]

In contrast, propositional thinking is post-evolutionary. It became possible
only after the historical invention of a range of devices for which Merlin Donald has provided the useful label 'external symbolic storage' (ESS) – devices that
range from the notepad I'm now writing on to the computer to which I will later
transfer these words. The human brain is not designed for logically disciplined
and non-narrative thought: the brain can only produce this kind of thought –
or rather, help produce it – as part of a larger complex of cognitive machinery.

Why is the contrasting evolutionary status of narrative vs. propositional
thinking important for the study of political doctrine? A successful political

---

1   For an argument that 'a good story and a well-formed argument are different natural kinds',
    see Jerome Bruner, *Actual Minds, Possible Worlds* (Bruner 1986, p. 11).
2   Frederic C. Bartlett, *Remembering: A Study in Experimental and Social Psychology* (Bartlett
    1932); Roger C. Schank, *Tell Me A Story: A New Look at Real and Artificial Memory* (Schank
    1990); Roger Schank and Robert P. Abelson, *Scripts, Plans, Goals, and Understanding: An
    Inquiry into Human Knowledge Structures* (Schank and Abelson 1977); Donald E. Brown,
    Human Universals (Brown 1991, pp. 134–5); John A. Robinson and Linda Hawpe, 'Narrative
    Thinking as a Heuristic Process', in *Narrative Psychology: The Storied Nature of Human Con-
    duct*, ed. Theodore R. Sarbin (Robinson and Hawpe 1986, pp. 111–25).
3   Merlin Donald, *Origins of the Modern Mind: Three Stages in the Evolution of Culture and Cog-
    nition* (Donald 1991, p. 257). The priority of narrative can also be observed in the language
    acquisition of the child; see Jerome Bruner, *Acts of Meaning* (Bruner 1990, p. 92).

doctrine unites a large and heterogeneous group of people: it is hard to imagine all these people truly sharing a set of theoretical propositions and much easier to imagine them sharing a story. Narrative's relative cognitive ease therefore suggests that the working part of a political doctrine will look less like theology and more like gospel: less like the hard-to-remember logic-chopping of Paul and more like Mark's attention-grabbing recitation of supremely important events.

Any ongoing political doctrine requires a repair process that assimilates anomalies and ratifies the doctrine's continuing authoritative status. This is done by constantly telling new stories, or rather, retelling old stories in ways that try to account for unexpected breaches and breakdowns while preserving the spirit of the inherited narrative. By proposing possible stories to fit our past conduct or to constrain the future conduct of others, we repair breaches in the social fabric and make concerted action possible. As Jerome Bruner puts it, 'Our sense of the normative is nourished in narrative, but so is our sense of breach and of exception.'[4]

This repair process occurs on an everyday, face-to-face level; it also occurs at a highly elaborated and institutionalized level. One such repair process – constitutional interpretation – offers a useful analogy to the function of the Bolshevik narratives presented here. The American constitutional tradition consists in large part of narratives that define, say, what free speech is and why it is important; it is up to judicial interpretation to apply these narratives with ongoing realities (is pornography free speech?).[5] In the case of the Bolsheviks as well, we find the rich ambiguities of constitutive narratives on one side and the unexpected challenges and anomalies of real life on the other. Only through some authoritative repair process could the gap between these two be provisionally closed.

2   'Shortcuts to Communism': A Case Study

The value of a narrative approach to political doctrine can be illustrated by using it to mount a challenge to a long-standing scholarly consensus about Bolshevik doctrine at the height of 'war communism' in 1920. During this year, we are told, the Bolsheviks as a whole believed that Russia was on the verge of a leap into socialism or even full communism. They saw the widespread use of

---

4   Bruner 1990, p. 97.
5   Edward Levi, *An Introduction to Legal Reasoning* (Levi 1949).

coercion and the super-centralization not just as a response to the emergencies of civil war and economic backwardness but as 'shortcuts to communism'.
Scholars have debated the reasons for this Bolshevik belief but not the fact of
its existence.

The best way to grasp this consensus about war communism is to look at
one of its earliest and most influential presentations: the concluding chapter of Isaac Deutscher's *The Prophet Armed*, published in 1954.[6] I shall quote
extensively from this chapter, first because variants of Deutscher's phrases
have echoed down the decades in the scholarly literature and second because
much of the influence of Deutscher's interpretation results from the savage
eloquence with which a hero-worshipper bashes his hero. Deutscher tells the
following story:

> The original cause of war communism was the civil war and the result-
> ing social and economic breakdown. 'The Bolsheviks strove to exercise
> the strictest control over scarce resources; and out of this striving grew
> their War Communism' (488). The Bolsheviks, however, saw it as some-
> thing more than an emergency programme: 'This set of desperate shifts
> and expedients looked to the party like an unexpectedly rapid realiza-
> tion of its own program ... The Bolshevik was therefore inclined to see
> the essential features of fully fledged communism embodied in the war
> economy of 1919–20. He was confirmed in this inclination by the stern
> egalitarianism, which his party preached and practiced and which gave
> to war communism a romantic and heroic aspect' (489).

This set of beliefs was of course a complete delusion: 'In truth, war communism
was a tragic travesty of the Marxist vision of the society of the future' (489).
What the Bolsheviks of 1920 failed to realize was that Marx's vision of socialist
society was incompatible with industrial ruin and constant hunger.

They also failed to see that an obvious solution existed for their economic
difficulties: using a tax to get grain rather than requisitioning. The Bolshevik
reluctance to adopt this obvious solution serves as a confirmation of the blinders that dogma imposed upon them: 'It was a sure sign of the Utopian character of war communism that it went on ignoring realities until it drove itself into
an impasse and could maintain itself only by ever-increasing doses of violence'
(490–1). Only in 1921, when the Bolsheviks finally replaced requisitioning with

---

6   Isaac Deutscher, *The Prophet Armed: Trotsky, 1879–1921* (first of three volumes) (Deutscher 1965
    [first published 1954]); page numbers in the text are from this edition. It should be noted that
    the term 'war communism' was not invented until after the introduction of NEP in 1921.

a tax, did they unwillingly leave this cycle of violence: 'Silently, with a heavy heart, Bolshevism parted with its dream of war communism. It retreated, as Lenin said, in order to be in a better position to advance' (514).

The story of Trotsky's individual fate brings home the moral failure inherent in the delusions of war communism. His story has an archetypal shape, as shown by the title Deutscher gives to his climactic chapter – 'Defeat in Victory' – and its opening sentence: 'At the very pinnacle of power, Trotsky, like the protagonist of a classical tragedy, stumbled' (486). Early in 1920, Trotsky proposed the obvious solution of a grain tax. When this was turned down by the Politburo, Trotsky became one of the most extreme war communists: 'On this occasion Trotsky, rebuked for his wisdom, plunged back into the accepted folly and persisted in it with an ardour which even the fools thought too foolish' (498). Trotsky's foolish ardour is exemplified by his defence of Bolshevik labour policies, which Deutscher describes as

> perhaps the only frank attempt made in modern times to give a logical justification of forced labour – the actual taskmasters and whippers-in do not bother to produce such justifications ... It was not the revolution's fault that, because of inherited poverty and the devastation of several wars and of blockade, it could not honour its promise. But the Bolsheviks need not have expressly repudiated that promise. This was what Trotsky appeared to do when he told the trade unions that coercion, regimentation, and militarization of labour were no mere emergency measures, and that the workers' state normally had the right to coerce any citizen to perform any work at any place of its choosing ... He told [people] that the workers' state had the right to use forced labour; and he was sincerely disappointed that they did not rush to enrol in the labour camps (500–1, 516).

Of course, in Trotsky's case, this foolishness was only an aberration. 'The policies which Trotsky now framed were incompatible with that *samodeyatelnost*, that political self-determination of the working class, which he had indefatigably preached for twenty years and which he was to preach again during the seventeen years of his open struggle against Stalin' (486).[7] Unfortunately, this

---

7 Deutscher may apologize for Trotsky's views in 1920, but Trotsky himself did not. When he republished *Terrorism and Communism* in his collected works in the 1920s, he wrote that he fully endorsed the views therein expressed; see also his prefaces to English and French editions in the 1930s (reprinted in *Terrorism and Communism* [Trotsky 1961, pp. xix–xlvii]). In the very short section of his autobiography devoted to 1920, Trotsky gives a highly qualified apol-

aberration had immense consequences: 'A decade later Stalin, who in 1920–1 had supported Lenin's "liberal" policy, was to adopt Trotsky's ideas in all but name. Neither Stalin nor Trotsky, nor the adherents of either, then admitted the fact' (515).

Did no one in the party protest against the perversion of both Bolshevik ideals and common sense? Yes, but the main protesters – the Worker Opposition – were in some ways the most deluded of all. It is true that they were 'high-minded, Utopian dreamers' who 'spoke the language which the whole party had spoken in 1917'. Nevertheless, they 'clamoured for the immediate satisfaction of the workers' needs, for equal wages and rewards for all, for the supply, without payment, of food clothing, and lodging to workers, for free medical attention, free travelling facilities, and free education. They wanted to see fulfilled nothing less than the program of full communism, which was theoretically designed for an economy of great plenty ... It was a sad omen that the people enveloped in such fumes of fancy were almost the only ones to advocate a full revival or proletarian democracy' (507–8).

This, then, is the story of war communism as told by a professed admirer of the Bolsheviks: a story of almost suicidal self-delusion. As I shall try to show in this article, there is little to support this thesis and much to refute it. Why, then, has it gained such unquestioned status? One reason for is Deutscher's status as Trotsky's great partisan. Why would he paint such an unflattering portrait of his hero unless compelled to do so by the facts?[8] And this leads to another powerful reason for the entrenchment of the Deutscher thesis. Although the shortcuts thesis was developed and propagated by scholars on the left (broadly speaking) of Soviet studies, nevertheless it was warmly embraced by more conservative writers and indeed elevated to a central place in the current conservative interpretation of Soviet history. And this is not surprising. The shortcuts thesis as presented by Deutscher is a thoroughly devastating portrait of foolish, violence-addicted utopians who betrayed their principles, inflicted great suffering on the Russian population through their delusional policies, and provided a direct precedent for the worst features of Stalinism.

In 1974, the shortcuts thesis received an influential endorsement from Moshe Lewin, a hero to some historians on the left. Lewin devoted a chapter to this topic in *Political Undercurrents in Soviet Economic Debates*, where he wrote: 'the majority of the party was led to believe that the war economy measures applied

---

ogy for his dispute with Lenin over the trade unions at the end of the year, but for nothing else (*Moia zhizn*, first published in 1930 [Trotsky 1991, pp. 437–46]).

8   For a comment on Deutscher's possible motives, see Pierre Broué, *Trotsky* (Broue 1988, pp. 15–16).

during this period [war communism] offered the shortcut to socialism that had been dubbed a childish "leftist" dream a short while before'. But Lewin's version made the Deutscher thesis even more damaging to the left. In his account, the disastrous delusion of war communism was directly motivated by a 'conception of a socialist economy' that was 'an old socialist doctrine, clearly stated by Marx and Engels and later accepted by the entire Marxist movement'. Of course, Lewin goes on to argue that Bolsheviks such as Bukharin later understood the necessity of market socialism.[9] Yet it is small wonder that conservative writers such as Robert Conquest and Martin Malia gratefully accepted the idea that the sufferings of Russia in 1920 were directly due to a mistaken Marxist consensus.[10]

The ironic outcome is that a thesis proposed by a Trotskyist writer in the 1940s has become a mainstay of the dominant conservative view of the Soviet Union in the 1990s. A critique of the Deutscher thesis is therefore not just a critique of one writer but also of an interpretation that has dominated post-war scholarship on early Soviet political history.

A final reason for the unchallenged dominance of the Deutscher thesis is a lack of appreciation for the crucial role of narrative in political doctrine. This is partly a matter of gathering relevant evidence. Looking for stories told by Bolsheviks will direct us to long available sources that have been completely overlooked by historians. An awareness of the narrative core of political doctrine also helps us state the issues more precisely, since the Deutscher thesis essentially concerns the story that the Bolsheviks told about themselves and the proletarian *vlast* in 1920.

According to Deutscher's version of this Bolshevik story, the purpose for which the *vlast* was exercised was immediate social transformation; in order

---

9   Moshe Lewin, *Political Undercurrents in Soviet Economic Debates* (Lewin 1974, pp. 77, 82–3). Lewin reaffirmed his thesis when he republished the book in 1991 under the title *Stalinism and the Seeds of Soviet Reform* (Lewin 1991). For Bukharin's actual views during NEP, see 'Political Testament' and 'Bukharin on Bolshevik Illusions' included in this volume.

10   Robert Conquest cites Lewin as his authority for the assertion that 'grain procurement by force' was 'regarded by the Party, from Lenin down, as not merely socialism, but even communism'; see *Harvest of Sorrow: Soviet Collectivization and the Terror-Famine* (Conquest 1986, p. 48). In his *The Soviet Tragedy*, Martin Malia bases his entire interpretation of Soviet history on the idea of a continual recurrence of the delusional maximalism of war communism; he takes this idea directly from Lewin, citing Lewin's own words to support his, Malia's, point: 'the Soviet historical drama [was] a two-act play, replayed several times with different sets and characters' (Malia 1994, p. 175). I once heard the distinguished historian Ron Suny admiringly describe 'Marxism-Lewinism' as the best alternative to the Malia interpretation, yet we see that on this crucial point Malia is actually following Lewin's lead.

to achieve this transformation, coercion was justified as a necessary and permanent way in which the *vlast* was to be wielded. The Deutscher thesis also describes what I earlier called a constitutional repair process: the original doctrinal story was altered to accommodate the unexpected realities of civil war policies. These changes can be summed up as an acceleration of the tempo of transformation and a fundamental revision in the role of coercion. Finally, Deutscher tells us that the only genuine counter-story came from the Worker Opposition and allied groups: they remained true to the 1917 version of the proletarian *vlast* as democratic and non-coercive even though they were even more swept up by the desire for immediate 'full communism'.

In order to test the Deutscher thesis, then, we need to look for authoritative stories told by Bolsheviks about the proletarian *vlast* and its vicissitudes in Russia. We will begin with a review of the canonical narrative inherited from pre-war Social Democracy. We will then look at the story as it was told by an authoritative party spokesmen – Nikolai Bukharin – in the months after the Bolshevik revolution. With this version as a benchmark, we shall look again at how Trotsky told the story in 1920 in order to see if the story has changed in the predicted ways.

Next we shall look for doctrinal narratives that bring out the basic issues at stake in the challenge symbolized by the Worker Opposition. After looking at stories told by Grigorii Zinoviev and Aleksandra Kollontai, we will discover instead that the source of the conflict was rather an unresolved tension in the inherited narrative – a tension that rose to the surface when the *vlast* turned from a dream into a day-to-day reality.

3   *The Inherited Narrative*

The Bolsheviks' central constitutive narrative was the one they inherited from pre-war Social Democracy: they used this narrative not only to justify their claim to power but even to explain what power meant to them. The Social Democratic narrative had three roots: the epic class narrative of the proletariat's 'world-freeing deed' provided by Marx and Engels, the image of inspiring leadership provided by Ferdinand Lassalle, and the successful struggle of the Social Democratic Party of Germany (SPD) against determined hostility.[11] These different elements were moulded into a consistent narrative by Karl Kautsky, a professional man of the theatre turned socialist theoretician.[12]

---

11   The quoted words ('weltbefreiende Tat') are taken from the final paragraph of Friedrich Engels, *Socialism, Utopian and Scientific* (Engels 1961–1968, 19:228).

12   Kautsky came from a professional theatrical family for whom he wrote and produced plays; his mother was a well-known socialist novelist; a George Sand novel was instrumen-

Kautsky had an immense impact on Russian Marxists; it was said of him that he was a more influential figure in the Russian party than he was in the German party.[13] This influence did not come from any particular originality or eloquence but rather from a grasp of the narrative core of Social Democracy. All quotations in the following description are taken from Kautsky.

The Social Democratic narrative hinges on the central event of the proletariat's conquest of political power (*Macht*) in order to introduce socialism. Under the surface, much of the emotional drama of this narrative arises from the theme of the leadership that enables that the proletariat to realize that its essential nature imposes a world-historical mission on it. Accordingly, the narrative falls naturally into three acts: the proletariat's realization of its mission, the road to state power, and the construction of socialism.

In Act I, 'it is the task of Social Democracy to bring to the proletariat an awareness of its position and its task'.[14] Act I portrays an expanding 'consciousness' or sense of mission that moves out in concentric circles from a sacred centre: Marx, Social Democracy, workers' movement, proletariat, toiling classes, mankind. The story of the expanding circle of consciousness can be told in melodramatic terms as the story of an inspired and inspiring leader: the Social Democratic activist who receives the good news – *ein neues Evangelium* – of the proletariat's identity and passes it on to ever wider circles.[15]

In Act II – the road to power – the central task was to preserve the sense of mission. 'Revisionism' was more than a theoretical position: it was the expression of the permanent possibility of backsliding and degeneration. If Lenin's Russian translation of the Social Democratic narrative has any distinctive features, it is his passionate fixation on the clash between the good leader who accepts his mission and the bad leader who evades these sacred obligations. This fixation became a titanic hatred after the outbreak of war in 1914, when Lenin condemned the newly revealed bad leaders who supported the war effort

---

tal in his conversion to Social Democracy; he himself wrote (unpublished) novels before writing socialist tracts (Gary P. Steenson, *Karl Kautsky 1854–1938: Marxism in the Classical Years* [Steenson 1978]). Detailed plot summaries of Kautsky's early plays and stories can be found in his *Erinnerungen und Erörterungen* (Kautsky 1960).

13   A German witticism reported with approval by Lenin in *State and Revolution* (Lenin 1975, p. 385). On Kautsky's influence in Russia, see Moira Donald, *Marxism and Revolution: Karl Kautsky and the Russian Marxists, 1900–1924* (Donald 1993).

14   Kautsky 1901, as cited by Lenin in *What is to be Done?* (Lenin 1958–1965, 6:38–9).

15   Kautsky, *Das Erfurter Programm* (Kautsky 1965, p. 230). This striking metaphor was dropped (along with much other important material) from the English translation; compare my earlier remark about gospel vs. theology in political doctrine.

and so betrayed everything Social Democracy stood for. It soon became apparent that Lenin took Kautsky's narrative more seriously than Kautsky did himself, with the ironic result that Kautsky was cast as the archetype of one kind of degenerate leader.

In Act III – the construction of socialism after the conquest of power – we see that the task of leadership continues in full force even after the proletariat becomes the ruling class. The three main class characters in the Social Democratic narrative are the bourgeoisie, the proletariat, and the toilers (exploited labourers such as poor peasants). The narrative imposes different leadership tasks on the proletariat in relation to these three characters, but state power is essential to all of them. The proletariat needs state power in order to deprive the bourgeoisie of a basic prop of their own power; coercion will be used to beat back any attempt of the class enemy to regain control of the state. The proletariat also needs state power as a tool of self-organization, especially since Kautsky emphasized that the whole proletariat would not be fully 'conscious' – aware of its mission – until sometime after the conquest of power. Finally, state power is needed to complete the task of class leadership of the toilers. The proletariat must reveal itself as the champion of the immediate interests of the toilers as well as successfully demonstrate that socialism is the only answer to their long-term problems.

A set of images ubiquitous among Social Democratic writers sums up much of the narrative thrust of Social Democracy: the path and the task. The point of revolution is to guarantee the possibility of traveling down the only path that leads to socialism; the mission of the proletariat imposes on it the task of opening up this path and then leading society toward the promised land. Bourgeois class power is a road-block that sits athwart the new road: it can and must be removed in a relatively short space of time. Any violence involved in this process will be entirely the fault of the elites threatened with loss of power: 'out of fear of revolution they want to provoke civil war'.[16] But even though 'a socialist revolution can at a single stroke transfer a factory from capitalist to social property, it is only step by step, through a course of gradual, progressive development, that one may transform a factory from a place of monotonous, repulsive, forced labour into an attractive spot for the joyful activity of happy human beings'.[17] A revolution defended by coercive means is needed to make peaceful evolution possible.

---

16   Kautsky, *The Road to Power* (Kautsky 1996, p. 37). The quoted words are taken from an 1893 article reprinted by Kautsky in this work of 1909. For more on *The Road to Power*, see Lih 2018b, 'Tasks of our Times'.

17   Kautsky, *Die Soziale Revolution* (Kautsky 1902, p. 12).

When we look back now at Marxism and Social Democracy, we tend to locate their source of drama in the struggle between capital and labour. Just as important or more so to Social Democrats of Lenin's generation was a narrative that portrayed the way in which inspired and inspiring leadership led to the recognition of the class mission. This is the drama invoked in the closing words of Kautsky's *The Road to Power*, his last important pre-war work and one that was enthusiastically endorsed by Lenin. Here Kautsky presents a dramatically charged version of the expanding circle of consciousness, starting with the leadership vanguard and then moving out to proletariat, toilers, and ultimately all humanity:

> The elite of the proletariat today forms the strongest, the most far-sighted, most selfless, boldest stratum, and the one united in the largest free organizations, of the nations with European civilization. And the proletariat will, in and through struggle, take up into itself the unselfish and far-sighted elements of all classes; it will organize and educate in its own bosom even its most backward elements and fill them with understanding and the joy of hope. It will place its elite at the head of civilization and make it capable of guiding the immense economic transformation that will finally, over the entire globe, put an end to all the misery arising out of subjection, exploitation, and ignorance.
>
> Fortunate are those destined to take part in this sublime struggle and share in this glorious victory![18]

4 Coercion and Transformation

The 'shortcuts to communism' thesis about Bolshevik doctrinal narratives in 1920 cannot be adequately assessed without a clear idea of the stories the Bolsheviks were telling about themselves at the time of the revolution. And yet on a closer look we see that the shortcuts thesis rests on a certain fuzziness about Bolshevik beliefs in 1917–18. One the one hand, we are told that the 'language of 1917' was the direct precursor of the idealistic but super-utopian Worker Opposition, but on the other hand we are also given to understand that 1917 and early 1918 was a period of relative moderation and realism. This fuzziness only serves to strengthen the shortcuts thesis, since both images of 1917–18 serve to picture

---

18   Kautsky 1996, p. 91.

war communism as a moral and political fall from grace. In one case, the fall is from democratic idealism to repressive coercion; in the other case, from realism to delusion.

This same fuzziness makes it difficult to obtain a focused image of Nikolai Bukharin during this early period. Since in early 1918 he was a leader of the Left Communist faction that was a direct ancestor of the Worker Opposition, many scholars assume he had millennial hopes of instant socialism. Neil Harding writes: 'Throughout 1917 both Bukharin and Lenin believed that the socialist Revolution signified the leap out of the stultifying and bloody dictatorship of the imperialist bourgeoisie directly into the realm of freedom'. Bukharin therefore did not see the new *vlast* as a dictatorship of the proletariat, since this was a transitional form that provided no 'alternative to the prison and charnel house of the contemporary state'.[19] This and similar descriptions of Bukharin's views during this period directly conflict with Bukharin's many pronouncements on the absolute necessity of a proletarian dictatorship and his insistence on the gradual pace of transformation.

This resulting fuzziness comes into focus when we see that Bukharin is telling the story of the new *vlast* as an instance of the canonical Social Democratic narrative that we have just described. This narrative background allows us to see that Bukharin's 'leftism' consists of his hard-line fierceness on matters of class power. In his aggressive polemics with moderate socialists who denied that the canonical narrative could be applied to Russia, Bukharin did not argue that Russia was ripe for instant socialism; he claimed it was ripe for a proletarian *vlast*. There is no contradiction between this position and his views on the gradual pace of transformation – indeed, as we shall see, the two go together.

The sources on which the following account is based do not come from factional debates within the party: Bukharin is addressing (or picturing himself as addressing) a non-party audience to whom he expounds party doctrine. There is no reason to assume that these works were not accepted as authoritative statements.[20] It is therefore all the more remarkable that they have been almost

---

19   Harding 1992, p. 102.

20   Bukharin, *Programma kommunistov (bol'shevikov)* (Bukharin 1918b); *Ot krusheniia tsarizma do padeniia burzhuazii* [From the Collapse of Tsarism to the Fall of the Bourgeoisie] (Bukharin 1918a); *Na podstupakh k Oktiabriu* (Bukharin 1926) (this is a collection of Bukharin's articles and speeches from 1917 and early 1918). The *Programma* was published abroad in many languages until it was superseded in late 1919 by the *ABC of Communism* that Bukharin co-authored with Evgenii Preobrazhensky. Note that the material in the Bukharin 1918a and Bukharin 1926 were republished in the mid-twenties, a time when Bukharin had denounced his Left Communist episode.

entirely overlooked by scholars. One reason for this neglect is a lack of appreci-ation of the narrative core of political doctrine. For example, *From the Collapse of Tsarism to the Fall of the Bourgeoisie* is a narrative history of 1917 written as events unfolded by the party's leading theorist. It should be one of our cen-tral sources for understanding the Bolshevik self-image during this period – instead, it has been forgotten.

Bukharin tells the following story: 'In all countries except Russia after the October turning-point – and before October in Russia as well – capital has the *vlast*.[21] In Russia, there is now a people's *vlast*, in which the revolutionary pro-letariat (and the party of the revolutionary proletariat) clearly plays the role of leader. If revolutions are the locomotives of history, then the proletariat is now the only qualified driver.[22] Since a proletarian state power will open the road to socialism, the violence that will undoubtedly be needed to obtain and defend proletarian power is 'sacred'.[23] Still, 'the socialist revolution *does not complete, but begins* "socialist development",' and so the path to socialism will be long and difficult, at least in Russia.[24] Progress along this path will require all of the pro-letariat's organizational and leadership resources; severe self-discipline will be required within the ranks of the 'army of labour'. Progress down this path will be 'gradual but unremitting'.[25]

In Bukharin's narrative, the identity of the class that holds the *vlast* decides everything else. If, for example, anyone other than a worker-peasant state – even moderate socialists – tried to regulate production, the result would be the same extraordinary exploitation observed in the other belligerent countries. On the other hand, if the new worker *vlast* resorts to violence and even to ter-ror, one should not equate it morally with tsarism or the imperialists. Such a comparison illegitimately equates the enslaver and the liberator.[26] Thus if the wrong class is in power, the best actions are subverted, and if the right class is in power, the worst actions are ennobled.

Since there are only two paths, one leading back to capitalism and the other leading forward to socialism, 'a complete and decisive victory of the workers, soldiers and peasants is the first condition of success. This task stands at the

---

21   This is the first sentence of the *Programma kommunistov* (Bukharin 1918b).
22   Bukharin 1918a, pp. 7–8.
23   Bukharin 1918b, p. 13.
24   *Kommunist*, No. 3 (Kowalski 1990, p. 174), Bukharin's emphasis. Bukharin is reviewing a book by Aleksandr Bogdanov, whose words are quoted. *Kommunist* was the organ of the Left Communists, although this article is a polemic against someone outside the party.
25   Bukharin 1926, p. 150 (30 October 1917).
26   Bukharin 1926, pp. 178, 183 (speech to Constituent Assembly in January 1918).

centre of everything. This task must be solved once and for all.'[27] Revolutionary violence that helps solve this fundamental task is not only justified but positively celebrated: 'We communists are for a *worker* government – one that is needed for the time being, until the working class has complete control over its opponents, thoroughly disciplined the whole of the bourgeoisie, knocked the conceit out of it, and eliminated any hope the bourgeoisie may have of again regaining the *vlast*.'[28]

If the task of ensuring class power is an all-or-nothing affair, the 'task of organizing economic life' is a more-or-less affair. As we might put it today, the class nature of *vlast* is digital, while social transformation is analogue. Bukharin, so fiercely radical and uncompromising on questions of class power, uses terms like 'gradually', 'step-by-step', 'little-by-little' when discussing social transformation. Indeed, Bukharin is at pains to emphasize the great difficulties facing the task of socialist transformation. He gives three main reasons: the damage caused by the war, the challenges posed by Russian backwardness and 'unorganized relations in the village', and the sabotage of the class enemy. Far from promising a leap into the realm of freedom, Bukharin's narrative emphasizes the length and hardships of the journey: 'Every revolution smashes what is old and rotten: a certain period (a very difficult one) must pass before the new arises, before a beautiful home starts to be built upon the ruins of the old pigsty.'[29]

More important than any specific transformational strategy are the leader-follower relations among the principal characters of the class narrative: activist vanguard, proletariat, and toilers. Organizations such as the trade unions educate the proletariat about the importance of labour discipline, while the workers as a whole will contribute their superior organizing ability to help the peasants transform their production relations. Bukharin's main answer to the charge that Russia is not yet ripe for a socialist revolution is to stress Russian industry's potential for economic leadership of the countryside – a potential ratified by the proletariat's political success: 'It was not for nothing that the working class was able to lead all the living forces of the revolution.'[30]

The proletariat's responsibilities as leader of the journey to socialism also give it the right to discipline individual workers who do not realize their new position as a ruling and leading class. Since proletarian power is still vulnerable and best by enemies, lack of conscientiousness is a crime and should be dealt

---

27   Bukharin 1926, p. 147 (27 October 1917).
28   Bukharin 1918b, p. 13.
29   Bukharin 1918b, pp. 55–6.
30   Bukharin 1918b, pp. 28–30.

with accordingly. In contrast to the central role assigned to coercion in conquering and defending a proletarian *vlast*, its role in the subsequent journey is
indirect and subsidiary: ensuring discipline while under attack. Its presence is
a sign of the difficulties of the journey and the immense distance separating
the travellers from the final goal.

Bukharin never lost his sense of a perilous and prolonged journey. Indeed,
the main point of *Economy of the Transition Period*, his magnum opus of 1920, is
that *any* socialist revolution will lead to a temporary but massive breakdown of
society.[31] In order to test Deutscher's portrait of 1920, however, the best source is
Deutscher's own central proof text: Trotsky's writings on labour policy in 1920.

In the course of justifying Bolshevik labour policies in 1920, Trotsky defended
a number of general propositions: compulsion (*prinuzhdenie*) is a basic socialist principle, as shown by the popular slogan 'He who does not work, neither
shall he eat'; socialist planning required central distribution of labour; 'repression for the attainment of economic goals is a necessary weapon of the socialist dictatorship'.[32] These and other similar arguments are the mainstay of the
Deutscher thesis: they seem to show by their very nature as general propositions that Trotsky was generalizing the policies of 1920 into the essence of
socialism.

The actual narrative framework used by Trotsky to justify policy cannot
in fact be deduced from any number of general propositions. For a spotlight
on this underlying narrative, let us turn to his pronouncements on a specific
aspect of labour policy: individual material incentives. Defenders of the shortcuts thesis have avoided any examination of these pronouncements and given
exclusive attention to egalitarianism and coercion. Lewin defines war communism as 'an ideological construct that mistook the egalitarianism of poverty and
wartime brotherhood not only for that of socialism, but also for that of communism'.[33] According to László Szamuely, author of the most detailed defence
of the shortcuts thesis, war communists such as Trotsky believed that 'the main
tool of building and controlling socialist economy [sic] is force, coercion by the
State'. Szamuely goes on to comment: 'This thesis can perhaps not be found

---

31   On the length of the path to socialism, see *Ekonomika perekhodnogo perioda* (Bukharin
      1920, pp. 151, 156). The famous chapter on 'extra-economic coercion' in this book is often
      used as proof of a 'war communist' leap mentality, but a comparison with the *Programma*
      of 1918 shows no essential change: coercion is needed to defend the revolution and to deal
      with the economic crisis caused by that defence.

32   *Terrorizm i kommunizm* (Trotsky 1925–1927, 15:143); English translation in Trotsky 1961,
      p. 149.

33   Lewin 1974, pp. 8–9.

expressis verbis in contemporary literature, but we can draw well-founded conclusions from the measures and methods that were discussed by the contemporary ideologues and from the methods that were *not* mentioned', that is, material incentives.[34]

Did Trotsky's support of compulsion/coercion in 1920 really mean that he rejected material incentives? The answer to this question is unambiguously 'no'. First, Trotsky argues that material incentives always remain the underlying reality: 'The effort and efficiency of labour is determined for the most part by personal material interest. For the toiler, what has decisive significance is not the juridical shell with which he obtains the fruits of his labour, but rather, what portion of them he receives.'[35]

Second, it was not socialist principle that led Trotsky to reject extensive reliance on material incentives but rather the practical unavailability of material that could be used in this way:

> In our hungry, exhausted and ruined country, with a disorganized transport and a statistical apparatus that is still extremely weak, Menshevism wants to regulate the distribution of the work force by means of a corresponding distribution of consumer items and goods. This is a complete and utter utopia. If indeed we had such a quantity of goods and the freedom to manoeuvre with them, then we could create centres of material attraction as we wished. In that case our position would be excellent.[36]

Third, poverty did not lead to egalitarianism and wartime brotherhood but just the opposite: 'As long as we are poor and beggarly, as long as we have insufficient food for supplying even a minimum of our needs, we are not able to distribute it equally to all toilers. We are going to direct consumer items to the central branches of labour and to the most important enterprises. And we are obliged to do this – obliged in the name of saving the toiling masses and the future of the country. We will be able to dress the worker more warmly, give him better nourishment, if he works conscientiously and energetically. That's why we are applying the bonus system [of differential wages].'[37] Trotsky stresses the offense not only to socialist principles but to elementary justice: 'We are forced to not grudge three rations for the [bourgeois] specialist, if he raises the productivity of the factory by ten percent. We are forced to go over to this kind of

---

34   Szamuely, *First Models of the Socialist Economic System* (Szamuely 1974, pp. 38–9).
35   Trotsky 1925–1927, 15:333.
36   Trotsky 1925–1927, 15:200; see also 181–2, 102–3.
37   Trotsky 1925–1927, 15:184–5.

crude and sharp individualization of the elite of the working class ... Without this injustice within the working class itself – without feeding some and letting others go hungry – we won't be able to cope.'[38]

Fourth, Trotsky brought out the implications of these policies for the length of the remaining journey to socialism: 'We have preserved the wage system and it will remain with us for a prolonged period. The further we go, the more its significance will consist in assuring all members of society with everything necessary – and just for that reason it will cease to be a *wage* system. But right now we're not rich enough for that. Our basic task is increasing the amount of what is produced and everything else must be subordinated to this task.'[39]

Trotsky's comments on individual material incentive create insuperable difficulties for the shortcuts thesis not only because they refute crucial assertions about egalitarianism and coercion but also because they point to the underlying narrative justification for policy. This narrative can be paraphrased as follows: the proletarian *vlast* has had to endure incredible costs in order to defend itself. These costs have taken us further away from socialism and impose on us the necessity for some very unpleasant policies. We need coercion not as a substitute for material incentives, but as a way of preventing a collapse that would make material incentives completely impossible. Nevertheless, these costs and these policies are justified by socialism, because socialism requires a proletarian *vlast*.

This implied narrative found explicit expression in a speech given on the third anniversary of the October revolution in 1920. Here Trotsky is not conducting polemics in support of controversial policies but trying to affirm his audience's sense of itself:

> We went into this struggle with magnificent ideals, with magnificent enthusiasm, and it seemed to many people that the promised land of communist fraternity, the flowering not only of material but spiritual life, was much closer than it has actually turned out to be ... The promised land – the new kingdom of justice, freedom, contentment and cultural uplift – was so near it could be touched ... If back then, three years ago, we were given the opportunity of looking ahead, we would not have believed our eyes. We would not have believed that three years after the proletarian revolution it would be so hard for us, so harsh to be living on this earth ...

---

38   Trotsky 1925–1927, 15:176–7.
39   Trotsky 1925–1927, 15:142 (Trotsky 1961, p. 149).

Three years have gone by – three years, during which the whole world of our enemies tried to hurl us back across that fateful historical threshold we had crossed. We defended ourselves, we did not retreat. We were not far from surrendering Petrograd, we retreated in the east and south with our back to Moscow, but we stood firm, we defended the first worker and peasant state *vlast* in the world. Our task has not been accomplished – each one of us knows this. The new society and new order for which we fought and are fighting still does not yet exist: the *narod* still does not live as one happy fraternal family, without inequality, without humiliation, without need and mutual offense. Every male worker feels this, every woman worker. Nevertheless – and this is our chief conquest – each male worker, each woman worker understands that there is no turning back.[40]

This eloquent speech has been entirely overlooked by scholars. Even though the 'shortcuts to communism' thesis is essentially about the stories the Bolsheviks told about themselves, scholars who are unaware of the narrative core of political doctrine have not been motivated to look for pure expressions of this story-telling. Nevertheless, one can argue on *a fortiori* grounds that this one citation does mortal damage to the Deutscher thesis: it comes from a speech that was delivered at a period (fall 1920) when the illusions of the Bolsheviks were supposed to be at their height, on an occasion when self-congratulation was in order, by a speaker who is supposed to be one of the most outspoken believers in a shortcut to communism. If the Deutscher thesis has merit, how is it conceivable that Trotsky said what he did say?

To conclude: war communism in 1920 is widely pictured as a fall from the revolutionary grace of 1917. There are no doubt many reasons for this, but we have just seen one of them to be entirely invalid: the alleged contrast between the doctrinal stories told about coercion and transformation. There is nothing new about the justification of coercion made in 1920: coercion was 'sacred' if it overcame the aggressive resistance of the class enemy; it was justifiable if it helped the workers and toilers mobilize resources against a common enemy; it was futile and reprehensible if it became a substitute for demonstrating the economic advantages of socialism. If this justification is a betrayal of the promises of the revolution, then they were already betrayed by early 1918.

We also do not observe the predicted acceleration of the tempo of transformation nor the imagery of leaps and shortcuts that scholars have taught us to expect. Bukharin was a leader of Left Communism in 1918; Trotsky was an

---

40   Trotsky 1925–1927, 17, 2, pp. 480–5.

extreme war communist – nevertheless, both assert the length and difficulty of the remaining journey to socialism. The main effect of the civil war on the narratives produced by these two leaders was to intensify the pathos of separation from the promised land.

5   Images of Degeneration: 'Soiling' and 'the Wall'

The narratives produced by Bukharin and Trotsky do not reveal the major narrative repair predicted by the Deutscher thesis. This does not mean that there were not real stresses and strains in applying the inherited narrative to post-revolutionary realities. These stresses and strains are most evident in the critique symbolized by the Worker Opposition of 1920 and early 1921. According to the Deutscher thesis, this critique was essentially over the question: what means shall we use to accomplish the leap into socialism? The Worker Opposition insisted even more fanatically than the rest of the party on the necessity of this leap – so Deutscher tells us – but at least they had faith in the masses and eschewed the use of coercion and super-centralization. In so doing, they acted as the conscience of the revolution and as the only ones who still spoke the language of 1917.

The influence of the Deutscher thesis has prevented us from seeing an elementary fact about the debate between the Worker Opposition and the party majority: it was a given for both sides that the policies of 1920 represented a retreat, not a leap. More precisely, each believed the military and economic emergency had enforced a series of compromises that carried a threat of party degeneration. Once we are aware of the consensus about the possibility of party degeneration, we can get to the real source of the doctrinal clash: opposing definitions of the meaning of 'degeneration'. It is this underlying clash – rather than the more notorious debate about the role of the trade unions – that best reveals the tensions hidden within the inherited narrative.

In Kautsky's peroration from *The Road to Power*, he gave two glorious tasks to the proletariat: to 'organize and educate' backward workers and members of other classes, and to 'place its elite at the head of civilization' in order to carry out economic transformation. The Bolsheviks saw their own *vlast* as committed to these two tasks but they also discovered that the day-to-day realities of an actual *vlast* created a tension between the two tasks. According to some Bolsheviks, carrying out the daily tasks of state power, especially in emergency conditions, threatened to create a wall between leader and follower – a wall that disrupted the task of transformative leadership. Others in the party worried more about another consequence of state power: the sustained contact with classes whose outlook had not yet been transformed by the spreading circle of consciousness. This contact meant that the party was soiled by alien elements. If it lost its class purity, it would no longer have the unique qualities needed to construct socialism. In this way, the same canonical narrative gave rise to two different conceptions of the degeneration lurking in the compromises in 1920.

In order to examine more closely the meaning of degeneration, we will turn to the pronouncements of Grigorii Zinoviev and Aleksandra Kollontai. Of all the spokesman on either side of the party divide, these two were the most inclined to make their points by means of narrative. We shall begin with Zinoviev, who was Lenin's closest companion in the years before the revolution, a member of the Politburo from the time it was formed, the party chief of Petrograd (later Leningrad) until he went into opposition in 1925–26, and chairman of the Communist International. His almost total neglect by historians has led to a serious gap in our understanding of Bolshevik doctrine.[41] One reason (among many) for this neglect is a bias in favour of propositional presentations of political doctrine as opposed to narrative ones. Zinoviev was extremely clumsy in propositional argument, a quality for which he was mocked by party critics at the time and by scholars since. On the other hand, his highly successful oratory was based in large part on his skill as a story-teller; he was also one of the first party historians.

The heart of Zinoviev's narrative was a confidence that sooner rather than later the spreading circle of consciousness would unite leaders and followers. For him, the outlying circles were not so much 'unenlightened' as 'not-yet-enlightened'. Thus, the good leader is one who sticks to his vision even when highly unpopular, secure in his confidence that the tide will soon turn and the message will again be received. The bad leader is one who allows a wall to grow up between him and the expanding circle. In an extensive study of the German SPD published just prior to the 1917 revolution, Zinoviev told how the German socialist leadership had degenerated into a self-perpetuating caste.[42]

Zinoviev saw the possession of the state *vlast* as a magnificent opportunity to accelerate the flow of consciousness: 'Only after the dictatorship of the pro-

---

41   Previous secondary literature devoted to Zinoviev consists of two insightful articles by Myron Hedlin: 'Grigorii Zinoviev: Myths of the Defeated' (Hedlin 1976) and 'Zinoviev's Revolutionary Tactics in 1917' (Hedlin 1975). See also 'Zinoviev: Populist Leninist', included in this volume.

42   'Sotsial'nye korni opportunizma' in Zinoviev 1920, pp. 292–335; portions of this work can be found in John Riddell, *Lenin's Struggle for a Revolutionary International* (Riddell 1984, pp. 475–96).

letariat has deprived the bourgeoisie of such mighty tools of influence as the press, the schools, parliament, the church, administrative machinery and so on – only after the decisive defeat of the bourgeois system has become evident to all – will all or almost all workers begin to join the ranks of the Communist party.'[43] But the mere possession of state power also led unexpectedly to a damming up of the flow of consciousness. Zinoviev was compelled to note that some party collectives 'have managed to fence themselves with a wall from the masses', so that 'people look at these collectives as if they were bosses [*nachalstvo*], instead of looking at them as people who lead'.[44] And in many cases this hostility toward the party was perfectly justified: 'Any person in the *narod* – the most backward little old lady, a toiling peasant – who regards us as in league with the devil [even though] they haven't read the party program and are not going to read it, they're not interested in the Third International and we can't expect them to be – in their hearts they are more of a communist than that communist in a leather jacket who looks down his nose at them'.[45]

Zinoviev's response in 1919 and 1920 might be called 'talk therapy': the best the leaders could do was to admit the situation, point to objective reasons, be frank about the sacrifices required, and promise to do better. The party's immediate task was not to accelerate transformation but to remove as much of the wall as they could:

> Up here in Petrograd, in connection with the recent disturbances, it was established that at the Nevsky gate cloth supplies were rotting away, while at the same time women workers who needed clothes were driven to thievery, for which we persecuted them and created conflict after conflict. There's no greater shame for us than that these supposedly small – but in reality not small at all – 'defects of the mechanism' are still around, that we still can't clothe a worker family or the mother of a worker, who would appreciate even the smallest improvement of their lot or some genuine love and concern for them.[46]

---

43   This passage is taken from Zinoviev's draft of a resolution of the second congress of the Communist International in 1920; see Zinoviev's *Istoriia Rossiiskoi Kommunisticheskoi Partii (bol'shevikov)* (Zinoviev 1924, p. 9).

44   *Vos'moi s'ezd RKP(b)* 1959, p. 294 (1919).

45   These words come from a speech of March 1919 first published in *Izvestiia TsK KPSS*, 1988, No. 8, pp. 185–97 (cited passage, p. 197).

46   *Vos'moi s'ezd RKP(b)* 1959, pp. 283–4 (1919).

According to Zinoviev's version of events, the party's relations with the workers reached their low point on the eve of NEP in early 1921 – the time of the Kronstadt rebellion and intense labour difficulties in Petrograd. In a speech given at this time, Zinoviev apologized for the guards at the factory gates, but asserted that it was the role of the 'conscious' leaders to make sure that waverings at a moment of intense strain did not lead to disaster.[47] After this crisis, things gradually became better. Of course, NEP still carried a 'danger of degeneration', but this was nothing new: 'we talked about this danger in 1919 and in 1921. We are obliged to repeat it, especially under NEP, with an even heavier accent'.[48] Zinoviev's basic response was again talk therapy:

> I mentioned the Putilov factory [in Petrograd] because not so long ago I went through an unpleasant experience there: after the end of one rally a young lad about 17 years old with a gloomy expression said to his neighbour but obviously so that I would hear it: 'Ekh, there's not one intelligent person in Soviet Russia' – clearly trying to say 'and you aren't so smart yourself'. When I started asking why he had such a gloomy, Schopenhauerian outlook on life already at age 17, it turned out that it wasn't from Schopenhauer at all, but because 'I have three unemployed at home, I'm the only worker and I can't provide for them. And what I'm usually receiving in the way of culture is next to nothing'. The figure of this young lad at the Putilov factory is not something exceptional and we have to pay attention to it. If we really have seventeen-year-olds in the factories that are subjected to such thoughts, then this is a serious danger.[49]

As we have seen, Zinoviev's talk therapy was based on an underlying confidence, but in 1925 it began to seem to the rest of the party leadership (particularly Bukharin) that his insistence on talking about difficulties was a manifestation of defeatism. Zinoviev and his comrade-in-arms Lev Kamenev were removed from leadership posts in 1925–26 and began their slow descent to

---

47 *Na poroge novoi epokhi* (Zinoviev 1921, pp. 40–1) (speech given in April 1921). (I learn from Barbara Allen's forthcoming Indiana University dissertation on Aleksandr Shliapnikov that many Bolsheviks, including Kollontai, felt that Zinoviev's own style of leadership had helped create the wall in Petrograd. I am grateful to Ms. Allen for letting me see her work in progress.) And see now Allen 2016, *Alexander Shliapnikov, 1885–1937: Life of an Old Bolshevik.*

48 Speech at the 11th Party Congress (1922), reprinted in *Odinnadtsatyi s'ezd RKP(b)* 1962, pp. 407–10.

49 *Odinnadtsatyi s'ezd RKP(b)* 1962, pp. 405–6.

humiliation and execution in 1936 after the first of the great show-trials of the mid-thirties. There is evidence that Zinoviev tried to interpret his political isolation as one more episode in the saga of the lonely leader who would eventually be vindicated. This time the tide never turned.

Kollontai's narratives of the revolution were designed to highlight the threat of a different kind of degeneration: the loss of purity. It is important not to understand this threat through the lens of our own canonical 'power corrupts' narrative. For Kollontai, it was not so much the temptations of power as its responsibilities that led to loss of purity. 'Tasks of a general state nature' meant dealing with a "heterogeneous" population – in other words, the unpleasant necessity of taking the interests of alien classes into account. 'Any party that stands at the head of a soviet state that is mixed in its social makeup is compelled willy-nilly to consider the aspirations of the "industrious [*khoziaistven-nyi*] muzhik" with his small-owner style of life and repugnance toward communism, as well as the numerous petty-bourgeois elements of former, capitalist, Russia.'[50] Kollontai therefore looked back with nostalgia to the time when the workers felt themselves to be the *only* force bringing communism [*nositel' kommunizma*]: 'the peasant had received the land but still did not feel himself to be a part of the soviet republic and a citizen with full rights in it'. Consequently, there was full unity in the party and no split between leaders and followers.[51]

Even more threatening than peasants or other 'petty bourgeois' elements were the 'bourgeois specialists' that the new regime was forced to use – indeed, to put into positions of authority over the workers. For Kollontai, this situation was a mockery of class power that constituted a threat to the very identity of the protagonist of the revolutionary drama: '*Spetsy*, with their origin in the past, closely and unalterably bound by their very essence to the bourgeois system that we are eliminating, began to show up everywhere in our Red Army, introducing their atmosphere of the past (blind subordination, servile obedience, distinction, ranks, and the arbitrary will of superiors in place of class discipline)'. Kollontai insisted that 'the Workers Opposition has

---

50   Kollontai is reacting in part to legislation in late 1920 that supported the 'industrious owner' (*staratelnyi khoziain*). See 'Bolshevik Sowing Committees of 1920', included in this volume.

51   *Rabochaia oppozitsiia* (Kollontai 1921, pp. 11, 16). Every time I look at this essay and read this quote, I feel compelled to look it up in Kollontai's pamphlet to see if I am distorting her argument. I am not: this comment comes after many pages of grumbling about the influence of the peasantry. Kollontai even casts shade on the slogan 'all power to the soviets', since precisely the soviets allow the petty-bourgeois psychology of the peasant to 'distort the class clarity [*chetkost*]' of government policies.

never anywhere objected to "using" technical and scientific specialists. But using is one thing – giving them *vlast* is another'.[52]

The opposition currents represented by Kollontai did not see the events of 1921 as a great turning point but merely as a *New Exploitation of the Proletariat* – the climax of a sorry record of 'compromise and bargaining'.[53] If NEP presented a special danger, it was that contamination was now more insidious and difficult to resist. Kollontai dramatized this danger in short stories written in the early 1920s. In a typical story, a pure woman of the people marries a party comrade who rises to a responsible post in the new order. After NEP, the husband begins at first by simply working with some plausible nepmen, but then starts taking long business trips, takes up with women from other classes, loses his idealism and generally goes to seed. 'However much she loved him, she seemed to understand him less and less. It was as if they were walking through a forest along two paths which diverged more and more the deeper they went in'. Despite her grief, she finally leaves her husband – just as the party's proletarian soul might grieve and leave.[54]

Deutscher criticizes Kollontai and other opposition groups because of their foolhardy demand for full communism and he compliments them on their devotion to democracy. Neither criticism nor compliment is deserved. There is absolutely no basis for Deutscher's charge that the opposition groups were blind to the economic crisis.[55] Although she drew a different moral, Kollontai told the same kind of story as Trotsky about the connection between revolutionary hopes of 1917 and the realities of 1920. The revolution had started off on a glorious note. Looking back in 1926, she recalled 'the first months of the Worker Government, months which were so rich in magnificent illusions, plans, ardent initiatives to improve life, to organize the world anew, months of the real romanticism of the Revolution'.[56] But by early 1921, Kollontai openly expressed her anger at being forced to put her dreams on hold: 'To our shame,

---

52   *Rabochaia oppozitsiia* (Kollontai 1921, pp. 12–13).
53   Berkman, *The Bolshevik Myth* (Berkman 1989, pp. 336–8). Berkman was an American anarchist exiled to Russia; these words are from a postscript to his diary of disillusionment. Verbal echoes show this paragraph to be a close paraphrase of Kollontai's 'Workers' Opposition'.
54   *Love of Worker Bees* (Kollontai 1978, p. 140).
55   Deutscher's charge rests on a misapprehension of a plank in the Worker Opposition platform that called for payment in kind. The real point of this plank was to ensure that amid general poverty the worker got first dibs on scarce items. The platform also made it clear that scarce items were to be used as individualized material incentives. The Worker Opposition proposed their scheme as a way out of the economic crisis, not as a demand for immediate full satisfaction of the worker's needs.
56   Kollontai, *The Autobiography of a Sexually Emancipated Communist Woman* (Kollontai

not only far out in the provinces but in the heart of the republic – in Moscow – working people are still living in filthy, overcrowded and anti-hygienic quarters, one visit to which makes one think that there has been no revolution at all'.[57]

The compliments to Kollontai's faith in democracy also need to be severely qualified. It is usual to see the essence of Kollontai's outlook in a romantic trust of the masses, in her insistence on worker initiative (*samodeiatelnost*) and freedom of criticism. Kollontai's doctrinal narratives reveal that her central concern was class purity. The insistence on class purity gave rise to some very practical recommendations: if the minds of party members who worked in the soviet apparatus were soiled (*zasoren*) by alien elements, then the solution was a cleansing process (*ochishchenie*) by means of a purge (*ochistka*) which would remove non-worker elements and give the party back its class purity (*chistota*).[58] Sympathetic commentators have not observed how the concern for purity undercuts the calls for party democracy. How do you combine bold initiative and criticism from the rank and file with a massive purge coupled with large-scale campaigns to 'educate' unreliable members? And not even all proletarians are reliable: some have been 'bourgeoisified' because of contact with non-worker elements in the party.[59]

Kollontai's insistence on worker initiative often seems motivated by fearful distrust of everybody else's initiative, particularly the peasant producers. Kollontai pictures the workers fighting on in heroic isolation against insidious influences from the outside world, unaided by all other classes who 'hanker after capitalism'.[60] Zinoviev was no more willing than Kollontai to contemplate real political self-determination for non-proletarian classes, yet he shows more real confidence than she does – and more connection with the outlook of 1917 – in his assumption that the walls would soon be breached and the transformative influence of the conscious working class allowed to work its magic. Zinoviev can be compared to a benevolent colonialist who fully intends to give the natives independence as soon as they are genuinely civilized. Both Zinoviev and Kollontai assumed along with Kautsky that the proletarian elite should be placed 'at the head of civilization'. But they stressed different dangers threatening the party missionaries who ventured out into the circles where conscious-

---

1971, p. 35). According to the editor, Kollontai removed the words 'magnificent illusions' from the galleys and substituted 'great aims and'.

57 *Rabochaia oppozitsiia* (Kollontai 1921, p. 18).
58 *Rabochaia oppozitsiia* (Kollontai 1921, pp. 24, 21, 41).
59 *Rabochaia oppozitsiia* (Kollontai 1921, pp. 42, 44, 46).
60 *Rabochaia oppozitsiia* (Kollontai 1921, pp. 45–6).

ness had not yet penetrated: Zinoviev worried that they would be seen as elitist and standoffish, while Kollontai worried that they would 'go native'.

Thus Deutscher is misleading when he suggests that one side in this clash was loyal to the language of 1917 and the other side was not. Both sides were inspired by the canonical narrative of pre-revolutionary and pre-war Social Democracy. Both saw the Bolshevik revolution as the long-awaited proletarian *vlast*. One side emphasized the part of the story that pictured the *vlast* as a magnificent opportunity to exert leadership; this side worried about the paradoxical wall that the very possession of the *vlast* put up between leader and follower. The other side emphasized the part of the story that pictured the *vlast* as an opportunity for the special nature of the proletariat to reveal itself in action; this side worried about the contamination that the very possession of the *vlast* seemed to bring to the world-historical creativity of the proletariat. Since both sides were indeed present in the inherited narrative and since the clash between the two was mainly a matter of emphasis, the tension between the two remained as long as the inherited narrative remained authoritative.

6   Conclusion

The Deutscher thesis about 'shortcuts to communism' in 1920 deserves to be refuted. It has dominated post-war scholarship on this crucial period and remains without serious challenge to this day. Yet its predictions fail to meet the challenge of the material presented here – material that we would have expected *a priori* to illustrate rather than disconfirm the thesis. To start with, it cannot account for the continuity between Bukharin's doctrinal narratives in 1917–18 and those of Trotsky in 1920, since the perceived relationship between coercion and transformation underwent no major change. The Deutscher thesis also cannot account for the actual contrast between these stories: instead of an accelerating leap into socialism we see a lengthening road.

Furthermore, the Deutscher thesis cannot account for the continuity between the doctrinal narratives of Zinoviev and Kollontai, since both are agreed that 1920 was a period of dangerous compromise, not of a leap into socialism. In particular, Deutscher cannot account for the view of NEP in these narratives. 'Silently, with a heavy heart, Bolshevism parted with its dream of war communism': this is how Deutscher describes the transition to NEP in 1921. In fact, Zinoviev and Kollontai saw NEP not as a dramatic reversal of war communism's uncompromising extremism but rather as a somewhat expanded version of the same type of compromise. Deutscher's thesis also cannot account for the contrast between Zinoviev and Kollontai, once we see that Kollontai is interested more in class purity than in democracy and that Zinoviev is in his way loyal to the language of class leadership that was spoken in 1917–18.

The issue of war communism thus needs reopening and rethinking. A narrative approach to political doctrine can help us in this quest. It allows us to formulate the issues brought up by the Deutscher thesis in a more precise way and points us to crucial but overlooked sources. Listening to stories told by Bolsheviks directs our attention back to the central themes of the canonical narrative inherited from pre-war Social Democracy: the proletariat's mission to conquer state power (*Macht, vlast*) in order to construct socialism, and, just as important, the inspired and inspiring leadership required first to accept and then to carry out this mission. This story is the real constitution of the Soviet Union; it is the real definition of what the *proletarskaia vlast* is all about. The legitimate uses of coercion and its relation to the pace of transformation can only be understood within the matrix of this story. The efforts at narrative repair that led to serious clashes about party degeneration must also be put in the context of the inherited narrative: they arose out of the hidden tensions and ambiguities that inevitably surfaced when the possession of state power became a day-to-day reality rather than a distant goal.

PART 3

Time of Troubles: Policies (1914–1921)

∵

Grain Monopoly and Agricultural Transformation: Ideals and Necessities

Part of the drama in any revolution is the clash between the long-range ideals of transformation and the pressing necessities imposed by the task of staying in power. For the Bolsheviks, a party of proletarian revolutionaries who came to power in an overwhelmingly peasant country, this clash was caused most fundamentally by problems of town-country relations.

According to the majority of Western scholars, during the years immediately following the Bolshevik takeover in October 1917, this conflict took the form of a militant imposition of proletarian ideals in the countryside. Only after the end of the civil war in 1921, it is argued, did the Bolsheviks realize the necessity of a more gradual approach.

There is a paradoxical contrast between this image and the criticism levelled at the Bolshevik leaders by socialist critics at the time. Karl Kautsky, the most authoritative Western socialist critic of Bolshevism, argued in *The Dictatorship of the Proletariat* in 1918 that 'it would have been dangerous for the Bolsheviks to interfere even slightly with peasant private property'. Owing to the impossibility of socialist revolution in backward Russia, Bolshevik concessions would inevitably end in a dictatorship of the peasantry rather than the proletariat. Within the Bolshevik camp, the left-wing Workers' Opposition made similar charges. As Aleksandra Kollontai put it in *The Workers' Opposition*, workers, who wanted a 'rapid advance towards communism', were being held back by the party's concessions to the 'petty-bourgeois proclivities' of the peasant.

How can we explain a critique of Bolshevik policy that seems so paradoxical today? Is there any way that the image of concessions to the peasantry can be made compatible with the facts supporting our current image of what some have termed a Bolshevik 'war on the peasantry'?

1   Bolshevik Axioms

The most informative exposition of Bolshevik goals during the first years after the revolution is still the *ABC of Communism* by Nikolai Bukharin and Evgenii Preobrazhensky (1919). Preobrazhensky, who wrote the chapters on agricultural and distribution policy, based his argument on what may be called the axioms of Bolshevik strategy:

- Large-scale centralized economic units are vastly more productive than scattered, small-scale ones.
- Only direct perception of material interest – not force – can induce people to adopt these higher economic forms.
- Lower economic forms should not be eliminated until higher forms are ready to replace them.
- Even in the best of circumstances, preparation of higher forms will take time, and the sacrifices imposed by the civil war have made this preparatory work yet more difficult and time-consuming.
- It will therefore be necessary to rely during the foreseeable future on lower economic forms such as single-owner peasant farms and market-mediated distribution.

Given Russia's economic backwardness, compounded by the peasant seizure of the large estates, the party will face incredible difficulties in convincing the peasants of the material advantages of socialist collectivism. The party must therefore devote much of its effort in the foreseeable future to improving small-scale peasant agriculture.

Preobrazhensky's remarks on small-scale trade also deserve to be cited: 'It makes no sense for the soviet authority to simply prohibit petty trade when it is not in a position to replace that trade completely with the activity of its own organs of distribution ... petty trade will continue to exist until large-scale industry in the towns has been restored and the provision of basic consumer items can be genuinely carried out by state monopolies.'

To sum up: the *ABC of Communism* expresses both great confidence in the superiority of 'higher' economic forms, and (contrary to its reputation) great caution about the pace of 'liquidation' of old forms. Thus on the programmatic level the Bolsheviks had a strong sense of where they were going but also gave themselves full license to compromise and improvise as they travelled towards their goal.[1]

2   Grain Monopoly

Preobrazhensky did not apply his 'slow and steady' strategy to the grain trade, the most strategic sector of town-country trade; instead, he put it into the category of large-scale trade that could be quickly nationalized. The story of the grain monopoly is partly the story of how this automatic assumption came to be viewed as a mistake.

---

1 For a more detailed discussion of the *ABC of Communism*, see 'The Mystery of the *ABC*', included in this volume.

It will be useful to introduce our discussion of policy by defining key terms. The core meaning of 'grain monopoly' is the elimination of private dealers and their replacement by a state-controlled apparatus. Even though grain monopolies had also been set up by 'bourgeois' governments such as that of Germany, a state monopoly could still be seen as a step in the direction of abolishing the private market altogether. But the mere fact of nationalization leaves a lot of questions unanswered: how were prices set? how flexible were they? were grain producers *obligated* to sell?

'Requisition' has a core meaning of forced sale, with the emphasis on 'forced'. A particular good or service is required by civil or military authority, and the owner is obligated to sell, at a price set by the state. It is an open question whether it is appropriate to extend the term 'requisition' from individual cases of forced sale to broad policies imposing an obligation (*povinnost*) on large sections of the population. The motive for this extension seems to be to emphasize the brutal and coercive enforcement that backed up these broader policies. Much is lost, however, if we blur the distinction between a general obligation and an *ad hoc* burden placed on unlucky individuals: you must shovel snow off this railroad track because there happens to be snow there and you happen to be living nearby. Individual requisitions were widely perceived as highly unfair and open to high-handed abuse of power. Indeed, one motive for imposing general obligations was to escape the petty arbitrariness of requisition.

If the state decides to impose a general obligation, it can choose between several methods for carrying it out. One method is a 'tax', whose core meaning is assessment by rates. Unlike a requisition, where the entire burden falls on the unfortunate owner of a required good, a tax shares the burden as equitably as possible. Unfortunately, a tax is information-intensive: in order to get to an acceptable level of fairness and comprehensiveness, a great deal of knowledge is required about each individual's wealth.

In order to cut down on information costs, a *razverstka* ('assessment') can be imposed. In the case of the 'food-supply *razverstka*' (*prodrazverstka*), an overall target was set by taking into account the needs of the state and overall harvest statistics. This overall obligation was shared out between provinces; the provinces shared out their assigned target to counties, and so on down to the individual household. This rough and ready method of sharing the burden was guaranteed to produce many inequities, but better methods may have been beyond the administrative resources available to the Bolsheviks.

'Sharing out' is the etymological core meaning of *razverstka*, but *razverstka* policies during the civil war were also based on the following logic: with equivalent exchange if possible and without it if necessary. Thus the *razverstka* can be identified as midway between monopoly at one end (at least a promise of compensation) and tax at the other (no compensation). As the economic collapse deepened and the Bolsheviks had fewer goods at their disposal to exchange for grain, the *razverstka* looked less and less like a grain monopoly and more and more like a tax.

Since requisitions, taxes and *razverstka* are all methods for imposing obligations on a population – methods that can be used by any type of government – they have no intrinsic connection to socialism or even the grain monopoly. If we examine the course of Bolshevik policy with these distinctions in mind, we will see a growing clash between the ideal of a grain monopoly vs. the practical methods required by the pressing necessity of collecting enough grain to stay in power and prevent complete economic collapse.

The Bolsheviks inherited the basic legislation setting up a grain monopoly from the Provisional Government, which in turn had merely completed the evolution of tsarist food-supply policy toward a state takeover of the grain trade. The monopoly legislation of March 1917 mandated fixed prices for grain, set up a network of food-supply committees, and imposed an obligation on producers to sell all their grain except for a stated norm for personal needs. The Provisional Government also recognized an obligation on its part to make industrial goods available to grain producers. A Ministry of Food Supply was established that later became the Bolshevik *Narkomprod* (People's Commissariat of Food Supply). Thus the legislation of March 1917 envisioned an ideal monopoly that would benefit both producer and consumer. This vision continued to inspire the Bolsheviks – even though they ultimately had no more luck than the Provisional Government in putting it into practice.

The Bolsheviks also inherited the repressive implications of the monopoly: the war against the sackmen (*meshochniki*). As the national economy continued to disintegrate and the government failed to make good its promise to provide goods, a flood of sackmen set off on long journeys to grain-producing villages to carry back a bag or two filled with food. *Meshochnichestvo* had already reached mass proportions by late summer 1917. It was a complicated phenomenon that included hungry city-dwellers, peasants from grain-deficit provinces, and ex-soldiers turned full-time 'speculators'.

After the October takeover, the Bolsheviks had their hands full getting their bearings and taking full control of the state food-supply apparatus. Their first major initiative came in spring 1918: a 'food-supply dictatorship' that attempted to enforce the monopoly through class-war methods. The term 'food-supply dictatorship' was borrowed from Germany and reflected the Bolshevik conception of the monopoly as part of a pre-socialist 'state capitalism'. The Bolsheviks' enforcement strategy was two-pronged: first, to enlist hungry workers and peasants from grain-deficit regions into 'food-supply detachments' that were sent to the villages; second, to incite 'class war in the villages' by setting up Committees of the Poor (*kombedy*). The class-war strategy was justified by demonizing the 'kulaks' (better-off peasants) as saboteurs responsible for the failure of the monopoly.

The results of this strategy were meagre and the costs prohibitive. The Bolsheviks found themselves forced to compromise on both the monopoly ideal and class-war enforcement methods. The search for a more viable policy began in summer 1918: at the centre there was an effort to control the excesses caused by the class-war rhetoric of the spring, and in the localities food-supply officials experimented with more effective methods of grain collection. The result was the *razverstka* system, which took shape by early 1919 and remained in place for the duration of the civil war.

Like the grain monopoly, the *razverstka* method was an inheritance from the past: it was first used by the tsarist Minister of Agriculture, A.A. Rittikh, in late 1916. (The origin of the term *razverstka* in tsarist bureaucratic practice would seem to exclude the possibility that the Bolsheviks equated it with socialism in any way.) A genuine monopoly required a detailed accounting (*uchët*) of the grain held on each farm; the *razverstka* method was a recognition that this information was unavailable and that cruder methods had to be used. A genuine monopoly was also supposed to provide a full economic equivalent for grain, whereas the best the *razverstka* could promise was to distribute whatever goods were available. The *razverstka* system also represented a compromise on the class-war enforcement strategy: the Committees of the Poor were disbanded, efforts were made to bring the food-supply detachments under better control, and village assemblies had more say in making assessments to individual households. Although the Bolsheviks compromised on both the monopoly ideal and class-war enforcement, they certainly did not repudiate either one.

From early 1919, the fate of the *razverstka* system can be traced on two curves, one ascending and the other descending. On the ascending curve there was a gradual improvement of the food-supply organization from totally unacceptable to barely tolerable. This curve continued past the civil war, since the food-supply tax of the early 1920s was collected by the same apparatus. The descending curve tracked the deterioration of the economy, which increased the relative burden of grain assessments and decreased the amount of material compensation the Bolsheviks could provide. As Aleksandr Tsiurupa, head of *Narkomprod*, said at the Tenth Party Congress in March 1921, the quantity of nails now being received by the village was less than the quantity of castor oil received before the war. Agriculture was so weakened by the burdens of seven years of war and civil war that a drought in the Volga region in 1921 turned into a devastating famine.

Ever since the end of the civil war, there have been attempts to come up with a statistical expression of the burden borne by the peasants. The effort to wring hard conclusions out of the shaky statistics of the period should not obscure two basic but contradictory realities. One reality is that the relative burden caused by the *razverstka* went up as the economy as a whole shrank and this led to fierce peasant resistance. The other reality is that something like half of the food received in the cities came there via the black market and the sackmen, which implies that the Bolsheviks collected nowhere near the full surplus (even without taking into account other voluntary uses for grain such as home-brewed liquor).

The glaring inadequacies of the food-supply organization were never denied even by the Bolsheviks. In order to collect the grain and enforce the prohibition against private trade, violence against both the grain producers and the sackmen was required and liberally applied. Huge wastefulness in storage, transport and retail distribution made *Narkomprod* almost as unpopular with consumers as it was with producers. Lack of proper information led to inequities in individual grain assessments that infuriated both peasants and state officials. Finally, abuse of power by local food-supply officials was endemic.

How we evaluate these facts depends on our view of the constraints facing the Bolsheviks (and their enemies in the civil war as well). If we believe that the Bolsheviks had the option of relying on a trained professional bureaucracy, adequate information, or fully equivalent exchange, then we are bound to condemn them for choosing the worse way. Some such reasoning seems to be the majority view among Western scholars. If we believe that the *razverstka* system was not itself the cause of these basic realities but rather an adjustment to them, then we are bound to condemn it less severely.

3   The End of the Razverstka System

The *razverstka* system came to an end when the Bolsheviks decriminalized the private grain trade in spring 1921. We still have no fully adequate account of the timing and significance of this crucial decision. One barrier to a full explanation is a number of widespread misconceptions. It is often asserted, for example, that the Bolsheviks thought they had achieved their ideal monopoly in 1920 and that this ideal consisted of taking grain from the peasants without providing economic incentives. Readers are also commonly informed that the Bolsheviks were living in a dream world in 1920, completely unaware of the immense economic and political danger caused by unrelenting pressure on the grain producer.

As sometimes happens, Soviet historians have contributed to this Western consensus about Bolshevik blindness, although for different motives. The over-riding aim of Soviet monographs about the end of the *razverstka* system seems to have been to reveal the insight of the great Lenin. In order to make their case, Soviet historians willingly emphasized the short-sightedness of everyone else, particularly the unpopular food-supply officials.

These misconceptions have been allowed to stand partly because of the genuine ambiguity of the *razverstka* system that by 1920 confused even the food-supply officials who operated it. The debate among officials during that year can be summarized by the question: was the *razverstka* system best thought of as a monopoly on crutches or a tax on crutches? A monopoly needs crutches if it does not have a substantial fund of industrial exchange items; a tax needs crutches if it does not have information about individual farms. The *razverstka* system was designed to collect grain in the absence of both requirements. As the economy began its long climb from near collapse, thus creating the opportunity for real improvements in collection methods, the question of the identity of the *razverstka* system became a vital one, since the answer would determine the direction of reforms.

In spring 1921, the decision was finally taken to improve the *razverstka* by turning it into a tax and to find other methods of moving towards an effective grain monopoly. Historians have traditionally been severe about the timing of the decision, judging it to be much too late. After the civil war wound down in early 1920, it is argued, the costs of continuing the *razverstka* system and the benefits of ending it should have been obvious to any rational person. Since the Bolsheviks waited for a full year to take the plunge, they must have been blinded by an irrational ideology.

In order to evaluate this argument, we have to examine more carefully the constraints under which the Bolsheviks at least thought they were operating. The party leadership had to answer three questions: do we need to collect a substantial amount of grain for centralized distribution? If so, can we afford to take the risk of changing methods? If we can relax our grip and make a significant cut in our grain collection targets, what changes should we make?

The answer to the first question was that the state needed grain under central control in order to distribute it to workers in industry and soldiers in the Red Army. The Bolsheviks judged that given the economic imbalance between industry and agriculture, it would be ruinous to throw industry on the mercy of the market. A subsidy financed by the *razverstka* (and later by the food-supply tax) was essential to stave off complete collapse.

The security motive behind the Bolshevik insistence on a burdensome grain collection has been even more neglected than the economic motive, partly because the Bolshevik leaders were loath to publicize their own vulnerability. Preservation of a fighting force was deemed essential even after the end of the war with Poland in summer 1920. Only after a determined forcing of the diplomatic pace by Lenin in early 1921 was it possible to contemplate the collapse of the Red Army that marked the early years of NEP.

Could the *razverstka* system be abandoned while collection targets remained relatively high? When the top leaders turned to their food-supply experts with this question in 1920, they got a resounding 'no'. The experts based their argument on their own weakness: the state did not have enough industrial goods for state-sponsored exchange, the bureaucracy was not good enough to make satisfactory individual assessments, and state collection efforts would be swept away by the black market (whether decriminalized or not) if grain producers had the right of free disposal over a significant part of the surplus. The reasoning of the food-supply officials is much more cogent than is usually realized: the experience of 1921 shows that it was indeed impossible to keep the free market within bounds and that under these circumstances state-conducted exchange could only obtain pitiful amounts.

Only after the top leaders made the decision to lower grain targets in early 1921 could they contemplate dismantling the *razverstka* system. Given lower collection targets, the food-supply establishment was able to go along somewhat grudgingly with the proposed changes. The most vocal protest came from *Narkomprod* official Moishe Frumkin, who accepted everything except the decriminalization of the market. Why abandon the monopoly ideal, he asked, just at the time when a reviving industry could begin to make state-conducted exchange a reality? But the consensus among Bolshevik economic experts was that it was pointless to adopt a tax system if free trade was still prohibited.

Frumkin need not have worried: the monopoly ideal was not abandoned. The Bolsheviks only revised their strategy for attaining it. Overgeneralizing from the wartime situation, they had earlier assumed it would only be possible to build up a genuine monopoly if it was protected from the competition of the private market by outright repression. When Lenin later referred to a crucial 'mistake' in the previous Bolshevik outlook, he seems to have been talking about this strategy (and not, as he is usually interpreted, the failures of the *razverstka* system as a wartime measure). After 1921, the Bolsheviks reverted to the logic of Preobrazhensky's 'slow and steady' alternative by tolerating the private market until it could be 'squeezed out' and replaced. In 1927, Bukharin remarked that 'the grain monopoly was repealed with the introduction of NEP. But now, on the basis of the growth of our economic organizations, on the basis of their competition with the private middleman, we have squeezed private capital out of grain procurements, and we have arrived, so to speak, at a state monopoly from the opposite direction and on a new basis.'

4   Agricultural Policy

Similar to Bolshevik attempts to realize an ideal grain monopoly, their attempts to transform peasant agriculture in a socialist direction revealed a growing clash between ideals of structural transformation vs. pressing political and economic necessities. In contrast to the grain monopoly, Bolshevik rethinking about peasant agriculture was conducted in the open and indeed with much fanfare.

It is hard to imagine that the Bolsheviks could have come to power in 1917, much less held on to it, if they had not given wholehearted support to peasant land hunger. From an orthodox socialist point of view, this was a dangerous concession, since it entailed breaking up the axiomatically more efficient large-scale estates and even the larger peasant farms. The Bolsheviks admitted that this policy pushed them back economically to a lower starting point, but they thought it was justifiable because it liquidated the landowners as a class and thus removed the main barrier to progress.

The Bolsheviks were confident in 1918 that the road was now open to rapid progress toward socialization in agriculture. The economic crisis would serve as a prod, while actual examples of socialist agriculture would serve as attractive models. A few landowner estates had been preserved intact from the flood of peasant revolution and turned into state farms or *sovkhozy*; these would demonstrate the advantages of large-scale production.

The Bolsheviks assumed that poor peasants would be in the forefront of the movement toward collective associations, and so great hopes were placed on the *kombedy* or Committees of the Poor formed in spring 1918. The main impetus for the creation of these committees was the food-supply crisis, but they also fit into a long-standing Bolshevik scenario about the political evolution of the peasantry. According to this scenario (worked out in greatest detail by Lenin himself), the peasantry as a whole worked together only in order to overthrow 'feudal' relations in the countryside. Once the common enemy was gone, economic evolution would lead to greater and greater conflict between peasants-in-the-process-of-becoming-proletarians and peasants-in-the-process-of-becoming-bourgeois. It was the task of the party to support the peasantry as a whole during the 'bourgeois' revolution against the landlords, but also to create special institutions for the poor peasants as soon as possible.

The Committees of the Poor of 1918 were based on this logic, but they proved to be an almost catastrophic disappointment: they came closer to uniting the village against the Bolsheviks than splitting it to their advantage. The Committees of the Poor were disbanded in late 1918; in later years the phrase *kombedovskii period* (the time of the Committees of the Poor) had a much more ominous ring than 'war communism' (usually dated 1918–21). The disbandment of the Committees of the Poor was part of a larger shift that can be called 'the discovery of the middle peasant'. The term 'middle peasant' (*seredniak*) was notably absent from Bolshevik revolutionary rhetoric until early summer 1918, but after that it became more and more central until it was enshrined in the party programme adopted at the Eighth Party Congress in 1919. Lenin's speech at this congress became the main source of 'pro-peasant' rhetoric throughout the 1920s.

For the most part, Western historiography has ignored the 1918–1919 shift toward the middle peasant; historians certainly have not been particularly interested in either its causes or its effects – perhaps because it conflicts with the overall image of proletarian militancy during the civil war. Yet it was arguably one of the most significant shifts in the outlook of the Bolsheviks after they took power. The shift was not in the characterization of the peasant, whom Marxists had long viewed as internally divided between a labouring soul and a property-owning soul. But until the shift in 1918–19, the Bolsheviks had assumed that they would either work with the peasantry as a whole or with peasants who had already chosen to identify themselves with their labouring soul. The vacillating middle peasant was thus less interesting for what he was than for what he would become. Only after the Bolsheviks took power and realized (as Preobrazhensky put it in *Pravda* on 7 November 1920) that victory in the civil war depended on the choice made by the middle peasant did they start to accept the fact that they would have to work out some long-term *modus vivendi* with the middle peasant, vacillations and all.

The next party-wide discussion of relations with the peasants came in late 1920 with the establishment of sowing committees (*posevkomy*). The sowing committees were primarily a response to a pressing emergency (maintaining production despite lack of usable incentives and preserving seed stores in the face of the approaching drought). The discussion sparked off by the new committees reveals some of the conclusions the Bolsheviks had drawn from their earlier disillusionment. The party economist Iurii Larin coined the term '*krekhozy*' for the ordinary, individual-owner, peasant farm, and insisted that the *krekhozy* must be the centre of attention in the foreseeable future (*Pravda*, 12 December 1920). The emphasis on the *krekhozy* was accompanied by an apotheosis of the 'industrious owner' (*staratelnyi khoziain*) and a condemnation of lazy peasants (*lodyri*). To critics inside and outside the party, it seemed as if the Bolsheviks had reversed their earlier fierce stand on the relative merits of kulak and poor peasant.

The fall from grace of the *sovkhozy* and other peasant collective experiments had become party orthodoxy by 1920. The attractive power of socialism was no longer expected to manifest itself by means of collective experiments within agriculture itself, but rather by the power and beneficence of state industry. In the short run, state aid was envisioned as a first repayment on the forced loan the Bolsheviks had extracted from the peasantry (the loan metaphor dominated Bolshevik rhetoric about the peasantry in 1920). In the long run, socialism would win over the peasantry via tractors and electrification.

At the time of the sowing committee legislation (late 1920), the Bolsheviks did not expect ever to decriminalize the grain market, and so they saw the winning-over of the industrious owner as a process occurring within a mandatory state-organized framework. The poverty of the state in 1920 also meant that for the most part it could only offer organization backed up by coercion, although the Bolsheviks assumed that the existing framework would slowly be filled with material content as industry revived. This scenario was revised in 1921 with the adoption of NEP and the emergence of a private grain market and the 'nepmen' who profited from it. The state now granted the private market a greater role in providing material incentives for increased production. Still, the revised scenario of NEP had the same basic plot as the scenario of 1920: the peasants will be won over to socialism via the might of socialist industry. But now the battle for influence over the peasantry was fought against a tolerated bourgeoisie rather than a bourgeoisie driven underground.

We can now identify three major changes in the Bolshevik conception of the path toward a transformed Russian countryside: the middle peasant replaced the poor peasant as the party's major companion on this journey; the task of demonstrating the advantages of socialism was taken away from *sovkhozy* and peasant collectives and given to industry; the bourgeois tempters of the vacillating middle peasant were allowed to emerge from the underground so that they could be 'squeezed out' more efficiently. None of these shifts challenged the Bolshevik axiom of moving to higher economic forms only by means of demonstrated material advantage – an axiom that was not violated on a large scale until Stalin's coercive collectivization, and even then shamefacedly and hypocritically. To overestimate the discontinuity that occurred in 1921 is to underestimate the more fundamental discontinuity that occurred in 1930.

5   Conclusion

We can now return to the two images of Bolshevik policy outlined at the outset: the one that sees Bolshevik policy as an aggressive attack on the peasantry
and the other that sees it as a series of concessions. We cannot choose between
them merely on the basis of our estimation of the brutality and material suffering caused by the civil war, since different observers put this suffering into
different overarching narratives.

According to Kautsky, the suffering was caused by the Bolshevik betrayal of
Social-Democratic teaching about the conditions needed for socialist revolution. Although Bolshevik leaders accepted most of Kautsky's Marxist presuppo-
sitions about agriculture, they wove them into a story of class leadership: policies that were economically regressive were justified if they shored up peasant
political support and thus ensured the survival of soviet power – the worker-
peasant *vlast*. For the Bolsheviks, even the suffering that arose directly from the
exactions they made was ultimately due to the counterrevolution that imposed
war and blockades on the country.

These contrasting stories by socialist participants converge on an image of
Bolshevik concessions to the peasantry. Today we know what observers at the
time did not know: the catastrophe waiting for the Soviet peasantry just around
the corner, the permanent failure of Soviet agriculture to make good its claim to
be a 'higher' economic form, and the final collapse of the whole Soviet experiment. Since we see the sufferings of the civil war as a rehearsal for the horrors to
come, we can hardly help seeing Bolshevik peasant policy as a story of national
tragedy.

Although we know more about the outcome than the participants themselves, we should not forget what they knew: the visions and unquestioned
axioms of Marxist revolutionaries. The more we understand these axioms, the
less we will see the policy changes of 1921 as a fundamental turning point: the
Bolshevik outlook contained about the same mixture of generosity and cruelty,
pragmatism and illusion, before as after. In our effort to tell the story of national
tragedy in all its human complexity, we should not simply reject the stories told
by participants but rather incorporate them into our own.

Bolshevik *Razverstka* and War Communism

Few would dispute the claim that the *razverstka*, the Bolshevik method of grain procurement, was a centrepiece of 'war communism'. Yet there exists no adequate treatment of the *razverstka* in the scholarly literature, and indeed there is widespread confusion about the nature and purposes of the *razverstka* policy as well as about the circumstances of its introduction and its replacement in 1921 by a food-supply tax (*prodnalog*). A closer look at the actual *razverstka* reveals some surprising features and in the end casts doubt on the validity and usefulness of the 'war communism' notion itself.

The *razverstka* was introduced in the second half of 1918 as a result of experience in trying to enforce a state grain monopoly by means of the food-supply dictatorship decreed in spring 1918. To understand the *razverstka* method we must first look at the more ambitious aims of the previous policy of a full-fledged grain monopoly. The grain monopoly had already been decreed by the Provisional Government in March 1917, and even this decree was only a step beyond the stage the tsarist government had reached by September 1916 when a fixed price had been made mandatory for all grain sales and when state officials were given de facto control over all grain transport. The Provisional Government's legislation declared that all grain above a fairly modest consumption norm had to be sold to the state at a fixed price. This measure was one of the most radical policies attempted by the Provisional Government.

The growing claims of the state over disposition of the nation's grain supply were of course a practical response to the intensifying food-supply crisis. But many also had ideological hopes pinned on the grain monopoly as a step toward full government control of the economy. These hopes were not confined to the Bolsheviks, as can be seen from the arguments of Vladimir Groman, the staunchest advocate of the grain monopoly both in tsarist governmental councils and in the Petrograd Soviet during 1917.[1] Lenin's own view of the matter is found in his 1918 doctrine of state capitalism, since the grain monopoly was a prime example of state capitalism in practice.

---

[1] During the Menshevik trial in 1931, N.S. Sukhanov stated that 'Groman was the author of War Communism. When did he proclaim it? He proclaimed it soon after the February Revolution … He took the Kadet Shingarev by the throat and squeezed out of him the basic element of War Communism, namely, the grain monopoly.' See Naum Jasny, *Soviet Economists of the Twenties: Names to be Remembered* (Jasny 1972, p. 100).

What Lenin meant by state capitalism in 1918 was not what the term came to mean later (a mixed-economy toleration of private capitalists), but rather a situation in which a bourgeois state – impelled by immanent capitalist development as accelerated by wartime demands – takes over actual control of the economy even while respecting legal ownership of the capitalists. Even before the revolution Lenin had argued in his 1916 pamphlet *Imperialism* that this situation was the threshold to socialism. In 1918 he argued further that the substance of this 'organizational task' remained the same even when a proletarian state had taken power. The grain monopoly in particular was a measure that had already been adopted by such advanced capitalist states as Germany but, in Russia, it could be enforced only over the vociferous opposition of the 'uncultured' petty capitalists and other assorted 'disorganizers' of town and country. Thus, in 1918, Lenin's goal of state capitalism was hardly moderate either in terms of its ideological ambitions or in the demands made on the Russian people.[2]

The practicality of the grain monopoly is also called into question by the extreme demands it made on state administrative resources. To properly carry out a grain monopoly, the state needed full information about everyone's grain holding so that a proper determination of each individual's surplus could be made. An organizational structure capable of receiving and distributing the grain had to be created, and material and coercive incentives had to be provided. The original plan of the Provisional Government relied almost completely on voluntary action for all three of these requirements – information, infrastructure, and incentives – and the predictable result was disaster.

The Bolshevik food-supply dictatorship of spring 1918 was an effort to supply these prerequisites. Information would be obtained through the village-splitting tactics embodied in the Poor Peasants Committees that were intended to be the 'alert eyes' of the food-supply apparatus.[3] This apparatus would be

---

2 See the discussion in chapter 10 of *Imperialism*, especially the passage at Lenin 1958–1965, 27:425. From the 1918 polemic with the Left Communists to which Lenin referred in 1921: 'We still have too little of the mercilessness necessary for the success of socialism. And not because of a lack of decisiveness ... But we don't have the ability to catch sufficiently quickly a sufficient number of speculators, predators, capitalists – destroyers of Soviet undertakings. And this ability can only come about as a result of the organization of registration and monitoring [*uchet i kontrol*]. [And] there is not enough firmness in our courts, where bribe takers are given six months in jail rather than being shot. Both of these defects have one social root: the influence of the petty-bourgeois element [*stikhiia*] and its flabbiness' (Lenin 1958–1965, 36:305).

3 This phrase was used by A.D. Tsiurupa in a speech at the Fifth Congress of Soviets in spring 1918 (*Piatyi Vserossiiskii s'ezd Sovetov 1918*, pp. 135–145).

based not on a voluntary hierarchy of committees, such as the one the Provisional Government had created, but on strict centralization supplemented by an infusion of new proletarian talent and dedication. The workers would also provide 'real force' in the form of requisition and blockade detachments that would supplement efforts to provide the village with industrial items at low fixed prices. Thus the food-supply dictatorship was not a rejection of Lenin's policy of state capitalism but an attempt to carry it out.

The food-supply dictatorship cannot be considered simply an improvised response to the deepening food-supply crisis of 1918, since it drew on a policy tradition that dated back even before the February Revolution. Top food-supply officials, then and later, argued that the methods of the food-supply dictatorship did not contain anything new in principle but were simply the logical culmination of methods already proposed.[4] While this argument may be exaggerated, it is true that the Provisional Government's Ministry of Food Supply was moving toward much tougher methods in the fall of 1917 and that the Bolsheviks did set themselves the same problem as their predecessors: enforcing a state grain monopoly.[5]

The genuine rethinking of the food-supply procurement problem came later in 1918 after the failure of the food-supply dictatorship set up in the spring had become evident. The village-splitting tactics embodied in the Committees of the Poor succeeded more in outraging the peasants than in obtaining grain; the workers were less pleased by the opportunity to take grain by force than irritated by the government's attack in the name of the monopoly on the independent grain-purchasing delegations sent by individual factories and towns; the lawlessness of the blockade detachments that enforced the monopoly exceeded all bounds. The political liability of a policy that created rebellion in the countryside and despair in the towns was made even less tolerable by the outbreak of the civil war. In early August Lenin demanded a change in direction and his proposals rapidly became legislative policy.

The extent of the retreat from the food-supply dictatorship can be gauged by looking at an appeal issued in May 1918 by the Council of People's Commissars. The appeal ended with these ringing words that set forth the principles of the grain monopoly:

---

4 Such arguments are made by A. Svidersky in *Chetyre goda prodovol'stvennoi raboty* (Svidersky 1922) and A.B. Khalatov in *Vnutrenniaia torgovlia Soiuza ssR za X let* (Khalatov 1928).
5 Material on the proposed changes by the Provisional Government can be found in the Central State Historical Archive, Leningrad, fond 1276, opis' 14, delo 483. For discussion, see Lih 1990 (*Bread and Authority*).

Not one step away from the grain monopoly! Not the slightest increase in fixed prices for grain! No independent procurement! All that is steadfast, disciplined, and conscious in a single organized food-supply order! Unhesitating fulfilment of all directives of the central authority! No separate actions! War to the kulaks![6]

But by September 1918 these brave slogans could not have been repeated. The fixed price for grain had been tripled. The grain monopoly had been officially relaxed to such an extent that workers in Moscow were temporarily allowed to go to the countryside to buy one and a half poods of grain for each traveller to the countryside – a measure referred to by disgusted food-supply officials as 'legalized sackmanism [*meshochnichestvo*]'. On a more permanent basis, the worker detachments were allowed to give half of the food they obtained directly to the organization that sent them; this practice was in reality heavily taxed independent procurement rather than state monopoly purchases. Although the kulaks were still treated as deadly enemies of the people, the emphasis of peasant policy had been switched very heavily to neutralization of the peasant producer, that is, the middle peasant who had not been so much as mentioned in the May appeal. Attempts had been made to restrain the blockade detachments that harassed the sackmen, and the Poor Peasants Committees were on the verge of being disbanded. The only plank that remained of the food-supply dictatorship was the insistence on a centralized food-supply apparatus.

The *razverstka* method that came to the fore in the second half of 1918 must be seen in the context of this general retreat from the grain monopoly strategy, so ambitious both in aim and method.[7] The *razverstka* method itself was not an invention of the central authorities but developed from the experience of

---

6 *Dekrety sovetskoi vlasti* 1959, pp. 353–4.
7 Because of this general retreat, it is misleading to see the *razverstka* as just a systemization of the food-supply dictatorship; see Alec Nove, *An Economic History of the USSR* (Nove 1969, p. 59). Silvana Malle notes the retreat in food-supply policy in the second half of 1918 but sees the *razverstka* as an indication of the failure of that retreat; see *The Economic Organization of War Communism, 1918–1921* (Malle 1985, p. 373). Malle stresses the ill effects of collective commodity exchange, an element of continuity in food-supply policy not discussed in this article. The distribution of scarce exchange items to those without a grain surplus was defended both as a welfare measure and as a material incentive for help in collecting the *razverstka*. Martin Malia is one of the few historians who see civil war food-supply policy as a retreat from earlier policy; see *Comprendre la revolution russe* (Malia 1980, pp. 132–4).

lower-level officials as they struggled to do their jobs. The *razverstka* supplied the requirements of information, infrastructure, and incentives in a more modest but practical way.

How did the *razverstka* work? The word is itself almost impossible to translate: perhaps 'quota assessment' is closest.[8] The method was essentially based on the old tsarist method of collective responsibility: an assessment was given to a collectivity, whose members were then free to decide how to divide the burden further. The outside authority was not concerned as long as the assessment was paid in full. This technique was applied from the top to the bottom of the food-supply hierarchy. At the top the People's Commissariat of Food Supply determined a total amount for the entire area controlled by the Bolsheviks. Quotas were then signed to the provinces through negotiations among top provincial officials. The provincial assessment was distributed in the same way among the *uezdy*, and so on down the hierarchy until the individual peasant household was presented with an assessment.

This method recommended itself to the Bolsheviks for the same reason it did to tsarist officials: it economized on administrative resources. Instead of the gleaming organization envisioned by the enthusiasts of the grain monopoly, the *razverstka* got along with the tried and true methods of collective responsibility. The same is true of information requirements. The grain monopoly had required all grain supplies to be put on register (*uchet*) so that the government could tell how much was surplus and how much was to be left to the individual producer. Here as elsewhere, the *uchet* became the battle cry of the state's drive for information as a prelude to full control. In translations of some famous passages in Lenin's *State and Revolution*, *uchet* is usually misrendered as 'accounting' and taken as a symbol of Lenin's naive view of the simplicity of modern economic management. This interpretation overlooks the fact that in 1917 and 1918 the *uchet* was seen as a major task and a basic political challenge. The *uchet* was central to socialist ambitions because the first task in nationalization was simply for the state to know what was going on.[9]

---

8 Sometimes *razverstka* or a translation is not used at all, and civil war food-supply policy is simply described with the term 'grain requisition' or with the redundant 'forcible requisition'. E.H. Carr, who barely alludes in passing to the *razverstka* itself as one of many 'constantly changing expedients', uses 'forcible requisition' in *The Bolshevik Revolution* (Carr 1950–1955, 2:150–1, 227–8). This term, however, is unfortunate because it completely slides over the question of the terms of the forced sale and, indeed, seems to be understood by some writers simply as confiscation. The term requisition is best restricted to individual acts of forced sale or provision of services, if only because the burden of these (as distinct from the general obligation of the *razverstka*) became a major source of peasant discontent on the eve of NEP.

9 In Bukharin and Preobrazhensky's *Azbuka Kommunizma*, it is asserted that 'the fulfillment

Sotsializm – eto uchet: Registration is socialism.[10] This statement may be typical Lenin hyperbole, but it does show the intimate connection between the practical demands of the grain monopoly, the nature of state capitalism ('all-embracing *uchet i kontrol*'), and the possibility of socialism. The task of actually putting grain supplies on register, however, proved to be an insurmountable obstacle to grain collection; as A.G. Shlikhter, one of the pioneers of the *razverstka* method, put it, 'either registration or grain'.[11] The monopoly had begun with a determination of the individual's needs with the residual going to the state. The *razverstka* economized vastly on information requirements by beginning with a determination of the state's needs with the residual going to the individual. In this crucial respect, the *razverstka* was closer to a tax than to a state monopoly.[12]

Given the fearsome reputation of the *razverstka* as the symbol of war communist radicalism, it is something of a shock to learn that when Bolshevik food-supply officials introduced the *razverstka* in late 1918/early 1919, they viewed it as a concession to the peasantry. The *razverstka* represented a switch from village-splitting tactics over to an attempt to work with the village. The original aim in 1918 was that even the amount of the assessment would be negotiated with peasant representatives, and, although this aspiration could not be maintained during the civil war, the *razverstka* still implied peasant control over at least distribution of the burden of the assessment. The *razverstka* was also supposed to include distribution of whatever industrial items could be spared, and the failure to do this was due simply to their unavailability.[13] The formula of the *razverstka* was: with material incentives if possible, without material incentives if necessary.

The *razverstka*, which became official policy in January 1919, was certainly no 'assault on full socialism' but rather was viewed by food-supply officials as a compromise adjustment to civil-war conditions and an enforced transitional measure to monopolization – itself only a first step toward a socialist organi-

---

of this task [of laying the foundations of a *planomernyi* economy] begins in practice with an *uchet*' (Bukharin and Preobrazhensky 1920, pp. 209–10). See 'The Mystery of the ABC', included in this volume.

10   Lenin 1958–1965, 35:63 (November 1917).

11   A.G. Shlikhter, *Agrarnyi vopros i prodovol'stvennaia politika v pervyi gody sovetskoi vlasti* (Shlikhter 1976, pp. 411–14). The cited statement was written in 1920.

12   The necessity of improving the statistical base through better registration was not forgotten, since state needs could not be the sole determinant of the *razverstka* total. On this see Iu. K. Strizhkov, 'Priniatie dekreta o prodovol'stvennoi razverstke i ego osushchestvlenie v pervoi polovine 1919 g.' (Strizhkov 1977).

13   N.A. Orlov, *Sistema prodovol'stvennoi zagotovki* (Orlov 1920).

zation of the economy. The word *razverstka* itself implies a lack of ideological ambition. For anyone associated with food-supply policy, the term *razverstka* recalled the tsarist minister of agriculture A.A. Rittikh, who introduced a *razverstka* policy in the last months of the tsarist regime. Rittikh's policy was based on a conscious rejection of the movement toward a state grain monopoly, and as such it was scornfully rejected by both liberals and socialists and abandoned by the Provisional Government the moment it took power. Thus the term *razverstka* was not associated with socialism or even with 'the highest stage of capitalism', but rather with 'reactionary' tsarist bureaucrats.

Of course, under civil war conditions the *razverstka* policy was even further distorted. The grain assessments were high relative to available supplies, the lack of industrial items removed any economic incentives for fulfilment, and local administrative abuses were a constant source of profound peasant irritation.[14] Bolshevik food-supply officials themselves were under few illusions about the inherent desirability of these methods and were little prone to utopian flights of fancy.

If anyone could represent the war communist bureaucrat in all his splendour, it would be A.D. Tsiurupa, the people's commissar of food supply, the man in charge of the *razverstka*. Tsiurupa was a hard-working official who rarely made public speeches, but he did lead the debate on food-supply policy at the Seventh Congress of Soviets in December 1919.[15] Perhaps we can learn something about the attitudes of the Bolsheviks during the civil war by examining his speeches. Tsiurupa made no bones about the necessity of the *razverstka*, the necessity of using force, or the necessity of taking 'surpluses' (a term that actually meant high grain quotas, given the scarcity of accurate information and the improbability of complete fulfilment). But his discussion hardly smacked of utopianism. Although he stated that the long-term goal was state procurement monopolies of all the major agricultural products, he noted that this must be done 'with extreme [*velichaishii*] gradualness and circumspection'. His defence of the goal of monopolization was that it was the only way to ensure even the possibility of correct distribution, since otherwise disorganizing speculation would get out of hand. Tsiurupa was confident, however, that awareness of the necessity of the *razverstka* was growing among the peasants, even if slowly.

14   The evolving nature of the *razverstka* is stressed by V.M. Andreev in 'Prodrazverstka i krest'ianstvo' (Andreev 1976).

15   Food-supply policy was not debated at any party congress until the Tenth in 1921. It evidently did not raise any matter for principled debate. The subject did come up regularly at the congresses of soviets, where the Bolsheviks tried to make contact with the non-party peasants.

What was this awareness based on? On the realization that in order to get needed industrial items, the peasant had first to give agricultural products to the city in the form of a loan – in other words, the logic of the peasant-worker alliance, the *smychka* under wartime conditions.

The complaints voiced in the ensuing debate by peasants and local officials about the incompetence and arbitrariness of the food-supply apparatus and the intolerable pressure of the assessments were strongly and uncompromisingly stated. It is these phenomena – completely undesirable from the point of view of the Bolshevik leadership – that were mainly responsible for the bad reputation of civil war policy (especially when they threatened to become a 'civil-war culture', a habitual and preferred mode of political work even in peacetime conditions). The response of Tsiurupa to these complaints was equally forthright. Tsiurupa admitted the many abuses and failures and went on to say:

> I can say about myself that I am at fault as well. I've worked for five years on food-supply procurement, but that is not enough in such a difficult moment. It must be admitted that we do not know how to work – but the fact that we are aware of this is also important.

Is this the *komchvanstvo*, the communist arrogance, that is often associated with war communism?[16]

Tsiurupa and his colleagues would only listen to specific complaints if the general line of the *razverstka* policy was accepted. One official, P.K. Kaganovich, admitted that the norm allowed for peasant horses (2 *funts* of oats and 12 *funts* of hay a day) was very low but responded that 5 *funts* a month for a working man was also too low. 'What do you think, the People's Commissariat of Food Supply does this for its own satisfaction? No, we do it because there's not enough food.'[17] The same with coercion: the people's commissariat would much rather have sent the food-supply detachments to the front rather than to the countryside, but it simply could not rely on the peasants sending in the grain by themselves. Both Kaganovich and Tsiurupa were perfectly aware of the damage done to the agricultural productive base, but they felt little could be done during the wartime emergency. In Tsiurupa's words: 'There are only two

---

16   Compare this to Victor Serge's portrait of Tsiurupa as a fanatic blind to reality in *Memoirs of a Revolutionary* (Serge 1965, p. 113). Tsiurupa's speech can be found in *Sed'moi vserossiiskii s'ezd Sovetov* 1920, pp. 121–31, 163–6; Serge's anecdote is quoted in 'Tsiurupa's White Beard,' included in this volume.

17   A *funt* is about four-tenths of a kilogram.

possibilities: either we perish from hunger, or we weaken the [peasant] economy to some extent, but [manage to] get out of our temporary difficulties'.[18]

In the latter half of 1920, the *razverstka* did become associated in the popular mind with policies that seemed to be based on ideological militancy: the closing of local bazaars and a supposed leap into a money-less economy. Had food-supply officials finally succumbed to utopian illusions?

For people living in Soviet Russia at the time, the renewed crackdown on local bazaars was a more vivid demonstration of Bolshevik ideological ambition on the eve of NEP than measures more familiar to historians, for example, efforts at economic reorganization such as VSNKh's nationalization decree of November 1920.[19] The crackdown was based on the long-standing prohibition of free trade in grain and the steadily increasing list of other agricultural products banned from private trade. But the prohibition against private trade was no more effective than liquor prohibition was in the United States, and the underground market in Russia was probably larger in total volume than legal state procurements.

In 1920, as the war came to a close, the Bolsheviks had to decide what to do about this immense black market. The Bolsheviks perforce had to tolerate this market since everybody, including government and party officials, relied on it in order to survive. As the sour parody had it, 'he who does not speculate, neither shall he eat'. The Bolsheviks hoped to eliminate the illegal market by combining 'administrative' persecution of the illegal market with a steady organizational and economic strengthening of the state food-supply apparatus. But the repression of the black market dwindled steadily in intensity until by 1920 there was almost de facto toleration.[20] This situation, however, was not satisfactory, if only because of the corruption and demoralization involved. Officials denied that the markets brought new goods into circulation, since the local markets thrived mainly on embezzled state property. Legalization of the grain trade was still not considered a possible solution.

Some voices in the People's Commissariat of Food Supply argued that even de facto toleration of sackmanism was no longer viable because the disorganization it created was proving stronger than the organizing influence of the food-supply apparatus. One official, Miron Vladimirov, advocated early in 1920

---

18   Kaganovich's speech is in *Sed'moi vserossiiskii s'ezd Sovetov* 1920, pp. 158–9.
19   Secondary accounts seldom mention this crackdown. The following description is based
      primarily on M.K. Vladimirov, *Meshochnichestvo i ego sotsial'no-politicheskoe otrazhenie*
      (Vladimirov 1920); A.M. Terne, *V tsarstve Lenina* (Terne 1922, pp. 253–9); A.E. Badaev, *X let
      bor'by i stroitel'stvo* (Badaev 1927, pp. 87–90).
20   S. Bychkov, 'Organizatsionnoe stroitel'stvo prodorganov do NEPa' (Bychkov 1923, p. 192).

that the illegal market be eliminated in one fell swoop in order to let the food-supply apparatus show what it could do when not faced with this corrupting competition. 'All it needs is the courage and daring to carry the experiment through, if only for the space of one month.'[21]

Later in 1920 A.E. Badaev, head of the Moscow food-supply organization, felt that circumstances allowed the closing of the famous Sukharevka market. According to his later account, he was motivated not only by the disorganization caused by the flourishing illegal market, but also by irritation with the popular argument that Moscow could not survive without it. The idea was then taken up by other urban soviets (with how much central prodding it is difficult to say). The policy was far from popular; in Rostov, for example, even after many of the tradespeople had been expropriated, the workers managed to keep the food bazaar open until the NEP turnaround.[22]

The crackdown on the bazaars showed that there was still some bite left to the Bolshevik commitment to the principle of a state monopoly of the grain trade. Given the refusal to compromise on this principle, a crackdown on corruption was necessary to make the system work at all (as Brezhnev's successors have found).[23] But it is hard to see the crackdown as evidence of an acceleration of ideological militancy, since it was not based on any new governmental legislation but on local enforcement of existing law. Even such officials as Vladimirov who advocated a renewed crackdown conceded it would be utopian to expect to eliminate 'the petty-bourgeois, huckstering, speculative outlook gripping wide sections of the population'.[24]

Were the food-supply officials also interested in eliminating money? Was the growing reliance on payment of wages in kind based on a commitment to a 'naturalized', money-less economy? Did officials actually believe that the financial chaos of the civil war was a prelude to full communism?

The absence of money was indeed seen as an essential feature of a fully socialist economy. This belief (securely grounded in the Marxist classics) was not affected by the transition to NEP and decayed only slowly. But it should be said that the reports of the death of the monetary economy in Russia in 1920–1921 are greatly exaggerated. Despite the general economic disorganiza-

---

21   Vladimirov 1920.
22   Badaev's account is in Badaev 1927, pp. 87–90. The events in Rostov are recounted in Terne 1922, pp. 253–9.
23   These words were written in 1986.
24   The sowing-committee legislation was explicitly based on the long-term predominance of the single-owner peasant farm (see 'Bolshevik Sowing Committees of 1920', included in this volume).

tion that led to a great volume of barter transactions, the Russian economy was at all times essentially a monetary economy. For the food-supply apparatus, the transition to payment of wages in kind was only one part of a much larger picture. Perhaps the point was best made by Evgenii Preobrazhensky, who is said to have 'hymned the virtues of inflation' in his book *Paper Money in the Epoch of the Proletarian Dictatorship*.[25] It is true that the book is dedicated to the printing press as an honoured weapon against the bourgeois economy, but this is the only compliment given to the inflation. Preobrazhensky demonstrates that, although the inflation was meant to act as an unpaid tax on the peasant, the real loser was not the peasant but the workers and the state employees who had to buy a significant amount of their sustenance on the free market. The state employees were especially hard-pressed for cash and were forced to moonlight, to register for fake jobs, and to accept bribes in order to get it. Even the peasant found he could not accumulate wealth, and the only real beneficiary from the inflation was the rapacious speculator whose entire aim was a quick turnover and high living. Far from advocating the abolition of money, Preobrazhensky argued for a silver-backed currency. He noted that the People's Commissariat of Food Supply was not likely to meet its *razverstka* target for 1920–1921, and this meant that, if the peasants lost their money illusion, the town dweller would be in a quandary.[26] Even if the state did collect enough grain to pay wages in kind, a more secure currency would still be necessary for the many products the workers had to obtain themselves.[27]

In 1920, food-supply officials repeatedly affirmed their loyalty to the *razverstka* as a basis for the further development of food-supply policy. This policy did not mean that they were also committed to the forced extraction of grain without equivalent exchange beyond the wartime emergency. The food-supply officials had always referred to the grain taken from the peasants as a loan and they were in fact looking forward to peacetime economic reconstruction so that the *razverstka* could work properly on the basis of equivalent exchange. Force was required only when proper exchange was not possible. In 1918, one food-supply official (D.E. Gol'man) contrasted the usual economic method of obtaining grain with the extraordinary 'revolutionary' methods of the food-supply dictatorship:

---

25   Carr 1950–1955, 2:345.
26   Lenin also worried about this; see Lenin 1958–1965, 41:146–7 (June 1920).
27   *Bumazhnye den'gi v epokhu proletarskoi diktatury* (Preobrazhensky 1920, pp. 48–58, 78–
       84) (for further discussion of this work, see 'Mystery of the ABC', included in this volume).

In order to receive grain by the economic method, we must get our industry in order, provide the market with a vast number of different commodities necessary for the peasant [and so forth]. When we have succeeded in getting to that stage, we can say with assurance that the peasants will bring grain voluntarily and turn it over to the state. [But] we need grain immediately, right now, and we must have all of it.[28]

Hostility to free trade was never hostility to equivalent exchange or to material incentives.

So far we have set forth the meaning of *razverstka* as seen by the professionals, but we should remember that those outside the ranks of food-supply officials had little understanding or interest in these technical developments. The disjunction between the *razverstka* as the symbol of civil war harshness and the *razverstka* as a method of food-supply policy was thus particularly great. The popular hatred of the *razverstka* was due to the burden that any collection method would have imposed under civil war conditions, not to any real appreciation of the technical logic behind the *razverstka*. When we hear our neighbour say 'this damned income tax', we do not suppose he is cursing the income tax as opposed to a sales tax or a capital gains tax, but simply the tax burden as such. The rhetorical aura of the *razverstka* became indelibly marked by civil war hardships – high grain assessments and lack of material exchange equivalents – that were not inherent in the method itself.[29]

This popular understanding of the *razverstka* would not have gone as unchallenged as it has been if the Bolsheviks themselves had not become interested in fudging some important distinctions. This occurred as a result of the policy changes of spring 1921. The exact nature of these changes is obscured by describing them simply as the replacement of the *razverstka* by a food-

---

28   Internal memorandum cited in Strizhkov, *Prodovol'stvennye otriady v gody grazhdanskoi voiny i inostrannoi interventsii, 1917–1921* (Strizhkov 1973, p. 106). In Bukharin's words, 'The exhausted towns cannot *at first* give an equivalent for grain and services [*povinnosti*] ... Therefore coercion is also here an absolute and imperative necessity'; see *Ekonomika perekhodnogo perioda* (Bukharin 1920, p. 146; emphasis added).

29   E.G. Gimpelson adopts this popular understanding of the *razverstka* as taking grain without compensation. Although he can easily show that this procedure was only a temporary necessity, his account cannot explain why Bolshevik officials defended the *razverstka* as such. He also goes too far in dismissing the monopoly principle, as well as the *razverstka* method, as merely a dispensable emergency response; see his 'Voennyi kommunizm' (Gimpelson 1973, pp. 48–56). Paul Craig Roberts also fails to distinguish between the monopoly principle and the *razverstka* method but draws the opposite conclusion: principled approval of the monopoly is used as evidence for similar devotion to the *razverstka*; see his '"War Communism" – A Product of Marxian Ideas' (Roberts 1970).

supply tax.[30] But, in and of itself, the substitution of a tax for a *razverstka* only meant that the government no longer recognized even a verbal commitment to provide industrial products in return for the grain assessment. Although the amount of the 1921 tax was lower than that of the 1920 *razverstka*, this comparison is somewhat misleading since the *razverstka* represented the total amount delivered to the state organs, while the tax represented only the unpaid part that was supposed to be supplemented by grain obtained through the cooperatives in exchange for whatever industrial items could be found (which would have been given to the peasants under the *razverstka* as well). The tax was still an extremely heavy burden in a year of famine and economic disorganization, and its collection required much coercion and loss of life. It is paradoxical that NEP should be symbolized by that part of the policy changes of 1921 that was most redolent of civil war conditions.[31]

Another feature of a tax system is the declaration by the state of an exact grain obligation so that the peasant could make his plans accordingly: once the peasant has fulfilled this obligation, nothing further would be required of him. The *razverstka* was midway between this system and a monopoly system that asserted a claim to the entire surplus, whatever it might be. On the one hand, even under the *razverstka* system, food-supply officials wanted to promise the peasant that if he paid his obligation, he would be left in peace.[32] On the other hand, there was still a rhetorical commitment to delivery of the entire surplus and many local officials were all too willing to translate this into reality through the supplementary requisitions and arbitrary exactions that irritated the peasants more than the *razverstka* itself.

Even so, however, the changes of 1921 were far from alien to the spirit of the *razverstka* as it was meant to operate under peacetime conditions. This fact is shown by the speech given at the Tenth Party Congress by a food-supply official, M.I. Frumkin, who supported all the proposed changes except one – the legalization of the free market in grain. Legalization was the real change not only from civil-war policy, but even from policy before the civil war and before October. The Bolsheviks were embarrassed by this change in policy, and with good cause. In 1919 Lenin had ringingly declared 'if you want freedom to trade in

---

30   The usual translation of *prodnalog* as tax-in-kind is in one respect unfortunate: the reader has a tendency to read it as tax-in-*kind*, that is, as opposed to a money tax. In 1921, however, the *prodnalog* was opposed to the *prodrazverstka*, so that the term should be read as *tax*-in-kind as opposed to a *razverstka*-in-kind.

31   Gimpelson is thus mistaken in pointing to the ineffectual civil war tax-in-kind as a forerunner to NEP. In reality, the *razverstka* itself, with its stress on using material incentives to the extent possible, is closer to NEP than this early tax-in-kind.

32   Iu. A. Poliakov, *Perekhod k NEPu i sovetskoe krest'ianstvo* (Poliakov 1967, pp. 94–6).

grain in a devastated country – then go back, try Kolchak, try Denikin! We will fight against this to our last drop of blood. Here there will be no concessions.'[33] In 1921 the country was economically in even worse shape and yet Lenin was making exactly this concession. To make matters worse, the Mensheviks and Socialist Revolutionaries had for a long time been calling for liberalization of food-supply policy and could now gleefully claim they had been vindicated. It was to cover up this embarrassment that the Bolsheviks tended to refer to the whole package of policy changes as 'introduction of a food-supply tax'. This euphemism was simply a way of referring to legalization of the market without actually saying 'legalization of the market'.

The confusion was compounded by Lenin's attempts to justify NEP through his characterization of the *razverstka*. Since Lenin was speaking to people not directly concerned with the details of food-supply policy, he mainly used *razverstka* in its popular sense of taking grain without compensation. Before 1921, he had seen this as only a temporary wartime necessity.[34] Lenin repeated this point in spring 1921: 'People represent the matter as if the transition were from communism in general to bourgeoisness [*burzhuaznost'*]. [But in reality] the food-supply tax is one of the forms of transition from a peculiar 'war communism', [a policy] compelled by extreme need, destruction and war, to sound socialist product-exchange.'[35] What is misleading in this statement, however, is Lenin's characterization of the views of his opponents. It is implied that people like Frumkin who saw the legalization of the market as a retreat did so because they saw the *razverstka* as something akin to full communism and saw the introduction of state-organized commodity-exchange as a form of *burzhuaznost*. It is not difficult to discredit opponents who advocate taking grain without compensation when there was no need for it and who refuse to give the peasants material goods that are actually available.

It is hardly necessary to comment on how unfounded are Lenin's accusations. No one held these views. The food-supply officials had always been in favour of providing material equivalents; under peacetime conditions they

---

33   Lenin 1958–1965, 39:408 (July 1919).
34   For example, see Lenin 1958–1965, 41:359–60 (October 1920). Moshe Lewin claims that during the civil war, Lenin saw the *razverstka* as the essence of socialism; see his *Political Undercurrents in Soviet Economic Debates* (Lewin 1974, p. 79). Lewin cites two texts from 1919 (Lenin 1958–1965, 39:167, 274). But the *razverstka* is not mentioned in either of these texts: what Lenin sees as essential to socialism is the replacement of free trade with state distribution – a position he never repudiated.
35   'O prodnaloge'; see Lenin 1958–1965, 43:219–23.

were now willing to grant the necessity of voluntary and individualized exchange – but why should this exchange not be restricted to the state and its authorized agents? Why abandon the ideal of a monopoly just when the state could actually look forward to acquiring some goods to trade with the peasants and thus make the monopoly a reality?

By the fall of 1921, the spread of market forms had gone too far to cover up with references to the introduction of a tax system, and so Lenin had to admit that NEP was a strategic retreat. He tried to make retreat palatable by claiming that the retreat was from an advanced position back to state capitalism. If the *razverstka* in its civil war form represented progress, then indeed most people would welcome a retreat.

> We decided that the peasant would give us the necessary quantity of grain according to the *razverstka*, and we would distribute [*razverstaem*] it to factories and workshops – and then we would have communist production and distribution ... The *razverstka* in the village – that immediate communist approach to the tasks of construction in the town – interfered with the increase in productive forces and became the basic reason for the profound economic and political crisis with which we collided in spring 1921.[36]

This statement shows not a development but a complete reversal of Lenin's position in the spring. In the spring, the *razverstka* was not an ideal but a bitter necessity; in the fall, it is said to be mandated by ideological extremism. In the spring, the *razverstka* was praised for preserving the Soviet republic in a time of crisis; in the fall it is responsible for a crisis that nearly toppled the republic. The only comment that can be made on the fall version is that it is an even worse distortion than the spring version.[37]

Lenin's obfuscations sealed the fate of proper historical understanding of the *razverstka*. The plausibility of Lenin's rhetoric has been enhanced by his air of admitting a mistake (although it is unclear to what extent Lenin included himself in the 'we' who made mistakes) as well as by the natural sympathy of most scholars for the NEP policies Lenin was defending. Even though the fall version with its 'strategic retreat' directly contradicts what was said in spring 1921 about the *razverstka* as a successful emergency measure, the two versions have lived in uneasy coexistence ever since.

---

36   Lenin 1958–1965, 44:157, 159 (October 1921). Even here Lenin does not claim that the *razverstka* itself was a communist method.

37   Compare Gimpelson's discussion of the fall version (Gimpelson 1973, pp. 229–33).

Does the concept of war communism help us put the *razverstka* into its proper context? We should remember that the Lenin texts we have just looked at are also the birthplace of the concept of war communism as well as of the term itself. It is dangerously anachronistic to imply that the concept played any role in attitudes and motivations before 1921.[38]

The term 'war communism' (strengthened by the image of the besieged fortress) almost inescapably suggests a coincidence between what was mandated by civil war pressures ('war') and what was mandated by ideological radicalism ('communism'). This possibility is reflected in the many accounts that point to a moderate policy of state capitalism that was disrupted by the outbreak of the civil war, which in turn led to a radicalization of Bolshevik policy.

In the case of food-supply policy, the actual relation between military necessity and ideological radicalism is the reverse of this supposed chain: the outbreak of civil war caused a conscious retreat from ideological ambitiousness. The phase of state capitalism could hardly be called moderate, either in its policy goal (a state grain monopoly) or its methods (the food-supply dictatorship). When war did break out in the summer of 1918, the immediate effect was to reinforce a retreat from the methods of the food-supply dictatorship that had already started. This effect is shown by two memorandums from Lenin in this period. On 26 May 1918 – the same day on which in distant Siberia the Czechoslovak soldiers rose in revolt – Lenin proposed: 'Change the War Commissariat into a War-Food-Supply Commissariat – that is, concentrate nine-tenths of the work of the War Commissariat on remaking the army for the war for grain and on conducting this war for three months.' In this statement Lenin thus puts a nine-to-one ratio between the urgency of food supply and the urgency of all other military pressures. Six weeks later, in early August, Lenin insisted that food-supply policy had to be revised: precisely because of the war it was necessary to 'neutralize the peasantry' (especially the newly discovered middle peasant).[39]

The other radical phase of food-supply policy – the crackdown on local markets in late 1920 – also came in a period when military pressures seemed to

---

38   For example, Lewin writes 'There was even a stronger sedative for whoever might have had qualms about ... harsh practices: the belief that something more than the war economy justified them. The term "war communism" implied that the most progressive system on earth was just installed *deus ex machina* by the most expedient, unexpected, but irreversible leap to freedom' (Lewin 1974, pp. 78–9).

39   Lenin 1958–1965, 36:374; 37:31–3.

be relaxed.[40] Thus the term war communism seems particularly inappropriate: the war part of the food-supply policy was not communist and the communist part was not appropriate for war.

The coincidence thesis is often put in subjective terms: the Bolsheviks themselves confused pragmatism and revolutionary vision, owing to a habit of baptizing necessary emergency measures with ideological labels.[41] But in the case of the *razverstka*, we see that the Bolsheviks were able to distinguish deeply held principle from temporary compromise. The commitment to a state monopoly was unswerving. Even bourgeois governments, such as Germany and the Provisional Government, had advanced to the point of adopting such a monopoly, and surely a socialist government could do no less.[42] The grain monopoly was part of a wider ideological programme of extending state organization over the economy as a basis for socialism – a programme that predated the October Revolution and survived the civil war. War conditions, particularly the scarcity of administrative resources and the lack of material exchange equivalents, made a proper grain monopoly impossible and so Bolshevik food-supply officials consciously accepted a practical compromise in the form of the *razverstka*. (Food-supply officials less willingly accepted a host of other compromises that must also be seen as part of civil-war food-supply policy.)

No one deceived themselves into thinking that the harsh emergency methods of the *razverstka* were actually socialism in disguise. Wartime conditions did indeed strengthen what we would now consider to be illusions about the efficacy of nonmarket methods of distribution, but they did so in a way opposite to that suggested by the concept of war communism. Precisely because wartime methods were so distorted and so far from socialist ideals, the food-supply officials had plausible grounds to believe that nonmarket methods would work according to expectation under proper peacetime conditions.

The use of war communism as an interpretive framework also leads to an overstatement of the contrast between the *razverstka* and the NEP policy that followed. War communism in general and the *razverstka* in particular are seen as expressing a principled disdain for peasant interests that was replaced by the *smychka* orientation of worker-peasant alliance.[43] This contrast cannot stand;

---

40   Similarly, the only attempts to conduct commodity exchange without money came in 1918 and 1921. M.I. Davydov, 'Gosudarstvennyi tovaroobmen mezhdu gorodom i derevnei v 1918–21 gg' (Davydov 1982, pp. 55–6).

41   Nove 1969, p. 47; Carr 1950–1955, 2:55.

42   Furthermore, the goal of an effective state grain monopoly was still operative during NEP; see 'Bukharin on Bolshevik "Illusions"', included in this volume.

43   Stephen Cohen, for example, calls the problem of the peasantry 'the blind side of war com-

it gains whatever plausibility it has only from the contrast between wartime deprivation and relative peacetime prosperity. The *razverstka* method was part and parcel of a general retreat from 'class war in the villages' to 'neutralization of the middle peasantry'. Undoubtedly, beneath the surface of official policy, anti-peasant feelings were exacerbated by the food-supply crisis – but these feelings also continued throughout the 1920s. At no time in the 1920s was the middle peasant as he was seen as a completely solid or reliable ally; the only question was how peacefully he would let himself be transformed. But transformed he had to be.[44]

Bolshevik food-supply officials never denied that the worker-peasant alliance required a material base in equivalent exchange. Here we may cite Iurii Larin, archetypal war communist, writing in 1920: 'The actual exchange of services and material values between the village and the town, between peasant and proletarian, is in general one of the basic problems of contemporary Russia, [and] one of the bases of the political union between workers and peasants as well'.[45] The assertion that during war communism the Bolsheviks not only took grain without compensation but approved of this procedure ideologically seems to result from a confusion between market exchange (which the Bolsheviks did oppose) and exchange in general, including state-organized exchange. Only this confusion can account for E.H. Carr's remarkable statement that the Soviet leaders were 'obstinately slow to recognize the hard fact' that 'the main difficulty in securing supplies of food for the towns was ... that no adequate return could be offered to the peasants' or for Alec Nove's equally remarkable assertion that 'the policy of requisitions and armed detachments' came to be seen as good in itself.[46] Bolshevik food-supply officials were so far from denying the importance of material exchange that in 1920 they were thrown into a panic by the imminent disappearance of even the meagre goods fund that had earlier been at their disposal.

---

munism'; see his *Bukharin and the Bolshevik Revolution* (Cohen 1971, p. 95). See also Merle Fainsod, *How Russia is Ruled*, 1st ed. (Fainsod 1953, pp. 93, 98) and Charles Bettelheim, *Class Struggles in the USSR, 1917–1923* (Bettelheim 1976, pp. 352–5).

44   In 1925, Bukharin distinguished between two methods for the overcoming (*preodolenie*) of bourgeois elements: towards the nepmen, the method would be crowding out, but towards the peasants, it would be reworking (*pererabotka*); see his *Kritika ekonomicheskoi platformy oppozitsii* (Bukharin 1926b, pp. 45–51).

45   Larin and Kritsman 1920, p. 23 (*Ocherk khoziaistvennoi zhizni i organizatsiia narodnogo khoziaistva Sovetskoĭ Rossii, 1 noiabria 1917–1 iiulia 1920 g.*, Moscow: Gosizdat).

46   Carr 1950–1955, 2:169; Nove 1969, p. 66. In similar fashion, Cohen argues that because Bukharin in 1920 rejected the commodity market, he was therefore reduced either to hoping that the peasants would volunteer grain out of revolutionary enthusiasm or to supporting 'a system of permanent requisitioning' (Cohen 1971, p. 95).

The contrast between war communism and NEP also suggests that the *razverstka* represented an attitude of coercive voluntarism aimed at immediate elimination of the market, as opposed to the gradualism of NEP. Certainly there is a switch of emphasis from the semi-persecution of the civil war years to the semi-toleration of the 1920s, but it should be remembered that 'crowding-out' (*vytesnenie*) of the free market was an axiomatic goal in both periods, whether the market was legal or illegal. The contrast between the two periods can be compared to two methods of conquering a continent. One way is to stick a flag on the coast, declare it the property of Queen Isabella or whomever, and then proceed to the slow work of making that control real. The other method is to regularize relations with the natives through various treaties and then proceed to the slow work of establishing hegemony and finally annexation. Despite the important differences involved, the choice is a matter of tactics and form. Before 1921, the grain market had been declared illegal at the outset, but the Bolsheviks were still aware that the market not only existed but flourished; they certainly did not believe that they could expediently abolish the market before the state was organizationally capable of replacing it. The food-supply officials – who better? – were aware of the immense difficulties they faced and the great distance they still had to travel through long and patient organizational work. The same criterion of expediency and the same difficulty in restraining overeager local officials remained throughout the NEP period.

It is tempting, but quite misleading, to see a continuity between the *razverstka* and Preobrazhensky's theory of 'unequal exchange' between town and country.[47] This comparison is unfair to both parties. On the one hand, food-supply officials before NEP did not base the need for coercion as opposed to material incentives on elaborate theories about the need to 'exploit' the petty-bourgeois sector, but on the clear and present danger of a collapse of the economy that would involve the peasant in its ruin along with everybody else. On the other hand, Bukharin's attempt in the mid-twenties to paint Preobrazhensky's proposal to use indirect taxation to support industrialization as a throwback to civil-war coercion was groundless. Bukharin's charge cannot be called an exaggeration, for there was no reality behind it at all. It is worthy of remark that many top pre-NEP food-supply officials (Tsiurupa, Frumkin, Vladimirov) were associated with the right during the 1920s.

In the case of food-supply policy, then, we have seen that the concept of 'war communism' originated in Lenin's obfuscatory rhetoric of 1921, that it suggests

---

47   Malle so argues (Malle 1985, pp. 453, 514). While it is true that fixed prices during the civil war were slanted toward the towns, a distinction should be made between manipulation of the terms of trade and a principled reliance on coercion as opposed to exchange.

a coincidence between emergency measures and militant principles that did not exist, and that it overdramatizes the contrast between civil war policy and NEP. In my view, there are no compensating interpretive advantages and the term 'war communism' should be dropped.

The genuine difficulty in interpreting the *razverstka* comes from its status as a holding operation for the state grain monopoly under the difficult circumstances of the civil war. There is no ambiguity about the Bolshevik commitment to abolish free trade in grain or about the sacrifices they were ready to impose in the name of that principle. Those critics within and without the Bolshevik party who called in 1920 for a replacement of the *razverstka* by a food-supply tax never went so far as to suggest legalization of the market.[48] But while the monopoly principle implied equivalent exchange, the *razverstka* method was designed to operate, if necessary, with only a minimum of industrial exchange items. This feature of the *razverstka* led to the contrast between the understanding of the food-supply professional and the understanding of everyone else. The non-professionals tended to identify the *razverstka* with the rigors of the civil war and to define it as taking grain without compensation. When the food-supply officials defended the *razverstka*, they were understood by others to be advocating taking grain without compensation not only as a temporary necessity but as a long-term principle. It is appropriate therefore to repeat the words of the food-supply official Kaganovich: 'What do you think, the People's Commissariat does this for its own satisfaction? No, we do it because there's not enough food'.

---

48   For example, David Dallin at the Eighth Congress of Soviets in December 1920 explicitly denied that his critique of Bolshevik food-supply policy was a defence of free trade. *Vos'moi vserossiiskii s'ezd sovetov*, stenographic report (Moscow, 1921), pp. 197–9.

Bolsheviks at Work: The Sowing Committees of 1920

In December 1920, on the eve of the introduction of the New Economic Policy (NEP), the Bolsheviks embarked on a crash campaign to avert an agricultural crisis. The Eighth Congress of Soviets passed legislation known by the name of one of its principal innovations, the sowing committees (*posevkomy*).[1] The usual view of this legislation is that it was a last binge of revolutionary inebriation before the sobering-up morning-after of NEP – a desperate attempt to use civil-war methods to undo the damage done by civil-war methods. The full record of the legislation and the debate surrounding it tell a different story.[2]

In the first half of this case-study, the overall goals of the sowing-committee legislation and the assumptions behind it are set forth. The Bolsheviks clashed over the best way to define the situation facing them: should they view their task in class-struggle terms or in class-partnership terms? The second half presents a more detailed picture of the legislative process as well as the concrete policies and new organizational forms that resulted. For the principal author of the sowing-committee legislation, N. Osinsky, the new organizational forms were an exciting innovation. This innovation was based on his own experience in work at the local level, an experience that gave rise to a grouping within the Bolshevik party that called themselves 'democratic centralists'. In conclusion, I argue that the sowing committees represent one more step in an evolution that began in 1918 and continued into NEP.

1   The Situation in 1920

Despite the flare-ups of armed conflict in Poland and the Crimea, the Bolsheviks had started to think in terms of post-war reconstruction by spring 1920. But even though the civil war was almost over, the economic emergency was

---

1   I would like to thank Daniel Field and the referees for *The Carl Beck Papers* for their generous and helpful comments.

2   The official name of the legislation is 'On Measures for the Strengthening and Development of Peasant Agriculture'. The text of the legislation can be found in *Dekrety sovetskoi vlasti*, vol. 12 (*Dekrety* 1986, pp. 73–87).

not. Lenin summed up the situation, giving the Donbass as an example: 'There is no bread because there is no coal, and no coal because there is no bread. ... We have to break through this damnable chain by using our energy, pressure [*nazhim*], and the heroism of the toilers, so that all the machines start turning'.[3] This meant that the extra-economic methods of the civil war could not be abandoned just yet; until 'the factories began to turn', the basis for normal economic relations between town and village simply did not exist.

Bolshevik thinking in 1920 was dominated by the search for ways to break the 'damnable chain' and take the final step from a time of troubles to a time of peace and reconstruction. The sowing-committee scheme was put forward in the autumn of 1920 as a way of taking that final step in agriculture. It was defended as an ingenious way of helping agriculture within the constraints imposed by the economic emergency. But the constraints were not only objective, for they included long-standing policy commitments of the Bolsheviks. Since these subjective constraints are widely misunderstood, we must examine them briefly before going on to the details of the sowing-committee legislation.[4] Three distinctions must be made:

1. Coercion versus exchange. At no time did the Bolsheviks believe that coercion was preferable to exchange as a basis for their dealings with the peasantry. The principled preference for exchange was symbolized by the metaphorical description of the grain levy – the *razverstka* – as a loan. Among the many Bolshevik statements on this point is from Trotsky in 1920:

> Had not the country been so exhausted, and if the proletariat had the possibility of offering to the peasant masses the necessary quantity of commodities and cultural requirements, the adaption of the toiling majority of the peasantry to the new regime would have taken place much less painfully. [So] the proletariat demanded of the peasantry the granting of food credits, economic subsidies in respect of values which it is only now to create ... But the peasant mass is not very capable of historical detachment.[5]

2. State monopoly versus free trade. All Bolsheviks in 1920 were firmly committed to the state grain monopoly, but since the grain monopoly and free trade

---

3 Lenin, *Polnoe sobranie sochinenii*, 5th ed. (Lenin 1958–1965, 42:364), 28 February 1921. All further citations by Lenin are from the Eighth Congress of Soviets unless otherwise specified.
4 The following is based on my book *Bread and Authority in Russia, 1914–1921* (Lih 1990) and my article 'Bolshevik *Razverstka* and War Communism' (included in this volume).
5 L. Trotsky, *The Defence of Terrorism* (Trotsky 1921, pp. 103–4).

in grain were simply two different ways of organizing exchange, this commitment says nothing about the role of coercion. What needs to be stressed here
is that the commitment to the grain monopoly was no aberration of 'war communism', since it predated not only the civil war but even the revolution. And
the same commitment continued into the NEP period.[6]

3. *Razverstka* versus food-supply tax. Although there was Bolshevik consensus on the grain monopoly, there was a lively debate on the relative merits of
the *razverstka* versus food-supply tax. Since the food-supply tax was introduced
in spring 1921 at the same time as the decriminalization of free trade, there is
a tendency to equate the two issues. Yet they are distinct, and in fact in 1920
no advocate of the food-supply tax publicly supported free trade. The *razverstka* was a method of enforcing the grain monopoly under the constraints of
a scarcity of exchange items and an undeveloped administrative apparatus.
It was designed to work with exchange items if possible but without them if
necessary. The food-supply officials insisted on the distinction between the
monopoly principle and the *razverstka method*. This meant that the commitment to the *razverstka* was much more conditional than the commitment to
the monopoly.

To these subjective constraints must be added the objective difficulties of
the devastated Russian economy. It is sometimes said that the main problem
for Russian agriculture was the Bolshevik insistence on taking the entire surplus production, thus removing any incentive for expanded production. This
is an oversimplified and misleading assertion. The agricultural crisis of 1920
went deeper than a matter of incentives: force can provide an incentive, if only
a blunt one. The crisis was caused in the first place, not by what the Bolsheviks took from agriculture, but rather by their inability – or, as the peasants
saw it, their refusal – to return anything. By 1920, the difficulty was not that
the peasants refused to produce a surplus – it was increasingly that they could
not produce one. Six long years of the absorption of industrial output by the
military, six years of using equipment without any renewal, had led to a fatal
weakening of agriculture's productive base.

As the civil war drew to a close, industry could once again begin to supply the
needs of agriculture. But the workers had to eat, and this required taking grain
from the peasants once again without compensation. This was the unpleasant situation from which N. Osinsky (Valerian Obolensky) proposed an escape
route in a series of articles in *Pravda* starting on September 5, 1920.[7] Osinsky is

---

6 See 'Bukharin on Bolshevik Illusions', included in this volume.
7 The articles were published as a book entitled *Gosudarstvennoe regulirovanie krestianskogo
   khoziaistva* (Osinskii 1920).

one of those second-tier Bolshevik figures that never come into focus as long as we use the clumsy categories of 'left' and 'right', or 'war communism' and 'NEP'. In 1918, he was one of the Left Communists, a Bolshevik grouping that some writers have seen as war communists *avant la lettre*. In 1920, he was one of the leaders of the 'democratic centralists'. This oppositional group is associated with protests against bureaucratic degeneration in state and party and the excessive power granted to 'bourgeois specialists'. Later in the year, Osinsky became the main proponent of the sowing committees, generally viewed as the apotheosis of the bureaucratic utopianism of war communism.

In spring 1921, Osinsky became an ardent supporter of NEP: he was the inventor of the phrase 'seriously and for a long time'. Lenin even felt it necessary to chide him for his excessively pessimistic view of the length of time before socialism would be possible.[8] Later in the year, he insisted that free-trade relations be extended to heavy industry, thereby earning the reputation of a leader of a 'bourgeois reaction' to the difficulties of early NEP policies.[9] From late 1931 to 1935, Osinsky was head of the statistical administration, and his tenure is still remembered as a brief respite from the Stalinist adulteration of statistical probity.[10] According to the normal stereotypes, Osinsky appears a very unstable fellow: now on the left, now on the right, now protesting against 'glavkism' (chief-committee-ism), now setting up new *glavki* for agriculture. A closer look and a different set of categories will bring the Osinsky of 1920–1921 into focus; we will see that from Osinsky's point of view, his advocacy of democratic centralism, of the sowing committees, and of NEP all fit together.

In his *Pravda* articles, Osinsky analysed the causes of the incipient agricultural crisis, reviewed the constraints imposed on any government response, and strongly urged an all-out campaign to ward off the crisis. At the end of October, the Politburo took up the suggestion and asked for legislation to be prepared in time for the Eighth Congress of Soviets in December 1920. Osinsky was at this time a member of the collegium of the Commissariat of Food Supply, and in general the food-supply officials were the most enthusiastic proponents of his scheme. The draft prepared by Osinsky met with some coolness

---

8   Lenin 1958–1965, 43:330, 340.

9   Bertrand Mark Patenaude, 'Bolshevism in Retreat: The Transition to the NEP, 1920–1922', PhD Dissertation, Stanford University (Patenaude 1987, pp. 280–1). This is an informative survey of public discussion during this period from which my essay has benefitted, even though we take different views of the significance of the sowing committees.

10   See the admiring discussion by two current reformers, Grigorii Khanin and Vasilii Seliunin, 'Lukavaia Tsifra' (Khanin and Seliunin 1987, p. 190).

from the Commissariat of Agriculture, however, and agriculture officials published criticisms of the legislation in a lively press debate prior to the Eighth
Congress.

The top Bolshevik leadership, and Lenin in particular, gave strong support
to the draft that evolved out of the consultation between the Commissariats
of Food Supply and Agriculture and then presented to the Eighth Congress.
Menshevik and SR spokesmen who were present at the congress challenged
the legislation's reliance on coercion and made this part of an overall critique
of Bolshevik food-supply policy, although they did not go so far as to advocate
legalizing free trade. There was also a revolt within the Bolshevik caucus, where
the majority felt that parts of the legislation would strengthen the position of
the rich peasants, that is, 'kulaks'. It took Lenin's personal intervention, plus
some concessions on legislative language, to beat back this revolt.

The sowing-committee legislation was duly passed by the Congress and
went immediately into effect. (The preamble to the legislation is translated in
the Appendix.) The transition to NEP did not end the agricultural crisis by any
means, and so the sowing committees remained on the job for another year,
trying to mitigate the effects of the drought and to ensure the largest possible
harvest in 1921 and 1922.

2   Two Approaches to the Peasantry

The legislation, like any initiative in agricultural policy, rested on a particular
view of the peasantry: its motivations, its internal relations, its prospects for
development. In order to put the views of Osinsky and his supporters into context, it will be helpful to describe two outlooks on the peasantry, which I will
call the 'class-struggle outlook' and the 'partnership outlook'. (See Chart 1.) In
their pure forms, these two views are two ends of a spectrum along which we
can locate the actual views of Bolshevik policy-makers.

According to the class-struggle view, the peasantry is divided (or is rapidly
becoming divided) into two groups: proto-proletariat and proto-capitalist. Because of the intensity of the struggle between them, political motivations take
primacy over economic motivations. If, for example, the peasants do not market their grain, it is interpreted as a 'grain strike' meant to choke the revolution
with the bony hand of hunger. This implies that pressing practical problems are
caused by sabotage; therefore, crushing sabotage is the basic method of solving these problems. In contrast, the partnership view portrays the peasantry as
homogeneous, with economic motivations dominant and objective difficulties
as the basic cause of practical problems.

CHART 1   Class-struggle outlook versus partnership outlook

Class struggle	Partnership
Peasantry is divided into rich/poor (or *kulak/bedniak*)	Peasantry is divided into industrious/lazy (or *staratelnyi/lodyr*)
Peasantry will soon dissolve into bourgeois and proletarians (*rassloenie*)	Peasantry will remain a distinct group for the foreseeable future
Political motivations	Economic motivations
Sabotage	Objective difficulties
Firm alliance only after socialist transformation	Firm alliance with present single-owner production relations
Socialist consciousness as goal ('conscious' or 'purposive' discipline of socialist worker)	State consciousness as goal (necessity of sacrificing for the common good)

Note: Material incentives versus coercion should not be included in this contrast. Material incentives can be used in class struggles – for example, the Committees of the Poor were promised a share of the grain they confiscated. Similarly, coercion can be part of a partnership strategy – for example, any compulsory tax to obtain a public good.

This central contrast leads to many others. What the class-struggle view regards as a division between evil rich and virtuous poor is seen by the partnership view as a division between the industrious peasant and the lazy one. The class-struggle view maintains that only socialist transformation will turn the peasant into a firm ally of the revolution, while the partnership view maintains that the peasantry's firm support is possible under present production relations. The class-struggle view aims at instilling a socialist consciousness among the peasantry, while the partnership view would be satisfied with a 'state consciousness' – that is, a realization that personal welfare depends on the general welfare and a willingness in consequence to make sacrifices in support of the general welfare.

If we apply this framework to the sowing-committee legislation, the first thing we see is a new peasant hero and villain: no longer the *bedniak* versus the *kulak*, but the industrious owner (*staratelnyi khoziain*) versus the lazy lout (*lodyr*). Osinsky argued that the aim of state regulation should be to uni-

versalize the standards of the industrious owner, and Lenin called the legislation a 'wager on the industrious' – a revealing allusion to the Stolypin programme.[11] The enemy within the peasantry was not so much the kulak as the
'the benighted, the backward, and the feckless', as a high official of the Commissariat of Agriculture, I.A. Teodorovich, put it at the Eighth Congress. Teodorovich went on to say that the time of division (*rassloenie*) was over, and it was
no longer a question of proletariat versus petty-bourgeois, but of partnership
with the 'middle labouring [*trudovoi*] peasantry'.[12] (The use of the adjective
'labouring' is significant, since it was associated with the SRs and had been
rejected with scorn by the Bolsheviks when they broke with the Left SRs in
1918.)

Although one aim of the legislation was to provide poor peasant households with seed in the interests of increasing sown acreage, the Bolsheviks
were at pains to disassociate themselves with any suggestion of class struggle, even to the extent of dropping the term 'poor' in favour of 'weak' (*mal-
omoshchnyi*).[13] V.V. Kuraev gave the following advice on how this part of the
legislation could be made palatable to the middle peasant who resented the
poor peasant because of the material burden he caused. The middle peasant
should be told that in loaning seed grain he is not helping the poor peasant
but helping the state, that is, the general interest in a restoration of the economy. The middle peasant had an immediate material stake as well: the chance
of lowering his personal burden in the *razverstka* of 1921. It is this sort of self-
interested appeal that will be 'comprehensible and convincing'. The agitator
should rely on the peasant's own distinction between the lazy lout vs. the worthy hard-working poor who simply had a bad break. The middle peasant should
also be assured that in the future the decisive figure in the village will be the
industrious owner.[14] Thus the Bolsheviks were actively advertising the outlook behind their legislation as a peasant outlook rather than a revolutionary
one.

Tied to the glorification of the industrious owner was a rejection of state
farms, collective farms and communes, as either a solution to the immediate
crisis or even as the high road to socialism in the countryside. Lenin sneeringly

---

11   *Pravda*, 4 November 1920; Lenin 1958–1965, 42:186.
12   *Vosmoi vserossiiskii s"ezd rabochikh, krestianskikh, krasnoarmeiskikh i kazachikh deputatov*
     (*Vosmoi* 1921, pp. 123–7).
13   Osinsky in *Pravda*, 5 September 1920. *Malomoshchnyii* later acquired a more precise statis-
     tical meaning and represented a category in between the poorest peasant and the middle
     peasant. During the sowing-committee debate, it was used with the rhetorical motivation
     of avoiding class-struggle overtones.
14   *Pravda*, 19 December 1920.

referred to the collective farms as alms-houses and asserted that 'we must rely on the single-owner [*edinolichny*] peasant – that's the way he is and he won't be different in the near future. To dream of a transition to socialism and collectivization won't do.'[15] Iurii Larin wrote that the state farms (*sovkhozy*) and the collective farms (*kolkhozy*) had to take second place to the *krekhozy* – his new coinage for the ordinary peasant [*krestianin*] farm: 'For today and tomorrow, in order to raise production *in the mass*, we must deal with the existing *krekhozy*, with the material and human resources now available ... Otherwise we will see nothing in 1921 or 1922 but confused experiments.'[16] In early 1921, official instructions for party propaganda drove the point home: 'Nothing could be more dangerous than if some overambitious agitator decided to explain it [the sowing-committee legislation] as a new way of communizing the peasantry. That would factually be incorrect, since the state's help is being given to the single-owner peasant enterprise.'[17]

Thus when Osinsky analysed the agricultural crisis of 1920, he pointedly did not include the absence of socialized production forms among the causes, but instead concentrated on objective difficulties such as the industrial collapse and the ravages of the civil war.[18] Prior to the end of the civil war, there had been a widespread feeling among Bolsheviks (and the urban population in general) that the peasants had gained more and suffered less from the revolution than the workers, but Bolshevik leaders admitted that by late 1920 the relative position of workers and peasants had been reversed.[19] In his discussion of the reasons for this reversal, Osinsky argued that the self-subsistent independence of the peasant economy was easily exaggerated and the peasant could not remain unaffected by industry's inability to supply his needs.

Osinsky also admitted that the pressure exerted through the *razverstka* had contributed to the crisis, especially in the long-suffering central agricultural region. Osinsky felt that the Bolsheviks were compelled to apply this pressure in order to achieve victory in a just cause, but still, 'facts are facts' – it was impossible to deny that civil-war pressures had caused grave damage to agriculture.[20]

---

15 Lenin 1958–1965, 42:180–1; see also 188. The Menshevik resolution at the Eighth Congress also asked for an end to privileges for the communes (*Vosmoi* 1921, pp. 199–200).

16 *Pravda*, 12 December 1920; see also Lenin 1958–1965, 42:181.

17 Cited in Ivan Iurkov, *Ekonomicheskaia politika partii v derevne 1917–1920* (Iurkov 1980, p. 179).

18 Osinsky's analysis can be found in *Pravda*, 5 September 1920.

19 For the earlier view, see Iu. Larin, *Pravda*, 24 March 1920; for the later view, see Osinsky, *Pravda*, 5 September 1920; Lenin 1958–1965, 42:306–9 (February 1921).

20 *Pravda*, 5 September 1920.

Bolshevik leaders were both proud of the accomplishments of the Commissariat of Food Supply and aware of the immense cost of this achievement. In Lenin's words:

> The real foundation of the economy is the food-supply reserve. And here the success has been great [and] we can now set about restoring the economy. We know that this success has been achieved at the cost of great deprivations and hunger in the peasantry [and] we know that a year of drought has sharpened these disasters ... For that reason we are putting primary emphasis on measures of help as set out in this legislation.[21]

Given this miserable economic position, Osinsky argued, the peasant felt two contradictory impulses: the 'healthy instinct of a business-like labourer [*khoziaistvenno-trudovoi*]' to fight the crisis, and the demoralizing urge of the lazy lout to exploit it.[22] Osinsky called the lazy lout's response 'sabotage', thus employing one of the key terms of the class-struggle outlook. But Osinsky was not trying to incite the poor against the rich, but to incite the hard-working taxpayer against the parasite who increased his fellow-villagers' material burden by refusing to sow (or doing so in a sloppy manner) and selling what grain he had on the black market rather than contributing to the village's collective *razverstka* obligation. In the words of a publication of the Commissariat of Food Supply: 'The person who is a lazy lout – who squanders his seed material and doesn't want to improve his working methods – who leaves his field unsown – will be considered a criminal hurting the common cause, and he won't be handled tenderly either by the state or by his more hardworking neighbours'.[23]

The partnership view did not expect the peasant to attain a socialist consciousness. Lenin argued that support for the sowing-committee legislation did not require a socialist transformation. On the contrary, the message that 'the labouring middle and poor peasant is a friend of soviet authority [*vlast*], and the lazy lout is its enemy' was 'the truth plain and simple, in which there is nothing socialist, but which is so obvious and indisputable [that it will be accepted]

---

21   Lenin 1958–1965, 42:150. For similar acknowledgements by Aleksandr Tsiurupa, see Lih, 'Bolshevik *Razverstka and War Communism*', included this volume.
22   *Pravda*, 5 November 1920.
23   *Kalendar-spravochnik prodovo/stvennika* (Moscow, 1921), pp. 120–2 (evidently a pre-NEP publication).

at any peasant meeting'.[24] No doubt even a state consciousness was in fact an unrealistic goal at the time (although many Bolsheviks convinced themselves otherwise), but accepting the necessity of compulsory sacrifice for the public good required much less of a break with peasant tradition than becoming committed socialists.

The Bolshevik leaders' explanation and defence of the sowing-committee legislation thus reveals a shift from the class-struggle view of the peasant to the partnership view. The replacement of poor/rich by industrious/lazy, the rejection of *sovkhozy* and *kolkhozy* in favour of *krekhozy*, the emphasis on objective difficulties rather than politically motivated sabotage, and the goal of state consciousness rather than socialist consciousness all attest to this shift. Of course, as the use of words like 'sabotage' showed, Bolshevik policy-makers did not make a clean break with the assumptions of their outlook of the recent past.[25] The Bolsheviks were able to explain their shift in perspective while retaining their vocabulary of class division by talking about the new prominence of the 'middle peasant [*seredniak*]'. But the objective process of 'middleization' of the peasantry was less important than the subjective shift in the Bolsheviks' own outlook.

The Bolshevik's new view of the peasantry corresponded to a new view of themselves as a national leadership rather than a class or revolutionary leadership. These two views of themselves could coexist or intertwine in various ways, but the agricultural crisis of 1920, like the civil war preceding it, tended to strengthen the national view. A remarkable manifestation of this tendency occurred in a *Pravda* article in September 1920:

> Hunger is the common enemy. It does not distinguish between parties and convictions. It tortures in similar fashion the worker, the intellectual, the communist, the Menshevik, and the non-party people .... Let all citizens of Russia close ranks behind the soviet *vlast*, and it will be able to defeat hunger as well.[26]

---

24   Lenin 1958–1965, 42:146–7; see also 5–6, 124, 139–40; Trotsky 1921, pp. 106–7; Lezhnev (speaker at the Eighth Congress) in *Vosmoi* 1921, pp. 141–2; Patenaude 1987, pp. 73–5.

25   For a passage that amalgamates poor/rich and industrious/lazy rhetoric, see Lenin 1958–1965, 42:174.

26   *Pravda*, 12 September 1920. In 1922, Osinsky described the legislation as a 'druzhnyi obshchii vsenarodnyi pokhod (kampaniia) protiv razrukhi' ('amicable, united, all-national crusade or campaign against economic breakdown'). Osinsky, *Vosstanovlenie krestianskogo khoziaistva v Rossii i nashi zadachi* (Osinsky 1922, pp. 13–14). See also Lenin 1958–1965, pp. 138–9.

3   Motivations

In their explanation and defence of the sowing-committee legislation, the Bolsheviks put an extraordinary emphasis on coercion (*prinuzhdenie*). This gave an excellent opportunity to the critics of the Bolsheviks; at the Eighth Congress, for instance, David Dallin called on the Bolsheviks to choose either coercion or partnership (*soglashenie*) with the peasants.[27] Lenin's response was exasperated:

> We certainly don't claim that we are doing things without mistakes. [But] neither the Mensheviks nor the SRs say, 'here is the need and misery of the peasants and workers, and here is the way to lift ourselves out of this misery'. No, they don't say that – they only say that what *we* are doing is coercion.

And if the peasants objected they were being made to 'work for Tsiurupa' (the Commissar of Food Supply), Lenin's response was 'quit joking, and answer the question directly: how would *you* restore industry?'[28] The Bolsheviks' assertion that coercion and assistance could be combined is theoretically better founded than Dallin's argument that a choice had to be made between the use of coercion and the partnership view.

This can best be demonstrated using the modern vocabulary of public goods. Economic recovery was a public good, which meant that everybody would benefit from it whether or not they contributed to its achievement. This leads to a paradox that should be familiar to anyone who has experienced fund-raising messages from Wikipedia: even though it would be in each individual's self-interest to make the sacrifice necessary to attain the public good, it would be even more advantageous to let other people make the sacrifice and enjoy the public good without cost. Besides, the individual's sacrifice will be useless unless there is some guarantee that enough other people will also make the sacrifice. The consequent reluctance to make voluntary sacrifices leads to the counter-intuitive conclusion that coercion may be necessary to achieve what is in everyone's direct material interest.[29]

---

27   *Vosmoi* 1921, pp. 197–9. See also Fyodor Dan's contrast between *nasilie* and *samodeiatelnost* (*Vosmoi* 1921, pp. 41–3) and remarks by the SR spokesman Volskii (*Vosmoi* 1921, pp. 48–51).

28   Lenin 1958–1965, 42:175, 180.

29   For an introduction to this topic, see Mancur Olson, *The Logic of Collective Action: Public Goods and the Theory of Groups* (Olson 1965).

It is necessary to review this logic, if only to emphasize that the conceptual vocabulary for demonstrating it in convincing fashion hardly existed in 1920 and was certainly not available to the Bolsheviks. Furthermore, many historians seem to share the idea that coercion *per se* is a bad thing – even though most of these historians support programmes of coercive taxation and regulation aimed at achieving public goods in their own societies.

Despite the rhetorical emphasis on coercion, Osinsky and his supporters knew from experience that coercion did not work efficiently in a vacuum. Osinsky intended the sowing-committee campaign to rely on a package of all three main types of motivation: coercion, material incentive, and persuasion. His dispute with his critics was not over what type of motivation to use, but over the most expedient way to combine these motivations in the difficult circumstances of 1920.[30]

Osinsky defined the problem as follows: 'how can we unite state procurement of food products and raw materials with single-owner peasant enterprise, given the weakness of our reserves of commodity goods [*tovarnyi fond*]?'[31] The first step was to supplement the available material incentives in every way possible. One way was to mobilize city workers to help with repairs, harvest labour, and other village activities. This campaign, started in spring 1920 under the name 'week of the peasant', was enthusiastically endorsed by Evgenii Preobrazhensky: 'We must demonstrate to the village that the Soviet authority takes the peasant's surplus, while giving for the present almost nothing in return, only because of its poverty ... The "week of the peasant" should be the beginning of this payment for grain and for labour services [*povinnosti*].'[32] Another possible method of strengthening material incentives was increasing the security of peasant property by ending frequent land redistribution.[33] In what turned out to be the most controversial provision of the legislation,

---

30   *Pravda*, 7 November 1920. Iurii Poliakov quotes Osinsky as rejecting the very idea of combining state regulation with economic stimuli. Poliakov, *Perekhod k NEPu i sovetskoe krestianstvo* (Poliakov 1967, p. 223). Osinsky's actual words were: 'It has been said that we must unite regulation with stimulation, and by this is meant that we must apply a food-supply tax according to acreage and stimulate *in this way*' (*Vosmoi* 1921, pp. 146–7; emphasis added). Osinsky's criticism was thus of a particular form of economic stimulation that he found inexpedient.

31   *Pravda*, 5 November 1920.

32   *Pravda*, 28 April 1920. The *subbotniki*, always a good indicator of urgent priorities, were used during the Peasant Week campaigns. William Chase, 'Voluntarism, Mobilisation and Coercion: *Subbotniki* 1919–1921' (Chase 1989, p. 122). This article also contains some useful reflections on the role of coercion during the Civil War.

33   Osinsky, *Pravda*, 5 November 1920.

incentives were also offered to the individual industrious peasant in the form of bonuses and an increased consumer norm (the amount left to the peasant after the *razverstka*).

A massive agitation campaign was also planned to convince the peasant that the demands placed on him would redound to his own benefit. Lenin was particularly interested in this aspect of the program, and he argued that unlike bourgeois governments, the dictatorship of the proletariat was strong because it knew how to combine coercion with persuasion (*ubezhdenie*). For his part, Osinsky stressed that agitational campaigns would be ineffective unless combined with material help and pressure on the lazy lout.[34]

The Bolshevik leaders had managed to convince themselves that coercion would be accepted as an integral part of this aid package. Lenin asserted that the essence of the legislation was that the measures of practical help consisted not only of encouragement (*pooshchrenie*) but coercion as well. In Lenin's vocabulary, there was a clear distinction between coercion (*prinuzhdenie*) and violence (*nasilie*). The violence used by the White Guard governments violated the interests of the peasant; the Bolsheviks would also be guilty of violence if they tried to force the peasants to enter the communes (*kommuniia*).[35]

On the basis of his experience in Tula province, Osinsky wrote in June 1920 that:

> no one can say now that the Soviet authority only takes grain from the village without a thought for the future and giving nothing in return. We are not only taking grain, we are organizing further production; even more, we are compelling the proper sowing of the land and cutting off any sabotage in that regard.[36]

If sowing to less than the fullest extent possible was 'sabotage', then ending this sabotage directly benefitted the industrious owner because of the restoration

---

34   *Biulletin Narodnogo Komissariata po Prodovolstviiu*, 30 November 1920 (hereafter cited as *Biulletin*); Lenin 1958–1965, 42:138–9, 146–7, 183. See also the remarks of Evgenii Varga in the introduction to the French edition of Osinsky's book, *La regularisation par l'état de la culture paysanne* (Varga 1921, pp. 5–10).

35   Lenin 1958–1965, 42:179, 139–40, 178. The main critic of the legislation, N.S. Bogdanov, had tried to use Lenin's 1919 statements on the communes as a weapon against the sowing committee legislation in *Ekonomicheskaia zhizn*, 19 December 1920. (Hereafter EZ.)

36   *Pravda*, 25 June 1920.

of industry and because of reduced individual shares of the 1921 *razverstka* burden. The pressure on the lazy lout also had psychological significance, since it showed the industrious owner that the soviet authority was on his side as well as weakening the demoralizing example of the lazy lout getting rich through speculation.[37]

Coercion also allowed the state to provide organizational help. Aleksei Sviderskii, a top food-supply official, argued that since the state would not be able for some time to provide the material preconditions of advanced agriculture such as tractors and electricity, the only means now available to lead the country out of economic ruin was the state's 'organizational strength'. The state did not itself have any seed reserves, for example, but it could gather up the scattered resources of the peasantry and redistribute the available seed to achieve the greatest effect possible.[38]

During the actual sowing campaign in spring 1921, Osinsky gave more concrete guidance on the application of 'reasonable coercion'. Even though the food-supply tax strengthened the possibility of a partnership with the peasants, it did not end the necessity for coercion. It was not the job of the sowing committees themselves to arrest or fine peasants; their job was rather to warn the peasants of the consequences of their actions and to check up on their performance. After the campaign was concluded, the officials would inform the courts that so-and-so had speculated with seed grain rather than sowing, that so-and-so did not use his own resources to their fullest because of laziness, and that so-and-so refused to sow a particular crop for self-interested reasons. The courts would go into the circumstances of each case openly (*glasno*). Osinsky realized that many enthusiastic local officials would find this advice rather feeble, but he felt that they needed to learn new ways.[39]

Osinsky seemed to think that the term 'coercion' had only positive connotations, and this led to some uneasiness even on the part of people who basically favoured the sowing-committee program. One food-supply official praised Osinsky's emphasis on the possibilities of state intervention, but objected that 'coercion' was a one-sided label that related only to external characteristics. Another writer felt that not enough emphasis was given in Bolshevik propaganda to demonstrating that coercion was applied only in order

---

37   *Pravda*, 5 September 1920.
38   *EZ*, 26 November 1920. My notes do not reveal any use of the term 'coercion' in Sviderskiy's discussion.
39   *Pravda*, 5 April, 7 April and 10 April 1921. See also Osinsky's article in *Pravda*, 7 November 1920. It would be interesting to find out how many cases of this kind were ever brought to trial.

to allow the state to repay its debt to the peasantry and that the consumer interest of the peasants remained paramount.[40]
The package on incentives contained in the sowing-committee legislation
was criticized both in the government press and at the Eighth Congress. The
most sustained critique was a series of articles by N.S. Bogdanov, an official in
the Commissariat of Agriculture. Since Bogdanov attacked the legislation from
a variety of angles, we shall be meeting him in later sections. We are here interested in his charge that Osinsky had overlooked available means of material
incentive. According to Bogdanov, Osinsky had been brought to admit during
the course of polemics that an improvement in 'the personal living standard of
the producers' was a necessary stimulus in the long run. But Osinsky seemed to
believe that this stimulus was not currently available. In response, Bogdanov
advocated that the *razverstka* be replaced by a tax, 'in accordance with the
unanimous desire of the village'. Under a tax, the peasant would give the state
a set amount; deliveries above this amount would be stimulated by individual bonuses (*premirovanie*). The tax was *not* a substitute for coercion, for it
would be collected 'with whips and scorpions'; it was simply a more expedient form of coercion. Bogdanov also felt that the tax was compatible with the
grain monopoly, 'the contemporary form [of the] market'.[41]
Osinsky argued (correctly) that the tax method was incompatible with the
grain monopoly in the conditions of 1920, but also (incorrectly) that without
the grain monopoly and the prohibition of the free market, there would be no
successful state grain collection at all. But Osinsky saw the force in the considerations advanced by Bogdanov and tried to get as many tax-like advantages
for the *razverstka* as possible. The sowing committees would help improve the
statistical base and thus ensure a more equitable distribution of the *razverstka* burden. Osinsky also stressed the importance of collecting the *razverstka*
as quickly as possible, so that at least after a certain date the state would let
the peasant 'live in peace'.[42] Finally, Osinsky defended individual incentives in
the form of higher 'consumer norms'. Osinsky gave the following hypothetical
example: one village sows 29 poods and another village only 22 poods. From
the first village 15 poods are taken, leaving 14, while 10 poods are taken from

40   Book review by N.M. in *Biulletin*, 20 November 1920; L. Mitrofanov in *EZ*, 21 December
      1920. See also N. Bogdanov, *EZ*, 2 December 1920.

41   *EZ*, 19 December and 16 October 1920. Similar proposals in favour of a food-supply tax (but
      not free trade) were made at the Eighth Congress by the Left SRs (*Vosmoi* 1921, pp. 120–2)
      and the Mensheviks (*Vosmoi* 1921, pp. 197–200).

42   *Pravda*, 4 November 1920. After the introduction of the food-supply tax, Osinsky argued
      that the sowing committees were needed to provide the statistical base of a fair tax distri-
      bution. *Pravda*, 25 March 1921.

the second, leaving only 12. Thus in the case of the first village, 'it turns out that the state receives more, *and* more is left with the industrious owner'.[43] This reasoning makes more plausible Osinsky's later claim that the sowing-committee legislation was the first step toward a limitation of state demands that was soon afterwards put in the 'clear and convenient form' of the food-supply tax.[44]

Bogdanov also argued that the few industrial items at the disposal of the government be used not just as a means of pressure for collective fulfilment of the *razverstka*, but as a positive stimulus for fulfilment of the sowing guidelines.[45] This idea was incorporated into the final legislation – evidently on the initiative of the Commissariat of Food Supply and over the objections of the Commissariat of Agriculture.[46] But the provision of industrial items to 'individual homeowners' (*domokhozaeva*, an unusual term) touched off a revolt among Bolshevik delegates to the Eighth Congress. An SR representative at the congress said he supported the wager on the industrious owner, but wondered how the policy differed from 'a rebirth of that very kulak against which a struggle was fought with such energy'.[47] Many Bolsheviks wondered the same thing, and giving means of production to economically strong individual peasants was too much for them to take. The Bolshevik caucus at the Eighth Congress voted to remove the provision about individual bonuses; the provision was saved only after Lenin himself appeared to defend it and to offer additional language intended to ensure that 'kulaks' would not be able to benefit.

Lenin's remarks on this occasion show the confusion created by the contradiction between the sowing-committee legislation and the class struggle outlook to which the Bolsheviks were officially committed. Lenin refused to answer a point-blank question on the difference between an industrious middle peasant and an industrious kulak; in response to this and all other difficult questions he responded simply by saying the locals should decide.[48] He insisted

---

43   Eighth Congress, pp. 146–7. Even prior to NEP, Osinsky stated that the unfair distribution
      of the *razverstka* burden among individual peasants was a major reason behind support of
      the food-supply tax by food-supply officials. *Prodovolstvennaia politika v svete obshchego
      khoziaistvennoi stroitelstve sovetskoi vlasti* (*Prodovolstvennaia* 1920, pp. 189–92). See also
      Patenaude 1987, p. 68.
44   Osinsky, *Vosstanovlenie*, pp. 13–14. Poliakov cites this passage and claims that Osinsky
      denied any real significance to the Tenth Party Congress. He misinterprets the passage
      because he equates the food-supply tax – which Osinsky refers to here – with the decriminalization of free trade. Osinsky did not deny the novelty of the latter decision (Poliakov
      1967, pp. 225–6, fn. 65).
45   *EZ*, 19 December 1920.
46   Lenin 1958–1965, 42:185.
47   *Vosmoi* 1921, pp. 48–51.
48   Osinsky struggled with this problem of differentiation in *Pravda*, 5 November 1920.

that the language of the new legislation ensured that the slightest use of 'kulak methods' would not be rewarded; he then spoiled the effect by asserting that practically every middle peasant resorted to kulak methods.[49]

Despite the confusion, the thrust of Lenin's remarks was clear. While he showed genuine concern about the use of 'kulak methods' and the growth of kulak influence, these took a decided back seat to the problem of raising productivity. In a backward and devastated economy, economic improvement required sustained effort: not to reward it was evident slavery (*perebarshchivanie*). Let people have as much land as they want, so long as they use it efficiently. Lenin reminded his audience that individual bonuses were being applied in industry – so why not in agriculture?[50] Lenin summed up by stating flatly that the Central Committee had unanimously agreed that 'we got carried away with the struggle against the kulak and lost all sense of measure'.[51]

An examination of the debates surrounding the sowing-committee legislation thus reveals that the emphasis on coercion was not a rejection of material incentives – indeed, it was coercion for the sake of material incentives. During the course of the debate, ways to strengthen material incentives that could be used within the framework of the state grain monopoly were taken up and incorporated into the legislation. The movement away from the class-struggle outlook went so far that it provoked a reaction on the part of rank-and-file Bolsheviks. They began to suspect what became painfully evident later on: the leadership had become much more interested in the practical solution of national problems than in revolutionary purity.

4   Goals and Methods

Having considered at length the general outlook behind the legislation, we may now turn to its goals and the methods envisioned to accomplish them. These goals can be divided into two categories: quantitative – the greatest sown acreage possible, and qualitative – an improvement in the methods used by the peasants.

The legislation made the greatest possible extension of the sown acreage into a state obligation. The programme's thrust was not to whip reluctant peas-

---

49   Lenin 1958–1965, 42:185–95. Lenin also gave contradictory guidelines about the individual versus the collective use of equipment.

50   In another place, Lenin remarked that there was nothing socialist about the use of such bonuses in industry. Lenin 1958–1965, 42:151.

51   Lenin 1958–1965, 42:195.

ants into sowing, but rather to use state mechanisms to enable the peasants to sow all available land by redistributing peasant resources. Various methods were to be employed: organizing 'mutual aid' to sow the land of 'weak' (*malo-moshchnyi*) or Red Army households, or even compulsory leasing of land left unsown by its owner.[52] But the basic method was to be the preservation, collection and redistribution of seed grain.

From one point of view, the seed programme was the least controversial part of the legislation. Some of the methods had already been used to mitigate droughts earlier in the year; it was Osinsky's experience with them in Tula that led to his original enthusiasm. Osinsky asserted that coercion would probably not have to be used very much to carry out this part of the legislation; indeed, the seed programme would reassure the peasants that the burden of the *razverstka* would not condemn them to inadequate sowing.[53]

From another point of view, seed redistribution was a very delicate operation, since seed was the peasants' 'holy of holies' and they were extremely touchy about any interference with it.[54] Osinsky and his supporters therefore stressed that methods had to be adapted to local circumstances. The least radical method was simply to put each peasant's seed grain on registration (*uchet*); this was an attempt to ensure that the seed grain was not eaten up and remained available for local redistribution. The next possibility was to preserve the seed grain in public warehouses – in sacks carefully labelled with the owner's name.[55] Finally, in regions with wide variation in local harvests, a seed *razverstka* might be applied for redistribution within *volosts* or *uezds*.[56]

In discussing the political preparation needed to carry out seed redistribution, Kuraev advised officials to make clear that it had nothing to do with any move toward *kommuniia* (this was the point of labelling individual sacks). Seed redistribution should not be seen as a revival of the Committees of the Poor, since seed grain was taken from the poor as well as the middle peasant. Based on the experience of food-supply work, Kuraev also stressed the importance of

---

52 *Na borbu s golodom* (*Na borbu* 1921, pp. 74–5).

53 *Pravda*, 25 June 1920; *Biulletin*, 30 November 1920; *Kalendar*, pp. 120–2. For the background to the sowing campaign, see Iurkov 1980, pp. 56–68.

54 V.V. Kuraev, *Pravda*, 19 December 1920.

55 A peasant delegate to the Eighth Congress from Riazan warned of abuses concerning these warehouses. Lenin 1958–1965, 42:384.

56 According to Svidersky, nine deficit provinces went the full route; five surplus provinces with harvest difficulties put seed grain on registration; for political reasons, Siberia and Ukraine rejected any seed redistribution. *EZ*, 22 December 1920. See also the editorial in *Pravda*, 24 September 1920.

working through the peasant village community (*obshchestvo*), since even the lowest level soviets were seen by the peasants as a 'higher organ'.[57]

If increasing sown acreage was the least controversial part of the program, using state coercion to improve agricultural methods was the most controversial. Osinsky included this idea in his proposals because of his perception that the agricultural crisis of 1920 had led to a qualitative as well as a quantitative decline: peasant sloppiness, while understandable, was leading to increased vulnerability from drought. He therefore argued that 'obligatory rules' of good farming practice should be part of the sowing-committee campaign. As could be expected, the obligatory rules were supposed to be inspired by the example of the local industrious owners.[58] In working out the details, Osinsky stressed again and again the danger of over-ambitiousness. The final legislative language gave much more attention to avoiding this danger – the rules had to be strictly coordinated with local conditions, they must not cause a 'radical break' in local farming practice, they must not subject the peasant owner to increased risk – than to the actual content of the methods.[59]

What concrete methods did Osinsky and his supporters have in mind? In all of the available material, the exclusive focus is on just two: early ploughing of fallow land and ploughing *na ziab*, that is, ploughing in autumn for spring sowing. According to Teodorovich, ploughing fallow land in April instead of June would double the harvest, and ploughing *na ziab* would lead to a 35 per cent increase.[60] The Bolshevik policy-makers were tempted by the possibility of a large harvest increase simply by mandating a couple of common-sense, easily implemented rules.

Osinsky later pointed to Tula province as an example of how these rules might be enforced. The Tula officials decided that if one-third of the peasants in a particular district wanted to carry out early ploughing, the rest would be compelled to do so. Osinsky felt that this showed how the state could strengthen the influence of the 'progressive industrious owner'. He only warned against coercing the consent of the one-third minority or of relying too heavily on peasants

---

57 *Pravda*, 19, 21 and 22 December 1920. Official instructions published in January 1921 also spoke of using the peasant *mir* (*Dekrety* 1958, pp. 151–8).

58 See Lenin 1958–1965, 42:179.

59 Osinsky proposed most of this language in his *Pravda* article of 5 November 1920; officials from the Agriculture Commissariat criticized the draft legislation because of its vagueness on the actual methods (*Biulleten*, 30 November 1920).

60 *Vosmoi* 1921, pp. 123–7.

without equipment who had no stake in the matter.[61] The interaction between officials and peasants described by Osinsky must have brought up memories of the Stolypin program.

This part of the legislation provoked an outcry from several quarters, based on the feeling that methods applicable to grain collection were being transferred inappropriately to grain production. In the words of a non-party peasant delegate to the Eighth Congress: 'I'll saw firewood under the stick. But you can't carry out agriculture under the stick'.[62] Bogdanov granted that coercion might help increase sown acreage (given proper technical back-up) but denied that it could do much to improve production methods. Production problems were so individualized and varied so much by locality that any coercive apparatus would be impossibly bulky.[63] More fundamentally, coercion only made sense if the reasons for neglecting the rules were backwardness and stubbornness, rather than economic constraints. But in reality the peasant failed to turn up fallow land early enough not because of ill-will but because of the pressure of other tasks and the absence of livestock.[64] This point was one of the most common criticisms of the legislation. Even a conditional supporter such as Iurii Larin called on the Bolsheviks to outgrow the habit of calling the peasant a fool and a poor farmer – the bottleneck was not stupidity, but possibility.[65]

In response Osinsky protested that there must be some rules to which these objections did not apply, for example, 'sow as early as possible without regard for holidays'.[66] Osinsky was impatient with agronomists of the old school who insisted on long preparatory propaganda and the most careful implementation by strictly voluntary means. The crisis in agriculture was too pressing to wait until an extensive agronomical network was set up.[67] But all in all, the Bolshevik leaders would have been well-advised to drop the attempt to improve agricultural methods through coercive regulation. It was the least important part of the actual programme, while at the same time it incurred a heavy political cost.

---

61   *Pravda*, 10 April 1921. Documents from Tula can be found in *EZ*, 10 and 11 December 1920. Osinsky also felt that a trained agronomist should approve the sowing rules.
62   Lenin 1958–1965, 42:384.
63   *EZ*, 16 October and 19 December 1920. A similar criticism was made by Dallin (*Vosmoi* 1921, pp. 197–9).
64   *EZ*, 2 December 1920.
65   *Pravda*, 12 December 1920. See also *Na borbu* 1921, pp. 92–5. Osinsky later criticized the Kaluga sowing committee for mandating methods without taking into account material constraints on the peasant (*Pravda*, 10 April 1921).
66   *Pravda*, 7 November 1920.
67   *Pravda*, 13 May and 17 May 1921.

This part of the sowing-committee programme is also mainly responsible for the programme's low reputation among historians.

Osinsky insisted on including the regulation of methods because he had a vision of the sowing-committee programme as the first step on a new road to socialism: the title of his September article in *Pravda* was 'The agricultural crisis and socialist construction in the village'.[68] The clash between him and Bogdanov was as much about this long-term perspective as about the practical specifics of the programme. Since Osinsky defended coercive centralized regulation while Bogdanov defended economic stimuli, and since Osinsky spoke of sabotage and attacked *kulturnichestvo* while Bogdanov spoke of 'growing-in' (*vrastanie*), it would seem that this is a clash between proto-Stalinist and proto-Bukharinist. But things, as is so often the case, are not quite what they seem.

For Bogdanov, state farms and collective farms should be the focus of the state's effort to bring socialism to the village. Granted, the state farms at present were somewhat parasitic, but after they received tractors and electricity, they would become potent sources of state influence. After a process of 'statization', there would be a 'growing-in of these socialist forms into the petty-bourgeois body of the village'.

The state's main tool in bringing this about would be 'the monopolized market', supplemented by the cultural influence of the agronomists. The ultimate goal was a 'production plan' encompassing agriculture. When this was achieved, Osinsky's urgent orders (*boevye prikazy*) might be useful. But until then, the state should be careful not to smother the independent initiative of the state and collective farms with coercive regulation.[69]

Osinsky rejected this strategy. For one thing, since the transition to collective farms would (as everyone knew) be a slow, patient process of persuasion, it could not be an answer to current problems. But Osinsky also sympathized with the peasant's suspicions about the whole strategy: 'It is not only the interest of the property owner at work here, but an instinct that is completely healthy from a socialist point of view ... Russia will not arrive at socialism through a gradual consolidation of a network of "grain factories".'[70]

---

68   *Pravda*, 5 September 1920. Historians who restrict themselves to this, the opening article of the series, will receive a misleading impression of the relative weight of short- and long-term priorities in Osinsky's outlook, since it is the only place where he goes into any detail about his long-term hopes.

69   *EZ*, 16 and 17 July 1920; 16 October 1920. See also the comment by S.P. Sereda recorded by Arthur Ransome, *Russia in 1919* (Ransome 1919, pp. 151–2).

70   *Pravda*, 5 September 1920; see also the article by V. Filippov, *EZ*, 1 October 1920.

It followed that any strategy of socialization had to accept the long-term existence of individual peasant farms. Osinsky was opposed to private (*chastno-khoziaistvennyi*) agriculture, which he contrasted to state regulation; he was not opposed to single-owner (*edinolichny*) agriculture, which he contrasted to collective and state farms. Private agriculture had been exposed as bankrupt, but not single-owner agriculture. Probably the most striking manifestation of Osinsky's faith in the viability of peasant farms was his interest in the possibility of electric plows that could be used on individual strips.[71] As opposed to implanting socialist cells from below, Osinsky's approach would 'take in the whole economy and gradually bring it by separate layers [*plasti*] up to a state setting'.[72] Osinsky never made this process extremely clear, but I assume the general idea is similar to Aleksandr Chaianov's idea of vertical concentration, whereby scattered peasant enterprises are brought up to the level of a state plan by means of 'a gradual, successive chipping off (*otshcheplenie*) of separate branches of individual enterprises and their organization into higher forms of large-scale undertakings'.[73]

Osinsky allowed that the two approaches were not mutually exclusive. Let the agronomist continue to use the collective farms as a base for *kulturnichestvo* – but this should not get in the way of a crash campaign to help the peasant by removing basic agricultural illiteracy. Indeed, the literacy campaign of *Narkompros* (Commissariat of Enlightenment) was a good model for combining short- and long-term perspectives in agricultural development. Osinsky's outlook allowed him to reject the dire warnings of Kautsky and the Mensheviks about a petty-bourgeois threat to the revolution; he felt confident that it would not take long before the peasants became an 'unshakable support' of the soviet authority, socialism, and the communist party.[74]

If 'Stalinist' implies support for a crash campaign of coercive collectivization based on the class-struggle outlook, then there were no Stalinists in 1920, for there was no one who so much as dreamed of such an option. On the other hand, both Osinsky and Bogdanov looked forward to a gradual approach to a planned, state-controlled agriculture dominated by a 'monopolized market'. If we are to assign honours for being forerunners of NEP, then Bogdanov deserves

71   *Pravda*, 5 September and 5 November 1920.
72   *Vosmoi* 1921, pp. 146–7. For further discussion, see *Pravda*, 5 September 1920.
73   Chaianov, *Osnovnye idei i formy organizatsii selsko-khoziaistvennoi kooperatsii* (2nd ed. reprinted in Chaianov 1967). The first edition was published in 1919 and was therefore available to Osinsky.
74   *Pravda*, 5 September 1920.

the credit he has received for his advocacy of the food-supply tax.[75] But Osinsky also deserves the credit that he has not received for his advocacy of a path to socialism based on acceptance of the viability of the single-owner peasant.

In the actual legislative process, complete confusion reigned about long- and short-term perspectives. Speakers at the Eighth Congress defended all possibilities: the legislation was only good for the short term, only good for the long term, good for neither, good for both.[76] Some praised what they saw as the legislation's long-term intent to replace single-owner agriculture with 'productive units' encompassing a whole village; others, who were paying closer attention, criticized the bill for basing future development on reactionary, splintered productive forms.[77]

The actual spirit of the legislation was best expressed by Kuraev at the Eighth Congress: while the legislation combined short- and long-term perspectives, all attention should be focused on the short-term effort to maximize sown acreage through the seed programme. 'We must crawl out of the quagmire of the agricultural crisis', for only this achievement would create a solid foundation for future socialization.[78] The preamble to the legislation reflected these priorities. (See Appendix.) Not a word was mentioned about socialism: the entire focus was on the current crisis and the effort to stave off disaster in the coming year. The sowing-committee legislation was no attempt at a great leap forward in the style of Stalin or Mao. Its aim was instead a small leap forward – out of the downward economic spiral of a time of troubles to the normal economic relations needed for future progress, no matter how defined.

5   Organizational Forms

Osinsky was very proud of the organizational innovations contained in the legislation: the sowing committees proper (*posevkomy*) and the village committees (*selkomy*). The sowing committees were designed to be a small, flexible and authoritative bureaucratic task force that would focus the energies of local

---

75   Advocates of the food-supply tax in 1920 did not support free trade as well, and Bogdanov for one seemed sincere in his defence of the state monopoly. In 1921, he criticized the first trial balloons in support of the food-supply tax as damaging the chances for collectivizing production (Patenaude 1987, p. 168, citing *EZ*, 5 March 1921).

76   Eighth Congress, pp. 10–45.

77   Deluded supporters: Tkachev in *Vosmoi* 1921, p. 139; Varga 1921, pp. 5–10. Critics: L. Mitrofanov, *EZ*, 21 December 1920; see also Lenin 1958–1965, 42:193.

78   *Vosmoi* 1921, pp. 132–4; Osinsky 1922, pp. 13–14.

officialdom on the top priority task of the sowing campaign. The village committees were designed to enlist the peasants themselves in the campaign.[79]
The logic behind the sowing committees proper was identical to what Osinsky
called 'democratic centralism'. The democratic centralists were an opposition
grouping within the Bolshevik party that tried to use Leninist orthodoxy to
legitimize their own concerns.[80]

These concerns actually had little to do with either democracy or centralism.
Osinsky went out of his way to argue that the collegiality he defended was compatible with the dictatorial power of a single individual – Lenin, for example.
He and his colleagues dissociated themselves from attempts to make collegiality a device for enlisting the broad worker masses. Their focus of attention was
not on the centre, but rather on the middle rungs of the state apparatus in the
provinces. 'Democratic centralism' was the protest of local officials against the
disruptive visits of central representatives, and its aim was to bring down the
'Chinese wall' that isolated local officials from central representatives and from
each other.[81] Osinsky said that it meant that 'the directives of the centre are not
given out from the top, straight down, through departmental pillars, but that
there exist horizontal bridges (*peremychki*), or hoops, that are called executive
committees. These create connections between the scattered departments.'[82]

The demands of the democratic centralists were thus motivated less by any
ideological principle such as democracy or socialism than by the desire for efficiency in the specific context of a newly emerging state apparatus. The new
officials should learn from each other rather than sinking into their own narrow bureaucratic specialties or, worse yet, fighting among themselves to the
point of mutual arrest No one individual – whether he was a bourgeois specialist or a 'red governor' – could make coherent decisions without extensive
consultations, so that the simplicity that one-man-rule seemed to promise was
illusory. Besides human limitations, the necessity for consultation arose from
the instability of the environment surrounding the fledgling state apparatus,
caused both by the economic breakdown and the unsettled nature of social
relations.[83]

---

79   For details, see *Dekrety* 1958, pp. 151–8 (10 January 1921).
80   This discussion of the democratic centralists is based on the presentation by Osinsky and
     his colleagues (T.V. Sapronov and V.M. Maksimovsky) at the Ninth Party Congress in March
     1920, and does not include their critique of internal party organization.
81   T.V. Sapronov in *Deviatii s'ezd RKP(b)* (*Deviatii* 1934, pp. 148–51). All three major democratic
     centralists had experience working in the provincial state apparatus.
82   *Deviatii* 1934, p. 131. The democratic centralists would have approved of Khrushchev's *sov-
     narkhoz* reforms.
83   Osinsky's reference to 'red governors' puts his critique into the context of a longstand-

Because of the economic emergency, the democratic centralists recognized the necessity of militarization. But here they made a distinction which I can best render as civilian militarization versus uniformed militarization. (The point can be made less clumsily in Russian by contrasting *militarizatsiia* with *voenizatsiia*.) Uniformed militarization implied deprivation of civil rights, blind reliance on military methods, and a power grab by the army bureaucracy. Civilian militarization implied all-out mobilization campaigns within the state apparatus to meet pressing emergencies.[84] In concrete terms, it required 'abbreviated collegia' – abbreviated both in terms of membership (three to five persons) and authority (a specific priority task). As an example, Osinsky described the 'provincial food-supply conferences' with which he had worked in Viatka province. This description reveals Osinsky's hopes for the sowing committees:[85]

We met every day or every other day, for two hours, in our three-member, stripped-down (*boevoi*) collegium, allowing only the shortest debates. Our resolutions were recorded to check up on their implementation. Each person was given a specific task and a specific deadline. At the beginning of the session the secretary announced the deadlines that had passed, and each person had to report fulfilment or to explain why he had failed. We carefully established links with the localities, kept a record of their work and checked up on it. We demanded regular visits with reports from representatives from the localities. We ourselves were always on a direct line with the *uezds*. Finally, we instituted disciplinary fines for carelessness and lack of fulfilment.[86]

The sowing committees were to bear the same relation to the local land sections (*zemskii otdely*) of the Commissariat of Agriculture as the food-supply conferences had to the regular food-supply organs. The sowing committees would have not more than five members: the chairmen of the local food-supply committee, land section, and soviet executive committee, plus a representative of

---

ing conflict within Russian political culture between what I have called the 'gubernatorial solution' and the 'enlistment solution'; for a detailed description, see Lih 1990, Chapter 2.

84   For Trotsky's view of *militarizatsiia*, see 'Our Position is in the Highest Degree Tragic', included in this volume.

85   For the food-supply conferences, see the article by S. Minkevich, *Pravda*, 24 November 1920, and Lih 1990, pp. 212–13.

86   *Deviatii* 1934, pp. 124–5. Osinsky did not repeat this argument when he referred to militarization in his article of 5 September 1920. ('Check up on fulfilment' was a favourite slogan of both Lenin and Stalin; see 'Stalin at Work', included in this volume.)

a higher-level soviet executive committee as well as a representative from the village committees. It would have no technical apparatus of its own, relying instead on the already existing staff of the local land sections and food-supply committees.

In an early draft of the legislation, Osinsky listed all the bureaucratic ills the sowing committees were supposed to cure: the committees would inspire local officials and counteract their lackadaisical attitude; they would cut through red tape, overcome interdepartmental squabbles, and put down bureaucratic sabotage.[87] This frank recital of defects was dropped from the final draft, and in general the bureaucratic rationale behind the sowing committees was played down in the propaganda supporting the legislation. But it was crucial for Osinsky, who gave the innovation of the food-supply conferences most of the credit for the relative success of food-supply work. This was the kind of task force needed to carry out a focused campaign with a political sensitivity missing from the normal workings of the local bureaucracy.[88]

Osinsky was known as a critic of the over-centralization symbolized by the industrial *glavki* and he resented the accusation that the sowing committees were just another *glavk*. On the contrary, he retorted, the *modus operandi* of a *glavk* was to send out a departmental representative with a 'three-foot mandate' who promptly disrupted local work. But in the case of the sowing committees, the visitor from the centre did not represent any one department but rather the Central Soviet Executive Committee (VTsIK), and the visitor's mission was to strengthen the authority of local organs and unify their efforts, not to replace them.[89]

Osinsky assured agricultural officials that the sowing committees were only temporary and not meant as a permanent replacement of the land sections.[90] As this indicates, the sowing-committee legislation was caught up in bureaucratic politics: most of the initiative for the legislation came from the Commissariat of Food Supply and most of the scepticism came from the Commissariat of Agriculture.[91] In the countryside, the two departments had settled

---

87   *Biulletin*, 30 November 1920.
88   The argument is spelled out by Kuraev, *Vosmoi* 1921, pp. 132–4; see also Teodorovich on pp. 123–7. Osinsky's rationale can be found in *Pravda*, 25 June and 9 November 1920. One speaker at the Eighth Congress, Karninsky, criticized the legislation for not being dictatorial enough (*Vosmoi* 1921, pp. 131–2).
89   *Vosmoi* 1921, pp. 146–7. Ironically, one critic on this score was Aleksandr Shlikhter, a food-supply official known as a super-centralizer.
90   *Pravda*, 9 November 1920.
91   See Sviderskii, *EZ*, 22 and 26 December 1920. On the other hand, the bill was presented to the congress by Teodorovich, an agricultural official.

down into a bad cop/good cop relationship: the Commissariat of Food Supply represented the state that put heavy pressure on the peasants while the
Commissariat of Agriculture represented the state that helped and defended
the peasant. Iurii Larin called for a combination of the two departments –
a *narzemprod* – that would avoid one-sided grain procurement without relation to agricultural needs and one-sided agronomy without relation to pressing
state needs.[92] One aim of the sowing-committee legislation was in fact to unite
the perspectives of procurement and production. In the meantime, impatient
food-supply officials felt that they represented the 'state outlook', for only they
grasped the urgency of improving next year's harvest and not simply preaching
better methods and collective production.[93] In response, agricultural officials
felt that the land sections, neglected by the centre in the past, were now being
unjustly blamed for the agricultural crisis.[94]

Separate from the enlistment of officials into the sowing committees was
the attempt to enlist the peasantry into the campaign by means of the village
committees. As with the sowing committees proper, the idea of enlisting 'the
will of the *mir*' in fulfilling state obligations was taken from the experience of
food-supply work.[95] Larin pointed out that the sowing campaign could not be
carried out only by applying pressure from outside, since the state did not have
adequate resources for either material incentives or coercion. The only hope
lay in activating the independent initiative (*samodeiatelnost*) and the moral
pressure of the village itself. Larin assured nervous Bolsheviks that the peasant committees would not become 'a base for counterrevolution', since their
sole purpose was to carry out a state assignment.[96] Accordingly, the village
committees were elected directly by the village community but headed by the
chairman of the village soviet; they were given responsibility for all the major
tasks of the campaign at the village level.[97]

The contradictory nature of the village committees – elected peasant representative and state organ – created some difficulty in giving them a name. The
original name was 'committees of assistance in the improvement of agriculture', but Kuraev objected that the committees were not assisting the authori-

---

92 *Pravda*, 12 December 1920; for similar remarks by Bogdanov, see *EZ*, 16 October 1920. See
    also M. Vladimirov, *Udarnye momenty prodovolstvennoi raboty na Ukraine* (Vladimirov
    1921, pp. 22–4).

93 Osinsky, *Pravda*, 5 September and 5 November 1920; V. Filippov, *EZ*, 1 October 1920.

94 Bogdanov, *EZ*, 2 December 1920; Eighth Congress, speakers Buianov (*Vosmoi* 1921, pp. 134–
    7), Lezhnev and Ishchenko (*Vosmoi* 1921, pp. 141–3).

95 See the Kuraev article in *Pravda*, 19 December 1920.

96 *Pravda*, 12 December 1920.

97 *Dekrety* 1958, p. 155.

ties but exercising authority themselves. Kuraev's suggestion was adopted and the word 'assistance' was dropped.[98] Whatever the name, the Bolsheviks were at pains to distinguish them from the Committees of the Poor. This was underlined in Osinsky's first draft, where the committees were to be recruited 'from the very best [peasant] owners'.[99] Osinsky later admitted that the peasants were suspicious of these committees unless they could be convinced they had nothing to do with the *razverstka*, the Committees of the Poor, or *kommuniia*.[100]

Critics of the legislation did not oppose the goal of enlistment and independent initiative, but they did attack the method proposed in the legislation. S.P. Sereda, the Commissar of Agriculture, suggested that the cooperatives offered a better framework for enlistment into the task of state regulation. This suggestion was overruled as 'politically incorrect'.[101] The political danger was underscored by the stand of the other socialist parties represented at the Eighth Congress. Calling the Bolshevik promise of participation an 'empty sound' to peasants deprived of their rights, they all insisted on freely elected cooperatives, where they presumably expected to do well.[102] Evidently the cooperatives could not be assigned the role now given to the village committees until this political danger was removed.

Many of the critics' suspicions about the sowing committees turned out to be justified. In spring 1921, Osinsky berated local officials who failed even to get a committee elected or who felt appointees were an adequate substitute. Even worse, officials tried to enlist the committees in the technical work of seed collection and the dirty work of applying coercion. The failure to give the peasants an independent voice was even more inexcusable after the introduction of the food-supply tax and the legalization of free trade, since these policy changes gave officials a 'common language' with the peasants. By the end of the spring sowing campaign, Osinsky felt that successful village committees had been instituted in many places, and advocated that they be given new tasks – including, perhaps ironically, setting up new cooperatives in the villages.[103]

---

98 *Vosmoi* 1921, pp. 132–4. Kuraev himself put forward the name 'observer committees'; Larin suggested 'peasant production councils'. The official title as 'peasant committees for the improvement of agricultural production'.

99 *Biulletin*, 30 November 1920.

100 *Sessii vserossiiskogo tsentralnogo ispolnitelnogo komiteta, VIII sozyva* (*Sessii* 1922, pp. 103–4), 20 March 1921.

101 Svidersky, cited in *Biulletin*, 30 November 1920.

102 See the resolutions presented at the Eighth Congress by the Mensheviks (*Vosmoi* 1921, pp. 199–200), the Left SRs (*Vosmoi* 1921, pp. 120–2) and the SRs (*Vosmoi* 1921, pp. 48–51).

103 *Pravda*, 5 April, 10 April, 13 May, 15 May, 26 May 1921. For a description of the problems

The opposition parties could easily point out the Bolshevik failure to combine genuine independent initiative with the heavy burdens the state had to
impose, but the underlying dilemma was insoluble. Much of Lenin's attention
at this time was occupied with trying to find ways around the problem. Lenin
was a strong defender of the sowing-committee legislation and of the idea
of using coercion to help the peasantry. His remarks stress the importance of
practical achievement rather than the application of 'Marxist methods'. Lenin
praised Osinsky for displaying this attitude and followed him in warning about
the dangers of trying to do too much.[104] But he was not greatly interested in
the details of the economic regulation of agriculture and tended to view the
sowing-committee legislation in the wider context of his search for mechanisms to handle the political challenge posed by the peasantry.

Lenin's immediate problem is illustrated by the remarks of non-party delegates to the Eighth Congress, transcribed by Lenin himself and sent around
to other Central Committee members. These remarks can only be properly
interpreted with a correct understanding of the point at contention, namely,
should the *kulak/bedniak* division be replaced by industrious/lazy lout? The
peasant speakers divided about equally on this question.[105] A closer look shows
that those who supported the industrious owner were not adverse to coercion
but were greatly upset by the burden of the *razverstka* and tended to support
a food-supply tax, while those who insisted on the existence of kulaks also
fiercely insisted on *razverstka* fulfilment. This second group of speakers also
viewed the label of the lazy lout as a code word for the poor peasant, arguing
that it was the devastation of the civil war that led to the difficulties of the poor.

What conclusion did Lenin draw from all of this? It was probably that (as he
himself remarked a few days later) the Bolsheviks had gotten carried away with
the struggle against the kulak, since it was the fixation on the kulak that was the
main obstacle to whole-hearted support of the sowing-committee legislation.
He might also have concluded that if the Bolsheviks were really going to throw
in their lot with the industrious owner, then something had to be done about
the *razverstka*.[106]

---

both of the village committees and the sowing committees, see the telegram of 4 April
     1921 in *Leninskii Sbornik*, 20:72–3.
104   Lenin 1958–1965, 42:144, 154, 178–80, 182–4, 191–2 and passim.
105   Lenin 1958–1965, 42:382–6. The meeting took place on 22 December 1920. In favour of
     the industrious category were speakers from Ivanovo-Voznesensk, Kursk, Tula, Kostroma,
     Novgorod, Perm; in favour of the kulak category were those from Cherepovets, Penza,
     Riazan, Dernianskii, Samara.
106   In the very first draft of the food-supply tax decision, Lenin called for using lowered tax

In the longer term, the problem of the peasantry was part of the larger problem of the 'non-party masses'. In time of war, these masses, whether worker
or peasant, could understand the necessity of sacrifices – but would they also
be able to grasp the same necessity in the more abstract case of economic
reconstruction? One solution was to emphasize the threat of war, and so Lenin
prophesied war and asserted in the accents later amplified by Stalin that 'we
are backward in relation to the capitalist powers and will remain so; we will be
beaten if we do not achieve the restoration of our economy'.[107] Another solution was to find mechanisms for the enlistment of the non-party masses. Lenin
defined his problem in terms that apply without change to Gorbachev: given
the fact that the masses have long lived in circumstances that crushed their
independent initiative so that they have trouble feeling like masters (*khozi-
aeva*), how can we organize them 'not for opposition to the *vlast*, but for its
support, [in order to develop] the measures of the worker *vlast* and to carry
them out completely?' The trade unions were one candidate for this job, and
the village committees were another. When the village committees did not pan
out, Lenin turned to the cooperatives in his final effort to square this particular
circle.[108]

In the very long term, Lenin believed that the only permanent solution to
the problem of state consciousness – recognition of the necessity of sacrifices
for the common good – was the advent of socialist consciousness. As noted earlier, the Bolsheviks did not have the conceptual vocabulary for discussing the
dilemma of public goods, and so, while they had a practical grasp of it, they
explained it by pointing to 'petty-bourgeois psychology'. They tended therefore
to assume that once peasants were given proper technical equipment and were
no longer isolated individualists, they would understand the necessity for sacrifices. But while Osinsky was upbeat about the possibility of achieving state
consciousness in the interim, Lenin was rather pessimistic during this period.
A leitmotif in his speeches was the Sukharevka (the open-air market in Moscow
that became a symbol of illegal speculation) residing in the soul of every independent peasant. In a moment of deep despair in early 1921, Lenin stated that
it would take years of re-education to undo the heritage of capitalism – until
then, many peasants would not understand that the worker-peasant govern-

---

rates as a way of rewarding the industriousness of the peasant (Lenin 1958–1965, 42:333,
8 February 1921).
107   Lenin 1958–1965, 42:142.
108   Lenin 1958–1965, 42:141–5; see also 5–6. For Lenin's dilemma in its widest context, see
Theodore Von Laue, *The World Revolution of Westernization: The Twentieth Century in
Global Perspective* (Von Laue 1987).

ment took grain only to improve the position of the workers *and* the peasants. And this meant that every spring there would be disorders and uprisings.[109]

6   Reflections

The principal defect of most earlier accounts of the sowing committees is that they do not place the debate in its full context nor examine the actual content of the legislation. After a closer look at the record, the following conclusions seem appropriate:

1. The sowing-committee legislation had no connection with any utopian 'leap into communism'; it was a small leap forward, or better, an attempt to crawl out of a quagmire. The Bolshevik perspective of 1920 is accurately summed up by an appeal issued by the Eighth Congress: 'Let us double our efforts and a reward will not be lacking to the toilers. A year will go by [and] we will no longer freeze in unlit homes ... Five years will go by and we will finally cure the wounds caused by the war to our economy.'[110]

This perspective applies not only to the content of the programme – seed redistribution, anti-drought methods – but also the organizational forms: the sowing committees were meant as a device for focusing the energies of offi- cialdom on a top-priority campaign. Osinsky and his supporters did stress the importance of keeping long-term perspectives in mind, but for the time being they warned primarily against over-ambitiousness.

2. By 1920, Bolshevik policy-makers had moved rather far along the spec- trum from the class-struggle outlook to the partnership outlook – far enough, in fact, to create difficulties with local activists. The substitution of industri- ous/lazy for rich/poor as the basic peasant division, the emphasis on objective economic difficulties, the rejection of collective productive forms as the main path to socialism, the call for sacrifices for the common good rather than for the revolution – all of these were intrinsic to the sowing-committee legislation.

The shift was not made with complete clarity. The continued use of the word 'sabotage' was ominous, even when it did not refer to class enemies but rather to demoralized peasants and negligent officials. Prescriptions for achiev- ing state consciousness still relied mainly on socialist strategies for remaking

---

109   Lenin 1958–1965, 42:363–4 (28 February 1921). This is almost the last speech in Volume 42; for a very similar formulation at the beginning, see 42:5–6. Lenin's diagnosis was picked up in *Kalendar*, pp. 120–2.

110   *Dekrety* 1958, pp. 118–20.

'petty-bourgeois psychology'.[111] Perhaps most dangerously, the kulak/bedniak class-struggle framework was not repudiated but only pushed into the background by the exclusive focus on the middle peasant. But although the class-struggle outlook went into abeyance, it did not die, and remained ready any time the Bolsheviks were again frustrated with the peasantry.

3. The rhetorical emphasis on coercion did not reflect an obsession born of civil-war militarism and/or communist fanaticism. The need for coercion arose from the grim realities of a situation where material incentives were low and where heavy burdens had to be imposed before the state could repay its debt to the peasantry. It was also a symbol of the moral right of the worker-peasant authority to impose obligations as well as of the contribution the state could make through its 'organizing strength'. We perhaps ought rather to compliment Osinsky for his eschewal of euphemism than to be shocked by the mention of a reality inherent in the situation.

At the ground level, where the state and peasantry met face to face, the distinction made by Lenin and others between illegitimate violence and legitimate coercion may have seemed remote. But despite the grubby realities of the application of power, I would argue that this distinction is a valid one in moral terms. There may even have been a perceptible political difference between force applied for transformational goals alien to the peasantry and force applied for understandable state interests. In any event, I would argue strongly that historians need to confront this distinction more explicitly in their description of the civil-war period.

The coercion of the sowing-committee legislation was designed as part of a broad aid package that included individualized material incentives. The use of coercion in the seed programme was not controversial nor does it seem problematical today.[112] The use of coercion to improve agricultural methods is less defensible, since it seems to have been based on an underestimation of the economic difficulties that prevented use of the methods. But in Osinsky's defence it should be mentioned that he continually stressed caution and gradualness and that the methods actually proposed were standard anti-drought measures. As it turned out, only the seed programme was of any importance and the crash campaign to improve agricultural methods did not prove viable.

---

111   For Bogdanov's insightful remarks on this issue, see *EZ*, 16 October 1920.

112   An anti-Bolshevik writer in Russia at the time wrote that the aims of the programme were rather ordinary; his criticism was reserved for Bolshevik incompetence in execution; see A. Terne, *V tsarstve Lenina* (Terne 1922, pp. 211–19).

4. In the bureaucratic battle between the Commissariat of Food Supply and the Commissariat of Agriculture, historians have tended almost automatically to side with the Commissariat of Agriculture – even when, or especially when, they are unaware of the existence of the departmental clash. In general, it is always easier for historians to adopt the role of oppositionist and criticize the powers that were for imposing heavy burdens. Although as a good North American I too am suspicious of both coercion and the state, I am willing to go so far as to argue that in fall 1920 the Commissariat of Food Supply did represent 'the state outlook' – that is, the common interest in combining a heavy procurement burden with a crash campaign to improve the upcoming harvest. There were obvious flaws in Osinsky's programme – many of them admitted and corrected at the time – but our criticism should be tempered with humility and even respect for people struggling to avert an overwhelming crisis with desperately few resources.

Although the sowing-committee legislation was only a passing episode, the account presented here has wider implications for our understanding of this crucial period as a whole. The sowing committees were not an apotheosis of war communism; indeed, the traditional stereotypes of war communism get in the way of recognizing the realities of the period.[113] It would take us too far afield to discuss all the different arguments subsumed under the label of 'war communism', so I shall discuss only the most plausible of these arguments, namely, that legislation such as the sowing committees reflected a state orientation that was unique to the civil war.

Writers both in the West and the Soviet Union point to a 'statization' of the Bolshevik outlook that was one of the sources of Stalinism. The sowing committees are cited as a vivid example of this process.[114] The Bolsheviks certainly

---

113   Two recent accounts that view the sowing committees in terms of 'war communism' are Poliakov 1967 pp. 213–30, and Silvana Malle, *The Economic Organization for War Communism* (Malle 1985, pp. 445–50). The reader of Poliakov and Malle is given the impression that Osinsky scorned all material incentives and proposed very ambitious and detailed socialist regulation as an answer to the agricultural crisis of 1920. Malle, for example, writes that 'the ultimate end of the law on the seed committees – through not explicitly stated – was the collectivization of land'. Such blatant misreadings of the record do not reflect credit on the stereotyped views about war communism that inspired them. Preferable to Malle are two earlier accounts in English: Michael S. Farbman, *Bolshevism in Retreat* (Farbman 1923, pp. 246–57), and Lancelot Lawton, *An Economic History of Soviet Russia* (Lawton 1927, 1:174–9).

114   For Soviet writings contemporaneous with the original publication of this study, see my article 'Perestroika Looks Back', included in this volume. Among Western scholars holding similar views are Moshe Lewin, *The Making of the Soviet System: Essays in the Social History of Interwar Russia* (Lewin 1985, especially p. 261); Stephen Cohen, *Rethinking the Soviet*

had great faith in the state, but this can hardly be ascribed to the civil war. The world war and the civil war did lead to a new emphasis on state regulation of society, but this antedated the Bolsheviks and encompassed almost the entire political spectrum. In 1917, a food-supply official quoted the arch-liberal Peter Struve as calling for 'the coercive regulation of basic economic processes'.[115] A look at the land committees of 1917 will also help put the sowing-committee programme into perspective. Already deeply worried about sown acreage, officials of the Provisional Government declared sowing a state duty and gave local land committees wide powers to deal with the problem, including the right to take over unsown land.[116]

The Bolsheviks themselves did not undergo a process of statization, since they were strongly pro-state from the beginning.[117] Their enthusiasm for the state derived both from their Marxist principles and the general Russian political environment. Lenin's talk about the 'withering away of the state' is no proof to the contrary. For purposes of this slogan, Lenin carefully and rather arbitrarily defined the state as a repressive apparatus alien to society. If the revolution succeeded in its aim of overcoming the gulf between state and society and uniting 'dual Russia', then of course the state in this restricted sense would wither away. But before, during and after 1917, Lenin was always pro-state when he was not using this specialized definition – that is, most of the time.

The Bolsheviks' state orientation remained in force during NEP. Both Osinsky and Bogdanov had wanted agriculture brought into the state sphere by means of 'the monopolized market', and this remained the ideal during NEP, when the 'crowding-out' of the private market was a matter of pride. Of course, this state orientation, which assumed rational economic methods in partnership with the peasantry, had only a passing resemblance to Stalin's state-building.

The real change in the Bolshevik outlook during the revolution and civil war did not occur in the area of state orientation but rather in the area of the class-

---

Experience: Politics and History since 1917 (Cohen 1985, especially p. 49); Robert Tucker, Political Culture and Leadership in Soviet Russia: From Lenin to Gorbachev (Tucker 1987, especially p. 61).

115   N. Dolinsky (a high food-supply official both under the Tsar and the Provisional Government) Izvestiia po prodovolstvennomu delu, No. 1, pp. 5–9. For a longer statement by Struve along these lines, see Richard Pipes, Struve: Liberal on the Right, 1905–1944 (Pipes 1980, p. 224).

116   For a discussion of this neglected aspect of the 1917 land committees, see Lih 1990, pp. 91–7.

117   The point is well made in the context of 1917 by S.A. Smith, Red Petrograd: Revolution in the Factories 1917–1918 (Smith 1983, p. 153).

struggle versus partnership outlooks. A common view of this question is that the Bolsheviks went through a moderate phase in spring 1918 but then were radicalized by the civil war, with a sharp break in attitude occurring only in spring 1921. This interpretation is strengthened by Lenin's own reference in 1921 to his writings of 1918 as a forerunner of NEP. The first time Lenin returned to spring 1918 as a model, however, was at the Eighth Congress of Soviets in December 1920. David Dallin was sceptical: had not the Bolsheviks relied on force in spring 1918 as well?[118]

Dallin's scepticism is justified: spring 1918 was not the moderate forerunner of NEP that Lenin claimed it to be. The class-struggle view reigned supreme in 1917 and the first half of 1918, when it found its sharpest practical expression in the Committees of the Poor (*Kombedy*). It was the failure of the Committees of the Poor to solve the food-supply problem that led to some hard rethinking in the latter part of 1918 and finally to the policy of cooperation with the middle peasant that became official party policy in 1919. The change in perspective was only imperfectly assimilated, especially at the local level, and it is easy to point to evidence of class-struggle attitudes in 1920 and 1921. But contrary to the stereotype of war communism, the class-struggle attitude represented the heritage of the past, while the partnership outlook was growing in strength.

Taking a step back, we might ask which interpretation is *a priori* more plausible: that a group of extremist revolutionaries took power in a year of tumult, preached moderation and then grew radical or that they came in breathing fire and learned moderation as they shed their inexperience and took on responsibility for complex national problems? I would say the latter. It was the experience of common catastrophe that pushed the Bolsheviks into asking people to make sacrifices like brothers (*po-bratski*) rather than in the spirit of class war.[119]

The sowing-committee legislation was hardly the high point of an evolution leading in a direction away from NEP, nor even (as some Soviet historians maintain) a harbinger of NEP's change of direction.[120] Rather it was one more step in an evolution that began in 1918 and continued into NEP. So far as I know, only one other historian shares this interpretation of the sowing committees, but his testimony is valuable because he did not like what he saw. Lev Kritsman argued that contrary to a commonly held view, the economic collapse did not lead

118   Lenin 1958–1965, 42:137–8; *Vosmoi* 1921, pp. 197–9.

119   V. Karpinskii, asking the lucky to help the unlucky with sowing, in *Na borbu* 1921, pp. 75–8.

120   E.B. Genkina, *Gosudarstvennaia deiatelnost V.I. Lenina, 1921–1923* (Genkina 1967); Iurkov 1980. These are the best published accounts of the sowing committee legislation.

to centralization but rather to decentralization and petty-bourgeois degeneration. As an example of the process, he cited the switch from class struggle to
the industrious owner.[121]

Neither Lenin nor Osinsky saw the sowing campaign as incompatible with
NEP. In his speech to the Tenth Party Congress in March 1921, Lenin asserted
that the introduction of the food-supply tax did not contradict the sowing
campaign, since it continued 'the line of maximum support of the industrious
owner'. Lenin also referred to the industrious owner at the Ninth Congress of
Soviets in December 1921, where he pronounced to sowing campaign a qualified success.[122] There was no suggestion that the introduction of NEP in and of
itself ended the need for emergency measures.

Osinsky was associated with NEP from the very beginning, since he was a
member of the first Politburo commission to draft the legislation on the food-
supply tax. Osinsky's change of heart about the food-supply tax seems to have
resulted from his experience trying to get the sowing campaign off the ground,
since he wrote immediately after the Tenth Party Congress that the tax would
help the campaign leave the 'extremely strained and uncertain position' in
which it found itself.[123] Osinsky could accept the tax more easily because no
vain effort was being made to combine the tax with a continued prohibition of
free trade. He had argued earlier that 'speculation' was one of the factors staving
off the agricultural crisis, so he was not being inconsistent when he argued that
free trade had picked up where the bonus system of the sowing-committee legislation had left off in activating the private interest of the peasant in expanded
production.[124]

When Osinsky wrote a pamphlet a year after the Eighth Congress he did
not regard the sowing committees as an embarrassment but rather as a praise-
worthy legislative milestone. The *razverstka* had been necessary when the economic breakdown prevented the soviet authority from giving much of anything
to the peasants, and so officials had gotten into the habit of listening only to
their own reasons and shutting out the peasants' voice. In contrast, the sowing-
committee legislation had not only recognized the priority of improving agriculture but had been the first state initiative based from the beginning on the
possibility of cooperating with the peasants.[125]

---

121   Kritsman, *Geroicheskii period russkoi revoliutsii* (Kritsman 1924, pp. 208–16).
122   Lenin 1958–1965, 43:80–1; 44:313–14; see also Lenin 1958–1965, 43:272–3.
123   *Pravda*, 25 March 1921.
124   *Pravda*, 5 April 1921.
125   For the consistency of Osinsky's outlook, compare *Deviatii* 1934, pp. 199 (1920); *Pravda*,
       5 April 1921; Osinsky 1922, pp. 13–14. In a short autobiography written in the late 1920s, Osin-

The 'extraordinary measures' of 1928 and the subsequent forced collectivization did not mean a return to the 'war communist' methods of the sowing
committees – on the contrary, the industrious owners were the first to suffer from the 'great breakthrough'.[126] Stalin used violence not to help repay a
debt but to exact tribute from the peasantry, not to increase the productivity of
single-owner agriculture but to transform the peasant's mode of production. If
Stalin's onslaught was a return to anything, it was to the class-struggle radicalism of 1917 and early 1918. The sowing-committee legislation did not represent
war communism or proto-Stalinism: it was instead an important milestone in
the evolution of a possible Bolshevik alternative to Stalinism.

Appendix: Preamble to 'On Measures for the Strengthening and Development of Peasant Agriculture'

The victorious but burdensome struggle of the workers and peasants with Russian and foreign landowners, kulaks and capitalists, demanded great sacrifices
from the labouring peasants. They endured the ravages of the pillaging White
Guards. They suffered from the mobilization of workers and horses for the Red
Army, the defender of worker-peasant freedom.

They have received too few machines, scythes, iron, nails and the rest from
the factories and workshops destroyed by Kolchak and Denikin and deprived
by them of coal and raw materials. The import of goods from abroad necessary for the peasantry was stopped by the foreign landowners and capitalists.
Despite all the efforts of the worker-peasant authority and its concern for the
toiling peasantry, sown acreage in the last years has shrunk, the cultivation on
the land has worsened, and livestock has fallen onto a decline.

---

sky says that while Lenin was very interested in Osinsky's plans, he energetically protested
against the element of coercion (*prinuditelnost*). Lenin went on to draw the conclusion
that war communism was no longer viable. When Osinsky began work in the Agriculture
commissariat in early 1921, he was forced to carry out, not an ambitious 'state regulation
of agriculture', but merely 'well-planned and organized campaigns' (*planomerno organizo-
vannye kampanii*). See *Deiateli SSSR i revoliutsionnogo dvizheniia Rossii: Entsiklopedicheskii
slovar Granat* (*Deiateli* 1989, p. 573).

Osinsky's retrospective comment must be taken with due seriousness. Still, the political pressure to give all the credit to Lenin may have led Osinsky to be unfair to himself.
The documents show that 'well-planned and organized campaigns' were always Osinsky's
uppermost concern.

126   Stephan Merl, *Die Anfange der Kollektivierung in der Sowjetunion* (Merl 1985, especially
pp. 119, 136, 146).

Due to the efforts of the heroic Red Army, the last dangerous internal enemy, General Wrangel, has been crushed. For a time the pressure of the external enemy has slackened. The soviet authority again turns its main attention to peaceful construction and in the first place to the strengthening and development of peasant agriculture.

While recognizing agriculture as the most important branch of the economy of the Republic and placing the responsibility of intensified and comprehensive help to peasant agriculture on all organs of the soviet authority, the worker-peasant authority declares at the same time that the correct performance of agriculture is a high state responsibility of the peasant population.

The worker-peasant *vlast* demands that the state make every effort to help agriculture with livestock and equipment, repair stations and granaries, seed material, fertilizer, agronomic advice, and the like. At the same time, it demands of all agriculturalists the full sowing of the fields, according to the tasks set by the state, and the correct cultivation of the land, according to the example of the best and most industrious owners – middle peasants and poor peasants.

The harvest failure that overtook the country in 1920, as well as the drought that threatens in 1921 according to the indications of science and other signs, have created the necessity for special intensity and for especially harmonious work in the preparation and implementation of the agricultural campaign in 1921 according to a united plan and a united leadership.

Source: *Dekrety* 1958, pp. 80–1.

PART 4

Time of Troubles: Outlook (1914–1921)

••

Bolshevism's 'Services to the State': Three Russian Observers

If you want a coalition with the bourgeoisie, then conclude an 'honest coalition' with the Kadets – but, if the Kornilov mutiny taught you what the party of the proletariat has been saying from the very beginning of the revolution, then you will say the following: the only salvation for revolutionary Russia, the only way to restore confidence [*doverie*] between soldiers and officers within the army, the only way to establish confidence on the part of the peasants that they will receive the land, the only way to give the workers the feeling that they live in a republic – the only method to do all this is to take the *vlast* into the hand of the worker, peasant, and soldier organizations themselves.

∵

Speaking at the Democratic Conference in September 1917, Lev Kamenev made a rather unexpected case for the Bolsheviks.[1] The focus was not on world revolution, socialist transformation, the evil deeds of the propertied classes, or even concrete immediate slogans such as a democratic peace. Kamenev instead argued that the only way to achieve a stable state system able to defend itself and to move forward economically was to create a *vlast* based directly on the *narod*, with all that entailed. In contrast, the Russian elites were *incapable* of achieving their own central goal: an effective and legitimate sovereign authority.

This perspective on Bolshevism's historical role remained an understated one.[2] Those who supported Bolshevism were inspired by its goals of revolutionary transformation or, less benignly, by long-standing class hatred. Those

---

1 Zlokazov and Ioffe, eds (2002), *Iz istorii bor'by za vlast v 1917 godu*, p. 155. Note Lenin's misreading of this passage: he criticized it as a 'constitutional' call for 'confidence in the government' (Lenin 1958–1965, 34:254).

2 Nevertheless, the Bolshevik message to the soviet constituency in September and October

who opposed Bolshevism did so precisely because they saw Bolshevism as an immensely *destructive* force that spelled the ruin of the historic Russian state. An air of paradox remained – perhaps to this day – about the argument that Bolshevism was the only force capable of doing what all the other king's men had so signally failed to do: put the smashed Humpty Dumpty of Russian statehood back together again.

The purpose of this essay is to present the arguments of three Russian writers who forcefully made exactly this case in the early 1920s. These three writers cover just about the entire Russian political spectrum: the nationalist right (Sergei Lukianov), the Bolshevik left (Nikolai Bukharin), and almost the exact middle, straddling socialism and liberalism (Alexei Peshekhonov). All the more fascinating is the extensive overlap in their respective apologies for Bolshevism.

The most familiar form of what might be called the conservative defense of Bolshevism is a focus on the Bolshevik achievement in gathering together most of the tsarist empire and giving Russia a renewed Great Power status. The three writers examined here are more interested in a less familiar aspect of 'the state services of the Bolsheviks', namely, the creation of a new *vlast* ex nihilo after the utter collapse of 'the historic *vlast*' in February/March 1917. We can define *vlast* as 'the energizing centre for both state and government'.[3]

Our three writers focus, each in their own way, on the unexpected and hard-to-grasp challenges created by the disappearance of the historic *vlast*, on the doomed efforts of the well-meaning reformers of 1917 to meet these challenges, and on the Bolsheviks' constructive achievement – an achievement admittedly hard to discern amidst the violence and chaos of the civil war. In the pages that follow, I shall give a straightforward paraphrase of each writer's argument.

1 Alexei Peshekhonov

Alexei Peshekhonov (1867–1933) was one of the founders in 1906 of the small party Popular Socialists (or 'enesy').[4] This party was generally considered to be

---

1917 pointed to the paralysis of the current *vlast* and strongly emphasized that only a *narodnaia vlast* based on the soviets would be stable and effective.

3   Lih 1990, p. xvi. I go on to comment: 'No single translation of *vlast* will do … "sovereignty" has been my first choice and "authority" or "political authority" my second choice. The difference between the February and the October revolutions is that the first gave rise to a *pravitelstvo* [government] and the second to a *vlast*.'

4   The full name of the party was *Narodno-Sotsialisticheskaia Partiia*; it merged with the Tru-

situated barely to the left of the great dividing line between socialist and non-socialist parties on the Russian political spectrum – just a step away from the left-wing of the Constitutional Democrats (Kadets). The relation of the Popular Socialists to the Socialist Revolutionaries is comparable to the case of the Social Democratic 'liquidators' – if the latter had ever summoned up the nerve to become an independent party.

During the February revolution, Peshekhonov helped establish the authority of the Petrograd Soviet in the capital city's Petrograd District. His engaging memoirs about his experience earned him a place in Solzhenitsyn's *March 1917*, where he is one of the few historical characters to emerge in a sympathetic light.[5] In May, he became the first head of Provisional Government's newly created Ministry of Food Supply and also one of the government's most ardent advocates of coalition. After his resignation in August, his public worries about economic collapse and government helplessness earned him sarcastic applause from Lenin.[6] The disillusionment he later expressed with the Provisional Government came from direct personal experience.

After the revolution, Peshekhonov participated in various anti-Bolshevik groups, but did not emigrate. He gradually moved closer to cooperation with the Bolsheviks and finally took on important government positions as a statistician in Ukraine and Moscow. In 1922, he was expelled along with other Russian intellectuals, a move he bitterly resented. He repeatedly asked for permission to return, but never succeeded in doing so until after his death. His ashes were buried in Leningrad, next to those of his mentor, the Narodnik pioneer, Nikolai Mikhailovsky.

Immediately after his forced removal from Russia, Peshekhonov wrote a small book entitled *Why I Didn't Emigrate*.[7] The aim of the book was to explain his position to other émigrés, many of whom regarded as a traitor anyone who stayed or, even worse, accepted work from the Soviet government. I first became interested in Peshekhonov while doing research on the politics of food-supply during the revolutionary period. When reading his little book of 1923, I was immediately struck by the section in the book in which he defiantly praised the 'services to the state' of the Bolsheviks. Peshekhonov's outlook chimed in

---

doviks in 1917. The party programme can be found at http://dlib.rsl.ru/viewer/01004097304#
?page=1. For useful articles on the party and on Peshekhonov by N.D. Erofeev, see Shelokhaev
1994 (*Politicheskaia istoriia Rossii v partiiakh i litsakh*), pp. 74–92, 145–73.

5 Hasegawa 1981, *The February Revolution: Petrograd 1917*, pp. 385–7; Solzhenitsyn 1986, *Mart semnadtsatogo*.

6 Lenin 1957–1962, 34:330–2.

7 Peshekhonov 1923, *Pochemu ia ne emigriroval*.

with the 'time-of-troubles' perspective that I employed in my monograph on food-supply politics and gave it the solidity of direct personal experience.[8]

Acting on my belief that Peshekhonov's essay presented a very valuable insight into the realities of the revolutionary period, I translated the relevant chapter some years ago in its entirety and circulated to colleagues at conferences and elsewhere. Recently I was pleased to discover that my high opinion was shared by Vitaly Startsev, who quoted the essay at a length quite unusual for a non-Bolshevik source.[9] I am glad to have this opportunity to make the essay publicly available. There is no need for further comment or paraphrase, since Peshekhonov makes his points clearly, concisely and vividly.

1.1   *The Bolsheviks and Effective State Authority [gosudarstvennost']*[10]

Soon after my arrival abroad, an article in one of the local papers – if I remember correctly, *Rul'* – cited an extract from the works of L.N. Tolstoy about Peter the Great. Characterizing Peter with the most horrific traits, Tolstoy at the same time mocked historians who invented and ascribed great services to the state to the credit of this monster and drunkard and in this way not only sought to justify but to glorify him in the eyes of posterity. After citing this extract, the article added some ironical commentary to the effect that perhaps people will be found that will invent and ascribe to the Bolsheviks some kind of services to the state in order to justify all their cruelties.

I consider myself obliged to respond to this challenge and say a few words about the 'services to the state' of the Bolsheviks. Of course, I do not do this in order to justify everything they have done nor because I find pleasure in being a devil's advocate. No! I am obliged to warn of the dangers that under certain circumstances could threaten Russia, if the 'services to the state' of the Bolsheviks are not acknowledged in time. And that this danger threatens us – that is clear already from the ironical commentary just cited and from many others that I have already had occasion to hear abroad.

Yes, I am convinced that the Bolsheviks have accomplished something great, and I will state it straight out: they re-established an effective state

---

8   Lih 1990 (*Bread and Authority*).
9   Startsev 1980 (*Vnutrenniaia politika vremennogo pravitel'stva*).
10   Peshekhonov 1923 (*Pochemu ia ne emigriroval*), pp. 50–60. For purposes of this selection, I have rendered Peshekhonov's key term *gosudarstvennost'* as 'effective state authority'. The chapter is translated in its entirety; all ellipses are in the original.

authority. 'How's this? – they're the ones who destroyed it!' – undoubtedly, many readers will respond in this way. I don't deny it. Yes, the Bolsheviks – not only they, but they for the most part – destroyed an effective state authority, but they are also the ones who recreated it. Let's recall how things were ...

On February 27, 1917, the old state *vlast* was overthrown. The Provisional Government that replaced it was not a state *vlast* in the genuine sense of the word: it was only the symbol of *vlast*, the carrier of the idea of *vlast*, or at best its embryo. The Provisional Government was not in a position to become a genuine state *vlast* or in any event did not succeed in becoming one – explain it how you will. The fact remains that during this period a state *vlast* was not established.

Together with the overthrow of the old state *vlast* also began a rapid destruction of the mechanism by which it maintained itself and without which no state *vlast* could exist. In Petrograd this happened at the same time as the overthrow of the autocracy. The machinery of state administration was thrown immediately out of kilter; those parts which were most vital from the point of view of the existence of a state *vlast* were completely destroyed. Courts, police, and other organs of state coercion were swept away without trace. Along with them vanished another foundation of state *vlast*: the Petrograd garrison troops emerged from the changeover utterly unable to serve as a support for the *vlast* – indeed, they were more of a threat. This process of destruction quickly spread to all local organs, down to the lowest, and to the army, in the rear and in the front.

The realization that the state *vlast* had vanished did not, of course, spread to the broad masses of the population right away. In the village this realization came about only in May, and in remote spots even later; at the front the situation revealed it with complete clarity in the second half of June [at the time of the full-scale military offensive]. If any state order at all continued to maintain itself, this was for the most part by inertia. The forces needed to support it with compulsion were simply not there.

The new apparatus of state administration was formed very slowly. Why this happened, I cannot now say. The fact remains that organs of local administration did not exist in the rural localities even in the fall, and organs of state coercion had also not been brought into any kind of system. No steps at all were taken toward the creation of new armed forces on which a state *vlast* could rely – up to the end people lived in the hope that they would manage to keep the old army from disintegrating.

In this process of destruction, the Bolsheviks played an outstanding role. They were also the main obstacle for the establishment of a new

state order. With their takeover, they so to speak finished off any effective Russian state *vlast*: they decisively destroyed the army and swept off
the face of the earth even those rudiments of a new state apparatus that
the Provisional Government had tried to create. The country was thrown
literally into anarchy.

There was in reality no legislative, no judicial, and no administrative
vlast. Anyone who wanted could legislate as best suited him. The Litovskii
regiment, quartered in the Vasileostrovskii section of Petrograd, issued
decrees for all of Russia – but of course, even in Vasileostrovskii, where
these decrees were posted, their actual force was doubtful, to say the least.
The legislative *vlast* of Smolny [where the central organs of the new Soviet
government were housed] was just a little bit stronger. It wasn't always in
the position to get its decrees posted in public places. Even in Petrograd
we would stroll at first into the revolutionary tribunal as into a theater
where a new and merry farce was playing. Even the tribunal was evidently
far from sure of its strength and at first limited itself mainly to 'public cen-
sure'. I could illustrate the powerlessness of administrative *vlast* during
these first months of with a series of episodes from my own life, but the
following shows it best. In March or April 1918, that is, something like six
months after the Bolshevik takeover, I happened to meet in Moscow the
chauffeur who had driven me when I was a member of the Provisional
Government. We greeted each other like old friends.

'Well', I asked, 'how are you getting along? Once you drove the Tsar
around, and now who?'

'There's no way around it', he said, 'I have to work for the Bolsheviks …
But you know I don't submit to them all that much. Yesterday Comrade
(and he named one of the People's Commissars) sent for an automobile, and I, as the secretary of our organization, answered him in writing:
there's a *vlast* up there, but there's also a *vlast* down here – we won't give
you an automobile!'

When the *vlast* at the bottom is no less strong than the *vlast* at the top,
then one can say that there is no *vlast* at all. And so for this reason even in
Petrograd it was then easy not to acknowledge the soviet *vlast* – although,
of course, not so easy as for people now living abroad.

But having finished off an effective state authority – which, from their
point of view, was nothing more than the organization of the class domination of the bourgeoisie – the Bolsheviks were immediately compelled
to begin work on its recreation in the interests of their own domination.
Here they showed unheard-of energy, stubborn stick-to-it-iveness and an
uncanny inventiveness. They stopped at nothing. The most irresponsible

demagoguery, brazen frauds, inhuman cruelty – these were their main tools. They created a mass of absurdities, led the people to unbelievable hunger and impoverishment, and covered the country with blood ...

But an effective Russian state authority was recreated. In the course of the past five years the Bolsheviks have re-established the fullness of a state *vlast* and again stretched it across the giant territory from the Dniestr to the Pacific Ocean and from the Arctic Ocean down to Afghanistan.

Most difficult of all of course was the recreation of the army, which in the final analysis is the chief support of a state *vlast*. I remember that in the middle of 1918 I had a conversation with General Boldyrev, to whom the Union of Regeneration [a left-wing, anti-Bolshevik government in Siberia] had given the assignment of thinking through this task. He was finding it exceedingly difficult. Indeed, one can find several hundred or even thousand men who for the sake of an idea, for ambition, or for material advantage will submit to discipline and even to risk their lives. But you need not hundreds and not thousands and even not tens of thousands, but hundreds of thousands and possibly even a million men – and men who are willing to go to their death. And this army is to be recreated not in peaceful times, but in the midst of enemies pressing on all sides. Where is there a guarantee that the state *vlast* – and remember, one that has just been born, still weak and unrecognized – will succeed in mobilizing these tens and hundreds of thousands of men? Where is the guarantee that once they are gathered and hastily trained they will submit to the commands of this *vlast*? Wouldn't they prefer simply to go off to their homes or into the forest, rather than go to their death? Of course, one can gather up others, but where is the guarantee that the same thing won't happen again? This could go on forever, like the story of the white steer [a children's game of infinite repetition]. Or everything could fall apart at once. Before running off to their homes, the troops might just overthrow the *vlast* itself. If the old army, under the pressure of the age-old conviction that there is no hiding from the state *vlast* and no escaping it – if this army finally mutinied even while facing the enemy, then how do you create a new army? An army that knows that the state *vlast* can be overthrown and includes among its members many who themselves participated in this overthrow?

The Bolsheviks overcame these boundless difficulties. They didn't succeed right away in creating an army worthy of the name – there were more than a few failures. Laughable as it was, one didn't feel like laughing when they sent their 'Red Guard' to the front to fight the Germans. With the Red Guard one could 'nationalize' banks or even disband the

Constituent Assembly, but of course they were no match for the German army in numbers, in organization, or in discipline. Whole units of
Red Guards fled at the sight of one German. And the Germans continued their triumphal march right up to Petrograd. The Bolsheviks didn't
let themselves get upset. They signed the 'shameful peace' and received a
'breathing space'. And meanwhile they found Latvians, Hungarians, Chinese, and with their help began to administer Russia and create a Russian
army. This force was sufficient to spread the bloody doings of the Cheka
throughout all of soviet territory and even to catch a sufficient number
of deserters and turn them into Red Army men, but it wasn't enough to
hold together the army created in this way. It took a while to succeed in
holding the army together with the internal cement of mobilized communists. The army continued to disintegrate, and more than once it seemed
on the verge of falling apart. The future historian will probably stand in
bafflement before the vicissitudes of our civil war. How can you explain
it – first the Whites rout the Reds, and then the Reds rout the Whites, and
not just once but many times and on all fronts. But the secret is simple:
first the Red Army would fall apart, then the White Army, and then start
to flee helter-skelter. And then once more you would whip together an
army and again lead them into attack. The Bolsheviks' nerves proved to
be stronger, they showed more persistence, and also at the top there was
more unanimity. And finally they conquered on all fronts. The soviet *vlast*
came out of the struggle with an army that hadn't fallen apart and that in
some of its parts was even hardened. Under the conditions of peacetime,
it was incomparably easier to secure the necessary command staff, to provide necessary material and to maintain discipline.

And they undoubtedly have achieved this task to a significant extent ...
It is difficult to judge from the side lines. But I must say that soviet troops
give in recent times a far from disheartening impression with their bearing, their discipline and their external appearance in general. Of course,
this army has no assurance against collapse – but again, what army in our
days has full assurance against this? But it seems to me that the state *vlast*
can already rely on this army without excessive risk in internal matters,
and under certain circumstances in external struggles as well.

The Bolsheviks had to take even longer to re-establish the state apparatus than to recreate the army – and not because this task was inherently
so difficult, but because they had no idea of how to go about it. It was no
help that they tried for so long to give the state apparatus a class character.
In each and every part, they would time without number build and pull
down, again build and again pull down. The observer was forced to say:

'no matter how much you practice, you'll never be musicians'. And indeed there were no experienced 'musicians' in their number whatsoever. But bit by bit they learned, and among them some talent even became evident. They [at first] imagined that the essential truth was that they could not do without 'specialists' [middle-class experts]. The Communists had not always been able to evaluate the specialists or to understand them, but in any event the specialists were not the basic problem – they were even enlisted in excessive numbers. And in general the apparatus was built up to bulky dimensions beyond the capacity of the country to support. Then mostly under the pressure of material difficulties, the soviet *vlast* began to squeeze and simplify the apparatus. This operation is not yet complete. And in other respects the state apparatus cannot be called complete: there is much that is clumsy, unnecessary, inexpedient, and even absurd.

Yet it is in no way as ridiculous as it was in the beginning, and even in its present condition it fulfils its function in a satisfactory enough fashion. It is adequately differentiated and specialized in its separate spheres of life and throughout the whole territory, reaching all the way down to the lower depths. The separate parts have gotten used to each other and work together; there is no longer (almost) that lack of coordination between them – especially the lack of coordination between the central institutions and the local organs that for a long time was characteristic of the soviet apparatus. The state *vlast* can rest assured that its orders will go out without any special distortion to any point in its territory and almost everywhere there will be organs that will observe these orders and carry them out.

The activity of these organs has already been brought into a certain framework and is regulated by a whole series of decrees, regulations and instructions. There was a time when Mr. Stuchka [People's Commissar of Justice] could propose for his direction of the courts only the courts' own revolutionary consciousness and the minimum programme of the socialist parties. At the present time, as you know, criminal and civil codes are in place, forms of court procedure have been established, and so on. The same thing in other areas – take, let's say, legislative activity. Of course, if it is necessary, the Central Committee of the Communist Party can carry through a decree that it needs in several hours. But now as a general rule every draft law goes through regular channels, receives the opinions of the various departments, and so on. This is already a guarantee that at least decrees won't be published whose effects are unexpected surprises even for the soviet *vlast* itself. Of course, in the norms that direct the work of soviet institutions, there is much that is not covered, or more often, there is excessive regulation; the norms themselves are badly coordinated and contain much that is absurd, even illiterate, but even so one must admit that the giant work of regulating the work of state organs has now been accomplished.

Also accomplished is another task that is perhaps even more important and difficult in the matter of recreating an effective state authority: the coercive force of the state *vlast* has been re-established in the popular consciousness. I admit that when I was a member of the Provisional Government I viewed this task – of course, one of the most urgent – with fear. Who will compel the population to carry out the orders of the *vlast*, and how? In particular, who will compel it to contribute taxes and fulfill state-imposed obligations? You can't do this with admonitions alone. A systematic persistence that does not stop before repressions is required. Would the new *vlast* [established in February] exhibit the stern decisiveness for taking on this 'dirty business'? Or would it just put it off day after day? Well, in that case it would clearly never be a genuine *vlast* ... Of course, there were reasons for being dilatory: one must wait until the revolutionary flames cool down; an apparatus must be created first; it would be best to await the true master of the Russian land, the Constituent Assembly ... In a word, there wasn't enough of the necessary decisiveness.

The Bolsheviks found this stern decisiveness in themselves. More than that: they showed an unheard-of and completely excessive cruelty. And they attained their goal ... I noted above that Bolshevik decrees were far from completely carried out at first and sometimes hardly at all. This was because on the one hand they were primitive, absurd, unrealizable, and on the other hand, the soviet apparatus was not in a position to reach all those who refused to obey. But those it reached were shown no mercy. As that apparatus was perfected, the possibility and therefore the inclination not to obey became less and less. And now one can say that the Bolshevik decrees are not simply written in vain: they are carried out almost as a law should be. In particular, taxes are collected promptly enough.

An effective Russian state authority has been re-established ... Oh, I am not at all a supporter of the methods by which the Bolsheviks did this. And this effective state authority of the Bolsheviks is in my view not only still imperfect, but much worse than the one they destroyed. I continue to think that, with the aid of incomparably milder measures, incomparably better results could have been attained. But even so, I am not going to deny the 'services to the state' of the Bolsheviks.

More than that – I am ready to turn to any of the claimants who calculate on taking the place of Lenin and say: don't destroy what the Bolsheviks have already done! Don't tear apart the soviet army – it would be better to control it, if you can. Don't break up the soviet apparatus: better to remake it according to taste. And do not undermine yet again the prestige of the state *vlast*, because you may not be able to re-establish it anew.

2   Sergei Lukianov

Sergei Lukianov was born in 1888 into a well-off intelligentsia family; his father was at one time chief procurator of the Holy Synod.[11] Before the revolution, he showed Kadet sympathies but otherwise was not politically involved. Cosson describes him as a historian of art, a translator, and a journalistic essay writer. In late 1920, he made his way to Paris, where he gave what was considered a rather scandalous lecture in February 1921 that called on émigrés to adopt a more positive attitude toward the Soviet Union. This lecture inspired Iurii Kliuchnikov to pull together the collective of writers who published *Smena vekh* in Prague in late 1921.[12] The title, 'Changing Signposts', is a direct reference to the famous 1909 collection of essays *Vekhi*, in which a group of prominent liberal intellectuals denounced traditional intelligentsia revolutionism.

In the secondary literature on the *Smena vekh* movement, most attention has gone to the editor, Iurii Kliuchnikov, or the collection's most prominent contributor, Nikolai Ustrialov. The themes of greatest interest to scholars have been admiration of the Bolshevik achievement in preserving Russia's status as a great power, the hopeful search for signs of an evolution in Bolshevism toward moderation, and the call for the Russian émigrés to reconcile with the Soviet Union. These themes are present in Lukianov's essay, but they are far from central. As a result, his essay has been marginalized in the literature, with only scattered and not highly representative comments quoted.

Academic observers also marginalize the *Smena vekh* writers as a group by reducing their outlook to the vagaries of exotic Russian intellectual traditions.

---

11   Biographical data is taken from Hilda Hardeman 1994, *Coming to Terms with the Soviet Regime* and Yves-Marie Cosson 2005, *Le Changement de Jalons*. In case of disagreement, I have adopted Cosson, the later source.

12   *Smena vekh* (Kliuchnikov et al. 1921).

In particular, the concern with social breakdown and anarchy is explained as a manifestation of a 'statist tradition' in Russian historiography. It seems that only those imbued with 'the mystique of the state' would share these concerns.[13] This kind of pigeonholing explanation actively discourages taking any of these essays seriously as valid observations or intellectually challenging interpretations.

After the publication of *Smena vekh*, Lukianov moved to Berlin and worked for a couple of years as an editor and contributor to various offshoots of the *Smena vekh* movement. In 1924, he returned to Paris and worked even more directly with Soviet-inspired initiatives, leading to his expulsion from France in 1926–1927. He then returned to Russia, where he was treated fairly well for a number of years – in fact, he became the first editor of the French-language weekly of the Foreign Affairs Commissariat, *Le Journal de Moscou*. Nevertheless, he was caught up in the repression that followed the Kirov assassination in 1935 and died in the camps in 1938.

In my view, Lukianov's article deserves serious attention as a hard-hitting interpretation of events. I hope to bring out these qualities by taking the article out of the context of *Smena vekh* itself and placing it alongside Peshekhonov and Bukharin. In 2005, a French translation of the entire collection appeared.[14] Only recently have substantial excerpts of *Smena vekh* been reprinted in Russian.[15] Since the text of the article is not easily available, I will give a close paraphrase with numerous excerpts. I have, however, skipped over Lukianov's long analysis of the original 'time of troubles' in the seventeenth century.

According to Lukianov, the Russian *vlast* has always needed a strong social base that would not only provide support for it but also help carry out its fundamental tasks of external independence and internal order. By the early twentieth century, the social base of the autocracy – the landowning gentry – had lived past its expiry date. It was no longer of much use in meeting the country's challenges; on the contrary, the autocracy was prevented from undertaking any effective response by the selfish class interests of the gentry.

After the collapse of the autocracy, two paths were open: the way of the responsible and realistic reformers and the way of the irresponsible and pro-

---

13 Hardeman 1994, pp. 80–2; see also Jane Burbank 1986 (*Intelligentsia and Revolution*) and Mikhail Agursky 1987 (*The Third Rome: National Bolshevism in the USSR*).

14 Cosson 2005; Lukianov's essay is on pp. 87–103.

15 *Smenovekhovstvo: pro et contra* (Bazanov (ed.) 2021). This entry in the long-running 'Pro et Contra' series contains a wide variety of contextual documents; I regret that I have not been able to consult it for this essay.

foundly unrealistic demagogues. The grim paradox was that the demagogues – precisely because of their demagoguery – proved to be the most realistic and the most responsible.

> At that time, who would have entertained the idea that the bitter opponents of 'war to final victory', those who preached extreme internationalism, people who started with calling for one hundred percent taxation and ended by calling for complete elimination of the bourgeoisie – that these elements, seemingly anti-state and anti-national through and through, could serve as a genuine foundation for a future Russian *vlast* that was imbued with the state principle and was thoroughly national?

Let us examine, through Lukianov's eyes, the dilemma of the responsible reformers, that is, the liberals and moderate socialists who formed the Provisional Government of 1917. The liberals had distinguished themselves before the revolution by their drive to *limit* power, not to create it. The tsarist establishment had not bothered to cooperate with them precisely because they were so evidently unable to provide significant social support to risky reform efforts. Corresponding to the vain liberal wish to create an 'above-class' *vlast* was what Lukianov calls the 'pseudo-class *vlast*' of the moderate socialists, who 'wished to rely on a specific class but spoke a language alien to its sense of the economy and its sense of justice'.

These reformers had several possible paths toward solving the problem of social support – all of them doomed. They could continue their pre-revolutionary project of preparing the *narod* for self-rule by working (and waiting) for 'the progressive raising of the cultural level of the peasants and transferring the *vlast* to them only after their thorough re-education'. But this project foundered on the post-revolutionary impossibility of asking the peasant and the proletariat to wait patiently until their betters thought they were ready.

The unrealistic hopes placed in the Constituent Assembly sprang from a partial grasp of this unsolvable dilemma. The hope was that a promised election based on 'universal, equal, secret and direct suffrage' would generate a legitimacy with the magic power of convincing the masses to wait for reforms throughout 1917 and then afterwards to accept the orderly decisions of the Assembly, while undergoing the sacrifices needed to carry them out. But 'the shameful fiasco – both material and moral – of the Constituent Assembly should have opened the eyes of even the most incorrigible of optimistic dreamers about the nature of the revolution and its *vlast*'.

As intelligentsia reformers moved past wishful thinking about relying on 'the confidence of the masses', they felt the need to throw in their lot with other elite classes such as the industrial bourgeoisie and the progressive landowners. But this 'realism' was based on the further illusion that these other elite classes had any intention of carrying out the reforms desired by the intelligentsia. Ultimately, in fact, this path led to total reliance on the one non-soviet source of real power, namely, the reactionary officer corps.

The history of the White movement showed just how little influence the intelligentsia had in any such alliance with former elites – and all to no avail, as the White movement itself was unable to find stable social support. The Whites (and even the Provisional Government!) saw the need for a firm hand (*tverdaia vlast*) and a strict dictatorship, but they were incapable of actually creating one.

There remained another path for the responsible reformer: carry out the reforms desired by the *narod* and by this means gain the confidence needed to stabilize the situation. Some voices in the Provisional Government advocated this path [and still today, I might add, some historians regret this path not taken]. But it was one that the reformers could not take, precisely because of their sense of responsibility. According to Lukianov, they reasoned as follows: 'Reforms are indispensable, but they mustn't weaken the economic, financial and military strength of the country, nor destroy cultural and legal values, even if these values are alien to the majority of the *narod*'. He goes on to comment: 'This prudence [*ostorozhnost'*] of the political leaders of the first half of 1917 was their principal and unpardonable failure – their crime against the Revolution and, as a consequence, against Russia.'[16]

In this passage, Lukianov is harsh on the responsible reformers of the Provisional Government, but elsewhere he shows more sympathy into the inescapable double bind that they faced:

> We cannot demand a prophetic clairvoyance from people, and none of the members of the Provisional Government could have committed themselves in an organic manner on the remaining alternative path: the belief that a worker-peasant *vlast* could be established immediately. More: to install such a *vlast* inevitably implied that one had to plunge for a time into the murkiness of the arbitrary – of bloodshed and the destruction of material and cultural values.

Enter the Bolsheviks. The Bolsheviks were irresponsible, fanatical demagogues – and this was a good thing, because fanatical demagogues were just

---

16   Peshekhonov was one of the foremost spokesman for this attitude in 1917; his motto was 'as much prudence, as little rupture, as possible' ('pobol'she ostorozhnosti, pomen'she lomki'); see Shelokhaev 1994, p. 169.

what was needed. Only such people could look at the unruly mob of demobi-
lized peasants in uniform and see in them the elements of a stable and progressive 'worker-peasant *vlast*'. And only such extremists could be accepted by
the mob as their kind of people. This cultural coherence allowed the new post-
October *vlast* to bridge over its many false moves as well as the widespread
popular incomprehension of even its rational and necessary moves.[17]

The Bolsheviks had another advantage in accomplishing the necessary but
seemingly impossible project of building a stable twentieth-century *vlast* on
such an archaic popular base: the urban workers, who were more culturally
advanced than the peasants but who still retained psychological ties with them,
in contrast to Western European countries.

> There is no need to dilate at length on the reasons that not only made
> the urban proletarian masses useful in the establishment of a revolution-
> ary *vlast* in October 1917, but also made them strong enough to give this
> *vlast* some solidity, after it had been organized ... True, during the last
> few years, the internal contradictions between countryside and town have
> often placed the soviet *vlast* in a very difficult position – but precisely this
> challenge has forced the *vlast* to be much more flexible and open to an
> evolution in tactics, as well as constrain the *vlast* to concern itself with
> the preservation of the town and its intellectual and artistic culture.

I do not know if Lukianov was aware that his argument about the role of the
urban workers is a version of Bolshevism's long-held scenario of 'hegemony'.
In fact, Lukianov's whole approach can be seen as a sceptical and 'realist' version of this scenario. Its basic logic came from the Bolshevik assertion that
the socialist proletariat was the natural leader in achieving the nation's *short-
term* goals precisely because of its fervent commitment to the *long-term* goal of
socialism. Lukianov was much more interested in the short-term goals than the
long-term socialist utopia that he no doubt dismissed as unrealistic dreaming.
He nevertheless argued for the essential role played by such fantastic dreams.

Lukianov is ready to rebut fellow émigrés who explained Bolshevik success
by their ruthless mass terror. Even the ability to organize a terror showed that
they had more solid roots in social reality than their opponents. Furthermore,
'the violence that at a precise historical moment took the inevitable (but none

---

17   Lukianov's argument on this point is supported by political scientist Harry Eckstein's 'con-
      gruence theory', which states that political stability requires cultural congruence between
      society and the forms of government. See Eckstein 1961, *A Theory of Stable Democracy* and
      Eckstein, ed. 1998, *Can Democracy Take Root in Post-Soviet Russia?*

the less horrifying for that) form of terror was indispensable during the period when the new base of national life and the *vlast* was still establishing and organizing itself'. Having gone so far in justifying mass violence, Lukianov hopefully points to the signs that the terror is now receding.

The Bolsheviks were not the only ones to evolve and to become more realistic. Lukianov points to a growing 'statization' on the part of the population. By 'statization' he means a greater appreciation of why a state is necessary and therefore why it requires support.

> After beginning with the categorical negation of the state, the proletariat and the peasantry now recognize perfectly well that, under present conditions, the state as well as the state *vlast* are indispensable – indeed, that their viability is directly linked to the existence of each citizen taken separately. In truth, without realizing it ourselves, we are witnessing the birth of a genuine sense of Russian citizenship and of a Russian state indissolubly tied to it.

In particular, the success of the Red Army can be explained by the success of the *vlast*, and not the other way around:

> The success of the Red Army in the struggle against the White movement would be completely inexplicable if we tried to show that the peasantry did not have a massive preference for *its own* soviet *vlast* as opposed to the 'counterrevolutionary' *vlast* that was surrounded by generals, directed by intellectual circles that claimed to be liberal and sometimes even 'socialist', and that relied (and this is the root of the matter) on those elements of the old social base that had outlived themselves.

Not only the peasants but the workers changed their attitudes. The workers moved from purely selfish redistributive demands to an appreciation of the need to *create* national wealth. Furthermore, automatic hostility toward the intelligentsia had mellowed into a sense of its necessary contribution to the cause of the people [as we shall see, this theme finds an echo in Bukharin].

Lukianov thus ends on a rather optimistic note. Nevertheless, the main thread of his argument is to show the irrelevance of asking whether the price paid for these meagre accomplishments was too high:

> The Russian revolution inevitably had to acquire an extremist character, and this, in its turn, had just as inevitably to find its guiding element in Russian Bolshevism. The Russian revolution could not help being

accompanied by enormous losses, measured in human lives as well as cultural values. If the Bolshevik socialists had not existed, the elemental storm [*stikhiia*] of the revolution would have engendered something much more terrifying – less because of the murders and pillaging than because of the threat of a degeneration of the revolution into anarchy and riot [*bunt*], with their inevitable conclusion: a death-like restoration.

3   Nikolai Bukharin

In spring 1920, Nikolai Bukharin, one of the top leaders of the Bolshevik party who was regarded as its accredited theorist, published a treatise entitled *Ekonomika perekhodnogo perioda*. *Ekonomika* (as we shall henceforth refer to the book) has been translated into English, but this operation removed only the most superficial barrier to understanding Bukharin's argument.[18] Bukharin writes in a strange, highly abstract jargon of his own invention, made up of equal parts of Marxese, sociological terms such as 'equilibrium', and new locutions coined by Bukharin himself. A good example of this jargon is 'negative expanded reproduction', which can be defined as 'a spiralling economic collapse'.

This jargon is not the only unusual barrier to understanding. Bukharin's real subject is the collapse of the Russian economy between 1917 and 1920, plus the policies adopted by the Bolsheviks to restore a minimal 'equilibrium'. Bukharin described these concrete policies in highly abstract terms because he wanted to present them as instances of a *general* process characteristic of all social revolutions. This strategy, besides its strictly theoretical motivations, suited Bukharin's polemical aim of excusing the Bolsheviks by showing Russian economic collapse as an inevitable cost of *any* profound revolution.

A knowledge of actual Bolshevik policies during the civil war is thus essential background for the necessary operation of decoding Bukharin's argument and grasping the real point hidden behind the fancy language. Owing to these various difficulties, Bukharin's argument has been persistently misunderstood and in fact turned on its head. *Ekonomika* is presented as a manifestation of the alleged psychology of war communism, during which (in Martin Malia's words)

---

18   Bukharin, *Ekonomika perekhodnogo perioda*; page numbers in the text refer to this edition. For an English translation, see Bukharin 1979, *The Politics and Economics of the Transition Period* (edited by Kenneth Tarbuck, translated by Oliver Field). In 1921, Bukharin defended the *Ekonomika* against Bolshevik critics; see 'Bukharin on Bolshevik "Illusions": "War Communism" vs. NEP', included in this volume.

'in a veritable ideological delirium, the most colossal economic collapse of the century was transmogrified into really-existing Communism, the radiant future *hic et nunc*'.[19] In reality, Bukharin's book is one long excuse for the Bolshevik failure to deliver on their promises of prosperity and socialist transformation.

A closer look at the title of the book will clear away some possible misconceptions. *Ekonomika perekhodogo perioda* is usually translated as 'Economics of the Transition Period'. 'Economy' is a more accurate rendering of *ekonomika* and gives a better idea of Bukharin's actual focus. He is interested in the empirical fate of the economy during the revolutionary period rather than creating an original economic theory (the one section of the book that deals with such things was drafted by his friend Iurii Piatakov). In fact, his real focus throughout is *class relations*: how antagonistic class relations led to widespread social and economic breakdown and how a new set of class relations made reconstitution possible.

The term 'transition period' is also potentially misleading. This term is easily understood as referring to the long-term transition between capitalism and full socialism, and Bukharin does occasionally use the term in this manner. Nevertheless, the real meaning of 'transition period' in his 1920 treatise is the short-term revolutionary crisis that begins with the collapse of capitalist economic institutions and ends when the new proletarian *vlast* manages to restore the minimal economic equilibrium necessary for any real economic progress. As Bukharin puts it in his generalizing way:

> The communist revolution of the proletariat, like any revolution, is accompanied with a *lowering* of productive forces. The civil war – especially one that partakes of the gigantic dimensions of contemporary class wars in which not only the bourgeoisie but the proletariat are organized as a state *vlast* – is *economically*, from the point of view of *current reproductive cycles*, a pure loss … The costs of revolution and civil war will appear [in historical perspective] as the temporary lowering of productive forces that nevertheless created the base for a tremendous development, *reconstructing productive relations* on a new basis … (50)
>
> The disintegration and falling-apart of the old system and the organization of the new: this is the *basic* and most general regularity of a transition period (154).

---

19   Malia 1994, *The Soviet Tragedy*, p. 130. As an example, Malia cites Bukharin and Preobrazhensky's 1919 popularization *ABC of Communism*. In actuality, the *ABC* delivers the same message as *Ekonomika*. See 'The Mystery of the *ABC*', included in this volume.

I have discussed interpretive issues in more detail elsewhere.[20] For purposes of this essay, I shall paraphrase Bukharin's account without further justification. My focus will be less on Bukharin's general theory than his interpretation of the Russian revolutionary experience.

We can best grasp Bukharin's vision by looking at the concrete case of the breakdown and reconstitution of the Russian Army. The birth of the Red Army from the collapse of the tsarist army is a paradigm – an especially pure and vivid example – of the process that Bukharin sees throughout society and the economy as a whole.

The Red Army paradigm can already be found in the *Programma kommunistov* that Bukharin published in the summer of 1918.[21] Bukharin is rebutting the accusation made by the moderate socialists that the Bolsheviks destroyed the army. Bukharin agrees with his accusers that the breakdown of such an essential institution is in itself a bad thing. His defense is that this breakdown was *inevitable* and that the Bolsheviks showed the *only* path to the army's reconstitution. The tsarist army operated on the basis of a class hierarchy that reflected the outside society: officer corps recruited from nobles and bourgeoisie faced soldiers recruited from the lower classes, particularly the peasants. If this class hierarchy no longer functioned properly, neither did the army. And this is exactly what was happening even before February 1917:

It is evident that with the Revolution, the army entirely resting on the old Tsarist basis, the army driven to slaughter for the purpose of conquering Constantinople even by Kerensky, must inevitably have become disorganized. Do you ask why? Because the soldiers saw that they were being organized, trained and thrown into battle for the sake of the criminal cupidity of the bourgeoisie. They saw that for nearly three years they sat in the trenches, perished, hungered, suffered, and died and killed others all for the sake of somebody's money-bags. It is natural enough that when the revolution had displaced the old discipline and a new one had not yet had time to be formed, the collapse, ruin and death of the old army took place.

This disease was inevitable ... The soldiers' rising against the Tsar was already the result of the disorganization of the Tsarist army. Every revolu-

---

20   Lih, 'Bukharin's "Illusions": "War Communism" vs. NEP', included in this volume.

21   Bukharin 1918b, *Programma kommunistov (bol'shevikov)*. I quote from the contemporaneous English translation that I admire for its punchy vividness (Bukharin 1918); the translation can be found on the Marxists Internet Archive under the title 'Programme of the World Revolution'.

tion destroys what is old and rotten: a certain period (a very difficult one to live through) must pass until the new life is formed, until the building of a new beautiful edifice is begun upon the ruins of the old pig-sty.

Bukharin's challenge to his accusers is: *if* you want revolution, you must be prepared to pay this price. But his deeper point is: *if* you want an effective Russian army, don't wail about the inevitable collapse of the old army but set to work building a new army in the only way possible – on the basis of a new class hierarchy in which the workers and peasants have the *vlast*.

Two years after the 1918 *Programma*, Bukharin's main focus is on other things, but he still invokes the paradigm of the Red Army to explain, for example, his thesis about industrial administration. *Ekonomika* is frank about the politics of the army's death and rebirth. Like Peshekhonov and Lukianov, he portrays 1917 as a time of disintegration and demagoguery:

> In the place of strict imperialist subordination was put forward a broad application of the elective principle. Innumerable committees were created at every link in the army chain of command; army issues became the subject of very wide deliberation and discussion; the 'old *vlast*' in the army was decisively discredited and fell apart; new organs and through them new classes became the real nodes of the *vlast* [in the army].
>
> What is the objective meaning of this process? First and most important: *disintegration and destruction of the old imperialist army*. Second: *training* [vospitanie] *and preparation of the active organizing forces of the new proletarian army – a training purchased at the cost of the destruction of the old*. No one will affirm that the regimental committees made the army battle-ready. But you see, the objective task was *not* to support the battle-readiness of the old army. On the contrary, the task was to destroy it and to prepare forces for *another* chain of command [*apparat*] (117–8).

'Temporary "anarchy" is thus objectively a completely inevitable stage of a revolutionary process that manifests itself in the collapse of the old "*apparat*"' (48). But the proletariat quickly discovers it needs an army to protect its gains. Furthermore, the methods of a successful army are pretty much the same everywhere. In the case of the Red Army, the problem is compounded by the need to use former tsarist officers: even in a revolutionary army these officers stand above the rank and file and give them orders (66).

The solution is the assertion of class power, as represented both by the proletariat's central *vlast* and the network of worker organizations such as the political commissars. Not only does the proletariat surprise everybody by revealing that it is capable of creating a new army, but the course of the civil war also reveals that *only* the proletariat is capable of doing this: 'the old armies [including the White armies] disintegrated, because the whole course of events makes impossible any social equilibrium on a capitalist basis' (154).

We can now describe in more generalized terms the process at work not only in the particular case of the Red Army, but throughout all of Russia's social institutions. The old society was stable only because the lower classes accepted their subordinate place in the class hierarchy. At a certain point, however, the *narod* simply no longer followed the directives of those whom it regarded as class enemies. There occurred a 'breaking apart of ties' [*razryv sviazei*] and the old institutions no longer functioned.[22]

Because of this inevitable institutional breakdown, the Russian revolution could never be a smooth transfer of power from one social group to another. It had to involve a political, economic and social collapse – and the more profound the social revolution, the more profound the collapse. There was a rapidly escalating downward spiral – what Bukharin calls 'negative expanded reproduction'. As a result, Russia was faced with an existential crisis: the question no longer was, 'how can we improve production?' but rather, 'is economic production possible at all?'

It took all the constructive energy of a new 'Promethean' ruling class – the socialist proletariat – to avert this existential crisis and create the conditions for a new 'minimal equilibrium'. Institutions literally had to be put back together again. The functional logic of hierarchical subordination had to be reinstated, but on a new class basis. This task is a far cry from the dazzling perspectives of social progress that inspired the proletariat in the first place. Nevertheless, simply making normal social life possible was, under the circumstances, a great and heroic achievement.

This is the overall vision that informs the various case studies that make up *Ekonomika*. Bukharin gives much attention to the problem of industrial administration. As always, his primary focus is on class relations – in this case, the relationship between the 'technical intelligentsia' and the industrial working class. Similar to the army, the hierarchical relations within industry are based on the class subordination prevalent in the wider society. When class subordination loses its mystique, industry starts to disintegrate. Unlike the army, the industrial collapse is not a total one, since this would have meant the death of society. Nevertheless, the existential threat of complete and utter collapse determined

---

22   Sometimes the process of 'state failure' is presented as follows: institutional failure leads to lack of legitimacy which leads to revolt. For Bukharin, the logic of the process is rather: lack of legitimacy leads to revolt which leads to institutional failure.

all the policies undertaken by the Bolshevik party. Bukharin minces no words about the extent of the economic collapse and goes into detail about its myriad causes.

In 1918, Bukharin and his Left Communist comrades called for a collegial style of administration that would involve workers in a way that would give them a sense of class power, even to the detriment of efficiency. In 1920, Bukharin called for 'militarization' of industry and strict subordination to the *spetsy*. He denied any inconsistency, because 1918 and 1920 represented two phases of a single overall process. In 1918, the task was to establish a sense of class power, since the workers were simply not going to be productive under the orders of the class enemy. The analogy with the soldier committees of 1917 is explicitly drawn. By 1920, the workers could see that the *spetsy* were indeed under the thumb of a genuinely worker/peasant *vlast*. Just for this reason, the new *vlast* could call for strict labour discipline. Indeed, the workers could now begin to look on the technical intelligentsia as partners rather than as class enemies.

The 'culminating point' of the 'breaking of ties' that previously bound together Russian society was the mutual isolation of town and country – an isolation that directly threatened economic death for the whole society. Following Kautsky, Bukharin sees the capitalist town exercising economic hegemony over the countryside. After this class relation collapses, the question becomes, in Bukharin's words: 'In what forms can the organizing influence of the proletarian town be established? And how can we achieve a new equilibrium *between* town and village?' (83).

Whether the town is capitalist or proletarian, the foundation of its influence is economic: the availability of a real material equivalent for the goods delivered by the countryside. But the possibility of this economic influence is threatened by the collapse of industry. 'Since the rebirth of industry is itself dependent on a flow of goods needed for life to the town, the absolute necessity of this flow *no matter what* is completely clear. This minimal "equilibrium" can be attained by (a) using a part of the resources remaining in the towns and (b) with the help of state-proletarian compulsion' (84). Thus the force needed to extract resources from the village was not intended to *replace* material incentives: it is force *for the sake of* material incentives.

The use of force will only work if the peasants can see a direct material interest in the establishment of a minimal economic equilibrium. The peasant is not asked to believe in the wonders of socialism – this belief will come about, but only after the reestablishment of economic equilibrium makes possible the wonder-working powers of electrification to reveal themselves. But ending the mutual isolation of town and country is indeed in the peasant's immediate material interest. Thus Bukharin responds to Kautsky's criticism that the Bolsheviks are oppressing the peasant by taking surpluses for the town and the army: 'The "clever" Kautsky doesn't even understand the significance of the war against Denikin, does not understand what is understandable to the most benighted peasant' (83–4).

Obviously Bukharin is here taking the wish for the fact; he himself acknowledges inevitable resistance from the property-owning side of peasant psychology. But his sally is worth pondering still today. Among the general public and even among historians, there seems to be an automatic assumption that the force applied by the Bolsheviks to get grain from the peasantry was intrinsically evil and wrong-headed and therefore only explainable by dogmatic hatred of the peasant or by hallucinatory utopianism. Bukharin's whole discussion of town-country relations – written in 1920, at the height of so-called 'war communism' – shows that other and more understandable motives were at work.

We have gone through an overview of Bukharin's vision of the revolution, circa 1920. Is there really a significant overlap between the vision of a top Bolshevik party leader and the vision of originally anti-Bolshevik observers such as the moderate Peshekhonov and the right-wing Lukianov? To answer this question, let us first list the major themes of Lukianov's essay, almost all of which are shared by Peshekhonov:

- The revolution imposed huge and devastating costs on Russia.
- These costs could not have been avoided, because social antagonisms between the *narod* and the elite made the 'historic *vlast*' unworkable.
- 1917 was a year of accelerated disintegration, due in large part to the failure of elite reformers to face the deep realities of the situation.
- Looking at the revolutionary process as a whole – that is, including the civil war – Bolshevism has to be seen, paradoxically, as a necessary and constructive force.
- Why paradox? Because Bolshevism could play this role partly due to qualities seen by others – with good reason – as destructive and irresponsible.
- Not only the Bolsheviks but the masses went through a process of shedding illusions, making the *narod* a more secure foundation for a functioning *vlast*.
- By 1921, all the Bolsheviks had achieved was a return to a battered normality. But, under the circumstances, this was a great accomplishment.

All of these themes find their echo in Bukharin's vision of the revolution. He begins *Ekonomika* with an evocation of the 'world-historical tragedy' and 'inescapable torments' of the revolution and civil war (5–6). His aim is not to deny these costs, but to portray them as inevitable. He is so intent on this theme that he tells revolutionaries in other countries that they too must undergo titanic social collapse – hardly an advertisement for revolution!

Bukharin argues that growing social antagonism made earlier coordinating institutions unworkable. In his writings as a whole, the breakdown of the state *vlast* is primary. *Ekonomika* extends the same kind of analysis – social antagonism leading to institutional dysfunction – to explain the collapse of essential economic coordinating institutions.

Bukharin is of course a much greater partisan of Bolshevism than the other two writers and he portrays its 'Promethean' role without their irony and sense of paradox. Nevertheless, in his discussion of the soldier committees of 1917 and elsewhere, Bukharin comes close to admitting the destructive and demagogic role of Bolshevism.

Finally, Bukharin's use of the learned term 'equilibrium' conveys in his 1920 treatise the same sense of a return to a battered normality that we find in the other two writers. Bukharin does not explicitly admit that the Bolsheviks themselves lost some of their illusions, although I think he tacitly presupposes this outcome in a number of places. He does argue that other social groups such as the *spetsy* and 'backward workers' did come to a better grip of social realities.

Thus, despite many differences in evaluation and emphasis, we may legitimately group Bukharin with Peshekhonov and Lukianov: all three writers praise Bolshevism for its ultimately (but only ultimately!) constructive role in preventing Russia's complete breakdown and even social death.

4   Concluding Remarks

If, as I have tried to show, these three very different people share a common or at least highly overlapping perspective on the Russian revolution, a research question immediately arises: how widespread was such a perspective during the revolutionary era? The *Smena vekh* outlook was roundly condemned in the émigré community, and Bukharin's theories never became part of official Bolshevik propaganda. But perhaps if we looked below the surface, we would find many more people – including Bolsheviks themselves – who were ready to accept Bolshevism mainly for its 'services to the state', as manifested in particular for its creation of a *vlast* ex nihilo.

Of course, the historiography of the revolution does emphasize the success of the Bolsheviks in preserving the Russian state along with its main territorial base and something of its great power status. There seems to be much less attention given to the specific but central issue of the breakdown and reconstitution of the *vlast*, that is, the energizing heart of the state and government. The problems created by the sudden disappearance of the 'historic *vlast*', the challenges of creating a new *vlast* that could command the obedience of millions, and the inevitability of a period of breakdown: these are themes that are overlooked or not given due weight by many writers.

Some historians do make these issues a central feature of their interpretation. I have noted Peshekhonov's influence in my own work as well as in the magisterial account of Vitalii Startsev. Theodore van Laue's take on the revolution reveals many of the same themes, although he gives less emphasis to class antagonisms than to the subversive effect of invidious cultural comparison with Western countries.[23] Aleksandr Solzhenitsyn's *Red Wheel* cycle also advances similar themes, although in a passionately inverted manner that comes from the hindsight denied writers in the early 1920s. Solzhenitsyn's approach can be summarized as follows: How bad was it in Russia in 1917? It was so bad that the only force capable of creating a new *vlast* and keeping the country together was the despicable Bolsheviks.

The perspective outlined here also has a direct bearing on many historical issues still relevant today. For example, Michael Hickey writes that in the summer of 1917, 'moderate socialist leaders often placed the long-term needs of the state above the short-term expectations and aspirations of the lower classes, and as a result, risked alienating their own political base'.[24] This relatively benign view of the coalition government as statesmanlike is challenged by our three writers, who would argue that the responsible reformers of 1917 had their own brand of utopianism and self-deception that was ultimately destructive of the state values they wished to preserve.

The canonization of the Constituent Assembly as the symbol of the democratic path not taken is another issue on which the Peshekhonov-Lukianov-Bukharin perspective has a direct bearing. Lukianov speaks of the bankruptcy, both political and moral, of the Constituent Assembly. This judgement stands in dramatic contrast to the widespread view that sees the Bolshevik suppression of the Constituent Assembly not only as a betrayal of the revolution but also as the act that more than any other caused the civil war.[25] Perhaps the Constituent Assembly can legitimately be invoked as a valid symbol of democracy vs. dictatorship. Nevertheless, the case can be made that it could not possibly have responded to the challenges outlined by our writers. The legitimacy conferred by one election would hardly have sufficed to prevent further polarization of the kind that had accelerated all though 1917. Can we imagine the Constituent Assembly either signing a peace treaty (an act which ripped apart

---

23   Von Laue 1971, *Why Lenin? Why Stalin?*
24   Hickey 2011, *Competing Voices from the Russian Revolution: Fighting Words*, p. 78.
25   The case is presented by Rex Wade in *The Russian Revolution, 1917* (Wade 2000).

even the Soviet majority), or fighting the Germans with the old army, or creating a new one? And if the Assembly could not have coped with these and similar challenges, would it not have been irresponsible for the Bolsheviks and the Left SRs to hand over the *vlast* and retire gracefully, as so many writers retrospectively call upon them to do?

Our three writers all see something of an interaction between the *vlast* and the *narod* that led to a better understanding of each other by the end of the civil war. Current work by younger scholars on state-peasant relations in the early Soviet period – including Erik C. Landis, Tracy McDonald, Aaron Retish and Sarah Badcock – picks up this theme in a detailed empirical way.[26]

I have merely glanced at issues such as these to suggest the continuing relevance of the arguments we find in Peshekhonov, Lukianov, and Bukharin. For a variety of reasons, these arguments have languished in obscurity. But as evidence of an outlook that was probably more widespread than we suspect, as well as strong and challenging interpretations in their own right, their arguments deserve our attention.

---

26   Landis 2008, *Bandits and Partisans*; McDonald 2011, *Face to the Village*; Retish 2008, *Russia's Peasants in Revolution and Civil War*; Badcock 2007, *Politics and the People*.

'Our Position Is in the Highest Degree Tragic':
Trotsky and Bolshevik 'Euphoria' in 1920

'Russia – looted, weakened, exhausted, falling apart'. Thus reads the first sentence in the volume of Lev Trotsky's writings containing his speeches on economic issues during 1920 – a sentence that appropriately sounds the keynote of the sombre rhetoric of that grim year.[1] The world war and then the civil war had drained Russia's resources and ripped apart the interdependent pre-war economic organism, and yet a large military establishment still had to be supported. The transport system was on the verge of utter collapse. Industry had no goods to give the peasants for their grain. The peasants were understandably reluctant to part with their grain for nothing and indeed had less and less even for themselves. Inflation had destroyed the financial system. Disease, hunger and cold stalked the land. The lives of the workers had gotten worse, not better – the promises of the revolution were more distant than ever. No wonder Trotsky angrily asked how the newspapers dared to publish optimistic articles. Didn't they see that 'our position is in the highest degree tragic'?[2]

The Bolsheviks would hardly have been sane if they had not realized how grim the situation was. But wait – the most eminent scholars in the field, on both the left and the right, assure us that the Bolsheviks were in fact far from fully sane in 1920. The devastation caused by the war did not bother them, indeed, 'the mood of 1920 remained on the whole one of complacency'.[3] 'Complacency' is too mild a word for many historians who prefer 'euphoria'.[4] Russia in 1920 was 'a theatre of the absurd' in which the depressing reality was presented 'as if it were what it was supposed to be, as imagined by the Communist leaders'.[5] And what did the Communist leaders imagine reality to be? 'In a veritable ideological delirium, the most colossal economic collapse of the century was transmogrified into really-existing Communism, the radiant future *hic et nunc*'.[6]

---

1 Lev Trotsky, *Sochineniia* (Trotsky 1925–1927, 15:1, appeal written in April 1920).
2 Trotsky 1925–1927, 15:27–52, speech of 12 January 1920; 15:102, speech of 6 January 1920.
3 E.H. Carr 1950–1953, *The Bolshevik Revolution, 1917–23*, 3 vols, 2:196.
4 A word that occurs surprisingly often; for a recent example, see S.A. Smith, *The Russian Revolution: A Very Short Introduction* (Smith 2002, p. 82).
5 Vladimir N. Brovkin, *Behind the Front Lines of the Civil War: Political Parties and Social Movements in Russia, 1918–1922* (Brovkin 1994, p. 270).
6 Martin Malia, *The Soviet Tragedy: A History of Socialism in Russia, 1917–1991* (Malia 1994, p. 130).

No wonder Sheila Fitzpatrick finds that 'the Bolsheviks' perception of the real world had become almost comically distorted in many respects by 1920'.[7] Indeed, it is rather comical that most Bolsheviks believed that 'the war economy measures applied during this period offered the shortcut to socialism that had been dubbed a childish "leftist" dream a short while before'.[8] And no doubt when we read that grain requisitioning by force was 'regarded by the Party, from Lenin down, as not merely socialism, but even communism' – or that the entire party thought for a brief period at the end of 1920 that the Soviet countryside was already fully socialized – it is hard to suppress a smile.[9] Ultimately, though, it is not very funny, when we consider 'the millions of victims who had paid with their lives for the leaders' brief moment of frenzy'.[10]

If what the academic experts say is true, then the real question about the Bolsheviks in 1920 is not, what were they thinking?, but, what were they smoking? According to the standard view, 'war communism' – the name given ex post facto to the policies and the outlook that reached its apogee in 1920 – was essentially a *hallucination*. There is no milder word for it. One of the main supports for this academic consensus is none other than Trotsky, whose rather un-euphoric words we have already cited. Trotsky's speeches, appeals, directives and pamphlets from 1920 make up one of the most extensive and easily available sources of evidence for the Bolshevik worldview during 'war communism'. He wrote so much during this one year that one wonders how he found time to do anything else. We shall test the 'euphoria' consensus by looking at this body of material and establishing the connections Trotsky made between the national economic crisis, Bolshevik policies, and the socialist transformation of society.

One of the key issues in the centuries-long discussion over the French Revolution is the relation between the original aims of the revolution in 1789 and the radical outcome in 1793. Was the Terror a perversion of revolutionary aims, a natural outgrowth, or just a transitory necessity? 'War communism' has the same sort of implication for our understanding of the aims of the revolution in 1917. There is thus a parallel between the issues explored here and the debate

---

7   Sheila Fitzpatrick, *The Russian Revolution, 1917–1932* (Fitzpatrick 1982, p. 76).

8   Moshe Lewin, *Political Undercurrents in Soviet Economic Debates* (Lewin 1974, p. 33).

9   Robert Conquest, *Harvest of Sorrow: Soviet Collectivization and the Terror-Famine* (Conquest 1986, p. 48); Bertrand M. Patenaude, 'Peasants into Russians: The Utopian Essence of War Communism' (Patenaude 1995).

10   Kolakowski, *Main Currents in Marxism*, 3 vols (Kolakowski 1978, 3:28–9).

over the 'revisionist' interpretation of the French Revolution.[11] Yet there is also a striking contrast. The amount of documentation and sophisticated argument about the relations between 1789 and 1793 is staggering, because historians have always understood the importance of these links. The debate is at a correspondingly high level, whatever we may think of current trends. But this is not true in the case of the Russian revolution. As will become evident, the most elementary facts about the Bolshevik outlook in 1920 have *not* been established. 'Theatre of the absurd' is in reality a good description of debates about war communism, since all sides attribute views to Trotsky and other Bolshevik leaders that are the exact opposite of what they were trying to pound home to their audiences in speech after speech.[12]

The title of the present collection of essays – 'refuting revisionism' – also hardly fits the present essay, since the hallucinatory view of war communism is for all practical purposes an unchallenged consensus. The portrayal of war communism as nothing but a set of destructive fantasies plays a key role in discrediting the Russian revolution, if only because it provides a direct bridge between 1917 and the Stalin era. Yet as we shall see, it was not originally created by those hostile to the revolution – it was created and is still defended today by the left, and particularly by Trotsky loyalists. This essay will show that Trotsky in 1920 is too important a subject to be left to the Trotskyists.

1   *Militarizatsiia*: 'A Natural, Saving Fear'

'Russia's industry lay in ruins, there was barely any transport, and the one pressing problem was how to save the towns from imminent starvation, not how to bring about a Communist millennium.'[13] Leszek Kolakowski thus expresses the views of historians who have castigated the Bolshevik leaders for neglecting the national emergency of 1920 in favour of their ideological obsessions. Central to this charge is the set of policies adopted in early 1920 under the general label of 'militarization of labour'. These policies were predicated on the assumption that military hostilities were coming to an end and that economic reconstruction was the order of the day – and so (historians conclude) these policies cannot be dismissed as simply a response to the civil-war emergency. No, mil-

---

11   This essay was first published in *History and Revolution: Refuting Revisionism* (Mike Haynes and Jim Wolfreys, eds. 2007).

12   For a more detailed dissection of Isaac Deutscher's portrait of Trotsky in 1920, see '*Vlast* from the Past: Stories Told by Bolsheviks', included in this volume.

13   Kolakowski 1978, 3:29.

itarization is how the Bolshevik leaders now conceived of socialism or in any event Soviet Russia's long-term future. As the principal architect and defender of these policies, Trotsky is Exhibit A of this accusation – especially since his eloquent defence of labour militarization, contained in the grimly titled *Terrorism and Communism*, is easily available in English.

All this is very odd. 'Militarization' is a label for a rather disparate set of policies whose connecting link was that they were all meant as responses to an economic crisis caused or greatly exacerbated by the civil war. 'Militarization' *means* national emergency.[14] And no one was more insistent about this than Trotsky.

'Why do we speak of militarization? Of course, this is only an analogy, but one that is very rich in content.'[15] The core of this analogy for Trotsky was not any particular organizational feature of the army. It was rather that the army represented the supremacy of the whole over the part when a nation was faced with a life-or-death battle for survival. In speech after speech throughout the year, Trotsky tried to impress upon his audiences that this was exactly how they should perceive the economic situation: literally as a life-or-death crisis. The key word in his understanding of militarization is 'ruin' (*gibel'*). 'We must tell the masses that breakdown and ruin threaten all of Soviet Russia.'[16] This situation of mortal danger is the basis of the analogy with the army:

What is an army? The army is the one organization in the world in which a person is obligated to give his life unconditionally and fully. An army demands bloody sacrifices. It is not concerned with the sacred interests of the individual and it demands sacrifices in the name of the interests of the whole. Our economic position is like the military position of a country surrounded by an enemy that is two or three times stronger than it.

A habitual, normal regime – a habitual, normal method of work – will not save us now. We need an exceptional wave of labour enthusiasm, an unprecedented readiness of each one of us to sacrifice himself for the revolution, and we need an exceptionally authoritative economic apparatus

---

14 For the distinction made by the 'democratic centralist' group in 1920 between *militarizatsiia* (emergency methods) and *voenizatsiia* (letting the army take over civilian tasks), see 'Bolshevik Sowing Committees of 1920', included in this volume.

15 *Terrorizm i kommunizm* (Trotsky 1925–1927, 12:135). The English translation made in the early twenties has been reprinted as Leon Trotsky, *Terrorism and Communism* (Trotsky 1961). All citations to *Terrorism and Communism* are newly translated from the Russian, but references to the English edition are provided as a convenience.

16 Trotsky 1925–1927, 15:86–7, 6 January 1920.

that says to each particular person: it's tough for you, you're sick, I know it, but despite the fact that I know it's tough for you, I give you orders, I put you to work in the name of the interests of the whole. *This* is militarization of labour.[17]

What was needed was 'an internal militarization, based on complete understanding and dictated by a situation of fear – a natural, saving fear when faced with the ruin of the country'.[18]

There were two other qualities of army life that Trotsky consistently put forward as a model. One was 'exactness' (*tochnost'*), a word that pops up frequently in his speeches along with an entourage of hard-to-translate terms: *akkuratnost'*, *ispolnitel'nost'*, *formlennost'*, *iasnost'*. This bundle of qualities evokes a combination of the reliability of the ideal German with the get-up-and-go of the ideal American – in other words, the ideal organization man. Trotsky, like many Marxists of his generation, saw the modern world as a clash of large-scale organizations – which meant that these individual qualities were life-and-death matters for whole societies. The transition to NEP made no difference to Trotsky's views. In a *Pravda* article of December 1921 entitled 'Man, we could really use some exactness!', he insisted that 'exactness and accuracy [are] among the most necessary traits of an aware, independent, cultured human being'.[19]

Another common theme in Trotsky's speeches of this era is the claim that the Red Army was in many ways a mirror of Soviet Russia as a whole. Trotsky was certainly not saying that Soviet Russia in 1920 or socialist society in general was or should be a compulsory hierarchical organization. He was talking about the basic *class relations* of Soviet Russia. *All* armies (according to Trotsky) reflected the basic class relations as the larger society around them, and the Red Army was just one example of this. For Trotsky, the essential fact about the Red Army was that it represented a winning combination of the peasantry, the military *spetsy* and the 'advanced workers'. In contrast, the White armies reflected the class hostility between peasant and officer and correspondingly fell apart. The Bolsheviks won the civil war because 'the soviet regime created an army in its own likeness, and this army learned how to win'.[20] Thus Trotsky

---

17   Trotsky 1925–1927, 12:188–9, 9 April 1920 (this revealing passage was dropped from the version of this speech in *Terrorism and Communism*).

18   Trotsky 1925–1927, 15:423, 2 December 1920.

19   'Ekh, nam ne khvataet tochnosti!', Trotsky 1925–1927, 21:359–62; see also 21:5 (*Pravda* article of 10 July 1923).

20   Trotsky 1925–1927, 17/2:353–5, December 1919.

used the Red Army as a model of *class partnership*. (Of course, Trotsky was at pains to emphasize that this partnership could only work because of the monopoly position of a disciplined party.)

So much for metaphors – what actual policies lay behind them? The labour militarization policies can be summarized as follows. First, locate and mobilize scattered skilled workers. Second, organize in the most coordinated and expedient way possible the onerous 'labour duties' [*povinnosti*] already widely imposed on the peasantry. Third, put vitally important 'shock' enterprises on a 'war footing' in which food rations were more solidly guaranteed but also in which workers were officially tied down to the enterprise. Fourth, create 'labour armies' out of military units caught in between full combat readiness and full demobilization. Fifth, 'shake up' the trade-union leadership in the absolutely crucial transport sector. Sixth and most generally, install a regime of the strictest possible labour discipline.

We leave to one side questions about whether these policies were well thought out, whether they were implemented in a competent way or even whether they actually ended up improving the economic situation. Our concern here is what these policies tell us about how the Bolsheviks and Trotsky in particular viewed socialism in 1920. We note first of all that they do not give the impression of a leap into the unknown of a socialist utopia – rather, they seem to be responses to specific and very real problems. We note further that although the policies were defended under the rubric of 'universal labour duty', they are in fact constructed on the 'shock' principle of diverting resources into the most urgent sectors.

This 'shock' logic comes out particularly in the policy of putting crucial factories on a war footing. Some historians write as if the Bolshevik wanted to militarize all factories, but this would have contradicted the entire logic of the policy. 'The most important factor of success [in these crucial factories] is the increased ration, but this ration is given out together with a war footing status. Obviously, it would be senseless to put industry as a whole on a war footing, so it is necessary to select certain shock points such as the railroads and locomotive factories and concentrate our best workers there and send shock production groups to them.'[21]

To be placed on a war footing essentially meant a *privileged* position, with the result that workers actually petitioned for this status to be conferred on their factory. Indeed, although the Bolshevik leaders could hardly have realized it, this 'shock' priority policy was a step in the direction of NEP. To guarantee

---

21   Trotsky 1925–1927, 15:46, 12 January 1920.

the rations of some workers was to tell other workers to fend for themselves – and ultimately this fending could no longer be done in the semi-legal fashion tolerated in 1920.

A special mention should be made of the 'labour armies', if only to stress that they played a relatively unimportant part in the complex of labour militarization policies. The labour army concept was specifically tied to the existence of army units in an awkward transitional stage between combat readiness and demobilization. Some historians – fascinated, one suspects, by the scandalous term 'labour army' – have made these the centrepiece of Bolshevik economic legislation in 1920, asserting that Trotsky and Co. wanted to transform all of Russia into labour armies. In reality, Trotsky put least ideological weight on these policies and gave them the most cautious and empirical defence.[22]

Another feature of the labour militarization policies was that all of them assumed a readiness to apply compulsion to any extent necessary. This aspect hardly needs emphasis. What does need emphasis is the equally central role of material incentives, because historians have consistently ignored or even denied the existence of *any* role for material incentives. Trotsky argued at some length that lack of consumer goods meant that otherwise desirable policies of material incentive were not applicable. But the same "shock" logic implied a ruthless application of material incentives. The dire shortages meant that differential 'bonus' systems had to be applied despite their manifest unfairness ('the state should – this is of course obvious – put the best workers in the best conditions of existence by means of the bonus system'). We have seen this assumption at work in the increased ration given to 'militarized' factories.[23]

'Militarization' thus did not mean (as historians imply) a transfer to the civilian economy of a military model that ignored material incentives. On the contrary, Trotsky makes it quite clear that the labour armies themselves were using bonus systems that improved their productivity.[24] If anything, this kind of policy represents the civilianization of the army rather than the reverse.

Many readers have gained the impression that Trotsky was calling for the maintenance of 1920 levels of compulsion into the indefinite future. Actually, Trotsky explicitly says that compulsion will steadily decrease as the eco-

---

22 'Naturally, the army apparatus as such is not adapted to the leadership of the labour process. But we didn't try to interfere in this' (Trotsky 1925–1927, 12:145 [*Terrorism and Communism*]; English edition, p. 152).

23 Trotsky 1925–1927, 12:16 (*Terrorism and Communism*); English edition, p. 168. I discuss this issue at greater length in '*Vlast* from the Past' (included in this volume).

24 Trotsky 1925–1927, 12:149 (*Terrorism and Communism*); English edition, p. 156; see also Trotsky 1925–1927, 15:259.

nomic crisis receded into the past, the material situation improved and people understood the benefits of the new system better.[25] The contrary impression is partly an artefact of the way the key term *trudovaia povinnost'* is translated in the English edition of *Terrorism and Communism*. I have translated this as 'labour duty', that is, something that is both a moral obligation and enforced by the state. One support for this translation is the equivalent German term *Arbeitspflicht*. Other possible translations are 'labour service' and 'labour obligation'. 'Labour conscription' is sometimes seen and even 'forced labour', both of which I regard as tendentious. In the English edition of Trotsky's book, however, the term is translated 'compulsory labour service' (compare the German term *Zwangsarbeit*). This translation is perhaps defensible, given the realities of the situation. Nevertheless it thoroughly obscures Trotsky's views on the *relation* between 'compulsion' (*prinuzhdenie*) and labour duty. Trotsky argued that *labour duty* was a basic socialist principle that would always be valid, while the *compulsion* needed to back it up during the revolutionary crisis would steadily decrease until it disappeared. This may or may not be an acceptable position, but it becomes opaque when the English translation has Trotsky asserting that 'the very principle of compulsory labour service is for the Communist quite unquestionable' (135).

Another misunderstanding arises from the use of the word 'transition' in the rhetoric of this period. 'Transition' could refer to the whole era between the worker revolution and the final construction of socialism. But it could also refer to the short-term transition from a capitalist regime to a socialist regime – that is, as Marxists understood it, from a regime of bourgeois class sovereignty to a regime of proletarian class sovereignty.

It is this second short-term revolutionary transition that understandably preoccupied the Bolshevik leaders in 1920. Bukharin and Trotsky both wanted to get across the same basic thesis about *this* transition: just as the advent of a proletarian regime required the political upheaval of revolution and civil war, so it required an economic upheaval that manifested itself by what Bukharin rather pompously called 'negative expanded reproduction' on a gigantic scale. Compulsion was an essential aspect of the transition period not only because of the quasi-inevitable political crisis but also because of the quasi-inevitable economic crisis.

Thus Trotsky scoffed at Jean Jaures's idea that the transition to socialism could be accomplished by means of gradual democratization. 'In this connection he was deeply mistaken. History shows humanity another path – the path

---

25   Trotsky 1925–1927, 15:88–91, 6 January 1920; 15:107–14 (Theses for 9th Party Congress).

of the cruellest bloody clashes, of world imperialist butchery with civil wars to follow'.[26] It followed that a fall in productivity and in quantity of products was to be expected, 'given the transition of the national economy onto new rails'.[27] 'We know from experience and should have predicted from Marxist theory the inevitability of the deepest crises during the epoch of revolutions. [Society's development] is not a straight one but a zigzag one'.[28]

Looking back in 1922, Trotsky summed it up: 'Revolution opens the door to a new political system, but it achieves this by means of a destructive catastrophe'.[29]

It is this understanding of 'transition period' that informed Trotsky's polemic against Menshevik criticism. Trotsky pounced on a phrase in the Menshevik statement to the effect that compulsory labour was *always* unproductive under *all* circumstances. If this was the case, Trotsky retorted, then you could forget about socialism – because a worker conquest of power leads to a profound economic crisis that cannot be resolved without compulsion (among other things).[30] 'Over and over it becomes evident that for [the Menshevik orator] the tasks of the transition period – that is, the proletarian revolution – do not exist. This is the source of the utter irrelevance of his criticism, his advice, plans and recipes. We're not talking about how it will be twenty or thirty years from – then, of course, things will be much better – but how we can climb out of economic breakdown *today*.'[31] In other words: don't talk about the socialist utopia, talk about the national emergency!

Trotsky also reasoned as follows: a *socialist* regime has a particular right to apply compulsion for the public interest. Socialism means a universal obligation to work. No idle parasites! He who does not work, neither shall he eat! Furthermore, socialism implies the regulated distribution of labour according

---

26   Trotsky 1925–1927, 17/2:338, December 1919. Trotsky went on to praise Jaures's ideas about a militia system.

27   Trotsky 1925–1927, 15:103–6, 25 March 1920.

28   Trotsky 1925–1927, 17/2:368, 25 March 1920. The first sentence seems to be an allusion to Bukharin's *Economy of the Transition Period* that had just appeared and whose main claim to originality was its demonstration that profound economic crises were inevitable in revolutions. For a more detailed discussion of Bukharin's 1920 treatise, see 'Bolshevism's "Services to the State": Three Voices', included in this volume.

29   Trotsky 1925–1927, 12:327–31. On 'transition', see also Trotsky 1925–1927, 15:52–7 and 15:413 as well as many passages in *Terrorism and Communism*, including 12:133–6 and 12:161–6.

30   The rewording in *Terrorism and Communism* of the relevant passage in the original speech in April brings out the train of thought. Compare Trotsky 1925–1927, 15:179–80 (original speech) with 12:133 (*Terrorism and Communism*, English edition, pp. 138–9).

31   Trotsky 1925–1927, 12:161–2 (*Terrorism and Communism*), English edition pp. 170–1.

to plan – it stands for the right of the collectivity as against the rights of the individual. If, at any time, circumstances are such that labour is absolutely necessary and it cannot be attained in any other way, then, undoubtedly, a socialist government has the right to use physical compulsion. In making this argument, Trotsky was not admitting that physical compulsion was or even could be used against the labour force as a whole. He maintained that labour militarization would not be successful unless the large majority of the working class supported it. Physical compulsion was applied only to slackers. Nevertheless, the government should have no compunction about applying it.

Some people, including many socialists, find this argument shocking. Speaking as a historian, I will only say that Trotsky is not distorting the hostility of pre-war socialism toward non-working 'parasites'. Certainly this type of argument is not a product of 1920. Anyone who thinks otherwise should look at Bukharin's pronouncements on labour duty and labour discipline in early 1918, when he was in his Left Communist and allegedly 'libertarian' stage.[32]

The right to apply physical compulsion and the expediency of using it in any particular case are two different things: 'The element of material, physical compulsion can be greater or smaller – that depends on many things, including the degree of wealth or poverty of a country, the heritage from the past, the level of culture, the condition of the transport system and of administrative mechanisms – but obligation, and consequently compulsion as well, is a necessary condition of taming bourgeois anarchy, of the socialization of the means of production and labour and the reconstruction of the economy on the basis of a single plan.'[33]

This passage certainly implies that, say, as the transport crisis eases up, the need for out-and-out compulsion will correspondingly decrease. This implication is further strengthened by the one passage in *Terrorism and Communism* where Trotsky does take a long-term perspective. According to Trotsky, the crucial long-term task for the regime is to raise productivity. If socialism turns out to be less productive than capitalism, it is doomed. But the productivity of labour under capitalism was 'the result of a long and stubborn policy of repression, education, organization and incentives applied by the bourgeoisie

---

32   Bukharin, *Programma kommunistov (bol'shevikov)* (Bukharin 1918b). The chapters on labour duty and labour discipline are reprinted in Bukharin, *Izbrannye proizvedeniia* (Bukharin 1990b) (for further discussion, see '*Vlast* from the Past', included in this volume).

33   Trotsky 1925–1927, 12:134 (*Terrorism and Communism*); English edition, p. 140. The meaning of 'single plan' in this passage is discussed in the next section.

in relation to the working class'.[34] Despite fundamental differences, socialist labour productivity would share one basic feature with its predecessor: it would be the result of a long process (especially in Russia where capitalism hardly accomplished its own historic mission) that used a variety of means. Repression is one of these means, but a minor one compared to moral influences and material incentive.[35]

This discussion more than any other in *Terrorism and Communism* does give a flavour of the Stalin era and its 'politics of productivity', to use Lewis Siegelbaum's phrase.[36] 'A good engineer, a good mechanic, and a good carpenter must have in the Soviet Republic the same fame and glory as was enjoyed hitherto by outstanding agitators, revolutionary fighters and, in the period just passed, the most courageous and capable commanders and commissars' – such a sentence does have a 1930s feel about it. But historians have been so obsessed with saddling Trotsky with the cranky thesis that physical compulsion was the *only* short- and long-term method of socialist construction that they have entirely overlooked these genuine links.

To conclude, Trotsky's justification of the use of compulsion may be paraphrased as follows:

The economic ruin that threatens Russia and our limited resources means that compulsion is written into the situation. If backward elements of the working class do not understand the full gravity of the situation, we shall nevertheless ensure by whatever means necessary that they do their job. Of course, this compulsion could only work because the bulk of the working class *does* understand the gravity of the situation – in fact, the continuing heroism of the Russian working class is a standing rebuke to the slander of such as Karl Kautsky. Of course, this compulsion only works as one element in a broad array of measures based primarily on differential material rewards and campaigns to explain the nature of the national emergency. Of course, the element of compulsion will steadily decrease as we pull out of the present crisis situation, until it finally disappears in full socialism.

This is all true, but none of it should obscure the fact that we as socialists have the right and the duty to use compulsory methods in order to defend the proletarian *vlast'* and to get the economy on its feet again.

---

34 Trotsky 1925–1927, 12:140 (*Terrorism and Communism*); English edition, p. 146.
35 Trotsky 1925–1927, 12:138–44 (*Terrorism and Communism*); English edition, pp. 144–50.
36 Lewis H. Siegelbaum, *Stakhanovism and the Politics of Productivity in the USSR, 1935–1941* (Siegelbaum 1988).

The transition to socialism will always start off with the economic chaos and breakdown caused by revolution. If compulsory methods are *always* unproductive, as our critics claim, we will never get past this starting point.

Not only the Mensheviks but critics within our own party compare our use of compulsion – undertaken in order to prevent the collapse of the economy and the ruin of the country – with the use of compulsion to build Egyptian pyramids or to conduct Arakcheev's nutty 'labour colony' experiments under Tsar Alexander I. Are these critics liberals, are they pacifists, that they don't see the difference between compulsory labour used to satisfy elite whims and compulsory labour used to keep the masses from dying of cold and hunger? Harsh times require harsh measures, and we Bolsheviks are not the ones to flinch when the fate of the revolution and the country hang in the balance.

2   The Road to Socialism during a 'Caricature Period'

'Marx wrote that the proletarian revolution does not unfold with such dazzling fireworks or so brilliantly as the bourgeois revolution. Kerensky's historical story was over in nine months, but we attack, retreat and again attack, and we always say that we have not traversed even a small portion of the road. The slowness of the unfolding of the proletarian revolution is explained by the colossal nature of the task and the profound approach of the working class to this task.'[37]

Thus did Trotsky assess the situation in December 1920 (a period when the hallucinations of war communism were supposed to be at their height). The metaphor of a journey along the road to socialism was fundamental to Marxism since it differed from other varieties of socialism primarily in its vision of how and by whom socialism would be achieved. The better we grasp the implication of this and related metaphors, the better we can understand the Bolshevik rhetoric of 1920 (or any other time).

Even granting that they had travelled only a short distance of the journey, the Bolsheviks felt that they had much to brag about. The very possibility of travelling down the road was due to the daring conquest of political power in 1917. Despite adverse conditions, they had managed to travel some part of the journey. They were definitely headed in the right direction and progress would

---

37   Trotsky 1925–1927, 15:428, 2 December 1920. For an extended examination of the path metaphor throughout Soviet history, see 'The Soviet Union and the Path to Communism', included in this volume.

be quite rapid once the war was over and the country was united. Nevertheless, in another rhetorical context, a speaker who earlier had quite sincerely made all these positive points could put the emphasis on other aspects of the same situation: we are not yet a socialist society, we still have a long and difficult way to go, and at present we suffer from a combination of the breakdown of the old and the embryonic nature of the new.

The road metaphor can also help us grasp what the advent of NEP changed and what it did not change in the Bolshevik outlook. In a 1922 speech to the Comintern that defended the New Economic Policy, Trotsky claimed that 'none of us thought that having taken over the *vlast'*, it was possible to remake society overnight'. On the contrary, war communism was 'the regime of a blockaded fortress with a disorganized economy and exhausted resources' – methods that could not fail to damage the economy severely. War communism inevitably created a 'bureaucratic surrogate of socialist [economic] unification', since 'old methods of economic verification were removed by the civil war before we succeeded in creating new ones'. Obviously, 'there was no communism in Russia. There was no socialism here and there could not have been.'

Trotsky nevertheless admitted that the Bolsheviks prior to NEP had been over-optimistic on one point. They believed they could move forward out of the post-civil-war crisis of 1920 toward socialism 'without large economic shifts, shake-ups and retreats, that is, by a more or less straight ascending line'. Progress toward socialism would take place 'by means of corrections and changes in the methods of our war communism' (for example, an adequate exchange equivalent would be given to the peasants for their grain). This optimism was partly based on the hope that a European revolution would bail the Bolsheviks out, after which Russia would thankfully switch from the role of the locomotive engine of socialism to its caboose.[38]

The knee-jerk reaction of historians when confronted with passages of this sort is to say something along the following lines. 'Well, sure, Trotsky and other Bolshevik leaders claimed afterwards that they did not have utopian expectations of remaking society overnight, but this was just a cover-up. The Bolsheviks sang quite a different tune during war communism itself!' In point of fact, Trotsky has here described quite accurately both the sober and the uplifting aspect of what he and others were saying in 1920. This can be illustrated by Trotsky's thoughts on planning and the coordination of industrial enterprises.

---

38   Trotsky 1925–1927, 12:301–56, November 1922. Trotsky later recommended this 1922 report
      as an appendix to *Terrorism and Communism* (Trotsky 1925–1927, 12:1).

The evidence is confusing at first because the 1920 slogan 'single economic plan' had two quite distinct meanings. In speeches in the spring of the year and in *Terrorism and Communism*, 'single economic plan' referred to a basic strategy for overcoming the crisis: first solve the transport crisis, then go on to machine-building and so forth.[39] This was a plan for recovery rather than for coordinating ongoing economic activity. This 'single economic plan' properly belongs in our earlier discussion of the national emergency. Trotsky took the basic idea from a pamphlet by S.I. Gusev published at the beginning of the year. The brunt of Gusev's argument is: let's not get fancy here with high-falutin' socialist projects, but focus our attention exclusively on the most elementary and pressing tasks.[40]

There was nothing particularly socialist about the actual set of stages advocated by Gusev and Trotsky. At the Ninth Party Congress in spring 1920, Gusev's 'plan' was both attacked (by Rykov) and defended (by Bukharin) as a strategy appropriate to *any* devastated economy. Trotsky strongly defended Gusev's plan, but he was mainly interested in it as an agitational device for focusing energy and explaining to the workers why they needed to make sacrifices.[41]

When Trotsky resumed his discourse on economic matters at the end of the year, 'single economic plan' had taken on the socialist connotation of centralized coordination of economic activity in lieu of the market. Trotsky had discussed aspects of this issue throughout the year. What particularly exercised him was *glavkokratiia*, a term he invented that rapidly became a by-word in 1920. Each nationalized and amalgamated industry was headed up by a 'head committee' or *glavny komitet* – or, in common parlance, a *glavk*. *Glavkokratiia*, or rule by the Moscow 'head committees', was highly resented by just about everybody else in the Bolshevik establishment.

The essence of *glavkokratiia* was the absence of meaningful coordination, since each *glavk* controlled its own industry with only tenuous links to anyone else. The problem was most intense in the localities, where competing

---

39 This plan was the opposite of any 'leap' mentality: 'There is no point in trying to predict whether the first or the following periods will be measured by months or by years.' Trotsky 1925–1927, 12:150 (*Terrorism and Communism*); English edition, p. 158.

40 Gusev's pamphlet *Edinyi khoziaivstennyi plan i edinyi khoziaistvennyi apparat* is reprinted in *Ob edinom khoziaistvennom plane* (Gusev 1989). It is indicative that Gusev has disappeared in the secondary literature. Arthur Ransome mentions the debate over Gusev's plan in his reporting from Russia in 1920; see his *The Crisis in Russia*, pp. 46–7 (Ransome 1921).

41 *Deviatyi s'ezd* RKP(*b*) (*Deviatyi* 1960), pp. 127–32, 135–9.

representatives from the central *glavki* almost literally duked it out. Trotsky recited horror stories of how the localities were prevented from effective use of their own locally available resources while they waited months from some non-forthcoming permission from Moscow. Trotsky summed up a basic structural reason for the prevailing economic chaos: 'The centre doesn't know and the locals don't dare.'[42]

This inevitable combination of a broken-down old system and an embryonic new system meant that Soviet Russia was now in a 'caricature period' of transition.[43] One solution might have been to charge ahead to full centralized coordination. But Trotsky scotched that idea. An 'immediate leap' into full centralization was impossible and any such hope was a 'bureaucratic utopia'.[44] The difficulty was that 'our economy is oriented toward a single plan, but this single plan does not exist – in fact, there does not yet exist any apparatus for either working out or implementing such a plan'.[45] Some Bolshevik supporters may have a naïve expectation of the existence of a plan 'as something complete and whole. We haven't got that far yet and won't for a long time'. The task of national electrification just by itself would require ten, maybe thirty years. And this electrification was an essential prerequisite for bringing technical progress and culture to the peasantry. How can there be a single centralized plan so long as this great task remains unaccomplished – so long as 'the socialist economy is a series of isolated islands in the agricultural ocean?'[46]

Given the inadequacies of *glavkokratiia*, it was wrong to blame the locals when they responded to urgent needs any way they could. Trotsky made all these points in a speech of January 1920 to a party audience that was not published until the mid-twenties – understandably in view of its stunning frankness. The two greatest symbols of outlaw economic activity in 1920 were home-brewing (*samogonka*) and 'sackmanism' (*meshoshchnichestvo*). Home-brewing used precious grain to make vodka for local consumption while sackmanism channelled grain into the black market. Yet Trotsky was prepared to shock his audience by announcing that '*samogonka* is the protest of local needs against the centralism that does not satisfy them ... I am speaking about the semi-contraband or completely contraband production that occurs in the localities

42   Trotsky 1925–1927, 15:146–52 (9th Party Congress, March 1920).
43   Trotsky 1925–1927, 15:94–7, 6 January 1920; see also 15:146–52 (9th Party Congress, March 1920).
44   Trotsky 1925–1927, 15:10–14, December 1919; 15:94–7, 6 January 1920.
45   Trotsky 1925–1927, 15:218–21, December 1920.
46   Trotsky 1925–1927, 15:233–7, 4 January 1921.

and plays an enormous economic role, because otherwise the country will be ruined. How can one live without horseshoes, without nails? Either you steal them from the warehouses or you make them yourself with primitive methods.'[47]

Another obstacle to rational economic coordination was the collapse of the money system. Looking ahead, Trotsky assumed that in the not-too-distant future some sort of measure of labour would play the coordinating role that money had played under capitalism. But what was on his mind in 1920 were the difficulties created by the absence of either capitalist or socialist value measures. Back in the old days, he told his listeners, market competition had coordinated economic activity – in a primitive and barbaric way, true, but nevertheless it had ensured some sort of equilibrium. But money prices were incapable of playing that role now:

> In our work we have bumped up against the important question of how to compare the work of production in comparison with the results that we get. The old accounts are conducted in roubles – and everybody well knows how much our Soviet rouble is worth. ... If I told you that transport absorbed 3 billion or 15 billion roubles, you would greet both the one and the other figure with the same lack of surprise. We have to find a value instrument that answers to the needs of socialist society.[48]

The result, *hic et nunc*? 'The old significance of money is destroyed and a new apparatus of distribution is still not functioning. And, comrades, this helps to explain all our troubles, including the fuel crisis.'[49] Why, then, had the Bolsheviks destroyed the money system before they were able to replace it? Because revolutionary necessity demanded that they smash not only the state but the economy: 'There is no way of building [the new] without destroying the old, because you have to take power out of the hands of the bourgeoisie.'[50] These outbursts show why Trotsky was able to accept so easily – one feels, with relief – the return of a functioning money system under NEP.

---

47   Trotsky 1925–1927, 15:95, 6 January 1920. The same passage contains similar remarks on sackmanism. Sackmanism was a central feature of the Russian civil war; for a full discussion, see Lih 1990 and 'Grain Monopoly and Agricultural Transformation: Ideals and Necessities', included in this volume.

48   Trotsky 1925–1927, 15:434–5, 2 December 1920.

49   Trotsky 1925–1927, 17/2:369, 3 March 1920.

50   Trotsky 1925–1927, 17/2:369, 3 March 1920; see also 15:221–5.

Trotsky's sarcastic sallies against *glavkokratiia* and its manifold defects struck such a chord that by the end of the year he became frightened at his own success and tried to cool things down (possibly at the invitation of the Politburo):

> Much more serious [than opposition within party circles] is what's happening in the more profound strata, among the workers male and female and the peasants male and female. And there's no doubt about it – here there is dissatisfaction, completely natural and lawful dissatisfaction with the economic position, that is, with overwhelming poverty. This dissatisfaction can take sharp forms among the dark masses, it can express itself in elemental and stormy protests of indignation, strikes in factories by the more backward elements of the working class. And when we blame everything on the bureaucracy, then all we're doing is planting prejudices in the heads of the most backward, hungry and freezing labouring masses. They're going to start thinking that there is some sort of central monster called 'the bureaucracy' that holds material goods in its hands and doesn't give them to the masses. People will start relating to it as a class enemy, just as earlier the worker did to the capitalist.[51]

One can easily see from these speeches that the Bolshevik leaders were themselves weary of continually issuing calls for further sacrifice. 'War is a cruel trade and the organs of war are cruel ones; their work consists in the merciless impoverishment of all the living forces and means of the country. When the war approaches its end, then those elements of exhaustion and dissatisfaction that accumulated during the war make themselves known. And this is a good thing, because it testifies to the vitality of the organism itself'. Russian workers are understandably disillusioned after the collapse of their 'unrealistic expectations'. As a result, 'the wide mass still to this day does not feel in appropriate fashion what the soviet regime really is'.[52]

Maybe next spring, Trotsky mused at the end of the year, we could tear down some of Moscow's rotten, filthy, disease-ridden apartment buildings and

---

51 Trotsky 1925–1927, 17/2:502–3, December 1920. Note that this speech was published in *Pravda* at the time. See also Zinoviev's worries about 'the wall' in '*Vlast*' from the Past', included in this volume.

52 Trotsky 1925–1927, 15:401 (2 December 1920); 17/2:371 (25 March 1920); 15:437 (2 December 1920). For another eloquent Trotsky statement on the disillusionment of the masses, see Lih, '*Vlast*' From the Past' (included in this volume).

replace them with ones like those in New York City – buildings that included a bath, that provided gas and electricity and where the trash was collected every day. If we could build just one building like this, the response would be colossal. Because up to now the workers see the wheels turning but they don't see the economic machinery working.[53]

Such were the dreams of 'war communism' – whether modest or grandiose, the reader must judge.

3   Enter the Historians

We find in Trotsky's speeches of 1920 innumerable variations on two overriding themes. One is the austere 'blood, sweat and tears' evocation of the economic ruin facing the country unless extraordinary efforts were made. The other is an insistence on the manifold difficulties created by the breakdown of the capitalist system combined with the primitive, incomplete 'caricature' version of socialist institutions set up during the war.

When we turn to the historians, we find a next-to-unanimous portrayal of the Bolshevik outlook in 1920. We learn that the Bolsheviks ignored the national crisis in favour of ideological experiments. We further learn that the Bolsheviks viewed the institutions of 1920 as an embodiment of full socialism and as an admirable and workable long-term system. The principal body of evidence adduced for these assertions: the speeches of Lev Trotsky.

What is the origin of this astonishingly misleading interpretation of these particular texts? Why is it not only dominant but unchallenged? One fact answers both questions: historians on the left created the framework for it. Historians in the Trotskyist tradition – starting with Trotsky himself – played the major role in this process. Paradoxically – given the charge that Trotsky ignored the national emergency – the key theme of the framework developed by these historians is that there was no serious national crisis. An obvious and painless solution existed, namely, the early introduction of NEP and the legalization of the free grain market. Only ideological blinders kept the Bolsheviks from realizing this.

One of the earliest and most influential statements of this argument is Trotsky's memoirs, *My Life*, published in 1930. The four or five pages devoted to economic policies in 1920 in these memoirs are a disappointment for the histo-

---

53   Trotsky 1925–1927, 15:437–8, 2 December 1920. Trotsky was living in Brooklyn when the Russian revolution broke out.

rian. Trotsky does not even mention labour militarization, labour duty, labour armies, exactness, *glavkokratiia* or the other issues discussed in this essay. His entire aim is polemical: to explain away his conflict with Lenin during the 'trade-union discussion' of late 1920 and early 1921 and to show that he was actually much closer to Lenin than the 'epigones' (a.k.a. all the other leaders of the Bolshevik party).

As often with Trotsky, he tells a story to show that he was right all along. In March 1920 he proposed replacing grain requisitioning with a food-supply tax. If this proposal had been accepted, much suffering would have been avoided. Nevertheless, Lenin and the Politburo turned it down. 'Once the transition to market methods was rejected, I demanded a correct and systematic implementation of 'war' methods in order to attain real results in the economy.' Trotsky goes on to claim that his views on the trade unions grew out of the logic of these war methods. When Lenin finally caught up with Trotsky and advocated NEP, Trotsky instantly supported him – but he did not correspondingly change his views on the unions quickly enough. Only on this last point does Trotsky actually admit error.[54]

This little parable has had an immense influence on later views of 'war communism' as a set of unnecessary and destructive measures motivated by ideological blindness. Nevertheless, it is full of holes. It is not important for our purposes that Trotsky has strongly misrepresented his proposal of March 1920.[55] What concerns us here is Trotsky's suggestion that he adopted his labour policies only because his March proposal was turned down. But these policies were all in place and elaborately defended by Trotsky some time *before* he made his quasi-proto-NEP proposal.

Trotsky also does not explain how his March proposal would have addressed the pressing problems that gave rise to the various militarization policies. The only concrete policy he does describe in his memoirs is the effort to revive the transport system from its near-death experience. And here, oddly enough, Trotsky stresses how vital this work was and how necessary were the methods adopted. He sums up: 'These results were attained by emergency methods of administrative pressure that inevitably arose from the grave position of trans-

---

54 *Moia zhizn'* (Trotsky 1991, pp. 437–46). Trotsky writes that he made his proposal in February and this is the date given in the historical literature. According to the editors of the 1991 Russian edition of his memoirs, however, the proposal was submitted to the Politburo on 20 March 1920 (p. 581).

55 Compare the text in *Novy kurs* (Trotsky 1924) with the full text in Trotsky 1925–1927, 17/2:543–4. It is indicative that as far as I know the full text of this historic proposal is not available in English.

port.' (True, he then adds 'as well as the system of war communism itself' – but this tacked-on reference to 'war communism' seems supererogatory.)[56]

In any event, we know for a fact that Trotsky did *not* repudiate the labour militarization policies of 1920. Twice after the publication of *My Life*, Trotsky authorized foreign reprints of *Terrorism and Communism*. He warned the workers that this is what real revolutions look like and asserted:

> At the time of the civil war, when this book was written, the Soviets were still under the flag of 'war communism'. This system was not an 'illusion' – as the Philistines often maintained afterwards – but an iron necessity. The question was how the wretched resources were to be applied, mainly for the needs of the war, and how production, on however small a scale, was to be kept alive for these same ends and without any possibility of the work being paid for. War communism fulfilled its mission in so far as it made victory a possibility in the civil war.[57]

The influence of Trotsky's little parable presented in *My Life* can be seen in the changing assessment of 'war communism' by Trotsky admirer Victor Serge. Writing in 1922, Serge condemns the Kronstadt rising and defends Bolshevik policy.[58] In his book-length study from the late twenties, *Year One of the Russian Revolution*, Serge considers war communism at greater length and justifies it in terms that go well beyond the chronological framework of the book. Defining war communism as 'an ambitious attempt to organize socialist production', he argues that it was responsible for victory in the civil war and *not* responsible for the decline in production. He also asserts that if international circumstances had been more favourable the same methods might have achieved great success. In all this, he follows *Terrorism and Communism* and Trotsky's 1922 speech to the Comintern.[59]

In 1937, shortly after his release from the Soviet Union, the tone is strikingly different. In *Destiny of a Revolution*, Serge cites Trotsky's memoirs to show that in 1920 'by misfortune Lenin's clear-sightedness is defective this time, he doesn't see the possibility of quitting the road of war communism without

56　Trotsky 1991, pp. 437–46.
57　From the introduction to the 1935 English edition (see p. xliii of the Ann Arbor edition of *Terrorism and Communism*, which also contains the introduction to the 1936 French edition).
58　*The Serge–Trotsky Papers* (Cotterill 1994, pp. 15–20).
59　Serge, *Year One of the Russian Revolution* (first published 1930) (Serge 1972, pp. 350–72).

surrendering to the rural counter-revolution'.[60] The bitterness of his attack on war communism becomes even more intense in his memoirs written in the mid-forties. Here the definition of 'war communism' is expanded to include everything Serge disliked about the regime, including the party monopoly, the terror and requisitioning (that is, taking grain without compensation). These Bolshevik policies arose solely out of a stunning ignorance of what was really going on (Serge seriously suggests, for example, that Aleksandr Tsiurupa, the head of the food-supply ministry, thought the black market was completely unimportant). But now Serge adds an element that is *not* in Trotsky's memoirs: the claim that in 1920 the Bolshevik leaders thought that their policies were not transitory measures but communism *tout court.*[61]

This claim became the keystone of Isaac Deutscher's immensely influential chapter on war communism in the first volume of his Trotsky biography. This chapter – 'Defeat in Victory' – is the foundation text for all further academic discourse on war communism. Deutscher very explicitly argues that the crisis could have been solved without any unpleasantness:

To cope with [the crisis] one of two courses of action had to be taken. The government could stop the requisitioning of food from the peasant and introduce an agricultural tax, in kind or money. Having paid his taxes, the peasant could then be permitted to dispose of his crop as he pleased, to consume it, sell it, or barter it. This would have induced him to grow the surpluses for urban consumption. With the flow of food from country to town restored, the activity of the state-owned industries could be expected to revive. This indeed would have been the only real solution. But a reform of this kind implied the revival of private trade; and it could not but explode the whole edifice of war communism, in the erection of which the Bolsheviks took so much pride.[62]

It all seems so simple. Money was notoriously valueless, but a money tax would have provided the government with necessary resources. There were no industrial consumer items then available, but the peasants would have undertaken backbreaking labour in order to get them. The workers had no food, but they

60   Serge, *Destiny of a Revolution* (Serge 1937, pp. 140–1).
61   Serge, *Memoirs of a Revolutionary 1901–1941* (written in the mid-forties and first published in French in 1951) (Serge 1963, pp. 117, 113). For further discussion of Serge's memoirs, see 'Tsiurupa's White Beard', included in this volume.
62   Deutscher, *The Prophet Armed: Trotsky, 1879–1921* (first published 1954) (Deutscher 1965, p. 490).

would have gladly waited many long months until the extra grain hopefully sown in spring 1920 became available for exchange. The transport system was on the point of collapse, but massive new demands on the system created by a private market in grain would have repaired the locomotives and gotten snow off the tracks without harsh labour discipline and compulsory labour duties. Soviet Russia was still completely isolated and threatened with invasion, but the inability to feed a large army would not have created any security threat.

At the end of the passage, Deutscher suggests the motive for refusing such an obvious solution: the Bolsheviks' pride in the edifice of war communism. They *liked* taking grain without compensation. 'The Bolshevik was ... inclined to see the essential features of fully fledged communism embodied in the war economy of 1919–20.'[63] Having identified the Bolshevik view of socialism with the war economy, Deutscher proceeds to identify the war economy with Stalin's concentration camps. Trotsky argued that 'the workers' state had the right to use forced labour; and he was sincerely disappointed that they did not rush to enrol in the labour camps ... What was only one of many facets in Trotsky's experimental thinking was to become Stalin's alpha and omega'.[64]

The Deutscher scenario became even more usable for the right when Moshe Lewin and others decided to use war communism as a polemical weapon in their advocacy of 'market socialism'. Lewin puts the blame for the economic crisis of 1920 squarely on Marxist hostility to the market. War communism started when the Bolsheviks

> began to speed up the dismantling of [capitalist] mechanisms and to replace them with more direct controls and distributive administrative techniques, apparently as a deliberate implementation of a suddenly rediscovered theory. This conception of a socialist economy explains why the illusion could spread, why with undue obstinacy it was adhered to for far longer than the economy could bear, and why it was disastrous.[65]

In turn, the failure of war communism explains why Lenin, Bukharin and Trotsky began to rethink and redefine socialism as compatible with markets during NEP. Unfortunately there was a 'swing of the pendulum' under Stalin back to war communism and the original Marxist anti-market definition of socialism. Thus we see that the aim of Lewin's narrative is to draw the tightest possible

63   Deutscher 1965, p. 489.
64   Deutscher 1965, p. 516 (order of passages rearranged).
65   Lewin 1974, pp. 81–3 (republished under the title *Stalinism and the Seeds of Soviet Reform*, Lewin 1991).

link between the Marxist conception of socialism, the illusions of war communism, the disastrous state of the Russian economy in 1920, the tyrannical Stalin
era, and 'dogmatic' Soviet economists in the 1960s.

Lewin and others were so engaged in their fight for reform of the Soviet
system that they did not notice how effective their own narrative was in the
hands of the right. The right did understand these implications – that is why
writers such as Martin Malia and Robert Conquest happily cite Lewin as an
authority on war communism, even though Lewin's account is itself utterly
undocumented.[66]

The consensus on war communism created by Deutscher and Lewin is still
unchallenged today. The chapter on war communism in Orlando Figes' *A People's Tragedy* is so strongly derivative of Deutscher that Figes even uses the
same chapter title, 'Defeat in Victory'. Figes uses Deutscher's imagery to make
Deutscher's points. Trotsky was not particularly concerned with the national
emergency, but only with 'the bureaucratic fantasy of imposing Communism
by decree'. This shows his affinity with Stalin: 'Both were driven by the notion
that in a backward peasant country such as Russia state coercion could be used
to provide a short-cut to Communism.' The main difference with Deutscher is
that Figes adds a new – although, if we accept their shared view of the empirical situation, more plausible – moral: 'The perversion was implicit in the system
from the start.'[67]

In essential agreement with Figes about Trotsky in 1920 is a recent book by
S.A. Smith. Smith is a representative of the left as that term is understood in
academic Soviet studies, that is, someone who is not organically incapable of
mentioning that the Bolsheviks were sometimes hemmed in by objective constraints. In his *The Russian Revolution: A Very Short Introduction*, for example,
we find an innovative discussion of the real dilemmas driving food-supply policy. Yet when it comes to 1920, Smith reverts to form. We are again introduced to
Trotsky, 'the most enthusiastic exponent of the idea that "obligation and compulsion" could be used to "reconstruct economic life on the basis of a single
plan".' True, 'not all Bolsheviks were enamoured of the idea of the labour army
as a microcosm of socialist society'. (Although Smith notes here that 'not all
Bolsheviks' had these crazy ideas, he is uninterested in what these presumably
more sane Bolsheviks thought, probably because Trotsky's alleged nuttiness
makes better copy.) After a mention of illusions about money, Smith concludes:
'Over the winter of 1920–21 such euphoria was rapidly dispelled.'[68]

---

66   Conquest 1986, p. 48; Malia 1994, p. 175.
67   Orlando Figes, *A People's Tragedy: The Russian Revolution 1891–1924* (Figes 1996, pp. 722–3).
68   S.A. Smith, *The Russian Revolution: A Very Short Introduction* (Smith 2002, p. 82).

This description is, as advertised, very short and yet it packs in a great many misconceptions. As we have seen, Trotsky tied the use of compulsion strongly to the economic crisis and had no intention of relying on it exclusively even under those circumstances. The 'plan' mentioned here is a broad set of priorities for getting out of the pit of economic breakdown and not a socialist plan that replaced the market – Trotsky insisted that a plan in this sense was many years away. Trotsky described the army (*not* the 'labour army') as a microcosm of contemporaneous soviet (not 'socialist') society in the same sense that any army reflects the society that produced it, and the specific point Trotsky wants to make with the comparison is the possibility of class collaboration.

The corpus of Trotsky's pronouncements in 1920 is a crucial source for any engagement with the big questions of the Russian revolution. The aims of the revolution, their relation to pre-war revolutionary and socialist traditions, their role in determining the ultimate outcome of the revolution, the role of the Bolshevik party in leading and/or repressing popular revolt – none of these issues can be seriously debated without a firm grasp of Trotsky's reaction to a crisis that he regarded as an inevitable companion to revolution. And Trotsky is only one of the voices of 1920, albeit among the more voluble and authoritative of them. This essay has not aimed at tackling the big questions themselves but rather at making such a discussion possible. We have to know that we do not know the basic elements of the Bolshevik outlook during these years. This salutary realization will not occur as long as historians who disagree on so much else join hands in affirming the reality of the will-o'-the-wisp that is Bolshevik 'euphoria' in 1920.

Zinoviev: Populist Leninist

What we need to do is get to the point where the widest circles of the masses of the *narod* understand that a communist is not someone who wears a leather jacket and sneers at everybody (applause) ... Any person in the *narod* – the most backward little old lady, a toiling peasant – who thinks we're in league with the devil [even though] they haven't read the party program and are not going to read it, they're not interested in the Third International and we can't expect them to be – in their hearts they are more of a communist than the communist in a leather jacket who looks down his nose at them.

ZINOVIEV, March 1919

• • •

The worst thing that can happen to a revolutionary party is to lose its [revolutionary] perspective.

ZINOVIEV, May 1925

• •
•

In terms of historical reputation, G.E. Zinoviev undoubtedly would have the right to repeat the words of the old song: 'I've been 'buked and I've been scorned'. No one seems to have a kind word for him. Among the many charges laid against him is intellectual and political inconsistency. Trotsky summed it up in a memorable wisecrack: 'Luther said, Here I stand – I can do no other. Zinoviev says, Here I stand – but I can do otherwise.'

Zinoviev was not in the least a systematic thinker who could state a coherent outlook in propositional form. On the other hand, he was an inspirational speaker who very often told stories – small anecdotes from daily life, large narratives about the revolution as a whole – in order to impress his audience. An assessment of the coherence and consistency of his outlook therefore requires a systematic survey of his many speeches during his time in the top leadership of the ruling Bolshevik party.

Using Zinoviev's speeches as basic material, this essay examines his out-look as revealed in two interconnected themes: the relationship of the party to the working class as a whole, and the battle Zinoviev thought was being waged for the soul of the peasantry. I have found a striking and demonstra-ble consistency in Zinoviev's outlook in the period 1918–1925, manifesting itself in rhetoric, focus of attention, and policy preferences. The transition from so-called 'war communism' to NEP did not lead to any fundamental changes in the way Zinoviev presented the basic Bolshevik message. In my view, Zinoviev's relatively populist version of Bolshevism has its attractive features. I am thus willing to join the small group of observers with something positive to say about Zinoviev (the only others I know in this select group are Anatoly Lunacharsky and Myron W. Hedlin).[1] (Update: I can now add the insightful contributions of Clayton Black and Ben Lewis.)[2]

I should reassure my readers that I am not going to challenge the general impression that Zinoviev was far from *vozhd* material. On the contrary, my investigation has brought home to me his anti-charisma, his tactical errors, and his inability to present his views in organized fashion. I am not going to argue anything like 'if only Zinoviev's views had been taken seriously …' I take it for granted that his solutions to intractable problems were simplistic and would not have worked. This simplistic outlook was one reason – but not the only one! – for the political ineptitude that was revealed in the Bolshevik infighting of the 1920s.

Two comments by Lunacharsky seem to me to hit the right note: he called Zinoviev a 'person who had a profound understanding of the essence of Bol-shevism' and one who was 'romantically' devoted to the party.[3] I will present Zinoviev as someone who was under the spell of the Leninist drama of hege-mony, but with a decided populist bent.

Lenin's drama had three basic characters: the proletarian vanguard, the hegemonic rivals, and the wavering classes. The best description of the van-guard is in Robert Tucker's classic article 'Lenin's Bolshevism as a Culture in the Making'. I will cite Tucker at length in order to give the Leninist context for Zinoviev's outlook:

---

1 Lunacharsky wrote sympathetically about Zinoviev in 1920, as reprinted in Lunacharsky, Radek and Trotsky, *Siluety: politicheskie portrety* (Lunacharsky 1991). Myron Hedlin wrote two excellent articles on Zinoviev that appeared in the 1970s: 'Grigorii Zinoviev: Myths of the Defeated' (Hedlin 1976) and 'Zinoviev's Revolutionary Tactics in 1917' (Hedlin 1975).

2 Clayton Black, 'Regionalism or Clientelism? Explaining the Zinoviev-Leningrad Opposition of 1925' (Black 2019); Ben Lewis, *Zinoviev and Martov: Head to Head in Halle* (Lewis 2011).

3 *Siluety* (Lunacharsky 1991, pp. 296, 298).

To understand Lenin's political concept in its totality, it is important to realize that he saw in his mind's eye not merely the militant organization of professional revolutionaries of which he spoke, but the party-led popular *movement* 'of the entire people'. The 'dream' was by no means simply a party dream although it centred in the party as the vanguard of conscious revolutionaries acting as teachers and organizers of a much larger mass following in the movement. The dream was a vision of an anti-state popular Russia raised up by propaganda and agitation as a vast army of fighters against the official Russia headed by the tsar; and of this other, popular Russia as an all-class *counter-community of the estranged*, a mass of people trained to revolutionary consciousness by its party tutors and dedicated to the goal of a revolution that would rid Russia of its 'shame and curse', as Lenin called the autocracy.[4]

To get the full dramatic structure of Lenin's outlook, we need to introduce two other characters. The first is the petty bourgeois with his or her 'two souls', one leading toward proletarian socialism and the other toward capitalism; the conflict between these tendencies produces the key feature of the petty bourgeois, namely, wavering (*kolebanie*). The other character is the hegemonic rival, the alternative leadership trying to lead the waverers down the wrong path.

The word 'populist' is used here in its American sense: someone who has genuine concern for the problems of ordinary people, who has a simplistic tendency to blame those problems on the machinations of elites, and who sees full democratization as the ultimate solution to all issues. We shall examine Zinoviev's message on three levels: the overall historical narrative or background story, the implied definition of specific stages of the Russian revolution, and the policy recommendations that flowed from his definition of the situation. [Comment from 2023: 'Populism' is now a considerably more charged political term than it was at the time this essay was written, so please heed the definition just given specifically for purposes of this essay.]

1   Party and Class: Civil War

We should start with Zinoviev's background story: what he thought was the *natural* course of events, the way things should go without disturbances, the story

---

4   Robert C. Tucker, *Political Culture and Leadership in Soviet Russia* (Tucker 1987, p. 39).

created by deep historical forces. According to this story, the party was in the vanguard not so much in the sense of a permanent officer corps but in a stricter sense: it was the first to go where the rest of the working class would soon be going. Zinoviev assumed that the influence of the party would be steadily growing and that the proletarians and semi-proletarians who didn't join today would be joining tomorrow. A category essential to his outlook – the 'non-party' worker or peasant – could really be labelled as the 'not-yet-party'. At any one time, the bourgeoisie might have influence over a certain portion of the masses, but all in all there will be a steady movement away from bourgeois influence. This fundamental assumption is set out in a resolution Zinoviev drafted for the Comintern in 1920 that he later often referred to with pride:

> Before the conquest of power and during the transition period, the Com-
> munist Party – given favourable circumstances – can make use of an
> undivided ideological and political influence on all proletarian and semi-
> proletarian strata of the population, but it cannot unite them organiza-
> tionally in its own ranks. Only after the dictatorship of the proletariat
> has deprived the bourgeoisie of such mighty tools of influence as the
> press, the schools, parliament, the church, administrative machinery and
> so on – only after the decisive defeat of the bourgeois system has become
> evident to all – will *all or almost all workers begin to join the ranks of the
> Communist party.*[5]

Just as the party is the most coherent organizational expression of basic class interests, so the party programme is just a more sophisticated expression of class instinct. It was good for the party to spend time on its programme in 1919, because each party member 'wants to have his own view on things, he wants to know how our world came to be, he needs an integral and thought-out worldview'.[6] But knowledge of the programme should not be a necessity for participation in the soviet system. Zinoviev wanted VTsIK (All-Russian Execu-tive Committee that played the role of legislature in the Soviet system) to have fewer commissars and more representatives of the people: 'Let peasants come to us from somewhere out on the Volga or from the Ukraine and other places – peasants who do not yet grasp all the inner secrets of communism, who know

---

5   Text taken from Zinoviev's self-quotation in 1924; see *Trinadtsatyi s'ezd RKP(b): Stenografich-eskii otchet* (*Trinadtsatyi* 1963) (Zinoviev's emphasis).
6   Grigory Zinoviev, 'Ob itogakh VIII S"ezda RKP(b)' in Zinoviev 1989 (remarks of 29 March 1919 to a meeting of party *aktiv* in Petrograd).

only the basics, that they are against the rich, that the land should belong to the peasants and not the *pomeshchik*, and so on.'[7]
As the last citation shows, Zinoviev's background story led to an optimism that made him always come down on the side of expanding membership of the party and 'enlisting' (*privlekat'*) 'non-party elements'. He assured his party audience that expansion did not mean that 'our party dissolves into fragments and stops consisting of a single whole'.[8]
The party's expanding influence did not manifest itself merely in passive assent but in active popular participation in government. This participation promised benefits for both state and population. For the population, it ultimately offered a cheap and transparent state apparatus: one of the key promises of the revolution. For the state, it offered the only long-term solution to inefficiency and bureaucratism. Thus the end result of the party's steadily expanding influence would be not only a party that embraced the entire working class, but the commune-state (*gosudarstvo-kommuna*).[9]
We now turn to Zinoviev's analysis of what Mary McAuley has labelled 'the wall': the barrier that seemed inevitably to grow up between the vanguard party and its constituency, much to the distress of the former.[10] Zinoviev himself used this imagery when he stated that even some party collectives in Petrograd 'have been able to fence themselves off from the masses with a wall'.[11] The wall also grew up within the party itself, leading to the 1920 crisis of the 'lower-downs vs. the higher-ups' [*nizy i verkhi*]. Zinoviev's analysis of the wall cannot be understood without keeping in mind the background story I have just discussed. The wall was a betrayal of the vanguard's mission of leadership, so that 'people look on these [party] collectives as the bosses [*nachal'stvo*] rather than looking on them as the advanced people'.[12] Thus the expectations that arise from his background story are what prompt Zinoviev's concern with the wall; they also form the basis of most of his solutions.
Based on work he had done before the war, Zinoviev had a ready-made and detailed model of the dangers of the wall in the German Social Democratic

7   Zinoviev 1989.
8   Zinoviev 1989, pp. 196–7.
9   Zinoviev used the term *gosudarstvo-kommuna* throughout the civil war for example, at the Eighth Congress of Soviets in late 1920.
10   Mary McAuley, *Bread and Justice: State and Society in Petrograd, 1917–1922* (McAuley 1991, p. 402). The last two chapters of the book and McAuley's conclusion contain an insightful analysis of the phenomenon of the wall. For a discussion of differing Bolshevik responses to the wall in 1920, see 'Vlast from the Past', included in this volume.
11   *Vosmoi s'ezd RKP(b)* 1959, p. 294.
12   Ibid.

Party (SPD).[13] He interpreted the SPD as an originally revolutionary party that unbeknownst to itself had allowed the leadership stratum to become a closed caste. The result was degeneration (*pererozhdenie*) of the party organism. This was a warning to the Communist party: it should not simply feel superior to other parties and ignore 'the beam in its own eye'. There was a definite possibility that it too would end up dominated by a 'stratum of state-employed intellectuals, soviet *chinovniki*, soviet and party bureaucrats'.[14]

Of course, Zinoviev denied that the wall was inherent in the soviet system as such (witness his speech at the Eighth Congress of Soviets in 1920), but he did analyse some of the deeper causes of the phenomenon. (In reading over Zinoviev's analysis of the situation in 1919 and 1920, keep in mind the standard stereotype according to which the Bolsheviks were then in the grip of a euphoric ideology of 'war communism' that led them to believe that socialism was just around the corner.)

One set of reasons arose from the fundamental fact that the party was now in power and had the responsibility of administering a vast state. If you were in your office administering a department, or off on a *komandirovka* in the provinces, you were physically unable to maintain a living link with the workers in the factory. Another set of reasons was the sacrifices caused by the war and the *razrukha*. What kind of communist paradise could there be if Russia had to be looted in order to serve the front?[15] No wonder that political life in the soviets died away. Poverty led to strict prioritizing and this is turn was the underlying reason for *glavkokratiia* (rule by *glavki*, the boards that ran the highly centralized industrial sector). The party also had to be on a war footing, with strict centralization, which meant that practices such as *naznachenstvo* (appointment from above) and *perebroska sil* (centralized distribution of scarce party forces) had to be tolerated.[16]

Another war-related factor was the need to deny political freedoms. Zinoviev affirmed the necessity for this denial, but he leaves the impression that it was anomalous and he looked forward to its gradual disappearance. At the eighth party congress in 1919, he noted that in practice a much wider group had been deprived of electoral rights than the Soviet Constitution itself had

---

13   See Zinoviev, 'The Social Roots of Opportunism', in John Riddell, ed., *Lenin's Struggle for a Revolutionary International* (Zinoviev 1984, pp. 476–95).
14   *Vosmoi s'ezd RKP(b)* 1959, pp. 279–80.
15   G. Zinoviev, *Na poroge novoi epokhi: kommunisty i bespartiinye* (Zinoviev 1921) (speech given to non-party conference in April 1921).
16   For more on *glavkokratiia*, see 'Our Position is in the Highest Degree Tragic: Trotsky and Bolshevik Euphoria', included in this volume.

mandated. The Bolsheviks should strive to extend electoral rights (when circumstances permitted) instead of waiting for the Mensheviks and the SRs to
get the credit.[17]
    Another fundamental reason for the appearance of the wall was the cultural
gap between the leadership of the party and the mass membership. This led
to reliance on *spetsy*, the so-called 'bourgeois specialists' – a reliance that was
not only bad in itself, but threatened an infectious degeneration on the part
of the communists who worked with them. Attempts by the workers simply to
replace the *spetsy* created chaos in government, as the workers 'get tangled up
in the state *apparat* in the same way that a child will sometimes get tangled up
in the coat of his father'.[18]
    All of these factors together – the need to administer the state, the perma-
nent emergency of war and *razrukha*, the monopoly of political power, the
cultural gulf between leaders and followers – meant that too great a burden
was placed on the thin layer of the party leadership. These leaders were spread
too thin, bone-tired, and loaded down with an 'accumulation of power' and
offices that boded nothing good.[19]
    The wall was like a dam that interrupted the otherwise natural flow of hearts
and minds into the Bolshevik camp. There were bad consequences on both
sides of the wall. On the leadership side, there were flagrant abuses of power
and privilege. Among those mentioned by Zinoviev were cases of privileged
distribution of expropriated goods such as apartments and an alarming case of
incipient anti-Semitism in his home town of Elizavetgrad.[20] On the side of the
workers, there was natural and justified anger at these abuses. One of the key
promises of the revolution had been equality, and nothing did the party more
harm than indifference and greed on the part of the party's leadership. 'People
do not realize that they deal a blow to our party with this sort of thing that no
single whiteguard would be able to do.'[21] Even if there were no abuses, the wall
led to resentment on the part of those left behind:

---

17 *Vosmoi s'ezd RKP(b)* 1959, pp. 290–1. Note the assumption, still not dead, of genuine party
    competition.
18 'Pometki V.I. Lenina v tezisakh G.E. Zinov'eva' (Lenin 1990). This image is taken from a
    draft Zinoviev wrote for presentation to the 8th Congress of Soviets in late 1920. Lenin was
    somewhat taken aback by it, writing '??' in the margin. (In '*Vlast* from the Past', included
    in this volume, I argue that fear of 'infectious degeneration' was more characteristic of
    Alexandra Kollontai and the Worker Opposition.)
19 *Vosmoi s'ezd RKP(b)* 1959, pp. 279–80.
20 Zinoviev 1989, pp. 190, 197.
21 Zinoviev 1989, p. 197.

The worker is jealous, he envies his fellow worker who is a member of a soviet, who dresses a little better, who eats a little better, and therefore he hates him worse than he earlier hated a *burzhui*. Yes, the worker has this trait ... If the worker doesn't see the one he elected for three months, he starts to regard him as part of 'them' [*chuzhoi*] and as no longer his representative.[22]

All of this led to a situation where alternative leaderships – the Bolsheviks' rivals for hegemony – had a greater chance. Zinoviev gave the example of one Federov at the Putilov factory: a 'petty crook' that the workers trusted more than their own elected representatives, simply because he was always there in the factory.[23]

If the main reason for the wall was objective conditions such as the war and material poverty, then ultimately the only way to break down the wall was to remove those underlying causes: end the war and improve productivity. At the beginning of 1920, Zinoviev looked forward to steady improvement in the standard of living, but this proved premature, since 1920 turned out to be another year of war and sacrifice. In the meantime, the party leaders had to be frank about the sacrifices they demanded and show that they realized the cost of victory. Furthermore, objective difficulties should not excuse inaction. The party's own incompetence – its 'lack of skill, sloppiness, lack of culture and carelessness' – had greatly contributed to the problem.[24] The most important thing was to improve the workers' lot in some minimal way:

Up here in Petrograd, in connection with the recent disturbances, it was established that at the Nevsky gate cloth supplies were rotting away, while at the same time women workers who needed clothes were driven to thievery, for which we persecuted them and created conflict after conflict. There's no greater shame for us than that these supposedly small – but in reality not small at all – 'defects of the mechanism' are still around, that

---

22   Zinoviev 1989, p. 195. This statement may give the impression that Zinoviev was justifying this inequality, but at the 9th party conference in September 1920 he discussed these same problems (position of a worker elite) at length and made clear that equality was a key value of the revolution; see *Deviataia konferentsiia RKP(b)* (*Deviataia* 1972, pp. 145–52). In 1925, the party majority gave Zinoviev a very hard time when he insisted that equality was a key revolutionary value.
23   Zinoviev 1989, pp. 194–5.
24   See Zinoviev's speech at *Vos'moi s'ezd Sovetov rabochikh, krest'ianskikh, krasnoarmeiskikh i kazachnykh deputatov* (*Vosmoi* 1921).

we still can't clothe a worker family or the mother of a worker, who would appreciate even the smallest improvement of their lot or some genuine love and concern for them.[25]

Another basic antidote for degeneration was workerization (*orabochenie*), or bringing the workers (and after them, the toilers in general) into the party and the soviets. The accent here is more on the workers' role in curing the party than on spreading the party's influence. Workerization includes bringing workers into the party, non-party toilers into the soviets, and turning Rabkrin into a tool for improving the state apparatus. It also meant bringing party members closer to the workers: Zinoviev persistently pushed measures to ensure that officials be regularly sent back to the factory floor.[26]

In particular, effort should be made to revitalize the soviets and extend party influence within them. Zinoviev recalled the hopes of 1917: 'the soviets as organs in which the creativity of the masses finds for itself the most free and most organized path, the soviets as organs that guaranteed a constant stream of fresh forces from below, the soviets as organs where the masses learned at one and the same time to legislate and to carry out their own laws'.[27] The net of enlistment should be thrown wide: in Petrograd a somewhat successful effort had been made to enlist 'craftsmen, laundresses, cabbies and lower-level civil servants' in order to free them 'from the influence and hegemony of the petty and large-scale bourgeoisie'.[28]

The converse of workerization was 're-registrations' or *chistki* (purges) to remove non-proletarian elements – or at least to impose a special check-up (*proverka*) on them. Finally, Zinoviev proposed some specific measures of abuse prevention: legal accountability of party members, a crackdown on favouritism and 'protectionism', and wide preliminary discussion of state decrees.

---

25   *Vosmoi* 1921, pp. 283–4.
26   McAuley comments: 'When faced with unrest, one response was to try to bring the government itself, physically, closer to the people; to create an immediate, personal link between leaders and led ... They repeatedly resorted to this strategy, described as one of restoring "links with the non-party masses", one which had its roots in old party practice (meetings were the place for gaining party support) and which fitted with notions of direct democracy, but one which was woefully inadequate as a means of connecting government and people' (McAuley 1991, p. 426).
27   Lenin 1990, p. 33. 'Revitalization of the soviets' became central to Zinoviev's rhetoric in the mid-twenties.
28   *Vosmoi* 1921, pp. 290–1.

2   Party and Class: NEP (1922–1925)

We now turn to the early NEP period when Zinoviev was the principal spokesman for Bolshevism. The basic story and the analysis of the wall remain more
or less the same, but updated to take into account the new circumstances of
peacetime. Zinoviev now adds some elaborations to his basic story of expanding influence. In 1922, he provided more detail to the story about the party prior
to the revolution. He claimed that in the pre-revolutionary years the party had
been able to create a 'reservoir' of sympathizers who provided the basic core of
new members after 1917.[29] In early 1921, the difficulties of the civil war reached
their height and the party's relations with the workers reached their low point.
In a speech given at the time, Zinoviev remember, he apologized for the guards
at the factory gates, but asserted that it was the role of the purposive (*sozna-
tel'nye*) leaders to make sure that waverings at a moment of intense strain did
not lead to disaster.[30]

    After this low point (Zinoviev continues) things gradually became better.
Although 1921–1923 were difficult years that allowed an unfortunate growth
in the influence of their Social Democratic rivals abroad, they also saw the
beginning of economic revival at home and the end of the 'declassing' of the
scattered and demoralized working class. The 'Lenin enrolment' of 1924 marked
the completion of the years of recovery and the beginning of a new chapter in
the story, one that would end with all members of the working class inside the
party.

    The task of Cassandra is now no longer carried out by the warning exam-
ple of the SPD's degeneration, but rather by what Zinoviev calls the 'clever foe'
(*umnyi vrag*): Russian émigrés who were looking forward to the party's degeneration. The clever foe was a basic rhetorical device for Zinoviev: he does not
just refer to such writers in passing, but gives very extensive citations from
their articles and indeed often frames his presentation around them. Among
the émigrés used in this way were Pavel Miliukov, David Dallin, Fyodor Dan,
Vladimir Nabokov (the father of the novelist), and Nikolai Ustrialov. It almost
seems as if Zinoviev is engaged in an inner polemic with these intelligentsia
critics.

---

29   *Odinnadtsatyi s'ezd RKP(b): Stenograficheskii otchet* (*Odinnadtsatyi* 1962, pp. 380–5).
30   Zinoviev, *Na poroge novoi epokhi*. Zinoviev was evidently deeply shaken by this episode;
      I have found two other references to it, both emphasizing the depth of the alienation
      between party and class at this point in time, but also praising the Bolsheviks for remain-
      ing true to their 'historical mission'. See Zinoviev, 'Zadachi nashei partii posle konchiny
      V.I. Lenina: Dva doklada' in *Krasnaia Nov'* (Zinoviev 1924a, p. 24) and Zinoviev, *Istoriia
      RKP(b)* (Zinoviev 1924, p. 200).

The wall that had grown up between party and class still existed, and the basic reason was still the clash between the responsibilities of power and the party's self-image as leader of the oppressed. On the one hand, the party member was told to 'learn to trade', to work closely with specialists, and to accept the need for inequality; on the other hand, he was supposed to be a representative of the class that was 'recently oppressed and that still today is economically the most downtrodden'.[31] This dilemma was not unique to NEP: 'The danger of degeneration of the social nucleus is real, we talked about this danger in 1919 and in 1921. We are obliged to repeat it, especially under NEP, with an even heavier accent.'[32]

The economic collapse was thankfully a problem that was gradually receding into the past: problems such as unemployment remained, but nothing like the crises of the recent past.[33] The revival of the economy presented a new challenge: handling the demands for political activity that were sure to come both from non-party elements (to be encouraged) and the new bourgeoisie (to be discouraged).[34] Zinoviev was adamant that there would be no 'political NEP', that is, no legalization of independent political activity. It is still possible to see hints that Zinoviev thought of this situation as an anomaly.[35] When he was accused in 1925 of advocacy of independent peasant councils, his fellow leaders seem to find the charge plausible.

In any event, Zinoviev went into detail about the dangers that resulted from the party's 'legal monopoly'. It was not so much open careerism that was the problem, since careerists could be removed with the relatively blunt instrument of the *chistka*. It was rather the mass, elemental phenomenon of the influence of unprepared party members, especially those from the Red Army. Zinoviev's discussion of this problem shows the tension in his outlook. He continues to praise the new recruits, point to their services, and emphasize their sincerity: it is not their fault that they do not know their own social nature and that they bring petty-bourgeois prejudices into the party.[36]

Nevertheless, the party is still faced with a cultural gap between leaders and rank-and-file. The low cultural level leads to endless squabbles (*skloki*),

31   *Odinnadtsatyi*, pp. 394–5.
32   *Odinnadtsatyi*, pp. 407–10.
33   *Trinadtsatyi s'ezd RKP(b): Stenograficheskii otchet (Trinadtsatyi* 1963, pp. 85–7).
34   Zinoviev 1924a, pp. 20–24.
35   *Odinnadtsatyi*, pp. 391–4.
36   *Odinnadtsatyi*, p. 390.

especially on the local level.[37] It is also undoubtedly true that decisions are often handed down ready-made from on high and that there is insufficient 'free discussion' in the party. Besides objective reasons for this situation, Zinoviev granted that inertia in party life from the days of the civil war was a factor. Finally, the party's responsibility to give political direction to the state put a tremendous strain on its internal unity. In a speech of January 1924, Zinoviev listed ten different categories of party membership: factory workers, peasants, Red Army officers, students, civil servants, administrators of the local soviets, economic officials, trade union officials, 'our merchants' and officials in the cooperatives.[38]

Some recently published archival material indicates that Zinoviev was genuinely worried about the possibility of the party turning into a 'mandarin sect'. On 6 August 1923, while vacationing in Kislovodsk, he wrote the following note to Stalin:

In one of the protocols of the Politburo I saw a decision ... to ease the enrolment of the children of high officials into secondary education.

In my opinion, this decision is a big mistake. It will only make the position of the children of high officials more difficult. And, most important, this kind of privilege closes the road to more gifted [applicants] and introduces an element of caste. This won't do.[39]

When speaking about the non-party workers on other side of the wall, Zinoviev revealed what appears to be genuine empathy with the difficulties of ordinary individuals and with the reasons why they would not always be completely thrilled with the party. For example:

I mentioned the Putilov factory [in Petrograd] because not so long ago I went through an unpleasant experience there: after the end of one rally a young lad about 17 years old with a gloomy expression said to his neighbour but obviously so that I would hear it: 'Ekh, there's not one intelligent person in Soviet Russia' – clearly trying to say 'and you aren't so smart yourself'. When I started asking why he had such a gloomy, Schopenhauerian outlook on life already at age 17, it turned out that it wasn't from Schopenhauer at all, but because 'I have three unemployed at home, I'm

---

37   For a civil-war discussion of *skloki*, see *Vosmoi s'ezd* RKP(*b*) 1959, p. 292.
38   Zinoviev 1924a, p. 12.
39   *Izvestiia TsK*, 1991, No. 4, p. 202.

the only worker and I can't provide for them. And what I'm usually receiving in the way of culture is next to nothing.' The figure of this young lad at the Putilov factory is not something exceptional and we have to pay attention to it. If we really have seventeen-year-olds in the factories that are subjected to such thoughts, then this is a serious danger.[40]

As we might expect, Zinoviev's basic wall-prevention measure was to end any 'massophobia' (*massoboiazn*) in the party and to accelerate workerization. An article dated 15 February 1924 – the beginning of the campaign for the Lenin enrolment – provides the fullest account of his hopes, and I will summarize it here.[41]

Zinoviev started by citing a Comintern resolution from 1920 (discussed earlier) in which he looked forward to the time when the party would embrace almost the entire working class. He then exultantly claimed 'we are now, in the USSR, in the most completely evident way, *beginning* to approach precisely this final phase ... The fragmentation, the de-classing of the proletariat is coming to an end.'

The foundation of the party had always been its 'stratum of old, long-time [*korennye*] worker-Bolsheviks'. The new worker members were also hereditary workers, so that the present enrolment was a case of 'potential energy turning into kinetic'. Everybody in the party should be taught to take for granted that they should take their cues (*ravniat'sia*) from the basic core of workers from the factory floor. Now that these new members have been enlisted, the party had to aggressively assimilate them (*perevarit'*). The basic method should be to give them state responsibilities: to help production through production conferences and the like, to assist the local Rabkrin in improving the state apparatus, and to strive for influence among the non-party elements. The new members must remember that the standards of the non-party people have risen, so that the basic party mission of leadership has become even more challenging. Zinoviev seems confident that the new workers will genuinely improve matters; he cites the testimony of 'our best red directors' that industrial production was now finally reviving.

Zinoviev then discussed some other ways to get the most out of workerization. There should be a party reorganization to get cells closer to the factory floor. Party democracy – especially in the sense of free discussion – should be intensified as the basic means of party education. The new workers with links to

---

40   *Odinnadtsatyi*, pp. 405–6.
41   This article can be found in Zinoviev's party history *Istoriia RKP(b)* (Zinoviev 1924b, pp. 5–21).

the village should be used to strengthen the *smychka*. The everyday living standard (*byt*) of the workers should be improved. Finally, massophobia should not
be allowed to stand in the way getting even more workers into the party: 'We
must plough the virgin soil ever deeper.'[42]

In presenting Zinoviev's outlook from this period, I have abstracted from
some dissonant notes that emerged in the struggle against Trotsky. His pronouncements reveal more and more emphasis on party unity and the imper-
missibility of any attack on it. Lenin's death made Zinoviev even more afraid
of splits within the party leadership. The audience response to this theme
was always foot-stomping approval – far more than to anything else he says.
Zinoviev also takes up the defence of the party *apparat* as a necessary tool in
disciplining the state *apparat*.

Despite these dissonant notes, I think we can conclude the following: from
at least 1919 to 1924, despite the end of the civil war and the introduction of NEP,
Zinoviev presented a consistent picture of the danger of the wall as well as some
possible antidotes. His main response is to urge the overcoming of 'massophobia' (his own, perhaps, as well as that of others). Despite the many objective
reasons for the existence of the wall, the party should strive to overcome it for
the sake of its own health as well as its need for social support. Zinoviev was
able to give a relatively lucid analysis of the wall and its consequences because
of his underlying optimism that the party and the class (and beyond it, the
mass) share an underlying unity of outlook that time will only make more clear.

3   The Peasantry: Hegemony and 'Who-Whom'

In the 1920s, Zinoviev often made a claim that stands in stark contrast to conventional wisdom about NEP: he presented it as just another manifestation of
the essence of Bolshevism, namely, the insistence on the mission of the working class to act as hegemonic leader of the peasantry. According to Zinoviev,
the insistence on this mission was Lenin's central contribution to Marxism
and had always separated Bolshevism from its socialist rivals. In 1924, he cited
the newly discovered manuscript of Lenin's *Who are the Friends of the People* from the early 1890s: 'The person of the future in Russia is the worker –
this is the thought of the Social Democrats.' He then paraphrased Lenin's formula in order to bring out the fundamental idea of hegemony: 'The person

---

42   Zinoviev 1924b, pp. 5–21; see also Zinoviev 1924a, *Zadachi nashei partii*.

of the future in Russia is the worker, *leading the peasant*.[43] According to this conception, the *smychka* of the 1920s has deep roots in Lenin's earliest writings.

In this way, Zinoviev fits the peasantry into his own larger story of hegemony: just as the party will eventually win over the working class as a whole, so will the working class win over the peasantry. The drama of the story is heightened, both because the peasants are more backward than the workers and because the kulak is a more formidable hegemonic rival than the urban bourgeoisie. Nevertheless, Zinoviev's drama of hegemony in the 1920s is still basically optimistic, since it is structured by an assumption of a *natural* hostility between the kulak and the majority of the peasantry: 'We have united with the working peasant against the kulak bloodsucker!'[44] When Zinoviev, Kamenev and Krupskaya protested against what they viewed as a whitewash of the kulak in 1925, they did so because they thought such a whitewash would offend *peasants* rather than party ideologues or urban workers. The *smychka* thus *required* hostility toward the kulak.

4   The Peasantry during the Civil War

By 1920, the revolution had given the peasants land and a countryside free from *pomeshchiki*, but very little else except heavy burdens and a deteriorating economy. The minimum (and perhaps the maximum) we can ask from the Bolsheviks is an honest avowal of these facts. Zinoviev (along with many other Bolshevik spokesmen) passes this particular test.[45]

In early 1920, Zinoviev admitted that although Russia had been in bad shape when the Bolsheviks took it over, it was in worse shape now. Yes, the peasants had received land. 'But you know, the peasant can't scrape the earth with his teeth. The peasant can't work the land because he has no horses. We declared mobilization after mobilization. The village is short of everything necessary.'[46] Taking peasants away from the field for two weeks at harvest time was

---

43   Zinoviev 1924b, p. 208.

44   G. Zinoviev, *Krest'iane i sovetskaia vlast'* (Zinoviev 1920c) (speech given 21 April 1920 to a non-party conference in Petrograd gubernia).

45   In reading the following, keep in mind the entrenched stereotype reflected, for example, in Robert Conquest's assertion in *Harvest of Sorrow* that 'grain procurement by force' was 'regarded by the Party, from Lenin down, as not merely socialism, but even communism' (Conquest 1986, p. 48).

46   *Novye zadachi nashei partii* (*ot voiny k khoziaistvu*) (Zinoviev 1920d), p. 11 (speech given 28 January 1920).

'appalling and a real torture. But still – it was unavoidable ... With a weary heart, we were forced literally to loot half of Russia, but achieve victory over the generals.'[47]

Added to the material burdens was arbitrary government by representatives of Soviet power. 'When I hear specific complaints – here they took your horse away, there they made an illegitimate arrest, the special tax was improperly levied – then I am amazed, not that examples [of peasant protest] occur, but that they are becoming ever fewer.' Given illiteracy, general backwardness, years of being divided from the workers, and the shortage of 'decent people and officials', such abuses could not be avoided.[48]

These are not isolated statements, or ones made only to peasant audiences. In Germany in late 1920, critics cited statements like these by Zinoviev as well as Lenin and Preobrazhensky to show how badly the peasants were faring in Russia. Zinoviev responded that yes indeed, he and the others had been quoted correctly, but they were doing their best to make things better. Besides, these statements showed that the Bolsheviks weren't afraid to talk about their problems.[49]

We next inquire whether we can find any doctrinal reflection about the importance of maintaining peasant support. We should remember that the Bolsheviks were criticized by orthodox socialists such as Karl Kautsky because they gave *too much* to the peasants: the break-up of the estates hurt large-scale agriculture and helped to entrench a village bourgeoisie. The Bolshevik response was to write the necessity of attracting peasant support into the 'twenty-one conditions' for membership in the Communist International – a document drafted by Zinoviev.[50]

In his speech in Germany in September 1920, Zinoviev maintained that neglect of the peasants was a cardinal reason for Bela Kun's failure in Hungary, and forecast the necessity for the German revolution to gain the support of

---

47   Zinoviev 1920c (*Krest'iane i sovetskaia vlast'*). Note that when Isaac Deutscher uses a similar phase, he implies that the Bolsheviks were highly content with the situation in 1920: 'Silently, with a heavy heart, Bolshevism parted with its dream of war communism' (see '*Vlast* from the Past', included in this volume).

48   Zinoviev 1920c, pp. 45–6 (*Krest'iane i sovetskaia vlast'*).

49   Zinoviev, *Dvenadtsat'dnei v Germanii* (Zinoviev 1920b, pp. 66 ff.); Ben Lewis's translation of Zinoviev's speech can be found in *Zinoviev and Martov: Head to Head in Halle*, edited by Ben Lewis and Lars T. Lih (Lewis and Lih 2011).

50   Hedlin shows that Zinoviev was the main author of the 21 conditions, despite their attribution to Lenin in the fifth edition of his works (Hedlin 1976). I can add a stylistic observation to Hedlin's discussion: the presence of the rare word *razzhizheniia* (rarefaction), one that I have run across only in Zinoviev's writings.

the *seredniak* (the middle peasant) in order to ward off counter revolution. In response to critics who said that the break-up of the estates signified a return to the Middle Ages, Zinoviev retorted that Russia could live five or ten years without socialism in the villages, but at least it would never go back to capitalism.[51] These statements by Zinoviev support his claim that, even during the period of so-called war communism, Bolshevism distinguished itself from Menshevism and other varieties of socialism by its willingness to attract peasant support even at the cost of slowing down the purely economic evolution of socialism in the countryside.

We now turn to Zinoviev's view of what was going on inside the peasantry. Here 'the kulak' can best be understood as a role in the drama of hegemony: the alternative leadership that struggles with the proletariat for influence over the swing vote, that is, the wavering mass of the peasantry. There is a certain inner contradiction prominent in this version of the hegemony story, since the alternative leadership is seen as both the oppressor loathed by the masses and the seductive rival with an enormous capacity to deceive the same masses.[52]

This is certainly the case for Zinoviev's view of the kulak. On the one hand, the kulaks are a small handful who 'hold the whole village in their tenacious clutches'.[53] The peasants know who these people are, and ultimately it is up to the peasants to deal with them. The kulak is somebody who lives 'at the expense of others' and thrives on usury, speculation and exploitation of labour. Zinoviev is frankly puzzled why the village does not declare open season on them and attributes this to village shyness or lack of organization.[54] Nevertheless, an enormous threat is posed by the kulaks as the most entrenched and rooted bourgeois class in Russia. Unlike the urban bourgeoisie, they're not leaving for Constantinople. On the contrary, they show great survival power: throw them out of a fifth story window, and they land on their feet. Some of them may see the need for a new life, but for the most part they remain dangerous enemies even if they don't take up arms (they spread rumours, wriggle into soviets and so forth). This is a long-term problem: kulakdom (*kulach'e*) isn't going to be extinct for a long time.[55]

---

51 He quickly added that it would be at least a century before the 'full practical realization of communism'. Later, during NEP, Zinoviev admitted that the Bolsheviks had underestimated the time factor.

52 For a discussion of the melodramatic essence of the hegemony narrative, see 'Show Trials in the Stalin Era: On Stage and In Court', included in this volume.

53 Zinoviev, *Pis'mo k krest'ianam: Zachem rabochie posylaiut prodovol'stvennye otriady v derevniu?* (Zinoviev 1918).

54 Zinoviev 1920c (*Krest'iane i sovetskaia vlast'*).

55 Zinoviev 1920c (*Krest'iane i sovetskaia vlast'*). Zinoviev's rhetoric about kulaks in 1920 is

Zinoviev's fierce rhetoric about kulaks must be put alongside the evidence that he took the worker-peasant union seriously. Perhaps this can best be seen by the very fact of the speech I have cited extensively: *Krest'iane i sovetskaia vlast*, given on 21 April 1920. Zinoviev made these remarks at a 'non-party conference' in Petrograd province. Here Zinoviev went before a peasant audience, admitted that the revolution had given little but imposed much, pleaded that the mutual victory not be spoiled by distrust, and tried to respond to the many vocal complaints. He couldn't understand why people in the audience were offended by his attacks on the kulak: 'There's no reason to be offended by what I said! ... If the kulak is offended, that makes sense. His turn has come. But there are no kulaks among you.'[56]

Zinoviev's confidence that deep down the peasants were on the side of the Bolsheviks is an extension of the same confidence he expressed in the case of the workers. The point of the soviets for both workers and peasants was to provide a means of 'bringing understanding to our backward brethren'.[57] Conversely the soviet mechanism would only benefit from enlisting peasants as well as workers. In 1919 he proposed that VTsIK bring in more peasants: 'We should see more leaders of the peasant poor there, who have not yet enrolled in the party, but who will do so in a month or maybe two.'[58]

As this last comment indicates, Zinoviev entered into the world of the peasantry from the proletarian door, that is, the *bednota*. These were the 'best people' in the village. Zinoviev was inclined not to be harsh about their mistakes: wasn't it time for them to triumph for once? He regarded the *seredniak* (middle peasant) somewhat condescendingly and put him in the same category as the 'lower middle-class intelligentsia' and the urban man-in-the-street (*obyvatel'*): all these groups could and should be won over, but only with time. The task of the party was thus to extend its influence in the villages so that it is possible to 'maintain the *vlast* [without military force]. To accomplish this will require a huge amount of work that will occupy a series of years.'[59]

---

    actually more moderate than his remarks in 1918; for examples, see Lars T. Lih, *Bread and Authority in Russia, 1914–1921* (Lih 1990).

56   Zinoviev 1920c, pp. 38–9 (*Krest'iane i sovetskaia vlast'*).
57   Zinoviev 1920b (*Dvenadtsat' dnei v Germanii*).
58   *Vos'moi* 1959, p. 288. See also the citation given earlier claiming that the peasant does not need a sophisticated grasp of the party programme in order to join VTsIK.
59   Zinoviev 1989.

5   The Peasantry during NEP

We now turn to Zinoviev's presentation of the logic of NEP in the years before he went into opposition in 1925. His understanding of it was summed up in the repeated phrase *kto-kovo*. Like most people, I had always thought that this phrase was a favourite expression of the hard-line Lenin: 'who (oppresses, beats, takes advantage of) whom?' It was something of a shock when some time ago I tried to track down its actual use by Lenin and found that (as far as I can tell) it was entirely confined to the NEP years and even then only employed to express the logic of NEP. Lenin used it in offhand fashion no more than a couple of times; it would no doubt have been forgotten without Zinoviev's frequent use of it in 1923–1925.[60]

As understood by Zinoviev, the phrase means something like this: who will gain the loyalty of the peasants, the proletarian state or the new bourgeoisie? Who will best take advantage of the opportunities presented by economic revival? Who will best represent the political interests of the peasant and best provide the peasant with goods and credit? Which *smychka* will prevail: the link with the proletarian or with the bourgeois? The answer to these questions will decide the fate of the revolution.

Thus, *kto-kovo* turns NEP into an on-going drama. We can best understand the further details of the NEP drama as understood by Zinoviev if we take seriously a terminological innovation he proposed in 1923 and 1924: to distinguish between NEP and the New Economic Policy. The acronym NEP had been turned into a term that conjured up the nepmen, the new bourgeoisie and the kulaks. Its negative connotations should not be transferred to the New Economic Policy, which was the only sensible policy for constructing socialism in a peasant country surrounded by capitalism. (The following discussion uses this distinction somewhat more systematically than Zinoviev did, but I am sticking closely to Zinoviev's own presentation of the logic of the New Economic Policy.)

According to Zinoviev, the New Economic Policy did involve a retreat, namely, the tolerance of NEP elements (*not* the concessions to the peasants). This retreat was necessary in order to revive the economy under conditions of the capitalist encirclement. The retreat was not all the way back to capitalism, but only to 'state capitalism', which included such uncapitalist things as a state monopoly on foreign trade. Once the economy had revived sufficiently, an advance was again possible. This advance would also be conducted under the

---

60   For a more extensive discussion of this famous phrase, see 'The Soviet Union and the Path to Communism', included in this volume.

terms of the New Economic Policy: its aim would be to replace the economic services now provided by the nepmen with the state's own superior economic structures. Until the advance was successfully completed, the question of *kto-kovo* would still be open. NEP could therefore be read as the *Necessary Economic Policy*; later, when state economic structures were in place, it would become the *Needless Economic Policy*.[61]

In the case of the party's relation to the workers, degeneration manifested itself by an acceptance of the wall. An equivalent degeneration in the case of the New Economic Policy would be forgetting about *kto-kovo*: welcoming economic revival in and of itself, without asking which direction it was going, and thus refusing the challenge of directing economic development down the proper socialist channels. This is the outcome predicted by the clever foe: pragmatic abandonment of socialist goals.

In his 1924 political report to the 13th party congress, Zinoviev asked two questions. The first was 'did the state's economic performance mean that it was moving out of the elementary class of economic competence?' The second was *kto-kovo*: who is gaining the loyalty of the peasants? A generally positive answer was given to the first question, but Zinoviev emphasized that an unambiguously positive answer was not yet possible for the second question. His speech is sprinkled with warnings about the dangers of forgetting about *kto-kovo*:

> We shouldn't delude ourselves: there is a real danger of degeneration, and the danger of a more then proportional growth of the bourgeoisie is also real – and of course this bourgeoisie is starting to emerge out of the village. This is the reason that we are much less confident and final in our response [to questions about the success of *kto-kovo*]. Here much depends precisely on the subjective efforts of our party, and what we need to do is not so much to underline the positive aspects but rather to show where we need to apply all our strength. The struggle between us and 'them' (the new bourgeoisie) is just starting.[62]

Zinoviev did not talk much about the kulaks until 1924; before then, 'NEP' meant primarily the urban nepmen. Even in 1924, he maintained that there was more danger from a revived Menshevism (interpreted as the political expression of the urban NEP) rather than from the SRs (the political expression of the village NEP, that is, the kulaks). But we find a familiar theme in his insis-

---

61   Zinoviev, *Russia's Path to Communism* (Zinoviev 1925) (speech given 20 May 1925).
62   *Trinadtsatyi* 1963, p. 88 (similar passages on pp. 99, 105).

tence that in the long run it would be the SRs who would prove most dangerous. Zinoviev's views rest on an assumption that he shared with others in the party opposition: the new bourgeoisie would eventually find political representation and expand their influence if the state was unable to render it economically superfluous. One might say that Zinoviev and the rest were stuck in pre-war conceptions of civil society and underestimated the power of their own repression. In contrast, Bukharin was supremely confident that the kulaks presented no threat, because his model was the wartime 'state capitalism' put into place by bourgeois states that was able (so it seemed to him) to co-opt all opposition.[63]

In his 1924 congress report, Zinoviev also put forth the idea of two possible deviations on the kulak question: trying to eliminate them by repressive means alone vs. denying their existence. He cited reports from the countryside that indicated the danger that the kulak would end up a greater support of the Bolshevik state than was the *bedniak*. Out of concern for the *smychka*, the party should be aware of peasant criticism on this issue.

It is hardly surprising that Zinoviev put heavy emphasis on the worker-peasant union during 1922–25, and I will not discuss this theme at length. I will cite here a few characteristic touches. In 1923, he rebuked the party by saying that even Mussolini was doing a better job of linking up with the peasants.[64] In his 1923 correspondence with Stalin, Zinoviev expressed his delight in the founding of a peasant international.[65] In a speech of early 1925, we find more evidence of Zinoviev's populism.[66] In explaining the new policies of the neo-NEP, he reviewed some statistics on peasant poverty and concluded: 'We are a government based upon the poor, but it is not our desire to perpetuate the poor; we want to improve their lot.' Later in the same speech he admitted that 'we know that often the non-party peasant knows our decrees, is almost invariably a better husbandman, better understands agriculture and sometimes is better educated than our village Communists'.[67] Zinoviev is still upset by abuses of power: 'The peasant will be sure that the bad "Communist" is not all-powerful when he feels free to lift his voice against him and sees justice meted out to him ... How, I ask ... are we to get the peasant to feel he has a right to speak up against bad Communists?'

If Zinoviev had an answer to his own question, he didn't give it in this speech.

---

63   See 'Bukharin on Bolshevik Illusions', included in the present volume.
64   *Dvenadtsatyi s'ezd RKP(b)* (*Dvenadtsatyi*, p. 6).
65   *Izvestiia TsK* 1991, No. 4, pp. 192–208.
66   Zinoviev 1925 (*Russia's Path to Communism*).
67   Lenin made exactly the same point during the civil war; see my short biography (Lih 2011).

6 Opposition in 1925: Flip-Flop or Continuity?

My original aim was to carry my analysis forward to the disputes of late 1925 when Zinoviev and Kamenev went into opposition, but this has proved to be impossible, since I would have to go into the policies of 1925's neonep, Bukharin's position, and the various doctrinal disputes that became intertwined with the main debate. I will only give the briefest outline of what I think was at issue. At present, the only full discussion of the debates of 1925 is by E.H. Carr. According to him, Zinoviev did a flip-flop on the question of NEP, moving from a strong defence of the neonep to a strong critique of NEP in a matter of months. With the background provided by this essay, the essential consistency of Zinoviev's position becomes apparent.

In my view, the essence of the party debate in 1925 was over defeatism vs. complacency. Bukharin's main polemical enemy had always been socialists such as Kautsky who argued that the Bolshevik revolution was doomed to failure because conditions in Russia were not ripe for socialism (the maturity [*zrelost'*] debate). If any Bolshevik talked too much about the difficulties facing socialist construction in Russia, Bukharin tended to conclude that he or she was a defeatist who secretly accepted Kautsky's argument and had lost faith in the possibility of socialism in Russia. In response, Bukharin himself tended to glide over the difficulties, and this pushed Zinoviev's buttons: behind Bukharin he heard the voice of Ustrialov and other clever foes who were predicting that the Bolsheviks would come to terms with capitalism, become complacent, and gradually forget their revolutionary aspirations.

Thus it was not the actual policy of neonep that led to Zinoviev's worries, but its interpretation by Bukharin and others. For Zinoviev, it was very important to see the legalization of various kulak practices as a retreat and to keep one's revolutionary perspective: the *kto-kovo* question was still an open one. Zinoviev had always said it would be a disaster if the *bedniak* came to see the New Economic Policy as a wager on the kulak, and now Bukharin with his 'get rich' slogan (April 1925) seemed to be going out of his way to give exactly that impression.

A related debate was over the status of state industry: was it 'state capitalism' or already socialist? Behind the mind-numbing citation-mongering on this issue we can perceive Zinoviev's concern that the party should take seriously the workers' dissatisfaction with low pay, bad working conditions, and abuses by the bosses.

7   Conclusions

the most important conclusion to emerge from this material is that Zinoviev
did in fact express a consistent outlook with some degree of intellectual and
political integrity (given standards appropriate for political leaders). This outlook was based on his understanding of Leninism as a drama of hegemony:
a battle with the class enemy for the souls of the masses. Zinoviev was especially concerned with the danger of degeneration: would the vanguard forget
its mission? Would it accept with complacency the wall that inevitably sprang
up between vanguard and masses? Would it forget about the drama of *kto-kovo*
made necessary by concessions to the new bourgeoisie? Indeed, degeneration
itself could even be defined as forgetting that hegemony *was* a drama, that is,
a struggle with no sure outcome. I can see no reason to dismiss this outlook as
mere rhetoric or as motivated by passing factional concerns. Zinoviev stuck to
it over a number of years, during both the civil war and NEP, he consistently put
forth policy suggestions based on it, and he used it as the basis of his platform
when he moved into opposition.

The particular features of Zinoviev's outlook seem to have been recognized
by his comrades in the Bolshevik leadership. For example, in spring 1919
Zinoviev was the speaker for the Central Committee at the Eighth Party Congress on issues of party organization and bureaucratism. He was also the main
spokesman on this question at the Ninth Party Conference in September 1920,
when the issue of bureaucratism was at the centre of a violent controversy
within the party. Zinoviev was also given the job of reporting on this issue at
the Eighth Congress of Soviets at the end of 1920.

Zinoviev's emphasis on the concept of hegemony makes one think of Anto-
nio Gramsci. As a foreign communist, Gramsci would have dealt more with
Zinoviev than with any other Bolshevik leader and must have been influenced
by his particular understanding of Leninism. Certainly it would be satisfyingly
ironic if the despised Zinoviev turned out ultimately to have more enduring
intellectual influence (via his talented pupil Gramsci) than any other top Bolshevik.[68]

I have been stressing some of the relatively attractive features of Zinoviev's
outlook, since it seems to me that this is the more surprising result of my investigation. Lest I seem unbalanced, I should add at least the following. Zinoviev

---

68   For the deep roots of the hegemony scenario in pre-war 'revolutionary Social Democracy'
      and in Lenin's outlook in particular, see 'The Proletariat and its Ally: The Logic of Bolshevik
      "Hegemony"' (part of Lih 2017, the series 'All Power to the Soviets!').

282

had very little concrete to say about the policy dilemmas faced by the Bolsheviks except what was implied by his hegemony scenario. Furthermore, when he went into opposition, all his weaknesses came into play and he was never able to make a coherent presentation of his case. His book *Leninism* and his speeches at the 14th party congress and the 15th party conference show him drowning in defensive logic-chopping and citation-mongering. It is largely (but not entirely!) his own fault that his message had to be excavated by obscure academics many decades later.

There is nevertheless something refreshing about Zinoviev's outlook, symbolized by the occasional presence in his speeches of the hungry mother and the Schopenhaurian teenager. To some extent, perhaps, this is just a rhetorical device – but if so, it is a refreshing one after the faceless abstractions that dominate the writings and speeches of other top Bolshevik leaders. My impression is that Zinoviev was genuinely concerned about the problems faced by ordinary people.

One reason that I undertook this research was scepticism about received understandings of 'war communism' and NEP. I have not stressed this aspect in the present essay, but I will make a couple of observations. Some of the things Zinoviev said during 1920 – especially about the problems of bureaucratism and the burdens placed on the peasantry – are simply not compatible with the standard stereotype of 'war communism' as the sanctification of wartime expedients into a permanent system or as a short-cut to full communism. In a less direct way, my Zinoviev material also presents problems for typical interpretations of NEP. There is first simply the consistency I have shown in Zinoviev's outlook: he was able to defend NEP by making the same kind of arguments that he made during the civil war.[69] Zinoviev's own understanding of NEP as typically Bolshevik also stands as a challenge to conventional views. Finally, his understanding of the retreat/advance metaphor shows that the 'advance' was not meant as a return to 'war communism' nor as a Stalin-style assault on the peasantry. In none of this is Zinoviev unique – he is simply another anomaly confronting the standard stereotypes.

The main purpose of this essay has been to complicate our understanding of the early years of Soviet power by presenting one authoritative and relatively populist rendering of the 'essence of Bolshevism'.

---

69   I make the same case vis-à-vis Bukharin in 'Bukharin on Bolshevik "Illusions": "War Communism" vs. NEP,' included in this volume.

PART 5

NEP (1921–1930)

∴

Political Testament: Lenin, Bukharin and the Meaning of NEP

Lenin's last writings have given rise to a surprising range of interpretations.[1] Despite this diversity, consensus holds that in these articles Lenin was striking new ground, extending his critique of war communism, and deepening his conception of the New Economic Policy. Another widely held view is that Nikolai Bukharin, inspired by the last articles, went further down the path opened by Lenin. Few agree about the content of Lenin's new direction, although one may note the following coincidence: Lenin is always seen as rejecting whatever the author in question does not like about original Bolshevism.

In the first half of this paper, I will argue that, on the contrary, despite some new details, the themes and concerns of the final writings faithfully reflect Lenin's long-term outlook. No critique of war communism or deepening of NEP can be extracted from these writings. This lack of originality does not detract from their importance but, rather, strengthens their position as Lenin's political testament. In the second half of the paper, I will argue, that, although Bukharin constantly referred to Lenin's final writings, they did not change his own outlook at any fundamental level.

---

1 This essay is dedicated to my teachers Robert Tucker and Stephen Cohen, who, long before perestroika, emphasized the importance of both Lenin's testament and Nikolai Bukharin to the Soviet reform tradition.

Under the rubric of 'last writings', I include the five final articles, the letter to the congress, and the draft for 'How to Reorganize Rabkrin'; all can be found in volume 45 of *Polnoe sobranie sochinenii*, 5th ed. (Lenin 1958–1965). Standard western discussions of the circumstances surrounding the final articles are found in Robert C. Tucker, *Stalin as Revolutionary: A Study in History and Personality* (Tucker 1973); Moshe Lewin, *Lenin's Last Struggle* (Lewin 1968); Robert H. McNeal, *Stalin: Man and Ruler* (McNeal 1988). On Bukharin, besides the standard works of Robert Daniels, *The Conscience of the Revolution: Communist Opposition in Soviet Russia* (Daniels 1960) and Stephen Cohen, *Bukharin and the Bolshevik Revolution: A Political Biography* (Cohen 1971), I have benefitted from the Marxist analyses of Michael Haynes, *Nikolai Bukharin and the Transition from Capitalism to Socialism* (Haynes 1985) and Christian Salmon, *Le rêve mathematique de Nicolai Boukharine, 1905–1923* (Salmon 1980).

For a useful collection of recent Soviet articles, see *Bukharin: Chelovek, politik, uchenyi* (Zhuravlev 1990). The student of Bukharin will benefit from three new Soviet editions of his writings: *Izbrannye proizvedeniia* (Bukharin 1988); *Problemy teorii i praktiki sotsializma* (Bukharin 1989): *Put' k sotsializmu* (Bukharin 1990). The last has an indispensable comprehensive bibliography of Bukharin's writings.

Lenin was a sick man when he dictated the final writings, a fact that is reflected in their unfocused, repetitive, and rambling organization. It is therefore useless to take up the articles one by one; we must adopt Bukharin's method and discuss each of Lenin's themes in light of all the references to it scattered throughout the writings.[2] For reasons of space, I will not discuss Lenin's view of nationality problems or the theme of Russia's international position between the tardy revolution in the west and the incipient revolution in the east. I shall also leave to one side the drama surrounding the Politburo's immediate reaction to Lenin's suggestions and his personal conflict with Stalin.[3] The three themes I will discuss are improving the apparatus, strengthening party authority, and the need for cultural revolution.

Lenin inveighed against 'bureaucratism' because he wanted an effective, centralized apparatus that would be an efficient tool in the hands of the worker's state. The Marxist aphorism about the 'withering away of the state' did not mean doing away with an administrative apparatus, but rather doing away with the separation between state and society – what Robert Tucker has called 'dual Russia'. The overcoming of this dualism would be achieved by full democracy, which would thus cleanse the apparatus of its 'bureaucratic' defects.[4]

Lenin's concern in the final writings is therefore not to do away with or even to limit the scope of the state apparatus but simply to improve it. According to Lenin, the defects of the apparatus stem entirely from the pre-revolutionary past: tsarist bureaucrats, bourgeois capitalists, petit bourgeois speculators. Bureaucratism is a *perezhitok starogo*, a holdover from the past.[5] Even though Lenin cautioned the Bolsheviks that in five years they could not expect to do very much to eliminate bureaucratism, he never suggests that war communism

---

2 'Politicheskoe zaveshchanie Lenina' in Bukharin 1988, pp. 419–36.

3 Recent Soviet discussions include V.P. Naumov, 'Leninskoe zaveshchanie', *Pravda*, 26 February and 25 March 1988; V.I. Startsev, 'Politicheskie rukovoditeli sovetskogo gosudarstva v 1922–nachale 1923 g'., *Istoriia SSSR*, 1988, no. 5, pp. 101–22; and Aleksandr Bek's interview with Lenin's secretaries, published in *Moscow News*, 1989, no. 17 (Bek's novel on this subject is being published). (2023: an internet search throws doubt on the existence of this novel.)

4 In 1922, Lenin wrote: 'The state = the working class, its vanguard, its crystallized organization and cultural power' (Lenin 1958–1965, 45:412). The attempt to combine high centralization with democratic enlistment is characteristic of a wider trend in Russian political culture I have termed 'the enlistment solution'. For discussion, see Lih, *Bread and Authority in Russia, 1914–1921* (Lih 1990).

5 Lenin 1958–1965, 45:383. See also pp. 347, 376, 385, 387, 405, 447. Lewin comments on the limitations of Lenin's analysis in Lewin 1968, p. 124 and in *Political Undercurrents in Soviet Economic Debates: From Bukharin to the Modern Reformers* (Lewin 1974, p. 64).

or the civil war had strengthened bureaucratism. Indeed, in one passage, intensified bureaucratism is associated with NEP in particular.[6]

Lenin does mention in passing that the party was also infected with bureaucratism, but the entire focus of his programme is to use the party to cleanse (or purge) the state apparatus.[7] The apparatus least infected by bureaucratism, the Foreign Affairs Commissariat, demonstrates this desired goal:

This apparatus is an exceptional component of our state apparatus. We have not allowed a single influential person from the old tsarist apparatus into it. All sections with any authority are composed of Communists. That is why it has already won for itself ... the name of a reliable communist apparatus, purged to an incomparably greater extent of the old tsarist, bourgeois and petty-bourgeois elements with which we have had to make do in other People's Commissariats.[8]

Lenin's proposal for improving the apparatus is to enlist the best and the brightest of young workers and peasants. (Peasants who are directly or indirectly associated with exploitation need not apply.) The evolution of Lenin's scheme can be traced from the letter to the congress to the first draft of 'How to Reorganize Rabkrin' to the final published article. During this evolution a number of substantive changes occur. When the proposal is first mentioned, it is assigned two aims of equal importance: preventing a split among the leadership and improving the apparatus. As Lenin works out the scheme, the first aim almost fades away and the second one becomes decisive.

At first Lenin wanted to put the enlisted workers on the Central Committee, but between the first draft and the published article he simply substituted the Central Control Commission for the Central Committee. Lenin did not explain why he dropped his plan for enlarging the Central Committee, but I assume it is because he saw the anomaly of having people on the Central Committee who would have 'full rights' and yet who would be confined to a specific task. The switch to the Central Control Commission is also consonant with a move away from elections and toward examinations as a way of selecting the enlisted workers.[9] In any event, the sudden switch shows that Lenin's focus is not on the reform of any particular party institution but on enlisting fresh forces.

---

6 Lenin 1958–1965, 45:397.
7 Lenin 1958–1965, 45:397. See also 308 (November 1922).
8 Lenin 1958–1965, 45:361. See also 45: 447, 405. For a similar strategy with Gosplan, see 45:351–52.
9 Bukharin put the emphasis on examinations (Bukharin 1988, p. 434). See also Lenin 1958–1965, 45:445–6.

The point of Lenin's scheme rests on the human – one might even say super-human – qualities of the enlisted workers. In the first mention of the plan, the main characteristic of these workers is the negative one of not having acquired the prejudices of the new Soviet civil service. But since Lenin wants them to be thoroughly versed in up-to-date administrative science, the source of the enlisted workers had to change. In the final version, Lenin is looking for candidates among experienced officials and students.[10] The enlisted workers will also be irreproachable Communists, conscientious, loyal, united among themselves. They will be fearless – unafraid of authority and never speaking against their consciences. They accept nothing on faith. They will inspire the confidence of the working class, the party, and indeed the whole population.

At times the enlisted workers will have to resort to craftiness. Since a major cause of the ineffectiveness of the apparatus was the semiconscious sabotage of the bureaucrats, the methods of intelligence work will be appropriate. These methods will 'sometimes be directed to rather remote sources or in a round-about way', and therefore Lenin advised the anti-bureaucratic crusaders to work out 'special ruses to screen their movements'. Lenin's call for unorthodox methods against class-inspired sabotage is perhaps the part of the testament closest to the Stalinist outlook.[11]

Lenin's aim is to 'concentrate in Rabkrin human material of a truly contemporary kind, that is, fully comparable to the best western European models'.[12] After training by 'highly qualified specialists' and party leaders, the enlisted workers will improve Rabkrin and, through Rabkrin, the entire state apparatus.[13] Bukharin called them a lever for reforming the apparatus and this appropriate metaphor reminds us of Lenin's famous paraphrase of Archimedes's lever in *What Is to Be Done?* ('Give us an organization of revolutionaries, and we shall overturn Russia!'). In his last articles, Lenin retreats to his dream of inspiring 'professional revolutionaries' whose total dedication and heroic leadership abilities will bring about miracles.[14]

---

10   Lenin 1958–1965, 45:347–8, 394–6.
11   Lenin 1958–1965, 45:397–400.
12   Lenin 1958–1965, 45:389.
13   Lenin 1958–1965, 45:354. See also the early mention of the scheme in May 1922, 45:181.
14   Bukharin 1988, p. 434. My understanding of *What Is to Be Done?* is based here on Robert
      C. Tucker, *Political Culture and Leadership in Soviet Russia* (Tucker 1988). (After writing
      this article, I embarked on a book-length commentary and new translation of *What Is to
      Be Done?* [Lih 2006]. For a short presentation of a central theme of this commentary, see
      'Ordinary Miracles: Lenin's Call for Revolutionary Ambition', included in this volume.)

'Our Central Committee has become a strictly centralized and highly author-itative group, but the work of this group has not been placed in conditions that correspond to this authority.'[15] While many of Lenin's remarks on this score bear on improvement of administrative routine, we shall focus on his remarks with broader political import. The most important consideration is the preven-tion of a schism. The fear of a schism and the insistence on unity is probably the aspect of Bolshevik mentality that is hardest for Americans to understand. The Bolsheviks felt deeply that in a hostile world the survival of the revolution depended on their own unity and the disunity of their opponents.[16]

Lenin discusses the possibility of a schism at two levels: among the individu-als of the top leadership and at the more fundamental level of the workers and the peasants. Lenin did not believe there was much chance of a peasant-worker split in and of itself. After noting the possibility of a lack of basic understand-ing between the classes, Lenin comments that 'this is too much [a matter of a] remote future and too unbelievable an occurrence for me [even] to talk about.'[17] Nor does the danger of a split in the top leadership result from any fear that his colleagues might underestimate the worker-peasant alliance; he did not fear any other potential serious policy differences. The danger that worried him was rather that a strictly accidental and personal split among the top leaders would lead to a loss of party authority and thus to failure in the battle for the loyalty of the peasant. Preventing a schism in the top leadership is also impor-tant because no one person can combine all the different qualities needed in a leader.

Despite his concern about a split in the leadership, Lenin does not mention factionalism, perhaps because he no longer saw factionalism as a threat, as he had in 1921. Another possibility is that Lenin saw factionalism arising from dis-putes among the elite rather than from rank and file pressures.[18] In any event, Lenin's scheme for enlisting the best and brightest workers was also designed to strengthen party unity. Those enlisted would reduce the chance of a per-sonal schism by improving the work routines of the top leadership. They will also provide the leadership with a 'tie to the masses', since these new recruits would gain authority from their closeness to 'the highest party institution [the

---

15   Lenin 1958–1965, 45:387.
16   Lenin 1958–1965, 45:344; see also pp. 360, 362.
17   Ibid. 45:344. After years of polemicizing with the opposition and then with Stalin, Bukharin insisted that Lenin used the testament to warn against the adoption of actively anti-peasant policies (Bukharin 1988, pp. 430–1). This emphasis is understandable, but it does not correspond to Lenin's own priorities.
18   Lewin 1968, p. 128; Igor Kliamkin, *Novyi mir*, 1989, no. 2, p. 211.

Central Committee] and from their equal standing with those who direct the party and through it the entire state apparatus'.[19] None of this seems to be a call for democratic pressure to limit top party leaders' freedom of action – on the contrary, the aim is to increase the effectiveness of what Lenin called in his last published sentence the 'highly authoritative party elite'.

In his early polemics with the Narodniki (Populists), Lenin had argued that capitalism was necessary to shake Russia out of its 'asiatic' sleepiness. At the end of his life, he still felt that, although capitalism itself was no longer necessary, this cultural task remained on the agenda. 'Proletarian culture' was impossible without the cultural revolution that capitalism had wrought elsewhere.[20]

Lenin's concern was prompted by his Marxist conscience that told him (in the person of Nikolai Sukhanov and other socialist critics) that a socialist revolution was not possible without the material base created by capitalism and its accompanying cultural attitudes. Another source of concern was the practical problem of dealing with the peasantry. Both concerns presented the same challenges: how to get present-day Russia to the position that a western country would enjoy the day after the revolution; how to find an enlistment mechanism that would transform the peasants' outlook so that they could participate in the building of socialism. Lenin's main response to these cultural concerns was the cooperatives, although *shefstvo* and the village school teachers can be seen as political equivalents.[21]

Lenin was not particularly interested in the economic advantages of the cooperatives; for him they were an answer to socialist criticism based on Russia's lack of culture.[22] The cooperatives would act as the functional equivalent of capitalism and transform the Russian peasant who at present had not arrived even at the level of a 'cultured huckster'. Lenin did not see the cooperatives as an extension of NEP, but rather as a tool for overcoming NEP:

> Under NEP we made a concession to the peasant as a merchant and to the principle of private trade; precisely from this (contrary to what is thought) flows the gigantic significance of the cooperatives ... We went

---

19   Lenin 1958–1965, 45:447; see also 45:384.

20   Lenin 1958–1965, 45:364, 389–92. Lenin's remarks on this issue should be seen in the context of his long-standing dispute with Aleksandr Bogdanov. For details see Zenovia A. Sochor, *Revolution and Culture: The Bogdanov–Lenin Controversy* (Sochor 1988).

21   Lenin 1958–1965, 45:366–8. (For an earlier confrontation of Lenin with this question, see Lih, *Bolshevik Sowing Committees of 1920: Apotheosis of War Communism?*, included in this volume.)

22   Lenin 1958–1965, 45:376–7. On subsidies for the cooperatives, see Lenin 1958–1965, 45:371, 373, 405.

too far, going over to NEP, not because we attached too much importance to the principle of free production and trade – we went too far because we forgot to think about the cooperatives.[23]

In other words, even though allowing private trade was a necessary concession, the Bolsheviks must remember that they have to transform the peasants so that they no longer require such a concession.[24]

To understand the nature of Lenin's testament, we must start with some of the things that are not in the final writings. No new definition of socialism can be found there. Today one of the most popular phrases from the testament is 'we are compelled to admit a radical change of our whole point of view on socialism'. Lenin immediately makes it clear, however, that he is referring to the shift from the task of taking power over to the task of peacefully construct-ing socialism. Lenin would have been seriously offended by recent claims that he had moved beyond Marx's definition of socialism.[25]

The testament contains no critique of war communism. The very concept is missing: Lenin continually refers to the five years since the revolution as a unit, with an occasional mention of the fact that intervention and hunger slowed down the pace of socialist construction. The source of all evils is the pre-revolutionary past and the petit-bourgeois environment. The civil war is not a corrupter of Bolshevism but a source of inspiring examples.[26]

---

23   Lenin 1958–1965, 45:370–1.

24   A western scholar writing in 1931 correctly expressed the role assigned to the cooperatives: 'It is upon the cooperatives, therefore, that the chief responsibility has had to be placed for bringing the wide masses of the population in touch with socialized production ... Upon the basis of these declarations of Lenin in regard to cooperation, the Party has counted upon it to aid in the maximum curtailment of the life of the New Economic Policy' (Calvin B. Hoover, *The Economic Life of Soviet Russia* [Hoover 1931, pp. 225–7]). Viktor Danilov describes Bukharin's outlook as a 'cooperative-market conception of economic develop-ment', but this expression is misleading, since the cooperatives were meant to overcome the market. See Danilov, 'Bukharinskaia al'ternativa' (Danilov 1990, pp. 82–130); Danilov's important article greatly aided the revision of my conference paper before publication. (For more on Bukharin and the market, see 'Bukharin on Bolshevik Illusions', included in this collection.)

25   Vladlen Sirotkin, 'Uroki NEPa', *Izvestiia*, 9 and 10 March 1989; Mikhail Antonov in *Nash sovremennik*, 1989, no. 2, pp. 125–30. The descriptions of Lenin's putative new definition offered by these two authors show almost no similarity – a fact that is not surprising since Lenin himself said nothing on the subject. For an indication of the emotional nature of the debate over Lenin's phrase, see A. Tikhonov, *Ogonek*, 1989, no. 5, p. 19.

26   References to five years of revolution are in Lenin 1958–1965, 45:376, 385, 390, 397, 443, 449; references to the civil war 45:347, 357, 401–2, 410; the inspiring examples of the civil war can be found in Lenin 1958–1965, 45:383, 372–3, and 302–5 (November 1922).

The testament contains no deeper, wider vision of NEP. Lenin defends NEP on the basis of the need for economic recovery and as a justifiable concession to the peasants' backward outlook, but otherwise his attitude seems negative. NEP is associated with bureaucratism, a low level of economic productivity, nepmen, and the Brest retreat.[27]

The political testament is not a critique of Stalinism *avant la lettre*. Despite Lenin's anger at Stalin personally, the testament contains no warning against coercive assaults on the peasantry or murderous purges of the party, simply because it never occurred to Lenin that such things were possible. He never hints at a rethinking of the party's role. Lenin saw the top party institutions as effective and authoritative, and he wanted to ensure that they became more so.[28]

While these remarks may seem to remove much of the drama of Lenin's final testament, they increase its significance as an expression of Lenin's basic outlook. One reason for this significance is the lack of tight editorial control that allows the tensions inherent in Lenin's outlook to surface directly. These tensions sometimes look like contradictions, but they reflect the real conflicts of a revolutionary statesman entering unknown territory. One such tension is the relation between 'west' and 'east'. Sometimes the west is a symbol of civilization, up-to-date science, and progress as opposed to the sleepy, backward, 'uncultured' east; in other places the west is oppressive, stodgy, and malevolent, while the east is a revolutionary giant just beginning to feel its strength.[29]

The attitude toward bourgeois culture and bourgeois specialists reveals a similar ambivalence. Lenin wants his readers both to look up to the specialists as sources of knowledge and as teachers and to look down on them as potential saboteurs. Related to this attitude is reliance on the virtue of the workers combined with suspicions about their lack of culture.[30]

Another tension is that between patience and impatience – between careful self-discipline and revolutionary daring. Lenin expressed this tension directly in his formula about combining revolutionary enthusiasm with the ability to be

---

27   Lenin 1958–1965, 45: 372, 397, 401, 387, 381.
28   Despite Lenin's discontent with Stalin, he seemed to envision an expanded role for the secretariat. See Lenin 1958–1965, 45:443, 449, 385–6.
29   Lenin 1958–1965, 45:397, 401–6. For other anti-west references, see 45:378, 379, 399–400; for other pro-west references, see 45:364, 389.
30   Sometimes the tension in his attitude toward specialists results in virtual incoherence, as in Lenin's remarks on a suitable textbook in Lenin 1958–1965, 45:395. On workers, see Lenin 1958–1965, 45:390–1.

an efficient trader.[31] It can also be seen in the split between the attention given to improvement of administrative routine vs. the denunciation of 'bureaucratism' – between the calls for patience vs. the sneers at timidity before established routine.[32] As with the bourgeois specialists, Lenin calls for a psychologically difficult attitude of contempt toward a source of necessary discipline.

A tension between the desire for centralization and the desire for mass participation leads to the instability of the scheme to enlist workers: Sometimes election is stressed, sometimes appointment – sometimes an unspoiled nature is emphasized, other times professional expertise is paramount.

A final, and perhaps basic, tension is between shame and pride in Russia – shame over its backwardness and tsarist past, pride in its people and revolutionary future:

We are speaking of the half-asiatic lack of culture, from which we have not yet extricated ourselves, and from which we cannot extricate ourselves without strenuous effort – although we now have every opportunity to do so, because nowhere are the masses of the people so interested in real culture as they are in our country; nowhere are the problems of this culture tackled so thoroughly and consistently as they are in our country; in no other country is state power in the hands of the working class which, in its mass, is fully aware of the deficiencies, I shall not say of its culture, but of its literacy; nowhere is the working class so ready to make, and nowhere is it actually making, such sacrifices to improve its position in this respect as in our country.[33]

1   Bukharin and Lenin's 'Testament'

Lenin's final articles seem to have had an extraordinary effect on Bukharin. He refers to them continually throughout his many writings of the 1920s; indeed, they are almost the exclusive source of his Lenin citations. Before examining what Bukharin saw in these articles, we need to look first at the overall evolution of his own thinking and then to the threats he saw to the proper Leninist course.

---

31   Stalin picked up this formula in his *Foundations of Leninism* (1924) with his phrase about combining Russian revolutionary sweep and American *delovitost*.

32   Lenin 1958–1965, 45:389, 399–401. Compare also the assessments of the five years since the revolution on pp. 390, 392, 395.

33   Lenin 1958–1965, 45:364–5.

Bukharin's outlook is informed by his understanding of the evolution of capitalism. The general line of this analysis remained consistent from 1915 onwards.[34] The immanent law of capitalist development was 'the law of centralization and concentration' that was replacing the capitalism of the competitive market. This trend was a progressive one, even though the various social contradictions of capitalism did not allow the complete rationalization of the economy. 'Under the shell of monopolistic capitalism has grown a system of concentrated means of production ... and an organization of social labour of vast power and scope, preparing the foundations of the rationalization of the whole industrial process.'[35]

Monopolistic 'finance capitalism' provided the empirical grounding for Bukharin's understanding of the dynamics of the transition to socialism in Russia. Bukharin's typical mode of argument is to say, 'look at what has happened under capitalism; the process with us is – in a *formal* sense – the same'. The similarity between monopoly capitalism and the Soviet economy was only formal because of the proletarian dictatorship, which transforms the class content of the process. The pressure of the masses, as expressed by the ruling Communist party, will prevent capitalist irrationality and parasitism.

A typical example of Bukharin's reasoning is the crucial chapter on town and country relations in *Economics of the Transition Period* (written in 1920). Bukharin first observes the danger of a growing disproportion between agriculture and industry. He then asks how capitalism deals with this life and death challenge (since 'agriculture – especially in a time of shocks – is the decisive branch of production'). Since, unlike industry, agricultural production is not concentrated, the 'organizational process' of state capitalism in this area takes the form of regulating 'circulation' – that is, exchange between town and country. Regulation takes place by means of the cooperatives and can include even the small peasant enterprise. (NB: even in 1920, at the height of so-called 'war communism', Bukharin stresses the role of the cooperatives.)

Later in the chapter Bukharin considers the central challenge to the Bolshevik revolutionary project: 'In what forms can we establish the organizing

---

34   For Bukharin's analysis of capitalism, see *Mirovoe khoziaistvo i imperializm, Problemy* 21–93; 'Toward a Theory of the Imperialist State' (Bukharin 1982, pp. 6–37) (both these works were written in 1915); *Azbuka kommunizma* (Bukharin and Evgenii Preobrazhensky 1920), pp. 88–91; *Ekonomika perekhodnogo perioda* (Bukharin 1920, pp. 7–26); 'The Theory of "Organized Economic Disorder"' in Bukharin 1982, pp. 331–51; 'Tekhnika i ekonomika sovremennogo kapitalizma' (Bukharin 1932, pp. 64–107).

35   Bukharin 1932b, pp. 106–7.

influence of the proletarian town? And how can we achieve a new equilibrium *between* town and village?' His answer: 'For the main mass of *small producers*, their involvement in the organizational apparatus is possible, for the most part, through *the sphere of circulation*, and therefore formally [sic] in the same way as under state capitalism.'[36] Under normal circumstances, the cooperatives will be the basic instrument in his process. Although *Economics of the Transition Period* is often regarded as the most vivid expression of 'war communist' ideology, Bukharin reproduced the substance of this argument more than once during the 1920s.[37]

When we understand the underlying structure of Bukharin's argument, we see that it is incorrect to assert that he was moving towards a conception of a 'socialist market' or 'socialist pluralism'. On the contrary, in 1925 as in 1920, Bukharin looked forward to an economy that would be a 'single organized whole' under the direction of a centralized state.[38] Yes, Bukharin vividly describes the many irrationalities of state-organized capitalism, attributes these irrationalities to the absence of 'the spur of competition', and mentions the danger of a similar degeneration under socialism.[39] Thus for a modern reader his analysis seems to imply the necessity of pluralism and the market, but Bukharin's outlook ensured that he himself did not move toward that conclusion. For him, the trend toward organization and concentration was the rational kernel of economic evolution; no remedy for bureaucratic degeneration that backtracked toward anarchic competition was acceptable to him. The only kind of competition that Bukharin accepted was between economic forms, that is, between socialism and capitalism: Socialism had to prove its superiority in deeds, not just in words. Even this type of competition was not desirable in itself; Bukharin wished to see it concluded triumphantly as soon as possible.

Bukharin's use of the analogy with finance capitalism also shows why his emphasis on the cooperatives had nothing to do with pluralism, if by that term we mean autonomy from a directing centre. In his famous 'Enrich yourselves!'

---

36   Bukharin 1920, pp. 73–87. Karl Kautsky is cited as an authority for the last statement.

37   Bukharin 1988, pp. 140–3, 171–5. The continuity in Bukharin's aims on this particular point is noted by Lewin 1974, p. 43 and Danilov 1990, p. 89. In 1933, Bukharin directly equated the withering away of the state with the withering away of society: 'Enlisting *everybody* into its immediate organization, the state stops being itself; by absorbing society into itself, it dissolves itself into society without trace' (Bukharin 1989a, p. 409).

38   Bukharin used the words 'single organized whole' (*odno organizovannoe tseloe*) both in 1920 (Bukharin 1920, p. 110) and in 1925 (Bukharin 1988, p. 175).

39   *Mezhdunarodnoe i vnutrennee polozhenie SSSR* (Bukharin 1927, pp. 35–7); 'Theory of "Organized Economic Disorder"' (Bukharin 1982).

speech of spring 1925, Bukharin began his discussion of the cooperatives by noting their dependent status under capitalism. He then went on to argue that a workers' state should be able to do even better:

> How will we be able to draw [the peasant] into our socialist organization? ... We will provide him with material incentives as a small property-owner. This isn't frightening at all, because in the final analysis, on the basis of this very same economic growth, the peasant will be moved along the path of our transformation of both himself and his enterprise into a particle of our general state socialist system – just as he grows into capitalist relations under a capitalist regime![40]

Within the socialist sector, political pressure – not competition – would ward off the degeneration that threatened any monopoly. Bukharin's vision of peaceful evolution was thus premised on the economic power and political unity of the state.[41] As he wrote in 1925: 'the general line of the proletariat during its dictatorship is a line toward *strengthening* the social whole, a line *against* schisms in society, a line for the consolidation of the state (until that phase when its "dying away" commences)'. In 1926, he insisted that factionalism within the party would aid the nepmen and the kulaks. In his 1929 article on Lenin's testament, he sets forth his view without ambiguity:

> In the last analysis, the state apparatus is the very lever, the very machine, through which our party, the victorious leader of the proletariat, will direct all of our politics; if we look from the point of view of the future, then our state apparatus is the very organization through which we must draw in millions, all the toilers without exception, and so attain a definite stage in the transition to the state-commune – from which, unfortunately, we are still very distant.[42]

---

40   Bukharin 1988, pp. 142–3. See also his objection to independent peasant organizations in *XIV s'ezd vsesoiuznoi kommunisticheskoi partii (b)* 1926, p. 131.

41   Bukharin 1927, pp. 37–8; Bukharin 1988, pp. 105–8. Bukharin did oppose over-centralization: see *Fourth Congress of the Communist International* 1923, p. 170, and Bukharin 1988, p. 417. The need to find a replacement for market competition was a commonplace of the period; see Hiroaki Kuromiya, *Stalin's Industrial Revolution: Politics and Workers, 1928–1932* (Kuromiya 1988). On the power and unity of the state, see Bukharin 1988, pp. 78, 138–9.

42   Bukharin 1988, pp. 433–4. For the other quoted statements in the paragraph, see Bukharin, *Kritika ekonomicheskoi platformy oppozitsii* (Bukharin 1926b, p. 47); Bukharin 1998, p. 264. Other references to the state include Bukharin 1988, pp. 71–4, 78–9, 139, 348–50, 358; *The*

When I began investigating Bukharin's conception of war communism and NEP, I assumed that he had tied his critique of war communism closely to his critique of the party opposition. To my surprise, I found that for the most part Bukharin separated the two critiques. Overcoming the remaining influence of war communism was a relatively minor problem for Bukharin; the serious threat to the proper Leninist course came from the party opposition.

To place these critiques in context, we must first chart Bukharin's conception of NEP. Some claim that any inclination to see NEP as a retreat was (and is) a sign of hostility to NEP and that defenders of NEP, such as Lenin and Bukharin, were moving away from this negative view. I believe that clarity on this matter is possible if we pay close attention to the content of the retreat and subsequent advance. We can do this by means of the four -*stups* (a root-word meaning 'step', appropriately enough for so dynamic a phenomenon as NEP): *otstuplenie, ustupka, dostupno* and *nastuplenie*. Bukharin's outlook can be paraphrased as follows: The retreat (*otstuplenie*) in 1921 was from a state trade monopoly to free trade – not from the *prodrazverstka*, a heavy wartime tax.[43] The decriminalization of free trade was a concession (*ustupka*) to the small individual owner-peasant that cleared the way for forms of advance understandable and accessible (*dostupno*) to peasants. As soon as economic recovery made it possible, the advance would start again (*nastuplenie*): private trade would be 'crowded out' by the combined forces of state trade and the cooperative apparatus, using peaceful economic measures. The 'crowding-out' policy was not in itself a new one, but rather that standard Bolshevik policy adapted to the new circumstances of a decriminalized market. Thus while including an undeniable element of retreat, NEP also entailed a subsequent advance toward a planned economy. The overcoming of NEP would be NEP's own doing.

Bukharin set forth this conception of NEP in 1921–1922. In the course of an extended comparison to the Brest peace – another retreat that made possible a later advance – Bukharin writes that once the Bolsheviks had built up the economy,

we will 'turn the rudder'. But this new reversal in the direction of the rudder will not, by any means, imply a return to the past, to *prodrazverstka* and the like ... The 'turn of the rudder' will involve gradual economic

---

Path to Socialism in Russia, ed. Sidney Heitman (Bukharin 1967, p. 178). See especially the refutation of anarchism in *Teoriia istoricheskogo materializma*, 9th ed. (Bukharin 1929, p. 345).

43   On the *prodrazverstka*, see 'Bolshevik *Razverstka* and War Communism', included in this volume.

liquidation of the large-scale private economy and [its replacement by] economic subordination of the small producer to large-scale industrial leadership. The small producer will be drawn into the socialized economy, not by measures of extra-economic compulsion, but, for the most part, by the economic benefits he will gain from tractors, electric lights, agricultural machines, etc. He will find himself enmeshed (to his own advantage) in *electric wires*, which bring life-giving energy to fertilize the economy.[44]

It is sometimes argued that Bukharin changed this conception as the 1920s wore on and he began to see the desirability of moving further in the direction of the original retreat. For political reasons, he could not be fully explicit about his change of heart and so he continued to talk about overcoming the market, but in reality this event was put off to the remote end of the transition period and even beyond. More and more (we are told) Bukharin realized that market relations had permanent positive value as a barrier to monopolistic degradation and the tyranny of a centralized state.[45]

I believe, on the contrary, that after the initial 'zig' of the decriminalization of the market, Bukharin looked forward to a steady, straight-line 'zag' toward the replacement of the market by a planned economy. It is true that in his polemics with Stalin in 1928–1929 Bukharin insisted on the necessity of preserving market relations for the time being. Bukharin argued that collective farms would not be able to replace individual peasant enterprises any time in the near future, and under these circumstances the market was the only available mechanism for managing economic relations with the peasantry. But in a comparative context, the market's association with the scattered and primitive individual peasantry meant that it was a badge of backwardness:

> The specific feature of the USSR is not NEP as such, but the *dimensions* of NEP and the *scope* of market relations ... The greater the industrial development of a country and the more it is industrialized, the smaller role will market relations play after the proletariat's seizure of power. From a dynamic point of view, [the more developed the country,] the faster we will be able to overcome NEP, that is, overcome market relations on the basis of those same market relations. Development in the context of mar-

---

44   Bukharin 1988, pp. 28–30 (translation in Bukharin 1982, pp. 105–6). See also 'The New Economic Policy of Soviet Russia' in *The New Policies of Soviet Russia* (Bukharin 1921); Lenin 1958–1965, 45:302 (November 1922).

45   Lewin 1974, pp. 46–7.

ket relations will be accompanied by the growth of the whole economic mechanism: The scope of market relations will be less, the tempo of its disappearance will be quicker, and there will be a quicker tempo of socialist development, from embryonic forms to a fully valid socialist economy, consisting of a single homogeneous organism.[46]

Bukharin's conditional tolerance of the market in the late 1920s did not imply any fondness for the private middleman or for competition within the state sector. In 1927, for example, he pointed with pride to the re-establishment of the grain monopoly that had been removed at the beginning of NEP. In 1928, one of his major remedies for inadequate grain procurement was to eliminate competition between state purchasing organs in order to create a 'single procurement front'.[47]

The analogy with capitalist evolution that was so integral to Bukharin's outlook also supports the sincerity of his hopes that NEP would 'negate itself'. Why not allow market forms, if they were politically or economically expedient? Just like capitalism everywhere else, the competitive market under NEP would evolve in the direction of a single organized whole.[48] It would be strange indeed if Bukharin's vision of the final goal included features (such as market competition) that he felt had already been left behind by the capitalist west.

Bukharin saw at least two threats to this vision of NEP: the illusions created by war communism and the party opposition's lack of faith in the possibility of constructing socialism without outside help. The influence of war communism was definitely the lesser threat.[49] While war communism had been a necessary set of measures, many in the party had erroneously absolutized the necessary methods of civil war. The end of the civil war and the introduction of NEP dissipated this error on the theoretical level, but moods and habits remained from earlier times, especially among students and 'our comrades in the villages'. These habits had to be combated, for example, by the measures introduced in

---

46   Speech to Comintern Congress in August 1928 (Bukharin 1989a, p. 213). The most explicit statement of Bukharin's differences with Stalin is his speech to the Central Committee in April 1929, published for the first time in Bukharin 1989, pp. 253–308. For Bukharin's views on the use of market forms after collectivization, see G.A. Bordiugov and V.A. Kozlov, 'Pozdnii Bukharin: Predstavleniia o sotsializme' (Bordiugov 1990, pp. 149–161). (For more discussion of Bukharin's changing attitudes toward Stalin's policies, see 'Bukharin's Bolshevik Epic: The Prison Writings', included in this volume.)

47   Bukharin 1988, p. 326; see also pp. 79, 192–8, 237, 325, 397, 405; Bukharin 1990a, p. 270.

48   Bukharin 1988, pp. 196–7, 447–8.

49   For more on Bukharin's rhetorical use of 'war communism', see 'Bukharin on Bolshevik "Illusions"', included in this volume.

early 1925 to allow greater opportunity for individual accumulation in the villages. By 1927 Bukharin seemed to think that this task had been more or less accomplished.[50]

Whatever the problems associated with war communism, it never led to any doubts about the worker-peasant alliance. Indeed, this alliance had been the basis of victory in the civil war. The bearers of war-communist illusions simply had to learn some new empirical answers to the same old question: how to vanquish the class enemy, how to build socialism by means of the worker-peasant alliance. As Bukharin wrote in an early philippic against Evgenii Preobrazhensky, 'up till now, *no one* has spoken against the worker-peasant bloc. [It is] an axiom in our ranks.'[51]

According to Bukharin, the party oppositionists had rejected this axiom both in theory and practice. In this way, Bukharin put the oppositionists into a polemical framework he had earlier constructed during the revolution and civil war, particularly in *Economics of the Transition Period*. This polemic was based on the issue of Russia's ripeness (*zrelost*) for revolution. The oppositionists were the most recent link in a long chain of capitalist and socialist critics who claimed that, as a 'petit-bourgeois peasant country', Russia was barren soil for a socialist revolution. The oppositionists were 'neo-Mensheviks' who had an exaggerated fear of degeneration of the revolution, owing to their panicky fear of the peasants. Their only solution in response to this fear was to build socialism on the ruination (*razorenie*) of the individual peasant or to wait for help from the victorious western proletariat. The symbol of the party opposition was not the overconfident war communist, but the defeatism and *dezertirstvo* of Zinoviev and Lev Kamenev in October 1917.[52]

Bukharin mainly used Lenin's final writings in his polemic with the oppositionists rather than with the war communists. The people Bukharin called

---

50 For discussions of war communism, see 'O likvidatorstve nashikh dnei', in Bukharin 1967, pp. 117–82; Bukharin 1988, pp. 122–45 (1925), pp. 316–23 (1927). Coercive emergency measures applied in a real emergency can be based on optimism about an underlying unity of interests. Emergency measures as a permanent system can only be based on a more pessimistic outlook. For this reason Bukharin accused Stalin in 1929 of an 'ideological capitulation' to the party opposition (Bukharin 1989, p. 266).

51 Bukharin 1988, p. 153; quotation on p. 97; see also pp. 75–7. Bukharin's accusation that Preobrazhensky attacked the worker-peasant alliance strikes me as a semi-deliberate misinterpretation.

52 Bukharin 1988, pp. 356–9. The most extended treatment is 'O karakhtere nashei revoliutsiia' in Bukharin 1988, pp. 277–315. At the fourteenth party congress, Bukharin accused Zinoviev of wanting to return to civil war methods; Zinoviev indignantly rejected the charge and Bukharin dropped the point (*XIV s"ezd* 1926, pp. 151, 427–9; Bukharin 1988, p. 244).

'war communists' were not guilty of ideological errors but only of insufficient practical flexibility; certainly they had always accepted the need for a worker-peasant alliance and, at least by the mid-twenties, they had been brought to see the practical necessity for a retreat followed by a more complicated advance. Lenin's final writings did not directly address these kinds of issues.

Lenin's testament, as expressed in his final writings, was a more useful weapon in the battle with the party oppositionists, since (Bukharin alleged) the oppositionists denied the axiom of the worker-peasant alliance as a path to socialism. Given this deeper challenge, Lenin's testament was needed not merely to show where the path could be found, but also to prove that such a path existed at all. In Bukharin's view, the main purpose of the testament was not to restrain revolutionary enthusiasm left over from the civil war (as often implied by historians), but rather to instil confidence and to refute the nay-sayers who magnified the difficulties of constructing socialism in one country. Even in 1929, on the eve of full-scale collectivization, Bukharin claimed that Lenin wrote these articles because he had foreseen attacks from the ranks of sceptics and pessimists.[53]

Any assertion that Lenin's testament led to real change in Bukharin's strategic plan is difficult to substantiate. Even before NEP, much less the appearance of the final articles, we see Bukharin answering his basic question 'in what forms can we establish the organizing influence of the proletarian town?' with the following elements: the primacy of circulation over production; the need to appeal only to the peasants' material interests; the cooperative's usefulness as a link in the chain of organization; the fear of bureaucratic degeneration; the eventual crowding-out of private trade; the long-term goal of an all-embracing, but democratic, central authority.

If the final articles had any real effect on Bukharin, they gave him permission to use his analysis of capitalist evolution as a framework for building socialism. The capitalists wanted civil peace to ensure a painless, crisis-free transition to organized production. The Bolsheviks had always denied and continued to deny that such a transition was possible – under capitalism. Lenin's testament gave Bukharin the authority he needed to argue that such a transition was possible *after* the revolution and that, therefore, the formal analogy with capitalist evolution was legitimate. The Bolsheviks would succeed in doing with the peasants what the capitalists had failed to do with the workers.[54]

---

53   Bukharin 1988, p. 420 (there is no mention of war communism in this article devoted to Lenin's political testament). See also Bukharin 1988, pp. 104, 305, 348–50.

54   For a schematic representation of Bukharin's perspective, see the charts added to *Ekonomika* (Bukharin 1920). These charts can also be found in Bukharin 1967, pp. 138–44.

In 1920, Bukharin argued that the cooperative network created by capitalism faced three possibilities: It would atrophy if town and country remained in economic isolation from each other; it would have to be destroyed if the kulaks used it as an instrument in a class offensive against the proletariat; 'it can be drawn in to the overall socialist organization of distribution and gradually rebuilt (given the resurrection of the real process of product exchange and the decisive *economic* influence of the towns)'.[55] Bukharin obviously preferred the third alternative; Lenin's testament gave him the basis for believing it was possible.

NEP is often defined primarily in terms of its contrast with war communism. This contrast has also served as an interpretive framework for Soviet political history as a whole. Left and majority in the 1920s, 'general line' and 'right deviationists' during the Stalin period, dogmatists and reformists during the post-Stalin period – all these have been seen in terms of the original contrast between war communism and NEP.

The plausibility of this framework has been strengthened by the adoption of NEP as a legitimating symbol for the reforms of Mikhail Gorbachev. Lenin's testament in particular has been treated almost as a charter for perestroika.[56] Bukharin's own reliance on Lenin's testament, with his opposition to Stalin in the late 1920s, has provided further support for the idea that Lenin and Bukharin were united in seeing the chief danger to the party as a resurgence of war communism (read 'proto-Stalinism').

A close reading of the texts in question does not support this interpretation. Neither Lenin nor Bukharin saw the civil-war period as a source of possible degeneration for the party. The illusions created by the necessary policies of war communism had been for the most part overcome.[57] Lenin saw no need to discuss this kind of illusion in his final articles, and Bukharin did not use Lenin's testament to prove the necessity of the original retreat. The main threats to the party lay elsewhere: the infection of the petit-bourgeois environment, the danger of a party schism, and the defeatism of pseudo-Marxists frightened by Russian backwardness.

My reading also points to the possibility that NEP had a less fundamental effect on the strategic outlook of Lenin and Bukharin than is often suggested.

---

55   Bukharin 1920, pp. 86–7.

56   Gorbachev has called the testament 'a revolution within the revolution, no less profound, perhaps, than October' (*Pravda*, 21 April 1990). (For more on this topic, see my article 'Perestroika Looks Back', included in this volume.)

57   Lenin 1958–1965, 45:302 (November 1922); Bukharin 1988, p. 128.

These leaders did not point the way to any 'deepening of NEP' but insisted rather on NEP's eventual self-overcoming. If true, my reading weakens the claim that Lenin or Bukharin directly expressed major reform ideas of today (1991). On the other hand, it strengthens the central contention of those who see a discontinuity between Bolshevism and Stalinism. Lenin's testament and Bukharin's interpretation of it remain an eloquent expression of the basic Bolshevik outlook betrayed by Stalin.

Bukharin on Bolshevik 'Illusions': 'War Communism' vs. NEP

'The transition to the new economic policy was the collapse of our illusions' – so asserted Bukharin in 1924. 'Collapse of our illusions' – this seems to be a very strong phrase, and so the natural tendency is to give this remark a maximalist interpretation. According to this interpretation, Bukharin's use of the word 'illusions' points to a whole series of impressive contrasts between war communism and NEP: from a 'leap into socialism' to an acceptance of a long and gradual path, from a glorification of coercion to a repudiation of violent class struggle, from a denial of the role of material incentives to an appreciation of the market, from an emphasis on statist centralization to a pluralist reliance on competition, from a radical and repressive attitude toward the peasantry to an acceptance of the peasants as allies. These shifts in outlook are exemplified most dramatically by Bukharin himself, who (we are told) moved at top speed from the left extreme of the party to its extreme right. In 1920, he wrote a book that many consider to be the apotheosis of the war communist outlook, *Economy of the Transition Period*. Only five years later, he wrote *The Path to Socialism and the Worker-Peasant Alliance*, the most extended and spirited defence of NEP produced by the party leadership.[1]

When we turn to Bukharin's own elaboration of his 'illusions' formula, a surprising fact emerges: Bukharin devised the formula in order to *minimize* the contrast between war communism and NEP. Indeed, if Bukharin could see the picture of him current today – painted by friends even more than by foes – he would be outraged: the views attributed to him are precisely those he vehemently attacked. Bukharin never repudiated the main theses of *Econ-*

---

1 An influential statement of this standard view is Moshe Lewin, *Political Undercurrents in Soviet Economic Debates* (Lewin 1974) (Lewin republished the book in 1991 under the title *Stalinism and the Seeds of Soviet Reform*). Stephen F. Cohen's magisterial *Bukharin and the Bolshevik Revolution* (Cohen 1971) also gives support to the scenario of Bukharin's rethinking of Bolshevism, although in a more historically grounded and nuanced way. From a Trotskyist perspective, Donny Gluckstein's *The Tragedy of Bukharin* correctly denies that Bukharin was moving toward market socialism, but also affirms that Bukharin's infatuation with NEP meant that 'with a stroke of the pen all the arguments of *The Economics* [sic] *of the Transition Period* were consigned to the dust as though they had never existed' (Gluckstein 1994, p. 80).

omy of the Transition Period: he aggressively defended them throughout the 1920s. Bukharin never viewed the transition to NEP as a defeat and an occasion for serious rethinking: rather, he attacked the critics and the 'secret sceptics' who claimed that such rethinking had taken place. Bukharin's NEP-era formula 'overcoming the market through the market' was not an expression of a sneaking admiration for pluralism and competition: Bukharin was supremely confident that a centrally-organized planned economy was in the works. And Bukharin indignantly rejected any insinuation that he himself saw NEP as a semi-permanent condition rather than as a transitional phase.

My original aim for this essay was to discover what Bukharin meant by 'the collapse of our illusions' by looking at his pronouncements on war communism during the 1920s.[2] I soon discovered that Bukharin's portrayal of war communism could not be disentangled from his portrayal of NEP. Bukharin did not have an academic interest in historical questions: he brought up the issue of war communism only when he wanted to explain and justify the ongoing policies of NEP. Conversely, he rarely talked explicitly about NEP without contrasting it to war communism. Thus the 'collapse of our illusions' remark turns out to be one end of a thread that leads us to an investigation of Bukharin's conception not only of war communism but also of NEP and indeed the Bolshevik revolution as a whole.

I shall focus on two revealing episodes where Bukharin addressed himself to the relation between war communism and NEP. In 1921, he responded to a sharp attack from a fellow Bolshevik who argued that *Economy of the Transition Period* was already outmoded. In 1924, Bukharin launched his 'collapse of our illusions' formula. Although Bukharin's pronouncements were always closely attuned to his immediate polemical aims, these two episodes as well as other polemical disputes during NEP show that he remained loyal to his basic outlook with a truly stubborn consistency.[3]

---

2   In other essays included in this volume, I argue that 'war communism' is a misleading construct that should be abandoned for purposes of historical analysis. To that end, I usually put the term in scare quotes, but I feel that doing so in this essay would be overly distracting.

3   Two further episodes revolved around the same set of issues. In 1925, the government introduced measures that granted economic freedoms to village kulaks and Bukharin invoked the spectre of war communism in his defence of these measures. In 1928, the Comintern debated the universal significance of war communism and NEP for revolutions around the world; Bukharin and Stalin used the occasion to carry on a muffled debate about the dangers of the 'extraordinary measures' adopted in response to the crisis in grain procurements. These later episodes are treated in more detail in the original publication of this essay (Lih 2000).

1   1921: Should Bukharin's Face Have Been Red?

In 1920 Bukharin published his theoretical magnum opus *Economy of the Transition Period* (henceforth ETP). This book contained not only a wide-ranging theoretical argument about the nature of proletarian revolution but also a belligerent justification of actual Bolshevik policies. In spring 1921, immediately after the introduction of NEP, a long-time party member named Mikhail Olminsky attacked ETP as 'revisionism from the left': theoretical nonsense that was a testimonial to the foolishness of sections of the party in 1920. A response considerably longer than Olminsky's original review was immediately penned by Bukharin and Georgii (Iurii) Piatakov (Piatakov had provided the first draft of one chapter of ETP).[4]

According to the few scholars who have looked at this exceptionally revealing exchange, the introduction of NEP gave Olminsky such an advantage that Bukharin and Piatakov barely bothered to fight back.[5] This impression rests on and helps to confirm the idea that ETP was an apotheosis of war communism and, as such, literally indefensible after the transition to NEP. In reality, the joint Bukharin-Piatakov response was an extremely angry and aggressive defence of the ETP's central arguments. They dismissed Olminsky's critique as an unrecognizable parody of their book.

Olminsky's review was indeed wildly inaccurate about the actual content of ETP. Unfortunately, the Olminsky interpretation won out and it now provides a keystone in the edifice of the scholarly consensus about war communism. Bukharin's vigorous rebuttal of Olminsky is simultaneously his challenge – fifty or sixty years ahead of time – to current academic accounts of his own outlook during 'war communism'.

In their 1921 defence, Bukharin and Piatakov announced that 'the central idea of the book is (a) the working apparatus of society inevitably falls apart

---

4   Both Olminsky's review and the response of Bukharin and Piatakov were published in *Krasnaia nov*, 1921, No. 1 (June), pp. 247–51, 256–74; Bukharin and Piatakov also took the occasion to respond to other critics of ETP. The entire exchange is reprinted in Bukharin, *Izbrannye proizvedeniia* (Bukharin 1990b, pp. 208–39); references are to this edition. This volume of selected works by Bukharin, devoted solely to economic writings, should be distinguished from a similar volume published in 1988, also entitled *Izbrannye proizvedeniia* (Bukharin 1988). (For further discussion of the ETP, see 'Bolshevism's "Services to the State": Three Voices', included in this volume.)

5   Stephen Cohen writes: 'With war communism then in the process of being dismantled and discredited, Olminsky scored some easy points ... Bukharin responded in a light vein, reprimanding Olminsky for his charges of "revisionism"' (Cohen 1971, p. 96); for similar remarks, see László Szamuely, *First Models of the Socialist Economic System: Principles and Theories* (Szamuely 1974).

during the transition period, (b) reorganization presupposes temporary disorganization, and (c) a temporary fall in productive forces is therefore an immanent law of revolution'.[6] This is an accurate statement of the main thesis of ETP
but it does not bring out the emotional tone of Bukharin's passionate book.
These qualities are immediately evident in Bukharin's thesis statement from
the book's opening pages:

> The old society in both its state and its productive guises splits apart, *falls
> apart to its very depths, to its uttermost foundations.* Never has there been
> such a grandiose breakdown. But without such a breakdown there can be
> no proletarian revolution, which takes the elements that have fallen apart
> and – with new links, new combinations, new principles – constructs the
> foundation of the future society ...
>   [He who does not see the necessity of this process] recoils in horror
> from the world-encompassing tragedy that humanity is undergoing. He
> is incapable of looking through the smoke of fire and thunder of the civil
> war to see the solemn and triumphal outlines of the future society. He will
> always remain a pathetic philistine whose intellect is as cowardly as his
> 'politics'.[7]

Bukharin's starting point was thus the realization that the economic collapse
of Russia during the civil war was a human tragedy that seemed to mock the
hopes inspired by the revolution. His response was not to deny the facts but
rather to insist that a collapse of similar dimensions was an inevitable even
though horrifying price to pay for the establishment of proletarian class power.
He wanted to convince his readers – and perhaps himself – that socialist writers
such as Karl Kautsky were 'pathetic philistines' when they pointed to Russia's
economic collapse as proof that the Bolshevik revolution had been premature.

It is strange that such a book is so often used as proof of a 'shortcut' mentality among Bolsheviks in 1920. Far from arguing that Russia was on the verge
of full socialism, Bukharin argued that a period of 'disequilibrium' and chaos
intervened before *any* constructive work was possible. Indeed, it seems to me
that Bukharin's fellow Bolsheviks should have criticized the book, not for its
non-existent 'leap into socialism' utopianism, but for its off-putting pessimism

---

6 Bukharin 1990b, pp. 217–18 (Bukharin response).
7 *Ekonomika perekhodnogo perioda* (Bukharin 1920, pp. 5–6 [emphasis in original]). The entire
   text is reproduced in Bukharin 1990b, pp. 81–207; page numbers in my citations are taken
   from the Prideaux Press reprint (Letchworth-Herts, England, 1980) of the 1920 edition. The
   title is usually translated as '*Economics* of the Transition Period', but *Economy* is correct.

about the immediate costs of revolution. What an enticing propaganda line for workers in more advanced countries! – don't think that you'll avoid a Russian-style collapse when you have your own revolution, because this kind of tragedy is a *universal law of revolution*.[8]

How did this rather glum book get transmogrified into a paradigm of the hallucinatory optimism alleged to be dominant among Bolsheviks in 1920? Olminsky's review provides a model for this operation, which proceeds as follows: Give absolutely no attention to the 'central idea' of ETP. Limit your attention explicitly to the last three chapters, particularly those devoted to the special topics of economic categories and revolutionary use of force. Seize on scandalous-sounding sentences and use them to draw out implications that clash directly with the book's central idea. Hold the resulting nonsense up to scorn and dismiss it as explainable only by the atmosphere of 1920.[9]

In the antepenultimate chapter of ETP, for example, we read that Marxist categories applicable to capitalism 'instantly ... begin to misfire' after the break-down of the capitalist system and the onset of proletarian rule.[10] For Olminsky, these outrageous words meant that Marxism was reduced to a memory:

> Given the instant decision about the instant death of Marxist categories, Bukharin doesn't even feel the need to pose the question of the degree of the control of production on the part of the proletarian 'conscious regula-tor': for him the complete triumph of this regulator begins, evidently, from the moment of the birth of bureaucratic institutions set up to master pro-duction. Who cares if *spetsy* are sitting in these institutions – yesterday's enterprise owners or stock-holders and their hangers-on, high adminis-trative and technical personnel of bourgeois enterprises? Who cares if these institutions 'control' not so much production as the destruction of productive forces by means of hidden sabotage, or if the overwhelming

---

8   In *The Bolshevik Revolution*, E.H. Carr writes that in ETP Bukharin 'had treated war com-munism as a process of transition, appropriate to the special Russian conditions, from capitalism to socialism' (Carr 1950–1955, p. 274). In fact, this is a succinct statement of the position Bukharin sets out to disprove.

9   For an example of an Olminsky-type parody of ETP's argument, see Alec Nove's immensely influential *Economic History of the Soviet Union* (Nove 1969), p. 66.

10   Bukharin 1920, pp. 124–5. Bukharin and Piatakov felt that categories devised for a society ruled by capitalists who aim to reproduce capitalism were inappropriate for a society ruled by a proletariat that aims to destroy it. Much of their discussion in ETP assumes, not full socialism, but the chaos and breakdown attendant upon the revolution. Bukharin contin-ued to assert during the twenties that economic categories like 'wages' or 'wage worker' were not fully appropriate to workers in state industry under a proletarian dictatorship.

mass of the population in the country consists of small-scale producers, producing up to now the great majority of goods? All this is unimportant to Bukharin: for him the concepts of commodity, value, wages, the concept of money as a universal equivalent have instantly stopped working.[11]

In reality, sabotage by *spetsy* and a breakdown in vital exchanges between city and village are discussed at length by Bukharin, who sees them as principal reasons for the inevitable collapse of production. Thus Olminsky's summary of Bukharin stands the book's actual argument on its head.

The penultimate chapter of ETP is devoted to the topic of 'extra-economic compulsion'. The sentence which most offended Olminsky from this chapter is probably still the one most frequently cited out of the whole book: 'From a larger point of view, from the point of view of a grander historical scale, proletarian compulsion in all its forms, beginning with shooting and ending with labour service, is – paradoxical as it sounds – a method of creating communist humanity from the human material of the capitalist epoch.'[12] Strangely enough, though, Olminsky himself is prepared to justify Bolshevik policies of revolutionary violence:

Of course, it would be stupid and destructive to the revolutionary cause to refuse to use violence and compulsion during the period of sharp civil war (whether open or hidden). It would repel a communist conscience to feed able-bodied parasites. Here – especially in the case of active enemies – we have to go by the rule: 'Shoot the enemy if you don't want him to hang you.' In such moments it is possible – and sometimes necessary – to have compulsory mobilization of the working people for work that from a social point of view cannot be delayed.

But as the struggle abates, as the proletarian system is solidified, it will be essential to shrink the area of coercion and to soften its forms, since compulsion is not at all a method of creating communist humanity, but rather an act of self-defence. And one can hardly rely on communists that are forced into communism by the threat of shooting.[13]

---

11   Bukharin 1990b, pp. 211–12 (Olminsky review). Note that in the first sentence of this passage, Olminsky says 'evidently': he cannot come up with a smoking gun where Bukharin actually asserts the idiocies attributed to him.

12   Bukharin 1920, p. 146.

13   Bukharin 1990b, p. 214 (Olminsky review). To Olminsky's credit, it should be noted that he criticized the Cheka treatment of peasants in a *Pravda* article of 1918, according to Iu. V. Emelianov, *Zametki o Bukharine* (Emelianov 1989).

In this passage, Olminsky approves of the actual policies justified by Bukharin; conversely, he does not give a single concrete example of Bukharin's advocacy of an illegitimate use of force. Why, then, is he so upset by Bukharin's argument? Because he attributes to Bukharin the claim that compulsion is not *a* method but *the* method for creating communist humanity: 'To the question of the type of method for the creation of communist humanity, he gives a single answer: extra-economic compulsion.' Olminsky even implies that Bukharin justifies *all* violence, including armed robbery (*razboi*). It is not difficult for Olminsky to refute the views he attributes to Bukharin: 'Marxists are not at all inclined to limit [sic] themselves to the Bukharin method of forced labour [*katorga*] and shooting. This is the profound Marxist sense in comrade Lenin's constant emphasis on tractors and electrification.'[14]

Once again, Olminsky's analysis of a single sentence turns Bukharin on his head. In their response, Bukharin and Piatakov ask with understandable exasperation: how is it Olminsky missed our extensive discussion of the technical revolution? They might also have cited ETP's glorification of electrification in particular: 'The electrification of industry, the creation of huge power stations, and the creation of a mighty transportation network will radically revise the relations between town and village. Not only will it aid the transformation of scattered petty property-owners into social labourers, it rationalizes and radically revises the whole process of agricultural production.'[15]

Olminsky's final thrust against Bukharin comes from ETP's final chapter, in which Bukharin 'speaks of the future in the present tense, as if all the awaited conquests are already attained ... What the heart desires must be realized now, this minute. He doesn't want to know about the slow transitions of [socialist] construction from stage to stage.'[16]

What is the evidence for Olminsky's interpretation? In a long paragraph that takes up the last two pages of ETP, Bukharin does describe the communist future using the present tense: 'gigantic reservoirs of energy that previously went toward class struggle, wars, militarism, overcoming [economic] crises, competition and so forth now turn into productive labour', and so on. In their defence, Bukharin and Piatakov note that Marx and Hilferding also presented visions of the future in the present tense. But this stylistic observation doesn't

---

14 Bukharin 1990b, p. 213 (Olminsky review). Since Lenin gave his enthusiastic approval to the chapter on extra-economic compulsion, we may conclude that he himself did not read Bukharin as *limiting* himself to coercion.

15 Bukharin 1920, p. 103; Bukharin cites the Bolshevik engineer Gleb Krzhizhanovsky who also inspired Lenin in 1920.

16 Bukharin 1990b, p. 214 (Olminsky review).

really get to the heart of the matter, which is that even in this very paragraph Bukharin makes it painfully clear that what his heart desired would be a long time coming:

The state authority [*vlast*] of the working class necessarily grows to the extent that the resistance of capitalist groups grows. And since the process of the unfolding of capitalist breakdown and communist revolution is a whole historical era, a whole epoch that also includes a series of merciless class wars – not to mention civil wars – it is completely understandable that the state cannot die out under *these* circumstances.

But as soon as the world-wide victory of the proletariat is clear, the growth curve of statehood will turn sharply downward. The essential, basic task of state authority as such – the task of crushing the bourgeoisie – will then be completed.[17]

Olminsky's highly indignant and painfully inaccurate critique of ETP can be summed up as follows: Bukharin uses the words 'instantly begins to misfire'; therefore he rejects Marxism. He uses the phrase 'a method for the creation of communist humanity'; therefore indiscriminate coercion is Bukharin's only method. He uses the present tense in his discussion of communist society; therefore he thinks that communist society is already attained. While Olminsky obsesses about these purely verbal points, he ignores the substantive theories that dominate Bukharin's book: the inevitability of temporary breakdown, the tedious struggle to establish even a minimum 'equilibrium', and the painful delay in making good on the promises of socialist construction. No wonder he concludes that 'basically this book is not a scholarly production but mere literature that expresses the mood of a part of the party in the middle of 1920' (215).

This extended discussion of Olminsky's review is a necessary prelude to our examination of Bukharin's NEP-era views of war communism. Most scholars today believe that Bukharin argued in 1920 what Olminsky says he argued: indiscriminate coercion, leap into socialism, and all the rest. If Bukharin really did hold these views in 1920, a maximalist interpretation of his 'illusions' remark is almost mandatory: of course Bukharin (and any sane person) would have rejected *these* views as utter illusions. But since he never actually held anything like them, he didn't feel any need to repudiate them.

---

17   Bukharin 1920, pp. 156–7. As this passage makes clear, it is contradictory to accuse Bukharin *both* of glorifying compulsion *and* believing in immediate communism, since part of Bukharin's definition of full communism is the absence of compulsion.

Bukharin's rebuttal of Olminsky also shows that he had no intention of apologizing for the policies later subsumed under the label 'war communism'. Of course, Bukharin was careful to restrict his defence to the main tendencies of Bolshevik policy. He conceded that another critic of the book, Aleksandr Chaianov, was correct to point out that 'much' of the effects of social collapse in Russia was caused by avoidable Bolshevik policies. Nevertheless, 'does this refute the fact that *other* effects of social collapse – and those the basic ones – were completely inevitable? *This* is what you need to refute.'[18]

Bukharin's ultimate justification of Bolshevik civil-war policies was that they made higher productivity possible, even though their immediate result was to *lower* productivity. Bolshevik policies of compulsion were just one example of this paradox: 'Is an armed uprising really accompanied by perfected "means of production"? Does the red terror drive productive forces forward? Or does the civil war remind comrade Olminsky of the horn of plenty? ... Revolutionary violence *clears the road* for a future upsurge. And it is after this upsurge *begins* that violence loses nine-tenths of its rationale.'[19]

Bukharin's chain of reasoning ran as follows: if you want higher productivity, you need socialism. If you want socialism, you need proletarian sovereignty. If you want proletarian sovereignty, you need a proletarian revolution. If you want a proletarian revolution, you must accept civil war and other forms of social breakdown. It followed that the proletarian state – and only the proletarian state – had a right to apply compulsion. Thus anyone – Mikhail Olminsky, for example – who labels *proletarian* labour service (*trudovaia povinnost*) as 'forced labour' (*katorga*) is no more than a liberal who refuses to understand the *class* essence of the proletarian dictatorship.[20]

Bukharin's vigorous defence of ETP and Bolshevik civil-war policies was written in early 1921 when the outlines of NEP were faint and fuzzy indeed. Perhaps as time went on Bukharin grew more embarrassed by ETP or at least was content to let it slip into oblivion? Not so. As Stephen Cohen notes: 'it continued to be a highly influential (and controversial) work. In 1928, [Mikhail] Pokrovskii, the doyen of Soviet historians, cited it as one of the three great Bolshevik achievements in "social science" since the revolution.'[21]

---

18   Bukharin 1990b, p. 237 (Bukharin response).
19   Bukharin 1990b, p. 232. Olminsky had stated that Marxism only justified violence when it was 'accompanied' by perfected means of production.
20   Bukharin 1990b, p. 233 (Bukharin response).
21   Cohen 1971, p. 88. The other two achievements were Lenin's *State and Revolution* and Lev Kritsman's *Heroic Period of the Russian Revolution*.

Bukharin himself continued belligerently to defend the main theses of ETP. The best evidence for this is provided by his theoretical textbook *Historical Materialism*. Bukharin wrote this textbook immediately after ETP; it was published in 1920 and re-issued in many editions throughout the 1920s.[22] Some writers have seen it as the beginning of a profound rethinking of the assumptions that inform ETP. This line of thought is hard to square with the explicit defence of ETP within *Historical Materialism* itself. One whole chapter of Bukharin's textbook is devoted to setting forth the scenario of inevitable breakdown and reconstitution during the proletarian revolution. Naturally, ETP is quoted at length. Of particular interest to us is a digression in which Bukharin specifically responds to the criticism that NEP had made ETP irrelevant. In his response, Bukharin sets out the issues with such clarity that extensive quotation seems in order:

The critics say that in ETP we produced a highly partial justification (apology) for the Russian communist party, which smashed up everything for no good reason [*zria bit' posudu*]. And now, it is said, life has proven that we should not have destroyed this apparatus and we have now become as mild and gentle as the Scheidemannites.[23] In other words: the destruction of the capitalist productive apparatus was a *fact* of Russian reality but definitely not a general law of revolutionary transition from one form of society (capitalist) to another (socialist). This 'objection' clearly rests on a serene failure to understand the basic issues. The Russian workers could permit the capitalists, etc., *only* after the workers had *fundamentally* knocked the capitalists around and made their own selves secure – that is, after the conditions of a new social equilibrium had at least been sketched out.

Our critics want to put the end before the beginning. Even in the state apparatus (for example, the army), we are [now] admitting large numbers of the old officer corps and putting them into command posts. But should we have tried to leave them there at the *beginning* of the revolu-

---

22   I do not have access to all editions of the book and so I am not sure when the material described below is first found. All I know is that it was present in the third edition of 1924 and still retained in the ninth edition of 1929; *Teoriia istoricheskogo materializma*, ninth edition (Bukharin 1929); *Historical Materialism* (Ann Arbor: University of Michigan Press, 1969) (translation of third edition).

23   Philipp Scheidemann was chancellor of Germany in 1919; he and the other figures mentioned below are symbolic of western socialists who failed to bring about a socialist revolution despite their participation in government.

tion? Should we have tried *not* to destroy the old *tsarist* army? In that case, the workers would not have told the officers what to do, but the officers would have told them what to do. For proof of this, look at the experience of Ministers Scheidemann and Noske in Germany, Otto Bauer and Renner in Austria, and Vandervelde in Belgium.

Furthermore, nine-tenths of the new economic policy in Russia is due to the peasant character of the country, that is, to specifically *Russian* conditions. Finally, it goes without saying that we are talking about the *typical* course of events. Under *special* conditions there could be a situation which does not involve destruction: for example, if the proletariat is victorious in the most important countries, then [in a later revolution] the bourgeoisie with all its apparatus might possibly surrender completely and without a fight.[24]

Should Bukharin's face have been red? Should he have repudiated the argument advanced in ETP, written at the height of war communism? The Bukharin who was conjured up by Olminsky should indeed have been ashamed of what he wrote – not just in 1921 after the coming of NEP but in 1920 or any other time. But Olminsky's version of ETP bears very little resemblance to the real book, with its complicated argument about the inevitable costs of proletarian revolution. It is not within our brief to comment on whether Bukharin should have been proud or embarrassed by the cogency or lack thereof of his actual argument. We merely point out that in reality Bukharin was *not* embarrassed: on the contrary, he was proud of ETP's contribution to Marxist theory – in 1921 and in all following years.

2   1924: The Newly Economic Policy

In their riposte to Olminsky, Bukharin and Piatakov stated defiantly: 'When comrade Olminsky says that "our party got completely carried away", we can "hint" to him most politely: speak for yourself, comrade!'[25] These words were written in spring of 1921, during the brief phase of proto-NEP that Bukharin

---

24   Bukharin 1929, p. 297; Bukharin 1969, p. 261. All emphases by Bukharin except for 'beginning'. Note that Bukharin argues here that civil war policies were a *general* characteristic of proletarian revolutions, while NEP is only a *special case*.

25   Bukharin 1990b, p. 234. I cannot find in the published review the exact words attributed to Olminsky by Bukharin and Piatakov – '*u nas (u partii) zakruzhilas golova*' – and they perhaps overstate Olminsky's actual thesis.

later labelled 'the system of free trade at the local level'.[26] In 1924, when NEP was approaching its apogee, Bukharin told a different story: 'the transition to the new economic policy was the collapse of our illusions'.[27] These words bespeak a new willingness to admit that the party and he himself had suffered from illusions. Doesn't this mean that NEP caused Bukharin to do some serious rethinking?

Yes, it does – but we need to look closely in order to judge the *extent* of this rethinking. The maximalist interpretation is that NEP caused Bukharin to adopt 'a radical modification of our view of socialism'.[28] In fact, Bukharin was engaged in damage control: his aim was to *minimize* the significance of the post-civil-war change of policy. His polemical target was what he called the 'collapse of communism' theory. Bukharin summarized this widespread critique of Bolshevism as follows: 'the Russian Bolsheviks, having made an unsuccessful attempt to realize genuine socialism, quickly became disillusioned with this attempt, since it demonstrated that a socialist order was completely unrealizable. They called on the aid of the very bourgeoisie that they wanted to annihilate and in so doing acknowledged their utter powerlessness.'[29] According to these same critics of Bolshevism, other retreats quickly followed:

Concessions [to foreign capitalists] and loans are further steps in the direction of capitalism. In this way, we see a capitalist degeneration of the soviet state, of the sovereign authority [*vlast*] and the Communist party: a clear betrayal of the proletariat. Illusions were scattered to the winds and the prose of life remained – and this prose is the *prose of capitalist exploitation*. Not only a growth of poverty, but an ever greater transition to capitalist positions: this is the meaning of the whole historical era and the whole evolution experienced by Bolshevism.[30]

---

26   Bukharin 1988, p. 124 ('at the local level' = *v mestnom oborote*). These words are taken from Bukharin's speech of 17 April 1925 entitled *O novoi ekonomicheskoi politiki i nashikh zadachakh*. This speech became notorious because it included the phrase 'enrich yourselves' addressed to the peasants, and is therefore identified in citations as 'Enrich'.

27   Bukharin 1990b, p. 253, in *O likvidatorstve nashikh dnei*, henceforth identified in citations as 'Illusions'.

28   This phrase from Lenin's article 'On Cooperation' (1923) was taken by many observers, especially during the perestroika era, to mean that Lenin had changed his views about the content of socialism. In actuality, Lenin meant that the tasks of constructing socialism looked different *after* taking power than they had *before*. See 'Political Testament: Lenin, Bukharin, and the Meaning of NEP', included in this volume.

29   Bukharin 1988, p. 194, in *Put' k sotsializmu i raboche-krestianskii soiuz* (1925), henceforth identified in citations as 'Path'.

30   Bukharin, *Mezhdunarodnaia burzhuaziia i Karl Kautskii, ee apostol* in *V zashchitu prole-*

Observe how closely the 'collapse of communism' theory as outlined by Bukharin resembles the maximalist interpretation of Bukharin's own 'collapse of our illusions' remark. According to this interpretation, the Bolsheviks unsuccessfully tried to implement a version of full communism and the failure of this attempt led Bukharin to see much merit in various standard operating features of capitalism such as the market. The maximalist interpretation thus tends to equate Bukharin's formula – 'the collapse of our illusions' – to the formula 'the collapse of communism'. But Bukharin put forward his 'illusions' formula in order to *refute* the 'collapse of communism' theory.

After setting up the 'collapse of communism' as a target, Bukharin elaborates on his own 'illusion' formula as follows (I have italicized key sentences):

What really 'collapsed'? 'War communism' as a system collapsed, and the ideology of 'war communism' collapsed, that is, those illusions that existed in our party. *This doesn't mean in any way that the war communist system was fundamentally incorrect for that period. Under the conditions of external and internal blockade we were compelled to act as we did.* But the fact of the matter is that we didn't perceive just how relative the war communist policy was.

Then we thought that our peaceful organizational work, our economic policy, the construction of our economy, would be a *further continuation* of the centralizing planned economy of that era. And since during that time lots of things were indeed centralized, the idea naturally followed that we were close to a securely established socialist planned economy. In other others: we understood 'war communism' not as 'war-related', that is, useful only at a certain stage in the development of the civil war, but as a universal, general and so to speak 'normal' form of the victorious proletariat's economic policy. *Simple rationalized forms for the strictest economy during a plunge in productive forces were taken as rational forms of a peacetime economic policy.* And this constituted the fundamental *illusion* of that period.

These illusions inevitably dissipated as soon as the norms and ideology of wartime fell away. Then immediately we confronted a sea of new questions about actual economic policy; a whole gamut of economic forms stepped out into the open, talking – and, in places, screaming – with the

---

tarskoi diktatury (Bukharin 1928, p. 62). This 106-page work, originally published in *Pravda* in summer 1925, has been strangely overlooked, although it is in many ways a more sophisticated presentation of Bukharin's views at the apogee of NEP than is the more famous *Path to Socialism*. It will be henceforth identified in citations as *Karl Kautsky*.

voices of their class representatives. *The illusions of war communism burst in the very hour that the proletarian army took Perekop.*[31]

By 'simple rationalized forms for the strictest economy', Bukharin means primarily the *prodrazverstka* and the prohibition of the grain trade. These policies allowed enough control over grain distribution that it became possible to feed the army and prevent the utter destruction of the urban working class. Bukharin does not apologize in any way for the policies themselves. Indeed, he belligerently asserts that 'the system of war communism fulfilled its historic role': it effectively distributed the dwindling stock of existing resources at a time when actual economic growth was out of the question.[32] Bukharin indignantly refutes critics who saw these policies as something to be ashamed of:

Yes, we had horrifying years – years of immense, monstrous poverty. Kautsky remembers this fact, but why does he forget precisely in this connection even to *mention the intervention?* ...

But (we will be told) the system of war communism itself hardly aided the growth of productive forces. That's right – it didn't. We openly admit it. But, respected 'critics', without war communism we could *not have 'beaten off the White Guards'* ... The system of war communism – inevitably reducing the basis of productive forces – *was itself a function of the war*, that is, a function of *intervention* with all its charms.[33]

As these words show, Bukharin's war-communist illusion should not be equated with a 'leap into socialism' mentality. This phrase is used by scholars to imply that the Bolsheviks in 1920 were so convinced they were on the threshold of full socialism that they were blind to such realities as the horrifying poverty of the country, the need to apply material incentives, the existence of a vast black market and the economic weight of small-scale peasant agriculture. During both war communism and NEP, Bukharin stressed that only a very few steps on the road to socialism during the civil war; he explicitly denied

---

31   Bukharin 1990b, pp. 254–5 (Illusions). Perekop is the isthmus that connects the Crimea to the mainland; its capture by the Red Army in November 1920 led to the prompt evacuation of the last White Army under General Petr Wrangel.

32   Bukharin 1990b, p. 124 (Enrich); see also Bukharin 1988, p. 152 (Path); *Karl Kautsky* (Bukharin 1928, p. 64).

33   *Karl Kautsky* (Bukharin 1928, pp. 51–3).

that any leap had taken place.[34] But one thing *had* been accomplished – or so the Bolsheviks thought at the time: a centralized *framework* had been set up that would allow steady progress in the future. Because they had set up this framework 'right away' [*srazu*], Bukharin and the rest of the party saw the road ahead as a straight one of steady organization. They then realized that they had to take a detour [*obkhodnyi put*] – but when people take a detour, they do not change their mind about their ultimate destination, they are simply taking into account some unexpected obstacles on the main path. They drive as fast as they can so that they can get back to the main road and proceed on their way as planned.

Bukharin thus defined the war-communist illusion as an over-generalization of certain features of policies such as the *prodrazverstka*.[35] One striking feature of these policies was the pressure and the material burdens placed on the peasantry, but the Bolsheviks in 1920 were certainly not under the illusion that *these* policies could be continued indefinitely. On the contrary: they stated their intention to ease the pressure on the peasantry as soon as conditions allowed.[36] What was at issue was the *institutional framework* by means of which the Bolsheviks intended to go about the task of restoring normal economic links with the countryside and then organizing the peasants into a unified socialist framework. Bukharin's war-communist illusion can therefore be defined in this way: *the mistaken idea that the strictly controlled distribution of resources by the cen-*

---

34   For Bukharin's views prior to 1921, see Lars T. Lih, 'The Mystery of the *ABC*' and '*Vlast* from the Past: Stories Told by Bolsheviks' (both included in this volume). Even during the 'Left Communist' stage of 1918, Bukharin brought out the costs of revolution; his appreciation of the scope of these social costs grew between 1918 and the publication of ETP in 1920 – the very years when Bukharin and much of the party are popularly supposed to have embraced a 'leap into socialism' mentality. Bukharin's evolution in this regard was typical rather than exceptional. (For Bukharin's evocation of the costs (*izderzhki*) of revolution in the context of Stalin's revolution from above in the early thirties, see 'Bukharin's Bolshevik Epic: The Prison Writings', included in this volume.)

35   For various formulations of this definition of the war-communist illusion, see Bukharin 1990b, pp. 254, 256 (Illusions); Bukharin 1988, p. 126 (Enrich) and pp. 195–6 (Path).

36   For example, Karl Radek, speaking in late 1919: 'If in the more or less near future the Soviet Republic is unable to change over to a peacetime production, so that food can be obtained from the peasants in exchange for goods, then it is clear that the working class, weak in numbers, will finally disappear through loss of blood even if it is victorious on the field of battle' (*Piat' let Kominterna*, Radek 1924, p. 164). Radek's comments are not incompatible with illusions about the *framework* used to conduct this exchange. For further evidence on this issue, see Lars T. Lih, *Bread and Authority in Russia, 1914–1921* (Lih 1990). For further discussion of food-supply policies during the civil war, see 'Bolshevik *Razverstka* and War Communism', included in this volume.

tre and aggressive prohibition of private trade provided a straightforward frame-work to accomplish 'our peaceable organizational work [and] the construction of our economy', even under the special circumstances of NEP.[37]
When we look closer, we see that the principal characteristic of the war-communist illusion in Bukharin's telling of the story is that it was *costless*. First of all, the illusion was a strictly limited one: it concerned one subset of economic policies only. Bukharin never asserts that any other feature of the civil-war outlook – for example, the immediate policies of terror, class policy toward the peasants, or the ultimate goal of a completely organized and highly centralized economy – was tainted with illusion. On the contrary, as we shall see.

Second, Bukharin's 'illusions' formula is not a belated endorsement of Olminsky's claim that the party (or sections of it) was seized in 1920 by a utopian fever that blinded them to reality. Bukharin's formula does not concede that he or any other Bolshevik was under the impression that Russia was on the verge of the socialist paradise in 1920, or that the economy could dispense with material incentives and rely indefinitely on force and enthusiasm, or that peasant agriculture was already organized in socialist fashion, or any other of the bizarre opinions associated with war communism by Olminsky and by modern scholars. According to Bukharin, war communism had given rise to some mistaken ideas about the proper *framework* for tackling the long-term task of transforming peasant agriculture, but the Bolsheviks had never been under any illusion that the *task* itself had even been properly begun:

> What changes in economic relations can be effected by means of the lever of politics depends on the previous condition of economic relations. We can best explain this with the example of the Russian proletarian revolu-tion. In October 1917 the working class took the *vlast* in its hands. But it couldn't even think about, for example, centralizing and socializing the petty-bourgeois economy and the peasant economy in particular. And in 1921 it became clear that the Russian economy was even more stubborn and that the forces of the proletarian state machine were capable of keep-ing only large-scale industry socialized, and not even all of that.[38]

---

37   In the laudatory article on Bukharin published in the *Bolshaia sovetskaia entsiklopediia* in 1924 by his disciple D. Maretsky, the only defect of ETP is that 'regularities of the process of restoring [economic] ties that had fallen apart and of the movement toward social-ism "on the rails of NEP" were not correctly and exactly projected' (see Emelianov 1989, p. 15).

38   *Teoriia* (Bukharin 1929, pp. 300–1); *Historical Materialism* (Bukharin 1969, p. 265).

Third, the illusion concerned only the *future application* of certain features of policies that were appropriate under prevailing circumstances. As soon as circumstances changed, the Bolsheviks realized their mistake and made the necessary modifications. Neither during the civil war nor afterwards, then, did the war-communist illusion have an adverse effect on actual policy. Indeed, the illusion was discarded without fuss as soon as the civil war came to a halt. Bukharin does not mention any delay in switching policies, any turmoil in the party, any false starts. Indeed, he insists on swift party unanimity and solid support for the new economic policy.

Conclusion: the Bolsheviks have nothing to apologize for. On the contrary, they can be proud of the ruthless self-criticism characteristic of proletarian revolution.[39] The war-communist illusion came and went without ever endangering the safety of the revolution or harming the well-being of the Russian people.

Bukharin's illusion formula is thrown into relief by a contrast with Lenin who in 1921 had used the word 'mistake' to make somewhat similar points about civil-war policies. Many party members objected to Lenin's choice of words, *not* because they were in principle opposed to NEP or because they hankered after a return to war communism, *but* for the straightforward and sensible reason that Lenin's choice of words seemed to justify the Mensheviks and other critics of actual Bolshevik civil-war policies. This was not Lenin's intention – he always stressed the basic correctness of civil-war policies – but his 'mistake' formulation certainly seemed, at the time and ever since, to be an admission that the critics had been right. In 1924, Bukharin is silently substituting a more acceptable formula: not a costly 'mistake', but a costless 'illusion'.[40]

The very name *'new* economic policy' points to the *discontinuity* between war communism and NEP. Bukharin needs to give an account of this discontinuity, and he does so with his 'illusions' formula – a formula that was aimed at minimizing its significance and extent, in explicit contrast to the 'collapse of communism' theory and in implicit contrast to Lenin's 'mistake' formula. In fact, Bukharin fundamentally saw NEP, not as a repudiation of war communism, but as its *continuation*. For him, the essential feature of both war communism and NEP was not the illusions that fell away but the insight that lived on.

---

39   Bukharin 1990b, p. 253 (Illusions).

40   In 1925, Bukharin toned it down even further and referred to 'the collapse of some errors and incorrect notions about the course of our development toward socialism' (Bukharin 1988, p. 195 [Path]).

Bukharin's sense of continuity comes from the overarching Bolshevik narrative: the revolutionary seizure of state authority by the proletariat as a class in
order to build socialism. Bukharin needs to show that both war communism
and NEP are legitimized by virtue of being episodes in this story. He does this
by affirming that in each case the proletarian protagonist had the same basic
strategy and the same basic goal. The basic strategy is the class struggle of the
proletariat in alliance with the peasantry. The basic goal is the abolition of the
market and the creation of a completely organized and unified society.

In the 'illusions' article of 1924, Bukharin pictures NEP as a continuation of
the same class struggle that animated the civil war:

During the period of the civil war we worked with clear political categories: beat the bourgeoisie, look for allies among the peasantry, repulse
the kulak rebels. These basic problems of class struggle now wear economic clothing – but they are no less problems of class struggle for all that:
state industry against the capitalist, *smychka* with the peasantry against
the merchant; cooperatives and electrification as weapons in the struggle
for a gradual overcoming of small-scale property. In other words: previously the class struggle had primarily a military-political, 'shock' character; now it has taken on a peaceful-economic-organic look. Victory in this
type of class struggle (we abstract here from problems arising from outside [the country]) *is* the final victory of socialism.[41]

The metaphor 'economic clothing' implies that the novelty of the new economic policy was relatively superficial: the same individual first wore military
clothes and then civilian clothes. Indeed, we will better understand Bukharin's
outlook if we read 'NEP' to mean the 'Newly Economic Policy': *one* underlying
policy of moving toward socialism via class struggle and class leadership, but in
two different forms – military and economic – corresponding to two different
phases of the revolution.

For Bukharin, the peasant policy of the civil war was not a regrettable folly
but a sterling object lesson that answered the question 'Why have we been victorious up to now?' In a chapter of his *Path to Socialism* that has this question
as its title, Bukharin elaborates:

The internal reason for our victory was the strong *military union between
the workers and peasants of our country* ... It goes without saying that this

---

41   Bukharin 1990b, p. 256 (Illusions).

military union did not hang in the air – it rested on the linkage of basic interests. When the peasantry fought the enemy, it was defending the land recently wrested away from the landowners ... And when peasant sons – soldiers of our Red Army, experiencing hunger and cold, suffering from typhus, without shoes – protected the frontiers of the Soviet land and fought off the enemy with bayonets, they were defending the magnificent cause of liberation *from the yoke of the landowner*.[42]

Civil-war policies such as the *prodrazverstka* that placed burdens on the peasantry did create difficulties between the workers and the peasants.[43] But this is an example of *peasant* illusions, not Bolshevik ones. The peasants found it difficult to grasp the necessity of harsh policies that were fundamentally in their interest:

True, the burdens of that time – when it was necessary with exceptional firmness to gather up all that was needed to feed the Red Army, to support the front, to support the workers remaining in the hungry towns – the burdens of that time made several strata of the peasantry waver more than once and more than twice. More than once and more than twice these strata of the peasantry, worn out by the burdens of struggle and not understanding the necessity of tremendous sacrifices, fled over to the side of the enemy: to the Whites, to the *uchredilovtsy*, to Kolchak. But the severe experience of civil war showed them every time that salvation couldn't be found in the camp of the Whites, because this was the camp of the cursed enemies not only of the working class but the peasantry as well.[44]

Bukharin's narrative reveals that the main class actors and their relationship to each other remained the same during both civil war and NEP. Furthermore, these class actors have the same basic task: the construction of socialism. For Bukharin, this task always meant the construction of a mono-organizational society explicitly hostile to any pluralism.[45] The NEP-era formula 'overcom-

---

42   Bukharin 1988, p. 151 (Path).
43   For a description of this policy, see 'Bolshevik *Razverstka* and War Communism', included in this volume.
44   Bukharin 1988, pp. 151–2 (Path). The *uchredilovtsy* were former SR delegates to the 1918 Constituent Assembly who briefly set up an anti-Bolshevik government in Siberia.
45   I take the term 'mono-organizational society' from T.H. Rigby, 'Stalinism and the Mono-Organizational Society' (Rigby 1977, pp. 53–76). Rigby uses the concept as a heuristic

ing the market through the market' outlined a strategy for achieving this goal. Bukharin was confident this strategy would work *because capitalism had already done it*:

Depending on the speed of the development of productive forces (and there is a good chance it will proceed at an 'American' tempo), the 'rational', *plan* principle will develop more and more, and the role of specifically market relations (after a certain point) will become less and less. Just as there is a tendency in the capitalist system (within the boundaries of a 'national economy') to overcome the market through the market, insofar as *competition* turns into *monopoly* – just so, under the system of the proletarian dictatorship, there proceeds an organization of small-scale peasant economies through the market and through the process of circulation, all under the economic leadership of an ever more organized state economy.[46]

Bukharin's understanding of capitalist dynamics is a radical version of Rudolf Hilferding's vision of monopolized capitalist economies dominated by centralized trusts. His entire strategy for NEP is based on his analogy between this Hilferdingian 'state capitalism' and the proletarian dictatorship. The 'illusion' article of 1924 sets out the logic in admirably concise form:

Under the capitalist regime we have a struggle between [economic] forms of the greatest variety. But the general tendency of development is this: large-scale production defeats its small-scale opponent, squeezes it out, overcomes it and, in the final analysis, becomes the economic dictator of the land. At the *limit* we have here state capitalism (in the west European rather than our Russian understanding of the word).[47]

---

device for understanding Soviet politics; I use it to refer only to an *image* Bukharin had both of state capitalism and the proletarian dictatorship. A graphic representation of his comparison can be found in Chart IV at the end of ETP.

46   Bukharin 1928, p. 86 (*Karl Kautsky*).

47   Bukharin 1990b, p. 256 (Illusions). Bukharin makes a distinction between Russian and West European understandings of 'state capitalism' because Lenin (rather irresponsibly) had used this term to describe a much different situation in Soviet Russia. See also Bukharin's comment in a speech to the Central Committee in 1929: 'I have been reproached with the fact that I allegedly preach a "capitalist market" for us in Russia ... The free market, I repeat, exists no longer even in the countries of monopolistic capitalism, in those branches and sections of the economy where there is a monopolistic concentration of industry' (Bukharin 1989, pp. 293–4).

After setting up this model of state capitalism, Bukharin makes his basic theoretical move: '*Formally* the same thing happens with us as well – but with this principled and most essential difference: in our case, large-scale production is in the hands of a *proletarian* state.' He then lists the various methods by which proletarian forms of property will 'squeeze out' private capital in Russia. Since large-scale, centralized forms are ultimately more efficient, the proletarian forms are sure to win:

> To the extent that we are successful in centralizing the economy and cooperatizing the peasantry (all these processes being regulated and directed by the dictatorial *vlast* of the working class), to the same extent will the economic plan become more real and all the sooner be transformed into a genuine plan of *social production as a whole*. At the limit we have, not state capitalism, but *socialism*. ... Thus, our current competitive struggle – which is externally extremely similar to the struggle that large-scale capital directs against small-scale capital – *in essence, that is, from the point of view of classes*, has a sharply defined proletarian, anti-capitalist, socialist character.[48]

We can call this the 'same but different' strategy: the proletarian dictatorship follows the same trajectory as Hilferdingian state capitalism, but the social meaning is totally different since a different class is running the show. If there is such a thing as Bukharinism, the 'same but different' analogy between the proletarian dictatorship and Hilferdingian state capitalism is at the heart of it. Pick up a pronouncement by Bukharin at *any* stage of his career and as likely as not you will find a version of 'same but different'.

We have explained the paradox by which Bukharin's constant analogies with capitalism signifies an affirmation of his fundamentally anti-market, anti-pluralist and anti-competition outlook.[49] Discarding the war-communist illusion and adopting the strategy of 'overcoming the market by the market' was thus simply a matter of finding the best way to construct the mono-organizational society: 'For the war period the centre of gravity lay first of all in rational *consumption*, while for the peace period it lies in maximal *production*. If the

---

48   Bukharin 1990b, pp. 256–7 (Illusions).
49   Bukharin realized that monopolies had their dangers, but he had no intention of solving those problems through the outmoded method of competition, but rather through top-down political pressure – or, in his idiosyncratic jargon, 'the constant pressure of the regulating principle of the state authority of the working class'. Bukharin 1990b, p. 255 (Illusion) ('regulating' = *uporiadochivaiushchii*).

war period called forth the illusion that it was possible to organize the peasant economy by doing violence to commodity exchange, then later experience
demonstrated that this must and could be done, in the first place, *through commodity exchange*.'[50]

This point and much else about Bukharin's 'illusion' can be illustrated more
concretely by the central example of the state grain monopoly. There were two
complementary tasks to overcoming the market in a peasant country like Russia: creating a state apparatus capable of replacing private trade, and organizing
the peasants by drawing the many millions of independent producers into a
unified framework. Obviously, organizing the peasantry was the task that was
more fundamental, more difficult and more long-term. Until this fundamental task was accomplished, the most that could be done was setting up a state
grain monopoly – that is, having the market operate through state/cooperative
institutions rather than private capital.

Bukharin seized on the subordinate task of setting up an effective grain
monopoly as a way of showing that NEP was not only constructing socialism,
but was doing it more effectively than war communism. He made this case in a
chapter of his 1925 polemic against Kautsky entitled 'The so-called "collapse of
communism" and private capital in trade'. In this chapter, Bukharin relates how
the efforts during the civil war to construct a genuine grain monopoly had been
a failure. 'Under the system of war communism, when almost all functions of
production and circulation *legally* belonged to the state and private trade was
prohibited, in actual *fact* this same private trade had the greatest significance.'
Bukharin illustrates the point with figures about the enormous size of the black
market during the civil war.

The first two or three years of NEP had also been unpropitious for accomplishing the task of setting up a truly effective grain monopoly: 'After the transition to the New Economic Policy, a situation arose in which the state found
itself face to face with the non-existence of its own *apparat* for distributing
commodities at just the same time as there was unleashed a million-headed
private-trade hurricane [*stikhiia*]'. But what the critics and nay-sayers who saw
NEP as a retreat overlooked were the feverish efforts to bring this state apparatus into existence.[51] By 1925 the proletarian state was in a position to begin a
successful 'offensive on the trade front'. Bukharin flourished figures to show the

---

50   *Karl Kautsky* (Bukharin 1928, p. 64; 'commodity exchange' = the market).
51   Bukharin always considered the cooperatives to be an integral part of this state apparatus,
      since 'in our system they have special rights and advantages and they work with the tight-
      est connections to the economic organs of the proletarian state' (*Karl Kautsky*, Bukharin
      1928, p. 75).

increasing relative weight of state plus cooperative trade and then exultantly crowed: some 'collapse of communism' this is!

Of course, Bukharin saw this 'offensive on the trade front' as a peaceful exercise in purely economic 'squeezing out' of petty private trade. Still, his use of military imagery is striking: 'Before a combined economic attack from all sides, private capital is compelled to move from one area to the other, retreating step by step further and further into regions far behind the economic front. But the economic detachments of the new order will fight their way through even in those places. In this way the victorious socialist offensive unfolds and moves forward.'[52]

Two years after the polemic with Kautsky, Bukharin claimed that the offensive on the trade front was nearing completion:

[In the last two years,] cooperative and state trade have effectively become *monopolistic merchants* in the area of grain procurements. The grain monopoly was repealed with the introduction of NEP. But now, on the basis of the growth of our economic organizations, on the basis of the competition with the private middleman, we have squeezed private capital out of grain procurements, and we have arrived, so to speak, at a state monopoly from the opposite direction and on a new basis.[53]

In 1927, Bukharin still saw the market as the main economic link between the peasants and the state: the peasants voluntarily decided how much grain to deliver on the basis of price signals. Thus the great work of organizing the peasantry still lay ahead.[54] Nevertheless, this was a market dominated by the state – a market without competition and without autonomous price formation. An important step toward the mono-organizational society had been successfully taken under the auspices of NEP.

'We have arrived at a state monopoly from the opposite direction' – this assertion eloquently symbolizes the relation of war communism and NEP in Bukharin's outlook. Part of the war-communist illusion of 1920 had been the

---

52   *Karl Kautsky* (Bukharin 1928, pp. 69–77).

53   Bukharin 1988, p. 326 (1927). This comment is not just propaganda; Bukharin reiterated the point *in camera* to the Central Committee in 1929 (Bukharin 1989, p. 286).

54   In *Karl Kautsky* (1925), Bukharin wrote that 'great constructive and organizational work – the most characteristic trait of our times – does not yet encompass sufficiently our backward village, scattered in tens of millions of households. Therefore it is completely natural that the process of economic organization here will be a *long* one' (Bukharin 1928, pp. 75–6).

mistaken idea that aggressive prohibition of private trade was a proper framework for creating an effective grain monopoly. But the mistake had consisted in the fact that the replacement of private trade had been *premature*. Now, a mere six or seven years later, Bukharin felt that private trade had been successfully squeezed out of grain procurement.

As an authoritative spokesman for the party leadership, Bukharin needed to refute the 'collapse of communism' theory held both by foreign opponents and (more dangerously) by 'secret sceptics' at home.[55] This theory pointed at NEP as evidence of a great defeat – a great reversal of previous Bolshevik policy. To paraphrase the old song, Bukharin's response was to accentuate the continuity and eliminate – or at least minimize – the discontinuity. The 'collapse of our illusions' formula turned the war-communist illusion into something rather spectral – a mistaken opinion that never adversely affected real policy, one that was effortlessly discarded when circumstances changed. The *continuity* between the two phases of the revolution was much more fundamental: war communism and NEP were both necessary ways of moving toward the same ultimate goal. They both relied on the same class policy: a worker-peasant alliance aimed at overcoming the bourgeoisie in its various guises. The creation of a truly effective state grain monopoly was vivid concrete proof that this class alliance was still going down the path toward socialism. 'NEP' was really no more than the Newly Economic Policy – that is, a rational adjustment to changed circumstances and priorities. The critics and the secret sceptics were wrong: far from collapsing, communism was being built faster than ever.

3   1925 and 1928: Bukharin's Final NEP-Era Views

On two other occasions during the 1920s, Bukharin involved himself in polemics that brought up the relations between 'war communism' and NEP. The first of these arose from his defence of the new measures announced by the Soviet government in 1925 that further liberalized rural economic activity. His defensive polemics justifying these policies are an integral part of two large-scale literary productions of the mid-twenties, *The Path to Socialism and the Worker-Peasant Alliance* and *The International Bourgeoisie and its Apostle Karl Kautsky*. In 1928, the mutual relations between 'war communism' and NEP arose once again in debates over a new programme for the Comintern. Both Bukharin and

---

55   'Secret sceptics', especially among students, were a principal target of Bukharin's 1924 'illusions' article.

Stalin wanted to have the programme include generalized definitions of 'war communism' and NEP in order to pronounce on their universal significance for communist revolutions around the world. Did these two labels merely signify episodes in the history of the Russian revolution? Or did proletarian revolutions everywhere have to go through essentially the same phases?

The ins-and-outs of these polemical battles are complicated and not very edifying. Specialists in the politics of the NEP era who are interested in more thorough case studies can consult my article as originally published in *Russian History*.[56] For this volume, I have extracted the material most relevant to answering the question 'what was Bolshevism?'. There are three main takeaways about Bukharin's views on the topic of 'war communism' vs. NEP during this period. First, as Bukharin saw things, what united these two phases of the revolution was much more fundamental than any contrast. Different external circumstances led to different but equally adaptive methods in service of the same strategy of class leadership. Second, during this period Bukharin dropped any talk about any 'illusions' of war communism and justified the distinctive polices of the civil war without apology as necessary and justified. Third, the market – the defining feature of NEP – was in his eyes a badge of backwardness to be left behind as soon as possible.

At the Sixth Comintern Congress in 1928, Bukharin got into a dispute with Eugen Varga, a Hungarian communist who maintained that war communism was a truly inevitable phase. In this debate, 'war communism' referred to harsh emergency measures of economic pressure. Bukharin responded: what about all the mistakes made by you Hungarian communists during their 1919 revolution? A central reason why you couldn't resist foreign intervention was that you alienated the peasants and the petty bourgeoisie. If the population had basically been on your side, you could have subverted the invading armies. This is how we won *our* civil war: our victories depended to a huge extent on the disintegration of enemy armies, and this is an essential means to victory back then and in future wars. You overemphasize war communism because you underestimate the mistakes you made in class policy.[57]

Bukharin's rejoinder to Varga is an eloquent restatement of his view of the Russian civil war as a time of underlying solidarity between workers and peasants. (It is worth noting: neither Varga nor any other communist supported war communism as a transition strategy for constructing socialism – only as a response to civil war and intervention.) A common view pictures the time of

---

56   Lih 2000.
57   *Problemy*, pp. 248–50. Henceforth citations from Bukharin's speeches to Sixth Comintern Congress in August 1928 are identified as 'Comintern'.

'war communism' as a time when the Bolsheviks were relatively anti-peasant and NEP as a time when they were relatively pro-peasant. Bukharin certainly cannot be invoked in support of this way of looking at things. For him, both period were equally based on the scenario of proletarian leadership of the peasantry that lies at the heart of Bolshevism. During the civil war, the main task was *military*: defending the very existence of the worker-peasant *vlast*. During NEP, the main task was *economic*: bringing the peasant into the ever-expanding sphere of centralized socialist organization.

Accordingly, the central policies of each period are equally valid, given the contrasting challenges facing the Bolsheviks. In these polemics from 1925 and 1928, Bukharin no longer bothered to talk about possible 'illusions' arising from civil-war policies. Instead, he insists that the Bolsheviks were not be condemned but rather commended for vigorously applying policies essential to victory in the civil war. In *Path to Socialism* (1925), Bukharin asserts that the application of pressure was the essence of 'war communism'. Putting pressure on peasant agriculture and on the peasant himself was a necessary task during the civil war and for several years thereafter. Bukharin mobilizes the resources of the Russian language to evoke its use: *nazhim, zazhim, prizhim*. The aim of government policy in the mid-twenties was therefore to depressurize the pressure (or, as Bukharin puts it, *razzhimat' nash zazhim*).[58]

But loosening up on the pressure was only possible *after* victory in the civil war. Yes, 'the methods of confiscation and requisition were completely habitual during that time – [but] it all resulted from the unbelievably cruel civil war that was foisted on the working class and the peasantry under conditions that were torturously difficult'.[59]

In 1918, a symbol of this economic pressure were the Committees of the Poor, the kombedy (Kom*itety* bed*noty*). The central purpose behind these committees was to split the village and enlist peasant help in extracting grain from so-called kulaks. They were disbanded at the end of 1918 as part of a shift toward more stable and more productive relations with the middle peasant. Speaking rather loosely of civil-war policy in general as 'the kombedy policy', Bukharin writes: 'The kombedy policy in the village basically resolved two tasks that were then top priority: first, the task of struggle against the resistance of the kulaks, and second, the task of collecting grain by means of the *prodrazverstka*, which was absolutely necessary for feeding the army'.[60]

---

58   Bukharin 1988, p. 189 (*Path*).
59   Bukharin 1988, pp. 207–8 (*Path*).
60   Bukharin 1988, pp. 197–8 (*Path*). For details of the rise and fall of the kombedy, see my
      Bread and Authority (Lih 1990) as well as the essays on civil-war policy included in this

Bukharin's defence of 'requisitions and confiscations' is mirrored by his broader defence of revolutionary terror. His chapter on this topic in his 1925 polemic with Kautsky should be put alongside better known works from the civil-war period such as Trotsky's *Terrorism and Communism*. Bukharin saw Bolshevik terror as analogous to Jacobin terror: a necessary response to counter-revolutionary intervention that in no way implied a lack of wide popular support. Even during the worst of times – 1918 and 1919 – both workers and peasants supported the soviet *vlast* 'with enthusiasm'. It follows that 'terror was a weapon of the broad masses of workers and peasants against the White Guards. Terror was a weapon of the revolution in its defensive war against reaction.'[61]

Political pressure was just as necessary as economic pressure during the civil war. Since the local soviets operated under conditions of a besieged fortress whose main task was to repulse the enemy, they inevitably shed their democratic forms and temporarily became organs of a 'military-proletarian dictatorship':

> This form of the soviet *vlast* did not cease being an expression of the interests of the laborers; it was *necessary* for that period, it was expedient for that time, when all palavering, all discussion, had to be reduced to a minimum – when it was necessary sometimes even to ignore the task of educating the masses – and when it was necessary to act, to act and again to act, on the field of armed struggle against the enemies of the labouring people.[62]

Furthermore, the need to apply these harsh policies was well-nigh inevitable. Bukharin remained loyal to the argument set forth in his most original work – *Economy of the Transition Period* (1920) – about the inevitable costs of proletarian revolution everywhere, not just in Russia. His loyalty to his magnum opus is strikingly revealed in an outburst during the debate on the Comintern program. The issue at hand was whether or not it was necessary to give land to the peasants immediately after the revolution. A certain comrade Dengel sug-

---

volume. In particular, 'Bolshevik *Razverstka* and War Communism' shows that Bukharin is misleading when he equates the *prodrazverstka* introduced in 1919 with the *kombedovskii period* of 1918. For Bukharin's views in the 1930s about 'the task of struggle against the resistance of the kulaks', see 'Bukharin's Bolshevik Epic: The Prison Writings', included in this volume.

61   *Karl Kautsky*, pp. 24–33 (cite from p. 30).
62   Bukharin 1988, p. 207 (*Path*). The phrase 'military-proletarian dictatorship' is not a result of hindsight; Bukharin used it both in ABC *of Communism* and ETP (1920).

gested that the political purpose of enlisting peasant support would be better served by providing agronomic help. Bukharin exploded:

Com. Dengel! *That's exactly what it is impossible to do right away*, and precisely because during the first phase of the revolution's development you will be facing *a fall in productive forces, a civil war*; you will face a situation such that we, the poor USSR, will be compelled to help *you* economically, and not the reverse. I'm sure of it. For a certain period of time you will be desperately fighting, you won't be in a position to get your industrial culture working, you won't be in a position to provide agricultural improvement programs and so on. This is almost inevitable during the first phase of the revolution's development. It would be great if there weren't any sabotage and so forth. *If* – and if wishes were horses, then beggars would ride.[63]

Bukharin concluded that there should be no 'illusions' about the possibility of immediate economic help for the peasants. In other words, by 1928, the most dangerous illusion did not arise from the use of 'war communist' measures, but rather from the pious hope of dispensing with them.

The market policies of NEP were justified by Bukharin in exactly the same way as the earlier policies of economic pressure: *not* as something good in itself, but as something otherwise unpleasant but nevertheless justified under the circumstances. And the main circumstance that justified market policies was *peasant backwardness*, particularly as manifested by the dominance of small-scale (*melkie*) peasant farms. Markets – in contrast to exchanges conducted through state channels – were in fact a *badge of backwardness*, to be discarded as soon as expedient in the march toward the mono-organizational society.

This badge had already been discarded by and large in advanced capitalist countries. As Bukharin insisted in 1929: 'Even under monopoly *capitalism* there is no free market, insofar as there is a gigantic concentration and centralization of production.'[64] Nevertheless, no country and no future communist revolution will entirely be without this badge. According to Bukharin in the 1928 Comintern debates, there is only one reason why the proletariat in power might want to retain market relations: the challenge presented by 'the scat-

---

63   *Problemy*, pp. 245–6 (Comintern). The last cited sentence is actually: *No 'khorosha Masha, da ne nasha'*.

64   Bukharin 1989a, p. 293 (debate over the 'extraordinary measures' at the April Plenum in 1929).

tered labour of small-scale, individual, formally independent producers' – a.k.a. peasant agriculture. 'If you don't have any small-scale producers at all, then you can speak out with complete peace of mind against "NEP", against market relations and such-like things.' But no country, not even the most advanced, is in this position, and so, some form of NEP will be required in all of them. And when we shift our attention from the advanced countries to the world revolution, the universal relevance of NEP is even more apparent: 'Is the peasant periphery that surrounds the world revolutionary proletariat really any less [important] than the one that surrounds the Soviet proletariat?'[65]

Soviet Russia's heavy reliance on NEP policies therefore shows just how backward its economy still was:

> The specific feature of the USSR is not NEP as such but the *dimensions* of NEP, the *scope* of market relations. In another country, where the relative weight of small-scale producers is not so significant, the scope of market relations will also be different from the USSR ... [In such countries,] the scope of market relations will be less, the tempo of its disappearance will be swifter. Also swifter will be the tempo of socialist development from its embryonic form to its full form: a socialist society consisting of a unitary and homogenous organism.[66]

During NEP, Bukharin put great emphasis on the peaceful nature of socialist transformation and the utter inexpedience of violent class struggle (*bien entendu, after* the proletariat was securely in power). We do not need to posit any sneaking predilection for markets and pluralism to explain this part of his outlook, once we grasp his contempt for pluralism as an outmoded form being replaced everywhere by some form of the mono-organizational society. He praised cooperatives as an effective tool of peaceful transformation precisely because capitalist experience showed that they could never have any real independence and therefore they could be used to reinforce class power. As he put it in a classic example of his 'same but different' approach:

> The landlords and the bourgeoisie under conditions of capitalist domination use clever policies to construct a union with the peasants against the workers and achieve a situation in which half of the agricultural proletariat works together with the baron, the prince and the duke. We would

65   *Problemy*, pp. 212–13.
66   *Problemy*, p. 213 (Comintern).

have to be complete fools if *we* aren't able to establish a union with the peasantry – since, after all, we stand immeasurably closer to them than the barons do.

And if the peasant [under capitalism] is drawn into the system of industrial and bank capital by means of the cooperatives, then under our dictatorship, given the relations of our state *vlast* with agricultural institutions – and given the nationalization of land, a policy that doesn't exist in any other country in the world – the same peasant can gradually grow into the system of socialist relations *through cooperation*.[67]

And the same strategy that cancels any threat of actual economic independence on the part of the cooperatives also ensured a successful anti-kulak policy:

> In the cities we have a more or less well organized and organized 'commanding height' that serves as our heavy artillery in the struggle against the urban nepmen. But where do we find this kind of 'commanding height' in the village? What can we put in the village against its well-off elite? Where are those economic fists [*kulaki*] we can use – on the basis of an economic struggle – to rain on the backs of the kulaks?[68]

The answer is clear: the economic 'commanding height' in the village is the proletarian town itself, since the economically revived towns are now in a position to exercise economic hegemony over the village. State industry, state banks, state law-making power – *these* are the commanding heights that rendered the village bourgeoisie harmless. There is thus absolutely no danger involved in the transfer of NEP to the village. And for this reason, the party opposition is wrong to label the new government policies as a 'wager on the kulak'. 'Our real wager is on ourselves – a wager on the working class and the labouring peasantry, a wager on the growth of socialist economic forms, on the growth of state industry in the first place and agricultural cooperatives in the second place. The *smychka* [link] between these two basic forms is a necessary condition of our victory.'[69]

In 1928–29, Bukharin and his allies Alexei Rykov and Mikhail Tomsky became spokesmen for the 'right deviation' that opposed Stalin's 'extraordinary

---

67   Bukharin 1988, p. 142 (Enrich) (emphasis in the original).
68   Bukharin 1988, p. 190 (Path).
69   SW, p. 198 (*Path*); the entire passage is emphasized in the original.

measures' of forced grain collection. In his long and valiant speech at the Central Committee Plenum in April 1929, Bukharin asserted that 'the extraordinary measures and NEP are two contradictory things. The extraordinary measures are an abrogation of NEP, even though a temporary one, of course. The extraordinary measures as a *system* eliminates NEP'.[70]

Consistent with his earlier logic, Bukharin did not argue either that the extraordinary measures were bad in themselves nor that market relations were good in themselves. Rather, he argued that Stalin's new policy was inappropriate under the prevailing circumstances: they represented a return to civil-war policies in a situation that still mandated NEP policies. This way of arguing implies that if Bukharin changed his mind about the relevant circumstances, he might also change his mind about the extraordinary measures. As shown in the essay 'Bukharin's Bolshevik Epic: The Prison Writings', included in this volume, this is exactly what happened – at least as Bukharin himself presented his volte-face in early 1930.

Economic reformers in the Soviet Union, especially during perestroika, used 'war communism' as an icon of over-centralized planning and NEP as an icon of market socialism of some sort. From this point of view, 'war communism' consisted of bad policies that should be rejected and NEP consisted of good policies that should be accepted. Bukharin was enlisted almost as a patron saint by these late Soviet reformers. The historical Bukharin had a very different view of the matter. For him, neither set of policies was good in itself, yet each set of policies was justified by the main task of the moment. Far from being in any way a progenitor of 'market socialism', Bukharin saw the market as a true badge of backwardness that should be transcended as soon as expedient. These underlying attitudes are essential to keep in mind when we look at the final chapter in Bukharin's saga.

4   Conclusion

A handy mnemonic device for keeping in mind Bukharin's views on war communism and NEP is: *official Bolshevik policy is always correct*. During the dramatic Kombedy phase in 1918–1919, not only confiscation and requisition but mass terror was needed to repulse the counter-revolution. During the rest of the war-communist period, pressure methods helped feed the Red Army and keep industry alive. An illusion grew up during these years concerning the future

---

70   *Problemy*, p. 289 (transcript of Bukharin's speech to April Plenum of 1929).

direction of policy, but this illusion had no effect on ongoing policy and was rapidly discarded in 1921, when the Newly Economic Policy was introduced. Pressure methods were used in the villages for a few more years, since it would be have been highly imprudent to engage in level-playing-field economic competition before an effective state apparatus was in place. In 1925, the transfer of NEP to the villages put the finishing touches to the same old new economic policy.

For a while in 1928 and 1929, Bukharin thought that for once the Soviet government had adopted a fundamentally mistaken policy. But that was because (he later announced) he had misinterpreted that policy and defined it as the extraordinary-measures-as-a-system. By early 1930 he saw the error of his ways: Stalin's revolution was not an inappropriate reversion to war communism but a breakthrough to a post-NEP situation in which the war communism/NEP opposition had been transcended.

As this summary suggests, Bukharin's arguments always had a strong apologetic flavour. Nevertheless, they are based on a consistent outlook to which Bukharin was stubbornly loyal – in fact, he was prepared to go into opposition when he saw them violated. This underlying outlook was based on a narrative about the heroic mission of the proletariat: the proletariat conquered and defended a new state authority in order to be able to build a benevolent mono-organizational society by drawing peasant farms into a unified socialist framework. Civil war and social collapse were close-to-inevitable consequences of proletarian revolution: they imposed high but justifiable costs. After a new equilibrium had been painfully established, society could proceed more smoothly toward a completely organized and planned society. Bukharin later accepted Stalin's revolution because he convinced himself that it was a repetition in another key of this same pattern: a sharpened class struggle caused by kulak aggression that imposed huge costs but that also opened up huge possibilities of peaceful construction.

In 1920, Bukharin saw the struggle to overcome private capital as a war between *Narkomprod* (Food Supply Commissariat) and *Sukharevka* (notorious open-air market in Moscow) – that is, between an official and legal socialist economy and an underground, illegal, petty-capitalist economy. After 1921, he discarded the illusion that the best way to victory in this war was to drive the private market underground. But he remained just as committed to winning the war itself and bragged in his NEP-era writings about Bolshevik successes on the field of economic battle. He saw no particular paradox in 'overcoming the market through the market': the analogy with Hilferdingian state capitalism assured him that monopolies of some kind were fated to 'squeeze out' independent producers. If state *capitalism* was able to absorb the challenges that emanated from an oppressed and exploited society, what kind of fools would the Bolsheviks have to be if they were unable to do just as well or even better, given that they were *not* exploiters?

At the beginning of this essay, I remarked that the maximalist interpretation of Bukharin's 'collapse of our illusions' formula provided strong support for the standard picture of a huge contrast between war communism and NEP. We have now seen that Bukharin devised the 'illusions' formula specifically to minimize the rethinking associated with NEP. Does the more accurate minimalist interpretation of the 'illusions' formula along with Bukharin's other pronouncements on war communism and NEP cause any damage to the standard view? At the very least, it imposes a greater burden of proof on it. Bukharin's own outlook demonstrably shifted very little in fundamentals and even in details, with the significant exception of the 'war-communist illusion' that he himself defined fairly precisely.

Since Bukharin was the foremost party spokesman as well as an intelligent and honest man, I think we should also take his pronouncements very seriously as useful hypotheses about the nature of war communism and NEP. My own research leads me to support Bukharin on a number of points. Bukharin's conception of the war-communist illusion implies correctly that the main issue on which the Bolsheviks changed their mind was the use of non-market but still exchange methods in peacetime: they did not need to rethink any 'leap into socialism', 'shortcuts to communism', glorification of coercion or most of the other stereotypes attached to war communism, because these illusions never existed. There is also much to be said for a periodization that highlights the turn toward the middle peasant in 1919 and downplays the introduction of NEP in 1921. I take Bukharin seriously when he insists that NEP was neither a retreat nor a cause for serious rethinking but a strategy that was genuinely meant to overcome the market.

Of course, as we have seen, Bukharin's pronouncements always had an immediate polemical aim: they are very far from disinterested hypotheses. His 1925 defence of 'the transfer of NEP to the villages' clearly shows the strain. As everyone (including Bukharin) knows, NEP was introduced as a response to peasant discontent and as a way of throwing a bridge across the economic chasm between town and country. Yet Bukharin's need to defend the measures of April 1925 led him to picture NEP as originally an *urban* policy that was only now being transferred to the villages. Much current research also casts doubt on his picture of local officials addicted to 'pressure methods'. From the point of view of central party leaders, a greater problem seems to have been a tendency for local officials to cozy up to peasant elites.[71]

---

71   Chris Monty, 'The Smolensk Scandal of 1928', paper delivered at AASSS national conven-

Taken all in all, Bukharin's views support an interpretation of war communism and NEP that puts much greater emphasis on the *continuity* in the Bolshevik outlook during these two periods. Bringing out this continuity means showing that elements of the standard view of the war communist outlook continued to exist during NEP – but also that elements of the standard view of the NEP outlook already existed during the civil war. I have a feeling that the first of these propositions will be much easier for most scholars to accept than the second. Many people will be happy to accept that Bukharin remained anti-market and anti-pluralist and continued to justify mass coercion under appropriate circumstances. This sort of thing seems to be what people usually have in mind when they talk about the continuity of war communism and NEP. It is much harder to get scholars to take seriously the 'NEP' component of war communism, since it means admitting that 'war communism' was not defined by a 'leap into socialism' mood, a glorification of coercion as opposed to material incentive as the main method for socialist transformation, or a strategy of violent assault on the peasant way of life à la Stalin. The 'shortcut to communism' picture of war communism as a time of fierce utopian illusions strongly appeals to a wide range of political orientations.[72]

A final question remains: what does our investigation into Bukharin's 'illusion' formula tell us about Bukharin's illusions, without the quotation marks? The usual contrast is between the unrealism and extremism of *Economy of the Transition Period* (1920) vs. the pragmatism and moderation of *Road to Socialism* (1925). Long familiarity with these works has left me with a different impression. The main thesis of ETP – social breakdown as an inevitable component of a deep and wide-ranging revolution – strikes me as defensible, even common-sensical. Certainly the current [2000] social costs and temporary (?) disorganization associated with Russia's transition back to capitalism lends support to much of Bukharin's analysis.

In contrast, the strategy set out in *Road to Socialism* is based heavily on the analogy with Hilferdingian state capitalism, that is, on the assumption of an immanent dynamic in all modern societies toward the mono-organizational society. Bukharin always held this view, but it is more closely intertwined with his strategy for NEP than with his justification of harsh war communist meth-

---

tion, Denver, November 2000; Vladimir Brovkin, *Russia after Lenin: Politics, Culture and Society, 1921–1929* (Brovkin 1998, chapter 2); Roger Pethybridge, *One Step Back, Two Steps Forward: Soviet Society and Politics in the New Economic Policy* (Pethybridge 1990).

72   For an examination of the origins of the 'shortcut' interpretation of war communism, see 'Our Position is in the Highest Degree Tragic: Trotsky and Bolshevik "Euphoria" in 1920', included in this volume.

ods. This analogy gave Bukharin supreme confidence that the market would fairly soon be abolished via the market, that large-scale state and cooperative trading organizations would almost automatically outperform private capital, and that peasants could be smoothly 'drawn in' and integrated into a unified socialist economic framework. Today this NEP-era strategy is the one that seems utopian and unrealistic, rather than the desperate harshness of war communism.

To conclude: Bukharin shows us that the Bolsheviks did less rethinking than we realized. This calls for some serious rethinking on our part.

PART 6

Stalin Era (1925–1953)

..

CHAPTER 14

Stalin at Work: Introduction to *Stalin's Letters to Molotov*

– Do you dream about Stalin?
– Not often, but sometimes. The circumstances are very unusual –
I'm in some sort of destroyed city, and I can't find any way out.
Afterwards I meet with him. In a word, very strange dreams,
very confused.

V.M. MOLOTOV

∴

In 1969, the man whose long association with Stalin resulted in such eerie dreams, Viacheslav M. Molotov, turned over a packet of letters to party authorities. For the most part, Stalin wrote these letters to Molotov during the years 1925 to 1936 while away from Moscow on what appear to be rather frequent vacations. Although generally addressed to Molotov, the letters were often intended for Stalin's allies in the Politburo. In his memoirs, Molotov describes these letters as both personal and official; they contain musings on political events, arguments meant to persuade fellow Politburo members, and specific instructions.[1] Detailed, handwritten letters were evidently necessary given the lack of a reliable telephone link between Moscow and Sochi (where Stalin's Black Sea resort was located). We therefore have primitive communications technology to thank for a unique set of documents that throw a searching light on how Stalin approached his job of running the Soviet state.

The letters put us in the middle of many crucial episodes during a dramatic period of transformation. We see Stalin fighting against party rivals like Trotsky and Bukharin, trying to manoeuvre in the rapids of the Chinese revolution, insisting on the completion of all-out collectivization, and ordering the exe-

---

1 F. Chuev, *Sto sorok besed s Molotovym: iz dnevnika F. Chueva* (Chuev 1991, p. 277). Molotov's conversations with Chuev are available in English: *Molotov Remembers: Inside Kremlin Politics* (Chuev 1993). A biographical sketch of Molotov can be found in Roy Medvedev, *All Stalin's Men* (Medvedev 1983).

cution of scapegoats for economic failures. The value of the correspondence is greatly enhanced by the comprehensive annotation provided by the Russian editors, O.V. Naumov and Oleg Khlevniuk. They have elucidated much that would otherwise have remained mysterious and have also given us supplementary archival documents of the highest interest.

1   Stalin at Work

In 1925, when the Stalin-Molotov correspondence begins, Stalin had been general secretary of the Communist Party for several years. The official duties of the Secretariat concerned internal party matters that were supposed to be below the level of high policy, and the post of general secretary was not yet the unchallenged leadership position it later became as a result of Stalin's ascendancy. The letters sometimes reflect an almost conscious apprenticeship on Stalin's part: he extends his policy-making role into economic and diplomatic affairs with greater and greater assurance.

Molotov had actually held the post of party secretary prior to Stalin. A decade younger than Stalin, Molotov was renowned for his bureaucratic efficiency, but he did not have any independent political authority. In 1922 the party leaders decided it would be better to have a senior party figure head up the Secretariat, and Stalin was given the job. Molotov remained in the Secretariat and soon became a full member of the Politburo.

Molotov always seemed rather cold and unemotional, occasionally revealing a streak of aggressive pedantry that was extremely irritating to other party leaders. They called him Stone Bottom, a nickname that was dismissive and yet respectful of his huge capacity for work. His hero-worship of Stalin seems genuine enough, and his role as Stalin's right-hand man is evident from the letters. He would argue with his boss on occasion, but always in an effort to point out what would be in Stalin's best interest. Molotov was later rewarded for his loyalty with a number of important posts, including head of the government and minister of foreign affairs. Toward the end of Stalin's life, Molotov fell into disfavour. He was forced to participate in the Politburo meeting that approved the arrest of his wife (he abstained). Nevertheless, after Stalin's death, Molotov remained loyal to Stalin's memory, and his unreconstructed views led eventually to a falling out with Nikita Khrushchev and to his expulsion from the party. Molotov doggedly applied for reinstatement and was rewarded with a party card shortly before his death in 1986.

The present collection of letters begins at a time when the Bolshevik party was approaching a turning point. The decade from the beginning of World

War I to 1925 was a period of social and economic breakdown and reconstitution for Russia. The low point occurred in the winter of 1920–1921. The economic upswing made possible by the end of hostilities associated with the civil war was further strengthened by the New Economic Policy (NEP) that was introduced in the spring of 1921. The essence of the new policy was a short-term toleration of private capitalists and middlemen, combined with a longer-term acceptance of a regulated market as the key economic link between socialized industry and peasant farms. The Bolsheviks assumed that, at some future date, industry would be advanced enough to allow Russian agriculture to be reorganized into large productive units. In the meantime, industrial growth had to rely on the surplus produced by small peasant farms. By 1925, the economy was on the verge of reaching pre-war levels. This recovery was shaky and infirm, however, since the orgy of destruction and demoralization that had occurred from 1914 to 1921 could not be made up in a few years' time. Furthermore, the rest of the world had not stood still. Thus the Bolsheviks were left in an even weaker international position than previous Russian governments had occupied. Still, by late 1925 the Bolsheviks were preparing to make an advance beyond simple recovery under the guidance of a general strategy that had a number of optimistic assumptions built into it: the superior productivity of nationalized industry, the availability of marketed surpluses of agricultural goods, and a relatively benign international environment.

Perhaps because of this optimism, Stalin devotes little attention to economic questions in the letters from 1925, 1926, and 1927. He comments in 1926: 'I am not alarmed by economic matters. Rykov will be able to take care of them. The opposition wins absolutely zero points on economic matters' (letter 20). Although Aleksei Rykov was official head of the government in the mid-1920s, he was a relatively colourless figure whom historians have left in the background. Stalin's remark hints that his role may have been greater than we suspected.

In the letters from the mid-1920s, Stalin's principal economic concern is to ensure that the Politburo maintains control over economic questions, despite the resistance of planning specialists, 'monopolistic' state syndicates, and lower-level trading cooperatives. One item of particular interest is Stalin's sceptical attitude in 1925 toward the Dneprostroi project – a proposed hydroelectric station that later became a symbol of Stalin's industrial achievements (letters 2 and 3). We know that Stalin voted against the project in April 1926, but here we see that his misgivings date back to a much earlier stage. Stalin felt that a commission that had been established under Trotsky's leadership would be too hasty in beginning the project. (He need not have worried, for in fact Trotsky used his influence to slow it down.)[2] Stalin learned about the Dneprostroi commission from a newspaper article, and indeed this seems to have been his main source of economic information, at least while he was on vacation.

The mid-1920s were a turning point for Bolshevism politically as well as economically. The Bolsheviks had always felt that one of the reasons they were able to survive in an extremely hostile world was the unity of what they called the top leadership nucleus. Unlike their rivals during the years of revolution and civil war, the Bolsheviks had not allowed the inevitable dissensions and the clash of ambitions to drive the party apart. Everyone realized that this remarkable political feat stemmed from Lenin's unique position in the party and that things would be very different after his death. Since no one could duplicate Lenin's status, the remaining leaders had to develop new methods for ensuring unity. This process is reflected in the letters from 1925 through 1927, which are strongly preoccupied with the political battle within the Politburo against Trotsky and Zinoviev. Stalin's attitudes toward his rivals are reflected in many other letters throughout the collection. Taken together, the letters suggest the need to reconsider the way we look at the leadership struggles after Lenin's death.

By 1925, most observers felt that the country was run by a triumvirate consisting of Zinoviev, Kamenev, and Stalin, with Trotsky already relegated to the side-lines. Trotsky had been openly at odds with his Politburo colleagues for several years before 1925. By the end of 1923, he had managed to enrage the rest of his Politburo colleagues so thoroughly that they formed a shadow Politburo: the *semërka* (the seven), an institution that plays a large role in Stalin's letters from the mid-1920s. The seven's sole purpose was to conduct Politburo business without Trotsky's participation. Trotsky did not even know the seven existed until Zinoviev told him when they joined forces in 1926.

Stalin's letters to Molotov give us a close-up view of some dramatic episodes in this battle among the top leaders. In 1925 the Politburo took Stalin's suggestion and compelled Trotsky to issue a public refutation of a book written by his American admirer Max Eastman. The 'Eastman affair' has previously been described as a cynical cover-up in which the triumvirate forced Trotsky to tell conscious lies. The letters and other documents allow a much different interpretation.

Another split within the Politburo was dramatically revealed at the Fourteenth Party Congress in late 1925. For reasons of both policy and ambition, Zinoviev and Kamenev rebelled and called for Stalin's removal from the post of general secretary. Their effort failed utterly; during the winter of 1925–1926,

---

2   Anne D. Rassweiler, *The Generation of Power: The History of Dneprostroi* (Rassweiler 1988).

Zinoviev even lost control of his political base in Leningrad. Even though Zinoviev had formerly been one of the most prominent Trotsky-baiters in the leadership, he now felt it expedient to join forces with his erstwhile foe. Thus was formed the united left opposition, which openly challenged the Politburo majority until late 1927, when its leaders were thrown out of the party. Trotsky ended up in exile; Zinoviev and Kamenev recanted and were soon reinstated.

A large number of Stalin's letters in 1926 and 1927 deal with foreign policy, particularly with revolutionary stirrings in England and China. Stalin's intense involvement belies the image of an isolationist leader interested only in 'socialism in one country'. The letters show us that Stalin did not make a rigid distinction between the interests of world revolution and the interests of the Soviet state: both concerns are continually present in his outlook.

Although the British government had recognized the Soviet Union in 1924, the Conservative Party that returned to power at the end of the year was uncomfortable with any dealings with bomb-throwing Bolsheviks. Relations were further strained by the enthusiasm with which the Bolsheviks greeted the brief general strike of 1926 and the moral and material support they gave to the striking miners. Back at home, the left opposition attacked the Politburo for not being revolutionary enough. The optimism of 1926 did not last long: working-class militancy in England petered out and the Conservative government broke off diplomatic relations in 1927. When a Labour government was formed in 1929, it promptly extended recognition to the Soviet Union; still, revolutionary feeling among the British working class did not resurface.[3]

Relations with China were even more complex, since China was experiencing its own revolutionary upheaval in the mid-1920s. The movement against the imperialist powers was spearheaded by the government at Canton controlled by the Kuomintang, the nationalist party founded by Sun Yat-sen. Allied to the Kuomintang was the newly formed Chinese Communist Party. Thanks in large part to Russian political and military advisors, the Kuomintang was prepared in 1926 to undertake the Northern Expedition in an effort to unite a country rendered powerless by internal divisions. The Northern Expedition was a phenomenal military success, but it quickly led to divisions within the camp of the Chinese revolutionaries. By the middle of 1927, the Chinese Communists found themselves isolated and driven underground, first by Chiang Kai-shek and then by the so-called left Kuomintang government located in Wuhan.

The Bolshevik leaders viewed events in China with the hope that a nationalist and anti-imperialist government would unite the country and strike a blow

3   Daniel F. Calhoun, *The United Front: The TUC and the Russians, 1923–1928* (Calhoun 1976).

at the world power of Western capitalism. To this end, they counselled the Chinese Communist Party to work as closely as possible with the Kuomintang and later with the Wuhan government. The left opposition roundly criticized this 'rightist' policy of cooperation with the bourgeoisie that indeed led eventually to disaster for the Chinese Communists.[4]

Policy toward both China and Great Britain was thus a matter of intense dispute among the Bolshevik leaders. The dramatic Politburo showdown with Zinoviev in June 1926 involved policy toward the British trade unions. In spite of this partisan dimension, the letters reveal Stalin's genuine enthusiasm about revolutionary prospects in 1926 as well as his reaction to defeat in 1927. Particularly revealing are the letters from 1927 written at the moment when Stalin had to face up to the ruin of his China policy.

After 1927 the prospect of revolution elsewhere diminished, and Stalin's foreign policy concerns were confined to such issues as diplomatic recognition from Great Britain and the United States. His interest in China now focused on the Chinese Eastern Railway, which ran through Manchuria. This railroad, built during tsarist times, was of strategic importance to the Soviet government as the most efficient route to Vladivostok. The de facto ruler of Manchuria, a warlord named Chang Tso-lin, wanted complete control over the railroad. The dispute over the railroad culminated in a brief armed clash in 1929 between the Soviet government and Chang's son (Chang Hsueh-liang).[5] Even though the dispute over the Chinese Eastern Railway was entirely a matter of state, Stalin viewed it through the prism of revolutionary interests. He even outlined a scenario for retaining control over the railroad by instigating an instant revolution in Manchuria.

From 1925 to 1927, Stalin worked closely with both Nikolai Bukharin, editor of *Pravda* (the party newspaper) and principal party theorist, and Aleksei Rykov, head of the Soviet government and top economic administrator. There are no letters from 1928, which is a pity but which adds to the dramatic effect when the curtain rises in 1929 and we find Stalin and Molotov plotting against Bukharin and Rykov, their erstwhile allies. The reason for the conflict was Stalin's radical 'offensive along the whole front', which attempted to combine a frantic pace of industrialization with a policy of 'extraordinary measures' that put extreme pressure on the peasantry to ensure grain deliveries. Stalin's offensive meant the end of NEP and its use of the market to link

---

4 C. Martin Wilbur and Julie Lien-ying How, *Missionaries of Revolution: Soviet Advisers and Nationalist China, 1920–1927* (Wilbur and How 1989).

5 For background on the conflict over the Chinese Eastern Railway in 1929, see E.H. Carr, *Foundations of a Planned Economy* (Carr 1976–1978, 3:895–910).

the peasants with state industry. Bukharin and Rykov, who found this policy ill-conceived and dangerous, were condemned as leaders of the 'right deviation'.[6]

The letters from 1929 and 1930 touch on all aspects of this great transformation. Stalin's high-pressure industrial policies led to an upheaval in the economy that left the government struggling to maintain a semblance of control. The letters show Stalin's response to this emergency as he ceaselessly shuffles personnel in order to put the right person in the right position. A more destructive response to the unending stream of foul-ups and breakdowns was to assign all blame to enemies within the Soviet government itself. An ideology centred on 'wrecking' finds expression in the letters. For many observers, upward mobility via promotion off the shop floor (*vydvizhenie*) was a key source of support for the Stalinist system. It is thus ironic to find Stalin inveighing against *vydvizhenie* as disruptive (letter 69).

Only scattered passages in the letters show Stalin's attitude toward grain procurement and collectivization, but taken together they illuminate the mindset that gave rise to the momentous decision in late 1929 to combine all-out collectivization with massive repression of the kulaks (better-off peasants). The letters also show Stalin's intensely personal anger against the leaders of the right deviation. More surprisingly, we find the same anger, justified with the same rhetoric, directed against people who are usually regarded as far removed from the right deviation: the former Trotskyist Georgii Piatakov and the loyal Stalinist Sergo Ordzhonikidze. The letters thus force us to re-examine the political logic by which Stalin defined his enemies within the party.

The nature of the correspondence changes drastically after 1930, and we have only thirteen rather fragmentary letters from the years 1931–1936. The reasons for this change are unclear. Molotov replaced Rykov as head of the government in late 1930, and it could be that other means were found to transmit Stalin's instructions. It is also possible that Molotov later found it expedient to suppress incriminating material. Nevertheless, the letters from this period are not without interest. In September 1935, for example, Stalin gives a provisional outline of the new Constitution adopted the following year, thus documenting a strong directive role early in the drafting process (letter 83).[7] Stalin wanted the Constitution to reflect only 'what has *already*

---

6   Invaluable background for many of the issues discussed in Stalin's letters can be found in R.W. Davies, *The Soviet Economy in Turmoil, 1929–1930* (Davies 1989a).

7   J. Arch Getty, 'State and Society under Stalin: Constitutions and Elections in the 1930s' (Getty 1991).

been achieved'; he and Molotov evidently had somewhat macabre theoretical disputes over exactly what stage of socialism had been reached by the mid-1930s.

The list of topics covered in the letters is a long and varied one. Just as revealing are the patterns that emerge from the collection as a whole, which give us an unparalleled look at Stalin as leader. A complete analysis of Stalin's leadership would cover at least three dimensions. We need to consider Stalin as an *official* and examine the constraints faced by anybody in the position of top leader in a country undergoing revolutionary transformation. We need to look at Stalin as a *Bolshevik*, since the basic mental tools Stalin applied to his job were derived from the Bolshevik political culture in which he had spent his adult life. Nor can we neglect Stalin as an *individual* with his own particular psychological makeup and mental habits.

Stalin's letters fill in the gap between public speeches about the general direction of policy, on the one hand, and specific decisions about day-to-day matters, on the other; they are documents of leadership and persuasion aimed specifically at the top echelons of the Bolshevik party. As such, they throw valuable and much-needed light on all three dimensions of Stalin as a leader. Because Stalin is explaining his views on urgent policy questions, we observe him as an official, dealing with the whole range of problems that would confront any ruler of Russia. Because he is trying to obtain support in the Politburo, we can examine the arguments that Stalin thought would work with fellow Bolsheviks. Although we will never learn what Stalin said privately to himself, the letters provide us with the next best resource for learning about Stalin as an individual: how Stalin defined the world in confidential correspondence with his closest political friend.

Along with my commentary on specific topics, I shall advance a general interpretation of Stalin as a leader that is based on my reading of the letters. My argument, in brief, is as follows: Stalin had a conscious and coherent approach to governing that I shall call the antibureaucrat scenario. The constructive side of this scenario allowed Stalin to use his undeniable leadership skills to get things done and to maintain Politburo support. These skills were the original basis of Stalin's power. On the other hand, the antibureaucrat scenario also defined governing as a continual struggle with class enemies of various types and hues. The scenario thus gave expression to the angry and vindictive sides of Stalin's personality.

The suspicious and punitive features of Stalin's scenario were always present, but they became more pronounced in 1929 and 1930 when the country was plunged into the whirlwind of the general offensive. We observe Stalin's anger at those he perceived as enemies become increasingly intense. Indeed, the ring of enemies seems to close in on him: first the international 'capitalist encirclement', then domestic class enemies such as the kulaks, next the 'bourgeois specialists' working for the Soviet government itself, and finally some of his closest comrades. Although the correspondence fades out in the early 1930s, we are well on our way to the murderous 'purification' (*ochishchenie*) campaigns of 1937–1938. The same outlook that allowed Stalin to run the government for so many years also pushed him close to destroying it.

2   The Antibureaucrat Scenario

To understand Stalin at work, we need to understand his views on running a government. It is not difficult to discover these views, for this was a subject that mattered deeply to Stalin; he gave it considerable thought and set forth his conclusions on a number of occasions. His own summary of his views seems no more than a couple of banal platitudes: the need for proper 'selection of officials' and 'checking up on fulfilment' of policy directives. These bland slogans only reveal their full meaning, however, when set into the context of a dramatic and politicized scenario of class conflict and revolutionary transformation. The details of this scenario can be found in Stalin's published speeches; the letters to Molotov reveal how the scenario guided him in his day-to-day work.

Stalin's scenario can be summarized as follows: There is no objective obstacle to the successful construction of socialism in Russia. The soviet system of government, the state control of the commanding heights of the economy, and the natural resources of Russia itself – all of these provide the potential for successfully completing the revolution. Correct leadership thus becomes the crucial factor. The first task of leadership is to define the correct line. The core leadership of the party – its 'leading nucleus' – must accurately size up the situation and deduce the necessary tasks facing the party at any one time. The main threat to defining the correct line comes from wavering on the part of leaders who in their hearts lack faith in the revolution.

Defining the correct line is only the first step. Next it must be spelled out so that all other party members understand both the overall picture and their own role in it. This requires clarity in presentation and a careful selection of slogans and directives. But it would be criminal laxness to believe that the party line will be carried out automatically. Proper leadership requires unremitting attention to 'selection of officials' and 'checking up on fulfilment'. The main threat here is Russia's low level of culture, which forces the worker-peasant state to rely on many 'class-alien elements' in its government bureaucracy. As a result, 'vigilance' is one of the basic duties of each party member.

These are the bare bones of Stalin's outlook, stated in somewhat dry propositional form. In order to understand the emotional power of this view, we have to recast it in the form of the dramatic antibureaucrat scenario that portrays well-intentioned but naive Communists doing battle with sophisticated bureaucrats who try to fool and corrupt them. (Update: if I were writing this introduction today, in 2023, I would talk about Stalin's hostility toward the 'deep state'.) Stalin's attitudes emerge in vivid language taken from three speeches given at different stages of his career.

In 1920, Stalin was head of Worker-Peasant Inspection (Rabkrin). This agency was the descendent of the tsarist Ministry of State Control, which was devoted mainly to auditing accounts of other government agencies. Lenin had ambitious plans for the Worker-Peasant Inspection and saw it as an instrument of mass participation in government. Although Stalin was nominally the head of Worker-Peasant Inspection, his other duties during the civil war prevented him from giving much of his time to it. Stalin left the Worker-Peasant Inspection in 1922 when he took over the post of general secretary.

In October 1920, Stalin addressed a group of officials from the Worker-Peasant Inspection. He stressed the vital importance of progressing from the seizure of political power to genuine control over the state *apparat*: 'Comrades, the people who really run the country are not those who elect delegates, whether to parliament in the bourgeois system or to soviet congresses under the Soviet system. No, those who factually run the country are those who really master the executive *apparaty* [or, the *apparaty* of fulfilment], those who lead these *apparaty*'. This task was difficult because the workers and peasants did not have any pre-revolutionary experience in administration. One consequence of this situation was that 'although bureaucratism has been smashed, the bureaucrats have remained. Painting themselves as soviet officials, they have entered our state *apparaty*. Here they use the insufficient experience of workers and peasants who have just come into power; they spin out their old machinations in order to plunder state property; they introduce their old bourgeois morals.' As Worker-Peasant Inspection officials tried to do their job, they would undoubtedly run into opposition from 'overzealous bureaucrats, as well as some Communists who give in to the voices of these bureaucrats'. When encountering this, their motto should be: 'Don't spare individuals, no matter what position they occupy; spare only the cause [*delo*], the interests of the cause.'[8]

---

8   J.V. Stalin, *Sochineniia* (Stalin 1947–1952, 4:366–8). For more on Lenin's hopes for Rabkrin, see 'Political Testament', included in this volume.

For our second speech we turn to the XII Party Congress in 1923. This was the last party congress in Lenin's lifetime; he was already incapacitated by strokes and did not attend. In his speech, Stalin depicted himself as developing Lenin's outlook. In addition to political considerations, Stalin felt that there was a 'moral aspect' to Lenin's demand for an improved apparat: Lenin 'wanted to get to the point where the country contained not a single bigwig, no matter how highly placed, about which the man in the street could say, "that one is above control"'. Years later, in the mid-1930s, a murderous version of this populist rhetoric dominated the mass media. Another of Lenin's slogans was 'selection of officials'. Stalin explained this slogan by arguing that it was insufficient merely to give directives – you had to find officials who could understand these directives and regard them as their own. For this reason the Central Committee needed to know each high official through and through.[9]

Our final example comes from the speech Stalin gave at a meeting of the Central Committee in January 1933. Stalin argued that the period of revolutionary transformation was drawing to a close: it was time to make the new structures work in a productive and efficient manner. The main obstacle was still 'the enemy within' (to borrow a phrase from J. Edgar Hoover), portrayed in vivid and melodramatic fashion as crushed and resentful class enemies: 'Thrown out of their groove, and scattered over the whole face of the USSR, these "former people" [the elite disinherited by the revolution] have wormed their way into our plants and factories, into our government offices and trading organizations, into our railway and water transport enterprises, and, principally, into our collective and state farms. They have crept into these places and taken cover there, donning the mask of "workers" and "peasants", and some of them have even managed to worm their way into the party'. What did these class enemies carry with them into these places? – a feeling of hatred toward Soviet power, a feeling of burning enmity toward the new forms of economy, life, and culture. Inspired by this hatred, the alien elements set out to organize sabotage; certain professors, for example, went so far as to inject plague and anthrax germs into cattle. Stalin insisted that 'the task is to eject these "former people" from our own enterprises and institutions and render them permanently harmless'. Unfortunately some people within the party thought that the class struggle was dying down, since the enemy classes had been defeated in open battle. Such people have either degenerated or are two-faced; they must be driven out of the party and their smug philistine attitude replaced by revolutionary vigilance.[10]

---

9   Stalin 1947–1952, 5:197–2.22.
10   Stalin 1947–1952, 13:159–233. For a more detailed discussion of Stalin's attitude toward

These three speeches give an idea of the emotions Stalin invested in the antibureaucrat scenario. In spite of an increase in the violence and obsessiveness of the rhetoric, the fundamental outlook remains the same: the system is basically good; problems arise from hostile individuals within the system and their ability to fool otherwise dedicated revolutionaries; only a united leadership devoid of wavering can combat the bureaucrats.

Turning now to Stalin's correspondence with Molotov, we observe that the slogans 'checking up on fulfilment' and 'selection of officials' are ubiquitous. Some examples will show how Stalin applied these in practice. His efforts to improve the oil industry in the Urals demonstrate his attitude toward selecting officials (letters 42, 44, 46, 57). Given the decision to develop this industry, Stalin's contribution was to get a competent person for the top party post – someone who was a 'Communist/oilman'. Once this person was found, he was to be given the 'combat assignment' to develop oil, drive out incompetent 'wreckers', and protect the Urals from having personnel be 'looted' by other localities and institutions.

The shortage of 'big people' – energetic and talented administrators – is a constant complaint. In letter 60, Stalin wants to help the Commissariat of Trade by sending over Rozengolts from the Worker-Peasant Inspection, even though he realizes that Sergo Ordzhonikidze, the head of Worker-Peasant Inspection, will be upset. He ends with the typical Stalin sentiment: 'Do people pity Khinchuk [a trade official]? But the cause should be pitied even more. Do they not want to offend Sergo? But what about the cause – can such an important and serious matter be offended?'

Once having selected the man for the job and given him vast powers, Stalin had to worry about whether he would do what he was supposed to do. Hence the importance of the slogan 'checking up on fulfilment'. His obsessive concern is revealed in an exhortation about grain procurement in 1929 (letter 42):

> The Politburo has adopted my proposals concerning grain procurement. This is good, but in my opinion, it is inadequate. Now the problem is *fulfilling* the Politburo's decision. There is no need to insist that all procurement organizations (especially in Ukraine) will *evade* this decision ... Therefore, it is necessary to demand the following from procurement organizations, the OGPU, the Collective Farm Centre, and so forth:

---

masks and 'double-dealers' (*dvurushniki*), see 'Vertigo: Masks and Lies in Stalin's Russia', included in this volume.

a) copies of their instructions to subordinate organs concerning the *fulfilment* of the Politburo's decision; b) regular reports every two weeks (even better, once a week) about the *results of the fulfilment* of the decisions. The Worker-Peasant Inspection and the Central Control Commission should be involved in this as well. I don't know how you regard this matter and the outlook for grain procurement (Mikoyan probably thinks that since the decision has been reached, he now has 130 million poods of an untouchable reserve sitting in the grain elevators) ... And grain procurement this year will provide the basis for everything we're doing – if we foul up here, everything will be wiped out. And the danger of a foul-up will grow if we don't insist that the Central Committee's decision *be fulfilled* with unrelenting *firmness* and *ruthlessness.*

In 1930, Stalin dreamed of a Fulfilment Commission that would solve all his problems: 'Without such an authoritative and rapidly acting commission, we will not be able to break through the wall of bureaucratism and [improve] the slipshod performance of our bureaucracies. Without such reforms, the centre's directives will remain completely on paper' (letter 68). (This commission was actually set up in late 1930, but nothing came of it.) When Stalin wanted to give Molotov a pat on the back, it is no wonder that he paid him the ultimate compliment and praised his 'Leninist checking up on fulfilment' (letter 70).

When set into the context of the antibureaucrat scenario, Stalin's two Lenin-derived slogans have both a constructive and a destructive side. 'Checking up on fulfilment' is the task of any responsible administrator who wants to ensure that central policies are actually carried out. According to Stalin's antibureaucrat scenario, however, class-motivated hostility is the main reason bureaucrats do not follow directives. If conscious or unconscious sabotage is the problem, repression is bound to be at least part of the solution. For Stalin, 'selection of officials' did not mean simply choosing and promoting the most competent people. There was a moral dimension: Officials needed to be chosen who would look on party directives as their own and who would not be seduced by 'bourgeois specialists'. But if the selected officials proved less reliable than anticipated, this moral dimension could easily give rise to disappointment and vindictive anger.

Let us now consider how the antibureaucrat scenario fits into the three dimensions of Stalin as leader. First, Stalin as an official: any politician trying to run an unwieldy bureaucracy is likely to develop some sort of antibureaucrat scenario. Richard Neustadt's classic *Presidential Power* shows this process at work in the case of the American presidency.[11] In Stalin's case, we have to

---

11   Richard Neustadt, *Presidential Power: The Politics of Leadership* (Neustadt 1960).

add his position as top leader in a country undergoing a state-guided revolutionary transformation. Stalin had to run the country with the help of officials whose trustworthiness was dubious and whose competence was perhaps even more dubious. He was forced to grant enormous power to these people and to give them next-to-impossible tasks. Obsession with shuffling personnel and intense suspicion of appointees was built into the situation, and the antibureaucrat scenario reflected these structural realities.

But Stalin did not create his particular version of the antibureaucrat scenario in a vacuum, and so we have to consider Stalin as a Bolshevik. His scenario had roots in what might be called the popular bolshevism that arose during the civil war. Both before and after the October revolution of 1917, the Bolsheviks blamed the breakdown of the economy on the sabotage of capitalists and bureaucrats and presented themselves as the only force capable of crushing this sabotage. When the economic breakdown continued during the civil war, the population transferred this explanation to the Bolshevik state itself. The population invented a new category – the 'soviet bourgeoisie' – that Stalin took over and used for his own purposes.[12]

Stalin could plausibly claim Lenin's authority for his scenario, since Lenin also viewed public administration as a dramatic struggle against a class enemy. When Lenin insisted on the slogans 'checking up on fulfilment' and 'selection of officials' in 1922, he emphasized that they were part of 'the struggle between two irreconcilably hostile classes [that] appears to be going on in all government offices'. Lenin blamed his frustration with bureaucratic red tape on clever saboteurs: 'The vile bureaucratic bog *draws us* into the writing of papers, endless talkfests about decrees, the writing of decrees, and real live work drowns in that sea of paper. Clever saboteurs deliberately draw us into this paper swamp. The majority of people's commissars and other government dignitaries unwittingly "walk into the trap".'[13]

The antibureaucrat scenario was thus derived from experiences that all the Bolshevik leaders had lived through. Shared experience gave Stalin's perceptions a basic legitimacy within the party elite: what he said made sense to them, even when they disagreed with it. The letters show the use that Stalin made of the scenario when exhorting his Politburo colleagues.

In spite of its links with Bolshevik political culture, the antibureaucrat scenario must also be considered from the point of view of Stalin as an individual.

---

12   Mary McAuley, *Bread and Justice* (McAuley 1991, p. 400). For a wide-ranging discussion of the changing meanings of 'soviet' and the relation of this word to 'Bolshevik', see Anna Krylova, 'Imagining socialism in the Soviet century' (Krylova 2017).

13   Robert C. Tucker, ed., *The Lenin Anthology* (Lenin 1975, pp. 526–28, 717).

Stalin stood out among Bolshevik leaders in the attention he devoted to the problems of controlling the state. This point is usually made by emphasizing that Stalin was preoccupied with machine politics and with manipulating the state and party apparat. This is one way of putting it, and no doubt a valid one, but if we limit ourselves to this presentation, we risk underestimating Stalin in the same way his opponents did. An equally valid way of putting it is that no other Bolshevik leader took so seriously the basic problem confronting the Bolsheviks: how to run the country. Stalin's antibureaucrat scenario arose out of his reflections on that problem.

[Update: thanks to the recent critical edition of the famous *Short Course* of party history that came out in 1938, we now know precisely what passages were added by Stalin. I see it as a confirmation of my above remarks that he added an emphatic paragraph about the importance of 'checking up on fulfilment': 'In order to guarantee success, it was necessary to *put the right people in the right place*, people able to give effect to the decisions of the leading organs and to *keep a check on the fulfilment of decisions* ... Comrade Stalin said that the disparity between adopted decisions and the organizational work of putting these decisions into effect and of keeping a check on their fulfilment was the chief evil in our partial word.'[14]]

According to the anti-bureaucrat scenario, good government was an eternal battle in which noble intentions were continually thwarted by the ill will of saboteurs. Without going deeply into psychological speculations, we may conclude that this scenario would recommend itself to a person predisposed to see the world in angry, punitive terms. Furthermore, as Stalin's goals became more ambitious and as the chaos of the general offensive led to greater and greater frustration, the intensity of the emotions he invested in the scenario rose to a murderous pitch.

3   Political Opposition during NEP

In the letters from 1925 through 1927 Stalin is strongly preoccupied with the political battle within the Politburo against Trotsky and Zinoviev. These letters amply confirm some well-known images of Stalin. One is Stalin the Crafty Maneuverer. In 1925 Stalin seizes on a book published in the West as an opportunity to further discredit Trotsky, and in 1926 he directs a Politburo campaign to isolate Zinoviev and Kamenev. Another familiar image is Stalin the Catechist:

---

14   Brandenberger and Zelenov 2019, p. 581.

the Stalin who learned in his days at the Tbilisi Theological Seminary to sum up any question with cut-and-dried formulae. Yet even these familiar images require modification when we observe them in the context of relations within the Politburo. The Politburo majority (which included Zinoviev and Kamenev in 1925) relied on Stalin not just to do secretarial chores but to act as a leader: his influence within the Politburo was based on what his colleagues considered the cogency of his analysis and the soundness of his recommendations.

3.1   The Eastman Affair

The Eastman affair of 1925 provides an excellent case study of Stalin's leadership within the Politburo. This affair has usually been interpreted as a brazen cover-up of the existence of the document known as Lenin's Testament. In late 1922, a few months before his final stroke, Lenin dictated a short document that he termed a 'letter to the [party] congress'. In it, he characterized the top leaders; in a postscript added a few days later, he suggested that Stalin be removed from the post of general secretary of the party. Only Nadezhda Krupskaya, Lenin's wife, knew the full contents of this document until after Lenin's death in early 1924, at which time she turned it and related documents over to the Central Committee. The party leadership decided not to read Lenin's letter into the official record of the upcoming XIII Party Congress but rather to read it to each delegation off the record. Stalin offered his resignation as general secretary, but it was not accepted. The letter itself was not published.

Although this letter became widely known as 'Lenin's Testament', it should be noted that Lenin himself did not give it this label; it was in fact one of a series of dictations on various matters. By 1925, Bukharin and others had given the title 'Lenin's Testament' to the five articles Lenin published in early 1923, on the grounds that these final articles discuss matters of grand political strategy. For convenience, I will refer to Lenin's letter as the Testament, with the proviso that the appropriateness of this label is a matter of dispute.[15]

The Western scholars who have discussed the Eastman affair (Leonard Schapiro, Isaac Deutscher, and Boris Souvarine, among others) all tell a similar story: after Lenin's death, his Testament was suppressed. In 1925 Max Eastman, an American journalist, wrote *Since Lenin Died*, in which he revealed the existence of the Testament and gave an accurate description of its contents.[16] The

---

15   I now regret using this label, since 'Lenin's testament' is better used to label his final writings as a whole; for full discussion, see 'Political Testament', included in this volume.

16   Max Eastman, *Since Lenin Died* (Eastman 1973 [1925]).

ruling triumvirate – Stalin, Zinoviev, and Kamenev – were horrified at the whistle being blown on their cover-up and forced both Trotsky and Krupskaya to write letters denying the existence of the Testament. Thus constrained to deny what he and other informed people knew to be true, Trotsky utterly discredited himself.[17] (Trotsky's and Krupskaya's letters can be found in the appendix of *The Stalin-Molotov Letters*.)

This account needs to be reconsidered in the light of Stalin's letters to Molotov and the other remarkable documents presented by the Russian editors.[18] Chief among the new documents is Stalin's long memorandum detailing the misstatements made in Eastman's book and demanding that Trotsky publicly repudiate these misstatements. From letter 6 it appears that Stalin wanted to publish his memorandum. This fact in itself forces us to reopen the case and ask whether the Eastman affair was a cynical cover-up or whether the Politburo was making what it considered legitimate demands. Our general picture of Politburo politics in the 1920s will be strongly influenced by the answer to this question.

Previous Western interpretations have all accepted that Eastman's book 'correctly reproduced long extracts' of the Testament.[19] On reading *Since Lenin Died*, I was surprised to find this was far from true. Not only does Eastman give a highly distorted rendition of the Testament, but the distortions all clearly serve an explicit political purpose, unambiguously stated in the final sentence of the book: revolutionaries in other countries ought to remember that 'they did not pledge themselves to accept, in the name of "Leninism", the international authority of a group against whom Lenin's dying words were a warning, and who have preserved that authority by suppressing the essential texts of Lenin' (130).

Eastman interprets the Testament as a 'direct endorsement of Trotsky's authority' (31). In order to reach this conclusion, he had to remove the complimentary references to other leaders as well as the uncomplimentary references

---

17   Leonard Schapiro, *The Communist Party of the Soviet Union*, rev. ed. (Schapiro 1971, pp. 300–1); Isaac Deutscher, *The Prophet Unarmed: Trotsky, 1921–1929* (Schapiro 1959, pp. 201–2); Boris Souvarine, *Stalin: A Critical Survey of Bolshevism* (Souvarine 1939, pp. 414, 348).

18   For further background on the relationship between Trotsky and Eastman, see V.V. Shevstov, 'Lev Trotskii i Maks Istmen [Max Eastman]: Istoriia odnoi politicheskoi druzhby' (Shevstov 1990). Many important new documents that shed light on the Eastman affair can be found in Yuri Buranov, *Lenin's Will: Falsified and Forbidden* (Buranov 1994). Buranov's book is unfortunately marred by serious inaccuracies, many of which can be attributed to the very inadequate English translation.

19   Schapiro 1971, p. 300.

to Trotsky.[20] The blame for these errors should not fall primarily on Eastman, who relied on 'three responsible Communists in Russia' who had read the Testament and 'committed its vital phrases to memory' (30–31). In memoirs published in 1964, Eastman recalled that during the XIII Party Congress in 1924, Trotsky 'told me, drawing me into a hidden corner of the palace, the principal phrases of Lenin's "testament".'[21] (In a memorandum to Stalin reproduced here, Trotsky implies that he did not meet with Eastman during this period.) Before publication, Eastman showed his manuscript to Christian Rakovskii, one of Trotsky's comrades who was working in France at the time, and Rakovskii approved publication. The responsibility for the distortions therefore seems to lie with the Trotsky group itself.

To understand the following course of events, then, we must start with the realization that *Since Lenin Died* is an inaccurate, highly politicized account that contrasts Trotsky, with his 'saintly' devotion to the revolution (13), to all the other leaders of the party, who are nothing more than unscrupulous usurpers. After Stalin was alerted to the existence of *Since Lenin Died*, he must have been elated: all he had to do was send around a translation of Eastman's book to the Politburo (and later to local party officials) and Trotsky would be further discredited. What must Trotsky's colleagues have felt, for example, when they read a passage like the following: 'If you danced on the corpse of Vladimir Ilich, you would insult his spirit less than by clapping censorship on his own last words to his Party and juggling under the table, with the cheapest tricks of the demagogue, the conscientious thoughts of that man whom he designated as the best of you' (92).

Stalin's lengthy memorandum on the Eastman book is a good example of his catechistic style, with its numbered points and its repetitious use of the phrase 'Trotsky must be aware'. On the whole, though, it must have struck his Politburo comrades as rather moderate and restrained. He passed over all genuine political differences and stuck to issues where he felt there could be no argument about Eastman's errors. He did not ask Trotsky to deny the existence of the Testament or to affirm any particular interpretation of it. Stalin did not accuse Trotsky of breaking discipline and revealing party secrets; rather, he chose to take at face value Trotsky's assertion that he had nothing to do with the Testament's transmission to Eastman. Stalin's main point was that by keeping silent, Trotsky was giving de facto legitimacy to slanderous accusations.

---

20   My detailed listing of Eastman's distortions can be found in the appendix of *Stalin's Letters to Molotov* (Lih et al. 1995, pp. 242–3).

21   Max Eastman, *Love and Revolution: My Journey through an Epoch* (Eastman 1964, p. 425).

The demand that Trotsky disavow this open attack on the Russian Communist Party must have seemed perfectly legitimate to the Politburo. Trotsky complied with the request and wrote an open letter. A comparison of Trotsky's letter and Stalin's memorandum shows that Trotsky stuck fairly close to the points Stalin suggested. Trotsky also added some rhetorical flourishes that have caused confusion ever since:

> In several places in his book, Eastman says that the Central Committee 'hid' from the party a number of highly important documents that Lenin wrote in the last period of his life (letters on the national question, the so-called testament, and so forth); this cannot be termed anything other than a slander of the Central Committee of our party ... Vladimir Ilich did not leave any 'testament' and the character of his relation to the party, not to mention the character of the party itself, excludes the possibility of such a 'testament'. When the émigré, foreign bourgeois, and menshevist press uses the term *testament*, it usually has in mind a letter – in a form distorted beyond recognition – in which Vladimir Ilich gave advice of an internal party character. The XIII Congress gave this letter, like all the others, its close attention and drew the conclusions appropriate to the circumstances of the moment. Any talk of a hidden or violated 'testament' is a spiteful invention aimed against the real will of Vladimir Ilich and the interests of the party he created.[22]

This is the passage that has led scholars to assert that Trotsky consciously lied about the existence of the Testament. But Trotsky's point is that it is inappropriate to call Lenin's letter a 'testament', in other words, a literal statement of last wishes that the party was beholden to carry out. Krupskaya's open letter makes the same point. After noting that Lenin's letters [sic] to the Congress referred to both virtues and defects of various top leaders, she continues:

> As Lenin wished, all members of the Congress familiarized themselves with the letters. It is incorrect to call them a 'testament', since Lenin's Testament in the real sense of the word is incomparably wider: it consists of V.I.'s last articles and discusses the basic questions of party and Soviet

---

22   For the text of Trotsky's letter, see *Bolshevik*, 1925, no. 16: 67–70. The full text of this letter appears in the appendix of *Stalin's Letters to Molotov* (Lih, Naumov, Khlevniuk 1995, pp. 244–8).

work ... Taken together with what Lenin said previously, these articles will illuminate the path we must take for a long time to come. They have all been published. But Mr. Eastman is not interested in them.[23]

If Stalin was engineering a cover-up, he would not have insisted on publishing his own memorandum, for he discusses the Testament (under that name) at length. If we may judge from his comments to Molotov, Stalin even felt that instead of discrediting himself, Trotsky would actually gain in prestige by denouncing Eastman. In order to prevent this outcome, Stalin argues that his own memorandum should be published to show that Trotsky acted under Politburo pressure (letter 6). Later, Stalin opines that Trotsky 'saved himself' by his compliance (letter 9).

On this revised understanding of the Eastman affair, the Politburo did not ask Trotsky to tell obvious untruths, nor did he do so. If Trotsky was discredited, it was because he or his friends allowed the publication of an inflammatory broadside.

Even though the Western scholars who have written on the Eastman affair did not have access to Stalin's memorandum and his correspondence with Molotov, it is still puzzling why they chose to endorse the accuracy of Eastman's rendition of the Testament. One reason is that they were misled by Trotsky's rhetorical flourishes into the erroneous assumption that the Politburo wanted him to deny the very existence of the Testament. I suspect that another reason was their exclusive focus on Lenin's suggestion that Stalin be removed from the post of general secretary. This focus led them to overlook the political aims of Eastman's book and the distortions Eastman unwittingly perpetrated in order to serve those aims. These scholars were also comfortable with the level of cynicism they assigned to the Bolshevik leaders: according to their account, *all* the Politburo members, Trotsky included, were conscious liars blandly betraying their dead leader and denying the obvious. Painful as it may be to our preconceptions, it seems that, in this instance at least, the Politburo did not 'laugh at all honesty as a limited prejudice' (as Boris Souvarine writes in his account of the affair).[24]

The new light thrown on the Eastman affair, when combined with evidence in other recently published documents, makes it difficult to put Politburo politics in the framework of a Trotsky-Stalin duel or even a duel between Trot-

---

23   For Krupskaya's text, see *Stalin's Letters to Molotov* (Lih, Naumov, Khlevniuk 1995, p. 249).
24   Souvarine 1939, p. 414.

sky and the triumvirate (Stalin, Zinoviev, Kamenev). Trotsky was not defeated because of Stalin's growing power. As the Russian historian Valerii Nadtocheev among others has argued, the reverse is true: Stalin gained power because he was able to provide leadership in the Politburo's effort to neutralize Trotsky.[25] The Eastman affair shows how this worked. Stalin took the initiative, but he was able to convince his colleagues primarily because he had a good case. The rest of the Politburo agreed that Trotsky should make a public statement denouncing Eastman and used Stalin's memorandum as a basis for drafting the statement. Beyond that point, the Politburo majority broke up amid disputes on appropriate further action (with Zinoviev taking a harder line against Trotsky than Stalin did). In spite of the success of his memorandum, Stalin does not yet seem a fully dominant figure. A different impression is given in the following year, after Zinoviev and Kamenev went into opposition.

3.2   The Campaign against Zinoviev

By all accounts, Zinoviev was not a particularly attractive human being. Neither in power nor in opposition was his conduct inspiring. Unlike Trotsky and Bukharin, Zinoviev has never been celebrated in a major biography as a symbol of resistance to Stalin, and Western political parties never transformed him into an icon. From the evidence of the letters, however, the leaders of the party majority treated his opposition with greater seriousness than they did the attacks by Trotsky, who was more renowned but also more marginalized.[26]

Zinoviev and Kamenev openly challenged Stalin at the XIV Party Congress a few months after the Eastman affair in 1925. Stalin's forces moved quickly to dismantle Zinoviev's political base in Leningrad. In spite of his former hostility to Trotsky, Zinoviev now found it expedient to join forces with him. Their alliance was formed soon after the defeat of the general strike in England, and since Zinoviev was still head of the Comintern (the international organization that united the Communist parties of the world), it was natural that the Politburo showdown took the form of a challenge to the previous policy of cooperating with the British unions. One of the first joint actions of the newly formed coalition was a stormy Politburo meeting in early June 1926. Because of the political tension that surrounded this meeting, there was a flurry of letters between the

---

25   Valerii Nadtocheev, '"Triumvirat" ili "semerka"?' in *Trudnye voprosy istorii* (Nadtocheev 1991).

26   For a more extensive discussion of Zinoviev, see 'Zinoviev: Populist Leninist', included in this volume.

absent Stalin and his political friends in Moscow, and we can follow the event in detail. In his biography of Trotsky, Isaac Deutscher pictures Trotsky forcing a hesitant and vacillating Zinoviev to reject the united front policies in England. With his usual flair for journalistic detail, Deutscher sets the scene: 'The battle was joined, partly on Stalin's initiative, in the first days of June. Immediately after Trotsky's return, Stalin met him at the Politburo' with a number of accusations.[27]

This picture is difficult to square with the train of events portrayed in the letters: Zinoviev prepares the theses condemning the united front and leads the fight at the Politburo session. If Trotsky was the leader of the coalition on this issue, the fact was kept carefully hidden from the rest of the Politburo. Stalin was vacationing at the time, so Bukharin and Molotov provided the leadership of the offensive against Zinoviev and Trotsky.

Thus the letters force us to make a considerable adjustment in our picture of the early days of the united opposition. The point is not Deutscher's pardonable error about Stalin's physical whereabouts, but rather the misleading image of the leadership dispute as essentially a duel between Trotsky and Stalin. As the letters show, the duel was in fact between Zinoviev and the Politburo majority. The next important clash between the newly united opposition and the Politburo majority occurred at a meeting of the full Central Committee in July. In preparation for this meeting, Stalin penned one of the more remarkable letters in the collection (letter 21). In it Stalin gives his reasons for considering the Zinoviev group as the leader of all schismatic tendencies in the party. He notes that previous opposition groups had stayed within definite bounds; furthermore, since Zinoviev occupied a much more central place in Bolshevik affairs than any previous opposition leader, he was better acquainted with the leadership's way of doing things. Another reason for worry was Zinoviev's potential power base as Comintern chief (Stalin does not mention Leningrad, which had been effectively taken away from Zinoviev earlier in the year).

Stalin recommends that Zinoviev and Trotsky be treated differently, with the brunt of the attack aimed at Zinoviev. This recommendation is partly justified by purely tactical considerations of divide and conquer, although it is possible that Stalin means what he says: Trotsky and his followers should be given a chance to return to the fold and work as team members. Stalin's recommendation was faithfully followed by his political friends, as shown by a statement Rykov made after the July Central Committee meeting, to

---

27   Deutscher 1959, p. 269.

the effect that Trotsky's actions do not require direct reprisal in the same way that Zinoviev's do, because 'Comrade Trotsky made no such attempt at a split'.[28]

Stalin's leadership amounted to more than the control over appointments that is usually considered the main basis for his power. In his memoirs, Molotov repeatedly stresses his admiration for Stalin's ability to size up a situation and extract directives for action.[29] The two episodes portrayed in the letters – the 1925 Eastman affair and the 1926 campaign against Zinoviev – show that the Politburo came increasingly to rely on these skills.

What we view as crafty manoeuvring may not have appeared that way to Stalin's Politburo colleagues. From their point of view, Stalin's proposal about Eastman's book was not an invitation to skulduggery but a legitimate demand that Trotsky disassociate himself from a scurrilous attack on the Russian Communist Party. Stalin's letter outlining the anti-Zinoviev strategy shows that he was no amateur at political infighting. But Stalin was not making any secret of his tactics: the letter is addressed to 'Molotov, Rykov, Bukharin, and other friends'. Stalin was eliminating a political rival, but he was also working toward a goal to which he and his fellow Bolsheviks accorded high legitimacy: preserving a united leadership team.

Stalin's catechistic style of exposition in his public speeches has struck many observers as the manifestation of a dogmatic mind. The letters show us that he employed the same dogged approach in his private correspondence. Yet his colleagues may have appreciated his conscious commitment to clarity in setting out his definition of the situation. In spite of (or perhaps because of) the numbered paragraphs and the litany-style repetitions, some of the letters are compelling expositions of complicated arguments. In the opening paragraph of his letter outlining the campaign against Zinoviev (letter 21), Stalin mentions that he reflected on the question a good deal but has now worked it all out – and thereupon follow the familiar numbered paragraphs. It would seem that the other Politburo members had come to rely on his ability to analyse a situation and devise a course of action.

According to Stalin's antibureaucrat scenario, the unity of the top leadership regarding the correct line was an essential precondition for the fight against the real enemies: the bureaucrats running the government. He therefore had no compunction about quashing Politburo colleagues who got out of line.

---

28   Robert V. Daniels, *The Conscience of the Revolution: Communist Opposition in Soviet Russia* (Daniels 1960, p. 279).

29   See, for example, Molotov's unfavourable comparison of Sergei Kirov to Stalin in Chuev 1991, pp. 307–13.

Yet despite the vigour of the political infighting in 1925 and 1926, and despite
Stalin's contempt for his rivals ('Really, Grisha's [Zinoviev's] brazenness knows
no bounds' [letter 20]), it is evident that he did not yet regard them as enemies
of the party and the revolution. It would take several years of conflict and frustration before Stalin arrived at the level of titanic anger and rejection we find
in the letters from 1929 and 1930.

4   The Outside World

Bukharin opened the XV Party Conference in 1926 with a speech that contained
these stirring words: 'The international revolution is now on the move in three
columns. It is moving in the East with the march of the Chinese people, with
its many hundreds of millions. It is moving in the far West with the measured
tread of the British coal miners; it is moving in the Soviet Union, with our growing offensive against the capitalist elements of our economy. These three forces
will become more and more decisive, and to them will be given the final victory.'[30]

What was Stalin's reaction to this enthusiastic picture of imminent world
revolution? Did he think it was mere verbiage, or was he genuinely caught up
in a moment of enthusiasm? Did Stalin dismiss world revolution in favour of
building up the Soviet state, or did he remain at heart a Bolshevik dedicated to
overthrowing capitalist society everywhere?

Observers have long puzzled over these questions. One point of view derives
from Trotsky's critique of 'socialism in one country' as a betrayal of the revolution. According to this view, Stalin decided early on that the chances of
revolution elsewhere were nil. By inclination as well as conviction, Stalin was
ready to turn his back on the rest of the world and devote his energies to building up a powerful Soviet state. Only when pressed by the critique made by the
united left opposition did he feel it necessary to make even verbal obeisance
to the icon of Bolshevik internationalism. He had only contempt for the Comintern, except perhaps as a minor tool of Soviet foreign policy. Some scholars
have even speculated that he did not want to see a successful revolution elsewhere: Who needs powerful socialist rivals?

Another view is that the question should not be put in either-or terms: either
the interests of world revolution or the interests of the Soviet state. We should
rather seek to understand how the two coalesced in Stalin's mind. Stalin was

---

30   *Piatnadtsataia Konferentsiia VKP(b)*, p. 45.

indeed deeply committed to the interests of the Soviet state, but we still need to examine how he understood those interests. Stalin was not hypocritical in his support for world revolution, since from his point of view no sacrifice of state interests was involved. His caution about revolutionary prospects in particular cases did not mean he dismissed all revolutionary prospects for the foreseeable future.[31]

The publication of Stalin's letters to Molotov gives us a chance to move toward resolving these issues, for several important episodes of both Comintern policy and Soviet diplomacy are treated in detail. In 1926 and 1927, Stalin is concerned with what appear to be revolutionary situations in England and China. After 1927, as the revolutionary tide ebbs, Stalin's attention in the letters turns toward problems arising from state-to-state relations. Since Stalin was talking in private with like-minded colleagues, there was little partisan pressure to sound more revolutionary than he felt. Let us review the clues provided by the letters before assessing the new evidence. We will first examine Stalin's feelings about the prospects for revolution in 1926 and 1927.

Policy toward the British trade unions was a priority issue in 1926. The Politburo majority's official line was that the situation in England was moving in the direction of revolution but that it would be unwise to break with the reformist trade unions in the ostentatious fashion demanded by Zinoviev and Trotsky. The united left opposition interpreted the policy of the united front as de facto collaboration with the reformist union leaders, and thus a betrayal of Leninist principles. Their particular target was the Anglo-Russian Committee that had been established as a link between the Soviet trade unions and the General Council of the British Trade Unions Congress. In response, the Politburo insisted that its only motive was to unmask the trade union leaders as the vacillating reformists that they were. Letters 13–19 contain Stalin's exposition of the majority point of view in preparation for the Politburo clash with Zinoviev in June. Stalin emphasizes his complete agreement with Bukharin and the others in Moscow. Given the highly partisan context, however, it is difficult to say whether Stalin's protestations are sincere.

Much more revealing are various remarks in letter 23, written in August 1926. Stalin first notes that a delegation from the British coal miners will soon arrive; they should be given an enthusiastic reception. More Soviet money needs to be collected for the striking miners. 'The situation in England is serious, and it obliges us to make serious "sacrifices".' The Americans had promised to give

---

31   For different points of view on Stalin's attitude toward revolution outside the USSR, see Isaac Deutscher, *Stalin: A Political Biography* (Deutscher 1949), chap. 10; Robert C. Tucker, *Stalin in Power: The Revolution from Above, 1928–1941* (Tucker 1990).

the miners a million dollars, and it would be shameful if the Soviet Union gave any less. (Stalin need not have worried, since in the end the Americans gave very little.)[32] Even sending money was an insufficient gesture: Stalin suggests following the wishes of the British Communists by imposing an embargo on coal imports.

Stalin then latches on to what he considers a missed opportunity for unmasking the British labour leaders as cowards: Didn't they go on vacation rather than account for their actions? He mentions that he is keeping up with the British Communist newspapers, so he knows they have not 'trumpeted' these facts as they should. Stalin's suggestion got a restrained response from Mikhail Tomsky, the leader of the Soviet trade unions. Tomsky had visited England and had acquired a greater sense of political reality; he doubted whether unmasking the reformist leaders' vacation trips would produce a serious political effect.[33]

Stalin goes on to ask how the Comintern Executive Committee is reacting to new, more radical slogans advocating new elections in England. The mention of the Comintern reminds him of a project to publish the Comintern's journal more frequently: Why isn't Bukharin pushing this matter more energetically? A weekly journal would greatly improve the work of the Comintern and its member parties. (On Stalin's attitude toward the Comintern, see also letter 82, from 1935.)

Let us consider a few other comments from 1926 before assessing the evidence. In letter 12, written before the outbreak of controversy within the Politburo, Stalin insists that a pamphlet documenting Soviet support for the striking coal miners be translated into all the major Western languages. In letter 26, we learn that Stalin preferred to loan rather than give the General Council the money they requested. His motivation: to show Europe that the Soviets were sober people who knew how to count kopecks. Finally, in letter 28 Stalin argues against unduly irritating the British reformists over their failure to protest their government's intervention in China.

Taken together, Stalin's remarks indicate that he was very involved in the British situation and genuinely hoped for a more radical outcome. The letters also seem to acquit him of any real interest in collaborating with reformists: unmasking always gets top priority. One would not deduce from these letters

---

32   Charles Loch Mowat, *Britain between the Wars, 1918–1940* (Mowat 1955), chapter 6.
33   For an account of this whole episode and Tomsky's role in particular, see Charters Wynn, 'Getting Together then Falling Apart: Tomsky and British Trade Unionists during NEP' (Wynn 2014); see also Wynn 2021 (*The Moderate Bolshevik: Mikhail Tomsky from the Factory to the Kremlin, 1880–1936*).

that he was contemptuous of the Comintern. On the other hand, he is certainly not above using a gesture of revolutionary solidarity as a way of burnishing the Soviet government's financial reputation. Stalin saw no anomaly in advancing both sets of interests simultaneously.

The other burning issue of the mid-1920s was the Soviet and Comintern role in the Chinese revolution. The course of events in China is inconceivable without the crucial influence of Russian political and military advisors like Mikhail Borodin and Vasilii Bliucher. Many books have been devoted to the rights and wrongs, the insights and mistakes, of Comintern policy and its disastrous outcome for the Chinese Communist Party, yet the letters shed new light on the attitudes of both Stalin and his Politburo colleagues. Let us restrict ourselves here to passages that help us understand Stalin's general attitude toward revolution outside the Soviet Union.

At the beginning of 1926, Stalin thought the Kuomintang government in Canton would be best advised not to attempt to unify the country with a risky enterprise like the Northern Expedition. In spite of his caution on the military front, he felt the Kuomintang would strengthen its political base and achieve a stronger anti-imperialist thrust if it carried out a thorough agrarian reform.[34] When Chiang Kai-shek went ahead and launched the highly successful Northern Expedition, Stalin was elated and assumed that a new stage of the revolution had commenced. He explains his feelings to Molotov when criticizing Lev Karakhan, the top Soviet diplomat in China at the time: 'He has outlived his usefulness: he was and *has remained* the ambassador of the *first* stage of the Chinese revolution and is entirely useless as a leader in the *current* new situation, both the Chinese and the international situation ... Karakhan will never understand that Hankow will soon become the Chinese Moscow' (letter 28). (Hankow was one of the cities in the Wuhan complex where the Kuomintang set up its capital during the Northern Expedition. His remark about a 'Chinese Moscow' reflects his view that the whole country would be united under one anti-imperialist government, not that there would be a socialist revolution in China.)

The crux of what Stalin called the new stage of the revolution was the opportunity for widespread agrarian reform. Stalin seems to have believed that giving the peasants land would strengthen the Kuomintang and that an implicit deal could therefore be struck on the following basis: the Kuomintang armies would provide military cover, and the Chinese Communist Party would stir up the

---

34   Stalin's views can be found in his addition to a memorandum written by Trotsky; the text can be found in Iurii Felshtinsky (ed.), *Kommunisticheskaia oppozitsiia v SSSR, 1923–27*, 4 vols (Felshtinsky 1988, 1:179).

peasant masses. A letter written in June 1927 shows that Stalin was willing to make considerable sacrifices to obtain political space for the Chinese Communists. By this time, the Moscow leaders had begun to realize that the 'left Kuomintang' government in Wuhan was on the verge of turning against the Communists. Stalin here gives his reasons for staving off the evil day by means of direct subsidies (letter 33):

> Losing Wuhan as a separate centre means losing at least some centre for the revolutionary movement, losing the possibility of free assembly and rallies for the workers, losing the possibility of the open existence of the Communist Party, losing the possibility of an open revolutionary press – in a word, losing the possibility of openly organizing the proletariat and the revolution. In order to obtain all this, I assure you, it is worth giving Wuhan an extra 3–5 million – only with some assurance that Wuhan will not surrender to the tender mercies of Nanking [headquarters of the right Kuomintang] with our money wasted for nothing.

The feared break between Kuomintang and Communists came only two weeks later, and Stalin had to face the ruin of all his hopes for revolutionary collaboration with the Kuomintang. After taking a day to read through all the documents sent down from Moscow, Stalin penned letter 36, a long series of glum reflections on the future of the Chinese Communists.

The letter contains political advice for the immediate future: the Chinese Communists should leave the government but not the Kuomintang itself. The Politburo quickly adopted this advice, and instructions to that effect were sent off to China even before Stalin returned from vacation.[35] Stalin insisted that the blame for the failure of Comintern strategy lay with the leaders of the Chinese Communist Party; this too became official policy. Stalin's charge against the Chinese leaders was that they failed to take advantage of the political space Stalin thought they had: they did not mobilize the peasants or infiltrate the army. He dismissed them in the same way he dismissed Karakhan: they had been recruited in the first phase of the revolution and were unsuitable for its second, more radical phase.

Stalin's letter is considerably more pessimistic than are his later public statements. He describes in vivid terms what the Chinese Communist Party will have to undergo as the tide of revolution ebbs away: '[going] underground,

---

35   Helmut Gruber, *Soviet Russia Masters the Comintern: International Communism in the Era of Stalin's Ascendancy* (Gruber 1974, pp. 494–500); C. Martin Wilbur, *The Nationalist Revolution in China, 1923–1928* (Wilbur 1983, p. 144).

arrests, beatings, executions, betrayals and provocations among their own ranks, etc.' Stalin's scenario for the Chinese Communists is derived from Bolshevik experience between the revolution of 1905 and the outbreak of revolution in 1917; Stalin thinks it likely that the Chinese Communists will have to wait a similar length of time before a new revolutionary outburst occurs in China.

In an article published only a fortnight later, Stalin mentions the pessimistic 1905–1917 scenario as *less* likely than the possibility of a swift return to the storms of revolution. From letter 38 it appears that Stalin's change of heart was the result of objections by Molotov and perhaps Bukharin. The more optimistic reading of the Chinese situation led to a number of abortive revolts by Chinese Communists that compounded the damage done during the Kuomintang alliance. Stalin no doubt reflected that his first instincts had been correct.

Another aspect of Stalin's letter not reflected in later public statements is his conception of future Soviet aid to the Chinese Communists. The proposed aid seems to consist of better Marxist literature and better advisors. 'We should regularly send to China, not people we don't need, but competent people instead.' These political advisors will play the role of 'nannies' for the present amorphous and weak Central Committee. 'As the revolution and the party grow, the need for these "nannies" will disappear.'

In the following letter, Stalin notes some misgivings on the part of some of his political friends about past policy but defiantly affirms: 'Never have I been so deeply and firmly convinced of the correctness of our policy, both in China and regarding the Anglo-Russian Committee, as I am now' (letter 37). As he did throughout his political career, Stalin blamed any unfortunate results on the failure of local leaders to understand the Politburo's correct policy.

To sum up: Stalin sees the success of the Chinese Communist Party as a matter of both state and revolutionary interest. Although by instinct he is cautious about revolutionary prospects, he can also be carried away by apparent success. He assumes that the Soviet model should guide the Chinese Communists, but he also assumes that Soviet 'nannies' are only a temporary necessity.

After 1927, the letters touch more on state diplomacy than on revolutionary strategy. This gives us the opportunity to observe Stalin's amalgamation of state and revolutionary interests from another angle: his insistence on imposing revolutionary considerations on normal diplomacy. Letter 44 (August 1929) provides several examples. By acting tough in state negotiations with England and China, the Soviet Union is also striking a blow for revolution:

> The point is not only or not even mainly how to resolve this or that 'conflict'. The point is really to use our tough position to *unmask* completely and to undermine the authority of Chiang Kai-shek's government, a gov-

ernment of lackeys of imperialism, for attempting to become the model of 'national governments' for the colonial and dependent countries ... [thus] making it easier to carry out the revolutionary education of the workers in colonial countries (and the Chinese workers above all).

Conversely, revolutionary success redounds to the Soviet state: 'This [unmasking] is a very important and necessary revolutionary task, which will, at the same time, raise the prestige of the Soviet government in the eyes of the workers of all countries (and above all in the eyes of the working class of the USSR).'

A version of the antibureaucrat scenario is at play here. Back in 1925, Stalin had warned that capitalist encirclement might corrupt the Soviet foreign service, leading the policy specialists to forget the cause of world revolution.[36] This seems to be the thought behind the repeated sneers directed at Maksim Litvinov, acting head of the foreign service. 'Litvinov does not see and is not interested in [the revolutionary aspect of policy]. But the Politburo [a party institution] should take all this into account' (letter 44). Litvinov is therefore associated with Bukharin and Rykov: 'These people don't see the growth of the power and might of the USSR, nor those changes in international relations that have occurred recently (and will go on taking place)' (letter 51; see also letter 45). This corruption by the outside environment is a typical symptom of the right deviation (discussed below in the section 'Right Deviation').

The most dramatic diplomatic event of 1929 was the armed intervention arising out of the clash over the Chinese Eastern Railway. This was a surgical military operation against weak resistance with little fear of intervention by other powers – in other words, something on the order of US interventions in Panama or Grenada. The war was not given wide publicity at home; one American journalist called it 'the war nobody knew'.[37] Still, Stalin was elated by its success: 'Let them know what the Bolsheviks are like! I think the Chinese landowners won't forget the object lesson taught them by the Far East Army' (letter 53). He also allowed that Litvinov's speech on the subject wasn't so bad; in this speech Litvinov mocked the Americans for their attempt at diplomatic intervention.

The strangest amalgamation of state and revolutionary interests occurs during the preparation for this intervention (letter 51). At one point, Stalin wanted to expand the operation from a limited incursion to a more grandiose revolutionary uprising. His projected scenario makes it seem so simple: Organize and

---

36   Stalin 1947–1952, 7:167–90.
37   Eugene Lyons, *Assignment in Utopia* (Lyons 1937).

equip two Chinese brigades and give them the task of fomenting a rebellion among the Manchurian troops; then have them occupy Harbin and declare a revolutionary state authority. After that, attract the peasants by smashing the landowners, organize soviets in town and country, and go on from there. This revolutionary daydream seems atypical of the cautious Stalin, and there is no indication anything was done with it. But perhaps we can see it as a first sketch of what has been called 'revolution from abroad', a term later applied to the countries on the USSR's western border.[38]

As the general offensive of the five-year plan came into full swing, the imperatives of Stalin's domestic revolution sometimes interfered with normal diplomatic relations. Several of the letters written after 1929 touch on this problem. In letter 72, for example, Stalin comments on a 1931 speech by Molotov defending the Soviet Union against charges of using forced labour. Stalin wants Molotov to argue that dekulakized peasants work only on a voluntary basis with the same rights as free labour. In letter 65, on the other hand, Stalin hoped to use the domestic campaign against 'wreckers' for diplomatic purposes: Since the government had confessions of sabotage by British nationals, why not publish them prior to upcoming talks with the British government about debts and concessions? It is not clear exactly what Stalin hoped to gain from this manoeuvre; it is probably just as well that someone appears to have talked him out of it.

Other scattered comments suggest Stalin's attitude toward relations with the capitalist world: he thought they were dangerous (because the capitalists are enemies who are ill-disposed toward the Soviet Union), unpleasant (because so many bourgeois politicians are just petty crooks), but necessary. American readers will be interested in his comments in 1932 on possible diplomatic recognition by the United States: 'United States – this is a complicated matter. Insofar as they want to use flattery to drag us into a war with Japan, we can tell them to go to hell. Insofar as the oil industrialists of the United States have agreed to give us a loan of 100 million roubles without requiring from us any political compensation, we would be foolish not to take their money' (letter 74).

Stalin's chip-on-the-shoulder defensiveness is readily apparent in a comment on yet another Molotov speech: 'Viacheslav! Today I read the section on international affairs. It came out well. The confident, contemptuous tone with respect to the "great" powers, the belief in our own strength, the delicate but plain spitting in the pot of the swaggering "great powers" – very good. Let them eat it' (letter 76).

---

38   Jan T. Gross, *Revolution from Abroad: The Soviet Conquest of Poland's Western Ukraine and Western Belorussia* (Gross 1988).

Having reviewed the evidence supplied by the letters, we can return to the dispute over Stalin's attitude toward the outside world. The letters refute the Trotsky-derived interpretation of 'socialism in one country' as an isolationist rejection of revolution elsewhere. To be sure, Stalin never ignored the interests of the Soviet state and he was often cautious to the point of pessimism about the prospects for immediate revolution. But the letters show that he was also capable of hope and enthusiasm when revolution seemed to be on the move and ready to put his money where his mouth was. The letters also document his unremitting hostility toward and suspicion of the capitalist world even when he was forced to deal with it. He was vigilant lest the foreign policy profession-als succumb to the disease of rightist degeneration and lose the ability to see the revolutionary aspect of diplomacy. All in all, Stalin comes out of the letters with his revolutionary credentials in good order.

Thus Stalin did not see state interests and revolutionary interests in 'either-or' terms. But this leaves open the question of exactly how he amalgamated the two in his mind. One key factor was the prestige of the Soviet state at home and abroad. The capitalist world would never accord even basic legitimacy to the Soviet Union, much less accept it as an equal or admire it. The Soviet Union could appeal only to the disinherited; only as an embodiment of the revolu-tionary idea could the Soviet Union acquire a leadership role worthy of a great power. Yet I do not mean to suggest that Stalin was interested in world revolu-tion only as a propaganda tool for the Russian empire. Because he identified himself with the prestige of the Soviet state, he also identified himself with its leading idea. As first servant of the state, he was also first servant of world rev-olution.

5   Grain Tribute and Collectivization

Starting in 1929, Stalin led the Bolshevik party and the Soviet state in a war against the peasantry – or, as Stalin's loyalists would say, against the better-off peasants (kulaks) who sabotaged necessary policies. The campaign had two theatres of conflict. One was a struggle over grain: Stalin insisted that the peas-ants had to pay what he openly called a tribute in order to help finance indus-trialization. The other area of conflict was a struggle over how the peasants ran their farms: Stalin wanted to transform the basic production units of the coun-tryside from small individual farms to large-scale collective ones (*kolkhozy*).

The amount of material in the letters that bears on these events is not large, but what exists is highly suggestive and illuminates key aspects of the thought processes that gave rise to some of the most important decisions in Soviet history. What connection did Stalin see between collecting the tribute and trans-forming peasant production relations? What lay behind the fateful decision in late 1929 to unleash all-out collectivization coupled with dekulakization? In what ways did Stalin prod state and party to embark on this campaign?

Obtaining the grain tribute and imposing collectivized production are sep-arate goals. It is quite possible to pursue each of them independently; in fact, they might even be seen as contradictory. During the civil war, the Bolsheviks felt compelled to exact a heavy tax from the peasantry, and for just this reason they found it expedient to move slowly in attempting to transform production relations.[39]

In the late 1920s and early 1930s, in contrast, the two goals were pursued in tandem. The usual interpretation is that mass collectivization was adopted in order to obtain the tribute, on the assumption that it is easier to apply state coercion to large-scale collective farms than to scattered individual farms. Yet, as Stephan Merl has cogently argued, this assumption is by no means self-evident.[40] The collectivization drive greatly disrupted production and alien-ated the peasantry, thus making it more difficult, not easier, to collect the trib-ute. By 1934 Stalin had taken so much grain from the peasants that he inflicted mass starvation (letters 74 and 77 give some indication of the pressure the Polit-buro was putting on the country in order to extract grain). Yet what was decisive in collecting the tribute was not the existence of collective farms but the mas-sive investment in repressive resources Stalin made in the early 1930s in order to make the system work at all. Given that the state prepared to stop at noth-ing, the same amount of grain could have been extracted from individual farms, perhaps even with considerably less coercion.

It thus remains an open question exactly why Stalin linked the two goals. If we turn to his speeches of 1928, when he was seeking to rally the party leader-ship behind his strategy, we find the following argument: This year we have had to apply coercive 'emergency measures' to get the grain we need to keep indus-trialization on track. We are all agreed that using such methods is costly and unsatisfactory in the long run. We cannot live forever with this continual war with the peasants, with no reserves, and with hunger threatening the city and the towns. (Stalin's obsession with a reserve fund can be observed in many of his 1929 letters, particularly letters 44 and 53.) Collective farms are the only route of escape from this chronic crisis. Since the collective farms will be supported by state economic assistance, the state will have a greater opportunity to ensure

---

39   For more discussion of this distinction, see 'Grain Monopoly and Agricultural Transfor-mation: Ideals and Necessities', included in this volume.

40   Stephan Merl, *Die Anfänge der Kollektivierung in der Sowjetunion* (Merl 1985).

deliveries by economic means. An expanding collective farm movement will also undercut the authority of the kulaks, whose sabotage is a principal reason for the difficulties we have encountered in grain collection.[41]

Thus Stalin did not publicly advocate collectivization as a necessary tool for coercing the peasants. Ironically, given the way things turned out, Stalin originally defended collectivization as a way of making up for the political and economic damage caused by collection of the tribute and of avoiding the permanent confrontation with the peasants implied by repeated use of emergency measures. The question is whether this public advocacy accurately reflects Stalin's private thinking. The clues provided by the letters are at least consistent with the thesis that Stalin did *not* see collectivization as a method for collecting the tribute. In his mind, these were two separate issues. Stalin's single-minded insistence on getting grain to export does come through loud and clear. Grain procurements are the key to everything; without exports there will be no new factories. The need is so urgent that it is impossible even to wait for better grain prices (letter 60). Yet, in letter 41 from August 1929, collective farms themselves show up as one of the main barriers to successful procurement. Later in the year he pronounces himself reasonably satisfied with the procurement campaign (letters 51 and 53), but his satisfaction did not stop him from giving the green light to the all-out collectivization campaign. His attitude in 1930 is similar: his anger at impediments to the collectivization drive in letters 61 and 63 is separate from his exhortations for better procurement in letters 57, 59, 60 (see also 67).

Turning now to the collectivization drive itself, we can ask whether the letters provide any clue to the decision in late 1929 to proceed with all-out collectivization, coupled with 'liquidation of the kulaks as a class'. The basic argument in favour of collective farms had always been their ability to make efficient use of up-to-date equipment. It was clear that Soviet industry was still in no position to provide this equipment (prior to December 1929 Stalin had never argued that collective farms would be able to increase production without new equipment).

All during 1929, regional officials tried to attract central attention and resources by accelerating the rate of collectivization in their areas. The most extreme case was Khoper county in the lower Volga region: local party officials announced in late August that they would complete all-out collectivization by the end of the five-year plan. A phenomenal rate of collectivization then fol-

---

41   For Bukharin's ultimate response to this reasoning, see 'Bukharin's Bolshevik Epic', included in this volume.

lowed. In June, only 2.2 percent of Khoper farms had been collectivized; by October, the total had reached at least 30 percent for the county as a whole, with much higher percentages reached in some areas.[42]

It is unclear to what extent local officials acted on their own initiative, but there is no doubt that central party officials gave much attention and encouragement to the frantic pace of collectivization in Khoper. Less sanguine were state officials responsible for administering the collective farm movement; they looked into the situation and sent back critical reports to Moscow. As a result, a commission under T.R. Ryskulov was sent out to Khoper in late October. By the end of November, this commission reported back to Moscow and dismissed the sceptics who argued that administrative pressure was behind the rush to form collective farms in Khoper. Ryskulov retorted that these sceptics were completely confused: the rate of collectivization should be accelerated, not reduced.

The goings-on in Khoper form the background for an excited passage from Stalin's letter dated 5 December 1929 (letter 53):

> The collective farm movement is growing by leaps and bounds. Of course there are not enough machines and tractors – how could it be otherwise? – but simply pooling the peasant tools results in a colossal increase in sown acreage (in some regions by as much as 50 percent!). In the lower Volga [where Khoper was located], 60 percent of peasant farms have been transferred (already transferred!) to collective farms. The eyes of our rightists are popping out of their heads in amazement ... [ellipsis in original]

In an important speech at the end of December, Stalin again used Khoper to show why collective farms brought tremendous advantages even without expensive new equipment. By simply banding together, the peasants were in a position to plough under virgin and abandoned land on a scale that lay beyond the powers of individual peasant farmers. In this same speech, Stalin announced the new slogan 'liquidation of the kulaks as a class'. He argued that it would have been irresponsible to liquidate the kulaks any sooner because they could not have been replaced.

With the clue provided by the letter of 5 December, we can surmise the following: Stalin regarded Khoper as a testing ground for all-out collectiviza-

---

42   For background on Khoper, see R.W. Davies, *The Socialist Offensive: The Collectivization of Soviet Agriculture, 1929–1930* (Davies 1980).

tion. In November 1929, high officials were still arguing about the results of this experiment, so Stalin waited for the report of the Ryskulov commission. The news he received excited him because it gave him the green light, not only for all-out collectivization, but also for dekulakization. Even without tractors, it was possible for collective farms to replace the kulak farms without damaging agricultural output.

The decision made in late December and in early January 1930 led to a wave of forced collectivization and other excesses that threatened to destroy the economy, so the leadership was forced to call a temporary halt in March 1930, when Stalin published his article 'Dizziness from Success'. A mass exodus of peasants from existing collective farms followed immediately. Stalin's determination to press on with collectivization is revealed in a 1930 letter written at the end of the summer (letter 61). The immediate occasion for his outburst was a campaign in favour of settlement associations, a new form of rural organization:

> You seem very unconcerned about the statute for settlement associations and the accompanying agitation in the press. Keep in mind that this ill-omened statute was offered to us as the *new* word, which claims to be *setting itself up against* the 'old' word, i.e., the statute for the agricultural *artel* [basic form of a collective farm]. And the whole point of the settlement (*new*) statute is the desire to give the individual the possibility of '*improving his* (*individual*) *farm*'. What kind of nonsense is this? Here we have the *collective farm* movement advancing in a growing wave, and then the clever ones from the Commissariat of Agriculture and from the agricultural cooperative societies want to *evade* the question of collective farms and busy themselves with '*improving*' the individual peasant farm! It seems to me that the rightists have achieved some sort of revenge here, sneaking in this statute on settlement associations, because people in the Central Committee, since they're overburdened with work, haven't noticed the little trick.

Stalin's practical conclusions show the emphasis he put on devising correct slogans and conducting educational propaganda in the press (letter 63):

> An illusion has arisen of a *retreat* from the slogan 'For the collective farms!' to the slogan 'For the settlement associations!' It doesn't matter what they want in Moscow – in practice there's been a *switch* from the vital and triumphant slogan 'For or against the collective farms' to the mongrel, artificial slogan 'For or against the settlement associations'. And all of this

at a time when we have a growing surge of peasants into the collective farms! ...

In my opinion, we should, *first*, give an *internal* directive to local party committees not to get carried away with settlement associations ... *In the second place*, it would be well to overhaul *Pravda* and all of our press in the spirit of the slogan, 'Into the collective farms' ... In a word, [we should] launch a systematic and persistent campaign in the press for the collective farm movement as the major and decisive factor in our current agricultural policy.

These remarks suggest that collectivization would never have been completed without unremitting pressure from the very top. The state bureaucracy was not a machine bent on achieving a single aim but a complex organism reflecting various currents and pressures. In this case, specialists in the Commissariat of Agriculture were trying to do their job – improve agricultural productivity – by giving support to individual farmers. Stalin realized that this policy opened up an alternative to the collective farms, and he moved to cut off the route of escape.

By 1929–1930, Stalin had immense power. It is striking, for example, how quickly press campaigns followed upon pronouncements in these letters. In August 1929 he complains about the lack of cooperation in grain procurement shown by collective farms; a press campaign follows in September. Immediately after his letter of 5 December on the breakthrough in Khoper, the press announces that tractors are not an inevitable prerequisite of collectivization. Finally, historians have observed a shift toward a harder line on collectivization in September 1930 – that is, immediately after the letter just cited on the danger of a slowdown.[43]

Yet Stalin's power to get his way on specific issues did not guarantee the success of his leadership in carrying out a revolutionary policy like collectivization. Guided by his antibureaucrat scenario, Stalin realized that he had to struggle continually against the bureaucracy and its tendency to follow the path of least resistance. This required energetic checking up on fulfilment: top party leaders should not allow incorrect policies to slip past them because of inattention. The antibureaucrat scenario also helped Stalin interpret the source of this bureaucratic resistance. In the case of the statute on settlement, it was a de facto alliance between the specialists working in the Commissariat of Agricul-

---

43   For background, see Davies 1980, pp. 372–81.

ture and the rightists within the party. In the next two sections, we shall look more closely at Stalin's dealings with these two sets of enemies within the state apparat and the party.

6   Wreckerism Rampant

The general offensive of 1929–1930 was accompanied by steadily mounting repression against any expert or bureaucrat who seemed to question the practicality of the industrialization and collectivization campaigns. Starting in late 1929, the Worker-Peasant Inspection, the agency that both Lenin and Stalin had seen as a weapon against bureaucratism, conducted a wide-ranging purge of economic bureaucracies. In this period, its task was to find any unused production reserves and to remove the bureaucrats who allegedly hid them. More and more engineers and other specialists were arrested for counterrevolutionary activity. As the superhuman pressure on the country created more frequent foul-ups and breakdowns, more scapegoats were accused of wreckerism. A particularly grisly execution came in September 1930: forty-eight specialists in the meat industry were executed after a secret trial in which they were found guilty of 'sabotaging the meat supply'. A public trial of engineers accused of forming an 'industrial party' devoted to wreckerism began in November; this was followed in the spring of 1931 by another trial devoted to a mythical 'Union Bureau' of Mensheviks.

These hysterical but deadly accusations of improbable conspiracies have often been called a witch-hunt. One challenge for observers in such cases is to probe the mixture of belief and cynicism that motivated the witch-hunters. Stalin's letters from 1930 provide rich material on this score. His cynicism is prominently on display. A striking instance is the execution of the forty-eight 'saboteurs' in the meat industry. Accounts by Western journalists from the period all stress how much this particular act of barbarity shocked Soviet society even amid the growing repression.[44] It appears from letter 65 that the decision to murder these unfortunate specialists resulted from a burst of vindictive anger by Stalin, impatient with Politburo foot-dragging: 'We must immediately *publish all* the testimonies of all the wreckers of the supplies of *meat, fish, tinned goods*, and *vegetables*. For what purpose are we preserving them, why

---

44   William Henry Chamberlin, *Russia's Iron Age* (Chamberlin 1935, p. 154); Lyons 1937, pp. 349–61; H.R. Knickerbocker, *The Red Trade Menace: Progress of the Soviet Five-Year Plan* (Knickerbocker 1931, p. 268); William Reswick, *I Dreamt Revolution* (Reswick 1952, pp. 294–8).

the "secrets"? We should publish them along with an announcement that the Central Executive Committee or the Council of Commissars has turned over the matter to the OGPU ... and after a week have the OGPU announce that *all* these scoundrels will be executed by firing squad. They should all be shot' (letter 65; see also letter 57). Less than two weeks later the executions were carried out.

For Stalin, judicial forms had meaning only as agitational theatre.[45] In letter 63, he muses whether or not it would be expedient to bring Kondratiev and his 'co-conspirators' to trial: 'By the way, how about Messrs. Defendants admitting their mistakes and disgracing themselves politically, while simultaneously acknowledging the strength of the Soviet government and the correctness of the method of collectivization? It wouldn't be a bad thing if they did'. In letter 65, he insists that accusatory documents be published with an appropriate 'interpretation' from the press underscoring the political moral to be drawn.

Stalin was thus cold-bloodedly set on maximizing the political exploitation of his victims. But another question is still unanswered: Was Stalin consciously framing innocent victims, or did he really believe in the guilt of the accused? Judging from the evidence of the letters, it would appear that he was a believer. Given the farfetched nature of the alleged crimes, this conclusion is very hard to credit – yet just for that reason, we should make the strongest possible hypothetical case in its favour before dismissing it. Even if we decide that Stalin must have been aware of what he was doing, it is still striking that he felt compelled to play the role of a believer in confidential correspondence with his closest political friends.

The basic mode of proof used by the secret police was the forced confession. Stalin expressed no doubts about the reliability of this method; on the contrary, he seems to have thought that prisoner testimonies were 'indisputable documents' (letter 65) that would convince anyone who read them. He continually urges that relevant testimonies be presented to elite and mass audiences (see letters 56, 57, 59, and 65). The introductory section for the year 1930 contains Stalin's remarkable letter to the head of the secret police, V.R. Menzhinskii, in which Stalin hopes that even Western workers will be impressed by the confessions.

There are other indications that Stalin took these testimonies quite seriously. If we compare letter 62 with the letter to Menzhinskii just mentioned, it appears that Stalin was genuinely concerned about the threat of intervention allegedly discovered by the secret police. Although Stalin gave strong hints to

---

45   See 'Show Trials in the Stalin Era: On Stage and In Court', included in this volume.

the police, he evidently did not simply dictate a desired scenario, and the testimonies did not show everything he wanted them to show. Even though he
is convinced that there is a 'direct line' between the arrested 'saboteurs' and
Bukharin, he is forced to admit that the police have not yet found any indication of it (letters 57, 67).

What the letters tell us about the so-called Syrtsov-Lominadze affair is also
revealing. S.I. Syrtsov was a fast-rising party official who had strongly supported
Stalin's line ever since the extraordinary measures were introduced in 1928. In
1930 he was head of government for the Russian republic, and many observers
felt he was being groomed to replace Rykov as head of government for the
Soviet Union as a whole. Yet in the fall of 1930, Syrtsov (along with V.V. Lomi-
nadze, a party official from the North Caucasus) was expelled from the Central
Committee and accused of forming an 'underground factional centre'. Most
analysts assume that the trouble stemmed from Syrtsov's publicly stated views,
particularly a speech he gave in August in which he obliquely criticized the
ferocious pace of the general offensive. The Syrtsov-Lominadze affair rounded
off the repressions of 1930 with evidence of a split within the Stalinist leadership group itself.

The letters raise the possibility that the affair was triggered by an informer's
report that Stalin received in late October. In the weeks prior to this report,
Syrtsov is mentioned a couple of times, not with great approval but not as
someone who was about to be removed (letters 64, 69). In letter 64, Syrtsov
is associated with the right deviationist Rykov, but only in the context of a
bureaucratic dispute over the use of forced labour. Stalin explodes in anger
only in letter 71, which was written after he received the informer's denunciation. Thus it seems that Stalin did not first choose Syrtsov as a victim and
trump up a case against him, but rather that Syrtsov's views were declared
beyond the pale after Stalin became convinced of his guilt. Many observers,
both at the time and later, have pointed out the numerous absurdities and
self-contradictions in the charges made in the newspapers and at the circus-
like show trials. Is it possible that anyone with minimum intelligence could
have been taken in by this nonsense for half a minute? But perhaps this is
not the right question to ask. Given a secure cognitive framework, all sorts of
anomalies can be ignored or explained away. In our society, we are aware that
our court system produces many absurdities and miscarriages of justice, yet
because we believe in its basic principles, we do not lose faith in the system as
a whole.

So it was with Stalin and his friends. They could explain away any anomalies in their system as a product of the same bureaucratism and wreckerism
in the secret police that existed in all other state agencies. They also consid-

ered it prudent to institute procedural safeguards in the more important cases. Prominent among these is the confrontation (*ochnaia stavka*), in which the accused met his accuser face-to-face in front of interested officials. The complete inadequacy of this safeguard may be apparent to us, but that does not mean it was apparent to the leaders of the Bolshevik party. (This hypothetical description of the Stalinist mentality is vividly illustrated by Molotov's memoirs.)

We should not be too hasty in dismissing the system of forced confessions as obviously unacceptable to any intelligent person. The use of torture has a long and distinguished history in Western jurisprudence. Historians have shown that torture was instituted for cases in which evidence was inherently hard to come by: witchcraft, for example, or adultery. It replaced trial by ordeal when rationalist criticism undermined the legitimacy of this method of pronouncing judgement in otherwise undecidable cases.[46] This history gives us a clue about the compelling power that the method of forced confessions had over the Stalinist leadership. The alternative to believing in forced confessions was simply *not knowing* – and this was intolerable in an atmosphere permeated by insecurity and struggle.

A dispute over foreign policy in 1929 illustrates Stalin's reaction to cognitive insecurity. When the Labour Party took over the British government after an election in spring 1929, the Soviet government expected a quick resumption of the diplomatic relations broken off by the Conservatives in 1927. The Bolsheviks were determined not to make recognition conditional on the resolution of such highly contentious issues as accepting tsarist debts or Comintern propaganda. Prior to recognition, therefore, they would discuss only the *procedure* for resolving the controversial issues, not their *substance*. This rather subtle distinction led to misunderstandings at a meeting in July between British Foreign Secretary Arthur Henderson and the Soviet ambassador to France, V.S. Dovgalevskii; according to a source close to Litvinov, the problem was also attributable to 'lack of a common language well-understood by both'.[47] The Russians received the impression that Henderson had insisted on substantive talks; Henderson later denied that he had done so.

The dispute within the Soviet government involved the best way to deal with the uncertainty surrounding Henderson's real intentions. Litvinov seems to have argued that it was a misunderstanding and that any move on the British side to clear it up should be met by a forthright Soviet response. Stalin was

46   Robert Bartlett, *Trial by Fire and Water: The Medieval Judicial Ordeal* (Bartlett 1988).
47   Louis Fischer, *The Soviets in World Affairs* (Fischer 1960 [1930], p. 604).

convinced it was a trap; even after Henderson made conciliatory statements in September, Stalin argued for a suspicious, go-slow attitude (letters 40, 42, 44, 47, 51).

This background makes letter 47 a revealing instance of how Stalin dealt with inherent uncertainty. Stalin was convinced that Litvinov's informants were unreliable; nevertheless, the only way to arrive at a correct interpretation was through the 'logic of things'. Stalin arrived at his own insight into Henderson's intentions by viewing the situation in the light of general considerations: the Bolsheviks were dealing with enemies, diplomatic politeness was only a 'masked' attempt to take advantage of the Soviets, left-wing bourgeois governments often tried to gain legitimacy by acting tough with the Soviets. In the welter of ambiguous signals, Stalin used maxims like these to give him the confidence to dismiss Litvinov's views in an aggressive fashion. Yet it seems clear that this aggressiveness arose from an underlying cognitive insecurity. As the top leader in revolutionary times, Stalin had no access to unbiased information and was condemned to permanent radical uncertainty. He had to fall back on his own sense of the 'logic of things'. If forced confessions seemed to confirm his logic, they undoubtedly acquired a compelling power in his mind.

Another circumstance that protected Stalin's belief in the guilt of his victims was the vagueness of the categories used to define it: 'sabotage', 'wrecking', 'faction', 'centre', and a host of others. 'Centre', for example, could refer to anything from a shadow government to a casual get-together of malcontents. Stalin's habit of running together names ('In addition, the disciples of Bogolepov-Groman-Sokolnikov-Kondratiev should be turned out' [letter 67]) is more than a rhetorical device: it manifests an outlook that seizes on almost any contact between individuals as a token of a purposeful organization. Because Mikhail Kalinin spoke to some of the arrested 'scoundrels', he is on his way to joining a counterrevolutionary organization: the Central Committee should be notified (letters 59 and 63). The reasoning recalls Stalin's earlier interest in discovering that Yevgeny Preobrazhensky had visited Trotsky in Berlin (letter 11 from 1926).

The people of the Soviet Union would probably have been better off if Stalin had been more cynical than he was. Robert Tucker has pointed out how much pain and suffering went into the mass production of confessions during 1937.[48] These confessions served no earthly purpose; they were promptly filed away and forgotten. Tucker speculates that Stalin insisted on these confessions as

---

48   Tucker 1990.

proof to posterity that his vision of a world filled with enemies was basically correct. It was a repetition on a grandiose scale of his insistence in 1930 that people read and heed the testimonies of arrested wreckers.

In this section we have seen the antibureaucrat scenario turn murderous. Bureaucrats are no longer merely a focus for exasperation; they are cast as evil wreckers. This outlook is not inconsistent with the cynical scapegoating that accompanied anti-wrecker campaigns throughout the 1930s. The Russian historian O.V. Khlevniuk has described the situation in 1937:

> If food was delivered in irregular fashion, this was because of enemies who had infiltrated the collective farms, and appropriate trials were already being organized. If the accident rate at work was high, a simple explanation was already at hand in the form of exposed wreckers. The housing problem was not solved for years, and even finished houses could not be lived in because of incomplete and unsound work: wreckerism again. Wreckers were active in trade, which worked incredibly badly. Wreckers in transport – that's the reason trains jumped the rails. In general, the Stalinist leadership used a means of manipulating public opinion that was simple but effective enough under the circumstances: everything good came from the party, from Soviet power, and from the leader; everything bad came from enemies and wreckers.[49]

This excellent description falls short of a complete explanation because it makes Stalin and his friends too cynical and knowing. The letters indicate that, at least in 1930, Stalin genuinely believed that the wreckers were guilty as charged. Not only did he himself believe, but he thought that others believed. His capacity for rational manipulation must have been severely limited by his own angry credulity.

7   **Right Deviation**

Up to now we have seen Stalin lashing out at various groups defined as enemies: capitalist governments, kulaks, and 'class-alien elements' employed by the Soviet state. In all these cases, Stalin's anger, however irrational, was directed against people toward whom Bolsheviks had long been hostile. In this section we shall examine a phenomenon that is much harder to understand: Stalin's

---

49   O.V. Khlevniuk, *1937: Stalin, NKVD i sovetskoe obshchestvo* (Khlevniuk 1992, pp. 81–2).

lashing out at fellow Bolsheviks, not just avowed rivals for the leadership like Trotsky or Zinoviev, but party comrades who protested their loyalty to Stalin's general line. Was this an aberration explainable only in terms of Stalin's individual psychology? Or was it based on a political logic that Stalin shared with his victims?

To answer these questions we must examine the phenomenon of the right deviation.[50] There is an air of paradox about the right deviation. On the one hand, it was an ephemeral political opposition, quickly called into being by Stalin's change of course in 1928 and as quickly defeated. On the other hand, it seemed to the Stalinist leadership to be a permanent enemy that could never be entirely rooted out, one that threatened to undo all of Stalin's work even after his death. In his memoirs, Molotov maintains that the right deviation was a permanent temptation that was much more dangerous than the left opposition.[51]

Clearly the Stalinist leadership had an expanded definition of the right deviation that encompassed more than the opposition to the extraordinary measures of 1928 and the breakneck industrialization of the first five-year plan.[52] The right deviation in this expanded sense was not just a right-wing counterpart to the left opposition. The left opposition can be defined by specific beliefs or policy commitments; the same cannot be said of the right deviation, since it was defined less by any specific set of beliefs than by the logic of Stalin's attitude. To understand this logic, we must return to the antibureaucrat scenario and look more closely at the relationship between the wily specialist and the naive Communist.

In expounding this feature of the antibureaucrat scenario, Stalin often used the imagery of infection. A vivid example of this imagery can be found in letter 66, when Stalin calls M.N. Riutin a 'counterrevolutionary scum [*nechist*]' who should be sent far away from Moscow. *Nechist* is a term taken from Russian folk belief; it means literally 'the unclean one' and refers to the devil or indeed to anyone with whom one should not share the same food and drink. Stalin's combination of foreign Marxist jargon and earthy peasant abuse is eloquent not only stylistically but also politically, revealing a concept of pollution that could only be removed by a 'cleansing' (*chistka*, usually translated as 'purge').

---

50   The standard study of the right deviation in the strict sense is Stephen F. Cohen, *Bukharin and the Bolshevik Revolution* (Cohen 1971).

51   For an example, see Chuev 1991, p. 171.

52   Evidence from the late 1930s reveals that one reason why the 'right deviation' loomed so large in Stalin's outlook was its scepticism about all-out collectivization. See 'Who Is Stalin? What Is He?', included in this volume.

Stalin's political epidemiology traced the infection of the right deviation through the following chain: starting with the surrounding 'petty-bourgeois' classes, moving on to lower-level bureaucrats, and from thence to bourgeois specialists, then Communist administrators, and finally party leaders. Once the party leaders were infected, they were a menace to the cause and could not be tolerated.

If the idea of infection is taken seriously, it presents two problems: how to deal with the lower-level bureaucrats who are the source of the infection, and how to deal with the infected leaders. The letters show Stalin acting to resolve both problems before and after the official discovery of the right deviation in 1928. They reveal that the logic that defined the right deviation was already in evidence during NEP, although there was an increase in emotional intensity after 1928.

If specialists and other lower-level bureaucrats are seen as wreckers, the response is straightforward: round them up and wring confessions out of them. If they are seen as a source of infection, the problem is more insidious: How can anyone work with them without losing one's Bolshevik immunity? In the long run, no doubt, the bourgeois specialists would be replaced by 'our people'. But this prospect did not solve the short-term dilemma. The letters show the methods employed by Stalin in response: pressure, reliable Communist administrators, and a united leadership front.

The need to exert pressure on state economic organs was part of official NEP doctrine. Bukharin argued that without the spur of competition, state industry was threatened by monopolistic degradation. The solution to this problem was not to reintroduce competition within state industry but rather to exert firm political leadership.[53] Stalin agreed: in letter 4 (28 July 1925), he writes: 'The syndicate's inertia is understandable: it doesn't feel like expanding production since expansion means more headaches – why bring on unnecessary headaches if the syndicate is doing fine without them? This ruinous inertia that arises from its monopoly position has to be overcome no matter what.'

Thus, nothing special is occurring when Stalin informs Molotov in 1926 that 'we are drafting immediate and *concrete* measures to reduce *retail* prices (we will put brutal pressure on the trade and cooperative network)' (letter 30). More uniquely characteristic of Stalin is his angry outburst in 1926 against lower-level cooperative and state procurement agents who 'violated' policy directives by offering prices higher than officially permitted (letter 27):

---

53   For more discussion, see 'Bukharin on Bolshevik Illusions', included in this volume.

An extremely bad impression is produced by the constant communiques in the press (especially in the economic press) about the complete violation of directives from the Commissariat of Trade and the party by the cooperatives and by the local and central procurement agencies. The virtual impunity of these obvious criminals is grist for the mill of the nepmen [private middlemen] and other enemies of the working class – it demoralizes the entire economic and soviet apparat, it turns our directives and our party into a meaningless toy. This can't be tolerated any further if we don't want to be captured by these bastards who claim to 'accept' our directives but in reality mock us.

Stalin insists that these violators must be arrested and a circular sent out to local party committees: 'These violators are enemies of the working class and ... the struggle with them should be merciless' (letter 27). (Stalin was still fuming about these violators in an impromptu speech given several months later in January 1927.)[54]

If this sort of pressure was considered appropriate even during NEP, it is hardly surprising that during the five-year plan Stalin would rely more and more on the security police (OGPU) to carry out economic tasks. An illustrative example from 1929 is letter 41 on improving grain procurements. The sources of difficulties include petty speculators, 'nepman elements' in the cooperative and state economic organs, and uncooperative collective farms. The answer in each case is to send in the OGPU – otherwise the government is limiting itself to mere propaganda. In the next letter, Stalin is still worried, even though the Politburo has adopted his suggestion: it is unlikely that either the procurement agency or the security police will carry out the directives without vigorous checking up on fulfilment by the top leadership.

In 1930 the 'OGPU-ization' of economic administration seems to take a step forward when Stalin feels that bank policy would be much improved if the hierarchy were cleansed of unreliable Communists and replaced with people from the OGPU and the Worker-Peasant Inspection (letter 63). Stalin uses the expressive and untranslatable phrase *proverochno-mordoboinaia rabota*. The closest American idiom I can think of is 'kick butt'; the general idea is 'checking up by punching people in the face'.

An alternative to crude pressure of this sort is to send in reliable Communists who will keep tabs on top-level specialists. Unfortunately, Stalin's fear that the specialists would subvert the party's control made the relationship between

---

54   Stalin 1947–1952, 9:158–9.

specialists and Communists inherently unstable in his eyes. His attitude can be documented by his references to one of the most important 'non-party specialists', Vladimir Groman, a former Menshevik whose contribution during the 1920s to the methodology of planning was so great that he probably deserves the title 'father of Soviet planning'. In July 1925, Stalin complains that the Politburo is losing control of important economic decisions to Gosplan (the state planning agency) – in fact, not even to Gosplan but to middle-level experts. The real leadership of Gosplan comes from 'Smilga and Strumilin ... plus Groman' (letter 5). As party members, Smilga and Strumilin were supposed to keep an eye on things, but were they really reliable? In letter 10, Stalin calls Smilga a 'fake' economic leader.

In 1929, while the general offensive is in full swing, Stalin demands reliability of a more violent and radical sort. He wants Mikoyan to '*smash* the nest of Gromans, Vinogradskiis, and other such bourgeois politicians ensconced in Gosplan, the Central Statistical Administration, and so on. Hound them out of Moscow and put in their place young fellows, our people, Communists' (letter 44).

By 1930 Groman is a wrecker who should be shot. But apart from his out-and-out wrecking, Groman is a source of infection. His example inspired the smaller fry: the cashiers, along with various other specialists (who should also be shot). No doubt if all were known, a 'direct link' (that is, a chain of acquaintances) could be found between Groman and the leaders of the right deviation. Groman also seemed to infect any Communist administrator who supervised him. In 1925, Piatakov was preferable to the 'sham' Smilga, but now Piatakov himself is a 'dubious Communist' who lets 'financial wreckers' get away with murder (letter 57).

As these remarks show, Stalin felt that lower-level elements were encouraged by infected leaders at the top – and therefore no wavering or dissension among the top leadership could be tolerated. A united front is needed in both economic and political spheres. If procurement agencies compete among themselves, grain holders will see their chance and hold out for a better price (letter 41). In the same way, if the party leadership is openly divided, the bureaucrats will rejoice. As Stalin warns Molotov in September 1929, even the appearance of reconsidering the self-criticism campaign will discourage the best elements of the party and gladden the hearts of bureaucrats everywhere (letter 49).

By these means – pressure, reliable watchdogs, united leadership front – Stalin sought to quarantine the source of infection, but with only partial success. What if a senior Bolshevik – a Politburo member – became infected? By what symptoms would you recognize the disease? What political consequences arise from the presence of the infected leader? Answers to these questions can be found in a speech Molotov gave at the Party Conference in 1926. We learn from letter 29 that Molotov asked Stalin to look over this speech before it was printed. We may thus infer that Molotov regarded the speech as an expression of their joint outlook.

Molotov's speech is a political sermon on the necessity of faith. 'Faith in victory, assurance about one's own forces, a genuine conviction about the correctness of one's line and the unwavering decisiveness in struggle that flows from it – this is what will decide the outcome [of our struggle].' If faith can move mountains, lack of faith is deadly. Lack of faith is not an unimportant matter, not just a psychological quirk – no, it stems from a whole 'ideology of unbelief'. Those party members who lack faith 'will waver, will wobble, will get confused, will not have a line, and will confuse everybody they can. This is the logic of things.' It is absolutely intolerable to permit waverers to remain in the leadership: 'In this period of undoubtedly tense and long-drawn-out struggle for victory, it is necessary that our hands not shake, that our will not waver, that our thinking not be paralyzed.'[55]

In other words, the symptom of the disease is lack of faith; if top leaders are infected, the result will be widespread wavering and confusion. In 1926 this analysis was directed against the left opposition, with the support of Bukharin and Rykov. In 1929, during the fury of the general offensive, it was turned against the right deviation. In their notes for 1929, the Russian editors have given us a Politburo statement from August of that year condemning Bukharin; it is instructive to compare this text to Molotov's earlier attack on the left. Bukharin is making 'masked attacks' against the party. A case in point: in a recent speech he cited Marx's dictum 'Doubt everything'. Doesn't this show that 'Com. Bukharin is engaged in spreading unbelief [*nedoverie*] in the general line of the party'? His struggle with the leadership arises out of the inevitable wavering of the petty-bourgeois stratum during a time of intense class struggle. And since Bukharin's sallies against the Central Committee destroy the appearance of a united leadership front, they 'nourish the illusions' of capitalist elements who hope that resistance might pay off. Bukharin has been infected by petty-bourgeois wavering, and the resulting lack of faith demoralizes the party and encourages the class enemy.

The letters supplement this political analysis by revealing Stalin's intensely personal anger with Bukharin. When describing his feelings, Stalin resorts to a revealing social imagery that associates Bukharin with the milieu of the specialists. In one of his outbursts of hard-to-translate invective, Stalin casts him

---

55   *Piatnadtsataia Konferentsiia* 1927, pp. 654–75.

in the role of a pre-revolutionary *intelligent*: he is a 'typical representative of the spineless, effete *intelligent* in politics, leaning in the direction of a Kadet lawyer' (letter 42). (The Kadets, or Constitutional Democrats, were the leading liberal party in the decade before the revolution.) Stalin's conflation of Bukharin with the educated specialist helps explain why he was so sure that Bukharin was somehow inspiring the bureaucrats to frustrate the party's aims: Bukharin would feel more at home in the left wing of a party of petty-bourgeois socialists than in the Communist Party, where he is a decrepit, rotten defeatist (letter 67).

We then observe the strange debate between Bukharin and Stalin in 1929, in which Bukharin protests that he has no differences with the general line and Stalin insists that he does. In a private conversation that someone reported to Stalin, Bukharin evidently claimed that his difficulties with the Central Committee stemmed from his personal difficulties with Stalin. Stalin would have none of it: 'If his disagreements with the present Central Committee are explainable by Stalin's "personality", then how does one explain his disagreements with the Central Committee *when Lenin lived?* Lenin's "personality"? But why does he praise Lenin so much *now*, after his death? Isn't it for the same reason that all renegades like Trotsky praise Lenin (after his death!)? Our lawyer has completely tied himself in knots' (letter 43).

Thus Stalin claimed that Bukharin's dislike of him arose from profound political causes and Bukharin claimed that it did not. It is ironic that Bukharin's present-day reputation rests on the assumption that Bukharin was wrong and Stalin was right.

For Stalin, Bukharin is thus the paradigmatic right deviationist. But according to Stalin's version of the antibureaucrat scenario, any party leader who worked closely with specialists risked infection. According to the usual categories of party history, Aleksei Rykov, Georgii Piatakov, and Sergo Ordzhonikidze belong in completely different slots: Rykov was a right deviationist, Piatakov a Trotskyist, and Ordzhonikidze a loyal Stalinist. Yet the letters reveal how Stalin lashed out at each of them in strikingly similar terms.

As long-time head of the Soviet government and top economic administrator, Rykov was the co-leader of the right deviationist group. In his memoirs, Molotov dwells on the disgrace of being called a Rykovite by Stalin as late as 1950.[56] Like almost anyone in a similar position, Rykov wanted to have efficient, business-like relations with the specialists working under him and was irritated by the systematic distrust that interfered with productive work. At the

---

56   Chuev 1991, p. 469.

same Party Conference in 1926 where Molotov delivered his sermon on faith, Rykov read aloud a long letter from a specialist of his acquaintance who was on the verge of quitting. The specialist gave a long list of all the reports he had to make to inquisitive government agencies and ended with a description of some petty harassment by the local OGPU officer. Rykov furiously scolded the security police for throwing its weight around just to show who was boss. He then drew the moral: 'Of course, together with good specialists, there are also bad ones. But the working class should be able to separate out the good from the bad, and to help the good in every way while punishing the bad.'[57]

This outburst by Rykov shows that Stalin's version of the antibureaucrat scenario was not the only one compatible with Bolshevik political culture. But Rykov's defence of specialists made him a prime target for Stalin's suspicion. Sometimes Stalin sounded as if Rykov's body had been snatched and he was no longer a Bolshevik but a specialist. In September 1929, Stalin was highly irritated by a recent speech in which Rykov evidently failed to denounce the right deviation. 'In my opinion, it's the speech of a *non-party soviet bureaucrat* pretending to take the tone of a "loyal" person "sympathizing" with the soviets' (letter 50).

After mentally expelling Rykov from the party in this way, Stalin insisted on removing him from key governmental posts in the name of ensuring effective party leadership of the government. He reasoned that only in this way could the rot in the top government agencies be effectively eliminated. Rykov and his infected associates could no longer be tolerated. 'If Rykov and Co. try to stick their noses in again, beat them over the head. We have spared them enough. It would be a crime to spare them now' (letter 67).

But if Rykov and company were removed, who would take their place while remaining immune from infection? A plausible candidate was Piatakov, who had always been known as a vigorous, perhaps too vigorous, party administrator. In 1925, Stalin preferred him over the 'sham' Smilga. Piatakov had joined the left opposition because of his desire for more energetic industrialization, but he was one of the first to recant and re-enlist when Stalin started his industrial push in the late 1920s. In 1930, Piatakov was head of the state bank.

It is not quite clear from the letters exactly why Stalin was angry at Piatakov in 1930. Many observers at the time felt that Piatakov was resisting the inflationary policies demanded by the party leadership. According to R.W. Davies, this is an unlikely explanation. Piatakov had recently presided over a complicated credit reform designed to ensure better central planning of credit. Owing

---

57   *Piatnadtsataia Konferentsiia* 1927, pp. 18–20.

to haste and lack of preparation, the reforms led to severe, unplanned inflation; as a result, a harsh deflationary policy was instituted soon after Piatakov's
dismissal in the autumn of 1930.[58] Another possible explanation for Stalin's discontent is suggested by Piatakov's memorandum reproduced in *Stalin's Letters
to Molotov*: some of his recommendations amounted to a de facto criticism of
the overall thrust of economic policy.[59]

Inflationary pressures were an inevitable result of massive industrialization;
the small-change crisis discussed in the letters was a passing episode confined
to the summer of 1930. Stalin's anger at the 'wreckers' involved is amply documented here, and visiting journalists were struck by the ferocity of the campaign against 'hoarders'.[60] Stalin may have held Piatakov responsible for this
mini-crisis. Most likely, Stalin was not for or against inflation, for or against the
credit reforms, but simply irritated at Piatakov when things went wrong.

More important for our purposes is Stalin's interpretation of Piatakov's sins:
Piatakov is a 'genuine rightist Trotskyist' (letter 65; see also letter 66). If the right
deviation was a set of policy positions like the left opposition, this description would be merely nonsensical. But holding Trotskyist opinions on industrial tempo is perfectly compatible with being a link in the chain of infection.
Piatakov is under the thumb of his specialists; he is 'a poor commissar alongside specialists' (letter 60). (The allusion is to the practice during the civil war of
attaching Bolshevik commissars to the army in order to keep an eye on former
tsarist officers.) Piatakov becomes 'the most harmful element in the Rykov-
Piatakov bloc plus the Kondratiev-defeatist sentiments of the bureaucrats from
the soviet apparat' (letter 65). The knotted prose of the Russian original conveys
an even stronger impression of an unbreakable conglomerate.

Both Rykov and Piatakov had blots on their escutcheons: their participation at one time or another in oppositional currents within the party. Perhaps
someone who had never wavered in supporting Stalin would better withstand
infection. In 1930, when plotting to remove Rykov from his governmental posts,
Stalin felt it was essential to get someone like Sergo Ordzhonikidze to do the
job. Alas! – in 1933, the conflict arose again, and this time with Ordzhonikidze
himself (letters 78 and 79).

Ordzhonikidze (known to everybody simply as Sergo) was a fellow Georgian
who had been a Stalin loyalist from the very beginning and yet had managed
to retain his independence in a way that people like Molotov had failed to
do. The letters show Stalin's great reliance on Sergo as well as his occasional

---

58   Davies 1989a, p. 431.
59   Lih, Naumov, Khlevniuk 1995, pp. 188–9.
60   Knickerbocker 1931, pp. 256–7.

impatience with his fiery temperament (see letters 25, 27, 31). The clash with Ordzhonikidze in 1933 is all the more revealing. By now, the scenario is familiar. An economic difficulty exists (this time it involves missing parts). Its cause is violation of party decisions by impudent enemies of the party. A punitive campaign against them is announced. Anyone who raises a warning hand about this campaign – no matter who – is acting in an 'anti-party' manner. The evil motives of the lower-level violators are clear enough, but Stalin is also aggrieved by Ordzhonikidze: 'For what reason [is he doing this]? Of course, not in order to rein in the reactionary violators of party decisions – rather to support them morally, to justify them in the eyes of party opinion, and, in this way, to discredit the party's unfolding campaign – which in practice means to discredit the policy of the Central Committee' (letter 79).

In early 1937 Ordzhonikidze committed suicide under circumstances that point to a growing conflict with Stalin over exactly this sort of issue. Ordzhonikidze's death removed one of the few remaining barriers to the purification campaign of 1937 that decimated the Soviet elite.

We began this section by noting the paradoxical quality of the right deviation: elusive yet fearsome. The imagery of infection helps account for its insidious power in the eyes of Stalin and Molotov. One is almost tempted to define the right deviation (in the expanded sense under consideration here) as the attempt to be a self-respecting Stalinist – more exactly, the attempt to combine loyalty with self-respect. A party leader assigned a difficult job would try to do it in the most professional way he could, and this meant establishing a working relationship with specialists and sometimes suggesting a local revision of the general line. But as soon as anything went wrong or otherwise irritated Stalin, the antibureaucrat scenario would come into play and Stalin would see his former comrade as infected by the class enemy, as a source of rot, and as an unclean spirit that had to be exorcised.

All three dimensions of leadership are needed to explain this result. As an official, Stalin was placed in a relationship that was bound to produce tension: the top party leader was exerting pressure on the economic bureaucracy. One's feelings about the specialists depended to a large extent on where one stood in this relationship. Ordzhonikidze changed his own attitude toward specialists in 1930 when he moved from the Worker-Peasant Inspection (used in this period as a party tool for prodding the specialists) over to the top post in the government economic bureaucracy.[61]

---

61   Sheila Fitzpatrick, 'Ordzhonikidze's Takeover of Vesenkha: A Case Study in Soviet Bureaucratic Politics' (Fitzpatrick 1985).

But an explanation based solely on the dynamics of bureaucratic politics is insufficient. Leonid Brezhnev confronted the same structural tensions Stalin faced but reacted quite differently. In part this was because the Soviet Union was no longer undergoing revolutionary transformation in Brezhnev's time. Brezhnev also had the advantage of many long years of experience with a system that was new and dangerously unpredictable in the early 1930s. For these reasons, Stalin's level of frustration and suspicion was bound to be much higher. The main reason, however, for the way that different people react differently to the same structural realities is that they interpret them differently in their own minds. For the source of Stalin's interpretation, we must turn to the other two dimensions of leadership: political culture and individual psychology. Stalin defined the problems he faced with the aid of the antibureaucrat scenario. He did not make up this scenario all by himself: some version of the scenario, and even much of the imagery of infection, was canonical within Bolshevik political culture. Even when Rykov was defending specialists, he had to admit that there were bad ones requiring police attention. The letters show that the essential logic that defined the right deviation was present and active already in the mid-1920s – before Stalin's radical change of course. It was common party property, and when Stalin invoked it he could expect his words to resonate even with his victims.

Still, not every Bolshevik would invest the scenario with the same emotional intensity, and so we must look at Stalin's own psychological makeup. The vivid invective of the letters belies the image of the cold-blooded Stalin. The antibureaucrat scenario in itself does not account for Stalin's certainty about Bukharin's guilt or his ability to suspect close friends like Ordzhonikidze of deliberately encouraging violation of party policy. The person who wrote these letters was a general secretary, a Bolshevik, and an exceptional individual.

8   Conclusion

When a large new body of material such as Stalin's letters to Molotov becomes available, it is always difficult to assess its significance. This is doubly difficult at the present time, because of the ongoing archival revolution in Soviet history. My own conclusions are offered here as hypotheses intended to promote discussion.

These letters show Stalin at work; they reveal how he saw his job and how he approached the problems on his desk each morning. I have argued that the antibureaucrat scenario provides an essential key to understanding Stalin's outlook. This scenario served as a bridge between his day-to-day work (deciding on policy and getting it implemented) and his descent into criminality (campaigns against wreckers and right deviationists). The mundane slogans 'checking up on fulfilment' and 'selection of officials' were embedded in a politicized drama of class conflict that pitted the revolutionary party against the specialists and bureaucrats. The bureaucracy arose from the petty bourgeoisie and, as such, provided a source of infection for party officials. Stalin interpreted the frustrations of his job as the result of sabotage, and he therefore lashed out with murderous anger.

The antibureaucrat scenario also formed a bridge between the Stalin of NEP and the Stalin of the general offensive. As early as 1925 and 1926, Stalin was angry at 'violators' of policy directives and worried about loss of Politburo control. The intolerability of any wavering within the party leadership was already explicit doctrine. But Stalin's application of the antibureaucrat scenario became steadily more violent during the general offensive when society threatened to spin out of control. The cognitive framework stayed pretty much the same; the emotional intensity became much fiercer.

Finally, the antibureaucrat scenario unites the three dimensions of Stalin's leadership. This scenario represents the resources of Bolshevik political culture applied to a particular job by a particular individual. Most top executives will come up with some form of the antibureaucrat scenario, but Stalin's version arose from the revolutionary experiences of the Bolshevik party and its collective reflection on them. Although Stalin's scenario thus made sense to his colleagues, it also acquired a characteristically angry and vindictive tone when he applied it. The letters reveal this vividly because they were written as immediate reactions to various problems confronting Stalin.

The picture of Stalin that emerges from the letters will have a profound effect on a number of scholarly debates. There have been two general approaches to deciphering the enigma of Stalin; each has been given classic expression by someone who worked with him and presumably knew him well. In 1928, after Bukharin broke with Stalin, he summed up his new view of Stalin to Kamenev: 'Stalin is an unprincipled intriguer, who subordinates everything to the preservation of his own power.'[62] Bukharin went on to complain that Stalin changed his views like a weathercock whenever it suited his interests.

This description has remained the basis of one popular interpretation of Stalin. It is not without foundation, for there is no doubt that Stalin was an adept intriguer; the Molotov letters provide some excellent examples. The question remains: Was Stalin an unprincipled or a principled intriguer? In con-

---

62   Robert V. Daniels, ed., *A Documentary History of Communism*, 2 vols (Daniels 1960b, 1:308).

trast to Bukharin's view in 1928 is a comment Nikita Khrushchev made during the 'secret speech' of 1956 in which he exposed many of the crimes of the dead tyrant: 'We cannot say that these were the deeds of a giddy despot. He considered that this should be done in the interest of the party, of the working masses, in the name of the defence of the revolution's gains. In this lies the whole tragedy!'[63]

In spite of its air of paradox, Khrushchev's portrait of a sincere Stalin has always had adherents. In my view, the letters weigh in heavily on Khrushchev's side of the debate: Stalin was a believer. This conclusion bears on another debate over Stalin: How much control did he have over events? To put the debate in oversimplified terms: Was Stalin powerful and committed enough to achieve what he wanted, so that we can deduce his intentions from the results? Or was he the creature of processes beyond his ken, avoiding decisions until his hand was forced? The letters suggest the need to pose the question in other terms. They reveal a very powerful Stalin who was aggressively confident about his own opinions. When he was committed to a policy, he selected officials and checked up on fulfilment until that policy was carried out. His insistence on the collectivization drive is the most eloquent example in the letters.

On the other hand, control over events implies cognitive control. To assume that we can deduce Stalin's intentions from the actual results is to assume that he knew what he was doing – in other words, that he had insight into the workings of state and society and that he understood the effects of his actions. Few readers of the letters will want to defend these statements. I have argued that much of Stalin's opinionated intolerance arose from cognitive insecurity; as top leader in revolutionary times, he had no access to unbiased information and was condemned to permanent radical uncertainty. The overriding mood of the letters is not the confidence of power but the anger of frustration.

Another long-standing debate over Stalin concerns his commitment to world revolution and the meaning of 'socialism in one country'. The letters show that Stalin did not see revolutionary interests and state interests in either-or terms: his genuine involvement in the revolutionary upswing in England and China did not contradict his fundamental loyalty to the power and prestige of the Soviet state. Finally, the letters show that by the mid-1920s Stalin's ascendancy within the Politburo rested to a large extent on his leadership skills and his ability to make a good case for his recommendations.

Each reader of the Stalin letters will come away with a conception of the person who wrote them. Here I offer my own impressions. Much of the correspon-

---

63   *Khrushchev Remembers*, trans. Strobe Talbott (Khrushchev 1970, p. 616).

dence is devoted to the rough-and-tumble of political infighting. Assuming that this was an inevitable part of the Kremlin environment, I find that Stalin's image of himself as a devoted, conscientious leader is not entirely without foundation. He plainly worked very hard trying to resolve genuinely intractable problems. His leadership skills are impressive. Although it is usual to scorn his catechistic style and numbered paragraphs, I have a feeling that if I were on a committee with Stalin and those prodigious memos came my way, I would find them difficult to ignore. On the other hand, the emotional range found in the letters is frighteningly narrow; it almost seems confined to anger, irritation, and vindictiveness. Praise, generosity, enthusiasm, humour – these, while not entirely absent, are in short supply. Robert Daniels's characterization based on Stalin's public writing is amply confirmed by the letters: 'an anxious, rigid, compulsive, combative mind'.[64]

Stalin was caught up in events beyond his comprehension (we are still struggling to understand them today), and his conceptual equipment was plainly inadequate for grasping the real causes of his problems or the effects of his actions. His ignorance and anger, amplified by his sincerity and his leadership skills, led to crimes of horrifying dimensions. It would take the powers of a Dostoyevsky to fully describe the combination of cynicism and belief, of manipulation and sincerity, that resulted in the tragedy of Stalin and his times.

---

64   Robert V. Daniels, *The Nature of Communism* (Daniels 1962, p. 115).

Bukharin's Bolshevik Epic: The Prison Writings

Roaming in thought over the Universe, I saw the little that is
Good steadily hastening towards immortality,
And the vast all that is call'd Evil I saw hastening to merge itself
and become lost and dead.

WALT WHITMAN, 'On Reading Hegel'

∴

Nikolai Bukharin was arrested in February 1937 and remained in prison for over
a year. He then stood trial in March 1938, followed by swift execution. During his
year in prison, he succeeded in writing a 258-page tract contrasting fascist culture with Soviet culture (*Socialism and its Culture*), an even more substantial
333-page work entitled *Philosophical Arabesques*, a poem cycle of more than
170 poems with the overall title of *Transformation of the World*, and finally a
novel/memoir *How It All Began*. This extremely impressive oeuvre has been
translated into English in its entirety.[1]

The present survey of Bukharin's prison writings focuses on two works: *Philosophical Arabesques* and the poem cycle *Transformation of the World*. My aim
is to set out the surface argument – the official message, so to speak – of these
works. This project may arouse surprise and even protest from some quarters. Many who write on Bukharin's writings of the 1930s feel strongly that
Bukharin's memory is dishonoured if we take too seriously his pro-Stalin effusions, since they are obviously the product of fear, coercion and psychological
torture. Others are interested mostly in decoding secret anti-Stalin messages

---

1 The prison writings (except for the poem cycle) are available in Russian in Bukharin, *Tiuremnye rukopisi*, 2 vols (Bukharin 1996) and Bukharin, *Vremena* (Bukharin 1994). For an updated
edition of the prison writings, see *Uznik Lubianki: Tiuremnye rukopisi Nikolaia Bukharina*,
ed. Gennadii Bordiugov (Bukharin 2008). As far as I know, there is no Russian edition of
Bukharin's poem cycle. For English-language editions, see *Philosophical Arabesques* (Bukharin 2005), *The Prison Manuscripts: Socialism and its Culture* (Bukharin 2006), the novel *How
It All Began* (Bukharin 1998), and *The Prison Poems of Nikolai Bukharin* (Bukharin 2018, originally published in 2009).

that they feel sure are embedded in his output. These objections raise serious issues to which we will return in the concluding section of this essay.

Nevertheless, even if these objections were valid, we would not be relieved of the responsibility to set forth Bukharin's views as directly stated in his writings of the 1930s and to consider how they fit into his long-term positions. If, after grasping Bukharin's explicit arguments in these writings, readers feel compelled to bracket them as 'not really Bukharin', they are entitled to do so. Nevertheless, there is absolutely no reason to ignore them – as scholars have done – just because they clash with our preconceived ideas about what Bukharin should have thought.

The prison writings look very different when put in the context of Bukharin's career-long corpus. Many themes that recur again and again in Bukharin's writings resurface in the prison writings. Nevertheless, there is also something new in his writings from the 1930s. Starting with an extensive *Pravda* article in February 1930, Bukharin consistently argued that Stalin's revolution from above – forced-tempo industrialization, dekulakization, mass collectivization – fulfilled the promise of the 1917 revolution and opened the doorway to a new stage of socialist transformation.[2] It will not do to dismiss these claims out-of-hand as nothing but coerced flattery or as cover for 'Aesopian' subversion. Bukharin's argument is too detailed, too carefully put together, too consistently maintained – too Bukharinian – to be dismissed in this way.

The prison writings are Bukharin's final iteration of the Bolshevik epic he defended throughout his career. And, if we open our ear to it, we will hear a vast, indeed apocalyptic, narrative of a struggle between good and evil that is rapidly approaching its climax. While Bukharin's Bolshevik epic may no longer be persuasive, it certainly is exhilarating.

1   Philosophical Arabesques

Philosophical Arabesques is Bukharin's penultimate prose work, with a poignant dating on the last page: 'November 7–8, 1937, the twentieth anniversary of the great victory'.[3] The highly dramatic circumstances under which Bukharin

---

2   Bukharin's *Pravda* article of 19 February 1930 'Velikaia rekonstruktsiia' was reprinted during the perestroika period in Bukharin 1990b. As we shall see later, Bukharin's article connects up with his prison poems in significant ways. In my view, this overlooked evidence creates severe challenges for many stereotypes about issues such as Bukharin's alleged opposition to Stalin's all-out collectivization.

3   Bukharin 2005, p. 376; further page references to this work are given in the text. This discus-

wrote *Philosophical Arabesques* give rise to a number of interpretive dilemmas. To what extent can we take Bukharin's argument at face value, given that he was fighting for his life? One's answer to this question depends in large part on one's reading of the prison writings as a whole and indeed of Bukharin's *oeuvre* as a whole. I will give my own provisional answer to this basic interpretive question later on, but first I will set out the official, so to speak, argument that binds together the 40 chapters of Bukharin's polemical exposition of dialectical materialism. Each of these short chapters has dialectical materialism square off with one of an intentionally dazzling array of theories, ranging from heavyweights such as Spinoza and Hegel to less intellectually respectable outlooks such as hylozoism (the view that all matter is animate) or racism. Nevertheless, an underlying story binds together what would otherwise be a string of disparate mini-essays. The story goes something like this:

Once upon a time, the bourgeoisie was itself revolutionary, and in consequence its highest philosophical expression was also revolutionary. But in the course of time the bourgeoisie became less and less revolutionary, more and more conservative. Hegel's philosophy was a reflection of this situation: revolutionary and dialectic in form, but used by Hegel to arrive at conservative, 'idealist' conclusions. Only the rising proletariat preserved the dialectical outlook by tying it to materialism.

In the present era, bourgeois society is moving beyond conservatism to complete ideological collapse. An underlying sense of pessimism and doom is giving rise to a recrudescence of unreason: mysticism, racism and overall irrationalism. Fascist ideology in particular tries to give itself a sense of a future by loudly proclaiming its own rejection of bourgeois individualism and laissez-faire in favour of a new mystical totality. All this aggressive nonsense barely conceals a panicked sense of doom.

Meanwhile, dialectical materialism has been going from strength to strength. Its basic predictions have been stunningly justified, particularly its insistence that the dictatorship of the proletariat is the only pathway to a socialist future. In the Soviet Union under Stalin, dialectical materialism is becoming the worldview of millions.

At the present time – the mid-thirties – there are two ideological worldviews starkly facing each other, each representing a different class principle: fascist

---

sion incorporates my review of *Philosophical Arabesques* published in *Science and Society* in January 2009.

philosophy as the most thorough expression of capitalism in desperate crisis versus dialectical materialism as the expression of the triumphant proletariat. Of course, fascist 'philosophy' is ludicrous – but it is supported by very real material force and in the end can only be defeated by a stronger material force. But refuting and rejecting fascist nonsense nevertheless makes a contribution to this material struggle. There is therefore a very political moral to be drawn from this cavalcade of clashing philosophies: 'Kantians, positivists, agnostics, phenomenalists, and others – make your choice! Time is running out' (38).

Such is Bukharin's anti-fascist story, a philosophical counterpoint to the similar stark confrontation between fascist and Soviet culture found in his other prison tract, *Socialism and its Culture*. The question immediately arises: can we take Bukharin's triumphalist picture of Soviet society in the mid-thirties as an expression of his actual views? One school of thought decidedly rejects this possibility and claims that by means of hints, doubletalk, and 'Aesopian language', Bukharin actually intended to convey an anti-Stalin message, or, at the very least, hoped to deflect Stalin's Russia from its disastrous path. This school presents Bukharin as a heroic *dvurushnik* or 'double-dealer', the label given by Stalin to mask-wearing enemies of the people, very much including Bukharin.[4] Bukharin's most passionate defenders agree with Stalin on this much: Bukharin's demonstrative loyalty was feigned, a cover-up for a consistent anti-Stalin message.

I find this reading unconvincing, not least because of a quality that is quite properly stressed by the defenders of Bukharin as heroic *dvurushnik*: his passionate anti-fascism. Bukharin wanted these writings published immediately (especially the book on culture) and made available to its target audience: Western intellectuals who he hoped would be a source of support for the Soviet Union in the coming struggle. If his book genuinely aimed at giving the impression that Soviet society was itself turning into a 'mirror-image' of fascism, the anti-fascist thrust of Bukharin's attempted intervention would be radically undermined.

I myself belong to the Horton school of Bukharin interpretation: like the Dr Seuss character of that name, Bukharin by and large meant what he said and said what he meant. I do not mean to apply this to every last bit of Stalin flattery, but I do think Bukharin had persuaded himself that, despite inevitable difficulties, Stalin's Russia was on the high road to socialism. The concluding section of this essay has a more detailed discussion of this highly contentious issue.

---

4   For an extended examination of *dvurushnichestvo* and mask-wearing during the Stalin era, see 'Vertigo: Masks and Lies in Stalin's Russia', included in this volume.

Here I will just point out some similarities between *Philosophical Arabesques* and Bukharin's recurrent style of argument throughout his *oeuvre*. By a revealing coincidence, the opening lines of one of Bukharin's first substantial works, *World Economy and Imperialism* (first published in 1915), and the opening lines of *Philosophical Arabesques*, his last theoretical work, both invoke the apocalypse. In each case, Bukharin says that the present era strikes many weak and philistine people as a time of apocalyptic disaster, while only revolutionary Marxism is able to keep its head and look reality in the eye. In order to give a sense of the continuity in Bukharin's outlook on this vital point, I will quote, not only the opening lines of the bookend works from 1915 and 1937, but also passages from 1920 and 1925.

Bukharin 1915, opening paragraph of World Economy and Imperialism: This grandiose global catastrophe, which to the superficial observer might signify the destruction of all laws of social development, closer to pages taken straight from the Apocalypse than the realities of a capitalist world, is, in actuality, simply a very sharp expression of the contradictions of contemporary society. And revolutionary Marxism, which had and still has the audacity to face up to the approaching storm, tirelessly predicted the inevitability of this catastrophe.

This circumstance proves yet again the immense value of Marxist doctrine as an explanatory tool. Marxism – a theory so many times ridiculed, so many times buried – receives now one more empirical confirmation. And this is the best possible guarantee that in future Marxism will undoubtedly play a colossal role in the working out of a new tactical line for the proletariat. We have absolutely no doubt that only revolutionary Marxism will be in a condition to work out this line and that only revolutionary Social Democracy will be capable of realizing it in practice.[5]

Bukharin 1920, from the preface to Economy of the Transition Period: He who thinks of the revolution of the proletariat as a peaceful transition of the *vlast* from one set of hands to another ... will recoil in horror from the world-encompassing tragedy that humanity is undergoing. He is inca-

---

5 Bukharin 1915, p. 21. *World Economy and Imperialism* is cited as originally published in a Bolshevik journal in 1915. In 1917, Bukharin's book was republished with additions and organizational changes. This version is the basis of English-language editions, for example, Bukharin 2003; the passage quoted here is found only in the original 1915 publication.

pable of looking through the smoke of fire and thunder of the civil war to the solemn and triumphal outlines of the future society. He will always remain a pathetic philistine whose intellect is as cowardly as his 'politics' ... The old society in both its state and its productive guises *splits apart, falls apart* to its very depths, to its uttermost foundations. Never has there been such a grandiose breakdown.

But without such a breakdown there can be no proletarian revolution, which takes the elements that have *fallen apart*, and – with new *links*, new *combinations*, new principles – *constructs* the foundation of the future society ... Humanity is paying a horrifying price for the sins of the capitalist system. And only a class such as the proletariat, the Prometheus class [*klass-Prometei*], will be able to carry on its shoulders the inescapable torments [*muki*] of the transition period.[6]

Bukharin 1925: [We must reject intellectuals whose personal decency did not prevent them from being] obstacles on the path of development for the simple reason that they do not understand the full historic scale of events. In those years of hunger, when the so-called privileged working class got only a potato a day, when things went as far as cannibalism, when even a superficial view of the cities presented a picture of a dying human society and to go outside the cities was truly frightening – it required a vast insight into the future to see the gigantic enthusiasm of the masses that would bring us to a new order.[7]

Bukharin 1937, opening paragraph of Philosophical Arabesques: Our age: an age of the great crisis of world history. The struggle of social forces has been raised to the highest possible tension. Apocalyptic times – as it seems to old ladies of either sex. The birth of a new world for mankind. An age calling on the highest heroism of the class called upon to transform the world [Время высокой героики для класса-преобразователя]. A twilight of the gods for the dying, departing order.

All the old values are crumbling and collapsing. An across-the-board re-evaluation of habits, norms, ideas, world outlooks is taking place; a demarcation, a polarization of all material and spiritual potentials. Is there anything surprising in the fact that *philosophy* as well is drawn into this whirlpool, this titanic struggle? Is there anything surprising in the fact

---

6 Bukharin 1920 (*Ekonomika*).
7 Bukharin, *Revoliutsiia i kultura* (Bukharin 1993), pp. 80–1 (March 1925).

that the philosophy of *Marxism* – about which professional philosophers a few years back spoke with such contemptuous sneers – has now risen to its feet and thrust its head up to the skies?[8]

The kind of 'dialectical' defence of Stalin's Russia that Bukharin mounts in *Philosophical Arabesques* is one he deployed continually throughout his career: despite all the disasters and the huge costs of a necessarily bloody and destructive struggle, the proletariat – the Prometheus class, the class that transforms society – is striding ahead. This reality presents itself only to those with eyes to see the *main* tendencies of the present era.

Another verbal echo between Bukharin's first and last work is his image of the final goal of socialism. Socialist society is pictured as organized by 'an organized collective, governed by a single will' (1915), or as 'the rational coordination of individual wills into a single whole' (1937).[9] This image of a totally organized society runs throughout Bukharin's writings (somewhat ironically, given Bukharin's reputation in some quarters as a defender of market socialism and pluralism). This is why he responds so fervently to the corresponding fascist claim to represent its own new 'totality'. An eloquent expression of Bukharin's goal of an all-embracing state power that 'impregnates every sphere of social life' comes from his 1933 work *Marx's Teaching and its Historical Importance*. His description here of the 'dictatorship of the proletariat' reflects his lifelong views:

> Bringing the whole administration of 'national economy' into its apparatus, enriching and varying to the greatest possible extent its tasks, placing itself on a foundation of socialist economy of ever-increasing planned character, the dictatorship of the proletariat rationalizes to the highest degree the vital process of society as a whole. The class struggle of the proletariat organized as the state power assumes a variety of forms, impregnating every sphere of social life, from technique to philosophy.
>
> This process of the transformation of society from a fractional-elemental [*drobno-stikhiinogo*] condition into a rationalized and organized one, this conversion of subjectless society into society the subject, fundamentally changes the very type of law of social development.

---

8 Bukharin 2005, p. 35.
9 Bukharin 1915, p. 77 (*World Economy and Imperialism*). The citation from *Philosophical Arabesques* was inadvertently dropped from the English edition (compare Bukharin 2005, p. 191 to Bukharin 1996, 2:166).

This lofty language had a practical application: 'Under the proletarian dictatorship the state merges more and more with economy. All the chief economic levers are in the hands of the proletarian state.' Bukharin draws the full conclusion from this logic: 'By drawing everyone into its direct organization, the state cease to be itself, and *absorbing society into itself*, itself dissolves into it without leaving a trace' (emphasis added). So, for Bukharin, the withering away of the state is logically equivalent to the withering away of society.[10]

Bukharin's evocation of a totally organized society that embodies a conflictless merger of individual and social strikes me, not as something modern, progressive, or humanist, but rather as something archaic – a reflection of still-potent traditional values. Consider this passage from Bukharin's prison essay on culture: 'Capitalist diversity *divides* people. It is an inharmonious chaos of sounds, roaring and squealing. Socialist diversity *unites* people. It is a triumphant symphony of creativity, a chorale ascending from earth to heaven.'[11] Speaking for myself, I would rather tolerate an inharmonious chaos than be trapped in somebody else's chorale. In the words of the great Polish epigrammatist Stanisław Lec, I prefer the sign that says 'No Entrance' to the sign that says 'No Exit'.

The English edition of *Philosophical Arabesques* is introduced by Helena Sheehan, author of a study of Marxism and the philosophy of science.[12] She states that the prison manuscripts 'must be read as a coded attempt to communicate covertly something sometimes utterly at odds with what he was asserting overtly', but she gives no concrete advice on how decoding might work in the case of *Philosophical Arabesques*. Given the extreme difficulties of translating such a determinedly erudite text and of accurately conveying so many abstruse arguments, the translator, Renfrey Clarke, can only be congratulated on the final result. I do have problems with one or two translations of technical terms. For example, *rassudochnyi* should not be translated 'rational', but rather 'rationalist' or 'rationalistic'. The present translation has Bukharin making a very confusing contrast between 'rational' thinking and 'dialectical' thinking, although the thrust of the whole work is to present dialectics as the height of

---

10   Bukharin et al., *Marxism and Modern Thought* (Bukharin 1935), pp. 82–3, 77–8. Bukharin himself suggested this volume of essays as appropriate for translation. For the Russian text of quoted passages, see Bukharin 1989, pp. 414–15, 409. Bukharin's praise of the mono-organizational society is not simply a reflection of the priorities of the Stalin era or a return to a pre-NEP outlook; see 'Bukharin on Bolshevik "Illusions"', included in this volume.

11   Bukharin 2006, p. 111 (*Socialism and its Culture*). For an idea of how such a triumphant chorale might sound, listen to the last movement of Sergei Prokofiev's *Anniversary Cantata* (1938), discussed in 'Who Is Stalin, What Is He?', included in this volume.

12   Helena Sheehan, *Marxism and the Philosophy of Science* (Sheehan 1993).

rationality (104–12). Occasionally Clarke misses out on a Russian idiom. For example, in his introduction, Bukharin is not really saying that fascist ideas need to be met with 'fixed bayonets', that is, physically repressed, but rather only that these ideas should be aggressively refuted (38).

Bukharin's prison writings give rise to so many historical and political questions that I have not said anything about the quality of philosophical argument deployed here.[13] While hardly an expert on such matters, I generally found myself on Bukharin's side (with the significant exception of his picture of the final goal). His dissection of racism and irrationalist mysticism is exhilarating, appropriately enough for a book whose bottom line is anti-fascism. All in all, *Philosophical Arabesques* is a highly significant historical document, and anyone interested in the Russian revolution and its fate owes a debt of gratitude to all those who were instrumental in recovering it from secret police archives and making it available in English.

2   *Transformation of the World*: Bukharin's Apocalypse

In the second half of 1937, at the same time that he was writing the *Philosophical Arabesques*, Bukharin composed a series of more than 170 poems. He intended these poems to be seen as a unified whole, and indeed they are: an epic that stretches back into ancient history and forward into a utopian future, with detours along the way to an almost pantheistic embrace of Nature with a capital N, along with some very personal loves and memories. But the heart of the epic – the core that unifies its panoramic scope – is Bolshevism as Bukharin experienced it from 1917 to 1937.[14]

The title Bukharin gave to the entire cycle is *Transformation of the World*. The central argument of the work as a whole is that the Soviet Union of the Stalin era – the land of the Five-Year Plan and of collectivization – is the fulfilment of the promise of the Bolshevik revolution. As such, it is a 'glorious turning-point' toward global transformation. One last, final battle with fascism's pure

---

13   For a full discussion of the ways in which *Philosophical Arabesques* contributed to Marxist theory, see '"Arabeski" Nikolaia Bukharina v kontekste ikh vremeni' (Ulig and Khedeller [Wladislaw Hedeler] 2008).

14   For a different view, see 'The Prison Writings of Nikolai Bukharin' by Howard Caygill: 'The collection of poems comprises two very distinct poetic projects: a revolutionary/historical epic of the rise of socialism and a pantheistic philosophical meditation on life and nature' (Caygill 2020). Caygill's essay has a useful survey of aspects of the poem cycle not treated here.

evil must be fought – and then humankind moves forward into a future with literally no limits. Even death will be overcome.

The drama set forth by *Transformation of the World* is thus apocalyptic in the strict sense defined by the biblical *Apocalypse* by John of Patmos (*Revelation*, the revealing of hidden realities, is just a Latinate version of *Apocalypse*). A new truth has entered the world, it has achieved a concrete historical presence, it is now beset by the assembled forced of demonic reaction aiming at a thousand-year kingdom, there will soon – soon! – be a cosmic battle between good and evil, good will triumph, and victory will usher in an untroubled, glorious future with a remade humanity.

At time of writing, only a few of Bukharin's prison poems are available in the original Russian.[15] Fortunately for readers of English, the late George Shriver has translated the entire series (with one important exception). His volume *The Prison Poems of Nikolai Bukharin* comes with a helpful analysis of the source texts and an explanation of obscure references.[16] Shriver's introduction also details the detective work and the bureaucratic politics deployed by Bukharin's widow Anna Larina and her ally Stephen Cohen as they successfully wrested Bukharin's impressive prison oeuvre out of the archives of the NKVD. Thanks to Larina, Cohen and Shriver, we are able to confront Bukharin's final answer to the question 'what was Bolshevism?'.

Transformation of the World is built up out of a number of smaller sections. Shriver has established that Bukharin had the following structure in mind:

Poema o Staline. Bukharin intended this poem, dedicated solely to Stalin, to lead off the collection. Unfortunately, this one poem has been suppressed and, as far as I know, is not publicly available anywhere in any form. Shriver reports that 'Larina decided, and I think quite rightly, that this fulsome *"Poema o Staline"*, the result really of pressure, extortion and abasement of the individual, should not be included in published versions of Bukharin's poetry' (xxii). Speaking as a historian, I regret the decision to suppress a significant historical document.

Precursors (13 poems). The opening cycle consists of snapshots of progressive rebels through the ages, including Spartacus, Pugachev, the French Revo-

---

The Russian text of a small number of Bukharin's poems can be found in Bukharin 1996 and Bukharin 2008.

Shriver's translation first came out in 2009. The edition used here is copyrighted by Seagull Books (Kolkata) in 2018; the full title is *The Prison Poems of Nikolai Bukharin: Transformation of the World (Verse about the Ages, and about People)*. The subtitle of Shriver's edition is Bukharin's own full title for his poem series.

lution, the 1848 revolution, John Brown, Chernyshevsky, and the Russian revolution of 1905. These rebels make up the genealogy of Bolshevism.

Civil War (16 poems). Bukharin starts the story of the Russian revolution immediately after the Bolsheviks come to power and finishes with Perekop, one of the final battles of the civil war. Thus his picture of the revolution lays heavy stress on the many enemies attempting to extirpate the fledgling worker-peasant *vlast* as well as the weighty sacrifices heroically accepted by its defenders. This cycle ends with a look ahead to what Bukharin calls 'the anti-kulak revolution' of 1929–30. Shriver moved this poem – 'Kulak Perdition' [*Kulatskaia pogibel*] – into the later section on Stalin-era society. As we shall see, Bukharin had his reasons for placing it here, as a coda to the civil war cycle.

Nature – Mother of All [*Pramater – Priroda*] (32 poems). Bukharin gives an exhilarating panorama of Nature in a variety of guises, from vultures in the Pamir mountains to electrons, from stormy avalanches to June bugs in the grass.

Heritage (28 poems). Another genealogy for Bolshevism: European humanism, as symbolized by its intellectual heroes, including Leonardo da Vinci, Shakespeare, Spinoza, Hegel, Pushkin, Darwin. Oddly enough, nowhere in Bukharin's epic is there a portrait of either Marx or Engels. Bukharin ends this cycle with a few poems about the descent into hysterical obscurantism, especially in Germany: a poetic version of the polemics in *Philosophical Arabesques*.

War of Worlds (*Borba mirov*) (28 poems). This section sets up the apocalyptic framework of an impending battle between good (the Soviet Union, plus Soviet beachheads elsewhere, for example, in China) and evil (capitalism, especially in its monstrously reactionary form in Germany). The stark contrasts deployed by Bukharin allow of no nuance whatsoever.

Lyrical Intermezzo (29 poems). These poems are very personal and mainly reflect on fleeting memories of his past life with Anna Larina. Nevertheless, I think there is also a political point to their inclusion in the epic of Bolshevism: as Bukharin states in his preface to the poems, Bolshevism is not *solely* political and combative, it also embraces humanity's relation with Nature, the humanistic tradition, and individual love and intimacy.[17]

Epoch of Great Works (*Epokha velikikh rabot*) (23 poems). This key section is nothing less than a hymn of praise to the changes wrought in Soviet society during the Stalin era:

The epoch's new feast
Is crowned by songs of triumphant glory,
A majestic hymn to immortal labour (397).

---

17   Bukharin 2009, pp. xlix–liii.

The Future (5 poems). A brief but exhilarating look into future communist society, as shown by the poem titles: 'The Universal Human Race', 'Laurel Wreaths of Brotherhood', 'Life-Creativity', 'Death and Life', 'Infinity'. In 'Death and Life', Bukharin predicts that human science will eventually find a way to defeat death.

3   The Role of Stalin

George Shriver did yeoman work in translating and annotating these poems, but his introduction fails to bring out the unity and the underlying message of *Transformation of the World*. The reason for this lapse is, I believe, an understandable reluctance to fully accept Bukharin's intention to write a hymn of praise for Stalin's Soviet Union – even though this praise is the linchpin that unifies the whole collection. Shriver's unease manifests itself in his apology for anything nice said about Stalin: 'The least attractive motif, which appears in a few of the poems, or passages in poems, has to do with the praising of Stalin.' These are all 'false and rather unpoetic curiosities' that might be better placed in an appendix (xx, 393). Shriver offers various excuses: vain hopes that the poems might be published, life insurance for his family, etc.

Unfortunately, we cannot censor Stalin as an individual out of these poems and still hope that what is left will be any more politically acceptable from an anti-Stalinist perspective. Some of Bukharin's poems about collective farms and the Stalinist factory are in themselves the verbal equivalent of over-the-top propaganda posters. If you celebrate dekulakization, collectivization, and the Five-Year Plan, you are also celebrating the leader who carried out these policies, whether or not you mention his name.

As with the choral works by Prokofiev and Shostakovich analysed in a later essay, we will get further in understanding what is going on in Bukharin's text if we can detach ourselves from our feelings about the empirical Stalin and reflect on how his image is being used here by Bukharin for his literary and polemical purposes.[18] Still, a few comments on Bukharin's attitude toward Stalin as political leader will be helpful. In 1937, Bukharin wrote two searingly personal letters, one composed on the eve of his arrest and addressed to 'the future generation of party leaders', the other to Stalin directly. In both letters, he affirmed with great evidence of sincerity that, from 1930 on, he approved of, defended and helped to carry out the party general line.[19] This affirmation of foundational

---

18   See 'Who Is Stalin? What Is He?', included in this volume.

19   In the letter to future party leaders, Bukharin states that the 'Bukharin organization' of

Stalin-era *policies* is the key point, and I see no reason not to accept it as sincere. It alone makes sense, not only of his prison writings as a whole, but of his earlier rationale for Stalin's revolution from above, as we will see later.

Owing to well-intentioned censorship, we do not have the introductory poem on Stalin – not even in an appendix – that Bukharin wanted to place at the front of the collection. But judging from what we have, 'Stalin' plays a significant but not overly obtrusive role in the cycle as a whole as the great leader who is responsible for the breakthrough to 'the epoch of great works'. One of the more elaborate mentions of Stalin comes from a poem about the Five-Year Plan:

> Thought flowing from the brain of Stalin
> Has been condensed in rows of figures.
> With his mighty iron hand,
> Authoritative, strong and firm,
> He led the people to new battles,
> To conflict hard and dangerous,
> And in that combat we've come out
> Victorious all along the line,
> Building a house of light-filled life
> And on the horizon's the communist future (399).

There are other reasons why removing Stalin or relegating him to an appendix would seriously hurt the intended political message of *Transformation of the World*. As in his other prison writings, Bukharin here urges the Soviet Union to gird its loins for a life-and-death battle with Nazism and mocks Hitler as a

---

which he was accused never existed, 'not only now, when already for seven years there has been no hint of any disagreement with the party on my part, but also back then, in the years of the "right" opposition ... I loved Kirov, I did not scheme [*zateval*] against Stalin.' (Shriver quotes Bukharin's attack on the secret police in this letter to prove that his praise of Stalin could not have been sincere [p. xx], but Shriver misses the political point about endorsing the party line.) From the letter to Stalin, dated 10 December 1937: 'I am saying the absolute truth: all these recent years I honestly and sincerely carried out the party line and learned, as is only sensible [*po-umnomu*], to value you and love you.' What is important for us is not the dubious profession of love but Bukharin's insistence that he fully supported the party line. The text of the letter to future generations can be found at http://www.famhist.ru/famhist/buharina/0008cbao.htm; the text of the letter to Stalin can be found at http://stalinism.ru/dokumentyi/predsmertnoe-pismo-buharina.html. Bordiugov and Kozlov quote an archival document from late 1937 or early 1938 in which Bukharin says that since 1933 at the latest, 'there was not even the slightest indication of doubleness [*dvoistvennost*] in my attitude toward the party and the party leadership' (Bordiugov and Kozlov 1992, p. 120).

grotesque clown. Having done so, he needed a great leader for socialism and for the Soviet Union to act as counterpoint. Furthermore, Stalin and only Stalin would be leading the socialist forces in the upcoming titanic battle. If Bukharin had not managed to persuade himself that Stalin was a great leader – rather than the disastrous leader seen by Bukharin's admirers today – wouldn't he have found it psychologically difficult to summon all humanity to a cosmic battle under Stalin's banner?

4   Themes of Bukharin's Epic

These considerations make it different for me to dismiss the presence of Stalin in *Transformation of the World* as merely the result of pressure or hypocritical flattery. But to repeat: agreement on this point is *not* necessary for an analysis of the themes of Bukharin's epic as he has given it to us, to which we now turn. As a historian, my interest is in the central political message that binds together the various parts of *Transformation of the World*. I will not be commenting on the aesthetic value of Bukharin's foray into poetry, except to say that Shriver's translations are highly readable and, I feel, trustworthy. I will add nothing further to what was said earlier about the highly lyrical poems in the sections devoted to Nature and to love, nor are we concerned with the sections on Bolshevism's genealogy (Precursors and Heritage). We thus concentrate on the sections that make up the heart of the epic: Civil War, War of Worlds, Epoch of Great Works, The Future.

As we have seen throughout the case studies in this volume, Bukharin answered the question 'what was Bolshevism?' with a consistent set of themes. These themes are bound together in a narrative that went something like this: a revolution inevitably involves enormous costs (*izderzhki*, the production-costs of revolution). Sceptics seize on these costs to discredit the socialist enterprise: the timid philistine, the *obyvatel*, cannot make out the shining goal through the fire and smoke. But the workers and peasants fight with unswerving faith for the revolutionary breakthrough, because they realize that current difficulties are the only way out of an otherwise disastrous dead-end situation – the only way to buy the possibility of rapid forward progress. After a new equilibrium is restored, society will leave behind chaos and conflict and move toward a mono-organizational society in which a central authority coordinates all social institutions.

Bukharin presented the logic of this narrative argument in *Economy of the Transition Period* (1920), where he applied it to the 1917 revolution and the ensuing civil war. The metaphor of *izderzhki* – the production costs of revolution – is explored at length in this work. Starting in early 1930, Bukharin inserted Stalin's revolution from above into the same framework. A little further on, we will look at his prose exposition of Stalin's revolution. Here we will look at four individual poems to show how these themes show up in the poetry of *Transformation of the World*.

In his civil war cycle, Bukharin dedicates a whole poem to the *Osmushka*, the slang term for the horrifyingly low bread rations given out during the most intense periods of the conflict. Here are some key stanzas:

> Remember the good old *Osmushka*, eighth of a pound
> Of black bread with orache and straw mixed in?
> Gloomy and angry, the regular 'man in the street'[20]
> Considered it a cursed blight from on high.
> In those days villains had us hemmed in tight,
> The hangmen of the workers, peasants' foes.
> They drew the noose of hunger round our weakened necks,
> As typhus' dark hurricane swept people away.
> Unheated factories and homes were blackened
> By death and disease. Our destiny seemed the grave.
> But hearts burned on, with an unyielding faith,
> Determined to achieve a feat of valour ...
> The enemy teased us, waving a loaf of white bread
> Before our starving eyes, saying 'Down on your knees!'
> The people answered the Whites, prancing in their 'Eden':
> 'You take your hateful power [*vlast*] and go to hell' ...
> Now labour's springs have flowed in great abundance,
> And well-fed life's in flower all around.
> The years of starving, strenuous exertion,
> The clash of stubborn battle – all were justified.
> And now when skies are shining we remember
> Amid the blossoms of a cloudless life
> That old *Osmushka* of those hungry times.
> Eighth of a pound, it fed our folk just fine (80–82).

'Osmushka' evokes the costs of revolution and civil war; the final pay-off for all these sacrifices comes only in the early thirties: 'We're at the glorious turning

---

20   The Russian original here is very probably *obyvatel*, that is, Bukharin's long-time bête-noire, the timid philistine.

point, The time of great change is here!' (402). I earlier expressed my personal discomfort with Bukharin's image of future society as 'a triumphant symphony of creativity, a chorale ascending from earth to heaven'. In the extensive poem 'Symphony of Cooperative Labour', Bukharin resorts to this musical imagery in grand style. The poem begins with Bukharin's essential assertion: 'An epoch of great works was opened up by victorious socialism.' He goes on to call on 'sculptors of human life ... artists of plants and fields ... millions of worker-warriors ... in a harmonious chorus of labour, seeking new solutions to riddles' (413–14). Stalin-era industry is presented as the marriage of vast technical projects with 'the intense free labour of people', as 'Thought come to life, components of the Deed, links in Action's chain' (416). The poem ends with a grandiloquent climax:

> The people are composing a great Symphony of Victories,
> A titanic Chorus of Cooperative Labour, a chorus of all the peoples,
> And a sentence of death for the Thousand-Year Evil (419).

Bukharin gives us a concrete case-study of the great turning-point in another extensive poem entitled 'Pearl Necklace (Song about Kabardá)'. Kabardá is a small region on the northern slopes of the Caucasus. Bukharin was evidently a frequent visitor there and a friend of the local First Party Secretary, Betel Kalmykov. The story of Kabardá is the story of the Soviet Union in miniature. The theme of the poem is announced in the first stanza:

> The difficult years have sunk, down deep in the River Lethe,
> And never can there be a turning back to the past.
> The civil war years were tough:
> The bloody years – their time has passed.
>   The struggle was a hard one ...
> The land was abuzz with bullets
> And blood flowed all around ...
>   A rigorous broom swept through the region,
> Though many died in those bitter fights (460–2).

Kalmykov's own father was killed by the White forces. But 'at last the concerns of battle passed':

> A lovely Leninist town has been built,
> Where everyone who can study
> Must put in their time for learning ...

Harmonious labour reigned everywhere
Along with comfort and good order (463–5).

Throughout, Party Secretary Kalmykov is described in familiar cult-of-personality terms: 'Father of his native land, Apprentice to the Leader of the Peoples, A constant source of energy', he 'introduced model order everywhere' (466). (Alas, unbeknownst to Bukharin, Kalmykov had been purged by the time these words were written.) Due to drought and the kulak threat, the struggle imposed great costs, but the *narod* under party leadership responded energetically and efficiently. The result is literally a transformed world:

The cockroach type of life has ended.
The expectant mother or the sick man
No longer knows any sorrow ...
Tell about the new life that has come.
Satisfaction has spread everywhere.
No trace is left of hoof prints of the past ...
Here culture grows not daily but every hour
Like a luxuriant forest of the tropics.
The honey's pouring right into your mouth,
Not off to the side and down your whiskers (469–71).

Nevertheless, there is one last battle, one last set of imposed costs, that is looming and must be faced before the whole globe can enter the new Eden. In 'Birth of Humanity' – the final poem in the section 'War of Worlds' – we learn that

The world today stands at a turning point
And fate's decisions now will be colossal.
A quarter hour is all that's left for Capital.
Thus toll the bells in towers of oblivion ...
The gods of black and gold will meet their twilight [a sarcastic reference to Wagner].
The final conflict history will see,
Marking at last the birth of humanity,
A single family united (323–4).

'Birth of Humanity' is one of the few poems available in the original Russian. In order to give the flavour of Bukharin's poetry, here are the two quoted stanzas:[21]

---

21   For available Russian texts, see Bukharin 1996 or Bukharin 2008.

На страшном рубеже весь мир стоит сейчас,
И колоссальны будут здесь судьбы решенья.
Бьет капиталу смертный без четверти час
На башнях вечного забвенья …
И черно-золотых богов затменье
В последнем историческом бою
Ознаменует человечества рожденье,
Объединенного в одну семью.

5   The 'Anti-kulak Revolution' in Prose

A key assertion undergirding Bukharin's Bolshevik epic is that Stalin's dekulakization campaign of 1929–1930 was a painful but necessary gateway to rapid
progress toward a modernized socialist agriculture. In fact, Stalin's 'anti-kulak
revolution' (Bukharin's label) was on a higher plane than Lenin's anti-kulak
'crusade' (Bukharin's label) during the civil war.[22] The civil war crusade was
necessary to protect the worker-peasant *vlast*, but in itself it did not signify
an advance toward socialist transformation – indeed, it led to an even greater
predominance of small peasant farms in Russian agriculture. In contrast, dekulakization was needed for a breakthrough to a higher land of socialism.

We will first look at Bukharin's detailed rationale, as set out in long newspaper articles in *Pravda* and *Izvestiia* in the early 1930s, and then show how
a poetic version of the same argument becomes an integral strand in *Transformation of the World* from 1937. In the late 1920s, Bukharin had come out
in opposition to Stalin's 'extraordinary measures' that put coercive pressure
on the peasantry in order to increase grain reserves. What worried Bukharin
was the prospect of the extraordinary measures turning into a semi-permanent
system (*chrezvychaishchina*) – an outcome that would constitute a premature
abrogation of NEP and an unjustified return to the *kombedovskii* period of 1918.
Bukharin was here evoking the period when Committees of the Poor (*komitety
bednoty*) took grain from the peasant kulaks in an atmosphere of heightened class struggle within the village. A decade later, the new extraordinary-
measures-as-a-system suffered from all the defects and high costs of the *kombedy* without the life-and-death crisis that justified them.[23]

---

22   This claim can also be found in the praise directed toward Stalin by his top lieutenants,
as shown in 'Who Is Stalin? What Is He?', included in this volume. In his 1990 biography
of Stalin, Robert Tucker emphasizes Stalin's desire, not just to follow in Lenin's footsteps,
but to outdo him (*Stalin in Power: The Revolution from Above, 1928–1941*).

23   Bukharin 1989, p. 289 (transcript of Bukharin's speech to April Plenum of 1929); for

By late 1929, the extraordinary measures had morphed into a grandiose revolution from above: a 'dekulakization' campaign and a determined drive to set
up (supposedly voluntary) collective farms. Paradoxically, perhaps, this radicalization allowed Bukharin to return to the fold. His rationale is set forth in
a long *Pravda* article published on 19 February 1930. This article and another
revealing discussion of the Soviet economy published in *Izvestiia* on 12 May
1934, were usefully republished during perestroika.[24] Our interest here is not
so much in Bukharin's detailed policy rationale for Stalin's revolution from
above as the way he fits his argument into his own long-held narrative framework.

In 1928–1929, Bukharin opposed Stalin's extraordinary measures because he
equated them to the *kombedovskii* period of 1918. But now, in February 1930, he
wrote that he realized that Stalin's 'anti-kulak revolution' – Bukharin's label for
dekulakization – had only an outward resemblance to the situation in 1918. In
reality, today's 'struggle against kulakdom is itself an "organic" component of
the great socialist *construction* in the village. This is the most crucial, the most
original feature of the present situation.' And this feature of the situation meant
that 'the meaning of the process, its objective significance, is, *in principle, radically* distinct from what happened in 1918'.

The repressive extraordinary measures looked quite different to Bukharin
after he managed to see them as necessary *izderzhki*, production costs of revolution: a painful but inevitable price for entering a higher stage of development:

For the first time in history, the deformity and backwardness of the agricultural economy is moving from its stationary point and beginning to
diminish; the most ignorant, the most oppressed, the most poverty-strick-

---

instances of the term *chrezvychaishchina*, see pp. 263, 279, 283–4. My understanding of the
issues involved owes much to articles from 1988–1989 by Gennadii Bordiugov and Vladimir
Kozlov collected in *Istoriia i kon"iunktura* (Bordiugov, Gennadi and Vladimir Kozlov 1992).
Note: these authors extend the term *chrezvychaishchina* to apply to the Stalin era as a
whole. While understandable in itself, this usage obscures Bukharin's use of the term to
apply specifically to the extraordinary measures in 1929, in contradistinction to collectivization in 1930.

24   'Velikaia rekonstruktsiia' (*Pravda* article of 19 February 1930) and 'Ekonomika Sovetskoi
strany' (*Izvestiia* article of 12 May 1934), reprinted in Bukharin 1990b, pp. 488–513. Quotations in the text are marked '1930' or '1934' as appropriate. The title of the *Izvestiia* article
might be an allusion to Bukharin's 1920 *Economy of the Transition Period*. See also his
joint statement with Rykov and Tomsky, sent to the Central Committee in November 1929
(*Dokumenty svidetel'stvuiut*, edited by V.P. Danilov and N.A. Ivnitskii [Danilov and Ivnitskii
1987, pp. 276–8]).

en sector of all hitherto existing societies is moving now – not without the torments [*muki*] of the transition period – along new paths. *This is a new page in human history* [1930].

'Torments of the transition period' is the same phrase we saw in Bukharin's Preface to *Economy of the Transition Period* (1920), as quoted earlier in this essay. *Muki*, the word translated here as 'torments', can also refer to the pangs of birth. In his 1934 *Izvestiia* article, Bukharin lists all the factors that led to a permanently higher tempo of growth in social productivity. Note the emphasis on a *continuing* 'harsh [*zhestokaia*] class struggle':

The emancipation of labour power and the unleashing of the creative energy of the laborers, the annihilation of parasitic consumption, the redirection of industry toward serving the needs of agriculture, the rationalization of agriculture combined with removing the fetters of private property, the practical application of the enormous and still expanding planning principle, the mass application of science, the ever-brighter growth of culture of all those who work for society, the overcoming in harsh class struggle all that is left over from capitalism as well as all efforts to 'resist through wrecking', the growing unity of an organized and centralized will combined with the simultaneous unleashing of the widest mass initiative, and so on.

Underlying these advantages of socialism is steady progress toward creating a mono-organizational society, that is, 'a single, organizing, centralized will ... The "monopoly status" [*monopol'nost'*] of the state now gives to the village machines, personnel, chemical fertilizers, on highly advantageous terms.'

In counterpart to these permanent advantages are the temporary *izderzhki*, the imposing start-up costs, of the 'agrarian revolution'. Bukharin spells them out in his 1934 article. The starting point faced by the collectivizers was unpromising: a low economic base, the exceptionally sharp resistance of the kulaks, the individualistic habits of millions of peasants, and the start-up costs of the collective farms. The Bolsheviks were thus faced with a multi-pronged challenge: they had to crush the kulaks, overcome the wavering of the middle peasants, and create a base for the socialist application of machinery – all at the same time. 'As a result, there were *very significant* "costs" [*izderzhki*] involved in this great process of reorganization' [Bukharin's emphasis].

Prominent among those costs of revolution is 'the struggle against us by our class enemies (kulakdom, the remains of the urban bourgeoisie, the wrecker bands, the agents of international imperialism)'. The suffering experienced by the dispossessed kulaks themselves is *not* counted as a cost – only the damage inflicted on others by their resistance. The coercion visited upon the kulaks is entirely their fault: 'The "sabotage" on the part of the kulaks turned into mad resistance to socialist reconstruction. The kulak fought like a beast, and under these circumstances you can only talk with him in the language of lead.' This brutal language finds a direct echo in *Transformation of the World.*

For Bukharin, 'liquidation of kulakdom as a class' – or, as he put it in April 1929, their 'decisive crowding-out [*vytesnenie*]' – was a desired goal even during NEP, but up to late 1929 he rejected the use of violence in accomplishing this task.[25] After this date, he consistently viewed violence as an integral part of this process. How did he rationalize this change of view? First, he labelled the kulaks themselves as the aggressors, and second, he welcomed the removal of a barrier to rapid 'socialist reconstruction':

> The slogan of the liquidation of kulakdom as a class is being given flesh and blood. This chief enemy of socialist reconstruction that threw itself with fury on its steel spears [*rogatina*] has received a mortal wound. The socialist sector in the village, the shrinking of the dimensions of NEP, the ever greater progress in contract relations between proletariat and peasant organizations, remove altogether the social oxygen needed by this class. It is in its death agony, but it still has a powerful bite [1930].

The last sentence justifies yet further violence against the kulaks in the immediate future. By 1934, Bukharin can talk about a '*qualitatively new* situation, created by the growth of industry, the collectivization of agriculture, the annihilation [*unichtozhenie*] of kulakdom'.

Very typical of Bukharin's individual inflection of Bolshevism, early and late, is the contrast between the 'basic tendencies of development' versus the costs that loom so large to the sceptic and the nay-sayer. This theme shows itself in the 1930 *Pravda* article, first, by a frank recognition of the scale of the costs:

> [Contradictions] express themselves in certain barriers that must be overcome by the most intense labour efforts, yes, and sometimes by a conscious refusal of immediate benefits for the sake of tomorrow, of a future day. It would be strange if we did not see all these difficulties – ones we will not outlive in just a month. It would be criminal if we did not concen-

---

25   Bukharin 1989, p. 285 (April Plenum, 1929).

trate our passionate attention on the toughest and most urgent problems facing us today.

Nevertheless, Bukharin continues to insist that these costs are only the shadow and not the reality. This reality – 'the basic tendencies of development' – can be found only in 'the contours of the future':

> But precisely to overcome these problems, we need to see the basic contours of the future. And these contours – they're not some abstract scheme, not a sad, platonic sigh, not just 'sweet dreams' of heaven that are doomed never to become real. The contours of the future can be found in *the real tendencies of life*, in the real creativity of the masses, who are remaking both the eternal foundations of economic existence and their own nature [1930].

Bukharin once again evokes the scoffing pessimists, from Oswald Spengler to Karl Kautsky to Pavel Miliukov, who point out real difficulties but portray them as impossible to overcome. In 1934, he added to this list the 'waverers and deviationists' who were 'frightened by such swift forward movement'. Bukharin did not need to spell out for his readers that he himself had for a time been such a waverer.

In both 1930 and 1934, Bukharin invokes the global context of the threat from international imperialism:

> The first among our enemies is *international imperialism*. But in this battle there will stand with us our glorious, heroic allies, 'the proletariat of all lands', who carry in their heart their gleaming red five-pointed star and who will explode the Babylonian towers of capitalism that stand in the way of the victorious communist armies [final sentence of the 1930 *Pravda* article].

The reference to 'Babylonian towers' is an appropriately apocalyptic touch (and in the poems as well, Bukharin recalls that 'Babylon was destroyed, its grandeur turned to ashes'). Victory against imperialism will open up the path to a world communist society:

> Of course, the imperialist attack on us will require economically unproductive efforts and will weaken the tempo of our development. But the metallic and fiery language of battles will transfer the whole 'historic conversation' into another region. The costs [*izderzhki*] of these battles will

be very great. But the class enemy will be beaten there as elsewhere. And the economy of socialism will begin a new movement, and this time not only inside the borders of our country [final sentence of the 1934 *Izvestiia* article].

A key section of the poem cycle *Transformation of the World* is entitled 'Epoch of Great Works': *Epokha velikikh rabot*. The organic link between Bukharin's prose articles and the poem cycle of 1937 is brought out by the use of the same phrase – 'great [or mighty] works' – in a summary formula of Bukharin's whole outlook on current Soviet society, taken from the final paragraph of his 1930 *Pravda* article: 'We will be fighting against all our enemies for this new way of life that in torments [*v mukakh*] is forging itself in our land and that already finds its reflection in a rough draft of a *general plan of great works* [*velikikh rabot*].'

6   The 'Anti-kulak Revolution' in Poetry

We are now in a position to return to *Transformation of the World* and extricate a continuing strand that helps to tie the poems together: the theme of the kulak. From what we have seen already, the excerpts given below will require little comment. Bukharin's underlying narrative is stark: The pre-revolutionary kulak was a symbol of village backwardness under tsarism. During the civil war, the kulaks fought fiercely against the new *vlast* but were brutally subdued. The kulaks also mounted armed resistance in 1929–1930, but their defeat now signified something much higher than in 1918. The new kulak-free collective farm is a place of rapid progress and human flowering.

> Before the October revolution, this is what we see:
>   The land! How much blood, how many salt tears,
> Have been shed over you, dear land of our birth.
> The blueblood landowner, a dangerous and predatory foe,
> Kept you held tight in his imperious hand,
> And the kulak kept you under his boot heel,
> As did the monastery, gold cupola and all ...
>   The evil seed of greed, of craftiness and grasping,
> Many times led to breaking a neighbour's skull (407–8).

The desperate struggle in 1918 shows the villainy of the kulak and his complete responsibility for the conflict and its costs. The poem 'For Bread!' is devoted to this struggle:

Hunger is choking the cities,
The blood barely stirs in the veins,
Hunger's bony black hand, tenacious,
Has fastened its grip on their throat.
   Proletarian detachments
Together with poor peasant folk
Are sent to the village for help,
For the requisition of grain.
   The kulak beasts are greedy:
'No grain, no flour', they say.
Deep pits they've dug to hid it
Beneath the hut and the barn.
   Hatred is choking the kulaks.
Against the poor, the shirtless,
They've organized plots and intrigues ...
   The tavern-keeper runs to the woods
With a sawed-off gun in his hands
To set an example with lead,
A model for the kulak crowd
Against the poor, the down and out ...
   In darkness they creep through the garden
And fall on the sleeping men.
They put the sleepers to death
And flee like so many badgers
Across the ravine by the stream ...
   The iron-strong detachments
Dig up the wolves' hidden pits,
The pitch-black magpies' nests,
And take the supplies of grain
Stored away by the evildoers (94–6).

The comparison to 'badgers' is probably an allusion to the excellent 1921 novel by Leonid Leonov, *The Badgers*, on the subject of peasant resistance during the civil war.[26] No wonder Lenin called for a crusade:

---

26   An English translation of Leonov's *Badgers* [*Barsuki*] is available (Westport, CT: Hyperion Press, 1973). For a discussion of how Leonov portrays peasant attitudes, see Lih, *Bread and Authority in Russia* (Lih 1990).

Lenin put out the call: 'Crusade against the kulaks!'
With iron hand he pointed the way forward.
We overcame the foe. He had to bow
His bloody, beaten, predatory head (81).

Bukharin wanted to end his civil war cycle with 'Kulak Perdition', a poem dedicated to the 'anti-kulak revolution' of 1930. The rationale for this decision is
found in the articles in *Pravda* and *Izvestiia* discussed earlier: Bukharin aims to
drive home his view that the full meaning of the civil war is revealed only by
the breakthrough of 1930. The 'crusade' against the kulaks in 1918 was fought
only for the grain needed to survive and not yet for the higher cause of socialist transformation. Lenin's crusade is therefore trumped by 'Stalin leading the
masses' in 1930.

'Kulak Perdition' is a central linchpin for the entire poem cycle and as such
it is worth quoting extensively:

The collective farms marching!
Tractors moving, rumbling,
Stalin's leading the masses.
The kulak's gone kaput! ...
It was fun to live that way,
Have know-how, be crafty, make profits,
Dupe people and cheat,
A lifetime of good living – knowing no grief.
But now, look around,
The shirtless ones have risen up.
They're pushing us kulaks back.
Don't even look at them!
Our house was full of everything,
They took it all for the kolkhoz,
A whole wagonload.
It's the time of Sodom again!
And the kulak picks up a gun,
And he shoots and he burns,
And expects from God
All kulak miracles.
    The villagers are restless.
They start to rise to power [*vlast*].
The bloodthirsty monster
Bares wide his greedy maw.

But his whole back is broken
By the people in struggle.
His turn has come. Time for
The kulak to meet his fate.
    He lives in penal camps
And his snout has been muzzled.
He's forever gone silent.
Else they'll chain him up ...
    The whole land is prospering
And in it all are studying.
For both father and son
Life's become truly full!
    An epic hero, a giant,
The people, strides forward,
The turbulent force of its battering ram
Knocks down every enemy wall.
    Life has grown grand and good!
When the kulak is gone,
Then the peasant can live,
A lifetime of good living – knowing no grief! (410–12)

Bad vs. good: the bestial kulaks chained up in penal colonies vs. the *narod* as 'an epic hero, a giant'. 'Giant' undoubtedly translates *bogatyr*, the word used by Lenin in *What is To Be Done?* and applied to ordinary Social Democratic *praktiki* (see 'Ordinary Miracles' included in this volume). The repression of the kulaks – their elimination as a class – can be celebrated in this epic fashion because it opened the doorway to a better world. The *narod* in Kabardá 'came down on [the kulak] hard and wiped him out', and *therefore* the *narod* 'flowed like a mighty river into the *kolkhozy*' (465).

The new, kulak-free village has 'weeded out the evil nettle of graspingness', the peasant producer can now 'stand at the wheel of a machine, at the helm of the Five-Year Plan'. The village is now a place of youth and vitality, as symbolized by emancipated women such as Sasha-*traktoristka*, Sasha the tractor driver, combative and thoroughly cheerful, ready if need be to fight the imperialists who threaten her country (439–40).[27]

---

27   The theme of the emancipated Soviet woman is a prominent one in the cycle; see, for
     example, 'Women' (Bukharin 2018, pp. 436–8).

The great Soviet breakthrough of the early thirties is accompanied by the same croaking chorus of sceptics, pessimists and nay-sayers that haunted Bukharin throughout his career. In a key poem entitled 'Conversation Between Two Worlds', Bukharin pits the world of doomed capitalism against the world of nascent socialism. At each stage, from the civil war to the Five-Year Plan, the sceptics prophesy with great relish that the Bolsheviks will fail the next challenge. At each stage, the Bolsheviks overcome the challenges, earning the right to assert confidently that 'History will judge us with its favour' (321). The prophets of doom sneer at the Bolsheviks in the following call and response about 'the kulak problem':

> *The kulak soon will show his sting.*
> *Just take a look around your land.*
> *What you've got is Sodom, that's all! ...*
> But in our country, we've won
> We have solved the kulak problem.
> With cheerful stride forever onward
> The toiling folk are marching! (319)

7   Conclusions

In early 1930, Bukharin sketched out a narrative that told how Stalin solved the problems necessarily left unfinished by Lenin. The great change made possible by industrialization and collectivization opened up new perspectives and allowed rapid progress. The 'anti-kulak revolution' – coercive dekulakization – was an integral part of the great change. If you are able to think dialectically, if you put the anti-kulak revolution into the big picture and concentrate on the fundamental tendencies determining the future, you will see it as part of the inevitable start-up costs of socialist transformation. *Izderzhki* leading to *velikhie raboty* – the costs of revolution buying the possibility of rapid progress – this is the narrative framework applied by Bukharin both to the October revolution and to Stalin's revolution from above.[28] Bukharin

---

28   A subject for further inquiry is the relation, if any, between Bukharin's early description of the anti-kulak revolution in his article of February 1930 as one that is 'organized, headed, and directed by the party and the government of the revolutionary proletariat' (Bukharin 1990b, p. 501) and Stalin's triumphalist label for it in the *Short Course* of 1938 as a revolution '*from above*, on the initiative of the state' (see text added by Stalin in Brandenberger

stayed loyal to this narrative even in the prison writings. Both *Philosophical Arabesques* and *Transformation of the World* tell the story of the great change wrought by Stalin's intervention. Bukharin compares Lenin and Stalin in the final peroration of the last chapter in *Philosophical Arabesques*:

> Standing in the way of the proletariat were conditions that had to be burst through, elements that had to be understood and overcome, and elemental forces that had to be organized. Under the leadership of Lenin, a mighty dialectical materialist and a mighty master of dialectical action, the victorious revolution of the proletariat brilliantly fulfilled its numerous and daunting tasks ...
>
> Lenin did not live long enough to see the final solving of the most important question of the revolution: *kto-kovo*, who-whom [will capitalist or will socialist tendencies win out in Soviet Russia?].[29] While he was alive, socialism was only a 'sector' of the country's economy. Elemental, anarchic forces [*stikhii*] remained strong in the economy and society. There was still a great deal that had not been subordinated to the socialist rationality of the plan ...
>
> The genius of Lenin has left us. The epoch, however, creates the people it requires, and, the new steps forward of history brought forth Stalin in Lenin's place. The centre of gravity of Stalin's thought and action was the next historical crossing [*pereval*], when, under his leadership, socialism became victorious forever.[30]

These concluding words are practically a prose poem in their own right, so we are not surprised to find the same story of 'the great change' being told in Bukharin's poem cycle. A short poem entitled 'The Lever of Archimedes' celebrates progress in industry and agriculture as symbols of 'the glorious turning point':

> The moss of routine is scraped away.
> The picture's not the same as before.
> On a tractor instead of a horse
> The flag of victory flaps in the wind.

---

and Zelenov 2018, p. 548). By any chance is Bukharin the essential originator of 'revolution from above' as a label for Stalinist collectivization?

29   For the unexpected history of this famous phrase, see 'The Soviet Union and the Path to Communism', included in this volume.

30   Bukharin 2005, pp. 375–6 (translation modified after consulting Russian text).

The end has come for the wooden plough;
The separate strip worked by each peasant.
An end has come to accursed miseries.
We're at the glorious turning point,
The time of great change is here! (402)

Is there any reason why we should deny that Bukharin wanted readers to take seriously this narrative and its supporting arguments, as found in writings composed and signed by him over a number of years? One plausible reason suggests itself. Given the oppressive atmosphere of fear and paranoia in the top rungs of the Bolshevik leadership during the 1930s, given the ubiquitous threat of arrest and execution that eventually became reality – are we not obliged to dismiss flattery of Stalin as self-protective hypocrisy?

This possibility cannot be excluded and certainly courtier-like flattery plays a role. Nevertheless, I find that this description does not square with my sense of the writings themselves. Bukharin's arguments are not a perfunctory, sullen 'Yeah, okay, Stalin's the greatest'. They are long, involved, detailed, and written with energy and verve. They dovetail with long-standing themes in Bukharin's outlook that occur and reoccur constantly in his oeuvre. Bukharin's narrative of the great change is maintained consistently from the time he first formulated it in *Pravda* in early 1930 all the way to his final writings in prison in late 1937. If all this is insincere flattery – the mask of a *dvurushnik* – it is a mask that is highly elaborate and lovingly sculpted.

But – some readers may ask – wasn't Bukharin the primary leader of the Right Deviation that defended NEP and opposed forced collectivization? This description of Bukharin's position is widespread, but it is not correct. Bukharin and the Right Deviation opposed the 'extraordinary measures' that put coercive pressure on 'kulaks' and peasant grain producers in general, measures that were put in place by Stalin's government in 1928–1929. Bukharin argued at the April Plenum in 1929 that the collective farms were still far in the future and they were therefore no solution for present problems. *Under these circumstances,* coercion was a dangerous and counter-productive substitute for a NEP-style market link with small peasant farms.

But when circumstances changed, when the drive toward mass collectivization swung into high gear in late 1929 and early 1930, Bukharin got on board. There is no evidence he disapproved of mass collectivization at any time – on the contrary. He not only accepted but enthusiastically endorsed the violence of the anti-kulak revolution. And, given what he evidently considered a real change in the empirical situation, his change of heart is not at all inconsistent with his argument in 1929–1929. If collective farms had really moved out of the future into the present, then the original protest of the Right Deviation against dekulakization and consequent abridgement of NEP lost much of its force. The 'extraordinary measures' were *not* turning into a semi-permanent system but leading to a qualitatively new system.[31]

In the end, the slanderous vitriol thrown at Bukharin by Stalin in passages that he personally added to the *Short Course* of Bolshevik party history (1938) has aided Bukharin's posthumous reputation much more than it harmed him. According to Stalin, Bukharin had a 'kulak soul' and his later protestations about loyalty and changed views were sickening hypocrisy.[32] For late- and post-Soviet society, what better recommendation could there be for Bukharin? He defended sturdy and efficient peasant farmers and he continued to be part of the resistance to Stalin, to the extent permitted by circumstances. But Bukharin himself was mortally offended by Stalin's portrait – and, from his point of view, correctly so.

Still, is it possible that Bukharin could be sincere when he praised the duplicitous tyrant who destroyed his life? Surely Bukharin was well aware of Stalin's evil nature? Perhaps so. Yet history shows no small number of murderous tyrants who at the same time – in the view of some informed observer or other – changed the course of history by instituting progressive change. Surely Bukharin could believe at one and the same time that Stalin was suspicious, vindictive, remorseless *and* a great leader capable of seeing the big picture and solving profound historical tasks. And when we look at the evidence, we see that while Bukharin wavered back and forth in his view of Stalin's personal characteristics, he never wavered in his support for the party line defined by Stalin.

Many of those who have written on Bukharin during this period are much more interested in decoding subversive messages than in ascertaining his explicit message. But, as I suggested earlier, using Aesopian language to undermine the Soviet Union's heroic self-image or even to equate Stalin's Russia with fascism is fundamentally incompatible with Bukharin's intensely emotional call for an anti-fascist crusade led by the Soviet Union.

---

31   One could certainly maintain that the *chrezvychaishchina* did in fact turn into a semi-permanent system of extra-legal coercion in Stalin's Russia. Nevertheless, this argument is not found in Bukharin's writings.

32   'The Party saw that the hollow speeches of these gentry [Bukharin, Rykov and Tomsky] were in reality meant for their supporters outside the congress, to serve as a lesson to them in *dvurushnichestvo*, and a call to them not to lay down their arms' (see Brandenberger and Zelenov 2018, pp. 526, 584–5).

Decoding secret messages runs into methodological problems, because the result often seems arbitrary and tendentious. The Russian writer B. Ia. Frezinskii cites the following passage from *Philosophical Arabesques* as an example of 'hidden allusions' to Stalin's misdeeds:

> It is possible to think in a restricted, formal manner, and on the basis of these limited (that is, one-sided and hence wrong) reflections of reality, to formulate tactics and act accordingly. In these circumstances errors, 'political errors', will be completely inevitable; they will proceed from the mistaken positions [*ustanovki*] with all the force of inevitability even in a favourable political conjuncture, and in an unfavourable one may serve to doom everything.[33]

According to Frezinskii, 'in these words of Bukharin is felt an echo of his struggle with the Stalinist program of practice of using violence to establish cooperative farms among the peasantry'.[34] In my view, however, Bukharin is not condemning Stalin but rather apologizing for his own 'one-sidedness' (*odnobokost*, a grave dialectical sin) when he opposed Stalin in 1928–1929. There is no way to judge which interpretation is correct simply from this particular abstract remark. We can only proceed from a larger reading of Bukharin's relevant writings.

All of the objections outlined above point to genuinely thorny questions of interpretation. I am far from certain about any of the arguments I have made above, but I am certain about this: whatever our views about Bukharin's sincerity or his hidden polemics with Stalin, we cannot evade the essential historical task of ascertaining what he explicitly argued and what he must have assumed most people would understand him to be saying.

We will never really know much about Bukharin's inner life. Still, I will allow myself one bout of speculation. In earlier essays, I suggested that perhaps Bukharin's fixation with sceptics who saw only the costs and not the historical big picture was an indication of his own inner struggle to keep his faith and confidence intact despite the ruin and social breakdown of the civil war. This determination to look pasts the *izderzhki* that otherwise could only horrify him may help account for some of his arguments in the 1930s.

This same lifelong war with scepticism and pessimism, however, may have led to an abiding sense of guilt over his own episode of nay-saying in 1928–

---

33   Bukharin 2008, p. 336 (translation modified after consulting Russian text).
34   Frezinskii, Introduction to *Philosophical Arabesques* in Bukharin 2008, pp. 220–38.

1929. At the April Plenum in 1929, Anastas Mikoyan scoffed at Bukharin's stand: 'all the time it's we're doomed, doomed!'[35] Bukharin ably defended himself in response, but nevertheless he must have felt appalled that *he* was being portrayed as what he most loathed: a defeatist, nay-saying pessimist.[36] He must have felt genuine relief when he could switch back to seeing the big picture and celebrating the rapid progress that justified the *izderzhki* of revolution.

Even when unjustly imprisoned, Bukharin remained true to himself. The same arguments, the same modes of thought, that he employed on the outside were reproduced inside the prison walls. Most of all, he remained loyal to his passionate, life-defining commitment to the mission of revolutionary Marxism – as incarnated in Russian and then world Bolshevism – to lead mankind to a better society and a better world. Standing on the edge of a precipice, Bukharin expressed his faith in terms as universal as possible. In time, he looks back to human origins and forward to a communist society that conquers death. In the realm of human experience, he evoked the intimate, the evanescent, the emotional, as well as political militancy and fervour. He surveyed Nature from micro to macro, from electrons to galaxies, from the familiar to the remote. In the realm of intellectual inquiry, he rushed to champion dialectical materialism against all comers, from the cranks to the seers.

Looking at the world around him, he assumed a prophetic stance and envisioned an almost cosmic clash in the near future. Like it or not, both Lenin and Stalin are part of this drama and they cannot be taken out: the great leaders, the embodiment of dialectical materialism in political action. A fervent Soviet patriot, Bukharin saw his country leading the way into the future. The prison writings are his monument and, I am sure, the way he wanted to be remembered.

---

35   Bukharin 1989, p. 227 (Mikoyan: *Gibnem, gibnem vse vremia*).

36   In his letter of December 1937 to Stalin, he writes: 'I am not a Christian. But I have my peculiarities. I believe that I am paying for the years when I really did lead a struggle' (that is, 1928–1929).

Show Trials in the Stalin Era: On Stage and in Court

Take for example the now famous stenographic report of the trial
of Bukharin and others. Don't regard it as a document, for it is not
a document; don't think about methods of investigation, about why
Krestinsky first offered one story and then others. Regard it as a work
of art. And you will agree that you've never read anything like it in all
of world literature. What well-defined characters! What a grandiose
plot, and how cohesive and integrated everything was. It's just too
bad that the characters were living people, otherwise you might be
able to stand reading it.

VLADIMIR VOINOVICH, *The Ivankiad*

∴

In 1935, the Soviet literary critic Abram Gurvich confidently predicted that
socialist reality would give rise to a new dramatic genre:

The old world created a magnificent genre of its own – tragedy – and can
justly take pride ... It is the highest monument of pre-socialist culture.
Nothing was as successful for that culture as a dramatic form which portrayed the path of man to ruin ...

In full correspondence to the new conditions of our reality, there arises
a completely new motif that is directly opposed to the old tragedy. Here
despair, decline, catastrophe appears as the starting point, and then these
are gradually overcome and bring the hero to self-affirmation, to a natural
and free existence. Man travels toward life. There we have death, here we
have birth.[1]

---

1 A. Gurvich, *V poiskakh geroia* (Gurvich 1938, p. 348). This essay was originally published in
2002 in *Imitations of Life: Two Centuries of Melodrama in Russia*, edited by Louise McReynolds
and Joan Neuberger (McReynolds and Neuberger 2002). Due to new information about this
topic and especially about Aleksandr Afinogenov, I have added an 'Update 2021' at the end of
the essay.

Gurvich called for a genre that would start with an acknowledgement of the trouble and strife in the world but then move toward a ringing affirmation of harmony. But as it happens, the 'old world' had produced just such a genre in the previous century: melodrama. Can the outlook and procedures of nineteenth-century melodrama and its subgenres help us understand the kind of mythic political narrative that Gurvich wanted to see reflected on the stage? Yes: melodramatic elements lay at the very heart of the constitutive myths of the pre-war Soviet Union.

By paying close attention to these melodramatic elements, important shifts in Soviet political myths can be mapped. In this essay, I will use two subgenres of nineteenth-century melodrama to analyse one such shift that occurred during the 1930s. Early in the decade, party-minded playwrights produced a type of drama I shall call political temperance drama. The label is taken from the temperance drama developed in the mid-nineteenth century by anti-alcohol activists in the United States. Political temperance drama portrays a struggle for the loyalty of 'the waverer' – the peasant, the intellectual, the backward worker – caught between revolution and counterrevolution. As the 1930s wore on, political temperance drama faded: the official myth was now that the waverers had all been convinced. One paradoxical consequence of this assertion was a sombre melodrama whose dynamics are very similar to the classical melodrama of Guilbert de Pixerécourt and his contemporaries at the beginning of the nineteenth century.

The narrative behind this new political myth can be traced directly to Stalin. Instead of the waverer, the spotlight was now placed on the slanderous villain that Stalin labelled the *dvurushnik* (usually translated 'double-dealer'). Soviet society was convulsed by an imposed melodrama whose climactic scene in the Moscow show trials was meant to definitively rip the mask off the *dvurushnik*. The relative confidence of political temperance drama was replaced by the barely controlled hysteria of Stalin's version of classical melodrama.

1   The Struggle for Recognition: Two Types of Melodrama

A bit of rapid-fire dialogue from a play by Pixerécourt with the evocative name *L'homme à trois visages* (1801) gives us the archetypal situation of classical melodrama: protest against a villain's slander. Vivaldi, a Venetian nobleman, has been successfully framed by the villainous Count Orsano. Rosemonde, who is secretly married to Vivaldi, defends him as she talks with her father, the Doge of Venice, who regards Vivaldi as a justly condemned traitor:

Doge:	So, the decree that condemns him ...
Rosemonde:	Is unjust.
Doge:	His crime ...
Rosemonde:	Imaginary.
Doge:	The proofs ...
Rosemonde:	Assumed.
Doge:	His accuser ...
Rosemonde:	A monster who sought revenge for my scorn by persecuting the most ardent soul and the most zealous servant of the republic.[2]

This excerpt illustrates the basic conflict that defines classical melodrama. It involves three basic forces: the villain, the slandered victim and her or his defenders, and the recognizer, that is, the basically good person who is tempted to believe the villain. The suspense of the plot derives from this question: will the recognizer see through the villain's mask of virtue and restore the victim's rightful place in the community?

The technical term in French theatre for the villain of melodrama is *traître*.[3] The term is useful because it shows that the villain's slanders are at the same time an attack on a virtuous community: by slandering a member of this community in good standing, the *traître* is also seducing the community into committing an injustice. In *L'homme à trois visages*, the *traître*'s threat to the community is made explicit: the slanderous Count Orsano is also preparing a coup d'état against the Doge. The *traître* is not motivated by any competing ideal or alternate conception of virtue. He represents the anti-community, whose mission is to destroy virtue by smearing it with 'infamy' (a key concept in classical melodrama). Thus the *traître* is not a self-righteous hypocrite who believes his own accusation: he is always perfectly lucid about his own evil motives.

The force that resists the *traître* is composed of the victim and her or his defenders. The vindication of the victim's virtue requires the active initiative of people who understand the vital importance of uncovering the truth and who are able to perceive it when clouded by false appearances. As in later Bolshevik conceptions of political leadership, moral leadership in the melodrama consists principally of dispersing false consciousness.

---

2 Pixerécourt, *Théâtre choisi*, 4 vols (Pixerécourt 1971, 1:199–200); my translations in text. Lack of space constrains me to give only a general acknowledgement of my debt to the many insightful observers who have written about melodrama from Pixerécourt's day to ours.

3 I will keep *traître* in French to mark it as technical term and distinguish it from 'traitor'.

Although the recognizer – the Doge in our example – is often a minor character, he nevertheless has the pivotal function of deciding the outcome of the battle between those who wish to maintain the virtuous community and those who wish to destroy it. In order to fulfil this function, the recognizer must be fundamentally upright but also vulnerable to being taken in by false appearances. The recognizer thus represents the community. The climax of classical melodrama is the community's moment of recognition of the truth about both the victim and the *traître*. The virtuous community is then reconstituted by casting out – purging – the *traître*.

Although the recognizer has a pivotal function in classical melodrama, he remains a secondary character: the main spotlight is on the clash between slanderous villain and wronged victim. In contrast, temperance drama puts the recognizer front and centre while the *traître* and the victim recede to the sidelines. The *traître* and victim now act as the two opposing poles of attraction who fight for influence through and within the recognizer: the seductive villain who represents the dissolute anti-community of Prince Alcohol vs. the weeping wife who represents the virtuous community of home and hearth. The suspense of temperance drama comes from the question: will the drunkard recognize the virtuous community as his true home or will he be seduced by the anti-community of the saloon and its disreputable denizens?

The key assumption of temperance drama is that the drunkard cannot stand still: he can travel in either direction but he must keep moving along the one-dimensional 'road to ruin' until he either ends up at complete ruin or makes the return journey to complete salvation. The drunkard is not really making choices based on his own individual psychology: he is the site of a struggle between virtue and vice, the prize for which they contend. He is thus trapped within a force-field that will not allow him either to stay in one spot for any length of time or to strike out in another direction altogether or even to think of his life as something other than a road between ruin or salvation. The temperance drama ends either by showing 'the fallen saved' in the bosom of his family or by showing the drunkard 'a bloated corpse ... in a lonely room'.[4]

Each of these two types of melodrama flirts with an hysteria in which unknown and deeply frightening forces are out of control. In classical melodrama, the potential hysteria comes from anxiety about masks: the double fear of being slandered and of being misled. Masks allow single individuals to do

---

4   William W. Pratt, *Ten Nights in a Barroom* (1858) in Michael Booth, ed., *Hiss the Villain: Six English and American Melodramas* (Booth 1964, p. 199); W.H. Smith's *The Drunkard, or The Fallen Saved* can be found in Richard Moody, ed., *Dramas from the American Theatre 1762–1909* (Moody 1966).

immense damage to the community. In temperance drama, the fear of other people's weaknesses and an exaggerated view of their eagerness to be seduced lead easily to hysteria and moral panic: take a single drink and you may end up a corpse upon the floor! In both cases, hysteria resolves itself into a view of the community under siege from hidden enemies within.

2   'The Waverer Redeemed': Political Temperance Drama

Soviet Marxism is sometimes said to have described the world in terms of vast impersonal forces. Vast, yes; impersonal, no. Pre-revolutionary Russian radicals debated the active forces (*dvizhushchie sily*) of the coming revolution: these forces interacted and struggled as the dramatis personae (*deistvuiushchie litsa*) of an epic world-historical drama. As heirs to pre-war 'revolutionary Social Democracy', the Bolsheviks saw the main characters of this drama as social classes struggling to impose their vision on society as a whole. A key theme in the plot of this doctrinal myth was leadership: the party's ability to lead the proletariat and the proletariat's ability to lead other classes.[5]

In a speech in 1933 on the tasks of Soviet drama, the Bolshevik 'commissar of enlightenment', Anatoly Lunacharsky, summed up one aspect of the Bolshevik myth of leadership in a pithy aphorism: *Proletariat – velikii klass-vospitatel.* A *vospitatel* is a teacher in a very broad sense. The noun *vospitanie* is usually translated 'upbringing': it signifies a blend of education, transformational leadership, behaviour modification and 'reforging'. I shall translate it as 'education'. Lunacharsky's dictum thus means: 'The proletariat's greatness is that it is a class that educates.' The proletariat's educational efforts are directed towards 'the waverer' (*kolebliushchiisia*), a key term in Bolshevik doctrine:

[The proletariat] educates the poor peasants and middle peasants, it educates the rural proletariat that is so close to it, it educates its own backward strata, it re-educates its own self, it educates the intelligentsia – which requires a great deal of education, right up to the most learned academic.[6]

The battle for the soul of the waverer is the central theme of three classics of Soviet theatre from the early 1930s that I call 'political temperance drama':

---

5 For further discussion of Bolshevik views of political leadership, see 'Ordinary Miracles: Lenin's Call for Revolutionary Ambition,' included in this volume.
6 Lunacharsky in *Sovetskie dramaturgi o svoem tvorchestve* (Pimenov 1967, p. 28).

Optimistic Tragedy (*Optimisticheskaia tragediia*) by Vsevolod Vishnevsky, *Bread* (*Khleb*) by Vladimir Kirshon and *Fear* (*Strakh*) by Aleksandr Afinogenov.[7] These plays were the product of a short-lived window of opportunity for serious dramatization of Soviet political myth. During the first decade after the revolution, committed Bolshevik playwrights were so absorbed by the titanic struggle of the Russian civil war that they gave scant attention to the problems of post-revolutionary society. After this period, they were no longer able to discuss real issues even for the purpose of assimilating them into myth: serious and honest myth-making became tawdry and evasive myth-making.

As in nineteenth-century temperance drama, these plays portray the struggle between virtuous community and anti-community. On one side stands 'models of socialist consciousness [whose] example will help in the socialist rebirth of those who have not yet freed themselves from the weight of the old slavish feelings, ideas and habits'. On the other side stand those who embody the pull of these slavish feelings.[8]

Waverers can only join the virtuous community by disciplining anarchic self-assertion and recognizing the virtuous community as an expression of their true individuality. This is the moral of Vishnevsky's *Optimistic Tragedy* – a moral expressed even better by the rejected title 'Out of Chaos'.[9] The central conflict in *Optimistic Tragedy* is over the self-identity of a band of anarchist sailors during the civil war: are they a self-governing 'detachment' or will they accept the discipline that befits a 'regiment' that is integrated into a larger whole? The waverers who will decide the outcome of the struggle are Aleksei, an anarchist sailor and Behring, a former tsarist naval officer. They are caught in a force-field set up by two opposing and mutually repellent poles: the sailor's anarchist chief, the Vozhak, vs. the female Commissar sent by the party. Vishnevsky's plot may remind today's readers of movies in which a gutsy female teacher civilizes a classroom of unruly juvenile delinquents.

The anarchist Vozhak, for all his influence over his fellow sailors, is ultimately only a parody *vozhd* (a Russian word meaning 'inspiring leader' that was regularly applied to Stalin in particular). When the Commissar comes on board,

---

7 For a discussion of actual temperance plays during the Soviet period, see Julie Cassiday's 'Alcohol is our enemy! Soviet temperance melodramas of the 1920s' (Cassiday 2002).

8 Lunacharsky in Pimenov 1967, p. 40.

9 *Optimistic Tragedy* was written in 1932 and published in 1933; it was then heavily revised for the Moscow production in late 1933. The revised version was published in 1934 and is now the canonical text. My analysis is based for the most part on the original version as published in 1933 (Vishnevsky 1933), since the contours of the underlying myth show up even more starkly than in the canonical version.

he says, 'Don't worry, we'll educate [*vospitat*] her'; of course, he fails miserably. Although in the past the Vozhak has earned his revolutionary credentials, he has degenerated and reveals his nihilist sentiments in a semi-aside to his henchman, after giving the sailor Aleksei a Judas-kiss:

> Don't trust either him or her [the Commissar]. (Wipes his lips with distaste and spits.) I've kissed a reptile. [His henchman asks: 'who should I trust? Only you?'] Not me either. We're all lying cattle. Everybody has been poisoned. We must cut at the root: the old life still lives on in each of us.

The self-contradiction underlying the Vozhak's anti-community stance is grasped by Aleksei in his moment of insightful recognition: 'You are a denier of power [*vlast*] who has seized power!'[10]

The party's outraged innocence is presented in standard melodramatic fashion by means of an attempted gang rape of the female Commissar (the Vozhak thinks that this would be an effective means of 'education'). The Commissar's first act of leadership and counter-education is to shoot down her attacker. The attempted rape shows the horrors that result when virtue is not accorded proper status: the horror is not that a *woman* is being raped but that a *party representative* is being raped. As the Commissar says, 'Well, who else wants to try out a commissar's body?'[11]

Political temperance drama typically reveals both confidence and a potential for hysteria. Vishnevsky shows confidence when he allows Aleksei and Behrens to voice genuine doubts about accepting Bolshevik discipline. The hysteria potential can be glimpsed in the final act of the play. The anarchist threat lives on – in devious cloaked form – even after the virtuous community has been established by the condemnation and execution of the Vozhak. The Vozhak's henchman Gravel-Voice (*Siplyi*) is a physical embodiment of the degenerating anti-community: syphilis is destroying his body just as alcohol destroys the bodies of its votaries. The community foolishly allows him to stay on after the Vozhak's execution, and he literally stabs them in the back: his murder of a sentry leads to the destruction of the whole community, including the Commissar. This is a parable of the dangers created by masked enemies posing as loyal members of the virtuous community.

In the literary polemics that pepper the first version of his play, Vishnevsky made clear his preference for a melodramatic approach. This helps to account

---

10   Vishnevsky 1933, pp. 22, 53–4.
11   'Ну, кто еще хочет попробовать комиссарского тела?' (Vishnevsky 1933, p. 15).

for his decision to give the roles of slandered victim and defender to a single female character. A melodrama victim was typically an unprotected woman who revealed the vulnerability of the community as well as its ultimate power to protect its own. In the same way, the Commissar dramatically reveals the power of the party that acts through her. She opposes Aleksei's male anarchism with the female schoolmarmism of the party. At the same time, she represents the party's secret feeling of self-pity as a slandered and misunderstood force for good. The dark unruly masses may try to rape the party, so it has to shoot back. But that's only to get their attention: soon the party's innate virtue will be recognized by all.

Vishnevsky pictured the civil war as a struggle for the loyalty of waverers. In *Bread* (1930), Vladimir Kirshon does the same for collectivization. Although an emergency grain collection is the explicit issue, the play's subtext is the mass collectivization drive that was underway in 1929–1930. Kirshon had earlier served his apprenticeship writing political melodramas of a lurid type, for example, relating the adventures of a daring group of Komsomol youths foiling the efforts of a gang of White Guard saboteurs. By 1930, he had become one of the pioneers of political temperance drama.[12]

Bread has two intertwined plots. In one, the waverer is the peasant village as a whole, forced to choose between two contending poles: the kulaks vs. the party. In the other plot, the waverer is a party leader who shows signs of incipient deviation and degeneration. The two plots drive each other: the degeneration of the party leader reveals itself in political mistakes that almost tip the balance in the village toward the kulaks. The most vivid character in the village story is the kulak leader Kvasov. I cite one of his speeches at length to show just how forcefully political temperance drama could allow its negative characters to speak:

> We have gathered here, dear guests, in secret. In our own home village, we must hide our heads from everybody. We must behave as if we were in the house of a stranger where we don't belong. Yet who are we? We are the foundation. The belly of Mother Russia is filled with our bread. It is we who clothe Moscow, we who provide shoes for her, we who feed her. But who orders us about? Ragged tramps, beggars, drunkards.
>
>   Those in Moscow are hardly worried about that. Russia for them is just a field for experiments. They want to raise a special brand of European

12   On Kirshon's early career, see L. Tamashin, *Vladimir Kirshon: Ocherk tvorchestva* (Tamashin 1965); for *Bread*, see Kirshon, *Khleb* (Kirshon 1933); Kirshon, *Izbrannoe* (Kirshon 1958); Eugene Lyons, *Six Soviet Plays* (Lyons 1934); A. Gurvich, *Tri dramaturgi* (Gurvich 1936).

herb on it. On that field we are the poisonous weeds – the broom-rape, the wild grass. They've begun to weed us out. By the roots they are weeding us out. They're mowing us down with a scythe. The hour has come when we must either lie down under the scythe or shout so that all Russia can hear us: 'You're wrong, you Moscow agronomists! We're not weeds – we're oaks!'[13]

This is explosive material: an accurate portrayal of a counter-myth that in the long run has proved more durable than the Bolshevik myth itself. Today this speech would be applauded rather than hissed. To undercut the power of this counter-myth, Kirshon uses devices from nineteenth-century melodrama to portray his villain. The kulak Kvasov relies on slander and defamation of the virtuous community consisting of the builders of socialism. He claims that the workers are living high on the hog while the peasants starve. On a more personal level, he lies to his own daughter after she begins to recognize the superior virtues of the party representatives: he tells her that the party people sneered at her. As the play draws to a climax, Kvasov uses vodka to incite a crowd of supporters who trample through the village – he is so carried away with the struggle that he gives orders to burn down a hut even though his own son is inside.[14]

Bread shows how the party's relations with the peasants could be structured as a melodrama: the party battles for the allegiance of the waverers, supremely confident that that proper leadership will be able to dispel the slander of the kulaks. The village plot thus shows relative confidence. The party plot shows more potential for stoking the hysteria that results when any and all members of the virtuous community itself are seen as potential masked enemies. Here the waverer is Raevsky, a party official who has taken the first steps down the primrose path toward deviation and opposition. Raevsky is not ill-intentioned, but his capacity for self-deception and his self-dramatizing nature come close to inciting a peasant rebellion. As the play ends, it is still unclear whether 'self-criticism' will be able to halt him on his road to ruin.[15] Like any waverer, Raevsky will keep moving until he ends up firmly ensconced in one of the two communities that are struggling in and through him. If he continues in the direction

---

13   Kirshon 1933, p. 72; Lyons 1934, p. 290.
14   A similar outcome is found in Meyerbeer's 1836 opera about religious civil war *Les Huguenots*.
15   *Bread* is a narrative version of Stalin's March 1930 article 'Dizzy with Success' (*Golovokruzhenie ot uspekhov*) calling for a halt in the excesses of the collectivization campaign – or rather, *Bread* reveals the underlying melodramatic structure of Stalin's intervention.

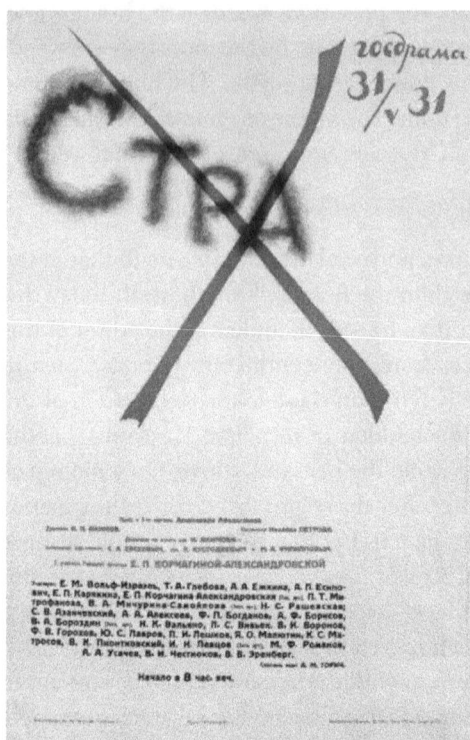

FIGURE 2
A theatrical poster evokes *Fear*
HTTPS://GOSLITMUZ.RU/POSTER/
9128/, LAST ACCESSED 11 JUNE
2023)

of the anti-community, he could very well turn into a masked *dvurushnik* with an enormous potential for stabbing the party in the back.

Aleksandr Afinogenov's *Fear* (1931) looks at waverers among the intellectuals. It allows its main character, Professor Borodin, to stand up and express the slanderous thought that Soviet reality was based entirely on fear. Borodin's indictment is so powerful that during the perestroika era Afinogenov was portrayed, quite unconvincingly, as a daring subversive critic of Stalinism – even though *Fear* was hailed immediately after its first production in 1931 as one of the outstanding successes of the new socialist theatre.[16] See the striking poster for a production of *Fear* (Страх) (Figure 2 above).

According to the categories of the time, *Fear* is a 'psychological drama' that deals with the inner conflicts of individuals. Yet Professor Borodin is less an individual than the site of a struggle between contending forces. He dominates

---

16   *Strakh* in Aleksandr Afinogenov, *Izbrannoe*, 2 vols (Afinogenov 1977, p. 243); Lyons 1934, pp. 468–9. For twenty-first-century discussions of Afinogenov, see 'Update 2021' at the end of this essay.

the play not because of his powerful personality but because he is the central waverer and, as such, the most visible expression of the play of forces. The plot is set in motion by Professor Borodin's distrust of the new standards of social promotion: his daughter doesn't win a sculpture contest, his student is not chosen to go abroad, he himself is forced to take on a young proletarian woman as an assistant and so forth. Feeling that virtue and status are growing apart from each other, he begins to gather material that will allow him to chronicle all the resentment felt by the losers under the system. He expresses their indictment in a great public speech of accusation.

But Borodin is not a slanderous villain like the kulak Kvasov: he is a waverer who can be still won over. The process starts with a counter-speech by Klara, an older woman who is a party member of long standing. When Borodin is taken away to GPU offices, he begins to recognize the true nature not only of Klara but of the people who had tried to make use of his speech for anti-Soviet purposes. These demoralized members of the anti-community betray each other as well as Professor Borodin. Borodin ends his wavering when he admits after his release that he had lost sight of the big picture: 'I joyously greeted every manifestation of fear and I failed to notice fearlessness. I welcomed the madness of Kimbaev, and I overlooked the growth of his reason.'[17]

As usual, the predominant note of confidence is accompanied by more unsettling images. The plot depends on the assumption that a band of conspirators and dupes could take over a scientific institute and use it for anti-Soviet purposes. Incipient hysteria can be heard in the suspicious remarks of Borodin's proletarian assistant:

On the surface it seems to be all right ... But then – then all of this material accumulated by us – the professor takes with him into his private study, where he locks himself in and works on it all by himself. We scientific workers are in the position of slaves who deliver the raw material to some mysterious factory. But we want to know now what is being manufactured in that factory – whether it's boots or wax candles, or poison gas.[18]

---

17   Kimbaev is a young Kazakh whose 'thirst for knowledge and intellectual zeal skirt the edge of the ludicrous' (Harold Segel, *Twentieth-Century Russian Drama: From Gorky to the Present* [Segel 1993, p. 242]).

18   Afinogenov 1977, p. 216; Lyons 1934, p. 432. Compare state prosecutor Andrei Vyshinsky in the Moscow show trial of 1938: 'Who else [but a high official like Chernov] could set up factories specially for the preparation of infections serums? He alone. And he did it. He has himself told us here that 25,000 horses were destroyed at his behest' (*Report of Court Proceedings in the Case of the Anti-Soviet 'Bloc of Rights and Trotskyites'* [*Report* 1938, p. 674]).

Like the other political temperance plays, *Fear* makes use of tried-and-true melodramatic devices. One such device is the angel-child, whose function is to see through the veils that we adults put over things and then to lead us to our better selves. Nineteenth-century angel-children such as Eva in *Uncle Tom's Cabin* or Joe Morgan's daughter in *Ten Nights* receive their special grace because they are close to death and to heaven. Afinogenov's angel-child is named Natasha. Although she is hardly mentioned in critical accounts of *Fear*, Natasha is actually quite important for the mechanics of the plot. Her special grace comes not from her closeness to death but from her connection to the future. In contrast to the villain who sings naughty Maurice Chevalier songs, Natasha sings pure and innocent Young Pioneer songs. She also lisps such sentiments as these: 'Papa, which is the greater menace – a Left deviation or a Right deviation? I think that the greatest menace is the *dvurushniki*.' Or this: 'Syeryozhka was expelled from our [Young Pioneer] detachment ... Our detachment leader [*vozhatyi*] said that if Seryozhka could deceive the detachment, he could deceive the working class ... And do you know who the most important leader [*vozhatyi*] is? You don't? Well, I know: it's the Party.'[19]

Thus out of the mouth of the angel-child comes the prevailing sentiment of the play: a horror of deception and masks. When Natasha eavesdrops and discovers her father has been covering up his bourgeois origins, she is devastated. Her horrified reaction signals his moral doom: 'Papa! where have you gone? You have deceived the working class. You have deceived the leader [*vozhatyi*].'[20] In contrast, Natasha seeks out the good characters and leads them into the virtuous community. In the play's final scene, she completes the rebirth of the chastened and lonely Professor Borodin, who begins to see life anew and to murmur, 'Ah, to be fourteen years old again!'

For these playwrights, melodrama was not just a way of popularizing a political outlook: it *was* a political outlook. They resorted to melodramatic devices not through clumsy inexperience but because these devices were tried and true ways of getting across the underlying doctrinal myth about the struggle to enlist the waverer into the virtuous community. The waverers – the anarchist sailors in *Optimistic Tragedy*, the peasants in *Bread*, the intellectuals in *Fear* – must learn to accept the discipline needed to carry out the tasks of the virtuous community. They must learn that the anti-community promises only an ultimately demoralizing false freedom. Each of these plays flirts with hysteria in ways that foreshadow the coming obsession with masked *traîtres*

---

19   Afinogenov 1977, pp. 197, 213; Lyons 1934, pp. 409, 428.
20   Afinogenov 1977, p. 215; Lyons 1934, p. 431.

within the virtuous community. But the dominant note remains one of confidence. If the virtuous community can overcome the doubts and hesitations
of its own members, it can then exert the kind of leadership that will put
the waverer in touch with his deeper and better self. The story ends with the
waverer's triumphant recognition of and acceptance by the builders of socialism.

3   'The *Dvurushnik* Unmasked': Stalin's Melodrama

In the mid-thirties, Stalin claimed that the virtuous community had triumphed
in real life, since the foundations of socialism had been laid in the Soviet Union
and the waverers had all been won over. Unfortunately, the curtain did not go
down at this point. Pushed front and centre was a new figure who was very
much like the slanderous *traître* of classical melodrama: the *dvurushnik*.

A Soviet dictionary defines *dvurushnik* as 'someone who, under the mask of
loyalty to someone or something, acts in the interest of the enemy'. The Stalinist textbook of party history, the *Short Course*, elaborates: 'political *dvurushnik*s
are an unprincipled gang of political careerists who, having long ago lost the
confidence of the people, strive to insinuate themselves once more into their
confidence by deception, by chameleon-like changes of colour, by fraud, by any
means, only that they might retain the title of political figures'.[21] In other words,
the *dvurushnik* can be called *l'homme à deux visages*.

The *dvurushnik* was the chief villain and driving force of a vast melodramatic narrative in which the Moscow show trials were only a single if climactic episode. A case can be made for regarding Stalin himself as the author of
this narrative, since it is presented with peculiar intensity in his speeches as
well as in authoritative pronouncements such as the *Short Course*. Stalin's justification for the trials and the purges of 1936–1938 is usually described as a
theoretical argument about 'the intensification of the class struggle in pro-
portion to the advance toward socialism'.[22] Stalin did come close to advancing a theoretical argument of this kind in 1928–30, on the eve of a genuine
intensification of what Bolsheviks called the class struggle. But as we shall see,

21   S.I. Ozhegov, *Slovar russkogo iazyka* (Ozhegov 1970, p. 149); *History of the Communist Party
       of the Soviet Union (Bolsheviks): Short Course* (*History* 1939, p. 291). The new critical edition
       of the *Short Course* reveals that this definition of *dvurushniki* comes directly from Stalin
       (Brandenberger and Zelenov 2018, pp. 517–21).
22   This particular formulation of a common interpretation is taken from Oleg Khlevniuk,
       Mekhanismy politicheskoi vlasti v 1930-e gody (Khlevniuk 1996, p. 194).

the *dvurushnik* narrative of the 1930s was actually based on quite a different premise: the triumph of the virtuous community and the resulting proliferation of masks.

The *dvurushnik* narrative covers the years 1932 to 1938. The following account is based directly on Stalin's own pronouncements; the passages in quotation marks are taken from his speeches as well as authoritative pronouncements by the party.

By 1933 the main struggle to establish socialism in the Soviet Union was over: the power of the opposing classes – kulak, hostile specialists, nepmen – had been broken in open battle. Their social roots had been destroyed and only shattered remnants remained. The great majority of the population supported the new socialist institutions such as the collective farms and nationalized industry. The time of major sacrifices and strained tempos was drawing to a close: the task was now to make the new institutions work.

But this new situation certainly did not mean that the class struggle had ceased. 'Thrown out of their groove, and scattered over the whole face of the USSR, these "former people" [members of the pre-revolutionary elites] have wormed their way into our plants and factories, into our government offices and trading organizations, into our railway and water transport enterprises, and principally into our collective and state farms. They have crept into these places and taken cover there, donning the mask of "workers" and "peasants", and some of them have even managed to worm their way into the party ... There is no filth or slander that these former people will not throw on the soviet power and use to mobilize backward elements' (13:207, 212).[23] These masked internal enemies were *dvurushnik*s.

The officers for this army of malicious malcontents are provided by the former party oppositionists who claim to have returned to the fold. The logic of struggle brings together a heterogeneous gang united only by hatred of Soviet socialism. Not only do the right and left oppositions – the Bukharinites and the Trotskyites – join forces: this combined bloc then links up with the security police of the fascist powers.

It is vital to recognize the difference between the *dvurushnik* and the class enemy of yore. Don't expect the kulak to flaunt his villainy and

---

23   References in the text are taken from Stalin, *Sochineniia*, 13 vols (Stalin, 1947–1952) as well as the additional three volumes in this series edited by Robert H. McNeal (Stalin 1967).

look like the caricature on a propaganda poster. Don't expect the new
wrecker specialists to be like Professor Borodin or the defendants in the
Shakhty trial of 1928.[24] Although Borodin and his ilk were openly alien
figures, they were comparatively honourable opponents whose class hostility was at least grounded in a well-developed world view. Don't expect
the two-faced former oppositionists to openly proclaim their views as former wreckers did. We face a new situation and a new type of danger: the
class enemy now has a party card.

The aim of the *dvurushnik*'s wrecking activities is not only to cause
direct damage but even more fundamentally to throw filth (*napakostit*)
on Soviet reality. Slowing down Soviet economic growth, lowering living
standards and causing popular discontent, bogging down the system in an
endless stream of mini-crises – the *dvurushnik* will do anything to slander socialism, make it look bad and reduce its innate attractive powers.
If the new system doesn't work as it should, despite the immense advantages of socialism, the main reason is the sabotage perpetrated by masked
dvurushniki.

The *dvurushnik*s are only a handful of degenerates: their power for
evil comes from the trust placed in them by myopic patriots who are too
engrossed in their own narrow sphere. The job of the true party leader
is to reveal what's really going on and to unmask the *dvurushnik*. These
true leaders can be at the top: the Central Committee has often given signals about the ubiquity of the two-faced wrecker. Or true leaders can arise
among the 'little people' – for example, Comrade Nikolaenko, a Ukrainian
woman who denounced corruption in high places and was expelled from
the party for her pains. In either case, the true leader exposes those who
try to throw filth on socialism: 'an essential quality of any Bolshevik under
present circumstances is the ability to recognize an enemy of the people,
no matter how well masked' (14:192).

It must be admitted that even the top leadership was late in understanding the full extent of the danger of the *dvurushnik* with a party card.
The murder of Comrade Kirov in 1934 was a wake-up call. Each of the
three major trials in 1936–38 revealed a more widely-flung conspiracy
than the last. Partly because of the looming danger of war, the time was
ripe in 1937 for a massive purification campaign.[25]

---

24   For background on 'wreckerism' (alleged sabotage by Soviet officials), see 'Stalin at Work',
      included in this volume.

25   'Purification' (*ochishchenie*) was the official label given to the events of 1937–38 that we
      usually call 'the great purge' or 'the great terror'. For examples of its use, see *Pravda*, 1 Jan-

But unfortunately, this mass campaign itself offered an opportunity to throw filth on the system. Careerist party officials used a mask of super-vigilance in order to protect themselves. Even more insidious was a new type of *dvurushnik*: 'still to this day, many of our party organizations and their leaders haven't learned to see through and expose the artfully masked enemy who attempts with cries of vigilance to mask his own enemy status ... and who uses repressive measures to cut down our Bolshevik cadres and to sow insecurity and excessive suspicion in our ranks'.[26]

Worst of all, *dvurushniki* infiltrated the NKVD, the organization dedicated to exposing *dvurushniki*. There they 'consciously distorted Soviet laws, committed forgeries, falsified investigative materials, investigated and arrested people on flimsy foundations or no foundations at all, created "cases" against innocent people for purposes of provocation, and using all these measures in order to hide and save from destruction their colleagues in this criminal anti-soviet activity'.[27] The danger represented by the *dvurushnik* will not be overcome until the slandered party loyalist is reinstated and the real *dvurushniki* exposed and eliminated.

Stalin's *dvurushnik* narrative marks a shift from political temperance drama to classical melodrama: the central figure is no longer the waverer/recognizer but the *traître* who is falsely trusted and almost succeeds in wrecking the virtuous community. The recognizer function is re-assigned to the community at large which must move from myopia (*blizorukost*) to vigilance (*bditelnost*). Suspense now revolves around the question: will the *dvurushnik* be unmasked before the community suffers mortal damage?

The key link between the political myths of the mid-thirties and classical melodrama is anxiety about masks: the fear of being slandered and the fear of relying on *traîtres*. This passage from a Pixerécourt play reads like one of Stalin's speeches about the *dvurushnik*:

---

uary 1938 (looking back over the achievements of 1937); Stalin, speech to the 18th party congress in March 1939 (Stalin 1967, 14:368–9).

26   Central Committee resolution of January 1938, as printed in Richard Kosolapov, *Slovo tovarishchu Stalinu* (Kosolapov 1995, pp. 148–9) (everything after 'expose' is underlined in original).

27   Government resolution of November 1938, as printed in Kosolapov 1995, p. 157. For further entry into the vertiginous world of Stalin, read Ezhov's tearful apology in November 1938 for allowing spies to infiltrate the NKVD in *Stalinskoe Politbiuro v 30-e gody* (Khlevniuk 1995, pp. 168–71).

Indeed, the more [Eloi's] life has been free from reproach – the more confidence and respect people have accorded him – the more he is guilty ...
You, Eloi, whom people have received with compassion, who has met with
the most generous hospitality, whose good behaviour and uprightness are
attested by all – you had nothing but the mask of virtue, and this misleading exterior hid the perverse soul of a villain [cette enveloppe trompeuse
cachait l'âme perverse d'un scélérat].[28]

A host of reasons – the Bolshevik underground experience, the devastating
social chaos of the revolutionary years, the repressions and denunciations of
the Stalin era, the imposed hypocrisy of the new centralized economic system – ensured that anxiety about masks would be a powerful presence in Soviet
culture. The specific melodramatic form given to this anxiety, however, was
due in large part to Stalin's insistence that the waverers had all been won over
and the virtuous community already established. In the old days of political
temperance drama, the waverer had helped make opposition understandable
and even acceptable (because hopefully only temporary). The waverer's doubts
could be explained by relatively objective social markers: there did in fact exist
anarchists, peasants and intellectuals with views roughly similar to the ones
ascribed to them. Because the waverer had comprehensible doubts, his ultimate conversion was also comprehensible – in fact, dispelling the waverer's
doubts was a central test of the party's leadership abilities. But now that the
virtuous community had been established, doubts were no longer legitimate
or comprehensible. Opposition could only be explained by unreasoning hatred
or by orders from powers outside the community. The doubter realized the virtuous community would reject him if he explained his real outlook, and so he
had to wear a mask. His slanders thus no longer took the form of open speech
but rather of covert wrecking. He could not be won over – he had to be rooted
out. The doubter had changed from a waverer to a *dvurushnik*.
   The anxieties accompanying life in a society of mobile strangers, intensified by revolutionary suspicions and the incomprehensible workings of the
new system, helped create a frightening and unstable world of masked *traîtres*
who were nowhere and everywhere. The only way to preserve one's sanity in
a world of masks was to rely on the top party leadership who (in the words
of an Afinogenov character) could lead us 'by ripping off masks from many
highly-educated leaders who had unlimited possibilities and yet bankrupted

---

28   Pixérécourt 1971, 3:171; compare especially Stalin's concluding remarks to the Plenum of
      February–March 1937, in which he argues that successful economic performance may only
      be part of a wrecker's artful mask (Stalin 1967, 14:225–247).

themselves'.[29] But Stalin proved unwilling or unable to contain the vertiginous logic of his own narrative. This narrative, with justice, can be given the melodramatic title of 'The *Dvurushnik* Unmasked'. Unfortunately, 'The *Dvurushnik* Unmasked' represented melodrama gone mad.

4 'Millions Will Shudder': The Show Trial as Melodrama

One of the devices used by melodrama in the nineteenth century to escape vertigo and allay the anxiety it itself provokes is the climactic courtroom scene. Here all masks are torn off, and virtue and villainy are authoritatively accorded the status they deserve. The virtuous community, reassured that its honour has been protected, purifies itself by the condemnation and expulsion of the *traître*.

The courtroom as a forum for the recognition of slandered virtue is a direct link between melodrama and socialism. Heroic courtroom defences bulked large in the stories – both historical and fictional – that pre-war Social Democracy told about itself. One of Social Democracy's founding myths was Ferdinand Lassalle's defence in his trial for treason in 1848. Trotsky was much taken with Lassalle; in 1905 he published an analysis and translation of Lassalle's defence speech. A year later Trotsky got his own chance to star as a revolutionary hero in a courtroom drama. Russian revolutionaries had their own tradition of heroic courtroom defences. In one famous case, a Russian jury in 1878 acquitted Vera Zasulich, a woman who had openly tried to assassinate a tsarist official. Gorky amalgamated international and local courtroom traditions for his novel *Mother* (1908) – the prototype for Socialist Realism – in which one of the climactic scenes is a trial of dedicated revolutionaries.

Political temperance drama usually included scenes that functioned very much like courtroom scenes: public meetings that affirmed the victory of virtue over slander. In 1932, Kirshon went further and wrote a full-fledged courtroom drama called *The Trial (Sud)*. Kirshon's play was set in Germany, and this location points to a serious problem. The pathos of the trial in the Social Democratic narrative depended entirely on the defendant's heroic defiance of the powers-that-be. As in many other areas, the Bolsheviks faced a dilemma when they themselves became the power in the land: how can a political trial retain its pathos when the good guys are not the defendants but the prosecutors? The

---

29   A. Karaganov, *Zhizn dramaturga* (Karaganov 1964, pp. 305–6). This quotation is taken from Afinogenov's play *Lies (Lozh)*; for a detailed examination of this highly revealing drama, see 'Vertigo: Masks and Lies in Stalin's Russia', included in this volume.

first attempt at an elaborate show trial – the 1922 trial of leaders of the Socialist Revolutionary party – was a relative failure for just this reason: the Bolsheviks used all the resources at their command to impose the proper meaning on the trial but their massive campaign only increased the pathos of the lonely defendants.[30] Indeed, the 1938 Moscow trial itself is often seen by Western and post-Soviet observers as a subversive courtroom defence in which the heroic *dvurushnik* Bukharin manages to condemn the Stalinist regime even while pretending to plead guilty.

The basic solution to the dilemma of putting on a convincing show trial while in power was outlined by Stalin in a 1930 letter to Molotov about the possibility of bringing some 'wreckers' to trial: 'By the way, how about Messrs. Defendants admitting their mistakes and disgracing themselves politically, while simultaneously acknowledging the strength of the soviet government and the correctness of the method of collectivization?' If the defendants would cooperate by demonstratively unmasking themselves, then a state-sponsored show trial could reap the advantages of a traditional melodramatic courtroom scene.[31]

The show trials of the Stalin era were based on this logic. This is particularly true of 'the trial of the Right-Trotskyite bloc' in March 1938 – the third in the series of Moscow show trials and the only one that took place during the purification campaign of 1937–38.[32] In many ways, the trial was meant to be the climactic episode of the whole *dvurushnik* narrative. The official indictment and the summary speech by state prosecutor Andrei Vyshinsky about the bloc and its crimes can be paraphrased as follows:

The bloc of Rights and Trotskyites was formed at the behest of foreign masters: the *razvedka* [counter-espionage agency] of various hostile powers plus Trotsky. Deprived of any prospect of support from within the Soviet Union, the bloc rested its hopes on foreign aggression and covert wrecking. In order to get help from outside, the bloc agreed to restore capitalism and to dismember the Soviet Union. Domestic wrecking took various forms. Uprisings were fomented: this category of wrecking can

30 Marc Jansen, *A Show Trial Under Lenin: The Trial of the Socialist Revolutionaries, Moscow, 1922* (Jansen 1982).

31 *Stalin's Letters to Molotov* (Lih 1995, pp. 210–11).

32 For the full transcript of the trial, see *Report of Court Proceedings in the Case of the Anti-Soviet 'Bloc of Rights and Trotskyites'* (*Report* 1938). For extended analyses, see Stephen F. Cohen, *Bukharin and the Bolshevik Revolution* (Cohen 1971) and Robert Tucker's introduction to Tucker and Cohen, eds., *The Great Purge Trial* (Tucker 1965).

be further subdivided into kulak uprisings and uprisings in the national republics. Another major form of wrecking tries to foul up the soviet economic system in order to create popular dissatisfaction. Finally, the bloc in its desperation resorted to the murder of staunch Stalin loyalists such as Kirov and Gorky.

Twenty-one members of the bloc were brought to trial in March 1938. At the top of the list were the two leaders of the right opposition, Bukharin and Rykov, who fomented uprisings, approved political murders and gave general direction. Next came prominent Trotskyites such as Konstantin Rakovsky. The Trotskyites were part of a larger group of spies – paid agents of foreign *razvedka* services. Indeed, NKVD investigators revealed that the spying activities of Trotsky and his associates started in the early 1920s – even earlier than formerly realized. In general, the Trotskyites were more ruthless and aggressive than the Rights.

The rest of the bloc were mostly small fry: some wreckers from the economic commissariats, a group of three provocateurs from tsarist days, and the people directly involved in political murder. The murderers were all people whose betrayal of trust was especially heinous: doctors, Gorky's personal secretary, and the former head of the NKVD, Genrikh Yagoda, the man who should have been protecting the Soviet system.

Eighteen of the defendants were sentenced to be shot; the sentence was carried out immediately. The remaining three (including Rakovsky) received long prison sentences.

The trial of the Right-Trotskyite bloc was the continuation and climax of the previous political trials. While building on earlier revelations, this trial portrayed an even vaster and more comprehensive conspiracy. The bloc included Mensheviks, Socialist Revolutionaries, bourgeois nationalists and provocateurs from the tsarist secret police as well as Rights and Trotskyites *sensu strictu*. 'Implicated in this "case" are the remnants of *all* anti-soviet forces, groups and organizations, and, as has been exactly established by the trial, at least four foreign intelligence services – the Japanese, German, Polish and British.'[33] The trial threw a searching light into the past: 'It is just these crimes that explain the real course of developments, the real logic of the events, and the struggle that brought two worlds face to face, two blocs.'[34]

---

33   *Report*, p. 629 (emphasis added).
34   *Report*, p. 633.

The foregoing summary of the indictment shows how this trial fit into the larger melodramatic story of the clash between the bloc of Soviet patriots vs. the bloc of *traîtres* – the virtuous community vs. the anti-community. In order to examine the dramatic structure of the trial itself, we shall look at how it was packaged and presented on the pages of *Pravda*. The newspaper's characterization of the forces in conflict fit neatly into the framework of classical melodrama: recognizers, victims and their defenders, and *traîtres*.

The recognizer was the trial's audience, an audience hardly confined to those physically present in the courtroom – it included all of Soviet society and progressive humanity: 'Hundreds of millions of workers, peasants and honest intellectuals throughout the world will shudder from indignation and loathing, when they learn of the monstrous conspiracy' (28 February).[35] *Pravda* used many devices to ensure that the audience was an active character in the drama of the trial. The extended audience from around the country made its presence felt by means of resolutions that demanded the death sentence, expressed gratitude to Ezhov and promised vigilance. As the title of one resolution put it: 'the entire people steps forth as accuser' (4 March). These resolutions filled at least half a page of *Pravda* each day.

Just as frequent were photographs showing the audience in its many forms: in the courtroom itself, in factories hearing newspaper reports, in barracks listening to comrades who had seen the real thing. The audience in all these shots looks at the speaker with attentive and unsmiling concentration. The climax of this series of photographs showed Vyshinsky giving his final summation: in a large photo spread at the top of the first page, we see Vyshinsky on the left facing a panoramic shot of the courtroom audience on the right (12 March).

Pravda also had a regular section entitled 'from the courtroom', sometimes written by journalists and sometimes by ordinary citizens. These audience reports often bring out the trial's resemblance to melodrama. A journalist reports that some of the defendants have an eerily familiar quality: if you take away their decent Soviet suits and picture them dressed in appropriate clothing – say, stereotypical dark glasses and overcoats – you would recognize them as tsarist secret police (4 March). A worker commented, perhaps a bit naively, about the same defendants: 'I had earlier seen such types only at the movies, on the screen, and now I had to look at them in real life. Disgusting' (6 March).

---

35   All citations come from *Pravda* for February and March 1938; the date of a particular citation is given in the text.

As the dimensions of the vast conspiracy become apparent, the audience understands that it had too easily given credit to slanders against Soviet power. The lesson is driven home with disarming forthrightness in an article on cooperatives:

> Now that the masks have been ripped off the fascist degenerates sitting on the bench of the accused, each collective farm worker, each worker, man and woman, sees who is to blame for the unsatisfactory work of the rural cooperatives and who withheld from the toilers such items as sugar, salt, tobacco – all of which exist in abundance in our country (6 March).

No wonder the audience reacts in appropriate 'hiss the villain' style. One journalist sitting in the hall reported that he wanted to jump up and grab the accused by the throats (3 March). Another observer shuddered to think: what if their wicked plans had succeeded (4 March)? A journalist pinches himself in order to realize that some of the grotesque scenes are not fantasy but the 'monstrous truth of class power' – a truth that would be too horrible to contemplate except for the 'happy and irrevocable fact' that the people and its vigilant *razvedka* won out in the end (9 March). At the end, the audience arises in just indignation and demands purification: 'outside the walls of the Dom Soiuzov, where the trial took place, a storm of popular anger raged. Rallies of many thousands and meetings demanded one thing: annihilate the cursed vermin' (16 March).[36]

The exciting trial that the recognizer/audience is watching is presented to the *Pravda* reader each day in the form of long excerpts from the official transcript. These excerpts read exactly like a play script: the prosecutor and the accused exchange their lines, with occasional dramatic interventions from the judges or from other defendants. In a manner entirely consonant with the norms of melodrama, *Pravda* surrounds the dialogue with commentary that leaves no ambiguity about who is slandered victim and who is faithless *traître*.

The main victim is the virtuous community, defined as 'socialism, the Bolshevik party and the Soviet people who are building socialist society' (28 February). The most visible vindicator is state prosecutor Vyshinsky, who 'rips off the masks' with 'annihilating force' (12 March). In the background but constantly mentioned are Ezhov and the 'valiant Soviet *razvedka*' who stand 'keen-eyed' [*zorko*] in defence of the Soviet people (28 February). Ezhov is victim as well as

---

36   *Pravda* was so eager for audience reaction that although the death sentence was announced at four o'clock in the morning, reporters still went out immediately to ask nightshift workers for their reaction (13 March).

vindicator: we learn that the villains were so afraid of the 'iron hand of the one sent by the Stalinist Central Committee' that they tried to kill him as well. Ezhov gallantly fought back at risk to his life and damage to his health (14 March).

Stalin himself had a very low profile in the coverage of the trial; he is mentioned only in passing as one of the intended victims back in 1918, along with Lenin and Sverdlov. While Stalin had very few speaking lines, he was a ubiquitous part of the environment in his adjectival form. The continual use of 'stalinskii' has an effect that is difficult to reproduce in English with its different rules about turning names into adjectives. *Stalinskii narkom* (Ezhov, People's Commissar of Internal Affairs), *Stalinskii Tsentralnyi Komitet, Stalinskaia Konstitutsiia, stalinskoe zadanie* ('Stalin assignment'): these and similar locutions make Stalin less an individual character and more of a ground of being for the virtuous community. As such, he is the number one victim of the assault against the community.

The villain of the piece was of course the Right-Trotskyite bloc. The twenty-one defendants were presented as a heterogeneous group united by only one thing: the *traître's* urge to 'slander' the virtuous community. Wearing masks followed from this basic motivation:

> The more their real face was uncovered before the whole people, the stronger their hatred toward the party of Bolsheviks. Wearing masks, playing the *dvurushnik*, using the most underhanded methods, the Trotskyites and Bukharinites turned into naked bandits, fascist murderers attacking from behind ambushes, spies, saboteurs (28 February).

All these enemies of Soviet power banded together because principled political opposition was impossible: 'They were spies *because* they were Rights and Trotskyites. The two categories are inextricably intertwined: one goes directly into the other' (5 March). The grandiose clash between good and evil portrayed by the show trials required an equally grandiose motivation and so *Pravda* emphasizes 'savage and inhuman hatred' rather than petty calculation (2 March). But the result is that the villain's motivations are disconnected from any objective basis.

Julia Przybos points out that in many ways the true victim of classical melodrama is the *traître*: it is he who is sacrificed, expelled from the community without compassion or remorse, so that the others can affirm their virtuous solidarity.[37] The *traître* as sacrificial victim certainly fits the Moscow show tri-

---

37   Przybos, *L'entreprise mélodramatique* (Przybos 1987).

CHAPTER 16

als. Strident calls for execution sound like a drumbeat throughout *Pravda*'s coverage. The accused must die in order to protect the purity of the virtuous community: they cannot expect to live among 'honest folk' on 'holy Soviet land' that has no place for 'contemptible vermin'.[38] The demand for purification gives rise to a strong filth vs. purity imagery in the rhetoric of the trial: 'a foul-smelling heap of human garbage' contaminates a land 'illumined by the sun of the Stalin Constitution'.[39] The trial reaches its grand climax in Vyshinsky's call for a rite of purification in which Stalin himself acts as high priest:

> Time will pass. The graves of the hateful traitors will grow over with weeds and thistle, they will be covered with the eternal contempt of honest Soviet citizens, of the entire Soviet people. But over us, over our happy country, our sun will shine with its luminous rays as bright and as joyous as before. Over the road cleared of the last scum [*nechist*] and filth of the past, we, our people, with our beloved *vozhd* and teacher, the great Stalin, at our head, will march as before onwards and onwards, towards Communism![40]

As poet Sergei Vasilev put it in an apostrophe to the accused: the nightingales will sing sweeter when you are dead (11 March).

For the most part, the *traître*/defendants dutifully played their role as self-accusers who now recognized the virtue of the community as well as their own evil nature. The only challenge resulted from the efforts of Krestinsky and Bukharin to depart from script. Although Krestinsky's direct denial of his pre-trial testimony was dealt with quickly, Bukharin's extraordinary defence became a major topic for *Pravda*. The following discussion is not an effort to discover what Bukharin was really up to but simply to examine the character of 'Bukharin' as portrayed by *Pravda*.

From the beginning, Bukharin was presented as the *dvurushnik par excellence*. This epithet was applied to him and not to the other chief criminals such as Trotsky, who, as head of the gang, disdained masks. The other labels attached to Bukharin – Jesuit, lawyer, sly, fox-like, two-faced, cry-baby – all strengthened Bukharin's basic characterization as a *dvurushnik*. Since many of these epithets

---

38   *Pravda*, 28 February and 1 March 1938. 'Vermin' is *gady*: an extremely emotive word that also has connotations of feces, reptiles and repulsive people.

39   *Report*, p. 631; *Pravda*, 13 March 1938.

40   *Pravda*, 12 March 1938; *Report*, p. 697. In Russian folk belief, *nechist* was the unclean one, the devil; for my comment on Stalin's use of this term, see 'Stalin at Work', included in this volume.

had been used much earlier by Stalin and his circle to describe Bukharin in private, it is even possible that Bukharin was the real-life original from which Stalin drew many features of his narrative's protagonist.[41]

When the dimensions of Bukharin's counter-trial became evident, the *Pravda* commentators used this basic characterization as a way of keeping the story on track: see how the ultimate *dvurushnik* denies his guilt right up to the last minute. But it is clear that they (or more likely their boss) were infuriated by Bukharin's defence. As seen through the prism of their refutation, Bukharin's case was that he was a 'theoretician' who accepted only *political* responsibility rather than *criminal* responsibility for sabotage and assassinations. *Pravda* granted that the purely political responsibility that Bukharin did accept was heavy enough: his 'verbal poison of restorationist, bourgeois, kulak, fascist mini-ideas, formulae and slogans' was as dangerous as a terrorist bullet (7 March). But *Pravda* was also insistent that Bukharin should accept material responsibility for actual crimes – so insistent that it gave extra publicity to Bukharin's courtroom denial of criminal responsibility.

It is likely that the full meaning of this duel must be sought in the long-standing and highly intense personal relations between Stalin and Bukharin. For our purposes, we should note that Bukharin's resistance was partly a struggle against the genre of classical melodrama that Stalin wished to impose on him. Bukharin portrayed himself as someone like Raevsky, the erring party leader in Kirshon's *Bread*: a wavering doubter whose leadership mistakes pushed other waverers into the camp of crime. The angry insistence of Vyshinsky and the *Pravda* commentators that Bukharin was an out-and-out criminal was an attempt to keep Stalin's classical melodrama from turning into outmoded political temperance drama.

Stalin longed for 'clarity' in the state's messages to society; he detested a confusing diversity of voices (what he called *raznogolositsa*).[42] Yet having a centralized propaganda apparatus no more guarantees the abolition of the anarchy of meanings than having a centralized economic apparatus guaran-

---

41   According to *Pravda*'s pre-trial introduction of the main villains, Trotsky is a Judas, Rykov is a 'malicious enemy of the party and people' and Bukharin is a 'base Jesuit and contemptible *dvurushnik*' (1 March).

42   Stalin, Speech of 1 October 1938 to propagandists about the recently published *Short Course*, published in *Istoricheskii arkhiv*, 1994, No. 5, pp. 4–31; quotation from p. 27. The multiplicity of meanings was intensified by the other stories jostling together with the trial on the pages of *Pravda*: the heroic Arctic expedition of Ivan Papanin, the Nazi takeover of Austria, efforts to improve economic performance, and the inadequate attempts by local party bodies to implement the Central Committee resolution of January 1938 that called for rehabilitation of people slandered during the purification campaign.

tees the abolition of the anarchy of the market. To use another metaphor: Stalin
was like the producer of a large studio production. The main story idea behind
the show trial was his, the ultimate control was his, and yet there was constant
interference with his artistic intentions, caused by the wide variety of people
employed, the temperament of the actors in the major roles, the varying talents of the actual scriptwriters, the technical means of representation, and the
imperatives of marketing – not to mention contradictions and incoherence in
the original story idea.[43] The result was 'The Trial of the Right-Trotskyite Bloc',
an effective if lurid climactic scene for Stalin's melodrama 'The *Dvurushnik*
Unmasked'. And yet even in this highly scripted production we can see a clash
of meanings that was impossible to overcome.

5   Epilogue

I have argued that melodrama is not just a way of popularizing a political
outlook: it *is* a political outlook. The political temperance dramas by Soviet
playwrights are not simply dramatizations of political doctrine, they are accurate expressions of the same narrative myths that energized political doctrine. In many ways they more adequately express the myth than attempts
by party theorists to put it in abstract propositional form. Similarly, the heart
of Stalin's rationale for the terror campaign was not a theoretical proposition
about 'intensification of the class struggle' but a highly charged narrative about
a threatened virtuous community.

   What unites these expressions of doctrinal myth is an insistence that the
true community is constituted and maintained through a struggle for the recognition of virtue. But this common melodramatic outlook should not obscure
real changes in Soviet doctrinal myth. The switch from the relatively optimistic
focus on the political waverer to the vertiginous world of the *dvurushnik* narrative was a deep-seated one. It is ironic that Stalin's repressive narrative was built
around the assumption that the virtuous community of socialism had already
been established. It is tragic that he was able to force an entire society to act
out his melodramatic fear of masks and two-faced wreckers.

   It is fitting to end with a story of individual citizens who had to cope as best
they could with Soviet political melodrama. In 1937, two of the creators of polit-

---

43   Robert Tucker comments: 'In addition to acting by remote control as the [1936] trial's chief
     producer, Stalin took a hand in creating the script. In doing so he applied to serious polit-
     ical business a dramaturgical bent that was rooted in his self-dramatizing nature' (*Stalin
     in Power: The Revolution from Above, 1928–1941* [Tucker 1990, pp. 316–17]).

ical temperance drama, Kirshon and Afinogenov, were caught up in Stalin's *dvurushnik* narrative. Both were viciously attacked in an open meeting as minions of the deceased *dvurushnik* Averbakh (a prominent literary theorist and official in earlier years). Averbakh was sneeringly referred to as a literary *vozhd* who ruled by 'the Trotskyite-style methods of disintegration and disunion'. Kirshon evidently didn't realize he was trapped in a real-life melodrama: he tried to defend himself and eventually perished.[44]

Afinogenov quickly cast himself as an innocent who now realizes he is on the path to ruin. 'Afinogenov spoke of how the demoralizing atmosphere, both creative and everyday, that prevailed at RAPP [the writers' organization headed by Averbakh] drew him away from life, from the party, from honest and sincere people – how he descended into the filth of Averbakh's world, arrived at catastrophe, slid down into a bog in his own literary creation.' He had 'lost the qualities of an honest Bolshevik and Soviet playwright', but now he wanted to reform.

One observer, Nikolai Panov, noted bitterly that 'during Afinogenov's speech it was sickening to observe how, behind the melodramatic gestures of a "proper gentleman", stood a self-satisfied philistine'. Nevertheless, Afinogenov's invocation of a vulgar kind of political temperance drama allowed him to survive. He realized quicker than most that life was being forced to imitate bad art.

6   Update 2021

When I wrote this essay in the late 1990s, not much academic attention, inside or outside Russia, had been given to the theatre of the Stalin era, especially in comparison to the novels and films of 'socialist realism'. Since then, mostly in Russia, there has been much exciting discussion and new evidence on this gripping topic. I am happy to report that two scholars with a more detailed knowledge of Soviet theatre than I can claim – Boris Wolfson and Ilya Veniavkin – endorse (with qualifications) my overall interpretive framework of a politicized melodrama.[45]

---

44   All citations from this meeting come from *Literaturnaia Gazeta*, 1 May 1937.
45   Wolfson 2006 ('Fear on Stage: Afinogenov, Stanislavsky, and the Making of Stalinist Theater'); Veniavkin 2011 ('"Nebogatoe oformlenie": "Lozh" Aleksandra Afinogenova i stalinskaia kultur'naia politika 1930-kh'). Wolfson gives a usefully detailed plot summary for *Fear*. For another recent discussion of *Fear*, see Ilya Serman, 'Afinogenov i ego "Strakh"' (Serman 2005).

The most important new archival publication of the original version of the play that Afinogenov wrote immediately after *Fear*. Afinogenov gave his new work an even more provocative one-word title: *Lies (Lozh')*. Stalin personally edited the play in early 1933 but eventually rejected it; much fuller versions of his editorial comments are also now available. This new material inspired me to write an essay found elsewhere in this volume with the title 'Vertigo: Masks and Lies in Stalin's Russia'. Here, in this very partial survey of new evidence, I restrict myself to some thoughts on Afinogenov as a representative Soviet intellectual and on the production history of *Fear*.

Some of the new writing on Afinogenov calls our attention, not just to new archival evidence, but to previously unused material from memoirs and journalistic accounts. Thanks to Ilya Veniavkin, I became aware of the portrait of Afinogenov in *Crisis in the Kremlin* (1953), a late entry in the classic series of reports on Russia written by Maurice Hindus, an American journalist who had grown up in tsarist Russia and who was a personal friend of Afinogenov. Looking back now on Hindus' portrait of his friend – written right after Stalin's demise – we can see his keen sense of the roots of the later reform movement during Khrushchev's thaw and then during perestroika.[46]

In the decade between 1931 and 1941, Afinogenov experienced the highs and the lows of the Soviet intellectual experience. In the early thirties, he was perhaps the most outwardly successful artist in the Soviet Union. *Fear* was 'Afinogenov's most sensational success. It was performed in the leading theatres of the country and in more clubhouses than any other play of the time.'[47] This smash hit made him very wealthy by Soviet standards, and he was openly befriended by Stalin.[48] Nevertheless, he was denounced in 1937 and spent a year waiting to be arrested. He kept a diary during the year that has attracted much scholarly attention.[49] He was lucky enough to be exonerated and reinstated in the party. In 1939, he had another hit with *Mashenka*, a play that is still performed today. In fact, under the title *Listen, Professor*, this play was mounted in late 1943 on Broadway, admittedly, for a very short run.[50] Afinogenov died

---

46 *Crisis in the Kremlin* (Hindus 1953). I also found invaluable observations on the Soviet theatrical scene in Hindus' earlier book *The Great Offensive* (Hindus 1933).

47 Hindus 1953, p. 248.

48 Successful authors and playwrights 'enjoy a higher degree of prosperity than perhaps anyone else in the country, including high-salaried engineers ... A successful play like Afinogenov's *Fear*, or Kirshon's *Bread*, may be given simultaneously in over one hundred theaters all over the country, and each theater pays the author a definite percentage of its receipts' (Hindus 1933, p. 277).

49 Hellback 2009; Sarnov 2011; Veniavkin 2016.

50 For the Playbill issue for this production, see https://www.playbill.com/playbillpagegallery

in the line of duty in late 1941, age thirty-seven. For Hindus, these experiences only made his representative qualities more vivid:

> Though a believing communist, Afinogenov was always sensitive to the inner struggle of the intellectual of whom he was both a triumphant and tragic example, now feeling secure and happy in his adjustments, now bewildered and anguished by his failure to strike a balance between faith and duty, between his rapture over the sweep of new construction and new education and his grief over the price the people paid for both.
>
> If he was more honest with himself than other Soviet writers who, like him, were party members, then they too, despite outward submissiveness, did not escape the conflict between rapture and torment. Someday, when manuscripts now stored away in trunks and garrets find their way into print, we shall be astonished to learn how deep and widespread this torment was.[51]

Hindus' account makes clear something obvious and yet easy to overlook: Afinogenov and other party loyalists did not know what was happening next. They could see various forces acting around them and they tried to encourage some and discourage others. Stalin's speech about the new Soviet constitution of 1936 is a case in point. Another essay included in this volume ('Who Is Stalin? What Is He?') looks at Prokofiev's musical apotheosis of this speech. Hindus describes Afinogenov's reaction: 'I think that the happiest day of Afinogenov's life, as of other Soviet intellectuals I knew, was November 23, 1936, when Stalin delivered his address on the new constitution. Shortly afterward Afinogenov rushed into my room with a bottle of wine and exclaimed, "Let's celebrate!"'

Although, as Hindus details, the new constitution was 'flagrantly dishonoured', it nevertheless remained compulsory study throughout the country. Hindus predicted that the *concept* of human rights was 'destined sooner or later to exert a powerful impact on Kremlin absolutism. In all my conversations with Afinogenov, he never doubted it, and in a sense not only writers but ordinary citizens, especially high school graduates, have always been questioning and struggling Afinogenovs.'[52]

/inside-playbill?asset=00000150-aea3-d936-a7fd-eef7ad530002&type=InsidePlaybill&slide=2. Playbill supplies the following useful information: 'His name is pronounced: Ah-FEEN-eh-GEN-off – the G as in go.'

51   Hindus 1953, p. 250.
52   Hindus 1953, p. 251.

To say that Afinogenov was befriended by Stalin is hardly an exaggeration. Stalin was very invested in the theatre personally and politically: he saw it as a more powerful tool in the hands of 'engineers of human souls' than, say, novels. His public intervention saved Afinogenov's early play *Chudak* (*The Eccentric*, 1929) and ensured the success of *Fear* (as detailed below). In 1933, Stalin could be said in practical terms to be collaborating with Afinogenov on the script for his new play *Lies*. Kremlin logbooks show a long one-on-one meeting with Afinogenov on 17 April 1933 – an extremely rare honour for a writer.[53]

If *Fear* was a daring critique of Soviet reality, it was enthusiastically endorsed by the party establishment. Veniavkin describes the Moscow opening night:

> In fall 1931, theatrical and cultured Moscow lived in expectation of a signal event: the Moscow Art Theatre, the famous MKhAT, was going to produce a play by a Soviet dramatist. The dramatist was Aleksandr Afinogenov, and the play was titled *Fear*. The production was a fantastic success. There were nineteen curtain calls, the author was called on stage, along with the stage director and the whole troupe. Afinogenov was then invited into the loge where the party leadership was seated; they shook his hand and shared their impressions of the play.[54]

One reason for such a success was the stage production itself, not just the script. Boris Wolfson points out in his informative article about the staging of *Fear* that I base my own analysis solely on the written script and not on its embodiment in live performance, that is, not on the essence of theatre as such.[55] The point is very well taken. More recent writing has given us invaluable information on actual productions, especially in the country's two main theatres, the Leningrad Academic Theatre (Alexandrinsky) and the Moscow Art Theatre. Unfortunately, the accounts available to me do not quite mesh in all of their detailed observations, but this, I gather, is a general problem in theatrical history. With this caveat, I will outline the course of *Fear*'s stage production.[56]

In an earlier book, published in 1933 when *Fear* was still a stage hit, Hindus gives a striking account of the importance of live theatrical production (although I think he overstates somewhat the purely literary problems of Kirshon's *Bread*):

---

53   Veniavkin 2011.
54   Veniavkin 2011.
55   Wolfson 2006.
56   My two main sources for the following discussion are Wolfson 2006 and Vaniashova 2018.

FIGURE 3   The Moscow Art Theatre's Staging of *Bread*
KONSTANTIN RUDNITSKY, *RUSSIAN AND SOVIET THEATER, 1905–1932* (NEW
YORK: HARRY N. ABRAMS, 1988), P. 273

The outstanding playwright in point of popularity is a certain Kirshon, an
eminent member of Rapp. He is an unprepossessing young man of little
culture and with no feeling for the reality of character and personality, but
with an excellent knowledge of the stage and of his political catechism.
He has written the most popular plays of the Revolution, the most notable
of which is *Bread*, a play on peasant life. So false is the picture it gives of
the peasantry that even Communists with a trace of literary taste speak
of it with contempt. The characters are all complete heroes or complete
villains, with hardly a living person among them, puppets all, who speak
and act in accordance with the political need of the moment.

And yet in the hands of the Stanislavsky Art Theatre this inferior play
becomes a superb spectacle [see Figure 3]. The directors and actors have
blown into it a soul which the author never intended it to have. They have
lifted it to a height of dramatic beauty which makes it an overwhelming
theatrical triumph.[57]

The challenge in staging Afinogenov's *Fear* was to ensure that Professor Borodin – who delivers the stinging indictment of a social system based on fear –
is convincingly refuted. Borodin's indictment is one that many in the audience

---

57   Hindus 1933, pp. 267–8 (*The Great Offensive*).

would have readily accepted, in whole or in part. To give one more vivid contemporaneous comment by Hindus:

> When Afinogenov had his *Fear* ready for production, there was a loud murmur against it. Afinogenov is himself a Communist, and the play ends with a triumph for the proletarian and his cause, and in as important an intellectual a sanctuary as a famous university laboratory. But Afinogenov has dared to picture Russian intellectuals as men who have a real and deepseated grievance against the discriminations that had until recently been visited on them. His professors speak freely, vehemently and touchingly.
>
> For the first time since the Revolution intellectuals are permitted to give expression to their pent-up complaints, and what more natural than that pious Communists should find it blasphemous? But Stalin and his close associates over-ruled them, and now the play is one of the outstanding successes in Russia.[58]

The refutation on stage had to come either from the counter-speech by Klara, the Old Bolshevik, or from Borodin himself, by seeing the light in a convincing way. As M.G. Vaniashova points out, the speech written for Klara does not really take on Borodin's analysis of the current Soviet system, but rather goes back to the fearless Bolsheviks of the revolution and civil war.[59] For this and other reasons, a strong actress in the Klara role was essential to ensure the production avoided the highly dangerous accusation of 'giving a platform to the class enemy'.

In the original Leningrad production, this danger was only narrowly averted. During rehearsals, a reading of the play was given to a select audience at the prestigious Communist Academy. The reading was not staged except for the duel between Borodin and Klara, who were the only ones to stand and come forward to address the audience. Both parts had been given to strong and experienced actors: Illarion Pevtsov and Ekaterina Korchagina-Aleksandrovskaya. But (our sources tell us), as Korchagina-Aleksandrovskaya listened to Borodin give his confident indictment, she lost her nerve completely. As *Fear*'s stage director Nikolai Petrov remembered, 'I looked at Korchagina-Aleksandrovskaya and became very frightened. Instead of the angry, wise and calm Klara I saw a frightened and agitated eyes of Korchagina, and the closer came the time of her speech, the more agitated and upset she became.'[60] The result was a fiasco and

---

58   Hindus 1933, pp. 272–3.
59   Vaniashova 2018 ('"Unichtozh'te strakh". P'esy A. Afinogenova nachala 1930-kh godov').
60   Vaniashova 2018, p. 36.

the play's fate hung in the balance. Evidently, only the intervention of Sergei Kirov, the party boss of Leningrad, saved the day. And, in the manner of a Hollywood backstage musical, the threatened show went on to huge success.[61] (This familiar narrative arc is a warning to exercise caution while turning theatrical anecdotes into history.)

The Leningrad premiere took place on 31 May 1931, but the production at Konstantin Stanislavsky's Moscow Art Theatre was delayed until the fall. This delay was caused in large part by the search for ways to ensure that the proper political message was sent. At a certain point, Stanislavsky himself took over the production. The original actress cast for Klara was Olga Knipper-Chekhova, Chekhov's widow, whose career at the Moscow Art Theater went back to *The Cherry Orchard* in 1904. But the vulnerability she was able to display with great effect in her 1904 role was deemed inappropriate for Klara, so Stanislavsky replaced her with another actress.

Stanislavsky tried another method to ensure a satisfactory outcome of the duel scene: he put students on stage as an audience to the clashing speeches between Borodin and Klara, and their obvious sympathy for Klara gave her personage a serious morale-booster. My sources differ as to whether this device was part of the actual production or used only in rehearsal. As related in 'Vertigo: Masks and Lies in Stalin's Russia', Stalin made a very similar suggestion for Afinogenov's *Lies*.

The other angle of attack was to tweak the role of Borodin. We have a record of how the actor playing the role complained about its difficulties:

Leonidov: But look, there's just nothing positive about Borodin! He's a reactionary – until he gets kicked in the head. You yourself said that he should be arrested!

Stanislavsky: The author has proved to me that I was mistaken, that the Borodins should be re-educated rather than arrested. And I think that I was wrong and Afinogenov was right.[62]

In evaluating the final staged outcome, we have to rely on various subjective impressions, and these sometimes clash. The following methods seem to have been employed. First, Borodin was presented, not as the angry reactionary

---

61   According to Wolfson 2006, the unrealistic slanting set used in the Leningrad production
      was one reason that Korchagina-Aleksandrovskaya's Klara won out in the duel scene as
      seen on stage.
62   Wolfson 2006, p. 108.

of the script, but rather someone who was already in partial or unconscious sympathy with the manifestations of the new Soviet life surrounding him. He couldn't help smiling, say, at the effusions of the eager student Kimbaev. More emphasis was given to events that occur after the duelling speeches and especially to the reassessment forced on Borodin: he confronted (with the help of an OGPU interrogator) the unmasked anti-soviet villainy of those he thought of as allies but who were just using him. More drastically, the actor who finally took on the role of Borodin, L.M. Mironov, turned him into a bumbling, somewhat out-of-it, almost comic figure.

Whatever the methods actually used, the result was a great success. Stalin showed up on opening night, praised the production and talked to the author. His wife Nadezhda Alliluyeva, a theatre-lover, also appreciated the play, it is said.[63] From Leningrad and Moscow, the play spread across the country. The Leningrad Academic Theatre sent out 'theatre brigades' to help local productions – and sometimes to cajole local theatres who were scared of the political risks. *Fear* was even produced in the United States. In early 1934, the Experimental Theatre at Vassar College put on the play (Hallie Flanagan, the adventurous head of the theatre, had spent a year in Russia in 1926). Nikander Strelsky, an émigré who taught Russian language at Vassar, gave a talk on the new play in which he emphasized the battle of youth against age:

> The play is tense because Russia is tense. 'No time, no time', says Yelena. 'No time, no time', echoes little Natasha. They passionately go along and build a new state. There is no reason for old people in Russia, everything is youth. Every young child has the feeling that he is the Czar – they have no respect for old people; the future belongs to youth alone. The individual must adjust himself to the new conditions or die.[64]

According to Vaniashova, however, the huge success of *Fear* in 1931–1932 did not give it a secure place in the repertoire and it soon vanished from the boards.[65]

Even with all the new information, the essential puzzle of this episode in Soviet theatre history remains just as mysterious or even more so. Why were plays such as *Bread* and *Fear* so enthusiastically embraced by the party establishment and by Stalin personally? Were writers like Afinogenov daring dissenters or sincere loyalists – or both at the same time, a possibility suggested by Hindus' phrase 'daring propaganda plays'. What was the actual effect that these

---

63   Veniavkin 2011, citing a diary entry by a friend of Afinogenov's.
64   *Vassar Miscellany News*, 24 January 1934.
65   Vaniashova 2018.

plays had on their audience in the theatre? What were the reasons leading to the curtain dropping on this episode in Soviet theatre history – a turning point exemplified by Stalin's de facto endorsement of Afinogenov's new play *Lies* in early 1933 and his rejection of it at the end of the year? Why was *Fear* feted and *Lies* rejected? Some of these questions are further considered in my 'Vertigo: Masks and Lies in Stalin's Russia'. Let us take leave of Afinogenov by quoting his own statement: 'I am no Chekhov, we cannot afford Chekhovs now. I can only write plays that will help to transform our incredibly backward muzhik country into an industrialized and civilized society.'[66]

---

66   Hindus 1953, p. 247.

CHAPTER 17

Vertigo: Masks and Lies in Stalin's Russia

After the young and up-and-coming Soviet playwright Aleksandr Afinogenov scored a success in 1931 with his play *Fear*, he wrote another play with another provocative one-word title: *Lies [Lozh']*. After completing a first draft in early 1933, he confidently sent it out to a couple of formidable critics: Maxim Gorky and Iosif Stalin. Gorky was hostile to the play both politically and artistically, but Stalin gave general approval to the theme of the play and spent consider-able time making editorial comments. Based on what the playwright thought was a de facto go-ahead sign from Stalin, rehearsals for *Lies* at the Moscow Art Theatre were set in motion and its opening was eagerly awaited. In fact, the play had already been publicly staged to great applause down in Kharkov. The director of the Kharkov production, Nikolai Petrov (who had also directed the Leningrad production of Afinogenov's earlier play *Fear*), described opening night:

> I have never in my life seen such a success. The success of *Fear* at the Alexandrinsky theatre [in Leningrad] was nothing in comparison to *Lies* in Kharkov. At the end of the play the spectators crowded the stage, extended their hands to the actors and congratulated them. Shook up by the overwhelming success, the actors broke the usual procedure for cur-tain bows – they came right to the edge of the stage and responded to the spectators with their own loud applause.[1]

In November 1933, Afinogenov sent Stalin a revised version that responded to his earlier comments. This time Stalin's answer was short and not so sweet: 'I consider the play in its second version to be a failure. 10.XI–33I. Stalin.'[2] Stalin's disapproval ended any hope of further production. Although Afinogenov was deeply disappointed, his further career (despite some severe political ups and downs) was not permanently derailed.

When I wrote 'Show Trials in the Stalin Era: On Stage and In Court' (included in this volume) in the late 1990s, the only material available to me about *Lies* and Stalin's reaction to it consisted of summaries and a few quotes in secondary

---

1 Veniavkin 2011.
2 Violetta Gudkova 2014, *Zabytye p'esy 1920–1930-kh godov*, p. 944.

sources.[3] Since then, the first version of the play has been published along with extensive passages from Stalin's response.[4] The whole episode has stirred interest in post-Soviet Russia and given rise to some insightful analyses.[5]

I have difficulty judging the stage worthiness of *Lies*. The plot mechanics are a bit on the creaky side, but, as we have seen, it received an enthusiastic audience reception during its aborted 1933 run in Kharkov. Whatever its artistic merits, *Lies* is a remarkable historical document and well worth detailed attention. It is a comprehensive, hands-on, inside look at the enormous role of figurative masks in both the reality and imaginary of Stalin's Russia. Stalin's response to the play and to the problems it uncovered was also much more nuanced than a simple rejection of the play's implied social criticism.

In this essay, we will first look at the first version of *Lies* and its portrait of a vertiginous world of mask-wearing. We will then look at the responses to the play by Gorky and Stalin. Stalin's response is best understood within the larger context of his overall musings on plot mechanisms and character motivation, both artistic and political. As an appendix to this essay, I have translated a crucial passage from *Lies* and some relevant literary musings by Stalin.

1   Masks and Double Life in *Lies*

When Afinogenov sent the script of *Lies* to Gorky, he told the older writer that 'this play is for me a response to so many questions of my life as a writer'. And when Stalin sent back his own critical remarks to Afinogenov, he allowed that 'the idea of the play is a rich one'.[6] The subject of Afinogenov's play is how to live in a world of masks. This subject is spelled out in two major themes. The first is what Nina Kovaleva, the central character of the play, calls 'double life' (*dvoinaia zhizn*): the seemingly unbridgeable gap between public and private selves in Soviet society. The other theme that powers the plot is *denunciation* of

3 A. Karaganov, *Zhizn dramaturga* (Moscow: Gosizdat, 1964), still a helpful discussion.

4 For the text of the original version of *Lies*, along with useful notes and a discussion of Stalin's comments, see Gudkova 2014, *Zabytye p'esy*. For Afinogenov's revised version, see *Sovremennaia dramaturgiia*, 1982, No. 1, pp. 190–223; I was not able to consult this text while drafting this essay (but see the Update below at the end of my discussion of *Lies*).

5 My discussion owes much in particular to Veniavkin 2011. For further helpful analysis of *Lies*, see Vaniashova 2018.

6 Gudkova 2014, pp. 940–1. As pointed out in Veniavkin 2011, Afinogenov's recent travels in Western Europe had forced him to encounter critiques of the Soviet system to which he had not earlier been exposed.

wrong-doers to the authorities. Denunciation bills itself as an act of unmasking, but, as the play makes clear, it can itself be used as a mask. How to distinguish upright Bolshevik vigilance from careerist slander?

Lies stands at the crossroads of two subgenres of political melodrama.[7] I have given the name 'political temperance drama' to plays that present a struggle between the virtuous community – in this case, party members and sympathizers – and the villains who seek to undermine it. This type of melodrama – an outstanding of which is Afinogenov's own *Fear* – dominated Soviet theatre in the early 1930s. Later in the decade a new and more somber type came to the fore, both on stage in society at large, that was similar to the classic melodrama of the early nineteenth century. Here the plot revolves around exposure of *dvurushniki*, that is, two-faced villains who seek to undermine the virtuous community. *Lies* contains strong elements of both types. Let us first look at the plot strands that express the subgenre of political temperance drama.

This type of melodrama typically expresses itself in a contest for the allegiance of a waverer who is caught between the two polar forces. In the case of *Lies*, the waverer is Nina, a young woman who has recently joined the party and yet is crippled by doubts caused by the 'double life' she sees all around her. Representing the forces of the virtuous community are standard types in Soviet political drama: Nina's father-in-law, an older worker; the secretary of the factory party cell; and most importantly, an Old Bolshevik named Riadovoi who serves as a wise mentor to Nina. As both Gorky and Stalin complained with some justice, Afinogenov does not succeed in making these positive figures especially compelling.

As usual, the plot dynamics are driven by the forces subverting the virtuous community. The play concerns the Ivanov family, whose life revolves around a factory in a large town in Stalin's Russia. In the course of Nina's pilgrimage, we meet a number of characters, each propelled by a character with an interest in a particular type of deceptive mask. First is Nina's husband Viktor, who advocates and practices what observers of the Soviet economy used to call 'pro-plan violations'. In order to fulfil the plan targets given to him, he is willing to cut corners – indeed, to steal supplies shipped to other factories, including those needed by his own mother! His motto is 'if you don't cheat, you meet defeat [*ne obmanish – ne postroish*]'.[8] His shenanigans are exposed by the end of the play.

---

7   For full explication of these two melodramatic subgenres, see 'Show Trials in the Stalin Era: On Stage and In Court', included in this volume.

8   All quotations from *Lies* are my translations of the text given in Gudkova 2014.

Next is another member of the factory party collective, Maria Gorchakova. Gorchakova is the type of the rigid hardliner who publicly accuses everything and everybody of some kind of political incorrectness. Nina derisively gives her the nickname Ms. Shut-your-mouth (*Tsyts*). She is a force that drives all those around her into silence and insincerity – but we learn during the play that she herself is driven by her need to crush her own debilitating doubts.

Finally we have a thorough-going *dvurushnik* – an Old Bolshevik named Vasily Nakatov. Nakatov is a former oppositionist who has decided that the party general line is a lie and that the party therefore needs a shake-up (*vstriaska*). He is engaged in creating a secret group of malcontents. The interest of the play is not so much in his nefarious doings as in the ethical dilemma he presents to the other characters: to denounce or not to denounce?

Similar to Afinogenov's *Fear* and Vladimir Kirshon's *Bread*, *Lies* contains a long monologue setting forth an indictment of Soviet reality. This monologue is delivered by Nina, who has just been publicly denounced and excluded from the party due to the unscrupulous use of her diary by Ms. Shut-your-mouth. Greatly discouraged by an almost complete lack of support, she vents to her wise party father-figure, Aleksandr Riadovoi, about the suffocating atmosphere of ubiquitous double life. Like the corresponding speeches in *Bread* and *Fear*, Nina's speech will surprise many readers today by its unsparing frankness. As an appendix to this essay, I have translated the opening passages of the speech. Keep in mind when reading Nina's monologue that it was written by a young loyalist playwright, who confidently sent it to Comrade Stalin for editorial advice.

Rather than delving further into the intricacies of the plot, I will now set out the impressively comprehensive analysis of mask-wearing in Stalin-era society as set forth in the words of Afinogenov's characters. Part of the problem is generational. Nina is twenty-three years old, and she was therefore seven or eight years old at the time of the 1917 revolution. Her whole political life has been spent in the Soviet era. Looking back, she admires the Bolsheviks of pre-revolutionary times: 'In earlier days, Bolsheviks would go to prison to back up each word of their convictions, they would suffer in exile.' But times have changed. Nina's post-revolutionary generation grew up with a ready-made understanding of the world handed to them. She herself does not harbour any doubt about the substantive correctness of the party line, but she is troubled by the passive way she and her agemates imbibed their outlook and the consequent fragility of their convictions:

And us, the younger generation? We hardly even know what a firm conviction is. We've even come to joke about the old guys: here they go again, defining their 'tendency' and 'disassociating' themselves from this other tendency. – But it's not so funny, this is how we're growing up: not thinking, not feeling. Oh yes, you've seen us at demonstrations for all these years and we've expressed our confidence in you so many times – but it's superficial, it's all so fragile. And we'll sell you out just as easily as we exalt you, because that's how we've been raised ...

I'm just so tired of living this way, I want so much to be able to delve into issues myself and understand them in such a way that, if I am tortured by enemies of the revolution, I would still even then preserve my voice and remain steadfast.

And that's not the worst of it. Many people are simply indifferent. When chided about her ignorance of ideological differences, Nina's flippant sister-in-law answers: why should I worry about where these deviations come from? Yes, yes, I know: all deviations are bad. Isn't that enough? – Some of the party people are okay with this attitude on the part of non-party people. In the following exchange, Gorchakova (a.k.a. Ms. Shut-your-mouth) berates Nina:

GORCHAKOVA: Why – instead of crushing doubts in yourself and strangling your own waverings and hesitations – do you drag them out into the open? Why? You're reopening wounds that haven't yet healed in many people. You talk on these forbidden topics, and people listen to you – listen and remain silent. Silent – but they're thinking! And when a person thinks but remains silent – well! – who can know what they're thinking about!

NINA: Why don't they *stop* being silent? Why don't they speak and tell the truth?

GORCHAKOVA: The masses should *believe* in us, without asking if it's true or not.

NINA: So why bother writing articles in *Pravda*?

GORCHAKOVA: It's a historical tradition.

All this mask-wearing covers up a growing gap between private and public. But behind this problem, Nina sees a larger issue: a callous, uncaring individualism in Soviet society.

People are growing up deformed, unable to speak out, indifferent to everything. Let's say a streetcar crushes a woman – everybody curses, 'oh,

another blasted traffic hold-up'. We live a double life. So we comfort ourselves: this is the life we need, we're new people, we're good people, we
praise ourselves, we write such eloquent words, we hand out portraits and
medals – and it's all for show, all just an exterior advertisement. And everybody knows this.[9]

So far we have looked mostly at the larger Soviet public. But what about the
committed party people? All is not well with them either. Nina looks at the
way some of the older Bolsheviks behave now: the kind of Bolsheviks that 'we
have today – well, as soon as they get in a little bit of trouble, they instantly
write letters to renounce their whole past'. (See the Epilogue to 'Show Trials in
the Stalin Era', included in this volume, for Afinogenov's real-life reactions to
being denounced in 1937.)

Another illness that afflicts the party people in *Lies* might be called 'deviation fatigue'. In 1933, the Soviet Union was coming out of a decade filled with
what seemed to be continual deviations, now coming from the left, now coming
from the right. For many people, the experience led them simply to keep their
head down in order to avoid getting knocked out by the next pendulum swing.
But even those who were more committed became wearied by the parade of
deviations. As Nina says, 'we don't even know what the party's general line will
be tomorrow: what today is the party line is a deviation tomorrow'. The bullying
dogmatist Ms. Shut-your-mouth is pictured as belligerently denouncing others
as a way of crushing her own doubts:

All my life I've fought with deviations, only to be called a deviationist myself. Is there justice if something like this happens? You, Nina,
were right when you doubted everything ... I've wavered all my life. I
was confounded when we went over to NEP, I had doubts when we
exposed Trotsky, I went back and forth when we fought with the rightists – but all of this was inside, for myself. Nobody ever even suspected
me – but neither did anyone give me any medals for this desperate struggle.

At the end of the play, Ms. Shut-your-mouth is dismissed as someone who
would have been happy before the revolution as a prioress in a religious con-

---

9   In her 1929 book *The New Russia*, the American journalist Dorothy Thompson used stories
    by Mikhail Zoshchenko to illustrate 'the tragic contrast [between] the grandiose scheme for
    collective life [vs.] the pitiful meanness of the individual situation ... how trifling and yet how
    tragic the individual problems' (Thompson 1929, pp. 36–9).

vent. But Afinogenov's portrait of Ms. Shut-your-mouth identified a type that was not so easily dismissed from Soviet society.

Even more upsetting from Afinogenov's point of view is the way masks are used by people to aggressively game the system. Not even the worst in this category is Viktor (Nina's husband), who employs shady methods to fulfil his plan targets. Viktor explains his outlook to a horrified Nina:

> You, Nina, are searching for the truth, but I'm running a factory. I wouldn't steal a plugged nickel for myself – but I would steal whole trains for the factory, without hesitation. I've got special agents scouring around to find anything not nailed down. Nina, we're fighting at the front [of an economic struggle to build socialism]. And at the front you need spurts of speed, risk-taking, fraud – yes, my dear, fraud!

Here again, Afinogenov has identified a type of activity that had deeper roots in the Soviet system than he himself realized. The logic of the Soviet planning system ensured that Viktor remained a Soviet type to the end.[10]

Much worse than Viktor are those who denounce others for demagogic reasons. Ms. Shut-your-mouth advances herself by such means. The reaction by many others is cowed silence. Those who do stand up to her – Nina is an example – are painfully aware that their words can be ripped out of context and used against them. As Nina's father-in-law says about this obsessive search for disreputable ulterior motives, 'they don't want to understand Ninushka. Behind every word they search for hidden meaning, just as if she needed to be dekulakized.'

Other careerists are not so aggressively self-promoting as Ms. Shut-your-mouth, but are nevertheless keenly alert to who is winning and who is losing in the unceasing bureaucratic and political battles always in progress, with a view to attaching themselves to the victors. A young man named Kulik – who also makes rather cynical capital out of his proletarian origins – is the play's representative of this type. (Another motive for mask-wearing during the Stalin era was the need to cover up inappropriate social origins. Despite the play's otherwise comprehensive survey of mask-wearing, this motivation is not mentioned.)[11]

---

10   Afinogenov was reacting against *My Friend*, a recent play by Nikolai Pogodin that seemed to celebrate this kind of wheeler-dealer behaviour. For the built-in constraints of Soviet-style economic systems that inevitably lead to Viktor's outlook, see especially the classic account by Hungarian economist Janos Kornai (Kornai 1980, *Economics of Shortage*).

11   Hiding one's social origins is a significant theme in Afinogenov's earlier play *Fear*. This

After the play's long parade of waverers, doubters, careerists, and philistines, we are relieved to come across an authentic *dvurushnik*, that is, someone who wears a mask because he has conscious goals that require secrecy and deception. Nakatov, the *dvurushnik* in *Lies*, is more lucid about what he believes and what he needs to do than almost any person in the play. To call someone an 'authentic *dvurushnik*' may be on the verge of an oxymoron, but Stalin picked up on it when he complained that Nakatov was the only integral [*tselnyi*] character in the play. Nakatov takes Nina's experience one step further. For Nina, a passive reception of the correct line is painful. For Nakatov, the party line is itself a lie:

We became Bolsheviks in a constant struggle with powerful opponents. In order to choose our path, we had to assimilate an entire library of alien thoughts. A whole Vatican Library. But you [Nina and her generation] are growing up with off-the-rack slogans. You are given the choice: either take our word for it, or remain silent. Your mental baggage consists only of the truths [*istiny*] that are clothed as directives. We are supposed to consider this as *the* truth [*pravda*]. But what if this isn't the case? What if this 'truth' you believe in is at bottom just lies?

The world of masks is unstable and vertiginous enough without someone like Nakatov raising the possibility that the system as a whole is essentially a lie. Is revolutionary fervour, then, no more than another mask? To counter this existential destabilization, the wise party member Riadovoi struggles to find a secure anchor to guarantee the existence of a reality beyond masks. He finds this anchor in Stalin personally, the *vozhd* (leader) at the very top:

I'm talking about the Central Committee, I'm talking about the *vozhd* who leads us by ripping off masks from many highly-educated leaders – they had unlimited possibilities and bankrupted themselves. I am talking about a person who gets his strength from the granite-like belief of hundreds of millions of people in him. In all languages in the world, his name rings out as a symbol of the strength of the Bolshevik cause. And that *vozhd* is unconquerable, because our revolution is unconquerable. You know who it is I'm talking about.

---

dimension of mask-wearing is discussed at length by Sheila Fitzpatrick 2005, *Tear Off the Masks! Identity and Imposture in Twentieth-Century Russia*.

Stalin's comment on this passage: 'There's no point in going on and on about "the *vozhd*". It's not good and perhaps even indecent. The point is not "the *vozhd*", but the collective leadership in the party Central Committee.'[12]

Riadovoi's attempt to find a fixed point among all of reality's shapeshifting tells us a couple of things. One is a motive from below for the Stalin cult of personality: the desire to find, in a confusing and radically unreliable world of masks, a psychological guarantee of a correct line, a line that is grounded in a maskless reality. At the same time, the rest of the conversation between Riadovoi and the *dvurushnik* Nakatov immediately thrusts us back into a vertiginous, unstable world:

> NAKATOV: So that means everything is just fine up top? All the enemies
>   are down below?
> RIADOVOI: No, there were enemies in the Central Committee as well.
> NAKATOV: Enemies [in what sense]?
> RIADOVOI: Traitors.
> NAKATOV: There *were* enemies and traitors [but no longer]?
> RIADOVOI: And if any remain – we'll smash them!

In 1933, of course, Stalin could have said to Afinogenov about exposing traitorous *dvurushniki* on the Central Committee: you ain't seen nothing yet.

All of this mask-wearing leads to an atmosphere of easily triggered denunciations and mutual ripping off of masks. Some denunciations are clearly demagogic, such as those by Ms. Shut-your-mouth. Others are defensive: denounce before you are denounced. The final twist in the plot, however, treats a denunciation that in itself is presented as perfectly proper: Riadovoi, Nina's wise mentor, shows his Bolshevik vigilance by announcing his intention to denounce the villainous *dvurushnik* Nakatov. The dramatic question is: will Nina, the waverer who must choose between contending forces, accept the necessity and propriety of this denunciation?

2   Nina's Crime, Nina's Redemption

In the denouement of *Lies*, Nina is led by her doubts and wavering to commit a serious political crime: she shoots a prominent party leader, who later dies

---

12   For numerous examples of similar editorial interventions by Stalin in the first draft of the
       Short Course, the canonical textbook of party history, see Brandenberger and Zelenov 2018.

of his wounds. One would think that this killing was an unforgiveable political crime. Nevertheless, Nina is redeemed and sees the error of her ways. But a question arises: is she redeemed because of her truth-seeking – or because she learns to renounce her truth-seeking?

What led Nina to make her fatal pistol shot? Her desperate act shows how *Lies* looks ahead to the new dominance of melodrama that centred on exposing the criminal *dvurushnik*. Nakatov, the former oppositionist, is at it again: he has forged a secret group to obtain a revision of the party line by hook or (more likely) by crook. He tries to recruit Nina, who relays this information to Riadovoi under seal of confidentiality. Nevertheless, Riadovoi has no scruples about announcing his intention to denounce Nakatov. When Nina finds out about this, she is shocked for a number of reasons. She has always highly respected Nakatov, who has a very distinguished Bolshevik past, knows a lot about people and events, and shows himself able to form independent judgements. She feels guilty because she was the inadvertent source of the compromising information. And, finally, she knows (because Riadovoi tells her) that Nakatov once saved Riadovoi's life in heroic fashion during the civil war. Nina therefore sees Riadovoi's denunciation as a despicable betrayal. She lashes out at him:

> It seems I never knew your heart. I was mistaken: it's grown old and cowardly. It's gotten out of the habit of feeling pain for other people. Just so long as *you* are warm and cozy. And then you can get a good apartment, and a car, and a position. And young girls! And if you denounce a friend, then you'll get an even higher position.

Of course, Nina's accusation of careerism has no basis in reality – in the particular case of Riadovoi. But the idea that base material motives are behind many denunciations is in no way challenged by the play. So wrought up is Nina that she shoots Riadovoi in the chest. He is taken to the hospital, but before he leaves, he informs everybody that his gunshot wound is due to his own carelessness in cleaning his gun – and Nina the truth-seeker goes along with this story. The two most truthful characters conspire to propagate an out-and-out lie!

What is really going on is revealed in the final scenes of the play. Riadovoi's lie about his gunshot wound is actually an act of Bolshevik leadership that keeps open the possibility of redemption for a wavering soul on the brink of disaster. Nina's redemption comes in three stages. First, she sees the real value of her doubts when Gorchakova – Ms. Shut-your-mouth – endorses them:

GORCHAKOVA: You, Nina, were right when you doubted everything ...
NINA: I didn't doubt, I only ...
GORCHAKOVA: No, don't deny your past, I remember every word ...
              'Where is truth? Who is telling the truth? Or does truth
              even exist? We wear masks ... double life ... tenderness
              is lost' ... [She leaves.]
NINA: She believed what I said ... It would have been bet-
              ter never to have said these words than to see them
              reflected in such a mirror.

Next, Nina receives a letter from Riadovoi, still alive but languishing in the
hospital. Riadovoi thinks Nina has the potential to be a good Bolshevik, but
reads her a sermon to get her back to the strait and narrow. Again, the message seems to be less 'your doubts are not justified' than 'having doubts is not
justified':

> The party needs you to be a good Bolshevik (*bolshevichka*). And that's
> what you'll be, Nina, if you don't you fall in love with your own rectitude
> but instead meld your thoughts and actions into a single whole, so that
> the ideas and the will of the party become for you – not a hair-shirt you
> wear to mortify the flesh – but your own flesh and blood ...
>
> Nina, retain the party's confidence, don't deceive it, but don't run to it in
> hysterics, don't overdo things, find in yourself the courage to decide ques-
> tions in a way that preserves and multiplies the strength of the party –
> after all, you yourself are a small part of this strength.

Nina is grateful, even in a romantic way, for this act of Bolshevik leadership:

> Why do I love him? For his strength, his steel-like [*stalnaia*] toughness,
> for his manliness and tenderness, for his clear mind. And because he held
> me back when I was on the edge of a precipice and returned me to life
> as a Bolshevik. Amidst all the chaff he found, with great care, the grain in
> me.

The final step in her redemption is after she learns how despicable Nakatov
truly is: he is hoping to escape denunciation if Riadovoi dies in the hospital,
since no one will believe Nina just on her own say-so. So Nina decides to confess
to the shooting, simply as a way of giving credibility to her own information. (I
guess the logic is: why would I have shot Riadovoi unless he himself intended
to denounce Nakatov?) This confession eliminates the last untruth and con-

firms Nina's Bolshevik redemption. The play ends with a call from the hospital: Riadovoi has died from his wounds – but now Nina is ready to replace him in the ranks.

3   Stalin as Theatrical Collaborator

Stalin's treatment of Afinogenov's *Lies* gives us an entrée into his theatricalized, melodramatic outlook. Far from rejecting outright what we see as the play's sharp social criticism, Stalin acted as a self-appointed collaborator. His attitude is in strong contrast to Gorky's condemnation of the play politically and artistically. In a letter to Afinogenov written in April 1933, Gorky argued that the play was politically unsuitable, not necessarily because its critique of party mores was wrong, but because the frankness of the play would have a bad effect on an unenlightened audience:

> I think the play would indeed be very useful if it were possible to put it on in some closed theatre, before a thousand well-schooled Leninists, unshakably confident in the correctness of the general line [of the party] ... But your play is aiming at an audience of millions of Soviet citizens, and, as you know, socialists are still not predominant among them.

Nakatov, the former opposition leader, 'will interest the spectator more than all the other characters of your play, because a majority of these spectators are themselves "oppositionist".' In other words, Gorky says to Afinogenov what Ms. Shut-your-mouth says to Nina: you can't say that out loud because 'they' will overhear![13]

In contrast, Stalin's comments in spring 1933 imply that he assumed that the play would eventually be staged, since he made manifold suggestions for small improvements. The Russian historian Ilya Veniavkin gives a striking example. Nakatov rejected the 'Mahometan socialism' dominant in the Soviet Union. This description comes straight from the émigré press and is based on the aphorism attributed to an Arab conqueror showing that the Koran was all that is needed: if what you say is already in the Koran, it's superfluous, and if it isn't in the Koran, it's harmful. Stalin crossed out 'Mahometan'

---

13   Gorky 1963, p. 32; for a discussion of this letter in the context of Gorky's idiosyncratic views about truth, see Heller 1988.

and substituted *prikaznoi*, socialist beliefs based on orders from above.[14] Possibly Stalin thought that the political point of 'Mahometan' would not be sufficiently clear to an audience. Whatever the actual merit of this editorial correction, we see Stalin trying to help Nakatov make his case – in order, of course, to increase the dramatic impact of his later exposure as a *dvurushnik*.

Therefore, despite Stalin's harsh criticism of various aspects of the play, Afinogenov was greatly encouraged when he received these comments. We have valuable direct memoir evidence that Afinogenov saw Stalin practically as a collaborator. The Russian-born American journalist Maurice Hindus – a personal friend of Afinogenov – wrote in 1953:

> One evening Afinogenov outlined to me the theme of his next play, the most daring he had yet conceived. It was to be titled *Lozh* (*The Lie*) and in it, he said, he would dramatize the little lies which for one reason or another party men in the lower ranks of the hierarchy transmit to their superiors, until by the time they reach the upper ranks they become big lies and blow up into catastrophe. The more he talked, the more enthusiastic he became, and when I ventured the suggestion that the censorship would never pass the play because party bureaucrats would resent an unfavourable portrayal of themselves, Afinogenov sprang from his chair and, pointing a finger at me, said 'There is where you are wrong. I discussed the theme with Stalin, and he told me we need a play like that and to go ahead and write it. I am assured of its production.'
>
> Afinogenov wrote the play, and when the censors rejected it he sent the manuscript to Stalin. The dictator read it immediately and telephoned Afinogenov, complimenting him on the play but informing him that the time was not ripe for its presentation. When the manuscript was returned Afinogenov saw with amazement certain parts of the dialogue corrected in Stalin's own handwriting. To him it signified that Stalin was too interested in the play to ban its production.
>
> But Stalin's 'ripe time' never came, and the play was never produced. Disillusioned and frustrated, Afinogenov stopped writing 'protest' plays.[15]

---

14   Veniavkin 2011. *Prikaznoi* is a term with historical overtones of Moscovite Russia.

15   Hindus 1953, p. 249. Without access to documents, Hindus' account understandably garbles chronological details. For more of Hindus' fascinating discussion of Afinogenov as a representative Soviet intellectual, see 'Show Trials in the Stalin Era: On Stage and In Court', included in this volume.

Only this sense of having received tacit encouragement can explain why Afinogenov and his theatrical collaborators went ahead with major rehearsals of the
play as well as public staging in Kharkov without even waiting for official permission. All the more devastating, then, was the final prohibition in November
1933.

Why did Stalin change his mind between April and October 1933? Some
point to changes in the external political environment during this period.[16]
Stalin may also have had objections to the script itself which were not resolved
by the second version. I will mention here some of the larger problems Stalin
had with the play's construction – problems that ultimately Afinogenov was
unable or unwilling to fix. Stalin had two overarching problems with *Lies*:
absence of complete melodramatic clarity and the insufficient vividness of the
positive characters. He impatiently asked for more and sooner clarity about
good and evil. Kulik – the character who parlays his proletarian origins into
career advancement – should be counterbalanced by 'another worker, honest,
noble and wholeheartedly devoted to the cause (open your eyes and you will
see that such workers really exist in our party)'. Stalin also wanted some virtuous character to openly insult Nakatov the *dvurushnik* even before his unmasking: 'All you're capable of is acting like a *dvurushnik*.'

He also suggested the deployment of a time-honoured melodramatic device:
the public meeting or trial where, in the manner of a Perry Mason TV episode,
the characters publicly verify and eliminate any doubt about the location of
good and evil. So Stalin asked: why not 'have a meeting of workers in the play
that would expose Viktor, topple Gorchakova and establish the truth?' This
last suggestion was put into practice during 1937 by thousands of meetings of
denunciation all across the country.

The other overall source of Stalin's dissatisfaction with *Lies* was its failure to
make the positive figures more compelling. 'Is there a reason why *all* your party
people are shown as deformed, physically, morally, politically (Gorchakova,
Viktor, Kulik, Seroshtanov)? Even Riadovoi comes out at various points as not
all there, almost retarded.' This characterization was in stark contrast to how
the villain was shown: 'The only character that carries out a coherent and carefully thought-out line – namely, *dvurushnichestvo* – is Nakatov. He is the most
"integral" [*tselnyi*] character.'

---

16   Veniavkin 2011 argues that during 1933 there was still a balance of power in high party
circles between leaders who took what might be called a 'temperance drama' minded
approach vs those who took a '*dvurushnik* drama' approach. In this way, Veniavkin adopts
my melodrama framework for Kremlinological purposes.

Later we will look more closely at Stalin's attitudes about melodramatic clarity and the difficulty of bringing the positive characters to vivid life. But Stalin also had serious objections to the ending of the play ('it seems evident that the ending was rushed'). He was drastically put off by Nina's monologue about masks and her confrontation with Riadovoi. His reaction: 'What's the point of this gloomy and annoying gibberish [*tarabarshchina*]?' He also strongly objected to Nina's attempt to shoot Riadovoi: 'What's the point of the pistol-shot by Nina? All it does is confuse things and spoils [the play's] whole music.'

In his revised version of *Lies*, Afinogenov tried to meet Stalin's criteria for powerful political melodrama. In the original version, Nina is feeling her way to an understanding of a world in which all are trapped. Judging from passages quoted by scholars from the revised version, Nina now becomes more moralistic and judgemental, looking at the situation from the point of view of the *vozhd*. When she repudiates her husband Viktor's pro-plan rule-bending, she restricts the problem to his crooked ways: 'You stand for collectivization only at meetings, and in fact you exist as an isolated unit with a mask on your face in order to hide your thoughts. This mask is a petty, scoundrelly one: you should be a wheeler-dealer in America, you belong there, rather than leading a socialist factory.'[17] Even his mask is a paltry one. When she talks about 'human trash', Nina seems to channel Stalin's exasperation with the people he had to deal with:

> I stopped in front of the Mausoleum and thought – thought about everything. Most of all: do our *vozhdi* [note the plural] know how much human trash [*driani liudskoi*] we have, how many liars, scoundrels, frauds? At meetings they applaud the slogans but at home they give their own evaluation – a different one. And we reassure ourselves: this is what the new life is, we have to praise and write eloquent words, portraits, medals – but it's all on the surface, all outside show.[18]

Nevertheless, Afinogenov failed to respond to many of Stalin's objections.[19] Most importantly, Afinogenov felt himself unable to do away with Nina's pistolshot. His rewritten version tinkers with this dramatic device rather than replac-

---

17   Karaganov 1964, p. 326.
18   Karaganov 1964, p. 320. This passage seems to have replaced the more damning charge in the first version of general indifference to the suffering of the woman crushed by a streetcar, as quoted earlier.
19   See Veniavkin 2011 for discussion.

ing it with something else: Nina tries to commit suicide rather than intentionally shooting Riadovoi. She only wounds him by accident, and he does not die.

Why was the pistol-shot so crucial to Afinogenov, and why did Stalin find it so objectionable?[20] I will suggest as a possible answer that the pistol-shot represents an unsuccessful juncture between the two melodramatic subgenres, the temperance drama and the *dvurushnik* drama. One crude but effective way of melding these two subgenres was employed by Stalin in material that he personally added to the 1938 *Short Course* on party history.[21] In accounting for the origin and motivation of two-faced wreckers such as Trotsky and Bukharin, Stalin took tropes from temperance drama: the party oppositionists take their fateful first drink when they oppose the party line, and from then on they steadily degenerate: from oppositionists to self-pitying failures to vengeful mask-wearing has-beens to deep-dyed villains in the service of fascist spy-agencies. Once arrived at this final point, they have become fully-fledged *dvurushniki*, ready to be exposed by vigilant Bolsheviks. Thus the main use of the 'waverer' trope here is simply to provide an origin story for the *dvurushnik*.

Afinogenov tried another way of uniting the two subgenres. Nina, his wavering character, moves step by step toward criminality, ending up by shooting a party leader. Nikolai Petrov, the director first of Afinogenov's *Fear* (in Leningrad) and then *Lies* (in Kharkov), made this result the primary lesson of the play: 'Our task is this: as the spectator leaves the theatre, having witnessed a slice of the life of the Ivanov family, he has deeply taken in the fact that a person who looks on life from the point of view of truth for themselves alone can end up committing terrible mistakes.'[22]

But Afinogenov was too fond of Nina, it seems, to turn her into a rejected criminal, and he tried another way of combing the two subgenres. Like Professor Borodin, the wavering character in *Fear*, Nina would be made to see the error of her ways and thus be pulled back from the brink. In the first version of *Lies*, Nina is redeemed even after committing a serious political crime. The revised version retains the pistol-shot as the nexus between the ultimate degeneration of the waverer and her ultimate salvation – but, as we have seen, the gravity of her crime is lessened by making the pistol-shot a suicide attempt

---

20   Gudkova suggests that Stalin was upset by the very idea of someone who was modelled on Stalin being shot (Gudkova 2014).

21   Brandenberger and Zelenov 2018.

22   Veniavkin 2011.

that only accidently wounds Riadovoi, who survives. But this makeshift adjustment – it could be argued – weakens both the degeneration story and the
redemption story.

Perhaps Gorky was correct, and Afinogenov liked Nina too much: 'Just like
Nina, you yourself, Afinogenov, are somewhat too much "in love with your own
rectitude" [so that you] "stick your finger right on the sore spot" of the party'.[23]
The playwright's attachment to his main character meant that he could not follow Stalin's suggestions/instructions, since he could neither fully condemn nor
fully exonerate his Nina.

According to Maurice Hindus, Stalin told Afinogenov that *Lies* simply
needed to wait until 'the time was ripe'.[24] The authenticity of this report is
impossible to judge. Perhaps Stalin said something like this, perhaps it represents Afinogenov's wishful thinking, perhaps Hindus misremembered what
Afinogenov told him. But we do know that during the next couple of years
Afinogenov and his theatrical friends did not give up all hope of staging *Lies*.
Indeed, after Kirov's assassination in December 1934, they felt it had gained
extra relevance, since the play talked about former oppositionists turning into
dvurushniki, about underground anti-party conspiracies and consequent assassination attempts. Even in 1936, Afinogenov was reading the plays to friends
and remarking on its newfound relevance.[25] Thus, even at this late date, they
did not feel *Lies* was entirely out of Stalinist bounds. But despite its seeming
relevance, the play's structural defect – Nina's enormous crime vs. her flimsy
redemption – remained. Or so we may speculate.

[Update: After sending my book to press, I had the opportunity to read the
full revised version. While I feel that my comments based on secondary sources
are still valid, I would like to add my overall reaction to Afinogenov's reworking. Afinogenov essentially wrote a new play in which the characters have only
a passing resemblance to their counterparts in the original version. All the
gloomy political passion has been bleached out, and the void is filled with triv-
ialities, both political and amorous. Stalin was probably correct to reject this
new version – even though the criteria he imposed on Afinogenov are ultimately responsible for the disastrous result.]

---

23   Gorky 1963, p. 33. The first quoted phrase comes from Riadovoi's letter to Nina urging her
      to become a good Bolshevik; the second seems to be Gorky's inaccurate memory of Ms.
      Shut-your-mouth's comment to Nina ('You're reopening wounds that haven't yet healed
      in many people. You talk on these forbidden topics, and people listen to you – listen and
      remain silent. Silent – but they're thinking!').
24   Hindus 1953.
25   Veniavkin 2011.

4   Melodramatic Motivations in Film Screenplays

Stalin criticized the original version of *Lies* for lack of melodramatic clarity and for failure to make the positive characters more vivid and appealing. We can easily find evidence of Stalin's continuing frustration about these two issues. Here we will take a look at some of his comments about screenplays for Soviet films during the 1930s. In 1935, after seeing Friedrich Ermler's film *Peasants*, Stalin commented:

> It's not bad that the spectator is confused at the beginning and intrigued as they ask themselves: who is the enemy? But still, when the enemy is already exposed, the *narod* demands a clear attitude to him, demands defence measures against his undermining work and against his terroristic activity. But you resort to symbolism – this doesn't work.[26]

As we see, Stalin is willing to allow some suspense about the identity of the villainous *dvurushnik* in order to sustain audience interest. But he is not willing to countenance any lack of clarity about the villainy itself. Its political significance must not be hidden by the slightest ambiguity. In 1937, Stalin was asked to pass judgement on a politically sensitive screenplay about the Kirov murder. His recommendations:

> You need to put the matter in such a way that the struggle between the Trotskyites and the Soviet government does not look like a struggle of two parties for power, one of whom is 'lucky' in this struggle and the other 'unlucky' – that would be a crude distortion of reality – but as a *struggle of two programs*, one of which corresponds to the interests of the revolution and is supported by the *narod* while the other opposes the interests of the revolution and is rejected by the *narod*.[27]

Stalin's demand here is that the *narod* fulfil the function of the virtuous community that plays such an essential role in classic melodrama. The *narod*

---

26   Veniavkin 2011, citing *Kremlevskii kinoteatr, 1928–1953: Dokumenty* (Moscow, 2005). It is not clear to me whether this comment applies to the film as released or (more likely) to an earlier viewing at the Kremlin. *Peasants* (*Krestiane*) can be viewed on YouTube; Ekaterina Korchagina-Aleksandrovskaia, the original Klara in the Leningrad production of *Fear*, has a principal role. *Peasants* is about a kulak saboteur and as such bears comparison with Vladimir Kirshon's *Bread*, staged four years earlier. The movie also features some very charming pigs.

27   G. Mar'iamov 1992, *Kremlevskii tsenzor: Stalin smotrit kino*, p. 34.

must see – and must be seen to see – who the villain is and then must cast him out.

In 1940, Stalin grappled at length with another source of his uneasiness with *Lies*: the challenge of creating vivid positive heroes within the framework of socialist realism. In 1940, the film *Law of Life* [*Zakon zhizni*] was released with a script by the well-known writer Aleksandr Avdeenko. Stalin took such a dislike to it that a Central Committee session was held in September 1940 to discuss the film and its problems. During this session, Stalin expatiated at length on the problem of characterization and tried out a theory that would explain why so many Soviet writers failed to make their positive characters come alive. In the Appendix to this essay, I provide excerpts from this fascinating look into Stalin's mind.[28]

In his remarks, Stalin insisted that he had no objection to giving the villain admirable qualities in order to increase their dramatic interest. He rather surprisingly faulted Shakespeare, Gogol and Griboedov for their unnuanced portrayal of villains as totally evil. Finding a writer at a greater distance from socialist realism than Chekhov would be difficult, but nevertheless:

> There is a particular way of writing, one found in Gogol, say, or Shakespeare. They have larger-than-life protagonists, both negative and positive. When you read Shakespeare or Gogol or Griboedov, you find one particular protagonist with negative traits.[29] Every possible negative trait is concentrated in one person. I prefer another way of writing, Chekhov's style, who doesn't have outstanding protagonists, but simply shows us average persons who nevertheless reflect the underlying stream of life. This is another way of writing.

Stalin even applied this theory to people he considered to be real-life villains: 'Why should we portray Bukharin as if he were an unadulterated monster? – He definitely had some [admirable] human qualities. Trotsky was an enemy,

---

28   The text of Stalin's remarks is an uncorrected transcript, and I have taken the liberty of making some adjustments in order to reflect what I take to be Stalin's meaning, as indicated in brackets. For the Russian original, see M.V. Zelenov 2006, *Istoricheskaia ideologiia v SSSR v 1920–1950-e gody*, pp. 461–6. For valuable background to the *Law of Life* episode, see Evgenii Gromov 2003, *Stalin: Iskusstvo i vlast*'; for Avdeenko's own memoir account, see his *Otluchenie*, published in *Znamia*, 1989, Nos. 3 and 4. The movie itself can be found on YouTube.

29   Or perhaps Stalin's meaning is: 'you find maybe one positive hero who has any negative traits.'

but he was a capable person, no doubt about it. We should portray him as an enemy with negative traits, but also with some admirable traits, because these existed, no doubt about it.'

In discussing this problem, at one point Stalin – as it seems to me – resorted to an argument that we often find in Bukharin. At all points in his career, Bukharin insisted on the need to look past the horrendous immediate costs and focus on the shining future purchased by these costs.[30] Stalin also allowed that the high costs of some policies might have misled people: 'So, it's not because [Avdeenko] portrays our enemies in a good light, but rather that [the positive characters], the people who expose these enemies, are not shown as Soviet people. And this isn't so easy to do. In our case, for example, something like 25–30 million people went hungry, there wasn't enough grain, and now they're starting to live better.'

Stalin's remarks on redeeming qualities in villains throw light on his earlier critique of *Lies*. He was irritated that the only integral character in the play was the *dvurushnik* Nakatov. But (as we have seen) he did not ask for Nakatov to be a more one-sided character. Rather, he was disappointed that there was no sufficient counterweight to him among the positive characters. In his later remarks about Avdeenko's screenplay, Stalin suggests a reason for the annoying failure on the part of Soviet artists to give dramatic life to such characters: the writers themselves were alien to the Bolshevik world and failed to profoundly understand it. Try as they might, their inner sympathies were elsewhere.

In Avdeenko's works, the people who should be fighting are shown as pretty poor specimens, commonplace, mediocre – how could such people crush the enemy? Yes, Avdeenko's failing is that the guy on our side, the Bolshevik, is left by the author in the shade – for the Bolshevik, Avdeenko lacks vivid colours. Avdeenko has examined the enemy closely and knows him well enough to be able to portray him with his negative traits and his positive traits. But he hasn't examined *our* reality closely. Strange but true: he doesn't understand it, he doesn't really see it ...

There exists a milieu [in our country] that produces heroes. So why isn't there enough colour to portray good people? [Avdeenko] doesn't have adequate colours to help build the new life. Why aren't there enough colours for the portrayal of life? Because he doesn't sympathize with it.

---

30   See 'Bukharin's Bolshevik Epic: The Prison Writings', included in this volume.

In his critique of the original version of *Lies*, Gorky advanced a similar theory to explain Afinogenov's seeming inability to make his positive characters live:

> I'm not a party member, and I'm not really familiar with its internal life. But the Bolshevik as a type is something I've been familiar with for thirty years or so. It could be that I myself haven't been able to portray the Bolshevik properly. But still I have grounds to say that this type of person is not clear to you. I find it hard to say why this is the case. But I think that it's because of your youth and consequently your small acquaintance with the life story of the kind of Bolshevik who is important and interesting not because of his flaws but because of his strong qualities. His flaws are rooted in the past that he is tirelessly destroying, while his strong qualities are in his work for constructing the future.[31]

Stalin's remarks on writers like Avdeenko can be compared to his feelings about 'soviet' bureaucrats in his letters to Molotov. In each case, the failure of the Soviet system to work properly is blamed on the inherent loyalty of the personnel to a world in which they had grown up and could never spiritually leave.[32] And perhaps Stalin had a point. But with hindsight, we can also see that problems also arose from the inner logic of the system he himself had helped to create. Ultimately, the heroic qualities of positive characters consisted of no more than faithfully executing orders from the centre. Bolsheviks fighting *for* the revolution could take on vivid life. Bolsheviks fighting to achieve socialism *after* the revolution were in danger of becoming no more than heroic cogs.

5   Melodramatic Motivation in Real Life

Stalin sounded almost poignant when he interrupted Bukharin at the 1937 February–March Plenum. After Bukharin insisted on the utter implausibility of the monstrous crimes attributed to him, Stalin responded: 'You have to put yourselves in our position. Trotsky with his students Zinoviev and Kamenev once worked with Lenin, and now these people have got themselves all the way to an agreement with Hitler. Can you call these things "monstrous" after that? Not at all. After what happened with these gentlemen – former comrades –

---

31   Gorky 1963, p. 34.
32   For Stalin's anti-bureaucrat scenario, see 'Stalin at Work', included in this volume.

who got themselves all the way to an agreement with Hitler and to selling off the USSR, there can be nothing surprising in human life.'[33]

Did Stalin really believe what he was saying? Did he really experience this epistemological vertigo? Instead of trying to answer these questions, let us examine how Stalin helped build a world in which this vertigo was inevitable. Stalin's *dvurushnik* narrative was an attempt to impose a melodramatic clarity on the course of events: anything that went wrong was the result of evil actions of evil men who would soon be exposed. Perhaps paradoxically, the end result of his attempt was not clarity but heightened ambiguity, not epistemological confidence but an obsessive vertigo. Like the hero of Hitchcock's *Vertigo*, this was because Stalin lived – and forced others to live – in a world of masks and unreliable identities.

Stalin, it is clear, genuinely wanted plays and movies to reflect reality – in any event, what he saw as reality. And conversely, in trying to make sense of political reality, he made use of tropes from melodrama. Several documents from the 1930s show us Stalin directly struggling with the problem of working out a coherent characterization for the *dvurushnik*.

In a speech from June 1937 informing military officers about the recent arrests of the top command, Stalin openly searched for a convincing motivation for the conspirators.[34] *Chto eto za liudi?* – What kind of people are these? Stalin answered his own question by systematically removing objective and socially based motivations. Social origin? This is not a reliable clue, since many individuals from privileged classes serve the cause 'not worse but better than full-blooded proletarians'. Previous opposition activity? No: many good party people have 'wavered' in the past and dallied with the opposition, but afterwards they saw the light and even fought well against later oppositions. Stalin even expresses some admiration for such people: they differed from 'official' Leninists because they 'lacked a sufficient dose of cowardice to hide their wavering'.

Policy disagreements? Stalin refused to admit, either personally or politically, that opposition might come from genuine political disagreement, especially about the fundamental issue of all-out collectivization: 'The collective farms – does that have anything to do [with these conspiracies]? Well, you see, now they're all sorry for the peasants.' To show the hypocrisy of this claim that opposition to himself was motivated by the disaster of all-out collectivization, Stalin cites the case of Abel Enukidze, who cries about the peasants now

---

33   *Voprosy istorii*, 1992, No. 4–5, p. 36.
34   Speech of 2 June 1937, as published in *Istochnik*, 1994, No. 3, pp. 72–85.

but mistreated them back in 1918, a crime for which Stalin – defender of the muzhik – wanted him expelled from the party. Stalin's remarks show us that the disaster of collectivization was one of the underlying reasons why the narrative of the waverer with his legitimate doubts was banished in favour of the *dvurushnik* with his unmotivated and illegitimate ones.

Since the *dvurushnik*'s motivation could not be tied to objective criteria, Stalin was forced to trivialize it. The conspirators were disappointed in their careers or they were tricked into jumping on the counter-revolutionary bandwagon or they were blackmailed. Stalin even suggested that some of the officers had fallen into the clutches of a Mata Hari-type vamp, a beautiful Danish woman who 'very willingly went along with any male suggestion and then destroyed [her victims]'. Since people within the virtuous community could have no understandable grounds for complaint, the source of active villainy and energetic evil was projected outside to the Nazi Reichswehr and 'top spy' Trotsky. 'We're not dealing here with political disagreements ... These people were puppets [*nevolniki*] in the hands of the Reichswehr.'[35]

And yet it is necessary to unmask every last one of the political chameleons, including those who seem to the myopic eye to be doing an excellent job. Stalin told a spy story to show how a single individual – like Gravel-voice in *Optimistic Tragedy* – can do incalculable damage.[36] 'To win a battle in time of war may requires several corps of Red Army men. But to destroy that victory on the front, all you need is a few individual spies in the Army or even divisional GHQ who are able to steal operational plans and sell them to the enemy.'

If the source of evil is outside the community, then presumably we don't need repressive or punitive organs inside the community. And in fact (says Stalin, speaking in 1938) they are even now withering away, right on schedule. What we do still need is an organization that uncovers hidden things: the *razvedka*, a word for which 'intelligence agencies' is a very pallid translation. As Stalin explains:

> [Given the nature of capitalist encirclement], we need to have a *razvedka*, and then a counter-*razvedka* as well, and this implies a strengthening of Chekist organs [political police] within the country, because our enemies, they don't sleep, time and again they send different people to us to sound us out, maybe something can be done, perhaps they can blow up some-

---

35   *Istochnik*, 1994, No. 3, pp. 72–85 (speech of 2 June 1937). The dictionary definition of *nevolniki* is 'prisoners', but Stalin's imagery emphasizes the entire absence of will.

36   For Gravel-voice, a character in Vsevolod Vishnevsky's *Optimistic Tragedy*, see 'Show Trials in the Stalin Era: On Stage and In Court', included in this volume.

thing, do a little bit of wrecking. And in our party exists a type of person – this type does exist, yes it does and it will continue to exist – that's what capitalist encirclement means, that it sends people who corrupt our people, corrupt them: don't think we've purified everything.[37]

The removal of any objective basis for motivation greatly intensified the vertigo that was both expression and cause of the hysteria that marks this period of Soviet history. Thus, in Stalin's vertiginous world, a cowering speech was a call to arms: 'At the Seventeenth Party Congress [in 1934], Bukharin, Rykov and Tomsky made repentant speeches, praising the Party and extolling its achievements to the skies ... The Party saw that the hollow speeches of these gentry were in reality meant for their supporters outside the congress, to serve as a lesson to them in duplicity, and a call to them not to lay down their arms.'[38]

When Stalin reduced all party opposition to *dvurushnichestvo*, he created a situation that lacked any objective guide to political judgement. He insisted that 'contemporary Trotskyism' could not be considered a political movement because it hid its views – even from itself! 'When Radek and Piatakov insisted that Trotsky authorize a small conference of about 30–40 people in order to inform them about the nature of their platform, Trotsky forbade such a conference by saying it was inexpedient to talk about the genuine character of the platform even to a small cluster of Trotskyites, since an "operation" of this kind would create a schism.'[39]

Political trials were supposed to establish the truth and yet the *dvurushnik* could not be pinned down so easily. In the first trials after the Kirov murder, 'the Zinovievites simulated remorse in court; but they persisted in their duplicity even in the dock. They concealed their connection with Trotsky. They concealed the fact that together with the Trotskyites they had sold themselves to fascist espionage services.'[40] The trial of Zinoviev and Kamenev in 1936 uncovered more of the truth, but even here the defendants denied they had a political program. Of course they had one – they were just afraid to reveal it!

---

37   Speech of 1 October 1938 to propagandists about the recently published *Short Course*; for
      text, see Brandenberger and Zelenov 2014, *'Kratkii kurs istorii vкр(b)': Tekst e ego istoriia
      v 2 chastiakh, Chast' 1*, pp. 452–66 (quoted passage on p. 461). 'Purification' *(ochishchenie)*
      was the official label given to the events of 1937–1938 that we usually call 'the great purge'
      or 'the great terror'.
38   This language was added by Stalin personally; see Brandenberger and Zelenov 2018,
      pp. 584–5.
39   Stalin 1967, 14:200.
40   This language was in the original committee draft of the *Short Course* prior to Stalin's final
      editorial intervention; see Brandenberger and Zelenov 2018, p. 586.

While giving tips on how to uncover the *dvurushnik*, Stalin emphasized look-ing at the results of their work rather than their declarations. But he immedi-ately undercut even this seemingly solid ground: of course, no wrecker wrecks all the time – he has to have occasional successes. Even a wrecker will some-times fulfil and overfulfil the plan: hasn't it been shown that plan targets are almost always too low?

A further difficulty for the would-be vigilante is Stalin's condemnation of any slander of honest Communists. Already in 1937, at the beginning of the purification campaign, he was warning against calling someone a Trotskyite merely because he walked down the same street as a Trotskyite. In a return to the rhetoric of Soviet political temperance dramas, he warned against push-ing waverers toward the Trotskyites (usually the *dvurushnik* narrative does not include waverers of any kind). This warning from 1937 allowed Stalin to appear consistent in the two documents of 1938 that signalled the beginning of the end of the terror campaign: a resolution of the January 1938 Party Plenum and a government resolution of November 1938.[41]

These are remarkable documents; perhaps we might call them 'Stalin-style destalinization' or some such inadequate oxymoron. On the one hand, they set out the charges that have remained the core of the indictment against Stalin's terror campaign to this day: the manufactured hysteria against fictitious 'ene-mies of the people' and the massive violations of legality. On the other hand, these accusations are fitted smoothly into the existing *dvurushnik* narrative: now it is the turn of the unmaskers to be unmasked. Two types of duplic-itous unmasking must be exposed. First, careerist party officials: 'Instead of ripping the mask of false vigilance off "communists" like these and bringing them out into the open, party organizations and their leaders have themselves often given to them the aura of vigilant warriors for the purity of party ranks.' (One is reminded of Ms. Shut-your-mouth from Afinogenov's *Lies*.)

Second, a new breed of *dvurushnik* has arisen: 'All these facts show that many of our party organizations and their leaders still to this day haven't learned to see through and expose the artfully masked enemy who attempts with cries of vigilance to mask his own enemy status ... and who uses repressive measures to cut down our Bolshevik cadres and to sow insecurity and excessive suspicion in our ranks.'[42]

The crowning climax to the vertiginous world of masked unmaskers is the revelation that the *dvurushniki* have infiltrated the ranks of the professional

41   Kosolapov 1995, pp. 143–52, 154–60.
42   Kosolapov 1995, pp. 148–9; everything after 'expose' is underlined in original.

dvurushnik-catchers. The explanation for the massive violations of legality is that enemies of the people have infiltrated the central and local organs of the NKVD itself. These are the enemies of the people who have 'consciously distorted Soviet laws, created forgeries, falsified investigative materials, investigating and arresting people on flimsy foundations or no foundations at all, created "cases" against innocent people for purposes of provocation, and using all these measures in order to hide and save from destruction their colleagues in this criminal anti-Soviet activity'.[43]

The January 1938 resolution remarked irritably: 'It is time to understand that Bolshevik vigilance means the ability to expose the enemy, no matter how tricky and resourceful he is, no matter what costume he puts on; it doesn't mean expelling from the party whoever comes to hand, in batches of ten or a hundred, without discrimination or "just in case".'[44] In other words, the only truly vigilant person is someone who is always right and never wrong. But given the absence of any stable criteria for identifying enemies of the people, zealous vigilance could be transformed in the twinkling of an eye to masked careerism or even to a higher and more terrifying form of *dvurushnichestvo*.

In a famous still from Sergei Eisenstein's film *Ivan the Terrible*, one of his henchmen peers around an elaborate mask to cast a wary and suspicious eye on the surroundings (see Figure 4). Judging from this image alone, the person whom we see using the mask could either be a henchman of the tsar or a *dvurushnik* seeking to undermine him. It doesn't matter: all are constrained to wear masks and to peer into a world where everybody else is doing the same.

Why did Soviet citizens wear masks? Let Afinogenov count the ways: fear, doubt, careerism, system constraints, conscious deception, and on and on. The result was an all-encompassing vertigo that spared no one, rulers or ruled. Attempts to cut through the vertigo and impose melodramatic clarity only accelerated the process. Ripping off the mask of the class enemy had always been part of the Bolshevik narrative, but, under the name of 'Bolshevik vigilance', it lost any anchorage in objective reality and threatened to fatally weaken Soviet society.

---

43   Kosolapov 1995, p. 157.
44   Kosolapov 1995, pp. 151–2.

FIGURE 4
A Bacchanal of Masks in Eisenstein's *Ivan the Terrible*
HTTPS://JONATHANROSENBAUM.NET/2021/
06/HIGH-AND-LOW-EISENSTEINS-IVAN-THE
-TERRIBLE-TK/ (LAST ACCESSED 11 JUNE
2023)

Appendix 1: Nina's Monologue on Masks and Double Life, from *Lies* by Aleksandr Afinogenov

Our whole country is covered these days [of frantic construction] with a film of lime dust and cement. We say: We are building! But – the dust from all this activity prevents us from seeing life, so we don't see that people are growing up deformed, unable to speak out, indifferent to everything. Let's say a streetcar crushes a woman – everybody curses, 'Oh, another blasted traffic hold-up'. We live a double life. So we comfort ourselves: this is the life we need, we're new people, we're good people, we praise ourselves, we write such eloquent words, we hand out portraits and medals – and it's all for show, all just an exterior advertisement. And everybody knows this, everyone has gotten used to it, like that paper rouble on which you read: 'Obligatory exchange for gold on demand'. But nobody is actually taking the rouble to the Torgsin [foreign exchange stores]!

It's the same thing with all our slogans: we applaud them at public meetings, but at home we give our own evaluation, a different one. Why are there no strong convictions anymore? Because yesterday a person is a *vozhd*, everybody burns incense in front of him, and tomorrow he's removed and no one wants even to shake his hand. In earlier days, Bolsheviks would go to prison to back up each word of their convictions, they would suffer through exile, but the ones we have today – well, as soon as they get in a little bit of trouble, they instantly write letters to deny their whole past.

And us, the younger generation? We hardly even know what a firm conviction is. We've even come to joke about the older ones: here they go again, defining their own political 'tendency' and 'disassociating' themselves from other tendencies. – But it's not so funny, this is how we're growing up: not thinking, not feeling. Oh yes, you've seen us at demonstrations for all these years and we've expressed our confidence in you so many times – but it's superficial, it's all so fragile. And we'll sell you out just as easily as we exalt you, because that's how we've been raised.

We don't know enough to make comparisons, they don't let us make comparisons, and we don't even know what the party's general line will be tomorrow: what today is the party line is a deviation tomorrow. And they don't even write the whole truth in the newspapers. I'm just so tired of living this way, I want so much to be able to delve into issues myself and understand them in such a way that if I am tortured by enemies of the revolution, I would still even then preserve my voice and remain steadfast.

So now we have feet of clay. Oh, it's easy to be steadfast, when there's only one party in the country, and that party is as strong as iron. So we hide behind its back, but as isolated individuals we're weak and sickly, rushing about like chickens with their head cut off. And we lie, and we cheat, and we sneak around, and we all hate each other, like a hundred years ago – maybe even worse, I don't know, I wasn't there. After all, I was brought up in a Komsomol commune ... All I do is talk, but what we need to do is this: catch each liar and beat him about the head and shoulders, until he tells us, *who* taught him to lie like that.

[source: Gudkova 2014; my translation]

Appendix II: Why Stalin Preferred Chekhov to Shakespeare (Remarks from a Central Committee Meeting, September 1940)

There are several issues involved here – issues having serious significance for the development of literature. I would like to talk about an issue not directly relating to Avdeenko's book: how to approach literature in general. There exists a truthful, objective approach to literature. Does this truthful and objective approach mean that one can or should be detached and simply paint what's there or just photograph? Can we equate a living person, an author who wants to be truthful and objective – can we compare him to some photographic equipment? Not at all. This means that truthfulness and objectivity must be not detached but living. The author is a living person, he sympathizes with that person among his protagonists, he doesn't care for this other. This means that truthfulness and objectivity are truthfulness and objectivity that serves a particular class. Plekhanov said that literature cannot [but] appear as tendentious, and when we unpack this, we find that literature must serve some particular social milieu, some particular class, some particular society. Therefore, literature cannot be some sort of photographic equipment. Truthfulness cannot be understood in this way. Literature cannot exist without emotions, it sympathizes with this person and hates this person. I believe that this is the point of view we must use in evaluating literature: the point of view of truthfulness and objectivity.

The demand is made that artistic works must show us the enemy based entirely on the main thing about him [that is, his villainy]. Is this correct or incorrect? Incorrect. There is a particular way of writing, one found in Gogol, say, or Shakespeare. They have larger-than-life protagonists, both negative and positive. When you read Shakespeare or Gogol or Griboedov, you find one particular protagonist with negative traits. Every possible negative trait is concentrated in this one person. I prefer another way of writing, Chekhov's style, who doesn't have outstanding protagonists, but simply shows us average persons who nevertheless reflect the underlying stream of life. This is another way of writing.

I prefer that writers present enemies to us, not just as monsters, but rather as people who, even though they are hostile to our society, are not devoid of some human qualities. Even the absolutely worst villain has some human qualities: he loves somebody, he respects somebody, he is ready to make sacrifices for somebody. He has some sort of human traits. That's the way that I think enemies should be presented – enemies with some stature. What's the benefit if we make a lot of noise about the class struggle of capitalism with socialism, and all we do is smash midgets? And [although] our enemies do indeed make a lot of noise, they're not at all weaklings. You can't say that there aren't strong personalities among them. Why should we portray Bukharin as if he were an unadulterated monster? – he definitely had some [admirable] human qualities. Trotsky was an enemy, but he was a capable person, no doubt about it. We should portray him as an enemy with negative traits, but also with some admirable traits, because these existed, no doubt about it.

The problem with Avdeenko, then, is not that he accords some decency to the enemy. The problem is that he leaves the people on our side [*nash brat*] in the shade. Yes, we need truthfulness that portrays the enemy in the round, with positive traits as well as negative ones – positive ones such as, for example, stubbornness, stick-to-it-iveness, the courage to go up against society. These are attractive qualities, why not portray them? The fact that Com. Avdeenko puts the enemy in a decent light is not the problem, but rather that the people who win out, who smash the enemies, who lead the country after them – these people he leaves in the shade, he doesn't give them colour. That's the problem. Here we have the basic reason for lack of truthfulness, lack of objectivity
...

And now back to Comrade Avdeenko. You see, as I said before, that the problem isn't that he makes mistakes about the enemy – that he presents to us examples of enemies or of friends of our enemies and puts them in the best possible light, not as monsters, but as people who do have some good qualities, and there is not a single person who doesn't have such qualities. The most consummate villain, if you consider closely, has good qualities – he could, say, lay down his life for his best friend. So, it's not because he portrays our enemies in a good light, but rather that the people who expose these enemies, are not shown as Soviet people. And this isn't so easy to do. In our case, for example, something like 25–30 million people went hungry, there wasn't enough grain, and now they're starting to live better. Or take our enemies within the party, who made the false claim that we'll give this away to the Germans and that away to the Japanese, since we'll always have plenty of land – and how did it turn out? Just the opposite, we didn't give anybody anything, on the contrary, we extended the front of socialism. Is that a bad thing? Is it a bad thing from the point of view of the balance of forces in the world? We extended the front of socialist construction, and that's a good thing for humanity, for don't the Lithuanians, the Western Belarusians, the Bessarabians, whom we saved from the yoke of the landowners, capitalists, police force and all other kinds of scum, count themselves lucky? This is from the point of view of the peoples involved. And from the point of view of the struggle of forces on a global scale between socialism and capitalism, this is a big plus, because we are extending the front of socialism and reducing the front of capitalism.

In Avdeenko's works, the people who should be fighting are shown as pretty poor specimens, commonplace, mediocre – how could such people crush the enemy? Yes, Avdeenko's failing is that the guy on our side, the Bolshevik, is left by him in the shade – for the Bolshevik, Avdeenko lacks vivid colours. Avdeenko has examined the enemy closely and knows him well enough to be able to portray him with his negative traits and his positive traits. But he hasn't examined our reality closely. Strange but true: he doesn't understand it, he doesn't really see it ...

You get the idea that he sympathizes with one kind of person and doesn't sympathize with the other kind. I'd like to know, which of his protagonists does he sympathize with? In any event, not the Bolsheviks! If that isn't the case, why doesn't he have enough vivid colour for actual people? Where do people like Chkalov and Gromov [heroic and beloved Soviet aviators] come from? From where do they appear – they don't shoot up out of nowhere, do they? There exists a milieu [in our country] that produces heroes. So why isn't there enough colour to portray good people? Why isn't there enough colour to show [their good] traits? He doesn't have adequate colours to help build the new life. Why aren't there enough colours for the portrayal of life? Because he doesn't sympathize with it. You will say that I am exaggerating. I hope I'm mistaken, but in my opinion he barely can be said to sympathize with the Bolsheviks. Let's go back to 1934: we corrected him for the same sort of thing. Again in 1938: we corrected him, showed him the correct path. Nevertheless he continued to do his own thing. That's the camp in which he lives, while our camp is somewhere in the shadows.

[source: Zelenov 2006; my translation]

Who Is Stalin, What Is He?

The aim of this essay is not to give a direct answer to the title question, but rather to look at some answers given by others: *Life Magazine* and its photojournalist Margaret Bourke-White, Soviet composers celebrating Stalin in choral compositions, and Stalin's own comments on the notorious *Short Course* of party history – a visual, an aural, and a textual case study. These three topics have no direct connection beyond the fact that they all come from the Stalin era itself. Although each item in the series has its own peculiar interest, I hope that each gains from unexpected refractions from all the others.

After writing up the three mini-essays, I discovered an unexpected link that unifies them. In many times and cultures, the existence of a prosperous, united, independent and happy community is guaranteed by the presence of a legitimate ruler, one in touch with the sacred. Such a ruler benefits the community, not only or even primarily because he makes wise decisions (although 'happy is the people whose Prince is a sage man'), but because his alignment with the sacred means that the forces of nature work with and not against the community.[1] To those steeped in a Marxist perspective (but not only them), the sacred will often appear as the deep forces of history. In their different ways, each of the following case studies brings up this kind of theme: the legitimate ruler as guarantee of a community's moral and material prosperity, the importance of being aligned with the forces of nature, the laws of history as source of the sacred. A visible link is the presence in each case study of the episode where Stalin made his most explicit contact with the sacred: the oath he swore in the name of the Soviet community immediately after Lenin's death in 1924.

1 *Life Magazine*: Special Issue USSR, 1943

On the cover of *Life Magazine*'s 'Special Issue USSR', published on 29 March 1943, is a striking and effective portrait of Stalin by the great photojournalist,

---

1 The quoted words come from a sung text found in the mid-sixteenth-century Wanley Partbooks; my thanks to the Montreal early music group One Equal Musick for bringing this text to my attention.

Margaret Bourke-White. There is no need to ask ourselves why an American mass-market magazine owned by conservative Republicans would publish an entire issue favourable to the USSR in 1943. The Soviet Union had emerged triumphant from the battle of Stalingrad, and was a valiant, indeed necessary, ally for the USA in the war against Hitler.

The entire issue is a fascinating artefact in itself, not least because of the constant clash between the photographic evocations of Soviet life and the picture of American society that arises from the advertisements found on most pages. The advertisements appeal to insecurities of every kind, from bad breath to cultural tastes (see the ads for classical LP s). The editors, who were so skilful in creating photo layouts for the main articles, seemed to have no eye for, or no control over, the incongruities arising from this clash. The most grimly surreal example is on the two-page spread found on pp. 26–7. On the left side, a full-page black and white photograph of scattered corpses, with only the following text: 'Since 1941 violent death has come to 10,000,000 of Russia's people'. This is by far the most gruesome photograph in the issue. On the right side, a full-page colour ad for Campbell's Vegetable Soup: 'Build your wartime meals around soups like these ...' (ellipsis in original). Three large pictures of hearty soups, plus a smiling picture of happy civilians – fathers, mothers, and kids – each serving the war effort in their own way.

The main thrust of the issue is to celebrate Soviet achievements in modernizing the country. This message is set out in the introductory editorial:

[The Russians] live under a system of tight state-controlled information. But probably the attitude to take toward this is not to get too excited about it. When we take account of what the USSR has accomplished in the 20 years of its existence we can make allowances for certain shortcomings, however deplorable. For that matter, even 15 years ago the Russian economy had scarcely yet changed from the days of the Czars, and the kulaks of the steppes were still treating modern industrial machines like new toys. In 1929 the Soviet Union did not have a single automobile or tractor plant and did not produce high-grade steel of ball bearings.

Today the USSR ranks among the top three or four nations in industrial power. She has improved her health, built libraries, raised her literacy to about 80% – and trained one of the most formidable armies on earth. It is safe to say that no nation in history has ever done so much so fast. If the Soviet leaders tell us that the control of information was necessary to get this job done, we can afford to take their word for it for the time being. We who know the power of free speech, and the necessity for it, may assume that if those leaders are sincere in their work of emancipating the Russian people they will swing around toward free speech – and soon.[2]

Accordingly, photographic essays are devoted to industrialization, literacy, cultural and sports programmes, and collectivization. The photo essay on agriculture is entitled 'Collective Farms Feed the Nation'. The reader is informed that during collectivization, 'the wealthier farmers, called kulaks, were brutally liquidated by death, exile or coercion'. Nevertheless, the bottom line is that 'whatever the cost of farm collectivization, in terms of human life and individual liberty, the historic fact is that it worked ... Russia could not have built the industry which turned out the munitions which stopped the German army'.[3]

In an extensive photo-essay devoted to Lenin's life, he is presented as 'perhaps the greatest man of modern times'. 'Lenin was the rarest of men, an absolutely unselfconscious and unselfish man who had a passionate respect for ideas, but even more respect for deeds ... He was a normal, well-balanced man'. A normal, well-balanced man! How shocking such an assertion sounds today! In contrast, Trotsky was 'a thinker and a dreamer ... He went into exile, leaving behind a secret network of opposition which strove for years to undermine the government'. His rival, Joseph Stalin, was a 'strong, tough silent proletarian man of action' who proceeded to 'ruthlessly eliminate the so-called Trotskyist fifth column'. In a four-page spread, Stalin's top leadership team is presented as 'tough, loyal, capable administrators'. Lavrentia Beria, for example, heads the NKVD, identified as 'a national police similar to the FBI'. His assignment at the present time is 'enforcement of Stalin's scorched-earth policy and tracking down of traitors'.[4]

Until I sat down to describe this issue, I didn't realize how little it contained about Stalin himself – apart from, of course, the striking cover photograph. This photograph has a gritty realism that was conspicuously absent from visual images of the leader circulating in the Soviet Union. In particular, his pockmarked face was not hidden. For a foreign audience, these pockmarks added to the impressiveness. As Bourke-White herself wrote in a book published in 1942, 'his rough pitted face was so strong that it looked as if it had been carved out of stone'.[5]

---

2 *Life Magazine* 1943, p. 20.
3 *Life Magazine* 1943, p. 4.
4 *Life Magazine* 1943, pp. 29, 36, 40.
5 Bourke-White 1942, p. 213. The photograph of Stalin found in this book is not the one used for the 1943 *Life* cover. In his new book *International Communism and the Cult of the Individual: Leaders, Tribunes and Martyrs under Lenin and Stalin* (2017), Kevin Morgan discusses the role

The only eye-witness description of Stalin as a person in the *Life* issue is a little anecdote about the taking of this photograph: 'Joseph Stalin is properly on the cover of this Russian issue of LIFE. This portrait was taken by LIFE Photographer Margaret Bourke-White two years ago in the Kremlin. Stalin's granite face kept breaking into a grin at Miss Bourke-White's photographic antics. He seemed very tired and drawn, with a whole night's work ahead of him'.[6]

When we compare this anecdote to Bourke-White's own account in her 1942 book *Shooting the Russian War*, we find that the *Life* editors evidently added the details about the repeated grins and the 'whole night's work ahead of him' – Bourke-White just observed that he looked very tired. Her overall impressions of her subject match those of more than one observer:

> As I crouched on my hands and knees from one low camera angle to another, Stalin thought it was funny and started to laugh.
>
> When his face lighted up with a smile, the change was miraculous. It was though a second personality had come to the front, genial, cordial and kindly. I pressed on through two more expressions, until I got the expression I wanted.
>
> I got ready to go, and threw my stuff back into the camera case; then I noticed a peculiar thing about Stalin's face. When the smile ended, it was though a veil had been drawn over his features. Again he looked as if he had been turned into granite, and I went away thinking that this was the strongest and most determined face I had ever seen.[7]

From various scattered comments throughout the issue about Stalin's career, we gather that he was much more interested in Russian national strength than world revolution. Eliding the chaotic years from 1928 to 1933, the editors give the impression of a steady retreat from the alleged radicalism that marked the period of Lenin's death in 1924 (the middle of NEP is described as if it were an era of heightened class struggle). Other than these few remarks made in passing, there is remarkably little discussion of Stalin directly, whether praise or condemnation.

Nevertheless, Stalin casts a long shadow over the issue, because he is so much part of the visual landscape. We have a few other photographs of Stalin,

---

of photography and Bourke-White's photograph in particular; my thanks to Kevin Morgan for letting me see chapters in advance.

6   *Life Magazine* 1943, p. 8.
7   Bourke-White 1942, p. 217.

particularly at funerals (Lenin in 1924 and Sergo Ordzhonikidze in 1937). We see
him in various historical paintings (for example, shaking hands with Lenin at
their first meeting in 1905). A meeting hall has huge banners of Marx, Engels,
Lenin and Stalin. The Leningrad Public Library has two large drawings of Lenin
and Stalin on the wall. A group of smiling women athletes stand underneath
what seems to be a huge tapestry with Stalin's portrait. A gargantuan statue of
Stalin stands in the Agriculture Exhibit in Moscow, along with a more-than-
life-size portrait of Stalin made out of flowers. This last portrait contains a line
from Stalin's funeral oration that we shall be meeting again: 'We vow to you,
Comrade Lenin!'

Perhaps because of her professional flair for the visual, the effect of Stalin's
ubiquity is well described by Bourke-White:

> A striking innovation since my previous visits to the Soviet Union, in the
> early 1930s, was the appearance everywhere of gigantic statues of Stalin
> ... At any mass meeting the speakers stand against the backdrop on which
> the official portrait is reproduced on such a gargantuan scale that the
> human performers could comfortably fit into Stalin's eye.
>
> These representations gave me a curious feeling about Stalin. He is so
> seldom seen, so rarely heard, and yet so much quoted that one comes to
> think of him as an ever-present yet fleshless spirit, a kind of superman so
> big that no human force can hold him, so powerful that everything down
> to the smallest action is guided by him.[8]

We now see Stalin's iconic ubiquity as manifestations of the cult of personality,
but these various items are presented by the *Life* editors without comment and
without, I think, any intent to be satiric. The ubiquity of Stalin just seems to be
a fact of life about the Soviet Union, one that, if anything, shows a patriotic and
united society, and thus a worthy ally.

This issue of *Life* is a somewhat unsettling journey to a forgotten past. Perhaps the issue is even somewhat embarrassing, but why, and to whom? Is it
embarrassing to the USA business elite that showed it could whitewash Stalin's
crimes as well as any woolly-headed leftist fellow-traveller? Or is it a disturbing
reminder of the present-day cultural amnesia about the time when the Soviet
Union was a valued ally, when Soviet achievements were seen positively – and
thus a reminder of the fact that we in the Western democracies directly bene-

---

8   Bourke-White 1942, pp. 195–7. These observations parallel the impressions I received from
    reading press accounts of the Bukharin show trial in 1938; see 'Show Trials in the Stalin Era:
    On Stage and In Court', included in this volume.

fitted from the huge sacrifices of a society and a system that today excites little beyond condemnation and mockery.

2   Sacred Cantatas

The figure of Stalin plays a major role in three choral cantatas by the great composers of the Soviet era: Sergei Prokofiev's *Cantata on the Twentieth Anniversary of the Russian Revolution* (1938) and *Zdravitsa* (Birthday Ode to Stalin, 1939), and Dmitri Shostakovich's *Song of the Forests* (1949). These works stand out among productions of the cult of personality because they are the work of artists of the first rank. They pose an immense critical problem, since we cannot simply dismiss them as hackwork, and indeed all three still find appreciative audiences today (performances can easily be found on YouTube).[9] Three main approaches are evident. First, enjoy the stirring music and dismiss the Stalin connection as irrelevant. Second, defend the artistic merit of the cantatas, but show that they are not really productions of the cult. For example, they are not really about Stalin but about the people, or they avoid the usual musical clichés associated with other musical tributes. Third, deny that Prokofiev and Shostakovich even wanted these works to have any merit as integral artistic productions, since they could have had nothing but contempt and derision for the text, and so they torpedoed their own works. The main English-language academic articles on the Prokofiev cantatas seem to me to take this approach.[10]

I take a fourth line of approach. I count myself among the 'defenders, who stubbornly insist on [the] artistic value' of these works (in the words of Vladimir Orlov).[11] The Anniversary Cantata is a great work, the Birthday Ode is a very good work, and the Song of the Forests is more than listenable. These works achieve their artistic merit not in spite of the texts, but because of them. In particular, the works achieve their resonance *because* they are about Stalin, the incarnation of the great cause. Of course, the Stalin figure in these works has about as much to do with the empirical Stalin as Spenser's Faerie Queene had

---

9   Viewing these works in live performance best gives a sense of their potential power. Recommended for YouTube viewing is Valery Gergiev for the Anniversary Cantata (https://www.youtube.com/watch?v=7r1adsrxz5c), Gennady Rozhdestvensky for Birthday Ode (https://www.youtube.com/watch?v=xLg7cmqllno&ab_channel=newhope123), and Yuri Temirkanov for Song of the Forests (https://www.youtube.com/watch?v=KmZJeImdzog &list=PLEGKOC7mvop_oW2-s5lzaq5PomscA_wBp).
10   Morrison and Kravetz 2006; Orlov 2007; Orlov 2013.
11   Orlov 2013.

to do with the empirical Elizabeth I. The texts incorporate Stalin into a powerful myth of a national community that is aligned with the sacred and therefore able to attain prosperity and greatness. The composers could and did respond to this mythic level wholeheartedly.[12]

I hope someday to offer extensive analyses of these works. Here I will only point briefly to the underlying mythic framework by putting the cantatas into a context wider than the cult of personality of the Soviet era. A major theme – perhaps *the* major theme – of Russian opera and choral cantatas is the contrast between the community that is in contact with the sacred and the community that has lost this contact. This theme finds a seminal expression – where else? – in the work of Alexander Pushkin, and in particular his late masterpiece *The Bronze Horseman*. This work of 481 lines consists of two contrasting parts: a Preface in which the positive achievements of Peter the Great are extolled, and a narrative in which Peter's city is portrayed as a malevolent and anti-human force.

In the Preface (96 lines), Pushkin shows us Peter as he contemplates the savage forest that forms the site of the future Petersburg: 'On the shore of the desolate waves *he* stood, filled with great thoughts [*dum velikikh poln*]'. Pushkin then celebrates the splendour of contemporary Petersburg – a shining, vivid, prosperous community that is in line with the sacred – a status it enjoys in and through the wise founder who understands the direction of history. Thus the Preface shows us the community aligned with the sacred owing to a legitimate ruler who is himself aligned with underlying historical processes. In contrast, the narrative sections of the poem show us a community that has lost touch with the sacred, so that the cosmic forces of nature and history have become malevolent and demonic: Peter's equestrian statue comes to life and threatens to trample and destroy a poor, solitary and eventually insane inhabitant of the city. Thus the narrative part of the poem shows us a dysfunctional community in which enormous energy cannot find the proper sacred channels and becomes wasteful, chaotic and dysfunctional.

The first great Russian opera, Glinka's *Life for the Tsar*, continues the theme of Pushkin's Preface: a community in which sacred ruler and population are aligned.[13] The patriotic and patriarchal peasant Ivan Susanin explicitly ties the

---

12   Some of the ideas behind my analysis are taken from Marghescu 2014, *Pourquoi la littérature?* (despite the title, this book is mainly about nineteenth-century Russian opera) and Tertz 1965, *On Socialist Realism*.

13   *Life for the Tsar* was first performed in 1836; Pushkin's *Bronze Horseman* was completed in 1833 but only published in 1837, after the poet's death. I am not arguing for any direct and explicit influence of the *Bronze Horseman* on Russian opera composers, although this possibility should not be ruled out.

fertility of the community to the presence of the sacred ruler, since he refuses to sanction his daughter's marriage until a new dynasty is established by crowning a legitimate ruler, thus putting an end to Russia's Time of Troubles (the opera celebrates the founding of the Romanov dynasty in 1613).

Most of the great Russian operas that follow portray a community that has lost its touch with the sacred. The foundational work in this branch of the tradition is Mussorgsky's *Boris Godunov*. The ruler Godunov is not a bad man, but he is barred from genuine legitimacy because the ancient dynasty has collapsed and Godunov's attempts to found a new one are unable to re-establish the connection between the population and the sacred. Although Boris is himself an effective ruler, his reign is cursed by famines and other manifestations of a disordered cosmos. The rebellious forces that rise up to challenge his lack of legitimacy are themselves without a firm connection to the sacred and so they promise only further chaos. Other operas and choral works that portray the dysfunctional community are Rimsky-Korsakov's *Golden Cockerel* (1909), Prokofiev's *Love of Three Oranges* (1921), Shostakovich's *The Nose* (1929), and even the émigré Stravinsky's *Oedipus Rex* (1927), to name only some twentieth-century examples.

With this framework established, we can now put the Stalin-era cantatas into context. They represent a return to Pushkin's Preface and to Glinka's *Life for the Tsar*, a return to the community in alignment with the sacred and thereby flourishing. The connection with the sacred is channelled and guaranteed by the legitimate ruler, that is, one who is in touch with the deep currents of history. Each of the three cantatas presents this connection in different ways, but all end up in the same place: a mighty chorus of affirmation in C major, ending in long-held chords sung and played at top volume.

Prokofiev's Anniversary Cantata was composed in 1938 soon after the composer's return to the Soviet Union.[14] Prokofiev was strongly committed to the project and fought hard for it – that is, it was not some piece of hackwork assigned to him. He wanted to undertake the challenge of setting political prose to music, and so chose passages directly from the works of Marx, Lenin, and Stalin. In the literature on the Cantata, one often finds the assertion that the composition was banned because the idea of setting Stalin's actual words seemed sacrilegious to bureaucrats with control over its fate. There is no evidence for this claim, which seems to be one of those memes that flourish and

---

14   The score for the Anniversary Cantata has not been published. Thanks to the good offices of Julie Carmen Lefebvre, head of the Gertrude Whitney Performance Library at the Schulich School of Music, McGill University, I was able to examine a score provided by G. Schirmer, Inc.

cannot be stamped out because they sound right.[15] What is true is that the Cantata was not performed in Prokofiev's lifetime. It does not seem ever to have been directly banned, and more than one reason (for instance, the vast performing resources required) may have been responsible for the failure to reach an audience.

The Cantata consists of ten movements of interspersed choral and orchestral numbers. The opening orchestral prelude has these words as an epigraph: 'A spectre is haunting Europe, the spectre of communism'. The music is appropriately spectral. There follows a choral movement based on another famous statement from Marx: 'the philosophers have interpreted the world in various ways, but the point is to change it'. The text of the next three choral movements is taken from Lenin – and, speaking as a Lenin expert, I must say that the particular passages are well chosen and give a coherent and defensible vision of Lenin as Founder of the Soviet Union. The first Lenin movement is based on a passage from *What Is to Be Done?* (1902), a passage that was much better known in the Soviet Union than it is in the West, even among those who know something about the book. It starts off: 'We move in a tight little band'. In much more metaphorical language than is usual for Lenin, the passage goes on to describe the lonely and precarious position of the pioneers of what will become a mighty mass movement. Even few as they are, this little band of pioneers is in tune with the sacred – the underlying movement of history – and thus the force was with them (to allude to another popular myth).

The next Lenin movement is based on texts from September/October 1917, when Lenin was advocating an armed uprising; Prokofiev provides a tremendously driving, energetic and wonderfully pull-out-all-the-stops evocation of popular revolution. The texts for the final Lenin movement come from 1920, when the civil war was ending in victory and the immense job of reconstruction loomed before the country. These texts include appropriate images of ice breaking and spring returning to a devastated land, inspiring one of Prokofiev's gorgeous sweeping melodies (a similar one is found in the Birthday Ode).

All of the Lenin movements carry a great sense of forward movement, but the two Stalin choral movements are much more static. The chosen texts were already canonical within Soviet society: Stalin's oath, sworn to the deceased Lenin at his funeral, to continue the work of the great cause (we saw this oath before in a flower portrait of Stalin that appeared in *Life*), and his speech of

---

15   This cliché seems to go back to a passing remark made by Maksimenkov 1997, *Sumbur vmesto musyki*, and is endorsed by Morrison and Kravetz 2006. Maksimenkov is an archival historian, but in this case he provides no basis for an assertion that contradicts other known facts.

December 1936 celebrating the new Constitution as a summation of Soviet achievements. In between these two moments of renewed dedication is a propulsive orchestral movement that supplies the requisite dynamism to the final third of the Cantata.

Thus the Cantata as a whole has an epic sweep that starts with the prophetic words of Marx and ends with their triumphal embodiment in Soviet society. The only other production of Soviet art with this kind of epic sweep that I know of is Mayakovsky's long poem *Lenin* (1924), which perforce ends with Lenin's death.[16] The texts for the Anniversary Cantata do not describe the sacred in terms of socialist ideals, class struggle, and the like – rather, they take this content as given and describe instead the effort to create a community dedicated to realizing these ideals. The focus is on community solidarity, and enemies are mentioned only in passing (mostly in the Revolution movement). At the beginning, the sacred principle is disembodied, a spectre. It enters the empirical world in the guise of Lenin's 'tight band' of devoted revolutionaries. The Revolution movement shows us the sacred principle fighting its way to becoming a reality in the world as an established political community – and here as elsewhere, the emphasis of the text and the musical setting is much more on the 'we' of the community than on the exact nature of the enemy or even of the community's positive socialist ideals. The sacred principle becomes fully embodied in the final chorus of affirmation that looks forward to the world victory of communism – the ideal which we first saw as a disembodied spectre.

In this epic, Stalin appears as hierophant, as high priest, one who represents the sacred to the community and the community to the sacred. Stalin's oath at Lenin's death uses explicitly liturgical language and rhythm: 'In leaving us, comrade Lenin left us the behest' to accomplish various tasks, and in response, 'we vow to you, Comrade Lenin, that we shall honourably fulfil this your commandment'. Like a litany, Lenin's behests and the corresponding vows follow one after the other in call-response fashion. The behests cover the key points of the world-historical mission of the Soviet Union: dictatorship of the proletariat, alliance of workers and peasants, unity of the various Soviet nationalities, and finally the Communist International – that is, the sacred mission in its most global and abstract form. The religious overtones in Prokofiev's musical

---

16   I would now add to this list Bukharin's poem cycle *Transformation of the World* (as discussed in 'Bukharin's Bolshevik Epic: The Prison Writings', included in this volume) and also Vsevolod Pudovkin's trilogy of films *Mother, The End of St. Petersburg*, and *Storm over Asia*, recently made available in a DVD package from Flicker Alley (*The Bolshevik Trilogy: Three Films by Vsevolod Pudovkin, 1926–1928*).

treatment are more explicit here than in other movements, since the composer appropriately writes a funeral march and brings out the litany-like repetitions with his musical setting.

Prokofiev also preserves the call and response pattern of Stalin's text. The call texts – those starting off with 'In leaving us, comrade Lenin ...' – are not given to soloists (there are none in the cantata), but rather to one or to various combinations of the four choral parts (soprano, alto, tenor, bass). The response is usually given to the full SATB choir. In this way, the 'call' function is not given to a determinate voice or set of voices that might represent an officiating priest. Instead, they are distributed throughout the choral community, thus making the communal 'we' dominate for both call and response.

The orchestral interlude that follows depicts the renewed outburst of creative energy that follows this moment of rededication and affirmation of mission. The final movement uses Stalin's speech in December 1936 (and thus almost contemporary with Prokofiev's composition) about the adoption of a new Constitution (usually called the Stalin Constitution), an event given an enormous amount of publicity despite the document's remoteness from the realities of Soviet life.[17] The text begins: 'As a result of the path of struggle and suffering that we have travelled, it is pleasant and joyful [*priyatno i radostno*] to have our own Constitution that enshrines the fruits of our victories.'

The prose is somewhat ungainly, but it serves its purpose as a fitting end to Prokofiev's epic. It maintains the liturgical ambiance by the repetition of '*priyatno i radostno*' ['pleasant and joyful]' and 'eto' ['it is ...']. This almost incantatory reliance on anaphora (the use of a repetition as a rhetorical figure of speech) is the most striking feature of Stalin's personal style in general. The text talks about 'spiritual' rearmament and 'world-historical victories'. Stalin maintains his hierophantic stance by talking about the sacrifice of 'our people': he is spokesman for the community as he directs its gaze to the sacred.

This final movement is in the genre of the overpowering affirmative chorus that gradually pulls out all stops and ends with the enormous performing ensemble playing and singing together at top volume, holding triumphant C-major chords for as long as possible (all three cantatas discussed here end in C major, and their final pages look very similar.) In composing this sort of final chorus, Soviet composers could look to models such as Handel's *Messiah*, Beethoven's *Fidelio*, and Rossini's *Guillaume Tell*. The foundational Russian example, unsurprisingly, comes from Glinka's *Life for the Tsar*.

---

17   For the enthusiastic reaction by many Soviet intellectuals to this speech, see 'Show Trials in the Stalin Era: On Stage and In Court', included in this volume.

There is no direct praise of Stalin in the Anniversary Cantata, and he is not really presented as a political speaker delivering a message to an audience. Rather, he provides words *for* the choir: his use of 'we' and 'us' makes his text usable for the huge choir that stands for the united and joyful (after long battles) community. Of course, the empirical historical occasions on which these words were originally spoken are important – but they are important insofar as they point to a symbolical, mythical level that is itself detached from empirical realities.

Stalin is even more detached from empirical reality in Prokofiev's Birthday Ode, written only a year after the Anniversary Cantata but a very different sort of work.[18] Here we are less in the realm of Marx and Lenin than of Sir James Frazer's *The Golden Bough*. Stalin becomes a sort of vegetation god who guarantees fertility and growth. The libretto of the Birthday Ode labels itself as the folklore-like expression of the Soviet people (especially the more unsophisticated among them) as they contemplate their great leader. The style and content of the text is no doubt primitive and more than faintly silly. Yet it provides just enough entrée to a genuine mythic level to allow Prokofiev to write some very engaging music.

The 15-minute cantata is in one continuous movement that sets a number of distinct texts. An orchestral prelude has a sweeping life-force melody similar to the one heard in the Victory movement of the Anniversary Cantata, a melody that returns periodically throughout. In the first section of the text, we step immediately into vegetation imagery, with evocations of green fields and full granaries. This section ends: 'The sun now shines differently to us on earth. Know this: it is with Stalin in the Kremlin.' We then move directly to the fertility of the community itself: 'I sing, rocking my son in my arms: "You are growing like ears of grain among the purple flowers. Stalin will be the first words on our lips!"' In the following section, there is a return of the life-force melody, with particularly strong emphasis given to the words 'it bloomed' [*rastsveli*].

We next have our first evocation of youth and sex: 'If my eyes were flashing as they were at seventeen, if my cheeks were still rosy', I would go to Moscow to visit Stalin. The mention of Moscow triggers another theme: movement toward the sacred centre. When in Moscow, the principles of an orderly community are paraded in an alarmingly straightforward fashion: everybody gets rewarded for good work. A familial image of the community is manifested by the paterfamilias Stalin who is hospitable and asks after everyone's welfare. (I especially like

---

18   The score and text for the Birthday Ode can be found at this link: https://www.youtube .com/watch?v=Y6pl7apTMK4.

the rendition of the text provided by one English subtitle: 'And he personally gives you sensible guidance' – who could ask for more?)[19]

At the next stage, the community almost literally marries Stalin. The words say: We celebrate and dress our Aksina as a bride – although she isn't actually getting married, she's going off to visit Stalin. At this point, only one thing is lacking for a full and compete vegetation god: a portrayal of dying and rebirth. And we are given this by a reference to Stalin's sufferings under the tsar, when 'he took upon himself much torment for the sake of the people'. The Birthday Ode ends with a triumphant return of the life-force theme.

Watching a performance of the Birthday Ode on YouTube or DVD is a strange experience – much stranger than the other cantatas discussed here. On the one hand, the words are so over-the-top that one wonders how the performers keep a straight face (I am sure strict orders were given to not crack even the hint of a smile). On the other hand, conductor and chorus are clearly enjoying themselves, and it is a hard-hearted listener who is not swept along with the music. I will leave it as a possibility that Prokofiev responded to a mythic level hidden behind the surface silliness.

Shostakovich's *Song of the Forests* (*Pesn' o lesakh*) was composed in 1949 in celebration of one of the last of Stalin's grand schemes, a vast project of refor-estation.[20] The words were provided by a competent official poet, Evgenii Dol-matovsky, who had visited the steppes where reforesting was taking place. The work was awarded the Stalin prize, a much-needed gesture of official approval for the harassed composer. The libretto is at its best when it evokes a fairy-tale atmosphere around the 'marvellous garden' that will be created by the reforestation project: the blighted, drought-threatened land it will replace, the childlike enthusiasm of its builders ('Shostakovich himself asked to have a movement for children's chorus after reading in his daughter's school news-paper of the groups of young "Pioneers" involved in the planting project'), and the fabulous growth expected in the future.[21]

The passages devoted explicitly to Stalin are few in quantity but establish a strong framework. The first of seven movements shows Stalin (identified not by

---

19   The Russian text is 'sam daet sovety mudrye'. The subtitles are found on the performance conducted by Gennady Rozhdestvensky on the DVD *Notes Interdites* (Ideale Audience / ARTE France: 2003).

20   For the score and text of *Pesn' o lesakh*, see Shostakovich 1999. For the fraught circum-stances under which Shostakovich composed his cantata, see Marina Frolova-Walker, 'A Birthday Present for Stalin: Shostakovich's *Song of the Forests* (1949)' (Frolova-Walker 2016).

21   Quoted words are taken from the useful liner notes by Steven Ledbetter to the CD perfor-mance by Yuri Temirkanov for RCA Victor Red Seal.

name but only as 'the great leader', *velikii vozhd*) in front of a map, exchanging the red flags of war by the green flags of peace and reforestation. In the middle of the cantata (fifth movement) is a short but weighty couplet:

> We're simple Soviet people, communism is our glory and honour.
> If Stalin says: this will be, we reply: it exists!

The final movement ends with a *Slava* ('Glory') chorus with Stalin and the *narod* (the people) sharing top billing, with Stalin clearly in primary position: '*Slava* to Lenin's party! *Slava* to the *narod* forever! *Slava* to the wise Stalin! *Slava!*'

The text and music make clear references to the pre-revolutionary tradition discussed earlier. Pushkin's Peter the Great is evoked by Dolmatovsky's Stalin, who also stands in solitude and thinks great thoughts: 'In the Kremlin, morning flashed with dawn. The Great Leader, sunk in wise thoughts [*v razdume mudrom*], went up to the huge map'. The cantata also situates itself in the Russian opera tradition, especially *Boris Godunov*. Both Boris and Iosif gaze at maps that portray Russia. When *Song of the Forests* describes the bad old days of drought and devastation, it uses the image of a bent beggar travelling over Rus' (the poetic name for old Russia) with an empty bag. This image responds directly to the scene in the Mussorgsky opera in front of the Cathedral, where a hungry crowd begs for food in time of famine, but it also responds indirectly to all the portrayals of Russia on the move that fill *Boris Godunov*. Shostakovich's final *Slava* chorus recalls not only Boris's coronation but many other Russian operas: it is a rare Russian opera indeed without a *Slava* chorus of some kind.[22]

All these allusions are meant to point up contrast rather than continuity. Peter's great project is to remove a forest associated with darkness and primitiveness, Iosif's project is to build a forest associated with light and progress. Peter's motives are imperial, and Stalin's main motive in the cantata – 'happiness for the *narod*' – is absent from the tsar's calculations. Boris is a doomed tsar whose inability to connect with the sacred ensures that his realm is off-kilter with nature. Stalin's forests will end the suffering pilgrimages of Rus', and the movement of the people is now shown as purposeful, organized, and successful. Boris's enthusiasm for his son's map-making is shot through with irony, due to his complete failure to found a new dynasty. Shostakovich's *Slava* chorus is 'pure affirmation' without irony.[23]

---

22   The Russianness of *Oedipus Rex* is further confirmed by its 'Gloria' chorus.
23   I am again quoting Stephen Ledbetter's liner notes.

Thus, as a ruler, Shostakovich's Stalin trumps Pushkin's Peter and Mussorgsky's Boris Godunov at every turn. In *Song of the Forests*, Stalin appears as an imperial ruler whose connection with the sacred guarantees that the bounty of nature will bless the land. Stalin and Godunov faced a similar challenge: each had to establish legitimacy after the collapse of a centuries-old dynasty. If the Shostakovich cantata is to be believed, Stalin succeeded where the doomed tsar failed.

I will discuss only one feature of the musical setting, namely, Shostakovich's use of a children's choir. A choir is a good medium for representing the entire community fulfilling its sacred function, and not just because a choir *is* a human community. The articulation into men and women, and high and low, helps the choir symbolize the community as a whole. The addition of a children's chorus expands this symbolism even further. The Soviet imagery of 'young Pioneers' (the organization for children from ten to 15 years of age and mostly remembered for its summer camps) is mobilized by librettist and composer to provide a rather rare feature in this genre: charm.[24] Thus the turning point in the cantata is the beginning of the fourth movement, 'The Pioneers Plant the Forests': a little trumpet figure begins to pierce through the remnants of the Mussorgskian music of suffering. A page or so of coexistence between the two themes, and then the children's chorus enters and we are in a new world.

During the Stalin era, Glinka's *Life for the Tsar* was overhauled to remove all references to the tsar, a massive operation that entailed moving the date of the story (thus ensuring that the action did not take place in the physical and symbolic spring). The retitled *Ivan Susanin* portrayed sacrifices for the *narod*, rather than for the tsar. But 'the whirligig of time brings in its revenges' and the sanitizing Stalin era was itself sanitized: Shostakovich's *Song of the Forest* was destalinized for performance after the dictator's death. The overhaul was not as drastic as in Glinka's case, since the explicit Stalin references are quantitatively few (although it was also felt necessary to transform the 'Stalingradtsy', people of Stalingrad, to 'Komsomoltsy', the Soviet youth movement for those older than the Pioneers). Once again, the *narod* stood in for the previously sacred but now disgraced leader. Only after the collapse of Soviet rule do we find performances that present the original text for both Glinka and Shostakovich (although an American performance of *Song of the Forest* in 2009 still used the post-Stalin bowdlerization).[25]

---

24   For a look at how Soviet Pioneers were portrayed in films, see http://rbth.com/multimedia/
      video/2014/08/07/cinematryoshka_7_common_character_types_from_movies_about_pi
      _38827 (*Russia Beyond the Headlines*).
25   https://www.grantparkmusicfestival.com/music/season-archives/2009-season/bernstein

The three cantatas we have discussed are unique products of the Stalin cult because they are kept alive, not for political, historical, or nostalgic reasons, but because people enjoy them. We should not be too dogmatic about how to approach this phenomenon. Some people boycott these works for political reasons. Others respond to them as guilty pleasures and try to ignore the presence of Stalin. I do not see these reactions as illegitimate. In these remarks, however, I have tried to account for the undeniable power of the cantatas by taking Stalin into account. The Stalin figure found in these works is an entryway into myth – a symbol whose meanings can only be grasped through knowledge of the Stalin of history, but whose ramifications far transcend him.

3   Stalin and the Short Course

The years 1937–1938 saw the terrible series of events that I call Stalin's 'purification campaign': show trials at the top, mass arrests at the bottom, and physical elimination of various marginal categories. In the summer of 1938, the campaign was being allowed to wind down, and war was on the horizon, so for several months Stalin focused his main attention on … the massive rewrite and launching of a new textbook on party history! This astonishing choice of priorities led to the publication of *The History of the Communist Party of the Soviet Union (Bolsheviks), Short Course* in November 1938. The *Short Course* became a veritable bible of Bolshevism for the rest of the Stalin era and for some time afterward. Though mostly unread today, it still exerts a massive influence – all the more powerful because unperceived – on the historiography of the Soviet Union, very much including Western academic history and historians in the Trotskyist tradition.[26]

For a long time, Stalin's role in the creation for the *Short Course* was cloudy. His authorship of the famous section on dialectical materialism was generally acknowledged, but the book as a whole was officially credited to a 'commission of the Central Committee' and little was known beyond that. Over the last decade or so, archival research has filled out the picture, and a fascinat-

---

-waterfront. The other two Stalin cantatas discussed here also underwent bowdlerization of various kinds. For a detailed examination, see Jack Weiner, 'The Destalinization of Dmitrii Shostakovich's "Song of the Forests", Op. 81 (1949)' (Weiner 1984).

26   The full text of the *Short Course* can be found in the Marxists Internet Archive at this link: https://www.marxists.org/reference/archive/stalin/works/1939/x01/.

ing and unexpected picture it is. In early summer 1938, Stalin was given a committee-composed draft of a new textbook that had been in the pipeline for several years. Dissatisfied with this draft, Stalin embarked on a massive rewrite. Some sections he left untouched, he made numerous corrections to others, and he simply tossed out some crucial sections and replaced them with his own draft. These brand-new sections bear the unmistakable imprint of Stalin's very idiosyncratic style. Following the creation of a final draft, Stalin gave much attention to the launching of the new textbook in autumn 1938. He was rather impressively involved with the nuts and bolts of 'propaganda' (seen in the positive Soviet sense of inculcating a correct worldview in depth). He also expressed his personal and rather utopian vision of what he hoped the new textbook would accomplish, and more than once he expressed frustration with the incomprehension of the propaganda officials of his aims.

The scholars who have done the most to uncover and publish this material are the Russian historian Mikhail Zelenov and the American historian David Brandenberger. They have recently published a 'critical edition' of the *Short Course* that allows us to see the original committee draft and to track Stalin's multifarious changes (my thanks to the Yale University Press and to David Brandenberger for letting me see some of this material in advance).[27] The following speculative remarks are based primarily on the various rationales provided by Stalin in autumn 1938 and published in a 2014 volume edited by Zelenov and Brendenberger.[28]

One of the surprises that emerge from our new knowledge of the editing process is how much Stalin removed laudatory references to himself. One reason for this is that he did not want a textbook based on the heroic deeds of this or that individual (mostly himself in the committee draft), nor one that simply recounted events. The glory of the new textbook in Stalin's eyes was that it showed *theory* as realized in action. For Stalin, 'theory' was defined primarily as knowledge of the laws of history. Among these laws of history were the reasons why so many people opposed the party that best understood these laws, namely, the Bolsheviks. Thus the Bolsheviks were forced to make their way forever combatting this or that misunderstanding of 'theory', and their story was one long battle against ever recurring deviations. If people didn't understand the reason why all these battles were necessary, the Bolsheviks might appear as indefatigable squabblers.

---

27   David Brandenberger and Mikhail Zelenov, eds., *Stalin's Master Narrative: A Critical Edition of the* History of the Communist Party of the Soviet Union (Bolsheviks): Short Course (Zelenov and Brandenberger 2019).

28   Zelenov and Brandenberger 2014.

In Stalin's vision, the *Short Course* taught theory by living example, and this had a value for the present and future as well as the historical past. Stalin hoped that the new textbook would give party and state cadres the tool for orienting themselves (*orientirovka*) in any situation. He protested a fair amount in this period against a nihilist attitude toward the new 'intelligentsia', that is, the generation of state officials that had grown up under Soviet rule. The main benefit the new intelligentsia received from Stalin's positive evaluation was to become a target audience for the new textbook.

Besides the positive aim of orienting the new intelligentsia, Stalin was motivated by a drive to prevent the reoccurrence of a very unfortunate phenomenon: the degeneration of previously loyal party members and citizens into *dvurushniki* ('double-dealers', hypocritical oppositionists who mask their real views) and finally into traitors. In Stalin's view, this process of degeneration was generated in the first place by a misperception of the laws of history. Because the oppositionists do not know these laws, they reject the party line and predict disaster. When their scepticism is belied by the success of the party line, they turn sour and become more and more embittered. The presence of these embittered opportunists within the party and state bureaucracy led to the painful necessity of the purification campaign of 1937–1938 – or so Stalin saw it.

A snapshot of the process of degeneration can be found in the *Short Course*'s description of the oppositionists at the Seventeenth Party Congress in 1934, that is, after the main collectivization battles had been fought. All the material quoted here was added by Stalin himself to the final draft in 1938. The title of the section is: 'Degeneration of the Bukharinists into political *dvurushniki* (double-dealers). Degeneration of the Trotskyist *dvurushniki* into a White Guard band of murders and spies. Foul Murder of S.M. Kirov. The party's measures to strengthen the vigilance of the Bolsheviks.' Here we see two precisely delineated stages of degeneration: the opposition led by Bukharin that is now degenerating into *dvurushnichestvo*, in contrast to the Trotskyists, who are already *dvurushniki* but who now degenerate even further into a White Guard band of murderers and spies.

Instead of evaluating the success of the collectivization drive from the point of view of the people (the *Short Course* narrative continues), the oppositionists saw only the collapse of their own policies; they evaluated everything from the point of view of their own 'pitiful factional group and were cut off from real life and thoroughly rotten' (the supercharged language of abuse is a specialty of Stalin's prose). The oppositionists refuse to admit even the most evident facts. In order to revenge themselves on the party and the people, they resort to 'wrecking activities': arson, explosions, and the like. At the same time, they hypocritically toady up to the party. Their speeches of praise for the party and its leadership at the Congress were outright acts of defiance that instructed their followers outside the Congress *not* to lay down their arms but rather to become *dvurushniki* like themselves.[29]

Looking back in 1938, Stalin felt that some of these people could have been saved, since they had started off as 'our people' but then were misled by their leaders and their own ignorance of the laws of history (Stalin's remarks are from an uncorrected stenographic record):

> If we talk about wreckers, about Trotskyists, then keep in mind that not all of these people were Trotskyist-Bukharinist wreckers, not all of them were spies. The top leaders are the ones who became spies, calling it collaboration with fascist governments. But they also had, so to speak, their constituency [*massa*]. I wouldn't say that these people [who made up the constituency] were spies, they were our people, but then they lost their bearings [*svikhnulis*]. Why? Because they weren't real Marxists, they were theoretically weak.
>
> What is theory? It is knowledge of the laws of the development of society, and this knowledge allows us to orient ourselves in situations – but this ability to orient themselves is what they didn't have, they were poor Marxists, very poor – but we ourselves did a poor job of educating them. And this one reason, among others, why it is necessary to put the emphasis [in the new *Short Course*] on theoretical preparation of our cadres, on the theoretical Marxist orientation of our cadres. If some actual fascist appears, our cadres should know how to fight against him, not be frightened of him, not backtrack and kowtow before him, as happened with a significant portion of our Trotskyists and Bukharinists, who were formerly our people and then went over to the other side. And don't think that all these cadres, the ones who helped the Trotskyists and Bukharinists, were *their* cadres. Among them are our people who lost their bearings – and will continue to lose their bearings if we don't fill this lacuna in the theoretical preparation of our cadres.[30]

Stalin's scenario of degeneration is given vivid expression in the 1946 film *The Oath (Kliatva)*. *The Oath* is the first of a trilogy of films by Mikhail Chiaureli

---

29   *Short Course*, Chapter 11, Section 4.
30   Zelenov and Brandenberger 2014, pp. 429–30; see also p. 479, and p. 537 for the same idea in a published party resolution.

that portrayed Stalin at various points in his invariably heroic career. The oath of the title is of course the one made by Stalin after Lenin's death and later set to music by Prokofiev in his Anniversary Cantata. The film follows the fortunes of a family in Stalingrad from 1924 to the end of the war. At the beginning of the story, two young men are equally discouraged because the chances for Russia's economic growth seem so slim when they look at the poverty and backwardness around them and the power and wealth of the Western countries.

The paths of the two young men diverge, because one keeps his faith in Stalin's visions and plans even if he doesn't fully understand them, and the other cannot get past his scepticism and continues to scoff as the first Five-Year Plan gets underway in the early thirties. Bukharin himself makes a cameo appearance as a scoffer among the top leadership. Eventually the Stalingrad scoffer resorts to arson, as per Stalin's script, while his more optimistic friend ends up in the sort of mass reception at the Kremlin evoked in Prokofiev's Birthday Ode. Chiaureli was one of Stalin's favourite movie directors, and *The Oath* shows that he truly understood the leader's melodramatic scenario of degeneration vs. redemption.

When considering this problem of cadres who lost faith because they didn't grasp the laws of history, Stalin had one particular, paradigmatic case in mind: collectivization. Stalin regarded collectivization as his proudest achievement and his particular claim to greatness. An indication of his feelings is found in the mirror provided by a collection of tribute articles issued on the occasion of Stalin's sixtieth birthday in 1939 (published in English in 1940). The authors of these articles were the leader's top lieutenants who had been with him for many years. These red courtiers understood Stalin's self-image and reflected it back at him.

Yes (said the eulogizers), he led the industrialization drive, but this achievement, great as it was, merely carried out Lenin's plan. In contrast, collectivization was Stalin's brainchild. As Lazar Kaganovich described the collectivization campaign, using an overwrought 'locomotive of history' metaphor: Stalin 'had theoretically to plan the track and lay the rails so that the locomotive could move on other routes for which the theoretical rails had not yet been laid, and for which even the track had only been generally indicated'. We further learn from these tributes that the collectivization drive was theoretically innovative, a new kind of revolution from above that was equal to the October revolution, and a feat that made a truly socialist society possible. In fact, Kaganovich assures us, 'we, Comrade Stalin's immediate pupils, can say without exaggeration that there is not a field of socialist construction into which Comrade Stalin has put so much energy, labour and care as he put in the field of collective farm development'.[31] If Stalin knew that collectivization was deeply unpopular, it didn't faze him – he was happy to own it.

A question arises: if Stalin had it all planned out ahead of time, whence all the chaos, contingency, improvisation and repression? Yes, there was some of that, admitted the eulogizers, but it was entirely due to the class enemy: 'All the brutal remnants of capitalism, all the elements of ignorance and vileness left over from the old system were mobilized with the assistance of foreign imperialists to prevent the socialist reconstruction of our country ... There was not a crime that these monsters hesitated to commit: terrorism, the assassination of some of our best people, blowing up factories, train wrecking, incendiarism, poisoning cattle – everything was brought into play.'[32]

We cannot discuss here Stalin's rationale for collectivization nor whether the rationale was justified by Bolshevik tradition. Our focus is on the way Stalin used this issue to illustrate his scenario of the degeneration caused by incomprehension of the laws of history. As he explained in late 1938 in the course of his remarks on the *Short Course* and its ambitious goals:

> How do we explain that some of them [among the larger constituency of the Right Opposition] became spies and intelligence agents? I mean, some of them were our people and afterwards went over to the other side. Why – because they were politically ungrounded, they were theoretically uneducated, they were people who did not know the laws of political development, and because of this they were not able to digest the sharp turn toward the collective farms ... Many of our cadres lacked grounding politically, they were poorly prepared theoretically, and so they thought that nothing would come of [the collectivization drive], and because of this we lost a fairly significant number of cadres, capable people ... We have to lead the country through the government apparatus, and in this apparatus are many people foreign to us – people who followed us before collectivization and who went away from us during collectivization.[33]

Despite the triumphal language he used about collectivization, Stalin evidently still felt defensive about the critique of the Right Opposition – partly, I speculate, because in his heart of hearts he respected them more than he did the 'Trotskyites', and partly because he knew that their doubts were still shared by

---

31   *Stalin* (Molotov, Kaganovich et al. 1940, p. 45).
32   Molotov, Kaganovich et al. 1940, pp. 46–7.
33   Zelenov and Brandenberger 2014, p. 479. For more discussion of what I call Stalin's 'anti-bureaucrat scenario', see 'Stalin at Work', included in this volume.

wide circles in the party and among the people.[34] These painful realizations led
to a remarkable outburst, almost a *cri de coeur*, at a combined meeting of the
Politburo with propaganda experts in October 1938:

> You know that the Rights explained our sharp turn to the collective farms
> by pointing to some sort of peculiar ideological itch on our part – this was
> the reason that we decided to get all the muzhiks into collective farms.
> From the testimony of the Rights we know that they declared: the Rus-
> sian spirit has nothing in common with any sort of collectivization ...
> [Chapter 11 of the *Short Course*] is key: why did we go over to the col-
> lective farms? What was this? Was it the caprice of the leaders, the [ide-
> ological] itch of the leaders, who (so we are told) read through Marx,
> drew conclusions, and then, if you please, restructured the whole coun-
> try according to those conclusions. Was collectivization just something
> made-up – or was it necessity? Those who didn't understand a damn thing
> about economics – all those Rights, who didn't have the slightest under-
> standing of our society either theoretically or economically, nor the slight-
> est understanding of the laws of historical development, nor the essence
> of Marxism – they could say such things as suggesting that we turn away
> from the collective farms and take the capitalist path of development in
> agriculture.[35]

In 1938, half a decade after the collectivization drive, Stalin realized that the
peasants still needed to be convinced that economic necessity, not ideological caprice, lay behind collectivization: 'It is very important to explain this to
the muzhik'. After running through the economic rationale (the inefficiency of
small peasant farms, the tendency toward further division of the land, the need
for larger production units, the horrors of taking the capitalist path), Stalin concluded 'how much expense, how much blood would have been demanded if we
had taken the capitalist path! But the path of the collective farms meant less
blood: not the impoverishment of the peasants, but their unification ... All this
needs to be explained to the muzhik, he'll understand it.'[36]

Some historians have called the *Short Course* an autobiography of Joseph
Stalin. In support of this, they pointed to the many mentions of Stalin per-

---

34   I put 'Trotskyite' in quotation marks, because Stalin included leaders such as Zinoviev and
      Kamenev who are not usually categorized in this way.
35   Zelenov and Brandenberger 2014, pp. 494–5.
36   Zelenov and Brandenberger 2014, pp. 494–5.

sonally and his heroic exploits.[37] Archival research has vastly complicated this
picture of a self-glorifying Stalin, since we now know he removed a great many
references to himself and explicitly rebutted an inflated view of, say, his organizing activities as a young Bolshevik back in Baku. But there is a deeper sense
in which these historians are correct: the *Short Course* is indeed Stalin's autobiography.

The real hero of the *Short Course* is the Bolshevik party line. The party line,
based solidly on a knowledge of the laws of history, is forced to fight against
innumerable critics and scoffers from right and left and goes on from triumph
to triumph – this is the narrative of the *Short Course*. And as it happens, Stalin
was in fact almost always a conscious defender of the party line during Lenin's
lifetime (with a few small and unimportant exceptions). Of course, after Lenin's
death, Stalin was himself the principal architect of the party line. Stalin's attitude toward the party line was therefore the same as W.S. Gilbert's Lord High
Chancellor toward the law:

> The law is the true embodiment
> Of everything that's excellent
> It has no kind of fault or flaw
> And I, my Lords, embody the law.

Even during Stalin's lifetime, he was known to be the author of the *Short
Course*'s famous section on dialectical materialism. Looking past all the abstractions about quantity turning into quality and the like, we find the argument that any leader who does not align themselves with the laws of history –
no matter how talented, brilliant and popular these leaders are – will go down
to defeat and disgrace. Trotsky and Bukharin are just such leaders. In contrast,
a leader who aligns himself to these same laws will be carried by the tidal force
of history from obscurity to world leadership. How modest is a Christian statesman who piously explains his triumphs by saying, 'Not I, but God'? How modest
is Stalin when he describes himself – in my view, with complete sincerity – by
saying, 'I am not a theoretician [*teoretik*], but a *praktik* who knows theory'?[38]

---

37   Tucker 1990, pp. 532–6.
38   Zelenov and Brandenberger 2014, p. 420. Stalin goes on to say, 'these are the kind of people
      we want to have: *praktiki* with a knowledge of theory'.

PART 7

Perestroika (1984–1991)

∴

Perestroika Looks Back

1 A Note of Explanation

In 1987, a group of former students of Robert Tucker held a conference in Princeton, New Jersey, devoted to various aspects of the perestroika reforms. This conference, organized by Stephen Cohen and Michael Kraus, seemed an appropriate way to honour one of the few scholars in the Soviet field who, far from being flummoxed by perestroika, had long brought to our attention both the need and potential for reform in the Soviet Union.

My report at this conference was on the topic of the reformers' use of NEP as a legitimating symbol. The NEP theme proved to be an extremely rich guide to the debates swirling in the Soviet media that were such a hallmark of the Gorbachev years. Public opinion mutated at high speed during perestroika, and so, with a view to publication, my report was substantially updated at least twice. The final revision was made in the summer of 1990, but, at that point, events overtook us. As the Soviet Union crumbled and fell, the publication of a volume devoted to the problems of perestroika was no longer viable.

Enough time has now passed, however, to allow an out-of-date study of *current* events to turn into a useful study of a fascinating *historical* episode. Part of the historical value of my essay comes precisely from its time-bound perspective, so I have left it substantially unchanged from its 1990 rewrite. At that time, I added a final section entitled 'The Waning of NEP'. By tracking the use of NEP as a rhetorical theme, I was able to sense what, in hindsight, was the waning of perestroika itself.

I hope my article evokes the atmosphere of the Gorbachev years, a transitory, swift-changing and passionate period in Soviet history that is too easily overlooked today.[1] As before, 'Perestroika's Revival of NEP' is dedicated to my teacher and friend, Robert C. Tucker.

---

1 See the recent discussion of the 'historical amnesia' about perestroika in Stephen Cohen, *Soviet Fates and Lost Alternatives: From Stalinism to the New Cold War* (Cohen 2009).

2   Perestroika's Revival of NEP: A Contemporary Chronicle, 1985–1990

> Lenin said NEP was meant seriously and for a long time, but he never
> said it would last forever.
>
> JOSEPH STALIN, December 1929

•••

> We must build and renovate socialism. We must advance our soci-
> ety by relying on and using all the sap that comes to us from roots
> that go deep into our history, especially into socialist history, and
> by chopping off everything negative that comes from the 1930s and
> 1940s and from the recent stagnant period.
>
> MIKHAIL GORBACHEV, February 1988

••
•

As the year 1920 came to a close, Soviet Russia had endured a long slide into
economic and social disaster. Since Russia's entry into the world war in 1914,
the country had known invasion and intervention, bitter class and national
conflict, desperate improvisation by political leaders, and rapidly accelerating
economic disintegration. The end of the civil war had not brought the relief
everyone had hoped for. With no food for the workers or fuel for the machines,
urban life almost ground to a halt. The cities felt compelled to take what they
needed from the peasants by force; the peasants responded with a wave of
revolts that threatened the existence of the new Bolshevik state authority.

At the last moment the Bolsheviks found a way out of this deadlocked situation by rethinking a basic policy toward the peasants. The party had previously
assumed that if free trade in grain were allowed, state grain collection would be
impossible and the urban workers would starve. The peasants were therefore
told to deliver to the state all the grain they normally would have marketed; the
state promised goods in return but could not keep this promise. In one of his
last great acts of leadership, Lenin convinced the Bolsheviks to allow the peasants to freely sell their grain after they had fulfilled the demands of the state
grain collection. This policy was called 'the food-supply tax' and it enabled the
Bolsheviks and the cities to get sufficient grain without driving the peasants to
desperation.[2]

---

2   'Food-supply tax' is a more accurate translation of *prodnalog* than the usual 'tax-in-kind'.

The food-supply tax was the most dramatic of many new economic poli-cies that became widespread in 1921 and the years that followed. The policies were rapidly seen as a unity – the New Economic Policy (NEP) – that promised to provide not only a response to the crisis of 1920 but also a long-term strat-egy for constructing socialism. The essence of this strategy was to involve the peasants in their own transformation through appeals to material interest and through direct demonstration of the practical advantages of socialism. But today's Soviet Union was not destined to be built by the logic of NEP. 1929 became what Stalin called the year of the great breakthrough – a breakthrough to forced-pace industrialization in the cities and coercive collectivization in the countryside. Stalin's Soviet Union went on to its own disasters and triumphs, and the era of NEP seemed to recede into historical irrelevance.

In 1985 the society built during the Stalin era began to face up to the dimen-sions of the impasse to which it had been led by Stalin's methods. For those searching for a path out of the crisis, NEP suddenly seemed irrelevant no longer. At the 27th Party Congress in February 1986, Mikhail Gorbachev went back to the origins of NEP and called for a creative use of the food-supply tax as a guid-ing principle of reform. Later that year the official journal *Kommunist* called for renewed attention to Lenin's writings of the NEP period. The prominent reform journalist Fedor Burlatsky wrote a series of long articles in *Literaturnaia Gazeta* that provided a detailed, point-by-point comparison between NEP as conceived by Lenin and the aims of the new reform movement.[3]

This is not the first time the meaning of NEP has been at the centre of politi-cal debate. Lenin's own approach to NEP evolved considerably; his last word on the subject – five articles published in early 1923 and described by Gorbachev as 'a revolution within the revolution, no less profound, perhaps, than Octo-ber' – is regarded today as almost a charter for perestroika. After Lenin's death in 1924, the struggle within Bolshevism was in many ways a struggle over the meaning of NEP. Was NEP a retreat, a necessary compromise with the 'petty-bourgeois' peasantry, a 'path to socialism', or some combination of all three? According to Stalin, the retreat involved in the introduction of NEP had been

---

For full discussion, see 'Bolshevik *Razverstka* and War Communism', included in this vol-ume.

3 *Kommunist*, 1986, no. 12, pp. 9–10 (see also *Kommunist*, 1987, no. 7, p. 63); Fedor Burlatsky, arti-cles in *Literaturnaia gazeta*, 16 April 1986; 1 October 1986; 22 July 1987. Burlatsky had already made comparisons to NEP in an article in *Voprosy filosofii*, 1984, no. 6, pp. 23–39. For other early articles, see Evgeny Ambartsumov, 'Analiz V.I. Leninym prichin krizisa 1921 g. i putei vykhoda iz nego', *Voprosy istorii*, 1984, no. 4, and the reply by E. Bugaev, 'Strannaia pozitsiia', *Kommu-nist*, 1984, no. 14, pp. 119–26; see also 'Iskusstvo tochnogo rascheta', A. Kolesnichenko, *Pravda*, 28 October 1986.

made for the sake of a new offensive. He therefore claimed that his 'offensive along the whole front' in 1929 – which resulted in collectivization in the countryside and elimination of the private and cooperative sector in the towns – was thoroughly consistent with NEP.[4] Stalin's famous *Short Course* of party history published in the late 1930s dismissed his opponents with these words: 'Since the oppositionists were poor Marxists and complete ignoramuses in questions of Bolshevik policy, they understood neither the essence of NEP nor the character of the retreat undertaken at the beginning of NEP.'[5]

In actuality, Stalin's opponents – especially Nikolai Bukharin and Alexei Rykov – had never denied the necessity of an 'economic offensive', that is, an accelerating socialist transformation of the economy and especially of the countryside. The dispute was over methods: when Stalin switched from the gradualist use of material incentives to a coercive 'revolution from above', he had in effect repudiated NEP. While Stalin claimed he had brought NEP to a triumphal conclusion with the construction of a socialist economy in the 1930s, his opponents argued that he had deliberately killed it in the late twenties.[6]

Stalin's version was orthodoxy until very recently, and within its framework NEP was treated with great respect: 'Only a few examples can be found in history of any important political undertaking that justified itself so completely and thoroughly, had such an immediate effect and such a long-term historical role as the transition to NEP.'[7] According to Soviet scholars, NEP was a necessary phase in the development of any and all socialist revolutions. After the Second World War, a NEP phase became mandatory for the popular democracies in Eastern Europe, and Soviet specialists often advised third world countries to

---

4 *Istoriia VKP(b)* (*kratkii kurs*), 1938, p. 245. For Gorbachev on Lenin's last articles, see *Pravda*, 21 April 1990; 'Oktiabr i perestroika: revoliutsiia prodolzhaetsia' (*Kommunist*, 1987, no. 17, p. 9) and *Perestroika: New Thinking for Our Country and the World* (Gorbachev 1987), pp. 25–6.

5 [Update: Thanks to the recent critical edition of the famous Short Course of party history that came out in 1938, we now know precisely what passages were added by Stalin; we can therefore state definitely that this curt remark not only sounds like Stalin, but was written by him (Brandenberger and Zelenov 2019, p. 464).]

6 A party resolution from 1925 called for 'an economic offensive of the proletariat on the basis of NEP' (cited in *Voprosy istorii KPSS*, 1968, no. 12, p. 85). On the political struggles of the 1920s, see Robert C. Tucker, *Stalin as Revolutionary: A Study in History and Personality* (Tucker 1973), and Stephen F. Cohen, *Bukharin and the Bolshevik Revolution: A Political Biography, 1888–1938* (Cohen 1971). The question of dating the end of NEP was one part of an extensive discussion of historical periodization in preparation for a new textbook of party history. Contributions to this debate can be found in *Kommunist*, 1987, no. 12, pp. 66–79, and Maksim Kim, *Voprosy istorii*, 1988, no. 6, pp. 115–30, as well as issues of *Voprosy istorii KPSS* starting with 1987, no. 6.

7 Iu. A. Poliakov, V.P. Dmitrenko, N.V. Shcherban, *Novaia ekonomicheskaia politika: razrabotka i osushchestvlenie* (Poliakov 1982), p. 236.

use NEP methods. But one reason for all these compliments was to neutralize NEP as a critical alternative to the Stalin model. NEP was a pre-socialist phase that the Soviet Union had passed long ago; any of its valuable features had already been incorporated into Soviet institutions.[8]

Occasionally slogans from NEP found their way into official rhetoric. During the most ambitious attempt before perestroika to deal with Stalin's economic heritage – the reform measures of the 1960s – the NEP experience was used to strengthen the call for expanded market relations. Beyond official rhetoric, one scholar's careful reading of Soviet economic literature revealed 'undercurrents' that harked back to Nikolai Bukharin and his defence of NEP against Stalin.[9] Most of the themes of today's reform thinking were present during the post-Stalin period; the major difference is that today the anti-Stalinist implications of NEP are no longer an undercurrent – they have come forcefully to the surface.

The most striking manifestation of this change is the rehabilitation of Bukharin, not just as an innocent man unjustly accused by Stalin, but as the principal spokesman for the NEP alternative. In 1982, a popular book could be written on NEP that did not so much as mention him.[10] He was still, if not a criminal spy, then a 'right deviationist'; now he is a martyr for the ideals of the revolution. By 1988, one Soviet writer described the conflict between him and Stalin as the conflict between good and evil, between life and death, between Christ and Satan.[11] The widespread interest in Bukharin has led to a Soviet edition of the biography written by Stephen Cohen. While almost all of the defendants of the show trials of the 1930s have been legally rehabilitated, only Bukharin and other prominent defenders of NEP such as Rykov have received extensive and sympathetic coverage in articles, documentaries, and even exhibitions. In the 1930s, Stalin was called 'Lenin today': the perestroika reformers want to make Bukharin 'Lenin today'.[12]

---

8   *Bol'shaia sovetskaia entsiklopediia*, 1st ed. (1939) and 2nd ed. (1954), entries on New Economic Policy; I.V. Stalin, *Economic Problems of Socialism in the USSR* (Stalin 1972), pp. 12–13. For a statement by Imre Nagy on NEP as applied to Hungary, see Nicolas Spulber, *Organizational Alternatives in Soviet-type Economies* (Spulber 1979), pp. 130–5, and for an application to Nicaragua, see Sergei Mikoian, *Latinskaia Amerika*, 1980, no. 3, pp. 34–44. See also Zenovia A. Sochor, 'NEP Rediscovered: Current Soviet Interest in Alternative Strategies of Development' (Sochor 1982), pp. 189–211.

9   Moshe Lewin, *Political Undercurrents in Soviet Economic Debates: From Bukharin to the Modern Reformers* (Lewin 1979), especially Chapter 12. Lewin's book is essential background for understanding today's debates.

10   Poliakov et al. 1982, *Novaia ekonomicheskaia politika*.

11   As cited by Mikhail Antonov, *Nash sovremennik*, 1989, no. 2, pp. 125–50.

12   Two indications of the Bukharin revival: a Komsomol political club named after him,

Today's revival of the 1920s has many aspects; the period has been praised for its art and literature, its legal institutions, and even its statistics.[13] In many ways, the return to NEP is a recovery of a rich but forgotten cultural heritage. For Gorbachev and the reformers, it shows that there are alternatives to Stalin's socialism that are rooted in Soviet history; Gorbachev can therefore claim that he is no revolutionary trying to tear down the fundamental structure of the system, but a reformer calling on Soviet society's own unrealized ideals.[14]

3   'Socialist Property Needs Its Owner': NEP and the Meaning of Socialism

NEP can be used an alternative model to Stalinism only insofar as it had Lenin's blessing. Gorbachev and the reformers have concentrated on two symbols of Lenin's association with NEP: the new food-supply system that inaugurated NEP in 1921, and the short article 'On Cooperation' that he wrote in 1923 on the eve of his final debilitating stroke.

At first glance, the food-supply tax seems an inappropriate symbol for perestroika, since it was an extremely heavy burden imposed on the peasantry in a time of famine and economic disorganization. Lenin himself said in 1921 that the tax was the aspect of the new policy that represented the crushing heritage of the past. A tax paid in kind rather than in money also seems a strange rallying cry for economic reforms that reject the command economy in favour of a money-based market system.

Why, then, was the food-supply tax adopted as a symbol of the liberating heritage of NEP? The answer lies in the other half of the new policy, namely, the legalization of the free market in grain. The Bolsheviks were understandably reluctant to make the market a prime symbol of their policy, and so the

---

and Evgeny Evtushenko's poem dedicated to Bukharin's widow (*Izvestiia*, March 26, 1988). For background, see Stephen F. Cohen, 'Bukharin, NEP, and the Idea of an Alternative to Stalinism', in *Rethinking the Soviet Experience: Politics and History since 1917* (Cohen 1985), pp. 71–92. On manifestations of the current revival, see Julia Wishnevsky, 'Bukharin's Legacy in the USSR Today' (*Radio Liberty Research Bulletin*, 3, 16/88).

13   Many major literary works (for example, Evgenii Zamiatin's *We*) and painters (for example, Pavel Filionov) of the 1920s are being rediscovered. On legality, see Iurii Feofanov's somewhat unconvincing tribute to N.V. Krylenko in *Pravda*, 11 August 1987; on statistics, see Vasily Seliunin and Grigorii Khanin, 'Lukavaia tsifra', *Novyi mir*, 1987, no. 2, pp. 181–201.

14   On the distinction between revolutionary leadership and reform leadership, see Robert C. Tucker, *Politics as Leadership* (Tucker 1981).

tax itself came to be used as the label of the new hands-off policy of the state. Under the system symbolized by the food-supply tax, the state said to economic producers: do what you want in whatever way you want to do it – as long as the state gets what it needs, it will let you alone. In 1921, this message was given to pre-socialist peasant producers. Today Gorbachev wants to send the same message – in his words, 'the possibility of ending the enserfment of construc- tive energy' – to collective farms and state industrial enterprises.[15]

Gorbachev also uses the introduction of the food-supply tax to show that he is not the only Soviet leader who proclaimed a drastic change of orientation and then had to convince many sceptics within the party about the social- ist credentials of the new course. A centrepiece of Lenin's defence of his new course is the article 'On Cooperation', viewed by today's reformers as the key Lenin text, far outstripping *What Is To Be Done?*, *State and Revolution*, and other works more familiar in the West. The article was written by a sick man who had evident difficulty expressing his thoughts, but the overall message is clear: the peasants must be led to socialism by appealing to their material interest, and cooperatives are an adequate means of bridging the gap between the interests of the peasant and the interests of society as a whole. In his oft-cited words: 'Given social ownership of the means of production, given the class victory of the proletariat over the bourgeoisie, the system of civilized cooperators is the system of socialism.'[16]

The food-supply tax and 'On Cooperation' are complementary symbols of NEP today. The food-supply tax symbolizes the hopes that the liberated energy of material self-interest will revitalize the Soviet economy. 'On Cooperation' is interpreted today as a call for a diversity of economic forms based on initiative from below. (This view of Lenin article is in contrast to the past, when NEP was praised as a way of overcoming the heterogeneity of economic forms in pre- socialist Russia by moving toward a completely socialist society.) This diversity of economic forms – in Gorbachev's words, 'a mechanism for the realization of the whole spectrum of the interests of working people' – is not meant to weaken the state but to strengthen it by restricting it to its essential tasks and giving it useful partners in the form of independent social organizations.

---

15   'Oktiabr i perestroika: revoliutsiia prodolzhaetsia', *Kommunist*, 1987, no. 17, p. 8. Gor- bachev's term *raskreposhchenie* was used in 1921 as well.

16   'On Cooperation' and Lenin's other final articles can be found in Robert C. Tucker, ed., *The Lenin Anthology* (Tucker 1975), pp. 701–48. The scholarly consensus is that the last articles represent a break with Lenin's past thought; for a different reading, see my 'Political Tes- tament: Lenin, Bukharin and the Meaning of NEP' (paper presented to the October 1989 conference on NEP, Moscow, and included in this volume).

In trying to give this vision concrete substance in terms of today's challenges, the reformers have come right up against the problem of socialist ownership – or more precisely, the problem of the socialist owner. A Russian word that is central to this problem is *khoziain*. Although it can be translated as 'owner', it has richer connotations than the English term. It is etymologically related to words meaning peasant farm (*khoziaistvo*), the economy as a whole (*narodnoe khoziaistvo*, or people's enterprise), and mistress of the house (*khoziaika*). The word conjures up images of a hardy, canny, industrious and self-reliant peasant owner who manages his property in worthy fashion. Under the centralized Stalinist system, the ultimate *khoziain* was Stalin himself, and in fact this was his nickname (usually translated as 'the Boss') among those who worked directly under him.

The reformers' remedy for the cynical apathy inherited from the Brezhnev era is to create in each producer a feeling of being a genuine *khoziain*. As the reformist economist Gavriil Popov (later mayor of Moscow) put it in his campaign platform when running for the Congress of People's Deputies: 'Socialist property needs its owner [*khoziain*]'.[17] The ideology of the *khoziain* is a socialist version of the image of the citizen who knows how to protect himself and contributes to society from a position of independence.

In the state sector of the economy, this ideology has given rise to the reform slogan 'full *khozraschet*'. This term is short for *khoziaistvennyi raschet*: the usual translations – 'economic accountability', 'financial independence' – give only the palest reflection of what is meant by it. The technical meaning of *khozraschet* is indeed the budgetary independence of a state enterprise: it receives no subsidies and in turn has control over what it earns. But the depth of the hopes placed on *khozraschet* is better conveyed by a translation such as 'a true owner's calculation'. Under *khozraschet*, socialist producers will make economic decisions based on the calculations of an owner who suffers from bad decisions and gains from good ones. This will not only lead to better decisions but will give producers the feeling that they have a stake in the economy as a whole.

To understand the implications of *khozraschet*, we must grasp the double nature of the centralized economic system inherited from the Stalin era. On the one hand, basic economic decisions are made at the top and imposed on producers. This is the message of the label made popular by Gavriil Popov: 'the Administrative System'.[18] (In Russian, *administrirovanie* has connotations

---

17   *Moscow News*, 1989, no. 4.
18   Gavriil Popov, 'S tochki zreniia ekonomista (o romane Aleksandra Beka "Novoe naznache-nie")', *Nauka i zhizn*, 1987, no. 4, pp. 54 ff.

of ordering people around without regard for their interests.) But this familiar aspect of the system should not obscure the other side of the coin: the enormous pressure from below that is created when all resources come from the centre. The centre is surrounded by a thousand outstretched hands: if over-centralized decision-making is a curse on the system, so is *izhdivenchestvo*, which can be translated as 'dependence bordering on parasitism'.

The task of *khozraschet* is to lift both these curses: the managers of local state enterprises are not subjected to direct orders and physical allocation of products, but they also cannot expect the central authorities to bail them out with subsidies. Their decisions will have to be based on market indicators such as prices and profits, and so *khozraschet* implies the expanded use of 'money-commodity relations' (a Marxist term for an independent market).[19] Gorbachev's wager on democracy within the factory also requires *khozraschet*. Without genuine enterprise independence, elections of managers will have a closer resemblance to an American high school choosing a powerless class president than a board of directors choosing a chief executive. Advocates of full *khozraschet* and the expanded use of money-commodity relations look back to NEP as the golden age of 'khozraschet socialism'. The inventor of this term, Nikolai Shmelev, wrote in a famous article in the journal *Novy mir*: 'The directive instead of the rouble has reigned too long in our economy. So long that we seem to have forgotten that there was a time, there really was a time, when the rouble reigned in our economy and not the directive – that is, common sense and not arbitrary schemes thought up in offices.'[20] As Shmelev's words indicate, much of reform thinking can be described as a revolt of economics against politics. Shmelev has gone so far as to argue that 'all that is economically ineffective is immoral, and all that is effective is moral'.[21]

---

19   A. Malafeev, 'Tovarno-denezhnye otnosheniia i perestroika khoziaistvennogo mekha-nizma, *Komnunist*, 1986, no. 18, pp. 78–88; P. Belousov, 'K istorii tovarno-denezhnykh otnoshenii v SSSR', *Voprosy ekonomiki*, 1987, no. 1, pp. 95–104; V.I. Manuilov, 'Metodologiia leninskogo issledovaniia tovarno-denezhnykh otnoshenii v period stroitelstva sotsializma i sovremennost', *Voprosy filosofii*, 1987, no. 10, pp. 39–48.

20   Nikolai Shmelev, 'Avansy i dolgi', *Novyi mir*, 1987, no. 6, pp. 142–58. An extended discussion of the NEP economic model can be found in Shmelev and Vladimir Popov, *Na perelome: ekonomicheskaia perestroika v SSSR* (Popov and Shmelev 1989a); an English translation is available as *The Turning Point: Revitalizing the Soviet Economy* (Popov and Shmelev 1989b). For a discussion of the economic thought of the 1920s, see the debate over the report by V. Manevich, *Voprosy istorii*, 1989, no. 10, pp. 46–75.

21   *Moscow News*, 1988, no. 6, p. 10; see also Shmelev, *Moscow News*, 1988, no. 47: 'It's a kind of insanity! We haven't yet realized the simple truth that *the market is always right*.'

This statement goes way too far for many Soviet citizens (and no doubt for many in the West). Shmelev has been attacked as a 'proponent of nouveau-riche-ism who is unconcerned about the growing economic inequality in the country'.[22] The economist Mikhail Antonov has made himself the spokesman of those who feel that to let the rouble reign is to dethrone morality. According to Antonov, Lenin did not intend NEP to be 'an idyllic development of "*khozraschet* socialism".' Antonov strongly opposes the programme of the present-day 'heirs of Bukharin', a programme that he fairly accurately identifies as the unhindered operation of money-commodity relations, the replacement of the collective farms by capitalist-style farmers, a substantial weakening of the foreign trade monopoly, and full freedom of action for foreign entrepreneurs.[23] *Khozraschet* is far from being a new slogan; it is easy enough, for example, to find endorsements of it by Stalin himself.[24] The question today is rather whether *khozraschet* will be used as just another method of enforcing 'plan discipline' or whether it will be used as a gateway to genuine independence of state enterprises.

Outside the state sector, the reformers also want to see the emergence of a genuine *khoziain*, but in this case their hopes are placed on a revival of the cooperatives. During the civil war, most Bolsheviks were hostile to the cooperative movement, primarily because cooperative activists were politically on the extreme right wing of the socialist camp. Lenin tried to combat this prejudice because of the practical usefulness of the cooperative organizations. In 'On Cooperation', Lenin argued further that cooperatives could be used as a bridge from single-owner peasant forms to more advanced socialist forms.

During the 1920s, even though the cooperatives had lost all political independence, they expanded their operations into many different fields. But mass collectivization in the early 1930s put a halt to this activity, even though Stalin claimed to be fulfilling 'Lenin's cooperative plan'. The collective farms (kolkhozes) were indeed billed as agricultural production cooperatives, but all other forms of cooperatives – credit, marketing, consumer, craft – were elim-

---

For Shmelev's defense of his position, see Stephen Cohen and Katrina Vanden Heuvel, *Voices of Glasnost: Interviews with Gorbachev's Reformers* (Cohen and Vanden Heuvel 1989, pp. 151–6).

22   Anatoly Saliutskii, *Literaturnaia Rossiia*, 23 December 1989; English translation in Current Digest of the Soviet Press (CDSP), 41:8 (1989).

23   Mikhail Antonov, 'Na perelome: razmyshleniia o nravstvennom smysle razvitiia ekonomiki i ekonomicheskoi nauki', *Moskva*, 1988, no. 3, pp. 3–26; *Nash sovremennik*, 1989, no. 2; CDSP, 41:8 (1989).

24   For example, Stalin 1972, p. 19 (*Economic Problems of Socialism*). See the discussion by M.I. Piskotin, *Sotsializm i gosudarstvennoe upravlenie* (Piskotin 1984), Chapter 2.

inated or reduced to insignificance. The collective farms themselves quickly lost the distinguishing feature of a cooperative, namely, independent economic activity based on democratic self-government. Economic pressure from state demands and internal interference by the party reduced the kolkhoz's freedom of activity to a minimum.

The essence of today's agricultural reforms is not only to restore this freedom of action to the collective farm but to turn it into a 'cooperative of cooperatives' – in other words, put effective decision-making as close as possible to the peasant household. Through long-term leases of land to peasant families, the reformers are aiming at no less than 'to revive the peasantry' and to change the peasant's status from a hired hand in a state-controlled enterprise to a genuine *khoziain*.[25]

The reformers claim that during NEP the Bolsheviks fully sympathized with the desire of the peasants to become masters of their own land; only during the Stalin era were such aspirations rejected as petty-bourgeois individualism.[26] In reality, today's view of the peasant is a fundamental break with the Bolshevik heritage. No Bolshevik, no matter how sympathetic to the peasants' interests, doubted that the peasants had to be 'remade' in the image of the urban proletariat, and to lose their petty-bourgeois property instincts. Much closer to today's outlook are the views of Petr Stolypin, the tsarist statesman who tried to break up the peasant commune in the years after the 1905 revolution on the assumption that a secure feeling of individual ownership was a necessary precondition of agricultural progress. Stolypin has always been anathema to the Russian revolutionary tradition; the Bolsheviks would have been shocked to discover that his views carry more weight today than their own.[27]

The image of the peasantry as a national resource rather than an emblem of backwardness is the main reason for the new-found prominence of Aleksandr Chayanov, the most important agrarian economist of the 1920s. Chayanov was one of the founders of a school of economists that looked on the peasant family farm as a unique and viable economic form, one that defied the framework of both 'bourgeois' and Marxist economists. Although he was not a Bolshevik nor even a Marxist, he played an important role in public discussion of the cooperative movement and agrarian policy throughout the 1920s. He was arrested in 1930 on trumped-up charges of counterrevolutionary activity. His further fate

25   Gelii Shmelev, *Moscow News*, 1988, no. 43.
26   Mikhail Gorbachev, *Pravda*, 16 March 1989; Gennadii Lisichkin, *Moscow News*, 1988, no. 45.
27   See the comparison between Stolypin and Bukharin in a debate between the liberal critic Benedikt Sarnov and the conservative critic Vadim Kozhinov in *Literaturnaia gazeta*, 1989, no. 13.

was unknown until recently; we now know that after working in internal exile as an agricultural official in Central Asia, he was re-arrested in 1937 and shot in 1939.[28]

Although Chayanov and his theories were quickly forgotten in the Soviet Union, his work became extremely influential in the West and in the developing countries. Soviet society had thus been denied a legitimate source of national pride. Like much of the reformist outlook, the Chayanov revival has its roots in the Brezhnev era; for almost two decades, we are told, a group of scholars has 'collected and studied Chayanov's heritage'.[29] When Chayanov and other non-party scholars such as Nikolai Kondratiev were posthumously cleared of all legal charges in the summer of 1987, agricultural economists were instantly ready to present detailed expositions of Chayanov's views.

It is not Chayanov's examination of technical questions about the optimal size of cooperatives that accounts for his widespread popularity today, but his celebration of the peasant's double role as 'owner-worker [khoziain-rabotnik]'. As the chairman of a collective farm who called for the exoneration of the kulaks put it: 'We are just beginning to realize, as it was proved by our outstanding economist Chayanov, that independent farmers fully correspond to the development of socialism.'[30] It has even been asserted that Lenin's article 'On Cooperation' was inspired by Chayanov's writing.[31] In the 1920s, writers like Chayanov who wanted to combine the virtues of the peasant way of life with modern technology were scorned as 'neo-populists'. But today Gorbachev argues that 'the objective is to revive and encourage the best features of the traditional peasant character'.[32]

Perestroika's agricultural reforms enjoy wide support, but the same cannot be said about the cooperatives in the cities. The urban cooperatives are both perestroika's greatest success and its greatest failure. They are a success

---

28   Vladimir Kabanov, 'Aleksandr Vasilevich Chaianov', *Voprosy istoriI*, 1988, no. 6, pp. 146–67; Nadezhda Figurovskaia, 'K stoletiiu so dnia rozhdeniia A.V. Chaianova', *Voprosy ekonomiki*, 1988, no. 1, pp. 52–62; V. Gavrichkin, 'Aleksandr Chaianov – grazhdanin i uchenyi', *Izvestiia*, 19 January 1988. See also the comment by Viktor Danilov in *Voprosy istorii*, 1988, no. 3, pp. 21–4.

29   'Posthumous Justice', *Moscow News*, 1987, no. 33, p. 12; B. Surganov in *Moscow News*, 1988, no. 7, p. 4. The major works in English are A.V. Chayanov, *The Theory of Peasant Economy* (Chayanov 1966), and 'Journey of my brother Alexei to the land of peasant utopia' in *The Russian Peasant, 1920 and 1984*, ed. R.E.F. Smith (Chayanov 1977).

30   *Moscow News*, 1989, no. 10.

31   Vladimir Bashmachnikov, *Literaturnaia gazeta*, 1989, no. 7, p. 11.

32   Gorbachev, 'Potentsial kooperatsii – delu perestroiki', *Pravda*, 24 March 1988; English translation in *Moscow News*, 1988, no. 14, supplement.

because the cooperatives called into life by the reform legislation have genuinely changed the economic landscape in the Soviet Union and made a visible
impact on the daily life of its citizens; they are a failure because the hostility
they have engendered has weakened support for perestroika and given the old
guard its most persuasive talking point.[33]

The cooperatives will determine which image of NEP will be uppermost
in popular consciousness: the NEP where the liberated energy of economic
independence leads to personal and social prosperity, or the one where disreputable 'nepmen' (barely tolerated private entrepreneurs of the 1920s) flaunt
their wealth while honest workers barely eke out a living. Cooperatives began
playing a role in reform rhetoric in 1986, and in the fall of that year, 'individual
labour activity' – or more briefly, moonlighting – was given legislative protection.[34] In the spring of 1988, when a fully-worked out Law on Cooperatives was
passed, Gorbachev claimed that the application of the ideas of the new law 'will
signify a new qualitative stage in the development not only of the cooperative
movement, but also of the whole of Soviet society'.[35] The Law on the Cooperatives is one of the legislative milestones of perestroika; some have called it
the best enactment of the reform period and others have called it a bad mistake.[36]

Later legislation regulating the cooperatives reflected the difficulties of
assimilating independent economic enterprise into the command economy. In
the summer of 1988, legislation proposing high taxation rates for cooperatives
was announced, but – a sign of the times – it was withdrawn after a heated
discussion in the Council of Ministers. Legislation on taxes only appeared the
following year and even then the central government avoided difficult decisions by handing over the job of setting tax rates to local authorities. In 1989, the
cooperatives ran into trouble with another child of perestroika, the new popularly elected legislature. The legislature provided a forum for the deep popular

---

33   The number of people working in cooperatives grew from 156 thousand to 1.4 million
     in the space of a year (*Izvestiia*, 10 March 1989). For a description of the impact of the
     cooperatives, see Robert Cullen, 'Letter from Rostov-on-Don', *The New Yorker*, 12 June 1989,
     pp. 107 ff.

34   The text of the law can be found in CDSP, 38:46 (1986), pp. 6–8; see A. Iu. Kabalkin, 'Zakon
     ob individualnoi trudovoi deiatelnost – vazhhnyi rychag osushchestvleniia sotsialno-
     ekonomicheskoi politiki', *Sovetskoe gosudarstvo i pravo*, 1987, no. 3, pp. 12–21; Libor Roucek,
     'Private Enterprise in Soviet Political Debates', *Soviet Studies*, 40 (1988), pp. 46–63.

35   Gorbachev, 'Potentsial kooperatsii--delu perestroiki', *Pravda*, 24 March 1988.

36   The best: Boris Kurashvili, *Moscow News*, 1989, no. 12, p. 13. A mistake: Iurii Solovev, dis-
     cussing his election defeat in spring 1989, CDSP, 41:17 (1989).

hostility to cooperatives, especially those involved in middleman activities. The government responded to this hostility by introducing restrictive legislation.[37]

Despite the legislative stops and starts, the cooperatives had been launched with a broad ideological justification based on NEP. In Gorbachev's 1988 speech introducing the Law on the Cooperatives, the cooperatives were used as a symbol of how much Soviet society lost by the termination of NEP: 'As non-equivalent exchange began developing between the state sector and the cooperatives, as command-style methods of management came to be used more and more, as the democratic principles of society started losing ground, the very idea of cooperation began to be frowned upon ... The cooperatives could not exist without *khozraschet* and broad democracy.'

Gorbachev belligerently refuted those who claimed that 'cooperation is not a socialist form of management but a return to private enterprise'. On the contrary, 'cooperatives – a mass social movement of the working people in a society freed from exploitation and class antagonism – are by their nature fully in line with the goals of socialism'. The cooperative movement is also 'one of the more important levers for broadening the democratic process as a whole' and it should serve as a model for state enterprises on their way to *khozraschet* and democratic self-management.[38] The reformers' main hope is that the liberated activity of the new *khoziain* would infuse new energy into the economy and help the population shake off its passivity and its 'levelling' instincts. Sometimes the reformers sound as if they have been briefed by the Small Business Administration:

---

37   For material on earlier legislation about the cooperatives, see *Moscow News*, 1989, no. 3; CDSP, 41:1, p. 10 and 41:6, p. 25 (1989); *Kooperatsiia i arenda: sbornik dokumentov i materi-alov*, Kn. 1, Moscow, 1989.

38   Gorbachev, 'Potentsial kooperatsii'; see also Gorbachev 1987, pp. 95–6. For a full-scale presentation of this outlook, see the article by the noted agricultural expert G.I. Shmelev, '"Ne smet' komandovat'," *Oktiabr*, 1988, no. 2, pp. 3–26; L.E. Fain, 'Razvitie kooperativnoi formy sotsialisticheskoi sobstvennosti v SSSR', *Voprosy istorii*, 1987, no. 5. The debate on the socialist nature of cooperative property can already be seen, in somewhat muffled form, by comparing the conservative view in *Razvitoe sotsialisticheskoe obshchestvo: sushchnost, kriterii zrelosti, kritika revisionistskikh kontseptsii*, 1975, pp. 84–6, with *Razvitoi sotsializm: obshchee i spetsificheskoe v ego stroitelstve*, 1980, pp. 110–13. See also the 1969 article 'Che-lovek, kooperatsiia, obshchestvo', reprinted in Gennadii Lisichkin, *Ternistyi put k izobiliiu* (Lisichkin 1984). (Lisichkin is one of the few writers who could republish his articles from the 1970s without undue embarrassment.) The previously dominant view can be found in Richard Kosolapov's article in *Pravda*, 3 March 1983; today's view can be found in articles from *Voprosy ekonomiki* by T. Kuznetsova (1987, no. 4), L. Nikiforov (1988, no. 3, pp. 22–34), G. Gorlanov (1988, no. 3, pp. 43–41), and V. Marianovskii (1988, no. 5, pp. 92–101). See also the exchange of letters between Kosolapov and Anatoly Butenko in *Voprosy filosof ii*, 1987, no. 12, pp. 142–50.

It turns out that it is not only the [high prices] that are unacceptable, but the independence of the cooperator. In contrast to all others he is the master [*khoziain*] of his own affairs and to that extent free. By his very existence he presents a challenge to people's barracks psychology, their subordination and dependence. In other words, he 'thrusts himself forward', he 'must have more than the rest', and it is this frank, legalized nonconformity that is intolerable to the philistine.[39]

The cooperatives were also assigned an important role in the over-all strategy of *reform*. In the short run, the cooperatives were supposed to find hidden reserves and to provide the population with immediate improvements in the provisions of goods and services. In the long run, the small-scale services provided by the cooperatives will create an environment in which large-scale state enterprise can function properly. Soviet specialists have calculated that thirty-five to forty billion man-hours are wasted each year in lines for food, so that in effect 'every seventh able-bodied person does not work, but is occupied in searching and acquiring food products'.[40] This stunning social inefficiency not only demoralizes the consumer but also undercuts the possibility of technically advanced production. In the words of Gavriil Popov:

The future ... will not be determined in private cafes or individual workshops. This future is tied to success in information science, computers, robotic technology, in the opening up of Siberia and the oceans. But in order for our worker or technician, engineer or manager, scientist or student to be able to eat a hot roll in the morning without trouble and to avoid running around the stores for hours in search of available goods or standing in lines at a repair shop – [in order that] hundreds of thousands of heads and hands be freed from imaginary work in countless offices and administrations – in order to strike a powerful blow at the underground economy that is corrupting our society – we need a flourishing individual sector.[41]

If a high-minded image of NEP inspired the reformers who summoned forth the new enterprises, the reality of the cooperatives helped reinforce another image. In popular literature and movies, NEP has long been portrayed as a sort of Roar-

39   Gennadii Batygin, 'Vse, chto ne zapreshcheno', *Krokodil*, 1988, no. 17.
40   A. Nikonov, 'Razvitie kooperatsii i reshenie prodovolstvennoi problemy', *Voprosy ekonomiki*, 1988, no. 2, pp. 3–11.
41   G. Popov, 'Perestroika ekonomiki i individualnyi trud', *Nauka i zhizn*, 1987, no. 9, pp. 2 ff.

ing Twenties in which nepmen and other shady underworld figures loom large. According to rumour, a young man appalled by high prices at a new cooperative cafe picketed the cafe with a sign that said 'Down with NEP!'[42] The large income of many of the new cooperative members offends against several deepseated Soviet values. There is a moral indignation against 'unearned income' that is hard for a Westerner to understand. The official reformist line labels this attitude with the opprobrious term 'levelling' and insists that if the money is honestly earned, then it is sheer malignant envy to begrudge it. But can one honestly earn money simply by buying low and selling high? For many Soviet citizens, it is perfectly legitimate if a farmer goes to town and sells his own potatoes. But if the farmer hires someone to deliver and sell the potatoes, it is 'exploitation' of a worker for private profit. And if someone should buy the potatoes from the farmer and sell them for a profit in the city, it is 'speculation'. The roots of these cultural attitudes go deeper than Marxist propaganda. The hostility to speculation, for example, goes back to pre-revolutionary prejudices against middlemen shared by statesmen and peasants alike; it was reinforced by the recurrent bouts with famine that made profiteering seem particularly ghoulish.

These attitudes are translated into pledges to use taxes to insure social justice, as well as into a good deal of official inquisitiveness about the percentage of earnings devoted to salaries as opposed to reinvestment. High cooperative incomes have also created morale problems for the state sector. 'How come a steelworker earns less than a person who sells shashlik [a tasty kebab-type snack]?'[43] Economic managers complained about a talent drain from the state sector and about unfair tax privileges for the cooperatives.[44]

High incomes for cooperative owners are all the more irritating to the population at large because they seem to be derived from the high prices that are making life miserable for everybody else. When the retail consumer market collapsed in the latter half of 1988, it seemed that the cooperatives were exploiting and perhaps even creating the maddening shortages. There was some foundation for this, since cooperatives were often forced to buy their raw materials at the same retail outlets as the population. Consumers were outraged when a cooperative cafe bought all the coffee in the stores and sold it back to the population at inflated prices – especially since the rigid command economy

---

42   *Izvestiia*, 1 May 1987, p. 3. In Nina Andreyeva's famous anti-perestroika broadside, reformers in general were called 'descendants of nepmen' (*Sovetskaia Rossiia*, 13 March 1988).

43   *Moscow News*, 1988, no. 22, p. 4.

44   CDSP, 39:16 (1987), pp. 8–9; *Moscow News*, 1988, no. 42.

ensured that increased demand did not increase the supply of coffee.[45] The dream that the cooperatives would compete with the state to the benefit of the consumer was replaced by a more prosaic reality: the cooperatives were often used as a semi-legal way to raise state prices. Fully eighty percent of the cooperative cafeterias in Leningrad were merely substitutes for previously existing state outlets.[46]

The cooperatives are also associated in the public mind with a new explosion of organized crime. Before the cooperatives, it is said, the Soviet Union had no need of words like mafia, racketeering, and money laundering (even though protection rackets had actually grown up during the Brezhnev era when large-scale embezzlement and fraud made many state employees vulnerable). The cooperatives are not simply victims of organized thuggery; they have also become a home for ex-convicts and wheeler-dealers from the underground economy of yesteryear.[47]

All of the negative images of the cooperatives came together in the case of Vadim Tarasov, the 'soviet millionaire' who headed the Tekhnika cooperative. Tarasov hit the headlines in early 1989 and seemed tailor-made for opponents of the cooperatives: he had made obscene profits simply by selling unused waste material abroad, spending the foreign currency on computers and selling the computers at home for inflated prices. Critics charged that Tarasov was not really selling waste, but rather valuable raw material, and that he protected himself by putting high bureaucrats on the cooperative's governing board. Tarasov was stoutly defended by reformist newspapers such as *Moscow News*, but even other cooperative businessmen felt that the Tarasov case was a public relations disaster.

In 1990, Tarasov was outdone by a major political scandal caused by the ANT cooperative that was accused of selling Soviet tanks to foreigners. The directors of the cooperative claimed that they were set up, since they had purchased tractors and were surprised to receive instead some out-of-date tanks. The resulting scandal involved major politicians such as Anatoly Sobchak and Nikolai Ryzhkov, who were accused of authorizing ANT's alleged machinations. The whole uproar became grist for the mill of Ivan Polozkov, the emerging leader of Russia's conservative communists.[48]

---

45   *Ogonek*, 1988, no. 7, p. 4, letter from N.P. Mankov.
46   *CDSP*, 41:6, pp. 4–5 (1989).
47   *Literaturnaia gazeta*, 1989, no. 2, p. 11.
48   'Antgate: Who Stands to Gain?', Boris Balkarei and Yuri Teplyakov, *Business in the USSR*, 1:1 (May 1990), pp. 60–3. On the Tarasov case, see 'Kooperatsiia i biurokratiia: kto kogo', *Literaturnaia gazeta*, 1989, no. 18.

Thus the cooperatives, instead of smoothing the transition to the new economic system, have upset many people (especially women) and exacerbated tensions.[49] Conservative forces have not been slow to pick up the issue. An ideological platform has been put together: the activities of the cooperatives show the dangers of 'group selfishness' and of egoistic actions that hurt the community. The cooperatives are unpatriotic as well, even to the extent of exporting tanks. The cooperatives should be seen as a manifestation of the 'shadow economy' that rose to prominence during the era of stagnation. The new millionaires will use the money acquired by corrupt activities to buy up the factories after the reformers manage to privatize them and in this way dispossess the working class.[50] The anti-cooperative movement also has a solid class basis: the industrial workers, who are threatened both by the high prices of the cooperatives and the economic success of those who left jobs in the state sector. The most outspoken attack on the cooperatives at the Congress of People's Deputies in 1989 was from Viktor Shcherbakov, the head of the trade unions. Reformers noted grimly that the cooperatives were replacing the bureaucrats as the image of the enemy.[51]

Spokesmen for the cooperatives fought back as best they could. When the cooperatives first appeared, it was confidently claimed that competition would drive prices down. The rigidities of the system and the continued collapse of the consumer market made this prophecy sound less and less plausible. (One exception was flower-vending, where the cooperatives have had the hoped-for positive impact.)[52] The cooperatives then pointed out the many difficulties that added to their production costs: problems in obtaining registration and in leasing space, discriminatory prices for raw materials, vulnerability to corrupt pressures. The state sector has managed to use its power to prevent any real competition between cooperatives and state enterprises; state economic managers made it clear that they wanted the cooperatives to do no more than 'tighten up the nuts' for state industry. No steps have been taken to establish the promised wholesale market for raw materials, so that the cooperatives have

---

49   See the polls in *Moscow News*, 1989, no. 4 and 1988, no. 3, p. 9; see also *Literaturnaia gazeta*, 1989, no. 13; 'Eshche raz o kooperativakh', *Izvestiia*, 27 February 1988; L. Belikanova and P. Degtiarev, 'Kachestvo zhizni', *Literaturnaia gazeta*, 9 March 1988.

50   Anatoly Saliutskii, *Pravda*, 14 February 1989 (translated in CDSP, 41:6, p. 7). The paper *Literaturnaia Rossia* is a fertile source of anti-cooperative articles. For a sober view of the topic, see S.D. Golovnin and A.N. Shoklin, 'Tenevaia ekonomiia: za realizm otsenok', *Kommunist*, 1990, no. 1, pp. 51–8.

51   *Moscow News*, 1989, no. 12.

52   *Moscow News*, 1988, no. 45; 1989, no. 4 (Andrei Kuteinikov).

been forced into competing with individual consumers for supplies. In this and other ways, the cooperatives feel that they have been set up as a scapegoat for the overall failure of the economy.[53]

Cooperative spokesmen admit that many of the new entrepreneurs have criminal records, but they ask in response: isn't it understandable that during the Brezhnev era of stagnation, many enterprising people ended up on the wrong side of the law? One association of cooperatives has even set up a programme for helping young ex-convicts go straight.[54]

The top leadership no longer seemed anxious to associate the reform programme too closely with the disreputable urban cooperatives, and so their fate became tied up with the progress of reform at local levels. Unreconstructed local authorities seemed to measure their performance by the number of cooperatives they closed; newly elected reform officials (such as the Moscow city council in 1990) promptly reversed many anti-cooperative restrictions. Under these circumstances, the cooperatives were forced to band together and organize in order to make their case to the public as well as to ensure services needed by the fledgling cooperatives. In this way the cooperative movement is making an impact on the political system that matches its impact on the economic system, for we are witnessing the birth of openly conducted interest-group politics.

Thus the cooperatives are a source of creativity not only in the economic but the political sphere. But they are also vulnerable to pressure in both spheres. The less respectable the cooperatives are, the less anyone reputable wants to become a cooperative businessman, and the more difficult it is to shake the nepman image.[55] Shortages pose another dilemma: if cooperatives are given economic independence in an environment of general shortage, they will be seen as speculators – but if their activities are restricted, they will be forced to the shady side of the law in order to obtain supplies. In either case, they will be pushed to a marginal economic and political position. The private sector managed to break out of this marginal position in Poland, but at the cost of an unholy alliance with a corrupt economic bureaucracy.[56]

---

53   See Anatolii Rubinov, 'Nepravednye dengi', *Literaturnaia gazeta*, 15, 1988; *Moscow News*, 1988, no. 6, 10, and 43; *Literatunaia gazeta*, 15, 1987, pp. 10–11.

54   V. Sorokin, head of the Union of Cooperatives, in *Pravda*, 4 February 1989 (CDSP, 41:5, p. 24). See also Vladimir Iakovlev, head of Fakt, *Moscow News*, 1988, no. 47.

55   'Kooperativ na starte', Iu. Kazantsev, *Krokodil*, 1989, no. 5, p. 9. An article by a spokesman for the conservative United Workers Front ironically harked back to the 1920s as a time when criminal activities by cooperatives and nepmen were vigorously repressed (Aleksei Sergeev in *Nash sovremennik*, 1990, no. 4).

56   Anders Aslund, *Private Enterprise in Eastern Europe* (Aslund 1985); 'The Decay of Social-

All of these sources of vulnerability had their counterpart in the NEP-that-was and helped prepare its premature demise. The reformers are still hoping to activate the NEP-that-might-have-been: the cooperatives will help the whole economy by providing not only salutary competition, but also the work ethic of an industrious *khoziain*. But one lesson of the NEP-that-was is that independent cooperatives cannot survive in an atmosphere of economic crisis and political hostility, and so the future of the cooperatives depends on the overall health of the new NEP.

What connects all the aspects of the NEP alternative – *khozraschet* in industry, revival of the peasantry in the countryside, and urban cooperatives in daily life – is the wager on the new socialist *khoziain*. Gorbachev has proposed a man named Anatoly Volochensky as a model *khoziain*. When Volochensky informed Gorbachev of his reasons for going over to agricultural rental contracts, he 'emphasized the possibility of free and independent decision-making and of working and acting depending on the conditions, without having anyone order him about or interfere in his work ... There was no talk of profit or income, but just of a man finally seeing his potential as a farmer realized.'[57]

4   'Which Road Leads to the Temple?': NEP and the Road to Socialism

The profound crisis of Soviet society has given rise to some very troubling questions. If the system requires radical restructuring, perhaps the original construction plan was a bad one. Perhaps the October revolution and the triumph of the Bolsheviks was a tragedy for Russia. These devastating doubts are directly expressed in *Forward! Forward! Forward!*, a play published in 1988 by the path-breaking historical dramatist Mikhail Shatrov.[58] The cast of characters is made

---

ism and the Growth of Private Enterprise in Poland', *Soviet Studies*, 41:2 (1989), pp. 194–214. Aslund's views of the cooperatives of perestroika can be found in *Gorbachev's Struggle for Economic Reform* (Aslund 1991).

57   Gorbachev, 'Potentsial kooperatsii'.
58   Shatrov, *Dalshe... dalshe..., dalshe!*, *Znamia*, 1988, no. 1, pp. 3–53. For this and other Shatrov plays, see Mikhail Shatrov, *The Bolsheviks: Three Plays* (Shatrov 1990). For further discussion of Shatrov, see *Pravda*, 10 January 1988 and 15 February 1988; *Komsomolskaia Pravda*, 19 February 1988; *Moscow News*, 1987, no. 24, p. 9 (discussion between Shatrov and Stephen Cohen), and 1988, no. 10, p. 12; *Znamia*, 1988, no. 5, pp. 219–36; *Oktiabr*, 1988, no. 5, pp. 201–3. Many of these documents can be found with a discussion by Jane Burbank in 'The Shatrov Controversy', *Michigan Quarterly Review*, Fall 1989, pp. 580–603. The Shatrov debate is characteristically Soviet in that it focuses on literary works rather than works of historical

up of a striking range of Russian political activists who had some connection
to the Bolshevik revolution of October 1917: non-Bolshevik revolutionaries, liberals, White Guard officers, as well as Bolshevik supporters and opponents of
Stalin. Many of these characters have never appeared in Soviet political theatre, or only in the stereotyped form described by one critic: 'The Menshevik
Martov, who slobbers and drops his pince-nez; the SR Spiridonova, who is flat-
chested, hysterical, and carries a gun in her fur-muff; the lordly Plekhanov,
terribly distant from the people; Trotsky, who is either selling out Mother Russia in mysterious ambassadorial residences or who flops himself down on the
sofa with a French novel [at the height of the civil war]'.[59]

Shatrov's play jumps forward and backward in time, and allows the characters to comment freely on events and to confront Lenin with the consequences
of his decision to take power in 1917. The question is starkly presented: was
the October revolution a mistake? Given the horrors of Stalinism, were Lenin's
critics right to oppose him in 1917? Shatrov's answer is that Stalinism was a distortion and a betrayal of the revolution and that the genuine Bolshevik heritage
is represented by NEP. But this response gives rise to a further question: if NEP
represents an alternative to Stalinism, why was it rejected at the end of the
1920s? Was this rejection inevitable? Was it justifiable?

A Soviet writer has observed that 'perestroika has made all of us historians'.
It is not simply an interest in the past that has led to self-scrutiny so intense that
in 1988 all school examinations in history were cancelled. There is a widespread
feeling that Soviet society has been travelling on a road leading to a dead end:
in order to find its way, the society must go back to where the wrong turning
was made. The fundamental question is 'which path leads to the temple?' – the
temple dedicated to the best ideals of the Soviet past.[60]

The historical fate of NEP is central to this search for the correct path. Despite
the wide variety of competing answers in the Soviet newspapers and journals,
three general approaches can be distinguished (neo-Stalinist interpretations
are not included):

scholarship. A conference was held 27–28 April 1988 on this topic: see 'Istoriki i pisateli
o literature i istorii', *Voprosy istorii*, 1988, no. 6, pp. 3–114. An English translation with an
introduction by William Rosenberg can be found in *Michigan Quarterly Review*, Fall 1989,
pp. 549–79.

59   L. Ovrutskii, *Sovetskaia kultura*, 4 February 1988.

60   The phrase comes from Igor Kliamkin, 'Kakaia ulitsa vedet k khramu?', *Novyi mir*, 1987,
no. 11, pp. 150–88. The image of a road leading to a temple comes from the film *Repen-
tance*. For an extended examination of the path metaphor, see 'The Soviet Union and the
Path to Communism', included in this volume.

1. *The abolition of* NEP *was not inevitable, but justifiable.* In his pioneering critique of Stalin, Nikita Khrushchev did not shed any tears over the abandonment of NEP. 'Violations of socialist legality' occurred only some years after the great breakthrough:

> Let us consider for a moment what would have happened if in 1928–29 the political line of the right deviation had prevailed among us ... We would not now have a powerful heavy industry, we would not have the kolkhozes, we would find ourselves disarmed and weak in a capitalist encirclement ... It was precisely during the period of 1935–1937–1938 that the practice of mass repression through the state apparatus was born.[61]

This Khrushchev-era critique is represented by Anatoly Rybakov's *Children of the Arbat*, a novel begun under Khrushchev but published only under Gorbachev. The heroes of the novel – the fictional Sasha Pankratov and the historical Sergei Kirov – are supporters of the 'revolution from above' that destroyed NEP, and one of the principal negative characters (a pool shark named Kostya) is portrayed as an anachronistic nepman. The main drama of the novel comes from Stalin's degeneration and his descent into active criminality in 1934.[62]

In 1987, despite his favourable view of NEP, Gorbachev remained within the limits of Khrushchev's critique. In his speech on the seventieth anniversary of the revolution, Gorbachev stated that the abandonment of NEP led to bureaucratization and over-centralization, the end of glasnost and democracy, and the peasant's loss of the status of a true *khoziain*. But Gorbachev still criticized Bukharin and other defenders of NEP for overlooking the life-and-death importance of the time factor. The threat of imperialist aggression and the imperative of extremely rapid industrialization meant that collectivization was necessary, despite mistakes in its implementation.

Gorbachev has slowly but steadily moved away from even this conditional defence of the destruction of NEP. In a 1989 speech going over the same events, Gorbachev's condemnation was more stark: the destruction of NEP was 'a serious strategic miscalculation and a deviation from Marxist views': it led to the famine of 1932–33, the crime of dekulakization, and the creation of the 'administrative-command system' of managing society as a whole. His denun-

---

61   The text of Khrushchev's 1956 speech on Stalin can be found in *Khrushchev Remembers*, ed. Strobe Talbott (Khrushchev 1970), pp. 560–618.

62   Rybakov, *Deti Arbata* (Rybakov 1988a); for an English translation, see Rybakov 1988b. There are a few pro-NEP passages in the novel, and these were picked up by Soviet reviewers; see A. Turkov in *Literaturnaia gazeta*, 8 June 1987.

ciation of collectivization was balanced only by a mere nod in the direction of orthodoxy. Despite Gorbachev's studied vagueness on the objective and subjective causes of NEP's demise, he left no doubt that he no longer thought it was justifiable. On this issue, Gorbachev finally caught up with his supporters.

Gorbachev's interpretation of Lenin's testament also changed in accordance with his view of the priorities of the reform process. In 1990, when ethnic violence and economic crisis had led to increasing talk of civil war, Gorbachev saw Lenin's central message as the insistence on peaceful reform rather than violent confrontation.[63]

2. *The abolition of NEP was neither inevitable nor justifiable.* The intelligentsia supporters of perestroika agree that the abolition of NEP was not inevitable and that real alternatives existed. But in their view, the wrong alternative was chosen: the party took the wrong path, with tragic consequences for socialism and for Soviet society.

The basic postulate of this interpretation is that the rejection of NEP was also a rejection of Lenin's political testament. In 1987, Fedor Burlatsky published a one-act play entitled 'Political Testament'. Burlatsky's play is set in the late 1920s and shows a peasant father and his two sons, one of whom is a Bukharinist and the other a Stalinist. The Bukharinist son tells his father that the issue between the brothers is 'what will happen to NEP? Will it be prolonged, or rolled back? ... At the end of 1922, the sick Lenin dictated five articles. [It is this testament] that we're arguing about.'[64] It is clear the Burlatsky thinks that the Bukharinist son has much the stronger case. But, as Burlatsky's parable of two brothers implies, the argument over Lenin's testament was a schism within Bolshevism. The reformers have to provide an explanation for this fatal misstep without seeming to condemn Bolshevism as a whole.

One way to solve this problem is to blame the leaders, rather than the party. Lenin's 'Letter to the Congress' can be used for this purpose. (This letter by itself is sometimes also called Lenin's testament.) The letter was actually a series of notes dictated by Lenin in preparation for the party congress scheduled for

---

63 'Oktiabr i perestroika', *Kommunist*, 1987, no. 17, pp. 9–15; *Perestroika*, pp. 39–40; *Pravda*, 16 March 1989. Gorbachev's critique of dekulakization was still limited to the 'mistaken' repression against non-kulaks. For a scholarly article that follows Gorbachev's 1987 line, see L.F. Morozov, 'Leninskaia kontseptsiia kooperatsii i alternativy razvitiia', *Voprosy istorii KPSS*, 1988, no. 6, pp. 101–55.

64 *Literaturnaia gazeta*, July 22, 1987. Burlatsky's title is taken from Bukharin's 1929 article 'Lenin's Political Testament', first published in 1929 and reprinted in *Kommunist*, 1988, no. 2.

spring 1923. In these notes, Lenin made damaging remarks about all the top Bolshevik leaders; in a postscript he proposed that Stalin be relieved of the post of
general secretary. We now know that the contents of the letter quickly became
known to the rest of the Politburo, but only after Lenin's death in 1924 were
his suggestions made known to the wider party public.[65] Stalin duly offered his
resignation, but he was urged to remain on the job by his fellow leaders, if only
because they needed his services in the fight against Trotsky. The existence of
the letter was not a secret during Stalin's time in power. The interested student
could read in Stalin's collected works the following passage from a 1927 speech:
'They say that in this "testament" comrade Lenin suggested to the Congress
that in light of Stalin's "crudeness", it should consider the question of replacing Stalin as general secretary. This is completely correct.'[66] The full text of the
letter was finally published after Stalin's death.

   It is only natural that once perestroika was under way, Lenin's letter would be
endlessly discussed in the press, with an underlying message of 'if only we had
listened to Lenin'. Many felt that the failure of the Bolshevik leaders – particularly Zinoviev and Kamenev – to carry out Lenin's wishes and insist on Stalin's
removal was (in the words of Dmitri Kazutin of the *Moscow News*) 'precisely
apostasy'.[67] This explanation relies on the Lenin cult to drive out the Stalin cult.
One critic wrote that the argument seems to be that 'Lenin is right, because
he is Lenin; the will of Ilych [a familiar nickname for Lenin] is law that must
be carried out; anyone who doesn't carry it out is an intriguer and a political
hack'.[68]

   Another convenient scapegoat is Lev Trotsky, even though he was removed
from all positions of influence long before the rejection of NEP. Trotsky is
accused of starting a power struggle within the party because of his overween-

65   For the complicated circumstances surrounding Lenin's letter, see Robert Tucker, *Stalin
      as Revolutionary* (Tucker 1973); Moshe Lewin, *Lenin's Last Struggle* (Lewin 1968); Robert
      H. McNeal, *Stalin: Man and Ruler* (McNeal 1988), chapter 5. For the new information about
      the letter, see V.P. Naumov, 'Leninskoe zaveshchanie', *Pravda*, 26 February and 25 March
      1988; V.I. Startsev, 'Politicheskie rukovoditeli sovetskogo gosudarstva v 1922-nachale 1923
      g', *Istoriia SSSR*, 1988, no. 5, pp. 101–22; Egor Yakovlev, *Moscow News*, 1989, no. 4; Alexander
      Bek, *Moscow News*, 1989, no. 17.
66   Stalin 1947–1952, 10:172–7. An important article on the reception of the testament during
      the 1920s is S. Dmitrenko, 'Leninskoe "pismo k sezdu": pravda i vymysli', *Politicheskoe obra-
      zovaniie*, 1988, no. 8, pp. 32–45.
67   *Moscow News*, 1988, no. 2, p. 12. For typical articles on the letter, see *Moscow News*, 1987,
      no. 3, p. 13; Iu. Borisov, 'Chelovek i simvol', *Nauka i zhizn*, 1987, no. 9, pp. 62–4; 'Lenin-
      skoe zaveshchanie', *Pravda*, 26 February and 25 March 1988. For a more sceptical view, see
      Maxim Kim in *Pravda*, 2 February 1988.
68   L. Ovrutskii, *Sovetskaia kultura*, 4 February 1988.

ing ambition. This accusation draws strength from an anti-political attitude still current today that 'the struggle for power is always unprincipled, since it is for oneself and not for principles and the truth'.[69] Gorbachev lent his support to another popular theory that Trotsky was the originator of Stalin's policies of 'super-industrialization' and exploitation of the peasantry. According to this theory, all Stalin did was 'out-Trotsky Trotsky'. This theory was seductive because it requires the smallest possible break with the previous orthodoxy that cast the Left Opposition as a villainous faction. The condemnation of Trotsky also unites reformers with less liberal currents who see Trotsky as the 'anti-national' evil genius of the revolution.[70]

To blame the top Bolshevik leaders for not getting rid of Stalin implies that the major reason for the degeneration of the revolution was Stalin's abuse of power. Social philosopher Anatoly Butenko has put this conclusion in the form of a thesis on Stalin's 'usurpation of power': 'relying on the cadres selected by him and creating an administrative-bureaucratic pyramid, [Stalin] secured unquestioned one-man rule'. Thus the dictatorship of the proletariat ceased to exist, and the party as Lenin understood it was almost destroyed.[71] Butenko's usurpation formula expresses extreme moral revulsion from Stalinism as antisocialist, while at the same time removing most of the blame from the Bolshevik party and the Soviet people. Despite its focus on Stalin as an individual, however, the usurpation explanation cannot avoid a wider question: why did the party allow Stalin's usurpation to take place?

This question has set the framework for the serious historical investigations of NEP that began to appear in 1988. Historians have argued over the reality of the economic crisis of the late 1920s that gave Stalin his excuse for destroying NEP. One influential interpretation argued that mistakes in policy had made a crisis in town-country relations all but inevitable by 1925. Stalin's solution to the crisis was to apply 'emergency measures' on a permanent basis against kulak

---

69   M.P. Kapustin, 'Ot kakogo nasledstva my otkazyvaemsia?', *Oktiabr*, 1988, no. 4, pp. 176–93, and no. 5, pp. 152–3. Kapustin calls Trotsky and Stalin 'two bears from the same cave'. At the 28th party congress in 1990, Aleksandr Yakovlev said that the tragedy of the party occurred when it turned from being a party of an idea to being a party of power (*Izvestiia*, 3 July 1990).

70   For example, Apollon Kuzmin, 'K kakomu khramu ishchem my dorogu?', *Nash Sovremennik*, 1988, no. 3, p. 158. The story of the gradual rehabilitation of Trotsky among the reformist intelligentsia would require a separate study.

71   *Moscow News*, 1988, no. 9, p. 12; see also no. 22, p. 12; *Sovetskaia kultura*, 4 February 1988. For critical discussion of the usurpation formula, see 'Nekotoryi problemy razvitiia obshchestva v 70-e gody. Deistvie mekhanizma tormozheniia', in *Voprosy istorii KPSS*, 1988, no. 2, pp. 110–33.

sabotage, as well as wreckers and class enemies of all descriptions. This solution found support because of a long-standing tendency toward 'petty-bourgeois revolutionism' in the party.[72]

If these historians are correct that the Bukharinist alternative was genuinely rejected by the majority of the party, then explanations must go deeper than the mistakes of the leadership. In coming to grips with the party's tragic misstep, reformers most often look to the earlier period of 'war communism'. War communism is the name usually given to the economic policies of the period 1918–1921; its hallmark was the extreme concentration of all available resources in order to win the civil war and prevent complete economic collapse, with a consequent inability to use material incentives. The official line has always been that war communism was an enforced set of emergency measures that were abandoned when the emergency was over.

Most reformers, however, would agree with Roy Medvedev when he described Stalinism as 'a more horrific version of war communism'. Medvedev argues that the Bolshevik leaders who introduced war communism saw it as a regrettable but temporary necessity.[73] If this is so, then war communism's destructive effect on many Bolsheviks was a tragic circumstance that casts no shadow on the heart of the Bolshevik enterprise. In the words of one of Shatrov's characters (the non-Bolshevik revolutionary Maria Spiridonova): 'October was a pure stream; it was the civil war that muddied it'.[74] Matters are more serious, however, if war communism genuinely represented an alternative conception of socialism. The economist Vasily Seliunin has argued that Lenin resorted to terror during the civil war mainly because he was still in thrall to the utopianism of traditional socialism and did not understand that material incentives were needed to motivate producers. Seliunin is an insightful economic critic but not a very adequate historian; his article betrays very little feel for the civil war, a period in which material incentives were in extremely short supply.[75]

---

72   G. Bordiugov and V. Kozlov, 'Vremia trudnikh voprosov', *Pravda*, 30 September and 10 October 1988 (reprinted in Bordiugov and Kozlov 1992). The influence of this argument can be detected in Gorbachev's speech from 15 March 1989. For other discussions, see V.S. Leichuk and L.P. Kosheleva, 'Industrializatsiia sssr: vybor kursa', *Pravda*, 21 October 1988 and the round-table discussion in *Voprosy istorii*, 1988, no. 9.

73   *Moscow News*, 1988, no. 24, p. 12.

74   *Znamia*, 1988, no. 1, p. 34.

75   Seliunin, 'Istoki', *Novyi mir*, 1988, no. 5, pp. 162–89. For a critique of stereotypes about 'war communism' – stereotypes dominant among Western historians as well – see 'Tsiurupa's White Beard', included in this volume along with other essays on this topic.

If Seliunin criticized the Lenin of war communism, it was all for the greater glory of the Lenin of NEP. But the emphasis on NEP and the last articles has allowed many Soviet intellectuals to reject most of what the historical Lenin stood for, while claiming that they are not rejecting Lenin himself, since 'the evolution of Lenin's views graphically attests to his greatness and his political genius'.[76]

It sometimes seems as if the concept of war communism has expanded far beyond the civil-war policies of 1918–1921 to include all the revolutionary fervour and the ideological commitment that today's reformers find so distasteful in the Soviet Union's founding fathers.[77] The conflict between war communism and NEP then becomes a split within Bolshevism itself, one that continues in different forms right up to today: Left and Right in the 1920s, Stalinist and Bukharinist in the 1930s, 'dogmatists' and reformers in the 1960s, opponents and supporters of perestroika today.[78] The image of the two Bolshevisms struggling for the soul of the party is probably dominant today among those intellectuals who have not given up on Bolshevism altogether.

3. *The abolition of* NEP *was inevitable.* The reformist writers who see NEP as a viable alternative are all concerned to save the honour of the Bolshevik revolution, or at least the NEP wing of Bolshevism. There are many Soviet writers who do not feel any such loyalty to Bolshevism and who deny that NEP was a genuine alternative to Stalinism. Nationalists who detest intelligentsia reformers as much as they do Stalinism and Brezhnevism charge that intellectuals only turned away from Stalin in 1937 when the repression finally cut a wide swath in the educated classes.[79] As a consequence, the intelligentsia critique is not radical enough and ignores the larger social forces behind Stalin. If asked to give a concrete description of these large social forces, some writers in this camp will refer to shadowy world-wide conspiracies with a Judeo-Masonic tinge.[80] The poverty of their own explanations, however, does not exclude the possibility of insightful criticisms of the reformist version of events.

---

76 Nikolai Portugalov, *Moscow News*, 1989, no. 8. For a protest against this sort of 'vivisection' of Lenin into two Lenins, see 'Tvorcheskaia energiia leninizma', *Kommunist*, 1989, no. 7, pp. 3–11.

77 Vladlen Sirotkin, 'Uroki NEPa', *Izvestiia*, 9 and 10 March 1989.

78 See Iu. Apenchenko, 'Nedodelannye dela: opyt oktiabria i puti perestroiki', *Znamia*, 1987, no. 11, pp. 166–80; Anatoly Strelianyi in *Moscow News*, 1988, no. 42; Vasilii Uzun, *Literaturnaia gazeta*, 1989, no. 11.

79 Kozhinov, 'Pravda i istina', *Nash sovremennik*, 1988, no. 4, pp. 160–75.

80 See the discussion by Igor Vinogradov of Vasilii Belov's new novel in *Moscow News*, 1989, no. 18.

The principal spokesman for this trend, Vadim Kozhinov, has used Rybakov's novel *Children of the Arbat* as an example of how the intelligentsia critique trivializes the emergence of Stalinism by reducing it to an intrigue by a demented egomaniac and his unscrupulous hirelings. This type of explanation views the intellectuals only as victims and in particular does not question the pre-Stalin Bolshevik consensus found during NEP. In a widely discussed series of articles, Aleksandr Tsipko argued that NEP did not bring about any change in the most damaging Bolshevik tenets: the demand for a total break with the past, the condescending attitude toward the peasant, the refusal to accept the constraints of the rule of law, and the denial of religious values.[81] Tsipko makes an exception for Bukharin, but Kozhinov and others feel that the current deification of Bukharin is a good example of the limitations of the intelligentsia critique. Iurii Emelianov devoted an entire book to cutting Bukharin down to size. Assembling all the compromising material glossed over by admirers of Bukharin, Emelianov used Bukharin in order to condemn the Bolshevik leadership as a whole (with the exception of Lenin). The book combines a genuinely insightful discussion of the effects of civil war with the popular but dubious argument that Bukharin was in the grip of 'Russophobia'.[82]

At first this type of critique spared Lenin himself, but only at the cost of disassociating him completely from the rest of Bolshevism. The last articles were used as evidence that Lenin finally realized that progress was only possible through 'development of the best models of tradition and the results of *existing* peasant culture'.[83] But, alas, he was unheeded by the rest of the Bolshevik leadership; in fact, argues Kozhinov, Lenin was factually removed from power before his final collapse in 1923, since the rest of the leadership flouted all his wishes with impunity. Lenin's privileged status in perestroika polemics did not last, and nationalist critiques were soon more open in their total rejection of Bolshevism. As a result, the nationalist intellectuals did not see NEP as a real alternative to Stalinism – indeed (in the words of Apollon Kuzmin) '1929 was in no way a departure from the policies of the 1920s, but their natural development'.[84]

81 Aleksandr Tsipko, *Nauka i zhizn*, 1988, nos. 11 and 12; 1989, nos. 1 and 2. Tsipko's article was reprinted in *Surovaia drama naroda* (*Surovaia* 1989), pp. 175–257; an abridged English translation can be found in CDSP, 41:10, 11, 12, 13.

82 Kozhinov, 'Samaia bolshaia opasnost', *Nash sovremennik*, 1989, no. 1, pp. 141–75; Iu. V. Emelianov, *Zametki o Bukharine: revoliutsiia, istoriia, lichnost* (Emelianov 1989). Emelianov pays Stephen Cohen the compliment of devoting an entire chapter to his influence in the Soviet Union.

83 Kseniia Mialo, 'Oborvannaia nit': krestianskaia kultura and kulturnaia revoliutsiia', *Novy mir*, 1988, no. 8, p. 249.

84 Kuzmin, 'K kakomu khramu', p. 163; Fatei Shipunov, 'Velikaia zamiatnia', *Nash Sovremen-*

The nationalist anti-intelligentsia critique is not the only analysis to maintain that NEP was not a viable alternative to Stalinism. Igor Kliamkin, a writer who fully shares the values of the reformist intellectuals, has maintained that 'NEP, called forth to replace war communism, created the conditions for its revival and secure establishment'.[85] Kliamkin goes beyond the villainy of individual Bolshevik leaders and the illusions of socialist intellectuals to examine the sociological bases of Stalinism. One base was the newly-recruited industrial class, living in terrible conditions, uprooted from one culture and not yet rooted in another, intolerant of a minority's right to disrupt social unity. Stalinism's sacrifice of the present for the sake of the future, its heady mixture of enthusiasm and repression, was more understandable to these workers than the celebration of the market and private accumulation associated today with NEP. NEP's roots in the countryside were also vulnerable. Neither a European market system nor a European political system could take root in a country with scattered pre-capitalist villages dominated by communal traditions. The imperatives of national independence in a peasant country destroyed NEP and made the institution of some kind of autocratic rule inevitable.

Kliamkin agrees with the liberal reformers that the only solution for the Soviet Union is the market system and the virtues of the Protestant work ethic, but he criticizes them for their moralistic search for villains, coupled with a lack of understanding of the complex cultural preconditions of a successful market system. In the past, Russian intellectuals allowed their love of genuinely admirable European ideals to blind them to the reality of their own society. This is why the liberals failed, the non-Bolshevik socialists failed, and finally why the Bolshevik Old Guard failed. To some, Kliamkin's analysis seems like blaming the victim. But (he asks) can the Russian people really be blamed because history did not make them able to carry out European ideals? 'Can we repent of the fact that we are what we are?'[86]

Why was NEP the road not taken? This is the question that every reformer must address. The aim of the investigation into the defeat of NEP is not only to find out who is to blame, but even more importantly, to find out what is to be

nik, 1989, no. 12, pp. 153–6. Shipunov manages to discuss collectivization without mentioning Stalin and putting all the focus on the Commissar of Agriculture, Ia. A. Iakovlev-Elshtein.

85 Igor Kliamkin, 'Kakaia ulitsa vedet k khramu?', *Novyi mir*, 1987, no. 11, pp. 150–88; 'Pochemu trudno govorit pravdu', *Novy mir*, 1989, no. 2, pp. 204–38. Another important article that treats Stalinism as a tragic necessity is Boris Kurashvili, 'Politicheskaia doktrina stalinizma', *Istoriia SSSR*, 1989, no. 5, pp. 60–77.

86 Igor Kliamkin, 'Kakaia ulitsa vedet k khramu?' and 'Pochemu trudno govorit pravdu'.

done. Even writers like Kozhinov and Kliamkin who reject the idea of an alternative in the past feel that the Soviet Union today is in an era of great choices. Under these circumstances, the failure of NEP may be the best available guide to the success of perestroika.

5   The Waning of NEP

By 1990 the NEP image had run out of steam. To be sure, NEP was still invoked by prominent reformers and scholarly interest in the NEP period remained high.[87] But the scope of the reform process had clearly moved beyond the point where NEP would play a central role either as a guide or as a legitimizing symbol.

At the beginning of perestroika, the challenge was to show that the market was compatible with socialism. By 1990, the challenge was to show that socialism was compatible with the market. The deepening economic crisis, the full-speed-ahead market reforms in Eastern Europe, and the Communist Party's growing inability to police the boundaries of political discourse – all of these factors contributed to making 'khozraschet socialism' less inspiring than the demand for a 'normal' Western-style market economy, with all that this implied in terms of high productivity, the rule of law, and openness to the world. Cooperatives were now viewed as a stepping stone to private property:

> According to Andrei Orlov, vice-chairman of the Council of Ministers' State Commission on Economic Reform ... private property's need to hide out under an assumed name (i.e., cooperative, family, or collective property) is nothing but a concession to people still not ready to accept it. Orlov said that this should dispel Western businessmen's scepticism and fear.[88]

---

87   Two collections of articles by Soviet historians on previously forbidden topics are *Istoriki sporiat* (*Istoriki* 1988), and *Urok daet istoriia* (*Urok* 1989). Two book-length studies by Western scholars of the new debates in history are R.W. Davies, *Soviet History in the Gorbachev Revolution* (Davies 1989b), and Alec Nove, *Glasnost in Action: Cultural Renaissance in Russia* (Nove 1989). Discussions of NEP could also be found in particular in the journal *Voprosy istorii KPSS*. In October 1989, I participated in a conference on the 1920s at the Institute of History in Moscow. This was one of the first conferences in which American and Soviet historians came together to discuss a problem of Soviet political history.

88   Andrei Borodenkov, 'Giving Private Property a Good Name', *Moscow News*, 1990, no. 27. For an early expression of doubts on the workability of '*khozraschet* socialism', see L. Popkova, 'Gde pyshnee pirogi', *Novyi mir*, 1987, no. 5, pp. 239–41.

Back in the day, NEP meant the toleration of the market on the road to socialism; if the reformers of perestroika were indeed on the same road, they were
travelling in the opposite direction.

Another reason for the waning of NEP was the new political scope of the
reform movement. The shift from party to state began in 1988 when Gorbachev
announced plans at the 19th party conference for the creation of a new national
legislature. In 1989 the national legislature became the focus of political attention; in 1990 the Communist Party renounced its de jure right to a political
monopoly and at the same time revealed its de facto abdication of a leadership role in the reform process. These developments forced reformers to take
another look at the 1920s as the period when opposition within and without the
party was definitively outlawed. Articles in the reformist press began to stress
other sides of Lenin's heritage, such as endorsement of monolithic party unity
or his deportation of prominent representatives of the intelligentsia in 1922. An
article in *Argumenty i fakty* stated bluntly that 'the foundations of the future
Stalinist model of society were laid between 1922 and 1924'.[89]

The shift in perspective can be seen by comparing two remarks by Len
Karpinsky, a 'half-dissident' who had re-joined the party after 1985. In an interview conducted sometime before April 1989, when he was still ready to defend
the party, Karpinsky used the 1920s as an image of pluralism: 'we had [then] the
kind of diverse structures and pluralism toward which we are now striving'. But
by 1990 he was sufficiently disillusioned with the party to draw a different lesson: 'In the 1920s the party kept at bay a multiparty system, freedom of speech
and the press.'[90] The reformers' new scepticism about the political implications
of NEP had already been expressed by Fazil Iskander in 1988:

The awful thing is that, remembering the Party arguments of the time,
I somehow cannot remember one man who put forward a program for
the democratization of the country. There were arguments about inter-
party democracy but I don't remember any others. And we must recognize in this the spiritual guilt of all the revolutionary leaders of the time.
What was this? Disdain for so-called bourgeois democracy ... or fear of

---

89   A. Podshchekoldin in *Argumenty i fakty*, no. 27, 7 July 1990, p. 2. For articles on Lenin,
     see Leonid Radzikhovsky, 'Testament', *Moscow News*, 1990, no. 16; Tamara Krasovitskaya,
     'Waste Not, Want Not', *Moscow News*, 1990, no. 21. On the fate of opposition in the 1920,
     see Nikolai Gul'binskii, 'Oppozitsiia', *Ogonek*, 1990, no. 13, pp. 6–11; Boris Belenkin, 'Gan'ka',
     Ogonek, 1990, no. 21, pp. 18–21; Viacheslav Kostikov, 'Vremia ottaiavshikh slov', *Ogonek*,
     1989, no. 22, pp. 4–7 (on the origins of censorship in the 1920s).
90   The first quote comes from Cohen and Vanden Heuvel 1989, p. 302; the second quote
     comes from an article co-authored with Dmitri Kazutin in *Moscow News*, 1990, no. 27.

552 CHAPTER 19

new competitors? I think it was both. In such conditions Stalin, naturally, proved to be the best Stalinist, and won.[91]

The waning of NEP coincided with a generational shift in the leadership of the reform movement. The original intelligentsia spokesmen for perestroika came from the generation variously called 'the children of the Twentieth Congress' (where Khrushchev denounced Stalin in 1956) or 'the people of the sixties'. These were people who had committed themselves to the reforms of the Khrushchev era and saw perestroika as a continuation with better leadership and a better strategy. As the reform movement progressed and as new economic and political opportunities opened up, it was inevitable that a new generation would come forward – a generation that had matured during the Brezhnev 'stagnation era' and shared some of the characteristics of that era. Among these were an ahistorical dismissal of the past and a more and more open fascination with the Western world.[92]

It was hardly likely that members of this new generation would follow the example of Egor Yakovlev, the editor of the *Moscow News*, and actually read Lenin for inspiration. If they do read Lenin, it was more probably because they were searching for incriminating quotations.[93] Insofar as this new generation needed an intelligentsia spokesman, it would be someone like Aleksandr Tsipko, who simply dismissed the Bolsheviks along with the whole revolutionary intelligentsia as arrogant fanatics.[94] The relation between the two generations can be compared to the relation between the Old Bolsheviks who started the revolution and the vast mass of party members who signed up during the civil war. The older generation shared many assumptions with their opponents; their fiery polemics were partly aimed at convincing themselves. The younger generation that was recruited after the fighting had started was so distant from the heritage of the past that they were impatient with polemics when action was needed. Don't refute the apparatchiki – just get rid of them!

The great burst of historical interest had not died out completely, but it had moved back from the 1920s to the civil war and the revolution itself. Arti-

91 *Moscow News*, 1988, no. 28, p. 11.
92 A self-portrait of the older generation can be found in Cohen and Vanden Heuvel 1989 (*Voices of Glasnost*). A striking example of an ahistorical attitude is Boris Yeltsin's memoirs, where the reader of Yeltsin's life is hardly aware of what decade it is; see Yeltsin, *Against the Grain* (Yeltsin 1990).
93 Vladimir Soloukhin, 'Chitaia Lenina' (Reading Lenin), *Rodina*, 1989, no. 10. For Egor Yakovlev, see Cohen and Vanden Heuvel 1989, p. 221.
94 Besides the articles cited earlier, see Aleksandr Tsipko, 'Awakening Russia', *Moscow News*, 1990, no. 26.

cles in the popular press became less interested in Bolshevik martyrs such as
Bukharin and more interested in examining the historical alternatives to Bolshevism itself. Sympathetic articles appeared on the Mensheviks, the liberal
Constitutional Democrats, the peasant-based Socialist Revolutionaries and the
radical Left Socialist Revolutionaries who briefly shared power with the Bolsheviks.[95] More and more, the fatal misturning of Russian history was placed
in 1917 rather than 1929. The official defence of the revolution was just that –
a defence, rather than a celebration. This defence focused more on the tragic
necessities of a time of troubles rather than on any spirited identification with
Bolshevik values.[96]

The slogan of the NEP alternative will be seen by historians as an important but ultimately transitory phase of the reform movement. This should not
detract from its value, not only as a bridge from communism to a market economy, but as a set of political ideals with its own integrity. These ideals are
expounded by the Bukharin character in Shatrov's play *Forward! Forward! Forward!*:

[We stand] for a slow, decades-long process of growing into socialism
through the systematic growth of industry, through cooperatives, through
a thousand and one intermediary forms of cooperation, from the lowest
to the highest. We stand for replacing the slogan 'who beats whom' with
'who is allied with whom?' – for overcoming difficulties principally with
economic methods. We believe the economy should serve man, and not
man the economy. We are for soviet law, and not soviet arbitrariness; [we
want] a free and varied culture. We are for the political dictatorship of the
party, but a party that does not forget [Lenin's words on the dangers of a
party of obedient fools]. We want a sharp repulse to nationalism, both
the crude anti-semitic kind as well as the most subtle – Ilyich demanded
this as well. We stand for conscience – it does not (as some think) lose

---

95   On the Mensheviks, see Viacheslav Kostikov, 'Sled ot shliapy Iu. o. [Martova]', *Ogonek*,
      1990, no. 10, pp. 28–31; on the liberals, see Rem Petrov, 'Miliukov, ili biografiia kompro-
      missa', *Ogonek*, 1990, no. 14, pp. 18–21; on the SRs, see the interview with Ekaterina Tarasova,
      Moscow News, 1990, no. 12; for the Left SRs, see Vasilii Golovanov, 'Levye esery: sorvannyi
      urok', *Literaturnaia gazeta*, 4 July 1990, p. 13. The Constituent Assembly dispersed by the
      Bolsheviks in 1918 became a rallying symbol; see Iurii Gavrilov, 'Volia naroda?', *Ogonek*,
      1990, no. 11, pp. 21–4.
96   See Gorbachev's speech in honour of Lenin's birthday in *Pravda*, 21 April 1990. Gorbachev
      seems to be following the line of argument set out by the historians G. Bordiugov, V. Kozlov,
      and V. Loginov; see their two articles in *Kommunist*, 1989, no. 14, pp. 74–87 and *Kommunist*,
      1990, no. 5, pp. 61–76.

its validity in politics. We want this to be always remembered: just as dry water cannot exist, neither can inhumane socialism.[97]

The reformers' use of NEP shows how a real past can give rise to an ideal past which turns into an ideal future. Although the NEP ideal may not be the path that leads to the temple, it will be remembered for its service as an inspiration for the pioneers of perestroika.

---

97   *Znamia*, 1988, no. 1, pp. 40–1.

Bibliography

Afinogenov, Aleksandr 1977, *Izbrannoe* (2 vols), Moscow: Gosizdat.

Agursky, Mikhail 1987, *The Third Rome: National Bolshevism in the USSR*, Boulder, CO: Westview Press.

Allen, Barbara 2016, *Alexander Shlyapnikov, 1885–1937: Life of an Old Bolshevik*, Leiden: Brill.

Andreev, V.M. 1976, 'Prodrazverstka i krest'ianstvo', *Istoricheskie Zapiski*, 97: 5–49.

Andreu, Maurice 2003, *L'Internationale communiste contre le Capital 1919–1924*, Paris: Presses Universitaires de France.

Andreu, Maurice 2012, 'What Was Bolshevism? The Case of N.I. Bukharin', paper delivered at *Historical Materialism* Conference, London.

Angenot, Marc 1993, *L'utopie collectiviste: le grand récit socialiste sous la Deuxième Internationale*, Paris: Presses universitaires de France.

Aslund, Anders 1985, *Private Enterprise in Eastern Europe*, London: Palgrave Macmillan.

Aslund, Anders 1991, *Gorbachev's Struggle for Economic Reform*, Ithaca, NY: Cornell University Press.

Avdeenko, Aleksandr 1989, *Otluchenie*, in *Znamia*, nos. 3 and 4.

Badaev, A.E. 1927, *X let bor'by i stroitel'stvo*, Leningrad: Priboi.

Badcock, Sarah 2007, *Politics and the People in Revolutionary Russia: A Provincial History*, Cambridge: Cambridge University Press.

Bartlett, Frederic C. 1932, *Remembering: A Study in Experimental and Social Psychology*, Cambridge: Cambridge University Press.

Bartlett, Robert 1988, *Trial by Fire and Water: The Medieval Judicial Ordeal*, Oxford: Oxford University Press.

Bazanov, P.N. (ed.) 2021, *Smenovekhovstvo: pro et contra*, St. Petersburg: RKhGA. Full text available at: https://www.rfbr.ru/rffi/ru/books/o_2131275#1

Bebel, August 1891, *Die Frau und der Sozialismus*, 10th edn., Stuttgart: J.H.W. Dietz.

Berkman, Alexander 1989 [1925], *The Bolshevik Myth*, London: Pluto Press.

Bettelheim, Charles 1976, *Class Struggles in the USSR, 1917–1923*, New York: Monthly Review Press.

Black, Clayton 2019, 'Regionalism or Clientelism? Explaining the Zinoviev-Leningrad Opposition of 1925', *Canadian-American Slavic Studies*, 53: 50–71.

Black, Clayton and Alexis Pogorelskin forthcoming, *New Perspectives on the 10th Party Congress, March 1921: Commemoration of the 100th Anniversary*, Leiden: Brill.

Boffa, Giuseppe 1992, *The Stalin Phenomenon*, Ithaca, NY: Cornell University Press.

Bogdanov, Alexander 1984, *Red Star: The First Bolshevik Utopia*, edited by Loren R. Graham, Charles Rougle, and Richard Stites, Bloomington: University of Indiana Press.

Bordiugov, Gennadi and Vladimir Kozlov 1990, 'Pozdnii Bukharin: Predstavleniia o sotsializme', in Zhuravlev 1990.

Bordiugov, Gennadi and Vladimir Kozlov 1992, *Istoriia i kon'iunktura*, Moscow: Gosizdat.

Bordiugov, Gennadi and Katrina vanden Heuvel (eds) 2021, *His Way/Ego Put'*, Moscow: AIRO-XX.

Bourke-White, Margaret 1942, *Shooting the Russian War*, New York: Simon and Schuster.

Brandenberger, David and Mikhail Zelenov (eds) 2014, *'Kratkii kurs istorii VKP(b)': Tekst i ego istoriia v 2 chastiakh*, Chast' 1, Moscow: Rosspen.

Brandenberger, David and Mikhail Zelenov (eds) 2019, *Stalin's Master Narrative: A Critical Edition of the* History of the Communist Party of the Soviet Union (Bolsheviks): Short Course, New Haven: Yale University Press.

Broué, Pierre 1988, *Trotsky*, Paris: Fayard.

Brovkin, Vladimir 1994, *Behind the Front Lines of the Civil War: Political Parties and Social Movements in Russia, 1918–1922*, Princeton: Princeton University Press.

Brovkin, Vladimir 1998, *Russia After Lenin: Politics, Culture and Society, 1921–1929*, New York: Routledge.

Brown, Donald E. 1991, *Human Universals*, Philadelphia: Temple University Press.

Bruner, Jerome 1986, *Actual Minds, Possible Worlds*, Cambridge, MA: Harvard University Press.

Bruner, Jerome 1990, *Acts of Meaning*, Cambridge, MA: Harvard University Press.

Bukharin, Nikolai 1915, 'Mirovoe khoziaistvo i imperializm', in Bukharin 1989.

Bukharin, Nikolai 1918a, *Ot krusheniia tsarizma do padeniia burzhuazii*, Moscow: Gosizdat.

Bukharin, Nikolai 1918b, *Programma kommunistov (bol'shevikov)*, Moscow: Gosizdat.

Bukharin, Nikolai 1918c, *Programme of the World Revolution* https://www.marxists.org/archive/bukharin/works/1918/worldrev/ch18.html (accessed 18 March 2015).

Bukharin, Nikolai 1920, *Ekonomika perekhodnogo perioda* [Prideaux Press 1980 reprint], Moscow: Gosizdat.

Bukharin, Nikolai 1921, 'The New Economic Policy of Soviet Russia', in *The New Policies of Soviet Russia*, Chicago: C.H. Kerr.

Bukharin, Nikolai 1926a, *Na podstupakh k oktiabriu*, Moscow: Gosizdat.

Bukharin, Nikolai 1926b, *Kritika ekonomicheskoi platformy oppozitsii*, Leningrad: Priboi.

Bukharin, Nikolai 1927, *Mezhdunarodnoe i vnutrennee polozhenie SSSR*, Moscow: Pravda-Bednota.

Bukharin, Nikolai 1928, *Mezhdunarodnaia burzhuaziia i Karl Kautskii, ee apostol* in Bukharin, *V zashchitu proletarskoi diktatury*, Moscow: Gosizdat.

Bukharin, Nikolai 1929 [1921], *Teoriia istoricheskogo materializma*, 9th edn., Moscow: Gosizdat.

Bukharin, Nikolai 1932a, *Etiudy*, Moscow: Gosizdat.

Bukharin, Nikolai 1932b, 'Tekhnika i ekonomika sovremennogo kapitalizma', in Bukharin 1932a.

Bukharin, Nikolai 1935, *Marxism and Modern Thought*, London: George Routledge and Sons.

Bukharin, Nikolai 1967, *The Path to Socialism in Russia*, edited by Sidney Heitman, New York: Omicron.

Bukharin, Nikolai 1969 [1921] *Historical Materialism*, 3rd edn., Ann Arbor: University of Michigan Press.

Bukharin, Nikolai 1979 [1920], *The Politics and Economics of the Transition Period*, London: Routledge & Kegan Paul.

Bukharin, Nikolai 1982, *Selected Writings on the State and the Transition to Socialism*, edited by Richard B. Day, Nottingham: Spokesman.

Bukharin, Nikolai 1988, *Izbrannye proizvedeniia*, Moscow: Gosizdat.

Bukharin, Nikolai 1989, *Problemy teorii i praktiki sotsializma*, Moscow: Gosizdat.

Bukharin, Nikolai 1990a, *Put' k sotsializmu: Izbrannye proizvedeniia*, Novosibirsk: Gosizdat.

Bukharin, Nikolai 1990b, *Izbrannye proizvedeniia*, Moscow: Ekonomika.

Bukharin, Nikolai 1993, *Revoliutsiia i kultura: stat'i i vystupleniia 1923–1936 godov*, Moscow: Fond im. N I. Bukharina.

Bukharin, Nikolai 1994, *Vremena*, Moscow: Progress.

Bukharin, Nikolai 1996, *Tiuremnye rukopisi* (2 vols), Moscow: AIRO-XX.

Bukharin, Nikolai 1998, *How It All Began*, New York: Columbia University Press.

Bukharin, Nikolai 2003, *Imperialism and World Economy*, London and Sydney: Bookmarks.

Bukharin, Nikolai 2005, *Philosophical Arabesques*, New York: Monthly Review Press.

Bukharin, Nikolai 2006, *The Prison Manuscripts: Socialism and its Culture*, London: Seagull.

Bukharin, Nikolai 2008, *Uznik Lubianki: Tiuremnye rukopisi Nikolaia Bukharina*, edited by Gennadii Bordiugov, Moscow: AIRO_XXI.

Bukharin, Nikolai 2018, *The Prison Poems of Nikolai Bukharin*, London: Seagull.

Bukharin, Nikolai and Evgenii Preobrazhensky 1920, *Azbuka kommunizma*, Moscow: Gosizdat.

Bukharin, Nikolai and Evgenii Preobrazhensky 1966, *The ABC of Communism*, Ann Arbor: University of Michigan Press.

Bukharin, Nikolai and Evgenii Preobrazhensky 1969, *The ABC of Communism*, Harmondsworth: Penguin Press.

Buranov, Yuri 1994, *Lenin's Will: Falsified and Forbidden*, Amherst, MA: Prometheus Books.

Burbank, Jane 1986, *Intelligentsia and Revolution: Russian Views of Bolshevism, 1917–1922*, New York: Oxford University Press.

Burbank, Jane 1989, 'The Shatrov Controversy', *Michigan Quarterly Review*, 28, no. 4: 580–603.

Bychkov, S. 1923, 'Organizatsionnoe stroitel'stvo prodorganov do NEPa', *Prodovol'stvie i revoliutsiia*, nos. 5–6.

Calhoun, Daniel F. 1976, *The United Front: The TUC and the Russians, 1923–1928*, Cambridge: Cambridge University Press.

Carr, E.H. 1950–1955, *The Bolshevik Revolution*, 3 vols, New York: Macmillan.

Carr, E.H. 1969, 'The Bolshevik Utopia', in Carr, *October Revolution: Before and After*, New York: A.A. Knopf.

Carr, E.H. 1976–1978, *Foundations of a Planned Economy* (3 vols), New York: Macmillan.

Cassiday, Julie 2002, 'Alcohol is Our Enemy! Soviet Temperance Melodramas of the 1920s', in McReynolds 2002.

Caygill, Howard 2020, 'The Prison Writings of Nikolai Bukharin', in *Prison Writing and the Literary World: Imprisonment, Institutionality and Questions of Literary Practice*, edited by Michelle Kelly and Claire Westal, New York: Routledge.

Chamberlin, William Henry 1935, *Russia's Iron Age*, Boston: Little, Brown.

Chase, William 1989, 'Voluntarism, Mobilisation and Coercion: *Subbotniki* 1919–1921', *Soviet Studies*, 41, no. 4.

Chayanov, A.V. 1966, *The Theory of Peasant Economy*, edited by Daniel Thorner, Basile Kerblay and R.E.F. Smith, Homewood, IL: R.D. Irwin.

Chayanov, A.V. 1977, 'Journey of my brother Alexei to the land of peasant utopia', in *The Russian Peasant, 1920 and 1984*, edited by R.E.F. Smith, London: Cass.

Chayanov, Aleksandr 1927 [1919], *Osnovnye idei i formy organizatsiii selsko-khoziaist-vennoi kooperatsiia*, 2nd edn., Moscow: Gosizdat.

Chayanov, Aleksandr 1967, *Oeuvres choisies de A.V. Cajanov*, Volume 5, edited by B. Kerblay, La Haye: Mouton.

Chuev, Feliks 1991, *Sto sorok besed s Molotovym: Iz dnevnika F. Chueva*, Moscow: TERRA.

Chuev, Feliks 1993, *Molotov Remembers: Inside Kremlin Politics*, edited by Albert Resis, Chicago: I.R. Dee.

Cohen, Stephen F. 1971, *Bukharin and the Bolshevik Revolution*, New York: A.A. Knopf.

Cohen, Stephen F. 1985, *Rethinking the Soviet Experience: Politics and History since 1917*, Oxford: Oxford University Press.

Cohen, Stephen F. 2009, *Soviet Fates and Lost Alternatives: From Stalinism to the New Cold War*, New York: Columbia University Press.

Cohen, Stephen F. 2010, *The Victims Return: Survivor of the Gulag after Stalin*, Exeter, NH: PW.

Cohen, Stephen F. and Katrina vanden Heuvel 1989, *Voices of Glasnost: Interviews with Gorbachev's Reformers*, New York: Norton.

Conquest, Robert 1986, *Harvest of Sorrow: Soviet Collectivization and the Terror-Famine*, Oxford: Oxford University Press.

Cosson, Yves-Marie (ed.) 2005, *Le Changement de Jalons*, Paris: L'Age d'homme.

Cotterill, D.J. (ed.) 1994, *The Serge-Trotsky Papers*, London: Pluto Press.

Daniels, Robert V. 1960a, *The Conscience of the Revolution: Communist Opposition in Soviet Russia*, Cambridge, MA: Harvard University Press.

Daniels, Robert V. 1960b, *A Documentary History of Communism* (2 vols), New York: Vintage.

Daniels, Robert V. 1962, *The Nature of Communism*, New York: Random House.

Danilov, V.P. 1990, 'Bukharinskaia al'ternativa', in Zhuravlev 1990.

Danilov, V.P. and N.A. Ivnitskii (eds) 1989, *Dokumenty svidetel'stvuiut: Iz istorii derevni nakanune i v khode kollektivizatsii 1927–1932*, Moscow: Gosizdat.

Davies, R.W. 1980, *The Socialist Offensive: The Collectivization of Soviet Agriculture, 1929–1930*, Cambridge, MA: Harvard University Press.

Davies, R.W. 1989a, *The Soviet Economy in Turmoil, 1929–1930*, Cambridge, MA: Harvard University Press.

Davies, R.W. 1989b, *Soviet History in the Gorbachev Revolution*, Bloomington, IL: University of Illinois Press.

Davydov, M.I. 1982, 'Gosudarstvennyi tovaroobmen mezhdu gorodom i derevnei v 1918–21 gg', *Istoricheskie Zapiski*, 108: 55–56.

Deiateli SSSR i revoliutsionnogo dvizheniia Rossii: Entsiklopedicheskii slovar Granat 1989 [1927], Moscow: Gosizdat.

Dekrety sovetskoi vlasti 1959, t. 2, Moscow: Gosizdat.

Dekrety sovetskoi vlasti 1986, t. 12, Moscow: Gosizdat.

Deutscher, Isaac 1949, *Stalin: A Political Biography*, Oxford: Oxford University Press.

Deutscher, Isaac 1954, *The Prophet Armed: Trotsky, 1879–1921*, Oxford: Oxford University Press.

Deutscher, Isaac 1959, *The Prophet Unarmed: Trotsky, 1921–1929*, New York: Vintage Books.

Deviataia konferentsiia RKP(b) 1972, Moscow: Gosizdat.

Deviatii s'ezd RKP(b) 1934, Moscow: Gosizdat.

Donald, Merlin 1991, *Origins of the Modern Mind: Three Stages in the Evolution of Culture and Cognition*, Cambridge, MA: Harvard University Press.

Donald, Moira 1993, *Marxism and Revolution: Karl Kautsky and the Russian Marxists, 1900–1924*, New Haven: Yale University Press.

Drabkin, Ia. S. (ed.) 1998, *Komintern i ideia mirovoi revoliutsii: dokumenty*, Moscow: Nauka.

Dudintsev, Vladimir 1957a, *Ne khlebom edinom*, Munich: Izdatel'stvo TsOPE.

Dudintsev, Vladimir 1957b, *Not by Bread Alone*, New York: E.P. Dutton.

Dushenko, Konstantin 2006, *Tsitaty iz russkoi istorii: spravochnik: 2200 tsitat ot prizvaniia variagov do nashikh dnei*, Moscow: EKSMO.

Dvenadtsatyi s'ezd RKP(b) 1968, Moscow: Gosizdat.

Eastman, Max 1964, *Love and Revolution: My Journey through an Epoch*, New York: Random House.

Eastman, Max 1973 [1925], *Since Lenin Died*, Westport, CT: Hyperion.

Eckstein, Harry (ed.) 1998, *Can Democracy Take Root in Post-Soviet Russia?* Lanham, MD: Rowman & Littlefield.

Eckstein, Harry (ed.) 1961, *A Theory of Stable Democracy*, Princeton, NJ: Center for International Studies.

Emelianov, Iurii Vasilevich 1989, *Zametki o Bukharine*, Moscow: Molodaia gvardiia.

Engels, Friedrich 1987, *Socialism, Utopian and Scientific* (Die Entwicklung des Sozialismus von der Utopie zur Wissenschaft), in *Marx-Engels Werke*, Volume 19, Berlin: Dietz Verlag.

Fainsod, Merle 1953, *How Russia is Ruled*, 1st edn., Cambridge, MA: Harvard University Press.

Farbman, Michael S. 1923, *Bolshevism in Retreat*, London.

Felshtinsky, Iurii (ed.) 1988, *Kommunisticheskaia oppozitsiia v SSSR, 1923–27* (4 vols), Benson, VT: Chalidze Publications.

Figes, Orlando 1996, *A People's Tragedy: The Russian Revolution 1891–1924*, London: J. Cape.

Fischer, Louis 1960 [1930], *The Soviets in World Affairs*, New York: Vintage Books.

Fitzpatrick, Sheila 1982, *The Russian Revolution*, Oxford: Oxford University Press.

Fitzpatrick, Sheila 1985, 'Ordzhonikidze's Takeover of Vesenkha: A Case Study in Soviet Bureaucratic Politics', *Soviet Studies*, 37: 153–72.

Fitzpatrick, Sheila 2005, *Tear Off the Masks! Identity and Imposture in Twentieth-Century Russia*, Princeton: Princeton University Press.

Fourth Congress of the Communist International 1923, London: Communist Party of Great Britain.

Frolova-Walker, Marina 2016, 'A Birthday Present for Stalin: Shostakovich's *Song of the Forests* (1949)', in *Composing for the State: Music in Twentieth-century Dictatorships*, edited by Esteban Buch, Igor Contreras Zubillaga and Manuel Deniz Silva, Abingdon: Ashgate.

Gendlin, Leonard 1973–1985, 'Eskiz k portretu (A.N. Afinogenov)', https://biography.wikireading.ru/189318,

Genkina, E.B. 1967, *Gosudarstvennaia deiatelnost V.I. Lenina, 1921–1923*, Moscow: Gosizdat.

Getty, J. Arch 1991, 'State and Society under Stalin: Constitutions and Elections in the 1930s', *Slavic Review*, 50: 18–35.

Gill, Graeme 1990, *The Origins of the Stalinist Political System*, Cambridge: Cambridge University Press.

Gimpelson, E.G. 1973, '*Voennyi kommunizm*', Moscow: Mysl'.

Gluckstein, Donny 1994, *The Tragedy of Bukharin*, London: Pluto Press.

Gorbachev, Mikhail 1987, 'Oktiabr i perestroika', *Kommunist*, 17: 9–15.

Gorbachev, Mikhail 1987, *Perestroika: New Thinking for Our Country and the World*, New York: Harper and Row.

Gorky, Maxim 1963, *Gorkii i sovetskie pisateli: neizdannaia perepiska*, in *Literaturnoe nasledstvo*, t. 70.

Gromov, Evgenii 2003, *Stalin: Iskusstvo i vlast'*, Moscow: Algoritm.

Gross, Jan T. 1988, *Revolution from Abroad: The Soviet Conquest of Poland's Western Ukraine and Western Belorussia*, Princeton: Princeton University Press.

Grossman, Vasily 2009, *Everything Flows*, translated by Robert and Elizabeth Chandler, with Anna Aslanyan, New York Review Books.

Gruber, Helmut 1974, *Soviet Russia Masters the Comintern: International Communism in the Era of Stalin's Ascendancy*, New York: Anchor Books.

Gudkova, Violetta 2006, 'Osobennosti "sovetskogo siuzheta": k tipologii rannei rossiiskoi dramy 1920–x gg', *Toronto Slavic Quarterly*, 26.

Gudkova, Violetta 2014, *Zabytye p'esy 1920–1930-kh godov*, Moscow: Novoe Lit. Obozrenie.

Gurvich, A. 1936, *Tri dramaturgi*, Moscow: Gosizdat.

Gurvich, A. 1938, *V poiskakh geroia*, Moscow: Gosizdat.

Gusev, Sergei Ivanovich 1989 [1920], 'Edinyi khoziaivstennyi plan i edinyi khoziaistvennyi apparat', in *Ob edinom khoziaistvennom plane*, Moscow: Gosizdat.

Haimson, Leopold 2004, 'Lenin's Revolutionary Career Revisited', *Kritika*, 5, no. 1: 57–9.

Hardeman, Hilda 1994, *Coming to Terms with the Soviet Regime: The 'Changing Signposts' Movement among Russian Émigrés in the Early 1920s*, DeKalb, IL: Northern Illinois University Press.

Harding, Neil 1992, 'Bukharin and the State', in *The Ideas of Nikolai Bukharin*, edited by A. Kemp-Welch, Oxford: Oxford University Press.

Harding, Neil 1996, *Leninism*, Durham, NC: Duke University Press.

Hasegawa, Tsuyoshi 1981, *The February Revolution: Petrograd 1917*, Seattle: University of Washington Press.

Haynes, Michael and Jim Wolfreys (eds) 2007, *History and Revolution: Refuting Revisionism*, London: Verso.

Haynes, Michael 1985, *Nikolai Bukharin and the Transition from Capitalism to Socialism*, New York: Holmes and Meier.

Hedlin, Myron 1975, 'Zinoviev's Revolutionary Tactics in 1917', *Slavic Review*, 34: 19–43.

Hedlin, Myron 1976, 'Grigorii Zinoviev: Myths of the Defeated', in *Reconsideration on the Russian Revolution*, edited by Ralph Carter Elwood, Cambridge, MA: Slavica.

Hellbeck, Jochen 2009, *Revolution on My Mind: Writing a Diary under Stalin*, Cambridge MA: Harvard University Press.

Heller, Mikhail 1988, 'Gorkii i lozh', *Cahiers du Monde russe et soviétique*, 29, no. 1: 5–12.

Hickey, Michael 2011, *Competing Voices from the Russian Revolution: Fighting Words*, Santa Barbara, CA: Greenwood.

Hilferding, Rudolf 1910, *Das Finanzkapital*, Vienna: Brand.

Hindus, Maurice 1933, *The Great Offensive*, New York: Harrison Smith and Robert Haas.

Hindus, Maurice 1953, *Crisis in the Kremlin*, Garden City, NY: Doubleday and Co.

History of the Communist Party of the Soviet Union (Bolsheviks): Short Course 1939, New York: International Publishers.

Hobsbawm, Eric 1996, *The Age of Extremes: A History of the World, 1914–1991*, New York: Vintage Books.

Hoover, Calvin B. 1931, *The Economic Life of Soviet Russia*, New York: Macmillan.

Istoriki sporiat 1988, Moscow: Gosizdat.

Iurkov, Ivan 1980, *Ekonomicheskaia politika partiia v derevne 1917–1920*, Moscow: Gosizdat.

Jansen, Marc 1982, *A Show Trial Under Lenin: The Trial of the Socialist Revolutionaries, Moscow, 1922*, The Hague: M. Nijhoff.

Jasny, Naum 1972, *Soviet Economists of the Twenties: Names to be Remembered*, Cambridge: Cambridge University Press.

Joravsky, David 1994, 'Communism in Historical Perspective', *American Historical Review*, 99: 837–57.

Kalendar-spravochnik prodovolstvennika 1921, Moscow: Gosizdat.

Karaganov, A. 1964, *Zhizn dramaturga*, Moscow: Gosizdat.

Kautsky, Karl 1901, 'Die Revision des Programms der Sozialdemokratie in Oesterreich', *Neue Zeit*, 20, no. 1: 68–82.

Kautsky, Karl 1902, *Die soziale Revolution*, Berlin: Vorwärts.

Kautsky, Karl 1908, *Die historische Leistung von Karl Marx*, Berlin: Vorwärts.

Kautsky, Karl 1909, *Der Weg zur Macht*, Berlin: Buchhandlung Vorwärts (German text at https://www.marxists.org/deutsch/archiv/kautsky/1909/macht/index.htm).

Kautsky, Karl 1960, *Erinnerungen und Erörterungen*, edited by Benedikt Kautsky, The Hague: Mouton.

Kautsky, Karl 1965 [1892], *Das Erfurter Programm*, Berlin: Dietz Verlag.

Kautsky, Karl and Bruno Schoenlank 1899, *Grundsätze und Forderungen der Sozialdemokratie: Erläuterungen zum Erfurter Programm*, 2nd edn., Berlin: Vorwärts.

Khalatov, A.B. 1928, *Vnutrenniaia torgovlia Soiuza SSR za X let*, Moscow: Narkomtorg.

Khanin, Grigorii and Vasilii Seliunin 1987, 'Lukavaia tsifra', *Novy mir*, 2: 181–201.

Khlevniuk, Oleg 1992, *1937: Stalin, NKVD i sovetskoe obshchestvo*, Moscow: Respublika.

Khlevniuk, Oleg 1996, *Mekhanizmy politicheskoi vlasti v 1930-e gody*, Moscow: ROSSPEN.

Khlevniuk, Oleg et al. (eds) 1995, *Stalinskoe Politbiuro v 30-e gody*, Moscow: AIRO – XX.

Khrushchev, Nikita 1970, *Khrushchev Remembers*, translated by Strobe Talbott, Boston: Little, Brown.

Kirshon, Vladimir 1933, *Khleb*, Moscow: Gosizdat.

Kirshon, Vladimir 1958, *Izbrannoe*, Moscow: Gosizdat.

Klehr, Harvey, John Earl Haynes and F.E. Firsov 1995, *The Secret World of American Communism*, New Haven: Yale University Press.

Kliuchnikov, Iurii et al. 1921, *Smena vekh*, Prague: Politika.

Knickerbocker, H.R. 1931, *The Red Trade Menace: Progress of the Soviet Five-Year Plan*, New York: Dodd, Mead.

Kołakowski, Leszek 1978, *Main Currents of Marxism*, 3 vols, Oxford: Oxford University Press.

Kollontai, Aleksandra 1921, *Rabochaia oppozitsiia*, Moscow: Gosizdat.

Kollontai, Aleksandra 1971, *The Autobiography of a Sexually Emancipated Communist Woman*, edited by Iring Fetscher, New York: Herder and Herder.

Kollontai, Aleksandra 1978, *Love of Worker Bees*, translated by Cathy Porter, Chicago: Cassandra Editions.

Kornai, Janos 1980, *Economics of Shortage*, Amsterdam: North-Holland Pub. Co.

Kosolapov, Richard 1995, *Slovo tovarishchu Stalinu*, Moscow: Paleia.

Kowalski, Ronald (ed.) 1990, *Kommunist: Organ Moskovskago oblastnogo büro R.K.P. (bol'shevikov)*, New York: Kraus International Publications.

Kowalski, Ronald (ed.) 1989, 'Geroicheskii Period Russkoi Revoliutsii', in *Revolutionary Russia*, 2, pp. v–x, 1–13.

Kritsman, Lev 1926, *Geroicheskii period velikoi russkoi revoliutsii (opyt analiza t. n. 'Voennogo Kommunizma'*, 2nd edn., Moscow: Gosizdat.

Krylova, Anna 2017, 'Imagining Socialism in the Soviet Century', *Social History*, 42, no. 3: 315–41.

Kuromiya, Hiroaki 1988, *Stalin's Industrial Revolution: Politics and Workers, 1928–1932*, Cambridge: Cambridge University Press.

Landis, Erik C. 2008, *Bandits and Partisans: The Antonov Movement in the Russian Civil War*, Pittsburgh: University of Pittsburgh Press.

Lansbury, George 1920, *What I Saw in Russia*, New York: Boni and Liverwright.

Larin, Iu. and Lev Kritsman 1920, *Ocherk khoziaistvennoi zhizni i organizatsiia narodnogo khoziaistva Sovetskoi Rossii, 1 noiabria 1917–1 iiulia 1920 g.*, Moscow: Gosizdat.

Lassalle, Ferdinand 1899 [1862], *The Workingman's Programme (Arbeiter-programm)*, New York: International Publishing Company.

Lawton, Lancelot 1927, *An Economic History of Soviet Russia* (2 vols), London: Macmillan.

Lenin, V.I. 1926–1935, *Polnoe sobranie sochinenii* (3rd edn.), Volume 27, Moscow: Gosizdat.

Lenin, V.I. 1958–1965, *Polnoe sobranie sochinenii* (5th edn.), Moscow: Gosizdat.

Lenin, V.I. 1975, *The Lenin Anthology*, edited by Robert C. Tucker, New York: Norton.

Lenin, V.I. 1990, 'Pometki V.I. Lenina v tezisakh G.E. Zinov'eva', *Voprosy Istorii KPSS*, 6: 30–6.

Leonov, Leonid 1973 (1924), *Badgers [Barsuki]*, Westport, CT: Hyperion Press.

Levi, Edward 1949, *An Introduction to Legal Reasoning*, Chicago: University of Chicago Press.

Levidov, Mikhail 1925, *Oratory oktiabria: siluety, zapisi*, Moscow: Gosizdat.

Lewin, Moshe 1969, *Lenin's Last Struggle*, New York: Monthly Review Press.

Lewin, Moshe 1974, *Political Undercurrents in Soviet Economic Debates*, Princeton: Princeton University Press.

Lewin, Moshe 1985, *The Making of the Soviet System: Essays in the Social History of Inter-war Russia*, New York: Pantheon Books.

Lewin, Moshe 1991, *Stalinism and the Seeds of Soviet Reform*, London: Pluto Press.

Lewis, Ben and Lars T. Lih (eds) 2011 [1920], *Zinoviev and Martov: Head to Head in Halle*, London: November Publications.

Lidtke, Vernon 1985, *The Alternative Culture: Socialist Labor in Imperial Germany*, New York: Oxford University Press.

Life Magazine 1943, 'Special Issue USSR' (29 March 1943).

Lih, Lars T. 1990, *Bread and Authority in Russia, 1914–1921*, Berkeley: University of California Press.

Lih, Lars T. 2000, 'Bukharin's "Illusion": War Communism and the Meaning of NEP', *Russian History*, 27, no. 4: 417–60.

Lih, Lars T. 2002, 'Melodrama and the Myth of the Soviet Union', in McReynolds 2002.

Lih, Lars T. 2003, 'How a Founding Document was Found, or One Hundred Years of Lenin's *What Is to be Done?*', *Kritika*, 4, no. 1: 1–45.

Lih, Lars T. 2006, *Lenin Rediscovered: What Is to Be Done? in Context*, Chicago: Haymarket Books.

Lih, Lars T. 2007, 'Lenin and the Great Awakening', in *Lenin Reloaded: Toward a Politics of Truth*, edited by Sebastian Budgen, Stathis Kouvelakis and Slavoj Žižek, Durham, NC: Duke University Press.

Lih, Lars T. 2009, 'Lenin's Aggressive Unoriginality, 1914–1916', *Socialist Studies: the Journal of the Society for Socialist Studies*, 5, no. 2: 90–112.

Lih, Lars T. 2011a, 'The Ironic Triumph of Old Bolshevism: The Debates of April 1917 in Context', *Russian History*, 38: 199–242.

Lih, Lars T. 2011b, *Lenin*, London: Reaktion.

Lih, Lars T. 2012, 'The Non-Geometric Elwood,' *Canadian Slavonic Papers*, 54, nos. 1–2: 185–213.

Lih, Lars T. 2013, 'Campaignism: An Essential Theme in the History of the Left (Essay-Review of Kevin Callahan, *Demonstration Culture: European Socialism and the Second International*)', *The International Newsletter of Communist Studies*, 19, no. 26: 95–103.

Lih, Lars T. 2014a, '"A New Era of War and Revolution": Lenin, Kautsky, Hegel and the Outbreak of World War I', in *Cataclysm 1914: The First World War and the Making of Modern World Politics*, edited by Alexander Anievas, Leiden: Brill.

Lih, Lars T. 2014b, 'Fully Armed: Kamenev and Pravda in March 1917', *The NEP Era: Soviet Russia, 1921–1928*, 8: 1–12.

Lih, Lars T. 2015, 'Letter from Afar, Corrections from Up Close: The Bolshevik Consensus of March 1917', *Kritika: Explorations in Russian and Eurasian History*, 16, no. 4: 799–834.

Lih, Lars T. 2017, 'All Power to the Soviets!', online series beginning at https://johnriddell .wordpress.com/2017/03/23/all-power-to-the-soviets-part-1-biography-of-a-slogan/.

Lih, Lars T. 2018a, 'All Power to the Soviets: Marx Meets Hobbes', *Radical Philosophy*, 2, no. 1.

Lih, Lars T. 2018b, 'The Tasks of Our Times: Kautsky's *Road to Power* in Germany and Russia', *Studies in East European Thought*, 70: 121–40.

Lih, Lars T. 2019a, 'Campaignism and the Fate of Political Freedom in Russia', in *The Fate of the Bolshevik Revolution: Illiberal Liberation, 1917–1941*, edited by Lara Douds, James Harris and Peter Whitewood, London: Bloomsbury Academic.

Lih, Lars T. 2019b, 'Lenin-Kautsky Post-1914 Database', at https://johnriddell.com/2019/ 08/05/lenin-kautsky-post-1914-database/.

Lih, Lars T. 2020a, 'The Bolsheviks and Their Message in 1917', in *A Companion to the Russian Revolution*, edited by Daniel Orlovsky, Hoboken, NJ: John Wiley and Sons.

Lih, Lars T. 2020b, 'The Curious Case of Comrade Kamenev', *Weekly Worker*, 17 December.

Lih, Lars T. 2021, 'Lenin and the Bolshevik Message in 1917', *Weekly Worker*, 7 January.

Lih, Lars T., O.V. Naumov and Oleg Khlevniuk (eds) 1995, *Stalin's Letters to Molotov*, New Haven: Yale University Press.

Lisichkin, Gennadii 1984, *Ternistyi put k izobiliiu*, Moscow: Gosizdat.

Lukianov, Sergei 1921, 'Revoliutsiia i vlast'', in Kliuchnikov 1921.

Lunacharsky, Anatolii, and Karl Radek and Lev Trotsky 1991, *Siluety: politicheskie portrety*, Moscow: Gosizdat.

Lyons, Eugene 1934, *Six Soviet Plays*, Boston: Houghton Mifflin.

Lyons, Eugene 1937, *Assignment in Utopia*, New York: Harcourt, Brace.

Maksimenkov, Leonid 1997, *Sumbur vmesto muzyki: Stalinskaia kul'turnaia revoliutsiia, 1936–1938*, Moscow: Iuridicheskaia kniga.

Malia, Martin 1980, *Comprendre la révolution russe*, Paris: Editions du Seuil.

Malia, Martin 1994, *The Soviet Tragedy: A History of Socialism in Russia, 1917–1991*, New York: Free Press.

Malle, Silvana 1985, *Economic Organization of War Communism, 1918–1921*, Cambridge: Cambridge University Press.

Mar'iamov, G. 1992, *Kremlevskii tsenzor: Stalin smotrit kino*, Moscow: Gosizdat.

Marghescu, Mircea 2014, *Pourquoi la littérature?* Paris: Kimé.

McAuley, Mary 1991, *Bread and Justice*, Oxford: Oxford University Press.

McCannon, John 1998, *Red Arctic: Polar Exploration and the Myth of the North in the Soviet Union, 1932–1939*, New York: Oxford University Press.

McDonald, Tracy 2011, *Face to the Village: The Riazan Countryside under Soviet Rule, 1921–1930*, Toronto: University of Toronto Press.

McNeal, Robert H. 1988, *Stalin: Man and Ruler*, Oxford: Oxford University Press.

McReynolds, Louise and Joan Neuberger (eds) 2002, *Imitations of Life: Two Centuries of Melodrama in Russia*, Durham, NC: Duke University Press.

Medvedev, Roy 1983, *All Stalin's Men*, Oxford: Blackwell.

Merl, Stephan 1985, *Die Anfänge der Kollektivierung in der Sowjetunion*, Wiesbaden: O. Harrassowitz.

Miliukov, Paul 1962 [1903], *Russia and its Crisis*, New York: Collier Books.

Molotov, V.M., L.M. Kaganovich et al. 1940, *Stalin*, New York: Workers Library Publishers.

Morrison, Simon and Nelly Kravetz 2006, 'The Cantata for the Twentieth Anniversary of October, or How the Specter of Communism Haunted Prokofiev', *The Journal of Musicology*, 23: 227–62.

Mowat, Charles Loch 1955, *Britain between the Wars, 1918–1940*, Chicago: University of Chicago Press.

Na bor'bu s golodom 1921, Moscow: Gosizdat.

Nadtocheev, Valerii 1991, '"Triumvirat" ili "semerka"?' in *Trudnye voprosy istorii*, Moscow: Gosizdat.

Neustadt, Richard 1960, *Presidential Power: The Politics of Leadership*, New York: Wiley.

Nove, Alec 1969, *An Economic History of the USSR*, Harmondsworth: Penguin Press.

Nove, Alec 1989, *Glasnost in Action: Cultural Renaissance in Russia*, Boston: Unwin Hyman.

Odinnadtsatyi s'ezd RKP(b) 1962, Moscow: Gosizdat.

Olminsky, Mikhail 1921, review of *Bumazhnye dengi* by Evgenii Preobrazhenskii, *Proletarskaia revoliutsiia*, 1: 181–5.

Olson, Mancur 1965, *The Logic of Collective Action: Public Goods and the Theory of Groups*, Cambridge, MA: Harvard University Press.

Orlov, N.A. 1920, *Sistema prodovol'stvennoi zagotovki*, Tambov: Gosizdat.

Orlov, Vladimir 2007, 'Prokofiev and the Myth of Revolution: The Cantata for the Twentieth Anniversary of the October Revolution', *Three Oranges Journal*, 13: 14–21.

Orlov, Vladimir 2013, 'Prokofiev and the Myth of the Father of Nations: The Cantata *Zdravitsa*', *The Journal of Musicology*, 30, no. 4: 577–620.

Osinskii, N. 1920, *Gosudarstvennoe regulirovanie krestianskogo khoziaistva*, Moscow: Gosizdat.

Osinskii, N. 1922, *Vosstanovlenie krestianskogo khoziaistva v Rossii i nashi zadachi*, Moscow: Gosizdat.

Ozhegov, S.I. 1970, *Slovar russkogo iazyka*, Moscow: Gosizdat.

Pasvolsky, Leo 1921, *The Economics of Communism, with Special Reference to Russia's Experiment*, New York: MacMillan.

Patenaude, Bertrand 1987, 'Bolshevism in Retreat: The Transition to the NEP, 1920–1922', PhD Dissertation, Stanford University.

Patenaude, Bertrand 1995, 'Peasants into Russians: The Utopian Essence of War Communism', *Russian Review*, 54, no. 4: 552–70.

Peshekhonov, Alexei 1923, *Pochemu ia ne emigriroval*, Berlin: Obelisk.

Pethybridge, Roger 1990, *One Step Back, Two Steps Forward: Soviet Society and Politics in the New Economic Policy*, Oxford: Oxford University Press.

Piatnadtsataia Konferentsiia VKP(b) 1927, Moscow: Gosizdat.

Piatyi Vserossiiskii s'ezd Sovetov 1918, Moscow: Gosizdat.

Pimenov, Vladimir 1967, *Sovetskie dramaturgi o svoem tvorchestve*, Moscow: Gosizdat.

Pipes, Richard 1980, *Struve: Liberal on the Right, 1905–1944*, Cambridge, MA: Harvard University Press.

Piskotin, M.I. 1984, *Sotsializm i gosudarstvennoe upravlenie*, Moscow: Gosizdat.

Pixerécourt, R.-C. Guilbert de 1971 [1841–43], *Théâtre choisi* (4 vols), Genève: Slatkine Reprints.

Pogorelskin, Alexis 2000, 'Kamenev and the Peasant Question: The Turn to Opposition, 1924–1925', *Russian History/Histoire Russe*, 27, no. 4: 381–96.

Poliakov, Iu. A. 1967, *Perekhod k NEPu i sovetskoe krest'ianstvo*, Moscow: Gosizdat.

Poliakov, Iu. A., V.P. Dmitrenko, and N.V. Shcherban 1982, *Novaia ekonomicheskaia politika: razrabotka i osushchestvlenie*, Moscow: Gosizdat.

Popov, Vladimir and Nikolai Shmelev 1989a, *Na perelome: ekonomicheskaia perestroika v SSSR*, Moscow: Gosizdat.

Popov, Vladimir and Nikolai Shmelev 1989b, *The Turning Point: Revitalizing the Soviet Economy*, Tauris: London.

Pratt, William W. 1964 [1858], *Ten Nights in a Barroom* in *Hiss the Villain: Six English and American Melodramas*, edited by Michael Booth, New York: B. Blom.

Preobrazhenskii, Evgenii 1920, *Bumazhnye dengi v epokhu proletarskoi diktatury*, Moscow: Gosizdat.

Preobrazhenskii, Evgenii 1921, *Trekhletie Oktiabr'skoi revoliutsiia*, Moscow: Gosizdat.

Preobrazhenskii, Evgenii 1922, *Ot NEPa do sotsializma*, Moscow: Moskovskii Rabochii.

Prodovolstvennaia politika v svete obshchego khoziaistvennogo stroitelstva sovetskoi vlasti 1920, Moscow: Gosizdat.

Protokoly desiatoi vserossiiskoi konferentsii RKP (bol'shevikov) 1933, Moscow: Gosizdat.

Przybos, Julia 1987, *L'entreprise mélodramatique*, Paris: J. Corti.

Radek, Karl 1924, *Piat' let Kominterna*, Moscow: Krasnaia nov'.

Ransome, Arthur 1919, *Russia in 1919*, New York: B.W. Huebsch.

Ransome, Arthur 1921, *The Crisis in Russia*, New York: B.W. Huebsch.

Rassweiler, Anne D. 1988, *The Generation of Power: The History of Dneprostroi*, Oxford: Oxford University Press.

Razvitoe sotsialisticheskoe obshchestvo: sushchnost, kriterii zrelosti, kritika revizionist-skikh kontseptsii 1975, Moscow: Gosizdat.

Razvitoi sotsializm: obshchee i spetsificheskoe v ego stroitelstve 1980, Moscow: Gosizdat.

Reabilitatsiia: Politicheskie protsessy 30–50-kh godov 1991, Moscow: Biblioteka zhurnala Izvestiia TsIK.

Report of Court Proceedings in the Case of the Anti-Soviet 'Bloc of Rights and Trotskyites' 1938, Moscow: People's Comissariat of Justice of the USSR.

Reswick, William 1952, *I Dreamt Revolution*, Chicago: H. Regnery Co.

Retish, Aaron B. 2008, *Russia's Peasants in Revolution and Civil War: Citizenship, Identity and the Creation of the Soviet State, 1914–1922*, Cambridge: Cambridge University Press.

Riddell John (ed.) 1984, *Lenin's Struggle for a Revolutionary International*, New York: Monad Press.

Riddell John (ed.) 1991, *Workers of the World and Oppressed Peoples, Unite! Proceedings and Documents of the Second Congress, 1920* (2 vols), New York: Pathfinder.

Rigby, T.H. 1977, 'Stalinism and the Mono-Organizational Society', in *Stalinism: Essays in Historical Interpretation*, edited by Robert C. Tucker, New York: Norton.

Roberts, Paul Craig 1970, '"War Communism" – A Product of Marxian Ideas', *Slavic Review*, 29: 238–261.

Robinson, John A. and Linda Hawpe 1986, 'Narrative Thinking as a Heuristic Process', in *Narrative Psychology: The Storied Nature of Human Conduct*, edited by Theodore R. Sarbin, New York: Praeger.

Roucek, Libor 1988, 'Private Enterprise in Soviet Political Debates', *Soviet Studies*, 40: 46–63.

Rybakov, Anatolii 1988a, *Deti Arbata*, Moscow: Knizhnaia Palata.

Rybakov, Anatolii 1988b, *Children of the Arbat*, Boston: Little, Brown & Co.

Salmon, Christian 1980, *Le rêve mathematique de Nicolai Boukharine, 1905–1923*, Paris: Sycamore.

Sarnov, Benedikt 2011, 'Strakh', *Novaia gazeta*, 30 September.

Schank, Roger C. 1990, *Tell Me A Story: A New Look at Real and Artificial Memory*, New York: Atheneum.

Schank, Roger and Robert P. Abelson 1977, *Scripts, Plans, Goals, and Understanding: An Inquiry into Human Knowledge Structures*, Hillsdale, NJ: L. Erlbaum Associates.

Schapiro, Leonard 1971, *The Communist Party of the Soviet Union*, rev. edn., New York: Random House.

Sed'moi vserossiiskii s'ezd Sovetov 1920, Moscow: Gosizdat.

Segel, Harold 1993, *Twentieth-Century Russian Drama: From Gorky to the Present*, updated edition, Baltimore: Johns Hopkins University Press.

Serge, Victor 1937, *Destiny of a Revolution*, London: National Book Association.

Serge, Victor 1963 [1951], *Memoirs of a Revolutionary 1901–1941*, Oxford: Oxford University Press.

Serge, Victor 1972 [1930], *Year One of the Russian Revolution*, edited by Peter Sedgwick, London: Allen Lane.

Serman, Ilia 2005, 'Afinogenov i ego "Strakh"', in *Semiotika strakha*, edited by Nora Buhks and Francis Conte, Moscow: Evropa.

Sessii vserossiiskogo tsentralnogo ispolnitelnogo komiteta, VIII sozyva 1922, Moscow: Gosizdat.

Shatrov, Mikhail 1990, *The Bolsheviks: Three Plays*, London: Nick Hern Books.

Sheehan, Helena 1993, *Marxism and the Philosophy of Science*, New Jersey: Humanities Press.

Shelokhaev, V. V (ed) 1994, *Politicheskaia istoriia Rossii v partiiakh i litsakh* (2 vols), Moscow: Terra.

Shevstov, V.V. 1990, 'Lev Trotskii i Maks Istmen [Max Eastman]: Istoriia odnoi politicheskoi druzhby', *Novaia i noveishaia istoriia*, 6: 141–63.

Shliapnikov, Aleksandr 1992–1994, *Kanun semnadtsatogo goda, Semnadtsatyi god* (3 vols), Moscow: Gosizdat.

Shlikhter, A.G. 1976, *Agrarnyi vopros i prodovol'stvennaia politika v pervyi gody sovetskoi vlasti*, Moscow: Nauka.

Shostakovich, Dmitri 1999, *Song of the Forests. Oratorio, Op. 81*, edited by Koichi Owa, Tokyo: Zen-On Music Company.

Siegelbaum, Lewis H. 1988, *Stakhanovism and the Politics of Productivity in the USSR, 1935–1941*, Cambridge: Cambridge University Press.

Smith, S.A. 1983, *Red Petrograd: Revolution in the Factories 1917–1918*, Cambridge: Cambridge University Press.

Smith, S.A. 2002, *The Russian Revolution: A Very Short Introduction*, Oxford: Oxford University Press.

Smith, W.H. 1966 [1844], *The Drunkard, or The Fallen Saved* in *Dramas from the American Theatre 1762–1909*, edited by Richard Moody, Cleveland: World Pub. Co.

Sochor, Zenovia A. 1982, 'NEP Rediscovered: Current Soviet Interest in Alternative Strategies of Development', *Soviet Union*, 9, no. 2: 189–211.

Sochor, Zenovia A. 1988, *Revolution and Culture: The Bogdanov–Lenin Controversy*, Ithaca, NY: Cornell University Press.

Solzhenitsyn, Aleksandr 1986, *Mart semnadtsatogo*, Paris: YMCA Press.

Souvarine, Boris 1939, *Stalin: A Critical Survey of Bolshevism*, New York: Longmans, Green and Co.

Spargo, John 1920, *'The Greatest Failure in All History': A Critical Examination of the Actual Workings of Bolshevism in Russia*, New York: Harper & Brothers.

Spulber, Nicolas 1979, *Organizational Alternatives in Soviet-type Economies*, Cambridge: Cambridge University Press.

Stalin, I.V. 1947–1952, *Sochineniia* (13 vols), Moscow: Gosizdat.

Stalin, I.V. 1967, *Sochineniia*, vols. 14, 15, 16, edited by Robert H. McNeal, Stanford: Hoover Institution.

Stalin, I.V. 1972 [1951], *Economic Problems of Socialism in the* USSR, Peking: State Publishing House.

Stalin, I.V. 1994, 'I.V. Stalin o "Kratkom kurse istorii VKP(b)"', *Istoricheskii arkhiv*, 5: 4–31.

Steenson, Gary P. 1978, *Karl Kautsky 1854–1938: Marxism in the Classical Years*, Pittsburgh: University of Pittsburgh Press.

Steenson, Gary P. 1981, *'Not One Man! Not One Penny!' German Social Democracy, 1863–1914*, Pittsburgh: University of Pittsburgh Press.

Stites, Richard 1989, *Revolutionary Dreams: Utopian Visions and Experimental Life in the Russian Revolution*, Oxford: Oxford University Press.

Strizhkov, Iu. K. 1973, *Prodovol'stvennye otriady v gody grazhdanskoi voiny i inostrannoi interventsii, 1917–1921*, Moscow: Nauka.

Strizhkov, Iu. K. 1977, 'Priniatie dekreta o prodovol'stvennoi razverstke i ego osushchestvlenie v pervoi polovine 1919 g.', in *Oktiabr i sovetskoe krest'ianstvo, 1917–1927gg*, Moscow: Nauka.

Surovaia drama naroda 1989, Moscow: Gosizdat.

Svidersky, A. 1922, *Chetyre goda prodovol'stvennoi raboty*, Moscow: People's Commissariat of Food Supply.

Szamuely, László 1974, *First Models of the Socialist Economic Systems: Principles and Theories*, Budapest: Akademiai Kiadó.

Tamashin, L. 1965, *Vladimir Kirshon: Ocherk tvorchestva*, Moscow: Gosizdat.

Terne, A.M. 1922, *V tsarstve Lenina*, Berlin: A. Terne.

Tertz, Abram 1965, *On Socialist Realism*, New York: Vintage Books.

Thatcher, Ian 2000, *Leon Trotsky and World War One: August 1914 to February 1917*, Basingstoke: Macmillan.

Thatcher, Ian 2016, 'The Russian Revolutionary Constitution and Pamphlet Literature in the 1917 Russian Revolution', *Europe-Asia Studies*, 68: 1635–53.

The Central Committee Resolution and Zhdanov's Speech on the Journals Zvezda *and* Leningrad 1978, Bilingual edn., Royal Oak, MI: Strathcona Publishing Company.

The Road to Communism 1962, Moscow: Foreign Languages Publishing House.

Thompson, Dorothy 1929, *The New Russia*, London: Jonathan Cape.

Trinadtsatyi s'ezd RKP(b)*: Stenograficheskii otchet* 1963, Moscow: Gosizdat.

Trotsky, Lev 1919, *Terrorizm i kommunizm*, Moscow: Sochineniia.

Trotsky, Lev 1921, *The Defence of Terrorism*, London: G. Allen and Unwin.

Trotsky, Lev 1924, *Novy kurs*, Moscow: Gosizdat.

Trotsky, Lev 1925–1927, *Sochineniia*, Moscow: Gosizdat.

Trotsky, Lev 1961 [1919], *Terrorism and Communism*, Ann Arbor: University of Michigan Press.

Tucker, Robert C. 1965, 'Introduction', in *The Great Purge Trial*, edited by Robert Tucker and Stephen Cohen, New York: Grosset & Dunlap.

Tucker, Robert C. 1973, *Stalin as Revolutionary: A Study in History and Personality*, New York: W.W. Norton.

Tucker, Robert C. 1975, 'Introduction: Lenin and Revolution', in *The Lenin Anthology*, edited by Robert Tucker, New York: Norton and Co.

Tucker, Robert C. 1981, *Politics as Leadership*, Columbia, MO: University of Missouri Press.

Tucker, Robert C. 1987, *Political Culture and Leadership in Soviet Russia: From Lenin to Gorbachev*, New York: W.W. Norton.

Tucker, Robert C. 1990, *Stalin in Power: The Revolution from Above, 1928–1941*, New York: W.W. Norton.

Tugan-Baranovsky, Mikhail 1996, *K luchshemu budushchemu*, Moscow: Rosspen.

Ulig, Diter and Vladislav Khedeller [Wladislaw Hedeler] 2008, '"Arabeski" Nikolaia Bukharina v kontekste ikh vremeni', in Bukharin 2008.

Urok daet istoriia 1989, Moscow: Gosizdat.

Vaniashova, M.G. 2018, '"Unichtozh'te strakh". P'esy A. Afinogenova nachala 1930-kh godov', *Verkhnevolzhskii filologicheskii vestnik*, 1.

Varga, Eugen 1921, 'Introduction', in Osinski, N., *La régularisation par l'état de la culture paysanne*, Moscow: Gosizdat.

Veniavkin, Il'ia 2011, '"Nebogatoe oformlenie": "Lozh'" Aleksandra Afinogenova i stalin-skaia kultur'naia politika 1930-kh', *NLO*, 2.

Veniavkin, Il'ia 2016, *Chernil'nitsa khoziaina: sovetskii pisatel' vnutri Bol'shogo terrora*, Arzama: https://arzamas.academy/mag/309-afinogenov.

Veniavkin, Il'ia n.d., 'Afinogenov. Strakh', *Arzamas*, Kurs 41, Season 5.

Vishnevsky, Vsevolod 1933, *Optimisticheskaia tragediia*, 1st edn., Moscow: Gosizdat.

Vladimirov, M.K. 1920, *Meshochnichestvo i ego sotsial'no-politicheskoe otrazhenie*, Kharkov: Gosizdat.

Vladimirov, M.K. 1921, *Udarnye momenty prodovolstvennoi raboty na Ukraine*, Kharkov: Gosizdat.

Volkogonov, Dmitrii 1991, *Triumph and Tragedy*, London: Weidenfeld and Nicolson.

Von Laue, Theodore 1971, *Why Lenin? Why Stalin? A Reappraisal of the Russian Revolution, 1900–1930*, Philadelphia: Lippincott.

Von Laue, Theodore 1987, *The World Revolution of Westernization: The Twentieth Century in Global Perspective*, Oxford: Oxford University Press.

Vosmoi s'ezd RKP(b) 1959, Moscow: Gosizdat.

Vosmoi vserossiiskii s'ezd rabochikh, krestianskikh, krasnoarmeiskikh i kazachikh deputatov 1921, Moscow: Gosizdat.

Vysotsky, Vladimir 1981, *Pesni i stikhi*, New York: Literary Frontiers Publishers.

Wade, Rex 2000, *The Russian Revolution, 1917*, Cambridge: Cambridge University Press.

Walicki, Andrzej 1995, *Marxism and the Leap to the Kingdom of Freedom: The Rise and Fall of the Communist Utopia*, Stanford: Stanford University Press.

Ward, Chris 1993, *Stalin's Russia*, London: Edward Arnold.

Weiner, Jack 1984, 'The Destalinization of Dmitrii Shostakovich's "Song of the Forests", Op. 81 (1949)', *Rocky Mountain Review of Language and Literature*, 38, no. 4: 214–22.

Wilbur, C. Martin 1983, *The Nationalist Revolution in China, 1923–1928*, Cambridge: Cambridge University Press.

Wilbur, C. Martin and Julie Lien-ying How 1989, *Missionaries of Revolution: Soviet Advisers and Nationalist China, 1920–1927*, Cambridge, MA: Harvard University Press.

Wolfson, Boris 2006, 'Fear on Stage: Afinogenov, Stanislavsky, and the Making of Stalinist Theater', in *Everyday Life in Early Soviet Russia: Taking the Revolution Inside*, edited by Christina Kiaer and Eric Naiman, Bloomington, IL: Indiana University Press.

Wynn, Charters 2014, 'Getting Together Then Falling Apart: Tomsky and British Trade Unionists during NEP', in *The Russian Review*, 73, no. 4: 571–95.

Wynn, Charters 2021, *The Moderate Bolshevik: Mikhail Tomsky from the Factory to the Kremlin, 1880–1936*, Leiden: Brill.

XIV s'ezd vsesoiuznoi kommunisticheskoi partii (b) 1926, Moscow: Gosizdat.

Yeltsin, Boris 1900, *Against the Grain*, London: Cape.

Zelenov, Mikhail (ed.) 2006, *Istoricheskaia ideologiia v SSSR v 1920–1950-e gody: Perepiska s istorikami, stat'i i zametki po istorii, stenogrammy vystuplenenii*, St. Petersburg: Nauka-Piter.

Zelnik, Reginald 2003, 'Worry about Workers: Concerns of the Russian Intelligentsia from the 1870s to *What Is to Be Done?*' in *Extending the Borders of Russian History*, edited by Marsha Seifert, Budapest: Central European University Press.

Zhuravlev, V.V. 1990 (ed.), *Bukharin: Chelovek, politik, uchenyi*, Moscow: Gosizdat.

Zinoviev, Grigorii 1918, *Pis'mo k krest'ianam: Zachem rabochie posylaiut prodovol'stvennye otriady v derevniu?* Petrograd: Gosizdat.

Zinoviev, Grigorii 1920a, 'Sotsial'nye korni opportunizma', in Zinoviev, *Voina i krizis sotsializma*, 2nd edn., Moscow: Gosizdat.

Zinoviev, Grigorii 1920b, *Dvenadtsat' dnei v Germanii*, Peterburg: Gosizdat.

Zinoviev, Grigorii 1920c, *Krest'iane i sovetskaia vlast'*, Petrograd: Gosizdat.

Zinoviev, Grigorii 1920d, *Novye zadachi nashei partii (ot voiny k khoziaistvu)*, Petersburg: Gosizdat.

Zinoviev, Grigorii 1921, *Na poroge novoi epokhi: kommunisty i bespartiinye*, Petrograd: Gosizdat.

Zinoviev, Grigorii 1924a, 'Zadachi nashei partii posle konchiny V.I. Lenina: Dva doklada', *Krasnaia Nov'*.

Zinoviev, Grigorii 1924b, *Istoriia Rossiiskoi Kommunisticheskoi Partii (bol'shevikov)*, 4th edn., Leningrad: Gosizdat.

Zinoviev, Grigorii 1925, *Russia's Path to Communism*, London: Communist Party of Great Britain.

Zinoviev, Grigorii 1984 [1916], 'The Social Roots of Opportunism', in Riddell 1984.

Zinoviev, Grigorii 1989, 'Ob itogakh VIII s'ezd RKP(b)', *Izvestiia TsK*, 8: 187–91.

Zlokazov, G.I., and G.Z. Ioffe (eds) 2002, *Iz istorii bor'by za vlast' v 1917 godu: sbornik dokumentov*, Moscow: Institut rossiiskoi istorii RAN.

Analytical Table of Contents

Index of Proper Names

9 798888 903292